Informatik-Fachberichte

Herausgegeben von W. Brauer
im Auftrag der Gesellschaft für Informatik (GI)

16

GI – 8. Jahrestagung

Herausgegeben von S. Schindler und W. K. Giloi

Springer-Verlag
Berlin Heidelberg New York 1978

Herausgeber

Prof. Dr. Sigram Schindler
Institut für Softwaretechnik
und theoretische Informatik
Fachbereich Informatik (20)
Fachgebiet Betriebssysteme
TU Berlin
Ernst-Reuter-Platz 7
1000 Berlin 10 / BRD

Prof. Dr. Wolfgang K. Giloi
Institut für technische Informatik
TU Berlin
Einsteinufer 35/37
1000 Berlin 10 / BRD

AMS Subject Classifications (1970): 68A05, 68A15
CR Subject Classifications (1974): 2.1, 2.2, 3.34, 4.20, 6.3, 8.2

ISBN-13: 978-3-540-09038-0 e-ISBN-13: 978-3-642-67091-6
DOI: 10.1007/978-3-642-67091-6

CIP-Kurztitelaufnahme der Deutschen Bibliothek. *Gesellschaft für Informatik:* : GI-Jahrestagung. – Berlin, Heidelberg, New York : Springer. Bis 5. 1975 u. d. T.: Gesellschaft für Informatik: Jahrestagung / GI, Gesellschaft für Informatik e. V. 8. 1978. – 1978. Informatik Fachberichte : 16)

2145/3140 - 5 4 3 2 1 0

Vorwort der Herausgeber

Bei der Gestaltung der Jahrestagung 1978 der Gesellschaft für Informatik in Berlin sollen zum Teil neue Wege beschritten werden, um Tendenzen zu berücksichtigen, die sich seit einigen Jahren in den USA und neuerdings auch in Deutschland abzeichnen. Eine solche Tendenz ist die Zunahme spezieller Fachtagungen auf den einzelnen Gebieten der Informatik, die von den Fachausschüssen veranstaltet werden. Spezielle Fachbeiträge können damit vorwiegend in die Fachtagungen verlegt werden. Eine andere Tendenz erkennt man in der zunehmenden Diskussion um die gesellschaftlichen und wirtschaftlichen Implikationen der neuen Informatik-Technologien.
Dieser Entwicklung Rechnung tragend wurde vom Programmausschuß der GI 78 beschlossen, die Jahrestagung 1978 nicht mehr aus Sitzungen aufzubauen, die den einzelnen technischen Fachgebieten gewidmet sind, sondern sie um eine Vortragsreihe über gegenwärtig zentrale Probleme der Informatik zu organisieren. Der vorliegende Band faßt in erster Linie diese Vortragsreihe zusammen. Darüber hinaus enthält er Aufsätze zu einigen besonders akuten Themen, die anläßlich der Jahrestagung in Fachgesprächen erörtert werden. Aus verschiedenen Gründen - zum Teil, weil die Aufsätze bereits zur Publikation an anderer Stelle vorgesehen sind - haben nicht alle neun Organisatoren eines Fachgesprächs einen Beitrag in diesen Band eingebracht; auch diese Beiträge werden jedoch im Rahmen der Fachgespräche selbst zugänglich sein.

Wir möchten an dieser Stelle sowohl allen denjenigen danken, die zum Zustandekommen dieses Bandes beigetragen haben, als auch allen denjenigen, die auf andere Weise am Erfolg der GI 78 mitgewirkt haben, insbesondere

- allen Sprechern der Jahrestagung
- allen Förderern der Jahrestagung
- den Mitgliedern des Programmausschusses
- den Organisatoren der Fachgespräche
- den Sitzungsleitern

- den für die Organisation Verantwortlichen
- dem Springer-Verlag für die Unterstützung bei der Erstellung des Tagungsbandes.

Für ihre vielfältigen Bemühungen beim Zusammenstellen des Tagungsbandes und den anderen organisatorischen Dingen der GI 78 möchten wir hiermit Frau Ruth Mahler unseren Dank aussprechen.

Berlin, Juli 78

Sigram Schindler
Wolfgang K. Giloi

INHALTSVERZEICHNIS

ÜBERSICHTSVORTRÄGE DER GI-JAHRESTAGUNG

ÜBERSICHTSVORTRÄGE DER FACHGESPRÄCHE

x)
Diese Beiträge sind verspätet eingegangen und mußten aus technischen Gründen daher am Ende des Bandes plaziert werden.

Design of a programming language for a program transformation system

F. L. Bauer
Institut für Informatik
Technische Universität München

Introduction

The late sixties and early seventies - twenty-five years after the classical work of ZUSE and VON NEUMANN - have seen the first crisis in the proud development of computing: large software systems showed alarming deficiencies.

Gradually, it became clear that it was more difficult than expected "to master complexity"[1] (DIJKSTRA). The cause of the misdevelopment was found in the programming habits of the mass of programmers. These had been influenced by the existing programming tools or rather by the lack of appropriate ones. Programming tools had in turn been corrupted by the arbitrariness of existing hardware, which indeed ruled the profession. This analysis of the situation was given by DIJKSTRA at the Rome Conference on Software Engineering (1969) and subsequently led to a movement of establishing a discipline of programming.

Another crisis had developed in these years, not totally unrelated to the Software Crisis: the crisis of programming languages. Seeing 700 of those listed in SAMMET's book was certainly not what the international ALGOL effort had wanted to produce, but not the number was an alarming sign: it was the fact that these languages all pretended to be different from each other; their promotors did not want to understand each other, and language users seemed not to care for a common conceptual basis. Instead, doctrines were erected.

That the circumstances that led to the Software Crisis were also responsible for this aberration of the human mind, this I could observe even in the work of the group that developed ALGOL 68. The original ALGOL idea which RUTISHAUSER, SAMELSON, BOTTENBRUCH and I had propagated: a universal framework of concepts, taken from mathematics and cast into some language, an idea which had already been spoiled by FORTRAN abracadabra and other gimmicks in ALGOL 60, was now completely submerged. I was therefore relieved and started to have new hope when WIRTH said in 1969 [2] "I believe the art of programming is based on a relatively small number of fundamental concepts, most of these concepts are already present in mathematics in some form".

---

[1] This difficulty was frequently circumvented by additional programming efforts, which only increased the complexity. Apollo programming support, [1] p. 43

[2] [1] p. 20, p. 18, p. 21

WIRTH, however, took the extremely cautious course "to find a compromise which is as close to the machine as possible, while remaining machine independent". While it was certainly practical in the short run to have "features omitted from PASCAL because they appear to be too sophisticated for presently known methods of proof" - and the success PASCAL has had in the most recent years, rather in its middle age, demonstrates this - I was more inclined to look for a long range improvement and I was rather on the side of DIJKSTRAs remark:
"I would like to make a comment on Niklaus Wirth's story. I would like to point out that he starts from a tacit assumption which I wouldn't like to let pass unchallenged. His tacit assumption is that elegance or convenience on the one hand, and efficiency on the other hand, cannot go hand in hand ... I just don't believe it, and I would like to point out that from the point of view of Niklaus Wirth, his assumption is just a belief. If I have any interest in computing science at all it is based on my firm belief that very often the most attractive solution is the most efficient one."[1]
This was in 1969. Working with ALGOL 68, or rather a core of it which is, after all, not as bad as some people had expected from the report, I found therein a basis for a great educational challenge, the build-up of computer science (Informatik) in Germany as a university discipline. I found - and many people concurred - that a stock of concepts common in most of the prevailing programming languages could be conveyed under the notation and terminology of this core of ALGOL 68 as used in [2]. Needless to say that I saw the rough sides, too. They were centered around the ALGOL 68 doctrine of references, and by and large I understood that this, too, was the effect of misguidance by features of existing machines: ALGOL 68 was only masquerading as a high level language, but it is a machine oriented language as much as PASCAL, and was worse because it was unsafe - for example by allowing 'dangling references'.

A further event influenced my approach to a truly algorithmic language: The appearance of a mathematical semantics of programming languages. I had underestimated the importance of McCARTHY's early, however restricted, attempts, and I was appalled by the clumsiness of the so called Vienna Definition Language, but the work initiated by PETER LANDIN and DANA SCOTT made me think: This was a convincing theory of computation, and nevertheless a gap existed between its merely functional, "applicative" level, the level of the Lambda Calculus on the one side and the prevailing level of constructs with program variables, with its semantics implied by HOARE's 'axioms' (and later by DIJKSTRA's predicate transformers) on the other side.

Moreover, I was not fully satisfied with the idea of proving correctness of a program, i.e. proving that it fits into a problem description. Didn't the whole movement start from the observation that most programs were wrong, and would it make sense to try to prove the correctness of an incorrect program? Programs don't fall from heaven, nor are they the product of omniscient oracles (SINTZOFF). KLAUS SAMELSON and DAVID GRIES appeased me, saying that correctness proof and program construction should go hand in hand. But to me this meant that programming is a transformation process starting from the problem description. LANDIN's work [3] encouraged me in this direction. We will come to this later.

Another misgiving I had was concerned with data structures. Both ALGOL 68 and PASCAL disallowed recursively defined data structures; instead they have to be introduced as a plexus (Geflecht) implementation - sometimes called Lists - with the help of pointers. Although PASCAL provided safe tools using this, it meant a terribly clumsy way of expressing even the simplest operations with sequences, like sorting in of an element. Again, a clean theory of recursive object structures existed in the meantime (DANA SCOTT [4]), based on McCARTHY's ideas of 1962, and a transformation had to be found from this purely applicative level to the level of Lists. We will also discuss this later.

---

[1] [1] p. 18

Looking at objects and operations simultaneously, there was thus the procedural level of program variables using loops with goto's and of lists with pointers, and there was the applicative level of recursive definition both of composite operations and composite objects. But there was a third, still "higher" level, too: The level of implicit specification, the typical implicit specification of operations being done with the help of a characteristic property, a predicate to hold. This idea generalizes to the joint characterization of objects and operations by a set of properties, a subject that in the meantime has been studied by ZILLES and GUTTAG. Naturally, the problem is how to derive from such an implicit specification operative constructs. We will also come to this later.

So it was necessary to search for transitions between these levels. Such an approach was endorsed by COOPER having had success [5] in "removing" recursion in particular instances. In order to formulate such transitions, a notation was needed, and since transitions would always be used locally in the programming process, it was natural to use one single language throughout, a *Wide Spectrum Language* reaching from the top level of specification to the fourth, hitherto unmentioned level of data and program addresses.

Work on such a project started in 1972 within the Research Unit 49 of the German Research Council (SFB 49 der DFG) at the Technical University Munich.

The problem of a unique conceptual basis, which I had discussed around 1970 many times with G. GOOS, and on which I had published first in Russian in the proceedings of a Novosibirsk Meeting 1970 [6] as a result of ERSHOV's interest in these questions in connection with his Beta Compiler, were taken up again in my London lectures in fall 1973 and supplemented by the idea of a transformation system. DIJKSTRA had seen [1] a program (statically) as a "necklace of pearls". Going a little step further, I came to the conclusion that programming itself is nothing else than a transformation process starting from a problem specification, forming step by step a sequence of programs (corresponding to DIJKSTRA's necklace of pearls) and ending with a sufficiently efficient, sufficiently machine-oriented program.

Now, if a transformation system - a mental or a programmed one - supports this transformation process, using some wide spectrum language, then the design of such a language depends on, is guided by and has to take into account the conceptual meaning of these transformations.

Thus, we are not interested in a particular notation, and in order to demonstrate this I envisaged to have at least say an ALGOL-like version and a PASCAL-like version of one and the same Wide Spectrum Language. Establishing the necessary and worthwhile transformations can be done for a coherent family of languages that can all be used externally equally well; it will indeed be done for an abstract conceptual language, which is our present understanding of the ALGORITHMIC LANGUAGE. This is ALGOL in the original sense; "algorithmic language" is a use of words similar to "mathematical language", which also does not mean a specific notation. After all the injustice that has been done to ALGOL, SAMELSON and I claim the acronym, also in the spirit of RUTISHAUSER, for this general and original meaning.

---

[1] [1] p. 87

Giving the transformation of programs such an importance, it should not be surprising that transformation can be viewed also as defining the semantics of many of the constructs, which are mere extensions (in the sense the word was used e.g. in ALGOL 68). It can be expected to have the semantics of the full Wide Spectrum Language in such a way reduced to an applicative core ("transformational semantics"); some non-trivial investigations in connection with this aim, for example the equivalence with the FLOYD-HOARE-DIJKSTRA Semantics, will be studied in a forthcoming dissertation by PEPPER.

In the following, we shall discuss some particular aspects of a Wide Spectrum Language for Program Transformations and of the transformations themselves. Starting with a discussion of the aims of the process of program evolution, we shall first deal with the applicative core, on which language and transformation are to be based. Next, we go through some examples of usual programming language constructs that can be defined by transformations. We also study mechanisms for joint refinement of objects and operations including the introduction of pointers. In a final section, the techniques of verification versus transformation are discussed. My remarks on the programmed system that is to support the mechanical performance of the program development process will be short because actual work has started only recently, and because this part of the project lies in the hands of my friend and colleague KLAUS SAMELSON who will report about details in due course.

When in 1974 a group of people at the Institute of Informatics of the TUM started work along the ideas outlined above, the project has been given the pseudonym CIP, possibly standing for computer-aided, intuition-guided programming. The abstract Wide Spectrum Language is called CIP-L. Its dialect "Algolesian CIP-L" or ALGOL 77 for short, is usually the conversation language; at the time being "Pascalesian CIP-L" is catching up. (In the future, we will give examples in both dialects in order to prevent language prejudice to darken the issue).

The philosophy presented here is the result of long discussions and detailed studies of a group which started out with R. Gnatz, H. Wössner, U. Hill and H. Kröger; then joined by B. Krieg-Brückner, W. Hesse, F. Geiselbrechtinger on the language side, H. Partsch, P. Pepper, M. Wirsing on transformations, R. Steinbrüggen, F. Erhard, H.-O. Riethmayer, M. Luckmann on the system side; more recently M. Broy, A. Laut, B. Möller joined the group.

The aims of the process of program evolution

Programming lives on the contradiction between problems which are to be solved and the machines doing it. Both have their particular "languages" - the language of problems varying very widely, the language of machines showing relatively little differences [1]. No wonder that these languages usually do not match. But there are deeper reasons.

Problem oriented languages are not necessarily fully operative, but machine-oriented ones are. A 'problem' just tells what to find without telling how. Machines that directly elaborate existential quantifiers are in general intolerably inefficient, moreover restricted to finite domains (a search machine would not terminate if given the problem: "Find all natural numbers x such that $12x > x^2 + 33$ " and no further information).

Moreover, problem oriented languages are not necessarily deterministic, but most machines are. Problems usually say: " Find s o m e element such that ...". Moreover, frequently a problem is reduced to a 'simple' one by using some auxiliary problem of the kind above, e.g. 'find some root of a polynomial' helps to find them all. The sorting problem we will deal with later is of this kind.

Nondeterministic constructs are useful in the program development process, they allow to postpone design decisions. For example, quite a number of sorting and merging algorithms can be derived jointly in this way. There are more instruments that allow to delay design decisions. Working with abstract operations on abstract objects is one instance. Subtraction, for example, can be defined on abstract objects with two abstract operations, the unary operation 'successor' and the nullary operation 0,

```
funct sub ≡ (λ a, λ b) λ :
            if a = b then 0
                      else succ(sub(a, succ(b)))  fi
```

---

[1] At least in the class of von Neumann machines.

Let $\underline{\lambda}$ be a finite set and the mapping succ be expressed by a transition graph like

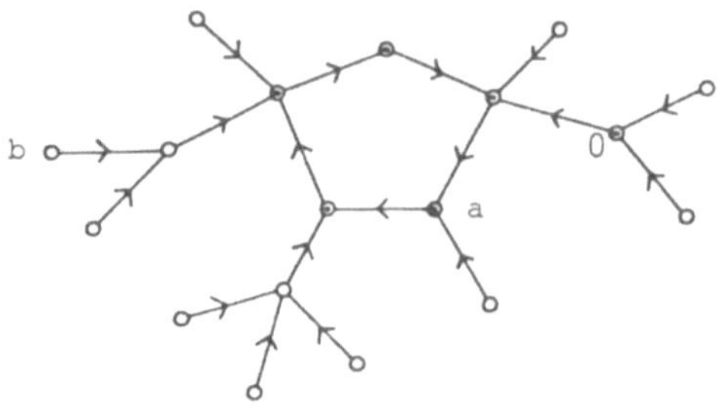

Recursion terminates, if and only if $a \geq b$ ('a' can be reached from 'b') and if so, the result is obtained by going 'as many steps' starting from 0 (the range is marked in the example by dotted circles). Only by introducing additional properties, the situation is restricted to common subtraction on the natural numbers.

Abstract objects and operations are comprised in an abstract type or abstract computation structure. Thus, *programming is based on expressing some abstract computation structure operatively in terms of another abstract computation structure*. The term 'operatively' means, that descriptive formulations are to be eliminated - this amounts to the elimination of certain quantifiers - and that non-determinism is eliminated.

But even then, an algorithm is frequently not efficient enough. *Programming also means to meliorate the efficiency of algorithms*. Frequently, appropriate development of the descriptive formulation leads directly to ameliorated operative solutions. Even fully operative and deterministic operations can often be improved. Sometimes, one has to go back to the abstract level and has to do mathematics, for example if one wants to accelerate the Fibonacci sequence by calculating F_{2j}, F_{2j+1} from F_j, F_{j+1} [7].

Another example is addition, defined similarly to subtraction above, which works too slowly. We shall find this later as an example of joint refinement both of operations and objects. *As a rule, meliorating an algorithm suggests or even requires a change in the object structure*. And it is clear that *the longer decisions are postponed, the easier it is to make them at the right moment with optimal operative gain.*

So far, it was not necessary to specify a particular class of machines to work with. Now we come to deal with reality. *Although for strictly applicative languages rather efficient machines can be built, prevailing machine languages are not applicative.*

Here we understand a strictly applicative language to be one in which existential quantifiers and non-determinism is disallowed and only recursion is left. Such languages are fully operative and CHURCH-complete. There exist, of course, theoretical text-replacement machines on this level for any given ensemble of primitive computation structures. Particular computation rules lead to the stack machine, which could be built quite economically [1], and there are other proposals for recursive machines [2].

Prevailing machines ('computers') have a number of restrictions. One is that their machine language does not cope with general recursion. This would not be so bad if they would deal at least with linear recursion, but even this is not so: repetitive recursion is all it can handle, and for doing it in the form of iteration, objects are put in containers, program variables are used.

Such an iterative machine - I would like to call it Babbage-Zuse machine - could still work with general applicative expressions determining the varying contents of the containers. Only techniques for simplifying the control flow of algorithms would be needed to bring algorithms to this level. Due to the fact that other aspects of the von Neumann machine dominate so much the scene, efforts aiming purely in this direction have started relatively late (COOPER [5]); a recent example is PARTSCH and PEPPER's dealing with a class of recursions to which the Towers of Hanoi problem belongs [8]. Some of these techniques look superficially like arithmetization of the control flow; in fact they amount generally to the introduction of suitable abstract computation structures for the 'computation' of the control flow.

We now come to the deteriorating aspects of the von Neumann-machine. They are: complete atomization and complete sequentialization. Atomization expresses the need to decompose objects and operations into atomic particles of some fixed kind or size, sequentialization the need to perform everything in a strict sequential order. Apart from being straightjackets, complete atomization and complete sequentialization amount to a loss of structure [3] and are harmful in the program development process. *The less atomized and sequentialized a program is, the more easily it is transformed for finding operative meliorations.*

---

[1] Why can a large computer not even have some of the devices a pocket calculator can have?

[2] Berkling, Magó, Hewitt.

[3] This is the reason for the difficulties of the decompilation process.

One way to keep people from passing too early to complete atomization and sequentialization is the use of a language that disallows them, followed by the use of a compiler. Every language, however, that provides fully for refinement of object and operation structures - which is needed for melioration - also allows to use these vehicles for complete atomization and sequentialization. So all we can do is to preach discipline. *To keep collateral constructs and the block structure as long as possible seems to be advisable.*

There is another dangerous aspect of the von Neumann machine, which is of quite subtle nature: organized store. On the applicative level, selective alteration of a component of a composite object is cumbersome: changing a stack at the remote end amounts to unraveling the whole stack, changing an array in some element amounts to building a new array piecemeal (c.f. DIJKSTRA [9], Ch. 11).

Having introduced variables, the step to organized store is done by replacing every variable for a composite object by a corresponding composition of variables for the elements of such an object. In connection with atomization this amounts to building every variable by composing containers for the atomic particles, called storage cells. This step makes selective updating a most trivial operation: the variable corresponding to the element to be changed is selected and is updated. Selection of this variable is done at the lowest level by an address, if the composition is an array of variables, or by a pointer. It allows tremendous operative meliorations. Its danger, which was recognized only lately (DIJKSTRA, HORNING, GRIES) lies in the fact that now variables are the result of a selection, i.e. a computing process, and therefore can coincide ('aliasing') without having the same name; assignments are then to be done with special care. This price is usually worth the operative gain, and we find organized store in all languages devoted to systems programming and in many other 'low level' languages, like ALGOL 60 (the Report speaks of 'subscripted variables') or PASCAL. Because of the limitations involved, the step to organized store (i.e. the use of selective updating) should be the last step in a program development before complete atomization and sequentialization (which then in most cases can be left to an (optimizing) compiler practically with little loss, or even sometimes with marginal gain).

Having outlined this philosophy of the program evolution process, the consequences for a language to support this process can be seen.

The applicative core of constructs for defining new operations and new object sets

As a matter of principle we treat object structures and operation structures simultaneously. The fundamental concept for doing so is the computation structure, a conglomerate of object sets and operations defined on these object sets - mathematically a (usually heterogeneous) algebra. In the extreme, the computation structure is specified only implicitly by its abstract type, i.e. by its signature and by properties of its operations (abstract computation structure). Usually, object sets and operations of a computation structure are defined, if not by enumeration, then in terms of other object sets and other operations, i.e. in terms of other computation structures which are said to be primitive with respect to the computation structure under consideration - a fundamental principle of modularization.

$\mathbb{N} \equiv (\underline{nat}, \mathrm{succ}, 0, \leq)$, the set $\underline{nat}$ of natural numbers together with the successor operation and 0 (a nullary operation) and the linear ordering $\leq$ is frequently met as a primitive and can be understood to be an abstract computation structure defined (uniquely!) by nothing but by the laws its operations obey. The same holds for $\mathbb{B} \equiv (\underline{bool}, \neg, \wedge, \vee)$, the Boolean algebra of truth values, which can, however, also be defined by enumeration.

McCARTHY discovered in 1962, that branching on condition - the if-then-else-construct - can play the role of the μ-operator of formal logic. This brings $\mathbb{B}$ into focus; $\mathbb{B}$ becomes a universal computation structure which will always be involved. Speaking of operations means that the fundamental concept of function application is available and that this application can be iterated to form general expressions. These two principles together with the principle of branching on conditions (defined with the help of boolean expressions) open already the level of recursive functions.

In practice, one rather dislikes partial functions. So-called assertions characterize the domain of definition of operations. Thus, an example is the assertion $a \geq b$ in

```
funct sub ≡ (nat a, nat b : a ≥ b) nat :
        if a = b then 0
                 else succ(sub(a, succ(b))) fi ,
```

based on $\mathbb{N}$ as a primitive.

Branching on condition, however, is only a (deterministic) special case of choice. Boolean expressions, together with the quantifiers $\forall$ ('for all') and $\exists$ ('there exists') can be used (as 'characteristic predicates') to characterize subsets to which the choice operator some can be applied.

$$\underline{\text{some}}\ \underline{\lambda}\ x : \text{succ}(x) = a$$

is such a choice, meaning intuitively

"some element from the set $\{ \underline{\lambda}\ x : \text{succ}(x) = a \}$ " .

some is undefined for the empty set, and it is convenient to have an operator that, too, which is only defined on singletons and coincides there with some .
Thus,

$$\underline{\text{funct}}\ \text{pred} \equiv (\underline{\text{nat}}\ a : a \neq 0)\ \underline{\text{nat}} :$$
$$\underline{\text{that}}\ \underline{\text{nat}}\ x : \text{succ}(x) = a$$

is the predecessor function, based on $\mathbb{N}$ as a primitive.

For later reference, we note that the equation for pred can be "solved" with the help of sub :

$$\underline{\text{funct}}\ \text{pred} \equiv (\underline{\text{nat}}\ a : a \neq 0)\ \underline{\text{nat}} : \text{sub}(a, \text{succ}(0))$$

Choices are non-deterministic, they comprise guarded expressions similar to DIJKSTRA's guarded commands:

$$\underline{\text{some}}\ \underline{\sigma}\ x : (p \wedge x \doteq a) \vee (q \wedge x \doteq b)$$

may be abbreviated to

$$\underline{\text{if}}\ p\ \underline{\text{then}}\ a$$
$$\square\ q\ \underline{\text{then}}\ b\ \ \underline{\text{fi}}$$

provided p , q are defined [1].

Choices do not define mappings, but only correspondences. The mathematical semantics of recursive definitions involving non-deterministic constructs can be based, however, on a fixpoint theory, too [10]. Such recursive definitions may even result in well-determined functions, as is shown by the example

$$\underline{\text{funct}}\ \text{pow} \equiv (\underline{\mu}\ a, \underline{\text{nat}}\ n)\ \underline{\mu} :$$
$$\underline{\text{if}}\ n = 0\ \underline{\text{then}}\ e$$
$$\square\ n > 0\ \underline{\text{then}}\ a\ \rho\ \text{pow}(a, \text{pred}(n))$$
$$\square\ n > 0 \wedge \underline{\text{even}}\ n\ \underline{\text{then}}\ \text{pow}(a\ \rho\ a, n/2)\ \ \underline{\text{fi}}$$

---

[1] $\doteq$ denotes the so-called 'strong equality', with $a \doteq b$ being true if both a and b are undefined or both are defined and equal, false otherwise.

with some computation structure ($\underline{\mu}$, ρ, e) where ρ is an associative binary operation and e an identity with respect to ρ .

Even essentially non-determinate routines may be useful. An example is given by [1]

```
funct diss ≡ (string a : a ≠ ◊)(string, char, string) :
      some (string u, char t, string v) : a = u o t o v
```

for the decomposition of a (non-empty) string into a string, a character and a string. It can be used to solve the following problem uniquely:

```
funct insort ≡ (string a, char x : isordered(a)) string :
      some string b : isordered(b) ∧
                 ∃ (string u, string v) : a = u o v ∧ b = u o x o v
```

which is nothing but a formalization of the usual verbal explanation of the sorting problem [2]. The predicate isordered is likewise defined by

```
funct isordered ≡ (string a) bool :
          if a = ◊ then true
                   else if rest(a) = ◊ then true
                                        else if top(a) > top(rest(a))
                                        then false
                                        else isordered(rest(a)) fi fi fi
```

All this is based on the primitive computation structure (string, char, o, top, rest, ◊) , where ◊ denotes the empty string.

A recursive solution for insort , based on diss , is

```
funct insort ≡ (string a, char x : isordered(a)) string :
          if a = ◊ then x
                   else if x ≤ t then insort(u, x) o t o v
                        [] x ≥ t then u o t o insort(v, x) fi
                        where (string u, char t, string v) ≡ diss(a)  fi
```

---

1 ◊ denotes the empty string.

2 Not all problems are *ab origine* defined by a characteristic predicate. In axiomatic number theory, for example, addition and multiplication are essentially defined recursively. In particular, it does not make sense to define a predicate by a characteristic predicate.

Such a solution is often found intuitively and then has to be supplemented by a correctness proof. It can, however, also be derived formally, and this requires just the same amount of labor since every formal derivation reflects a proof and vice versa.

The non-determinate function diss allows several well-determined implementations; anyone may be used and gives still a solution. They can be obtained by imposing further conditions, provided these additional conditions introduce no contradiction. In the example above, the requirement $u = ()$ gives linear sorting, the requirement $0 \leq \text{length}(u) - \text{length}(v) \leq 1$ gives binary sorting. In insort , one of the guards $x \leq t$ and $x \geq t$ can be restricted to $x < t$, $x > t$ resp. Non-determinism is a powerful tool for postponing decisions in the program development process.

This example shows us how "structuring a problem" is in the extreme done by replacing a descriptive expression by an operative expression in terms of some other descriptive expression.

On the other hand, "finding a solution" for a problem specified with the help of some (or that), ∀ and ∃ means finally the elimination of these quantifiers [1].

More general than the specification of a routine by a characteristic predicate is the specification of a whole computation structure by a (set of) characteristic predicate(s), i.e. the definition of an abstract type. To give an example:

```
type $tack ≡ (mode μ) stack μ, nullstack, isnull, top, rest,append :
     mode stack μ ,
     funct stack μ nullstack ,
     funct(stack μ) bool isnull ,
     funct(stack μ s : ¬ isnull(s)) μ top ,
     funct(stack μ s : ¬ isnull(s)) stack μ rest ,
     funct(stack μ, μ) stack μ append ,
     law A : ¬ isnull(s) ⇒ append(rest(s), top(s)) = s ,
     law R : rest(append(s,x)) = s ,
     law T : top(append(s,x)) = x ,
     law E : isnull(nullstack) ,
     law NE : ¬ isnull(append(s,x))                       endoftype
```

---

[1] There is no algorithm, no set of rules for doing this in the general case, and it is even hard to find useful classes for which it can be done mechanically. We consider any attempt to achieve this by heuristic methods, by "artificial intelligence", practically worthless.

The computation structure $\mathfrak{S}$tack (whose parameter $\underline{\mu}$ denotes some primitive object set) comprises the object set $\underline{\text{stack}\ \mu}$ and the operations isnull, append, top rest , nullstack and is characterized by the laws A , R , T , E, NE . The signature of $\mathfrak{S}$tack is expressed by a bipartite graph, the 'signature graph':

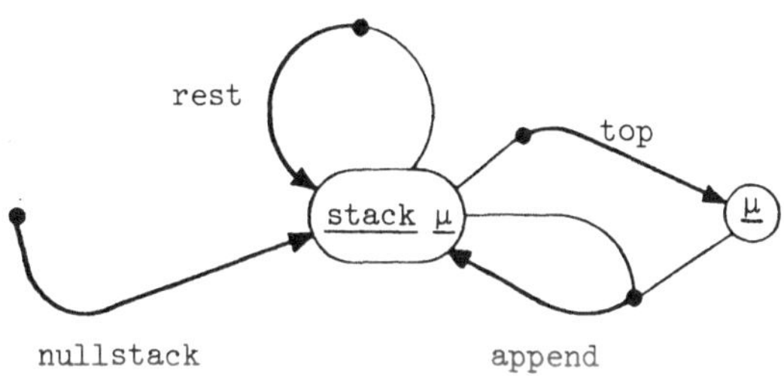

Apart from the requirement that the predicates be not contradictory, practical considerations suggest the requirement that, roughly speaking, the operations of the computation structure, based on nullary operations and primitive object sets, map *onto* the object sets of the computation structure, thus "freely generating" them ('generation principle', a requirement towards uniqueness), and *into* the primitive object sets (GUTTAG's completeness) [1]. In our example, the premise ¬ isnull(s) in A guarantees completeness, while without E , the definition is not monomorphic - although the generation principle selects the "smallest model".

Stacks and their variants: queues, decks, sequences , and object sets of cascade-type: LISP-like lists and trees have so far been the preferred examples of abstract computation structures; but there are many more interesting and practically important examples, like graph-building computation structures [11].

Abstract specifications of computation structures can be transformed into concrete definitions, replacing (partly or totally) the characteristic predicates by (in general recursive) definitions of object sets and operations.

---

[1] More precisely, one considers the set of all terms the outermost operation of which has as its range some object set of the computation structure or some primitive object set. In the first case, the object set in question is identified with the corresponding set of terms ('generated'), in the second case it is requested that equality of any such term with some object from the corresponding primitive object set can be derived from the postulated predicates.

To this end, MCCARTHY again has observed in 1963 that it suffices to have the operations of the (non-associative) direct product

$$(\underline{\mu}_1, \underline{\mu}_2, \ldots, \underline{\mu}_n)$$

of n object sets and of the (associative) direct sum

$$\underline{\mu}_1 \mid \underline{\mu}_2$$

of two (disjoint) object sets; with the nullary direct product, the 0-tuple, denoted by $()$, forming the universal object set mode empty ≡ { () } . Direct products and direct sums are used in mode declarations, for example non-recursively in

mode int ≡ (nat num, nat den)

which can be used to construct integers (together with defining an equivalence relation = on int), a rather trivial example. A recursive mode declaration is used in the following sample concretization of $Stack ($\underline{\mu}$) with $\underline{\mu}$ as a primitive:

```
⌈mode stack μ ≡ empty | (stack μ trunk, μ item) ,
 funct nullstack ≡ stack μ : () ,
 funct isnull ≡ (stack μ s) bool : s = nullstack ,
 funct top ≡ (stack μ s : ¬ isnull(s)) μ : item of s ,
 funct rest ≡ (stack μ s : ¬ isnull(s)) stack μ : trunk of s ,
 funct append ≡ (stack μ s , μ x) stack μ:(s, x)              ⌋
```

Here, trunk of and item of are selector functions, defined by the notation (stack $\underline{\mu}$ trunk, $\underline{\mu}$ item) for the direct product; stack $\underline{\mu}$:(•, •) is the corresponding constructor. Properties A , R , T , E , NE are wellknown properties of the direct product.

Less trivial examples are the bounded stack 𝔹stack ($\underline{\mu}$, n) or cascade-type ('tree-like') computation structures based on

mode casc μ ≡ empty | (casc μ left, μ node, casc μ right) .

A given type does by its signature Σ and properties E not always monomorphically characterize computation structures [1]; we may speak of a model of (Σ, E) as "some model of that type", which is again a non-deterministic construct. Again, non-determinism helps to postpone decisions in the design process.

---

[1] There are certain distinguished models, the "initial algebra" and the "terminal algebra"; if they coincide the type is monomorphic.

Constructs defined by transformations

A few kinds of basic transformations of constructs within the applicative core are to be listed. This is UNFOLD, the substitution of a call by the body of the function called, which has to be treated with care in non-deterministic situations, and reciprocally FOLD, which has to be handled carefully with respect to termination.

A further example of a basic (one-sided) transformation is RESTRICT, the restriction of the choice set :

$$\frac{\underline{\text{some}}\ \underline{\mu}\ x : p(x)}{\underline{\text{some}}\ \underline{\mu}\ x : q(x)} \quad \left\{ (\forall\ \underline{\mu}\ x : q(x) \Rightarrow p(x)) \wedge (\exists\ \underline{\mu}\ x : p(x) \Rightarrow \exists\ \underline{\mu}\ x : q(x)) \right.$$

which in the extreme allows transition to a choice the choice set of which is a singleton. This is the case where we may write

$$\underline{\text{that}}\ \underline{\mu}\ x : q(x) .$$

Guarded expressions are (see above) notational shorthand for some choices which are met frequently. This is the first example of a defining transformation.
The alternative (if-then-else-fi construction)

if p then a else b fi

is then defined as the exclusive choice

if p then a
▯ ¬ p then b fi

The commutativity of guarded expressions and the possibility to exchange the two branches of an if-then-else-fi - construction under negation of the condition follow from the definition, using properties of the universal computation structure $\mathbb{B}$.

The example of isordered suggests the introduction of McCarthy's sequential alternative in the form

```
if a = ()                        then true
elsf rest(a) = ()                then true
elsf top(a) > top(rest(a))       then false
                                 else isordered(rest(a)) fi
```

with an obvious defining transformation. Now commutativity of the branches is lost.

In recent years, we have even seen the treatment of most of the constructs of programming languages outside the applicative core by mathematical semantics ('denotational semantics') and thus a reduction of these concepts to the applicative core. If we wish to base programming on program transformation, it would be natural to define these constructs directly by transformations from and to the core.

Indeed, in a number of cases this is not only possible but quite simple and practical. An example is the introduction of a block structure through subordinate routines and auxiliary object declarations.

Let f and g be two different routines out of a system, and let the routine f have the parameters $x_1, x_2, \ldots, x_n$.

The parameter x_i of f is said to be *constant* if a call $f(a_1, a_2, \ldots a_n)$ leads to no other calls of f than ones which have the object a_i in the i-th parameter position. If now f is called in some expression within g , we can 'suppress' the parameter x_i of f and 'subordinate' (a copy of) f to the expression; x_i becomes 'global' for this 'scope', which is to be indicated by block parentheses begin end or rather ⌈ ⌋ for short. This process of parameter suppression is normally done subconciously by a programmer who is familiar with mathematical notation. In a similar way, a system of routines can be subordinated.

Take for example the system of two routines standing side by side (with ≤ , - and 0 as primitives)

```
funct gcd ≡ (nat a, nat b) nat :
    if b = 0 then a else gcd(b, mod(a, b)) fi ,
funct mod ≡ (nat c, nat d) nat :
    if c < d then c else mod(c - d, d) fi
```

Here, the second parameter d in mod is constant. If we subordinate mod to the body of gcd , d may be suppressed in a reduced mod' and replaced by a global parameter.

We obtain as body of gcd a *block with a routine declaration,*

```
funct gcd ≡ (nat a, nat d) nat :
            ⌈if d = 0 then a else gcd(d, mod'(a)) fi
             where funct mod' ≡ (nat c) nat :
                   if c < d then c else mod'(c - d) fi ⌋
```

or even more localised

```
funct gcd ≡ (nat a, nat d) nat :
            if d = 0 then a else ⌈gcd(d, mod'(a))
                                  where funct mod' ≡ (nat c) nat :
                                  if c < d then c else mod'(c - d) fi⌋ fi
```

On the other hand, using again for short ⌈ for begin and ⌋ for end , *a block with a collective object declaration* [1]

$$\underline{r}:\lceil (\underline{m}_1\ x_1\ ,\ \ldots,\ \underline{m}_n\ x_n) \equiv (E_1\ ,\ \ldots,\ E_n) \quad \underline{\text{within}}\ G(x_1\ ,\ \ldots,\ x_n) \rfloor$$

is by definition a shorthand for the application of the routine

$$(\underline{m}_1\ x_1\ ,\ \ldots,\ \underline{m}_n\ x_n)\ \underline{r}\ :\ G(x_1\ ,\ \ldots,\ x_n)$$

to the argument set $(E_1\ ,\ \ldots,\ E_n)$.

Note that the block with parameterless subordinated routines

```
⌈G(f1 ... fn)
 where funct f1 ≡ m1 : E1
       funct f2 ≡ m2 : E2
             :
       funct fn ≡ mn : En  ⌋
```

is by definition essentially different from the above construct; G may involve repeated calls of f_1 , ... f_n . It is, of course, always possible to replace an object by a (parameterless) routine, but the converse is only true if $E_1,\ldots,E_n$ are determinate.

---

[1] The mode specification $\underline{r}$: is usually suppressed.

Object declarations may be used to extract common subexpressions; in any case they can serve to express more explicitly the natural 'stream of evaluation' that results from a 'call by value' computation rule [1]. Iterated use of the transformation

```
f(g(x))
   |
 --+--
   ↓
⌈ λ y ≡ g(x) within f(y) ⌋
```

establishes isolation of nested calls. A notational convenience, somewhat similar to the 'sequential alternative', is to write (with an obvious defining transformation)

```
⌈real h1 ≡ a - 1 ; real h2 ≡ h1 × t - 3 ; real h3 ≡ h2 × t - 5 ; h3 ⌋
```

instead of the nested, right-aligning construct

```
⌈real h1 ≡ t - 1 within ⌈real h2 ≡ h1 × t - 3 within ⌈real h3 ≡ h2 × t - 5 within h3⌋⌋⌋
```

which isolates the Horner operations of $((t-1) \times t-3) \times t-5$.

The next logical step is the introduction of program variables as a sort of re-usable object names. This step leads definitely outside the applicative level. It can be done by a defining transformation, too. Details of this approach will be found in a forthcoming dissertation by P. PEPPER. It has to be demonstrated that this transformation allows to define the classical 'state-oriented' semantics of constructs with program variables, thus establishing correspondence to the FLOYD-HOARE predicate relations and to DIJSTRA's predicate transformation.

The crucial point is, of course, the phenomenon of repetition and the way it is reflected as iteration when working with program variables. The transformation

```
funct F ≡ (m A) n :                     |   funct F ≡ (m A) n :
  if P1(A) then F(E1(A))                |     ⌈var m a := A ; G where
  ▯  P2(A) then E2(A)    fi          <-+->     proc G ≡ n :
                                        |        if P1(a) then a := E1(a); G
                                        |        ▯  P2(a) then E2(a)          fi ⌋
```

---

[1] DE ROEVER [12] has given this alternative to the classical fixpoint theory as used by MANNA; in it the leftmost-innermost ('call by value') computation rule is a safe rule.

(where $P1 \vee P2 =$ true), shows the essential steps in going from a purely applicative, recursive construct for F to iteration: introduction of a program variable helps to isolate the call of F . Next, the constant parameter can be suppressed, which leads to the parameterless procedure G .

This is the essence of the metamorphosis, and what follows is merely notational. It is widely accepted to write iteration in the while -form; the obvious definitory transformation results in (*) below. Combining an idea of DIJKSTRA [9] with the leave -construct already mentioned in [13], an alternative notation (**) can be used:

```
    proc G ≡ n :                                 proc G ≡ n :
(*)  ⌈while P1(a) do a := E1(a) od ;      (**)    do if P1(a) then a := E1(a)
      E2(a)                           ⌋              ▯ P2(a) then E2(a) leave fi od
```

It offers more flexibility, in particular when the recursion occurs together with multiple branching; possible non-determinism is preserved. It comprises also the until -form of iteration and the " (n + 1/2) -times iteration". The while -form, on the other hand, is natural in the case of an if-then-else-fi -situation, i.e. if in the example above $P2 = \neg P1$. In general, the while -form (*) is a deterministic implementation.

The general do ... od -construct (**) above is a shorthand with the obvious meaning of repetition until leaving. This can be indicated also by interpreting the call of the parameterless procedure G as a jump to the beginning of G ; a further jump return , replacing leave , ends the procedure. Thus

```
           proc G ≡ n :
  (***)      g : if P1(a) then a := E1(a) ; goto g
                 ▯ P2(a) then E2(a) return          fi
```

This gives the loop - form of iteration, a return immediately before the fi being usually suppressed. In this way, systems of recursive definitions can be treated as well. Whichever of these three notations is used, recursion can be replaced by iteration fully if and only if every call of a procedure of the system is a *plain call* [1], i.e. the last action of the surrounding body. A jump is a notational variant of a plain call of a parameterless procedure - a special case where the calling mechanism can be utterly simplified (The BLISS compiler did already recognize this situation).

---

1 Germ. "schlichter Prozedurwechsel".

Systems which fulfil the aforementioned requirement are called repetitive. Non-repetitive systems can always be transformed into repetitive ones at the expense of introducing stacks; frequently one can do better, however. To discuss special techniques for this [14] is not possible in the frame of this paper.

Transformation of computation structures

Transformation of computation structures involves not only the modification of routines, but also the modification of mode declarations.

'Structuring the problem' may mean in the extreme to concretize some abstract computation structure in terms of some other abstract computation structure. An example with a situation quite similar to the above treatment of insort with the help of diss is the concretization of the abstract computation structure $\mathbb{N}$ ≡ (nat, succ, 0) (the characteristic properties of which, the "Peano axioms", are well known) with the help of the abstract computation structure $\mathbb{S}$tack(μ) for some one-element set : mode μ ≡ {|} ,

```
mode nat ≡ stack {|} ,
funct succ ≡ (stack {|} a) stack {|} : append(a, |)
funct 0 ≡ stack {|} : nullstack
```

Compared with the clumsy solution given above, pred can now be defined simply by

```
funct pred ≡ (stack {|} a : ¬ isnull(a)) stack {|} : rest(a)
```

In such a way, an appropriate change of object structure often simplifies operations. As another example, let us use a stack of binary elements {O, L} for the concretization of natural numbers.

Addition in $\mathbb{N}$at , which is defined by

```
funct add ≡ (nat a, nat b) nat :
     if b = 0 then a
               else succ(add(a, pred(b))) fi
```

uses pred, which works efficiently in the $\mathbb{S}$tack ({|}) implementation. However, with the help of a unary operation double ,

```
funct double ≡ (nat a ) nat : add(a, a)
```

and its inverse half defined for even a , using the properties (which can be proved formally)

double(add(m, n)) = add(double(m), double(n))

and commutativity of add , the number of recursive invocations of add can be decreased drastically:

```
funct add ≡ (nat a, nat b) nat :
     if b = 0 then a
     [] a = 0 then b
     [] b ≠ 0 ∧ a ≠ 0 then  if even(a) ∧ even(b) then double(add(half(a),half(b)))
                            [] ¬ even(b)         then succ(add(a, pred(b)))
                            [] ¬ even(a)         then succ(add(pred(a), b))     fi¹
```

This suggests a change from Nat to Stack({0, L}) , where the operation double , the predicate even, and the operation half are trivially implemented by

```
funct double ≡ (stack {0, L} a) stack {0, L} : append(a, 0) ,
funct even   ≡ (stack {0, L} a) bool : if isnull(a) then true else top(a) = 0 fi,
funct half   ≡ (stack {0, L} a : even(a)) stack {0, L} : if isnull(a) then a
                                                          else rest(a) fi
```

For the connaisseur, it should be remarked that not only Stack ({I}) is isomorphic to the term algebra of (succ, 0) , but Stack ({0, L}) is also related to the term algebra of (succ, double, 0) , as is demonstrated by comparing e.g.

```
succ(double(succ(double(succ(double(double(succ(0))))))))
     L           L           L       0      L
```

with LOLLL .

The abstract stacks used here may be concretized, on the other hand, by using McCarthy's recursive definition. This corresponds to replacing functions defined by a predicate by functions defined recursively.

---

[1] Note that with true instead of the guards ¬ even(b) and ¬ even(a) , the algorithm would be correct, too; the guards speed up the execution, however.

To give a more complicated example, we define an abstract computation structure 𝔊rex of aggregates [1]:

```
type 𝔊rex ≡ (mode μ, mode index) grex μ, put, get, init :
     mode grex μ ,
     funct (grex μ, index, μ) grex μ put ,
     funct (grex μ, index) μ get ,
     funct grex μ vac ,
     law S : get(put(a, i, x), j) = if i = j then x
                                    ▯ i ≠ j then get(a, j) fi ,
     law U : get(vac, j) = ω ,
     law E : put(a, i, x) ≠ vac ,
     law I : put(a, i, get(a, i)) = a                     endoftype
```

This structure describes a very archaic form of arrays, of indexed sets with vac being the vacuous set *ab origine*; put and get are operations which are in practice frequently used in connection with background storage (in data bank systems: 'direct access'). The domain of get is defined recursively by

```
funct isaccessible ≡ (grex μ a, index i) bool :
         if a = vac then false
         ▯ a ≠ vac then (grex μ a', index i') ≡ some grex μ b, index j :
                                       ∃ μ x' : a = put(b, j, x') within
                        i = i' ∨ isaccessible(a', i)                  fi
```

A structure 𝔽lex , which comprises in abstract form what one usually understands to be a (one-sided) flexible array, is defined as follows [2] (index is now a *well-ordered* set with least element min)

```
type 𝔽lex ≡ (mode μ, mode index) flex μ, init, isinit, ext, rem, hib, alt, sel:
   mode flex μ ,
   funct flex μ init ,
   funct (flex μ) bool isinit ,
   funct (flex μ, μ) flex μ ext ,
   funct (flex μ f : ¬ isinit(f)) flex μ rem ,
   funct (flex μ f : ¬ isinit(f)) index hib ,
   funct (flex μ f, index i, μ : ¬ isinit(f) ∧ i ≤ hib(f)) flex μ alt ,
   funct (flex μ f, index i : ¬ isinit(f) ∧ i ≤ hib(f)) μ sel ,
```

---

[1] Latin *grex*: flock. GUTTAG: Hoare-like array (HOARE 1973).

[2] For simplicity we use here the one-sided half of Dijkstra's ARRAYs: [9], Ch. 11

```
law I    : isinit(init) ,
law NI   : ¬ isinit(ext(f,m)) ∧ ¬ isinit(alt(f,i,m))
law HIB1 : hib(ext(f,m)) = if  isinit(f) then min
                           [] ¬ isinit(f) then succ(hib(f)) fi ,
law HIB2 : ¬ isinit(f) ∧ i ≤ hib(f) ⇒ hib(rem(f)) = pred(hib(f)) ,
law HIB3 : ¬ isinit(f) ∧ i ≤ hib(f) ⇒ hib(alt(f,i,m)) = hib(f) ,
law IR   : ¬ isinit(f) ⇒ isinit(rem(f)) = (hib(f) = min) ,

law SEL1 : ¬ isinit(f) ∧ i ≤ succ(hib(f)) ⇒
           sel(ext(f,m), i) = if i = succ(hib(f)) then m
                              [] i ≠ succ(hib(f)) then sel(f,i) fi ,
law SEL2 : ¬ isinit(f) ∧ i ≤ pred(hib(f)) ⇒
           sel(rem(f) , i) = sel(f, i) ,
law SEL3 : ¬ isinit(f) ∧ i ≤ hib(f) ∧ j ≤ hib(f) ⇒
           sel(alt(f,i,m), j) = if i = j then m
                                [] i ≠ j then sel(f, j) fi      endoftype
```

Now, a concretization of 𝔽lex in terms of 𝔾rex is possible; hib is carried along in the object structure explicitly:

```
⌈ mode flex μ ≡ (index p, grex μ d) ,
  funct init   ≡ flex μ : (ω , vac) ,
  funct isinit ≡ (flex μ a) bool : p of a = ω ,
  funct ext    ≡ (flex μ a, μ x) flex μ :
                 if isinit(a) then (min, put(d of a, min, x))
                              else (succ(p of a), put(d of a, succ(p of a), x))fi,
  funct rem    ≡ (flex μ a:¬ isinit(a)) flex μ :
                 if p of a = min then init else (pred(p of a), d of a) fi ,
  funct hib    ≡ (flex μ a) index : p of a ,
  funct alt    ≡ (flex μ a, index i, μ x : ¬ isinit(a) ∧ i ≤ hib(a)) flex μ a :
                 (p of a, put(d of a, i, x)) ,
  funct sel    ≡ (flex μ a, index i : ¬ isinit(a) ∧ i ≤ hib(a)) μ :
                 get(d of a, i)
```

In turn, a concretization of 𝕊tack in terms of 𝔽lex is possible: init , ext , rem , and sel applied to hib , resp., yield nullstack , append , rest and top, resp.. Bounded stacks can be implemented in this way, too.

Thus, several interesting types of "linear" object structures are reduced to 𝔾rex(μ, index) . Implementations 'in bounded homogeneous storage' can be obtained by first restricting

𝔾rex(μ, index)

to

Grex (μ, index [lwb .. upb])

and then passing to

index [lwb .. upb] array μ ,

the elementary rowing, i.e. to classical arrays (vac is represented by a row all elements of which are ⊖). However, this makes put and thus alt to complicated operations, since they involve now selective alteration.
In contrast to this "row" technique of implementing linear object structures is the "list" technique. It uses a representation for Flex in terms of Stack :

```
mode flex μ ≡ (index p, stack μ d) ,
funct init   ≡ flex μ : (⊖ , nullstack) ,
funct isinit≡ (flex μ a) bool : p of a = ⊖ ,
funct ext    ≡ (flex μ a, μ x) flex μ : (if isinit(a) then min
                                                       else succ(p of a) fi ,
                                          append(d of a, x)                    ) ,
funct rem    ≡ (flex μ a : ¬ isinit(a)) flex μ :
                 if p of a = min then init
                                 else (pred(p of a), rest(d of a)) fi ,
funct hib    ≡ (flex μ a) index : p of a ,
funct alt    ≡ (flex μ a, index i, μ x : ¬ isinit(a) ∧ i ≤ hib(a)) flex μ :
                ⌈(p of a, altl (d of a, p of a)) where
                  funct altl ≡ (stack μ s, index j) stack μ :
                        if j = i then append(rest(s), x)
                                 else altl(rest(s), pred(j))  fi ⌋ ,
funct sel    ≡ (flex μ a, index i : ¬ isinit(a) ∧ i ≤ hib(a)) μ :
                if i = hib(a) then top(d of a)
                              else sel(rem(a), i)             fi
```

The final step, which corresponds somewhat to the introduction of gotos in routines, is the implementation of recursive modes as Lists (with capital L in the sense of KNUTH) with the help of pointers. The transformation is done quite mechanically; we demonstrate this again for Stack :

We represent stack μ , defined by

mode stack μ ≡ empty | (stack μ trunk, μ item)

by pointers either to () or to a pair (stack μ trunk, μ item).

(A pointer to the 0-tuple () is universally denoted by nil).

We then have in two steps

```
mode stack μ ≡ pt stack' μ
mode stack' μ ≡ empty |(stack μ trunk, μ item)
```

Whenever a stack is formed by the constructor stack μ:(•,•) , we denote the generation of a pointer to that object by newpt , like newpt stack' μ:(a, x) . The transcription of append then reads

```
funct append ≡ (pt stack' μ a, μ x) pt stack'μ  : newpt stack'μ:(a, x) ,
```

top and rest are simply transcribed as

```
funct  top ≡ (pt stack' μ a : a ≠ nil) μ : item of a
funct rest ≡ (pt stack' μ a : a ≠ nil) pt stack' μ : trunk of a ,
```

nullstack is represented by nil and

```
funct isnull ≡ (stack μ a) bool : a = nullstack
```

becomes

```
funct isnull ≡ (pt stack' μ a) bool : a = nil .
```

The introduction of pointers, however, presupposes that another transition is made before: variables for composite objects are represented by a corresponding composition of variables for these objects. This means the introduction of containers, of organized store. It transforms selective alteration, which is a complicated operation on the applicative level, to selective updating, which is a simple operation. Selective updating, however, in connection with pointers can be used to replace certain recursions over composite objects by a simple operation. This can be demonstrated by the operation stalk ,

```
funct stalk ≡ (μ x, stack μ s) stack μ :
              if isnull(s) then append(nullstack, x)
                           else append(stalk(x, rest(s)), top(s)) fi
```

which raises a stack at the remote end. Thus, in the iteration

```
funct convert ≡ (nat A) stack {0, L} :
     ⌈(var nat a, var stack {0, L} s) := (A, nullstack) ;
      while a ≠ 0 do (a,s) := if even(a) then (a/2, stalk(0, s))
                                         else ((a - 1)/2, stalk(0, s)) fi od ;
              s                                                                ⌋
```

stalk would perpetually run up and down the stack. Using pointers, selective updating and a pointer variable ss for s as well as an auxiliary pointer variable tt , we can replace the particle s := stalk(x, s) by

⌈pt stack' μ f ≡ newpt stack' μ : (nil, x) ; next of tt := f ; tt := f ⌋

except for the first step, which is simply

⌈pt stack' μ f ≡ newpt stack' μ : (nil, x) ; ss := f ; tt := f ⌋

Finally ss delivers the result $f^{(1)}$, the pointer generated in the first incarnation,all other pointers being used only internally.
For a more detailed discussion, in particular of the pointer representation of 'infinite objects' like ring lists and doubly linked lists, see [15].
For the "row" technique mentioned above, the introduction of containers means transition to index [lwb..upb] array var μ . It turns put and alt into simple updating operations on the selected containers.

Verification versus transformation

Verification techniques, based on the FLOYD - HOARE semantics and DIJKSTRA's predicate transformers, generally work with program variables and usually require purely iterative situations. If the problem specification is given recursively by a repetitive system, then the iterative form is a mere transliteration of it. If such an iterative form falls from heaven, (or is given to a student as an exercise), then finding the proof amounts to finding "the invariant condition" and this may be quite a puzzle for the naive programmer. But real programs do not fall from heaven.

Clearly, the postcondition from which to start the verification process corresponds to the characteristic predicate of the problem description, and the precondition which stands at the end of the verification process corresponds to an assertion for the descriptive construct.

Moreover, if (as mentioned above) the program and its verification are developed step by step, there is a corresponding program transformation, too, and vice versa. It may depend on taste and prejudice what form one prefers. As in mathematics, verification of a result that is obtained somewhat informally can be technically shorter then the correct derivation. In particular, verifying that a program fulfils some assertion can be done 'streamlined', avoiding many corners and eddies into which the bulky program transformation mechanism is going.

We think, however, that derivation of a solution by program transformations, as sketched above, has its merits, too: not only can it be done in one and the same language, it naturally leads to structured solutions and should please the followers of structured programming. It allows in particular to follow several alleys to the solution, side by side.

Program development by transformations can be done mentally, supported by paper and pencil. A programmed support system, however, can be very helpful: it takes over the clerical work, including keeping a record of the development history. Its main advantage seems to be that all steps can be checked mechanically, and thus genuinely correct versions will be obtained. The effort may be too expensive when only a dirty one-time program (throw-away program) is needed - whatever use this may have. The effort is worthwhile for programs that run for a long time, in particular if their reliability is subject to public or economic requirements. This includes the fabrication of large programs which are to be placed on one chip in permanent superhigh-integration technique, one day big enough to comprise a small compiler or a building block of an operating system, not to speak of arithmetic units and storage communication units. The techniques we develop today may have some bearing on the production of quality software tomorrow. In the end, transformation techniques and verification techniques go hand in hand.

References

[1] J.N. Buxton, B. Randell(eds.): Software engineering techniques. NATO Scientific Affairs Division, Bruxelles, 1970

[2] F.L. Bauer, G. Goos: Informatik - Eine einführende Übersicht. 2 Vols. 2nd ed. Springer, 1973, 1974

[3] P.J. Landin: The next 700 programming languages. Comm. ACM 9, 157-166 (1966)

[4] D. Scott: Data types as lattices. SIAM Journal of Computing 5, 522-587 (1976)

[5] D.C. Cooper: The equivalence of certain computations. Computer Journal 9, 45-52 (1966)

[6] F.L. Bauer: Programming Languages under Educational and under Professional Aspects (Russian). In: Proceedings 2nd All-Union Conference on Programming, Novosibirsk, February 1970

[7] E.W. Dijkstra: In honour of Fibonacci. EWD654. In: Lecture Notes of the International Summer School on Program Construction, Marktoberdorf, 1978

[8] H. Partsch, P. Pepper: A family of rules for recursion removal related to the Towers of Hanoi problem. Institut für Informatik der Technischen Universität München, Rep. No. 7612, 1976. Also: Information Processing Letters, 5, 1974 - 1977 (1976)

[9] E.W. Dijkstra: A discipline of programming. Prentice-Hall, Englewood Cliffs, N.J., 1976

[10] H. Egli: A mathematical model for nondeterministic computations. ETH Zürich, 1975

[11] T.A. Matzner: Entwicklung eines Algorithmus für Depth-first-search mit einer einfachen Anwendung. In: Algorithmen und Objektstrukturen. Institut für Informatik der Technischen Universität München, Interner Bericht, 1978

[12] W.P. de Roever: Operational, mathematical and axiomatized semantics for recursive procedures and data structures. Mathematisch Centrum, Amsterdam, 1974

[13] W.A. Wulf, D.B. Russell, A.N. Habermann: BLISS: A language for systems programming. Comm. ACM 14, 780-790 (1971)

[14] F.L. Bauer, H. Partsch, P. Pepper, H. Wössner: Techniques for program development. In: Software Engineering Techniques. Infotech State of the Art Report 34. Maidenhead: Infotech International 1977, p. 25-30

[15] F.L. Bauer: Detailization and lazy evaluation, infinite objects and pointer representation. Lecture Notes of the International Summer School on Program Construction, Marktoberdorf, 1978

METHODEN DER PROGRAMM- UND SYSTEMKONSTRUKTION: EIN STATUSBERICHT

A. Endres
IBM Entwicklung und Forschung
7030 Böblingen/Württ.

KURZFASSUNG

Der Beitrag gibt einen überblick über das Spektrum der Methoden und Hilfsmittel, die heute dem Entwickler eines DV-Systems zur Verfügung stehen. Es wird besonders abgehoben auf die Veränderungen während der letzten zehn Jahre, sowohl was das Angebot an Methoden betrifft als auch die Anforderungen der Aufgabenstellung. Die betrachteten Methoden und Hilfsmittel werden eingebettet in einen typischen Projektablauf und bewertet nach ihrer Akzeptanz und ihrer relativen Bedeutung. Auf einige aktuelle Forschungsschwerpunkte und die dabei adressierten Probleme wird hingewiesen. Der Beitrag enthält ein ausführliches Literaturverzeichnis.

EINLEITUNG

Für die Methodendiskussion in Informatik und Datenverarbeitung bedeutet das Jahr 1968, rückblickend betrachtet, so etwas wie einen historischen Einschnitt. Es waren Ereignisse des Jahres 1968, die einige der bisherigen Grundsätze in Frage stellten und die einer nachfolgenden breitwirkenden Entwicklung Namen und Richtung gaben. Gemeint sind *Dijkstras* (1968a, b, c) grundlegende Veröffentlichungen zum Thema Strukturierte Programmierung und die Garmischer Tagung über "Software Engineering" (siehe *Naur/Randell* (1968)).

Laut Aussage der Veranstalter der Garmischer Tagung war damals der Begriff "Software Engineering" an sich als Provokation gedacht. Ob dieser Effekt erzielt worden ist oder nicht, sei dahingestellt. Tatsache ist, daß der Begriff anschließend als programmatischer Appel aufgefaßt worden ist, und zum Synonym wurde für eine ganze Reihe neuerer Methoden und insbesondere für den Versuch einer verfahrenstechnischen Integration dieser und älterer Methoden zu einem modernen Methodengebäude. Auch Dijkstras Adjektiv "strukturiert" wurde zum Schlagwort und zum Etikett für alle möglichen Dinge, die sich einen modernen Anstrich geben wollten.

Zehn Jahre nach Garmisch reizt es sehr, sich einige der damaligen Gedanken und Thesen noch einmal ins Gedächtnis zurückzurufen und sich zu fragen, was sich seither eigentlich geändert (oder auch nicht geändert) hat. Jemand, der auch die zehn Jahre *vor* 1968 auf demselben Tätigkeitsgebiet erlebt hat, ist natürlich bestrebt, auch den Weisheiten früherer Jahre ihren gerechten Platz nicht streitig zu machen.

Beide angedeuteten Themen beziehen sich schwerpunktmäßig auf Probleme der Programmierung. Daß ich für diesen Beitrag jedoch einen etwas weiteren Titel gewählt habe, folgt aus der Überzeugung, daß man *Programm- und Systementwicklung* als eine Einheit ansehen muß. Die Tätigkeit, mit der sich unsere Kollegen in der Praxis befassen, und auf die der Informatikernachwuchs vorbereitet werden muß, ist nicht nur die Programmerstellung, sondern die Konzeption, Entwicklung und der Betrieb von DV-Systemen. Ein *DV-System* entsteht durch das Zusammenwirken von Geräten, Daten, Programmen und organisatorischen Abläufen.

Man kann häufig die Ansicht hören, daß das Programmaterial (oder die Software) diejenige Komponente sei, die das ganze System zusammenhält und charakterisiert. Dem muß entgegengehalten werden, daß es heute immer häufiger Betriebsformen gibt, bei denen die Daten im Mittelpunkt stehen, wo die Programme von untergeordneter Bedeutung sind und sich an den Daten ausrichten (siehe *Bachman* (1973)). Daß Programmierer sich auf einen Problemkreis konzentrieren können, der unabhängig von der verwendeten Gerätetechnik ist, scheint auch nur der Ausfluß eines bestimmten Standes der gerätetechnischen Entwicklung und des dadurch besonders bevorzugten Stapelbetriebs gewesen zu sein. Ein modernes DV-System ist ein interaktives Datenbanksystem, das seine Leistungen auch geographisch verteilten Benutzern am Ort anbietet. Seine Konstruktion ist nicht denkbar, ohne daß die Art der Datenstationen, die Verteilung der Prozessorleistung oder die Verbindungen zwischen einzelnen Geräten in die Betrachtung einbezogen werden. Auch hier hat, von einigen Anwendern sicherlich mehr als von der akademischen Welt beachtet, vor zehn Jahren die Neuzeit begonnen.

Der organisatorische Rahmen, in dem die meisten DV-Systeme entwickelt werden, ist der eines Projekts. Einem *Projekt* stehen zur Verfügung, bzw. es verbraucht alle die Betriebsmittel, die erforderlich sind, um ein bestimmtes System*produkt* zu entwickeln.

Es ist das Ziel der jeweiligen Verfahrenstechnik, gleichgültig ob das Endprodukt ein DV-System, ein Flugzeug oder eine Autobahnbrücke ist, folgende drei Parameter zu optimieren:

(a) die Produktivität der Betriebsmittel

(b) die Qualität des Produkts und

(c) die Projektführung

Eine hohe Produktivität wird erzielt, wenn die relative Leistung bezogen auf die Gesamtheit aller eingesetzten Betriebsmittel hoch ist im Vergleich zu ähnlichen Projekten. Die Qualität des Produkts ist entscheidend für seinen späteren Nutzwert. Die Güte der Projektführung drückt sich aus als Kosten- oder Termintreue, oder allgemeiner als das Maß der Übereinstimmung zwischen geschätztem und tatsächlichem Verbrauch von Betriebsmitteln. Methoden, die das Risiko von Fehleinschätzungen reduzieren, unterstützen die Projektführung.

Eine *Verfahrenstechnik* ist ein Gebäude, bestehend aus Grundsätzen, Methoden und Hilfsmitteln. Innerhalb eines bestimmten Projektes kommt immer nur eine Untermenge von Methoden zur Anwendung, abhängig von den zu lösenden Teilaufgaben. In welcher Reihenfolge welche Teilaufgaben am besten gelöst werden, ist eine Frage, die wieder zur Verfahrenstechnik gehört.

Methoden sind systematische Verfahren und Vorgehensweisen, die angewandt werden können, um eine bestimmte Aufgabe zu lösen. Eine Methode ist dann *akzeptiert*, wenn eine signifikante Untermenge aller potentiellen Benutzer über einen längeren Zeitraum hinweg von einer Methode Gebrauch macht. Methoden beruhen häufig, aber nicht immer, auf anerkannten Grundsätzen oder Prinzipien. *Grundsätze* sind Denkweisen oder Überzeugungen, die als Ergebnis früherer Erfahrungen oder aufgrund von Nachdenken gewonnen wurden. Methoden werden häufig durch eigens dafür entwickelte *Hilfsmittel* oder Werkzeuge unterstützt. Der Nutzwert einer Methode und ihre Akzeptanz hängen oft von den zur Verfügung stehenden Hilfsmitteln ab. Im Falle von DV-Methoden haben Hilfsmittel sehr häufig die Form eines Programms. Wir sprechen dann von automatisierten Verfahren. Andere Formen von Hilfsmitteln können genauso nützlich sein, je nach Aufgabe.

Zu dieser Kategorie gehören Formelsammlungen, Tabellen, Prüflisten, Fragebogen, Formulare und Schablonen. Die Bedeutung einer Methode richtet sich nicht allein nach ihrer Akzeptanz. Andere Gesichtspunkte sind die Wichtigkeit der von ihr unterstützten Tätigkeit, der erzielbare Nutzen und die Vorhersehbarkeit oder Gleichmäßigkeit der erzielten Ergebnisse.

Für die Methoden der Programm- und Systemkonstruktion, über die wir im folgenden sprechen werden, muß man zugestehen, daß sie nicht alle auf denselben Grundsätzen beruhen, wobei hier vor allem zwischen Praktikern noch am ehesten eine Übereinstimmung zu erzielen ist. Da es selbst bei übereinstimmenden Grundsätzen mehrere Wege zum selben Ziel geben kann, sind wir heute mit einem unwahrscheinlich reichen Spektrum von Methoden konfrontiert, die alle in irgendeiner Weise relevant sind. Für Hilfsmittel gilt dasselbe.

Der für diesen Bericht zur Verfügung stehende Raum reicht natürlich nicht aus, um alle Methoden und Hilfsmittel zu beschreiben. Hierfür gibt es Broschüren und Handbücher, und mindestens pro Methode eins. Das beigefügte Literaturverzeichnis kann hier gegebenenfalls weiterhelfen. Da ich einen Eindruck vermitteln möchte für die Breite des Methodenangebots, sind im Tabellenteil mehr Methoden und Hilfsmittel erwähnt, als ich im Text diskutieren werde. Im Text werde ich mich auf die Methoden konzentrieren, die entweder in der Fachdiskussion der letzten Jahre eine besondere Rolle spielten oder deren Bedeutung ich für signifikant halte, ungeachtet einer eventuell fehlenden Popularität in der Fachliteratur. In der Gliederung folgt der Beitrag der typischen zeitlichen Folge eines Projekts, wobei außer den technischen Methoden selbst auch die Aspekte der Projektführung mit in die Betrachtung einbezogen werden.

PROJEKTPLANUNG UND -ORGANISATION

> "We build systems like the Wright brothers built airplanes - build the whole thing, put it off the cliff, let it crash, and start over again" *Graham* (1968)

Die Konstruktion eines DV-Systems ist eine risiko-behaftete und kostenintensive Tätigkeit. Es ist daher sinnvoll, von vornherein den Arbeitsablauf und den Einsatz von Betriebsmitteln so zu planen, daß man schon beim ersten Mal Erfolg hat.

Dies ist dann besonders schwierig, wenn aufgrund der Terminanforderungen ein hoher Grad an paralleler Arbeitsweise erforderlich ist und wenn außerdem das Projektziel ein vollständiges Systemprodukt ist.

Den Unterschied zwischen einem Programm für den eigenen Gebrauch und einem Systemprodukt hat *Brooks* (1975) wie folgt charakterisiert: Ein Programm wird ein System, wenn es alle Schnittstellenerfordernisse berücksichtigt und geprüft hat; es wird zu einem Produkt, wenn es hinreichend generalisiert, dokumentiert und verteilungsfähig gemacht worden ist. Jede der beiden Erweiterungen erhöht die Kosten und vergrößert das Risiko um einen Faktor 3. Ein Systemprodukt ist die Vereinigung der beiden Erweiterungen. Aufwand und Risiko erhöhen sich demnach um den Faktor 9.

Dieser aufwandsmäßige Unterschied von einer Größenordnung ist nur ein Aspekt des oft zitierten qualitativen Unterschieds zwischen der amateurhaften und der professionellen Seite dieser Tätigkeit. Leider ist es so, daß man immer wieder geneigt ist, die Erfahrungen und Methoden von nicht-produktorientierten Einpersonen-Projekten auf produkt-orientierte System-Projekte zu übertragen. Diese Kluft ist eigentlich die Hauptursache für Mißverständnisse und Widersprüche, wenn es darum geht, sich über Grundsätze zu einigen. Es gibt kaum gemeinsame Grundsätze für beide Projektarten.

Das organisatorische Schema, das den zeitlichen Ablauf eines größeren Projekts unterstützt, ist das *Phasenkonzept*. Das Prinzip findet seine Anwendung bei jedem zielgerichteten größeren Unterfangen und erhält für die DV-Systementwicklung nur eine ganz spezifische inhaltliche Ausprägung.

Ohne auf die vielfältigen Variationsmöglichkeiten oder auf alternative Bezeichnungsweisen einzugehen, wollen wir verlangen, daß jedes DV-Projekt zeitlich und inhaltlich aufgeteilt werden kann in folgende 6 Phasen: Definition, Entwurf, Implementierung, Test, Installation sowie Betrieb & Wartung. Die Abgrenzung der einzelnen Phasen erfolgt im wesentlichen durch die in Bild 1 angegebenen Arbeitsergebnisse. Das Ergebnis einer Phase ist Voraussetzung für den Beginn der nächsten.

Diese Phasen sind der Rahmen für jede Methodendiskussion. In jeder Phase sind andere Aufgaben zu lösen; es kommen damit andere Methoden und Hilfsmittel zur Anwendung.

Es ist die Aufgabe der *Projektplanung*, die zeitliche Dauer dieser einzelnen Phasen, sowie die Art und den Umfang der einzusetzenden Mittel möglichst genau abzuschätzen. Die für die *Kostenschätzung* angewandten Methoden lassen sich in folgende drei Gruppen einteilen:

(a) Vergleich mit ähnlichen Projekten
(b) Extrapolation von einer Tätigkeit
(c) Detailabschätzung aller Tätigkeiten

Diese Methoden unterscheiden sich ganz erheblich im Aufwand und damit im Zuverlässigkeitsgrad. Die Wahl sollte sich nach dem Umfang des Projekts richten, nach der Art der eingegangenen Haftung und nach der zur Verfügung stehenden Zeit. Die drei Methoden können sich gegenseitig prüfen und ergänzen.

Eine wichtige Rolle bei Kostenschätzungen bilden Daten und Faustregeln über die zu erwartende Produktivität je Tätigkeit. Abgesehen von der Diskussion um die Vergleichbarkeit von derartigen Daten (siehe *Jones* (1978)) hat sich im Prinzip an der Vorgehensweise in den letzten zehn Jahren wenig geändert. So gelten etwa die Faustregeln, die *Aron* (1969) für das Apollo-Projekt benützte, auch heute noch ohne wesentliche Abschläge. Sie wurden in anderen Großprojekten (siehe *Haslinger/Meßerer/Wolters* (1975)) anscheinend mit Erfolg angewandt und sind durch neuere Untersuchungen, etwa von *Wolverton* (1974) und *Walston/Felix* (1977) nur in Details verbessert worden.

Für das Problem der *Zeitschätzung* wird verschiedentlich von Methoden aus der Netzplantechnik Gebrauch gemacht, allerdings sehr sporadisch und schwerpunktmäßig nur bei bestimmten Projektsituationen.

Das Hauptproblem der Projektorganisation ist die *Arbeitsverteilung*. Hier haben die klassischen Formen der hierarchischen oder Matrixorganisation einige Konkurrenz bekommen, im wesentlichen durch die Vorschläge von *Baker* (1972) und *Mills/Baker* (1973). Gemeint ist das Konzept des *Chefprogrammierer-Teams*, durch das versucht wurde, eine der Programmentwicklung besonders angepaßte Organisationsform zu schaffen. Man kann eigentlich nicht sagen, daß sehr viele Gruppen die Mills-Bakerschen Grundsätze Punkt für Punkt übernommen haben. Es finden sich aber häufig abgewandelte Formen, die ebenfalls versuchen, den Nutzeffekt einer expliziten Rollenverteilung für sich zu gewinnen (siehe etwa *Schieferdecker* (1976)).

Auf die Probleme der Ablauforganisation und der Projektkontrolle im einzelnen einzugehen, würde sicherlich zu weit führen. Zwei Bücher, die in dieser Hinsicht ausführliche Anleitungen und Prüflisten liefern, sind *Metzger* (1973) und *Hice/Turner/Cashwell* (1974). Auch die Arbeit von *Daly* (1977) enthält nützliche Hinweise und Daten.

Projektplanung und -organisation haben zwar einen ersten Schwerpunkt in der Definitionsphase. Sie sollten jedoch als projektbegleitende Aktivitäten angesehen werden, die mit Fortschreiten des Projekts verfeinert bzw. angepaßt werden.

DIE PRODUKT-DEFINITION

> "A problem unstated is a problem unsolved" *Ross/Schoman* (1977)

Die Produktdefinition ist die erste Phase eines Projekts. Es ist die Phase, die dazu dient, Verständnis und Übereinstimmung dafür zu erzeugen, was eigentlich der Gegenstand des Projekts ist, welches Problem zu lösen ist.

Der Auslöser eines Projekts ist oft eine relativ vage Anweisung oder Aufforderung. Es bedarf dann einer gezielten Untersuchung, um festzulegen, welches die Grundsätze, Detailziele und Randbedingungen sind, die darüber entscheiden, ob der erwartete Nutzen erzielt werden kann.

Dieser Vorgang ist oft sehr mühsam und im Grunde nicht formalisierbar. Er hinterläßt daher selbst bei erfahrenen Praktikern oft einen etwas unbefriedigenden Eindruck. Für einen Theoretiker fehlt vielleicht sogar das grundsätzliche Verständnis für die Aufgabenstellung. Für ihn ist ein Problem oft erst dann existent, wenn es definiert ist.

Die Ansätze, um die Aufgaben der Definitionsphase in den Griff zu bekommen, liegen meist im Organisatorischen. Technische Hilfsmittel spielen eine sehr untergeordnete Rolle.

Der kritischste und damit entscheidende Ansatzpunkt ist die Kommunikation. Die Auftraggeber oder Benutzer des Produkts denken vielfach in Kategorien, die dem Entwickler nur oberflächlich vertraut sind, oder die überhaupt keine Relevanz haben zu den Kriterien, die für den Produktentwurf wichtig sind. Andererseits muß sich der Entwickler davor hüten, vorschnell bestimmte Benutzeranforderungen abzubilden auf Produktklassen oder Produktkriterien, die er zufällig kennt.

Die Produktdefinition ergibt sich (wie jede andere Phase auch) aus der Lösung mehrerer Teilaufgaben (siehe Tabelle 1). Die erste Aufgabe ist die *Bedarfsermittlung*. Sie ist eine Informationsaufnahme- oder -sammelphase. Mit der Dokumentation beginnt bereits die Klassifizierung und Abstrahierung. Je nachdem welche Form der Dokumentation gewählt wird, entscheidet darüber welche *Prüfungen* anschließend möglich sind. Die effektivsten Prüfungen sind die, die vom Auftraggeber oder Benutzer selbst gemacht werden können. Es wird deshalb ein großer Teil des Pflichtenheftes aus Text, Tabellen und Graphiken bestehen, da dies die Darstellungsformen sind, die einem möglichst großen Personenkreis zumutbar sind.

Es überrascht daher nicht, daß die später noch zu erwähnende HIPO-Methode gerade hier einige Erfolge erzielt hat. Sie erfüllt offenbar in idealer Weise die Anforderungen an ein Kommunikationsmittel, das von beiden Seiten verstanden wird und das für beide Seiten nützlich ist.

Es gibt in letzter Zeit eine Reihe von Vorschlägen, etwa von *Ross/Schoman* (1977), *Bell/Bixler/Dyer* (1977) und vor allem von *Teichrow/Hershey* (1977), die die Bedarfsanalyse mit maschinellen Hilfsmitteln unterstützen wollen. Aus der Gruppe um Teichrow gibt es eine Bedarfsbeschreibungssprache (PSL) und ein Analyseprogramm (PSA), mit dem sich auch mehrere Anwender in Deutschland bereits auseinandergesetzt haben. Diesen und ähnlichen Ansätzen liegt immer die Vorstellung zugrunde, daß sich etwa anhand eines graphentheoretischen Modells der Anwendung oder des Produkts gewisse Inkonsistenzen und Lücken leichter feststellen lassen als nur aufgrund von geschriebenem Text. Ob diese Modelle auch als Kommunikationsmittel einen Wert haben, ist jedoch fraglich.

Die Betonung der Bedarfsanalyse (Schlagwort: Requirements engineering) ist berechtigt, da Fehler, die in dieser Phase gemacht werden, einerseits oft die Grundkonzeption eines Systems betreffen können, andererseits aber erst sehr spät im Projekt, etwa zur Installationszeit, wieder aufgedeckt werden.

Über die Häufigkeit und die Art der Fehler, die in dieser Phase gemacht werden, geben *Bell/Thayer* (1977) einigen Aufschluß. Sie berichten auch über einen Versuch im Universitätsmilieu, der dazu diente, Studenten ein Gefühl für diese Problematik zu vermitteln. Dabei wurde für dieselbe vage definierte Aufgabe von mehreren Gruppen je ein Pflichtenheft entwickelt und anschließend verglichen.

Der Übergang zwischen Produktdefinition und Produktentwurf wird durch das *Pflichtenheft* sichergestellt. Genau wie jedes andere Projektdokument erfordert es einen kontrollierten Änderungsdienst. Für die inhaltliche Abgrenzung kann als Kriterium dienen, daß in dieser Phase nur das 'Was' gefragt ist, und nicht das 'Wie'. Im Grunde kann man sich ja nach der Definitionsphase noch dafür entscheiden, die gewünschte informationstechnische Leistung auch manuell zu erbringen.

DER PRODUKT-ENTWURF

> "We design until we think we understand" *Kinslow* (1968)

Der Entwurf eines DV-Systems ist die Antwort auf das Pflichtenheft; es ist eine Lösung des dort beschriebenen Problems mit den Mitteln der DV-Technik. Das Ergebnis des Entwurfs ist nicht das Produkt selbst, sondern eine technische Beschreibung der gewählten Lösung, incl. Begründung. Lediglich bei Programmen scheint es hier schon mal Begriffsschwierigkeiten zu geben. Hier wird mitunter, vielleicht wegen der Ähnlichkeit der Medien, der Entwurf eines Programms mit dem Programm selbst gleichgesetzt. Der Entwurf findet seinen Niederschlag in Spezifikationen.

Für die Vorgehensweise beim Entwurf eines DV-Systems gibt es viele Vorschläge. Das Schlagwort, das die meiste Popularität genießt, heißt *"Top-down-Entwurf"*. Wenn wir es nicht nur mit einem einzelnen Programm, sondern mit einem gesamten DV-System zu tun haben, ist mit Recht die Frage zu stellen, was dieses "oben" eigentlich ist. In diesem Falle sollte es sicher eher heißen, daß eine Vorgehensweise von außen nach innen gemeint ist. Das Außen ist die Architektur des Systems, das ist die Erscheinungsform, die der Benutzer sieht. Bei einem interaktiven System sind das die Dialoge, die Bildschirm- und die Listenformate. Bei einem Kompilierer ist es der Sprachumfang und die Aufruffolge im Betriebssystem. Diese Dinge entscheiden vor allem über die Akzeptanz des Systems. Die Entscheidungen, die hier getroffen werden, haben in der Regel auch äußerst langfristige Folgen.

Im Gegensatz zur Architektur ist die interne Struktur des Systems ein

Bereich, wo der Konstrukteur über Freiheitsgrade verfügt, die er sich möglichst lange offen halten sollte. Die interne Struktur ist maßgebend für das Leistungsverhalten, für die Wartbarkeit und für die Erweiterbarkeit. Typische Entscheidungen, die hier eine Rolle spielen, sind die Auswahl der Datei- oder Datenbankorganisation, die Zuordnung von Funktionen zu Gerätetypen, die Leistung und Kapazität von Geräten u. dgl.

Nicht immer kann der Konstrukteur davon ausgehen, daß alle Parameter frei wählbar sind. Die Vorgehensweise beim Entwurf wird daher auch bestimmt von dem, was bereits vorgegeben ist oder was von anderswo übernommen werden kann. Hier liegt einer der typischen Widersprüche.

Es besteht im Grundsatz vollständige Einigung, daß man vorhandene Bausteine benützt, wenn es irgendwie geht, und das auch in der Programmierung. Alle Entwurfsmethoden, die in der Diskussion sind, tun jedoch so, als ob man immer am Punkte Null anfangen könnte.

Beim Entwurf von Dialogen und Bildschirmmasken ist die Rückkopplung mit dem Benutzer oft von entscheidender Bedeutung. Hier gibt es die Möglichkeit mittels Dialogbeschreibungssprachen, wie sie im rechnergestützten Unterricht verwandt werden, sehr früh einen Prototyp zu erstellen und die Resonanz der Benutzer zu prüfen.

Für den Datei- und Datenbankentwurf gibt es eine derart große Anzahl von Hilfsmitteln, daß ihre Beherrschung schon fast zu einem Spezialgebiet geworden ist. Ein großer Teil dieser Hilfsmittel ist natürlich produkt- oder herstellerspezifisch. Es gibt aber auch recht beachtenswerte Ausnahmen (siehe *Raver/Hubbard* (1977)). Wie die Vorgehensweise beim Datenbankentwurf die übrigen Schritte der Entwurfs- und Implementierungsphase beeinflussen kann, zeigt Bild 2.

Der Programmentwurf im engeren Sinne ist das Gebiet, das in der Literatur der letzten zehn Jahre die größte Beachtung fand. Wie bereits in der Einleitung erwähnt, begann die Diskussion mit Dijkstra, aber die Beiträge von *Wirth* (1971a) und *Mills* (1971) sind fast im gleichen Atemzug zu nennen. Vor allem Wirth's Methode der schrittweisen Verfeinerung wird als typische Anwendung der Top-down-Vorgehensweise angesehen.

Bei seinen Beispielen argumentiert Wirth, daß man sich zuerst auf den Kontrollfluß konzentrieren sollte und die Datenstrukturen so lange unbestimmt lassen sollte wie möglich. Dies steht natürlich in Widerspruch zu der Vorgehensweise bei Datenbankanwendungen, wo die Datenstruktur das ist, was über mehrere Programme hinweg einheitlich geplant werden muß, d.h. als erstes festgelegt wird.

Auch die vielzitierte Entwurfsmethode nach *Jackson* (1975) geht von den Datenstrukturen aus. Hier ist es aber die Datenstruktur im Sinne der Satzgruppen und der Gruppenwechsel innerhalb einer sequentiellen Datei. Er benützt zur Beschreibung der Ein- und Ausgabedateien eine Art kontextfreie Grammatik. Das Programm wird dann abgeleitet als Abbildung zwischen diesen Grammatiken. Dieser scheinbar zwingende Zusammenhang zwischen Programm- und Datenstruktur, der daraus resultiert, besticht zwar. Die Methode ist aber eindeutig limitiert auf die sequentielle Verarbeitung von Dateien und erinnert etwas an die normierte Programmierung, wie sie in DIN 66220 beschrieben und in jedem Listprogrammgenerator implizit enthalten ist.

Zwischen diesen beiden Extremen liegt die von *Myers* (1975) und *Stevens/ Myers/Constantine* (1974) propagierte Entwurfsmethode (Composite Design). Die Grundvorstellung dabei ist die eines kontinuierlich veränderten Datenstroms zwischen Eingabe und Ausgabe. Die Aufteilung des Programms in Moduln erfolgt durch eine wiederholte Dreiteilung des Datenflusses in Noch-Eingabe, Umformung und Schon-Ausgabe. Dies ist ein anderes Beispiel für die Top-down-Vorgehensweise und ist im übrigen sehr gut verträglich mit der Entwurfsdarstellung durch HIPO-Diagramme.

Die Methodendiskussion scheint etwas abzulenken von einigen wesentlich fundamentaleren Fragen. Die erste lautet: Was ist eigentlich das Entscheidende, die Struktur des Produkts selbst, oder die Art, wie man zu dieser Struktur gelangte? Vor allem *Parnas* (1972a, b), aber auch *Stevens/ Myers/Constantine* (1974) haben Prinzipien herausgearbeitet, nach denen man eine Struktur beurteilen kann. Im wesentlichen ist es die Idee, daß eine Struktur dann besonders stabil ist, d.h. gegen notwendige Änderungen unempfindlich, wenn einerseits die interne funktionale Vollständigkeit der einzelnen Module sehr hoch ist, und andererseits der externe Verkopplungsgrad möglichst gering ist. Es ist dies eine Interpretation des Begriffs Modularität.

Die zweite Frage, die man stellen muß lautet: Welche Fehlerarten werden durch welche Methode verhindert? Über Fehlerarten gibt es inzwischen mehrere Untersuchungen, unter anderem von *Boehm* (1975), *Endres* (1974), *Goodenough/Gerhart* (1975) und *Gerhart/Yelowitz* (1976). Danach haben Entwurfsfehler typischerweise damit zu tun, daß ganze Funktionsteile vergessen wurden oder daß Fallunterscheidungen fehlen oder daß falsche Annahmen über Daten und Geräte gemacht wurden. Welche Entwurfsmethode welche Fehlerquellen adressiert, ist im Hinblick auf die bisher skizzierten Entwurfsmethoden noch nicht untersucht worden.

Demgegenüber drängt sich in diesem Zusammenhang ein anderes Verfahren immer wieder auf, nämlich die *Entscheidungstabellentechnik* (siehe *Strunz* (1977)). Sie hat offensichtlich Vorteile in solchen Situationen, wo die Komplexität des Problems sich haupsächlich aus der Anzahl der Fallunterscheidungen ergibt. Ein drastisches Beispiel dafür geben *Goodenough/ Gerhart* (1975), die vermöge einer Art von Entscheidungstabellen in einem von *Naur* (1966) als richtig dargestellten 20-Zeiler etwa ein Dutzend Fehler nachweisen.

Die *Dokumentation* des Entwurfs soll die Unterscheidung in Architektur und Struktur reflektieren. Man benützt dafür auch die Bezeichnungen externe und interne Spezifikation. Die Methoden der Dokumentation richten sich nach dem Verwendungszweck. Dieser ist unterschiedlich je nach Spezifikationstyp, aber auch nach Projekttyp und -organisation.

Der Adressatenkreis einer externen Spezifikation kann durchaus Nicht-Fachleute umfassen. Damit scheiden formale Darstellungsweisen fast immer aus. Anders bei den internen Spezifikationen. Die traditionelle Form der internen Entwurfsdokumentation ist das Flußdiagramm im Sinne von DIN 66001. Eine Alternative, die aber die Strukturprinzipien des go-to-freien Programmierens besser unterstützt, sind die *Nassi-Shneiderman* (1973)-Diagramme. Genau wie Flußdiagramme zeigen sie nur den Kontrollfluß. Zur Erstellung von Flußdiagrammen, aber auch für Nassi-Shneiderman-Diagramme gibt es diverse Hilfsprogramme. Ein Beispiel für die letzte Gruppe ist das COLUMBUS-System von *Witt* (1975).

Da für das Verständnis eines Programms der Datenfluß ebenso wichtig ist, fand die von *IBM* (1974) in Poughkeepsie entwickelte *HIPO-Methode* viele enthusiastische Anwender. Die HIPO-Methode hat den großen Vorteil, daß sie auch bei kurzer Betrachtung bereits einen guten Überblick gibt. Sie ist jedoch nicht besonders gut geeignet, um die Logik eines Programms im Detail darzustellen. Hierfür gibt es aber im Falle von höheren Sprachen nicht dieselben Anforderungen wie etwa bei der Assembler-Programmierung. Außerdem gibt es ergänzende Alternativen. HIPO-Diagramme sind trotz einiger komfortabler Hilfsmittel bei Programmierern nicht besonders beliebt. Der Zeichnungs- und Fortschreibungsaufwand ist eine Belastung. Ihr Wert liegt in der Kommunikationsrolle, die bereits beschrieben wurde.

Das Thema der formalen *Entwurfssprachen* ist so alt wie die Programmierung selbst. An Vorschlägen bestand kein Mangel. Eine große Bedeutung hat bis heute keiner dieser Vorschläge gewonnen. Der letzte Beitrag, der diesen Namen trägt, geht auf *Caine/Gordon* (1975) zurück. Im Grunde ist diese Sprache nichts anderes als das, was unter dem Namen Pseudokode auch von *Mills* (1971) bereits propagiert wurde.

Pseudokode kann als eine stilisierte Form von Kommentaren aufgefaßt werden. Er kann wie ein Programmtext manipuliert werden, und kann später die Rolle von Kommentaren übernehmen. Je nach dem wie etwa die Modulaufrufe oder die Parameterübergabe formalisiert worden ist, lassen sich auch anhand des Pseudokodes sinnvolle Konsistenz- und Vollständigkeitsprüfungen durchführen.

Pseudokode wird in einigen Umgebungen zusammen mit HIPO verwandt. Wir haben in diesem Falle eine verträgliche Kette von Methoden, nämlich HIPO für die Bedarfsdarstellung und den Grobentwurf, Pseudokode für den Detailentwurf und später als Kommentar im Programmtext selbst.

Die wichtigste Verwendung jeder Entwurfsdokumentation besteht in der *funktionalen Prüfung* des Entwurfs. Eine Prüfung des Entwurfs ist deshalb unumgänglich, weil die Fehler, die in der Entwurfsphase eingeführt werden, schwerwiegend sind und zahlreich. Sie haben nach den Fehlern aus der Definitionsphase die zweitlängste Lebensdauer und damit entsprechend hohe Kosten. Der Grundsatz, der die Entwurfsprüfung leitet, beruht auf der Erfahrung, daß der Autor eines Programms Entwurfsfehler kaum selbst findet. Es bedarf eines unabhängigen Prüfers, d.h. eines unabhängigen Nachvollziehens der dem Entwurf zugrundeliegenden Gedankengänge.

Während bei der Prüfung der externen Spezifikationen Benutzer oder Auftraggeber beteiligt sein sollten, ist die Prüfung der internen Spezifikationen eine Angelegenheit, die innerhalb des Projektes erledigt werden kann. Für diesen Teil gibt es eine Reihe detailliert ausgearbeiteter Organisations- und Arbeitsanleitungen von *Kohli* (1975) und *Kohli/Radice* (1976), die unter dem Namen *Entwurfsinspektion* bekannt wurden. Man kann ohne Übertreibung sagen, daß diese Verfahren, zusammen mit der später noch zu diskutierenden Kodeinspektion, wohl mehr zur Verbesserung der Programmqualität beitragen als irgendeines der anderen neuen Verfahren.

Nach der funktionalen Prüfung des Entwurfs ist die *Leistungsschätzung* der nächste wichtige Schritt vor Abschluß der Entwurfsphase. Auf diesem Gebiet gibt es in den letzten zehn Jahren kaum signifikante Neuentwicklungen, abgesehen vielleicht von einigen theoretischen Ergebnissen auf dem Gebiet der Warteschlangenmodelle. Eine gute Darstellung der relevanten Methoden und Hilfsmittel gibt *Graham* (1973).

DIE PRODUKT-IMPLEMENTIERUNG

"We should build on top of the work of others ..." *Hamming* (1969)

Die Implementierungsphase [1] ist die Realisierung des Entwurfs; sie überführt die Spezifikation in Programmoduln, Testfälle und Daten. Im Prinzip reichen in dieser Phase Schreibpapier und Bleistift noch als Medium und Werkzeug aus. Die Zielmaschine und alle E/A-Geräte müssen erst am Anfang der nächsten Phase zur Verfügung stehen. Benützen wir in dieser Phase einen Rechner, dann nicht als Träger des geplanten Systems, sondern als Entwicklungshilfsmittel. Solange man sich nur mit einem einzelnen Rechnertyp mit ausreichender Speicher- und E/A-Konfiguration befaßt, erscheint einem diese Unterscheidung als künstlich konstruiert. Sie wird zur Realität, sobald man es mit Spezialrechnern oder mit solchen geringer Leistungsfähigkeit zu tun hat, oder wenn aus irgendeinem Grunde das Angebot an Hilfsmitteln die Ansprüche nicht erfüllt (etwa bei neuentwickelten Rechnerarchitekturen).

DV-Anwendungssysteme waren traditionsgemäß Einzelanfertigungen, d.h. jede Installation hatte ein anderes System. Die Folge davon ist, daß die Vervielfältigung ganzer Systeme, also das was man anderswo Produktion nennt, kaum eine Rolle spielt. Auch fallen Prototyp- und Produktentwicklung meistens zusammen.

Beide Aspekte sind als Zeichen des vor-industriellen Standes unserer Disziplin beklagt worden. Ein Beispiel dafür ist McIlroy's Beitrag in Garmisch und Graham's herrlicher Vergleich mit der Frühphase des Flugzeugbaus (siehe *Naur/Randell* (1968)).

So schön derartige Vergleiche sind, sie enthielten auch vor zehn Jahren nur die halbe Wahrheit. Selbst wenn wir uns auf die Programment-

1) von lat. implere = ausfüllen

wicklung beschränken, so gab es schon früh eine Art Komponentenindustrie, d.h. es gab Standardbauelemente, die im Markt angeboten wurden, und die jeder benutzen konnte, der daraus ein System bauen wollte. Die Ebene, auf der die Integration stattfindet, lag damals jedoch bereits wesentlich höher als etwa von McIlroy gefordert. Es werden nicht lexikalische Abprüfer (scanners) für Kompilierer angeboten, sondern ganze Kompilierer, nicht Indexsuchroutinen sondern ganze Datenorganisationspakete. Dieser Trend hat sich in den letzten zehn Jahren erheblich verstärkt. Sieht man sich heute DV-Systeme an, die im interaktiven oder Datenbankbetrieb eingesetzt sind, so ist der Anteil des Standardkodes, der in einem solchen System ausgeführt wird, also des Kodes, der für mehrfache Verwendung durch die Software-Industrie hergestellt wurde, häufig im Bereich von 70-80% des Gesamtkodes. Nur etwa 20-30% des Programmaterials ist installations- oder anwendungsspezifisch. Dieser Trend ist durchaus richtungsweisend für einen großen Bereich der Datenverarbeitung. (Er ist es jedoch nicht für die gesamte Datenverarbeitung, wie wir später sehen werden.)

Der Kern der Implementierungsphase ist nach wie vor das Erstellen von Kode. Fast genau so wichtig ist es jedoch, daß man prüft, ob die Routinen, die man schreiben will, nicht schon vorhanden sind. Das setzt voraus, daß man weiß, welche Komponenten von wem angeboten werden, wie sie mit einander verknüpft werden können und welche Modifikationsmöglichkeiten vorgesehen sind, um sie speziellen Erfordernissen anzupassen.

Diese Schwelle zu überschreiten fällt manchem Programmierer schwer. Er sehnt sich oft zurück in die "gute alte Zeit", wo man bei jedem Programm so tun konnte, als ob nur es allein existiere und es für das Programm kaum andere Einschränkungen gab als die Größe des Adressraums der jeweiligen Maschine.

Man kann ohne Übertreibung sagen, daß hier eine Verschiebung von handwerklichen zu industriellen Implementierungsmethoden stattgefunden hat. Die dafür typischen Merkmale sind: Die Erstellung von Produkten ist arbeitsteilig; die Spezialisierung nimmt zu; es macht nicht mehr jeder alles. Die Vorinvestitionen, die man tätigen muß, selbst um kleine Dinge zu tun, sind unverhältnismäßig groß. Sie lohnen sich erst im Laufe der Zeit. Für jemanden, der mithalten will, reicht es nicht mehr, daß er nur die Grundtechniken beherrscht. Er muß lernen, mit komplexeren Hilfsmitteln umzugehen.

Hat man sich einmal mit dieser Veränderung in der Struktur heutiger Systeme vertraut gemacht, so erscheinen viele Dinge, die in der Fachdiskussion eine Rolle spielen, in einem etwas anderen Licht.

Das gilt als erstes für das Thema *Programmiersprachen*. Hier trat ebenfalls etwa 1968 ein Umschwung ein. Mit PL/I und Algol 68 war ein Weg beschritten worden, der in dieser Richtung nicht weitergegangen werden konnte. Beide Sprachen hatten versucht, zuviele Konzepte und Mechanismen in sich zu vereinigen. Das macht beide etwas unhandlich. Da außerdem ältere Sprachen wie FORTRAN und COBOL ein erstaunliches Beharrungsvermögen zeigten, blieb im Grunde nur die Wahl, neue Systemfunktionen möglichst sprachneutral anzubieten. Das hat die Motivation zur Sprachumstellung weiter vermindert.

Seit 1971 gibt es eine Reihe von Sprachneuentwicklungen, die zunächst didaktisch motiviert waren, wie PASCAL von *Wirth* (1971b). Andere versuchen, neuere Strukturierungsprinzipien zu unterstützen, wie CLU von *Liskov/Zilles* (1974), ALPHARD von *Wulf* (1974) und MODULA von *Wirth* (1977). Keine dieser Sprachen hat bisher die Schwelle zur breiten industriellen Anwendung überschritten. Im Bereich der Mittel- und Großsysteme werden neue Sprachen vor allem daran gemessen, wie sehr sie die Integration vorhandener Software erleichtern. Hierbei schneidet keine der gerade erwähnten Sprachen besonders gut ab.

Wenn neue Sprachen eine Chance haben, dann besteht diese am ehesten im Bereich der Mikroprozessoren. Hier besteht noch Neuland und zwar in vielerlei Hinsicht. Die Methoden, die hier für die Erstellung von Programmen angewandt werden, entsprechend etwa dem, was in der übrigen Datenverarbeitung um 1958 üblich war. Die zu erstellenden Programme sind relativ klein. Da es sich fast immer um neue Maschinenarchitekturen handelt, gibt es keine signifikante Basis an Programmen, die übertragen werden kann.

Anders ging es der Idee des *Strukturierten Programmierens*, wie sie vor allem von *Dijkstra* (1969) in die Diskussion gebracht wurde. Daß Programme nicht nur für Maschinen geschrieben werden, sondern daß sie auch für Kollegen lesbar sein müssen, ist eine Erkenntnis, zu der jeder Projektleiter sehr schnell kommt. Nur so sichert man sich gegen Personalausfälle, schafft die Voraussetzungen für eine spätere Prüfbarkeit durch andere Programmierer und erleichtert die Arbeit bei Erweiterungen und während der Wartungsphase. Es ist Dijkstras Verdienst, daß er die

Fachwelt überzeugt hat, daß Programme um so leichter lesbar und nachvollziehbar sind, je einfacher ihre Kontrollstruktur ist.

Für die Anhänger einzelner Sprachen war es ein leichtes zu zeigen, daß man ohne sehr viel Aufwand fast in jeder Sprache die Vorteile des Strukturierten Programmierens erreichen kann. Hierüber gibt es unzählige Veröffentlichungen und eine große Zahl von Lehrbüchern. Es kann sich heute kaum ein Programmierer diesen Argumenten entziehen und es ist offensichtlich, daß diese Grundsätze auch in fast jeder Umgebung praktiziert werden. *Elshoffs* (1977) Bericht ist das Beispiel einer Analyse, die auch Skeptiker überzeugen sollte.

Eine Technik, die sehr oft im engen Zusammenhang mit Strukturiertem Programmieren gesehen wird, ist das *Beweisen von Programmen*. Die Idee, die Korrektheit von Programmen durch einen mathematischen Beweis zu zeigen, geht vor allem auf *Floyd* (1967) und *Hoare* (1969) zurück. *Dijkstra* (1975) argumentiert dafür, daß man ein Programm am besten gleichzeitig mit seinem Beweis, sozusagen aus dem Beweis heraus, entwickeln sollte. Die Automatisierung von Korrektheitsbeweisen hat sich zwar als ein lukratives Forschungsgebiet erwiesen (siehe *Elspas* (1972) und *London* (1975)), die praktische Anwendung ist jedoch bis heute recht bescheiden geblieben. Der Hauptgrund dafür ist die Schwierigkeit für ein normales Programm, d.h. für etwas anderes als triviale mathematische Funktionen, die erforderlichen Zusicherungen zu finden. Zusicherungen (assertions) sind die formelmäßige Beschreibung der Abhängigkeiten zwischen Ein- und Ausgabewerten. Sie müssen vor allem unabhängig vom Programm selbst entwickelt werden, da sie sonst keine Aussagekraft haben.

Die Beschäftigung mit Korrektheitsbeweisen sollte eigentlich ein anderes Gebiet sehr stark befruchten, das in seiner Zielsetzung etwas bescheidener ist und daher eher einige Erfolge erwarten läßt. Gemeint ist das Thema der *semantischen Analyse* von Programmen. Wie in *Endres* (1977) gezeigt, gibt es hierfür, auch auf der Basis vorhandener Programmiersprachen, noch sehr viele Möglichkeiten.

Daß man sein Heil nicht allein in formalen Verfahren und komplexen Hilfsmitteln suchen muß, hat der Erfolg bewiesen, den die *Kodeinspektion* aufweisen kann. Die Kodeinspektion ist das Analoge zur Entwurfsinspektion, aber übertragen auf die Implementierungsphase. Obwohl dieses Verfahren sicherlich auch viel früher schon praktiziert wurde, erhielt es jedoch erst eine gewisse Formalisierung durch *Fagan* (1976) und seine Kollegen (siehe *Ascoli* (1976)). Eine Variante davon ist die Testinspektion, wie sie von *Larson* (1975) beschrieben wurde.

Die Kodeinspektion basiert, genau wie die Entwurfsinspektion, auf dem Grundsatz, daß sehr viele Fehler, die gemacht werden, vom Ersteller des Programms selbst nur sehr schwer gefunden werden können. Um die Kodeinspektion einzuführen, bedarf es natürlich einiger organisatorischer Voraussetzungen und Vorbereitungen. Ist jedoch die psychologische Barriere einmal überwunden, daß ein Programm nicht etwas ist, was man gegen den geistigen Einfluß anderer abschirmen muß, so eröffnen sich für die betreffende Gruppe eine Reihe von Vorteilen. Nicht nur, daß Fehler früher und mit wesentlich weniger Aufwand entdeckt werden, auch die Nebeneffekte, die dabei erzielt werden, sind ausgesprochen positiv. Es wird der gegenseitige Lerneffekt gefördert, das Bewußtsein für Qualität und gemeinsame Verantwortung sowie die Möglichkeit, schnell jemanden einzuarbeiten, wenn nötig. *Weinberg* (1971) nennt dies "ego-less programming".

Trotz der möglichen psychologischen Schwierigkeiten scheint die Kodeinspektion von allen modernen Methoden am stärksten Anklang gefunden zu haben. Ihre Ergebnisse werden einhellig als signifikant beurteilt (siehe *Holton* (1977), *Belford* et al. (1977) und *Walston/Felix* (1977)).

Der unmittelbare Einsatz des Rechners bei der Programmentwicklung und Programmverwaltung ist in der Diskussion seit weit über einem Jahrzehnt. Obwohl die technischen Voraussetzungen schon länger vorhanden waren, scheint sich das *interaktive Programmieren* erst in den letzten Jahren stärker auszubreiten. Seine Vorteile liegen eindeutig in der wesentlich reduzierten Umschlagzeit bei kleineren Programmänderungen und der Möglichkeit der sofortigen Syntaxprüfung.

Um die Vorteile voll zur Geltung zu bringen, empfielt sich die Kombination mit einem interaktiven Testsystem und einer Programmentwicklungsbibliothek. Offensichtlich stellt die Kombination dieser drei Hilfsmittel für viele Anwender noch eine zu hohe Investitionsschwelle dar, einmal wegen der organisatorischen Konsequenzen, zum andern wegen der befürchteten Interferenz mit den normalen Anwendungen.

Der Begriff *Programmentwicklingsbibliothek* umfaßt an sich ein großes Spektrum von Hilfsmitteln. Im einfachsten Falle ist es die übliche Programmbibliothek eines Betriebssystems, die in der Regel zwischen Quell-

und Objektprogrammoduln unterscheidet. Komplizierte Systeme, wie etwa das von *Brown* (1969) beschriebene CLEAR/CASTER System, unterstützen mehrere Versionen ein und desselben Moduls und erlauben temporäre und alternative Änderungen vermöge einer Baumstruktur der Bibliothek. Für die Statuskontrolle können Vollständigkeitsprüfungen und Vergleiche durchgeführt werden, es können Testdaten und Testergebnisse, Benutzerinformationen und Fehlerdaten gesammelt werden und viele andere Dinge mehr.

Die Anwendung solcher Systeme findet man hauptsächlich bei Herstellern von Systemprogrammen. Sie werden relativ selten in der Literatur beschrieben.

Die bereits mehrfach angesprochene Programmentwicklung für Mikroprozessoren geht in der Tendenz dahin, daß Programmverwaltung, Übersetzung und Simulation auf einem Großsystem durchgeführt werden. Da sich die vollen Kosten eines derartigen Großsystems nicht immer rechtfertigen lassen, wird dieser Service oft von Rechenzentren angeboten. Ein Projekt mit dem anspruchsvollen Namen "National Software Works" (siehe *Robinson* (1977)) macht derzeit in den USA von sich reden. Hierbei ist daran gedacht, ein heterogenes Rechnernetz (das ARPA-Netz) dafür einzusetzen, um sämtliche im Netz vorhandenen Hilfsmittel der Programmentwicklung an jedem Knoten verfügbar zu machen.

DAS TESTEN DES PRODUKTS

> "If we develop systematically, we can dispense with testing altogether"
>
> *Van der Poel* (1968)

Die Testphase unterwirft das fertige Produkt seiner beabsichtigten Verwendung, mit der Einschränkung, daß es sich um einen probeweisen Betrieb handelt und um eine weitgehend kontrollierte Produktumgebung.

Selbst wenn man zugesteht, daß es sich bei dem Ausdruck 'fertiges Produkt' um einen dehnbaren Begriff handelt, so wird man mit dieser Definition des Testens immer noch Widerspruch hervorrufen - aber auch mit jeder anderen Definition. Das ist kennzeichnend dafür, daß auf dem Gebiet des Testens kaum Übereinstimmung besteht hinsichtlich der Grundsätze und Ziele und daß, besonders zwischen Theoretikern und Praktikern, sehr häufig aneinander vorbeigedacht wird.

Von der Zielsetzung des Tests her muß man unterscheiden zwischen Funktionstest, Leistungsmessung und Hantierungstest. Ein *Funktionstest* hat das Ziel, durch Ausführung von Testfällen Auskunft über das funktionale Verhalten des Systems zu bekommen. Unterschiede zwischen dem erwarteten und dem tatsächlichen Verhalten sind Fehler, wobei man sofort hinzufügen muß, daß auch die erwarteten Ergebnisse ihrerseits fehleranfällig sein können.

Die Diskussion um Sinn und Zweck des Testens ist besonders beeinflußt worden von *Dijkstras* (1969) Hinweis, daß Testen zwar das Vorhandensein von Fehlern nicht jedoch die Fehlerfreiheit zeigen kann. Ansichten, wie die von Van der Poel sind sicherlich als Extremfall anzusehen. Dennoch fühlt sich der Kollege, der glaubt auf das Testen nicht verzichten zu können, etwas in die Defensive gedrängt. Der implizite Vorwurf, dem er sich ausgesetzt sieht, lautet etwa so: Wer glaubt, einen Test nötig zu haben, erwartet Fehler. Er hat also nicht genug getan, um Fehler zu verhüten, sei es in der Entwurfs- oder in der Implementierungsphase.

Dem ist entgegenzuhalten, daß selbst dann, wenn man das Menschenmögliche getan hat, Testen dennoch sinnvoll ist. Das Testen führt zum ersten Mal alle Komponenten eines DV-Systems zusammen, d.h. Geräte, Daten, Programme und organisatorische Abläufe. Hier kommt das Zusammenspiel zum Tragen zwischen tatsächlichen Geräten, tatsächlichen Daten und dem Programm. Falsche Annahmen, etwa über die Datenformate, kommen ans Licht. Das Testen erlaubt eine durchgreifende und unabhängige Prüfung aller Entwurfs- und Implementierungsergebnisse. Die Unabhängigkeit kommt herein, dadurch daß der Auftraggeber oder der Endbenutzer eher in der Lage ist, das Programm durch Testfälle zu prüfen als durch irgendeine andere Methode.

Die Aktivität, die für den Erfolg der Testphase den Ausschlag gibt, ist die Auswahl bzw. die Entwicklung von Testfällen. Diese Aktivität ist an und für sich Teil der Implementierungsphase und muß zu Beginn der Testphase abgeschlossen sein.

Wieweit zufällig existierende Testdaten benützt werden können oder welche Testfälle gezielt neuentwickelt werden sollen, ist eine Frage der Teststrategie.

Die *Teststrategie* ist das übergeordnete Konzept für die Vorgehensweise beim Testen und für die Anwendung bestimmter Methoden. Auch beim Testen gibt es die Frage, ob man oben oder unten anfangen soll. Im Falle, daß man oben beginnt (Top-down-Strategie), werden als erstes die das Programmsystem zusammenhaltenden Steuerfunktionen getestet, etwa die Systeminitialisierung, der Übergang von einer Aufgabe zur andern, von einem Transaktionstyp zum andern, und dgl. Es muß in diesem Falle gewährleistet sein, daß entweder alle Detailfunktionen umgangen oder durch einfache Operationen simuliert werden können. Es wird also unter Umständen für Testzwecke zusätzlicher Kode (Modulstümpfe) in das System eingebaut, der später wieder ersetzt wird.

Beginnt man unten (Bottom-up-Strategie), so hat man das Problem, daß man Testdaten generieren muß, die genau den von einem Modul erwarteten internen Parametern und Formaten entsprechen. Man schreibt also redundante Testfälle, die später im Systemtest nicht mehr benötigt werden, spart aber die Erstellung von redundantem Kode. Der Hauptvorteil, den man gewinnt, besteht darin, daß man auf den lokal geprüften Moduln wie auf Bausteinen aufbauen kann, vor allem dann, wenn es Moduln sind, die mehrfach benützt werden.

Die klassische, und auch heute noch am meisten angewandte Strategie ist das Testen von unten nach oben. Es werden dabei mindestens folgende drei Stufen unterschieden, die zeitlich hintereinander folgen: Modultest, Komponententest und Systemtest.

Für den Modultest ist in der Regel der Entwickler selbst zuständig. Er entwickelt auch die Testfälle. Für Komponenten- und Systemtest können die Testfälle von Dritten entwickelt werden, da sie den externen Daten entsprechen.

Für die *Auswahl von Testfällen* gibt es zwei grundsätzlich verschiedene Methoden, die beide ihre Vor- und Nachteile haben. Die am leichtesten anzuwendende Methode betrachtet nur die externe Architektur des Systems als relevant (black-box Methode). Testfälle werden ausgewählt anhand der Wertebereiche der externen Parameter, ohne Rücksicht darauf, wie diese intern behandelt werden. Wegen der Häufigkeit von Entwurfsfehlern sind die Testfälle am effektivsten, die von unabhängigen Dritten erstellt werden, die sich allein nach dem Wortlaut der externen Spezifikationen (oder der Problemstellung) richten und nicht davon beeinflußt sind, wie etwa der Programmierer die Spezifikation verstanden hat. Der Nachteil dieser Methode ist, daß man nichts dazu sagen kann, wieviele Testfälle man braucht und welche Testfälle wirklich aussagefähig sind, es sei denn man entschließt sich zu einem erschöpfenden Test. Ein *erschöpfender Test* deckt alle möglichen Wertekombinationen der Parameter ab, was sehr oft zu astronomischen Größenordnungen führt und aufwandsmäßig nicht realisierbar ist.

In einem solchen Falle muß man eine Untermenge möglicher Parametervariationen auswählen, also eine *Stichprobe*. Hierfür gibt es auch automatisierte Hilfsmittel, die entweder mit Zufallszahlen oder statistischen Wahrscheinlichkeiten arbeiten. Eines der universellsten Hilfsmittel in dieser Kategorie ist die Syntaxmaschine von *Hanford* (1970), die seit Jahren mit Erfolg eingesetzt wird. Sie hat sich insbesondere beim Erstellen von Diagnostik-Testfällen bewährt. Diagnostik-Testfälle sind ungültige Eingabedaten, die dazu dienen, die Robustheit eines Systems zu testen.

Die Methoden, von denen in letzter Zeit immer mehr die Rede ist, berücksichtigen die interne Struktur des Programms bei der Auswahl vo Testfällen (Schlagwort: *strukturiertes Testen*). Man sollte diese Methoden nicht unbedingt als Gegensatz zu den gerade beschriebenen sehen, da sie durchaus mit ihnen kombiniert werden können und sie sich im Prinzip ergänzen.
Die Frage, die hier am Anfang steht, lautet: Wenn ein erschöpfender Test nicht durchführbar ist, mit welcher Untermenge von Testfällen erhalte ich dann die zuverlässigste Aussage über ein Programm? Die Antwort erhält man, indem man sogenannte Abdeckungsmaße definiert (siehe *Huang* (1975), *Howden* (1975, 1976) und vor allem *Miller* (1974, 1977)).

Der einfachste Ansatz, und damit das schwächste *Abdeckungsmaß* ist dadurch gegeben, daß man verlangt, daß während eines Tests alle Instruktionen eines Programms wenigstens einmal ausgeführt werden. Ein stärkeres Maß ist eines, das verlangt, daß wenigstens alle Pfade eines Programms einmal ausgeführt werden müssen.

Ein Abdeckungsmaß ist stärker als ein anderes, wenn mehr Testfälle benötigt werden, um es zu erfüllen. Eine ausführliche Diskussion dieses Begriffs befindet sich bei *Miller* (1977).

Der Begriff eines *Pfades* spielt hier eine zentrale Rolle. Man spricht daher auch von *pfad-orientierten* Methoden. Allerdings sind die meisten Definitionen nicht sehr brauchbar, da selbst bei kleineren Programmen für die Anzahl der Pfade keine obere Schranke angegeben werden kann. Dieses Problem löst eine andere Definition des Pfadbegriffs, wie sie von *Endres/Glatthaar* (1977) angegeben wird. In dieser Arbeit sind auch andere Aspekte der pfad-orientierten Testmethode weiterentwickelt worden.

Es gibt inzwischen, zumindest in der Literatur, eine Vielzahl von Hilfsmitteln, die die pfad-orientierten Testverfahren unterstützen (siehe *Ramamoorthy/Ho* (1975), *Howden* (1975), *Osterweil/Fosdick* (1976) und *Miller* (1977). Welche praktische Bedeutung sie bisher erlangt haben, ist nicht bekannt. Auch gibt es keine Daten über ihre Wirksamkeit. Ich betrachte diese Entwicklungen dennoch als richtungsweisend, da hier die Vorteile des Beweisens mit denen des Testens zusammenfließen.

Die *Durchführung* von Tests ist die Aufgabe innerhalb eines Projekts, die an das Organisationsgeschick, die Erfahrung und die Geduld der Beteiligten die größten Anforderungen stellt. Das Spektrum der Methoden reicht vom einzelnen Programmierer an der Maschine, über den Stapelbetrieb zum interaktiven Testen. Soll eine einigermaßen optimale Ausnutzung der Betriebsmittel, insbesondere in der zur Verfügung stehenden Zeit, erreicht werden, ist der überlegte Einsatz von Hilfsmitteln unabdinglich. Hier sind Produktivitätsunterschiede um den Faktor 2-5 erreichbar.

Eine Schlüsselrolle spielen hier sicherlich die interaktiven Systeme. Zusammen mit einem interaktiven Programm-Editor und diversen Hilfsmitteln für die Testüberwachung kann der Modultest erheblich erleichtert werden. Interpretierende Sprachen oder die symbolische Ausführung von Testfällen (siehe *King* (1974) sind Beispiele von unterschiedlichen Ansätzen.

Für den Komponenten- und Systemtest kann ein Programmverwaltungssystem nützliche Dienste leisten. Die Abhängigkeit von bestimmten Gerätekonfigurationen löst ein System mit der Fähigkeit virtueller Maschinen, z.B. VM/370.

Hat man sich entschlossen, zwecks hoher Abdeckung des Kodes eine große Anzahl von Testfällen laufen zu lassen, so tritt sehr leicht das Problem auf, daß die *Auswertung* von Testläufen zum Engpaß wird. Wenn irgend möglich, sollte man alle Testergebnisse im vornherein ermitteln, sie maschinell speichern und während der Testphase einen automatischen Vergleich vorsehen zwischen erwartetem und tatsächlichem Ergebnis.

Je nach der gewählten Methode muß während des Tests eventuell eine *Kon-*

trolle des erreichten *Abdeckungsmaßes* vorgenommen werden. Hilfsmittel in dieser Kategorie sind oft sehr maschinenzeitaufwendig, es sei denn es werden Mikroprogramm- oder zusätzliche gerätetechnische Hilfen benützt.

Für die Projektführung stellt die Testphase einen sehr kritischen Abschnitt dar in bezug auf die *Erfolgskontrolle*. Hier müssen einerseits klar meßbare Ziele definiert werden und andererseits der entsprechende Datenerfassungs- und Kontrollmechanismus eingerichtet werden.

Die *Leistungsmessung* eines DV-Systems hat fast nur zufällige Berührungspunkte mit dem Funktionstest. Die Testfälle oder Systemlasten werden nach völlig anderen Gesichtspunkten ausgewählt. Auch die Durchführung der Tests verlangt eine spezielle Instrumentierung des Systems. Oft ist die Systemuhr das wichtigste Gerät, manchmal werden aber eigene Hardware- oder Software-Monitore benötigt. Gute Einführungen zu diesem Thema geben *Lucas* (1971) und *Gotlieb* (1973).

Der *Hantierungstest* soll Auskunft darüber geben, ob die Annahmen, die über die Mensch-Maschine-Schnittstelle gemacht wurden, in der Realität des Systembetriebs tragfähig sind. Einige Hinweise hierzu gibt *Komarnicki* (1971).

Da bei der Leistungsmessung wie beim Hantierungstest sich die Notwendigkeit für Änderungen des Systems herausstellen kann, ist es zweckmäßig, diese Tests so früh wie irgend möglich zu beginnen. Sie müssen jedoch bei jeder funktionalen Änderung des Systems wiederholt oder ergänzt werden.

Änderungen an einem System während der Testphase, etwa als Korrektur von Funktions-, Leistungs- oder Hantierungsfehlern, müssen in jedem Testplan mit vorgesehen werden. In welchem zeitlichen Zyklus überhaupt Änderungen eingebaut werden, ist eine Frage der Integrationsstrategie.

Eine *Integrationsstrategie* ist in der Regel ein Kompromiß zwischen dem Wunsch, Korrekturen sofort anzubringen, sobald sie vorhanden sind, und dem Begehren, eine möglichst hohe Abdeckung für eine gegebene Systemversion zu erreichen. Mit jeder neuen Integrationsstufe tritt außerdem das Problem auf zu zeigen, daß durch Änderungen keine neuen Fehler eingeführt wurden. Diesem Zweck dient der *Regressionstest*. Hierfür sind wenige, aber umfassende Testfälle das richtige.

DIE PRODUKT-INSTALLATION

"The real problem is the user,
since he needs the system..."
Samelson (1968)

Die Installationsphase überführt das Produkt in seine beabsichtigte Umgebung. Ein DV-System löst in der Regel eine Teilaufgabe innerhalb eines größeren Aufgabenkomplexes. Die übrigen Aufgaben werden von Menschen, Maschinen oder anderen DV-Systemen gelöst. Fast immer jedoch ist für diese eine gewisse Anpassung erforderlich, es ändert sich der bisherige Arbeitsablauf oder die Arbeitsweise.

Bei einem Anwendungssystem sind die Endbenutzer des Systems keine DV-Fachleute. Es stellt sich also in dieser Phase heraus, ob alle Annahmen bezüglich Sachkenntnis, Lernbereitschaft, Anpassungsfähigkeit und Ausdauer richtig waren. Auch tritt jetzt die tatsächliche Systemlast in Erscheinung, d.h. die Anzahl der Benutzer, der Betriebsmittelbedarf je Benutzer und die relative Verteilung des Daten- oder Arbeitsanfalls über die Zeit.

Bei einigen Standardprodukten sind die Endbenutzer zwar DV-Fachleute, dafür sind aber zusätzliche Personengruppen einzubeziehen, insbesondere solche, die für den Vertriebs- und Wartungsdienst benötigt werden.

Beide Situationen erfordern eine sorgfältige Vorbereitung, die in allen ihren Schritten und Aspekten geplant sein und konsequent durchgeführt werden muß.

In technischer Hinsicht gibt es einige konkrete Aufgabenstellungen, die in Tabelle 7 angegeben sind. Sie betreffen im wesentlichen die Umstellung oder Anpassung vorhandener Programme und Daten. Je älter die Datenverarbeitung wird, um so geringer wird die Wahrscheinlichkeit, daß ein neues DV-System ausschließlich manuelle Arbeitsabläufe ersetzt.

Für die *Datenumstellung* kommen verschiedene Methoden in Frage, je nachdem ob die bisherigen Datenträger beibehalten werden oder nicht. Ist sowohl eine Datenträgerumstellung als auch eine logische Reorganisation der Daten erforderlich, so kann die Umstellung kaum ohne spezielle Hilfsmittel und zusätzliche Geräte erfolgen.

Eine *Programmumstellung* ist immer dann nötig, wenn sich die Schnittstellen vorhandener Anwendungs- oder Systemprogramme ändern. Diese Schnittstellen sind mannigfacher Art, beginnend mit externen Sprachelementen bis zur relativen Lage einzelner Programmodule zur Ausführungszeit.

Für die eigentliche *Systemeinführung* stellt sich manchmal die Alternative zwischen Direkt- und Paralleleinführung. Bei der Direkteinführung erfolgt die Umstellung auf einen Schlag. Sie ist die kostengünstigere, aber risiko-reichere Methode. Die Paralleleinführung minimiert das Risiko, indem das alte System eine Weile neben dem neuen System betrieben wird und so eine Rückgriffsmöglichkeit erhalten bleibt. Dafür sind aber die Kosten des Parallelbetriebs wesentlich höher; manchmal können sogar technische Gründe diese Möglichkeit verhindern. Ein Kompromiß kann eine stufenweise Übernahme sein, d.h. es wird die mögliche Auswirkung eines Fehlschlags begrenzt. Für weitere Einzelheiten sei auf *Hice/Turner/Cashwell* (1974) oder *Wedekind* (1973) verwiesen.

Bei jedem komplexen System ist es sinnvoll, noch nach der Einführung die Möglichkeit der *Feinanpassung* (Tuning) vorzusehen. Gemeint ist damit, daß in der Entwicklungsphase einige Freiheitsgrade im System belassen wurden, die nach der Einführung verändert werden können, um die Leistungsfähigkeit dem tatsächlichen Bedarfsprofil anzupassen. Jedes moderne Betriebssystem bietet hier eine Reihe von Möglichkeiten, die jedoch nur ausgenutzt werden können, wenn sich das Anwendungsprogramm den entsprechenden Regeln unterworfen hat.

Bei einem Standardprodukt hat die Installationsphase zum Inhalt, daß ein Reproduktions- oder Verteilungszentrum in die Lage versetzt wird, Kundenbestellungen entgegenzunehmen und auszuliefern. Hierfür sind geräte- und programmtechnische Voraussetzungen zu schaffen, es müssen Arbeitspläne erstellt und Mitarbeiter ausgebildet werden.

BETRIEB UND WARTUNG

> "Three quarters of the total programmer time in our installation is spent in maintenance"
>
> *Elshoff* (1976)

Die Betriebs- und Wartungsphase ist die Endphase eines Entwicklungsprojekts. Hier zeigt es sich, ob die Qualitätsziele und damit der Nutzwert des Produkts erreicht werden.

Um den Betrieb eines DV-Systems sicherzustellen, sind mehrere Teilaufgaben zu lösen (siehe Tabelle 8). Sie umfassen die Ablaufsicherung, Datensicherung und Datenschutz und - im Falle eines Fehlverhaltens - die Rekonstruktion von Daten und Dateien. Die hierfür relevanten Methoden und Hilfsmittel gehören an sich zu einem anderen Themenkreis und sollen deshalb nicht weiter diskutiert werden.

Obwohl die Benutzung eines DV-Systems oft über viele Jahre gehen kann, plant man nur die ersten 2-3 Jahre nach der Installation als formelle Wartungsphase. In dieser Zeit konzentrieren sich die Aktivitäten, für die eine Wartungsdienst vorgesehen werden muß.

Bei der Diskussion um den Sinn und Zweck eines Wartungsdienstes findet man ähnlich kontroverse Meinungen wie beim Programmtesten. Ein Wartungsplan sei das Netz, das sich derjenige baut, der aufgrund unzureichender Entwicklungsmethoden weniger als ein qualitativ einwandfreies Produkt liefert. Obwohl bei Programmen der Faktor Verschleiß keine Rolle spielt, ist ein Programm ohne Wartungsunterstützung de facto nur die Hälfte wert. Außer der Behebung übriggebliebener Fehler dient ein Wartungsdienst auch dazu, dem Benutzer bei Schwierigkeiten mit dem Produkt zu helfen und eventuell notwendige kleinere Produktänderungen vorzunehmen.

Um den Arbeitsaufwand für die Wartung abzuschätzen, kann man Prognosen über die noch zu erwartenden Fehler mitbenutzen. Diese bauen entweder auf pauschalen Erfahrungswerten auf oder aber auf den konkreten, modulbezogenen Testergebnissen (siehe *Shooman* (1976)). Bei einem Standardprodukt gehen natürlich auch noch die Anzahl und die geographische Verteilung der Benutzer mit ein, da diese die Größe des Service-Netzes beeinflussen.

Bei der Organisation der Wartungsgruppe stellt sich die Frage, ob man eine gewisse Anzahl von Mitarbeitern ausschließlich mit Wartungsaufgaben betraut oder ob dies als eine Nebenaufgabe angesehen werden soll. Für das erste spricht das bessere Reaktionsvermögen, für das zweite eine teilweise bessere Arbeitszufriedenheit.

Zu den organisatorischen Aufgaben der Wartungsphase gehört die genaue Festlegung des Informationsflusses zwischen Benutzer und Wartungsgruppe, und zwar bezüglich Inhalt, Format und Verantwortlichkeit. Ähnlich wie in der Testphase ist eine sorgfältige Statuskontrolle von Vorteil, sowie eine Planung der Integrationsstufen. Als Hilfsmittel spielt wieder die Entwicklungsbibliothek eine zentrale Rolle, aber auch die Programmdokumentation und die Testdaten.

Je mehr Standardprodukte eingesetzt werden, um so mehr wird der Benutzer abhängig von nicht lokal gewarteten Programmen. Dies hat zur Folge, daß für alle Beteiligten die organisatorische Planung und Kontrolle zum zentralen Problem wird. Methoden, die hier von Nutzen sind, sind die maschinelle Buchführung über den Änderungsstand eines jeden Moduls, Vorkehrungen um Änderungen provisorisch einzubauen und wieder rückgängig zu machen sowie die Möglichkeit, Änderungen während des laufenden Betriebs vornehmen zu können. Gerade die lezte Möglichkeit gewinnt mit der Zunahme von interaktiven oder Echtzeitanwendungen an Bedeutung.

Welche funktionellen Änderungen noch im Rahmen der Wartungsphase abgedeckt werden sollen, oder wann es besser ist, ein neues Projekt zu beginnen, ist im Grunde eine Ermessensfrage. Die pragmatische Grenze dürfte sich dadurch ergeben, wie groß der Anteil des für die Wartung vorgesehenen Personals ist, der nicht für Fehlerkorrekturen in Anspruch genommen ist.

Die Geschichte vieler DV-Systeme kann man bereits in Zeiträumen von mehreren Jahrzehnten betrachten. Im Grunde muß man sogar eine unbegrenzte Lebensdauer annehmen. Als erste Autoren, die eine längerfristige Betrachtungsweise angewandt haben, sind *Belady/Lehman* (1971 , 1976, 1977) zu nennen. Bei ihren Untersuchungen von OS/360 betrachten sie nicht einzelne Veränderungen, noch die Gründe für diese, und kommen dennoch zu Aussagen über Gesetzmäßigkeiten, die vielleicht für alle großen Systeme gelten (Schlagwort: System dynamics).

ZUSAMMENFASSUNG UND AUSBLICK

In diesem Beitrag wurde das Problem der Programm- und Systemkonstruktion als die Summe zahlreicher Teilaufgaben dargestellt. Diese wurden in 6 zeitlich getrennten Phasen und einer projektbegleitenden Aktivität gruppiert. Das Programmieren im engeren Sinne, also das Erstellen neuer vollständiger Quellprogrammoduln, ist nur eine der vielen Teilaufgaben, wenn auch eine sehr zentrale.

Für die Lösung der einzelnen Teilaufgaben wurde eine Vielzahl von Methoden in Betracht gezogen. Dabei zeigte sich, daß je Aufgabe im Schnitt mehr als zwei Methoden in Frage kommen. Ähnlich sieht es bei den Hilfsmitteln aus.

Vorhandene Umfragen bei DV-Anwendern zeigen zwar, daß ihnen die Mehrzahl der hier erwähnten Methoden bekannt ist. Man hat sich in irgendeiner Form bereits mit ihnen beschäftigt. Die Zahl der tatsächlich angewandten Methoden ist ebenfalls recht hoch. Allerdings ist der Durchschnitt der Methoden, die bei all den Anwendern benützt werden, die dafür aufgrund ihrer gerätetechnischen oder anwendungsmäßigen Voraussetzungen in Frage kommen, sehr klein. Es ist noch vielfach eine Frage der subjektiven Präferenz, welche Methoden und welche Hilfsmittel benützt werden. Bei den praktischen DV-Anwendern fehlt es sicherlich nicht an der notwendigen Übereinstimmung in den Grundsätzen, dafür fehlt es jedoch an konkreten Daten über den Effekt einzelner Methoden, sowie an gezielter Unterstützung bei ihrer praktischen Anwendung.

Mehrere quantitative Untersuchungen über den Effekt einzelner Methoden liegen inzwischen vor, so von *Baker* (1975), *Fagan* (1976), *Walston/Felix* (1977) und *Black* (1977). Sie zeigen in der Regel einen Produktivitäts- oder Qualitätsgewinn je Methode von 50% bis 150%, d.h. der Effekt ist signifikant.

Abgesehen von möglichen psychologisch bedingten Veränderungen bei den Testprojekten (Stichwort: Hawthorne-Effekt), leiden die bisherigen Untersuchungen an folgendem generellen Problem: Beim Vergleich zweier Projekte können durchaus ungenannte Faktoren eine Rolle spielen, deren Auswirkung ein Vielfaches des oben erwähnten Wertes sein kann und die damit das Ergebnis stark überlagern. Ein Beispiel ist Bakers Vergleich zweier Raumfahrtprojekte (Apollo und Skylab). Er führt die Produktivitätssteigerung um einen Faktor von mehr als 3 auf die Verwendung von Strukturierter Programmierung und einer Entwicklungsbibliothek zurück, andererseits ist anzunehmen, daß die Vertrautheit der Programmierer mit der Aufgabenstellung einen gleichlaufenden Effekt haben muß. Laut Walston/Felix ist dieser ebenfalls mit einem Faktor 3 anzusetzen. Mit anderen Worten: Es ist sehr schwer, ein kontrolliertes Experiment durchzuführen, d.h. einen Vergleich zweier Projekte, bei dem der Einfluß aller Faktoren ferngehalten wird bis auf den einen, dessen Effekt man beobachten will. Andere experimentell arbeitende Wissenschaften haben durchaus dasselbe Problem und müssen auch irgendwie damit fertig werden.

Von den in diesem Bericht erwähnten Methoden sind etwa ein Viertel erst in den letzten zehn Jahren bekannt geworden. Das wird den überraschen, der annimmt, daß die letzten zehn Jahre eine Art revolutionären Durchbruch brachten. Neue Methoden erhalten naturgemäß ein Höchstmaß an Aufmerksamkeit. Die Aufmerksamkeit, die sie erhalten, ist jedoch nicht gleichzusetzen mit ihrer Bedeutung. Ich habe auch nicht den Eindruck, daß man bereits von einem geschlossenen Methodengebäude reden kann. Dies erreichen zu wollen, mag sogar eine Utopie sein.

Dennoch hat sich in diesen zehn Jahren eine wesentliche Änderung vollzogen. Die lebhafte, teils mit euphorischen Untertönen geführte Diskussion hat bewirkt, daß auch der Praktiker im Betrieb methoden-bewußter geworden ist und sogar bereit ist zuzuhören. Die Teilnahmeziffern bei entsprechenden Lehrgängen und Tagungen beweisen dies. Der Praktiker erwartet aber, daß ihm auf die Dauer bessere Entscheidungshilfen an die Hand gegeben werden als die subjektive Überzeugung einzelner. Hier haben sicherlich Hochschulen, Beratungsfirmen und Hersteller eine gemeinsame Aufgabe zu lösen.

Im gleichen Maße wie dies geschieht, wächst übrigens auch die wissenschaftliche Grundlage unseres Fachgebiets. Die Erfahrungen mit den Methoden von heute ergeben ja die Grundsätze von morgen. Nur wenn sich die Informatik im Sinne einer empirischen Wissenschaft um die Erfahrungen vieler kümmert, hat sie auch die Chance, eine Übereinstimmung in den Grundsätzen zu erreichen.

LITERATUR

Das nachfolgende Literaturverzeichnis enthält nur solche Arbeiten, auf die in diesem Beitrag Bezug genommen wurde. Eine nach Sachgebieten gegliederte Bibliographie, die das ganze Gebiet des "Software engineering" abdeckt, ist kürzlich von *Kleine* (1978) veröffentlicht worden. Einen ähnlich motivierten Statusbericht wie diesen geben *Boehm* (1976), *Gewald/Haake/Pfadler* (1977), *Infotech* (1977) und *Myers* (1978). Die drei ersten enthalten ebenfalls ausführliche Literaturangaben.

Aron, J.D.: Estimating resources for large programming systems, In: *Buxton/Randell* (1969)

Ascoli, J. et al.: Code inspection specifications, IBM Techn. Report TR21.630 (1976)

Bachman, C.W.: The programmer as navigator, Comm. ACM 16,11 (1973)

Baker, F.T.: Chief programmer team management of production programming, IBM Syst. J. 11,1 (1972)

Baker, F.T.: Structured programming in a production programming environment, IEEE Trans. Softw. Eng. 1,2 (1975)

Bauer, F.L. (ed): Advanced course on software engineering, Lecture Notes Economics and Math. Systems 81, Berlin: Springer (1973)

Belady, L.A. and Lehman, M.M.: Programming system dynamics, IBM report RC3546 (1971)

Belady, L.A. and Lehman, M.M.: A model of large program development, IBM Syst. J. 15,3 (1976)

Belady, L.A. and Lehman, M.M.: The characteristics of large systems, IBM report RC6785 (1977)

Belford, P.C., Donahoo, J.D. and Heard, W.J.: An evaluation of effectiveness of software engineering techniques, IEEE Compcon Fall (1977)

Bell, T.E. and Thayer, T.A.: Software requirements: Are they really a problem? Proc. 2nd Int. Conf. Softw. Eng. ACM/IEEE (1976)

Bell, T.E., Bixler, D.C. and Dyer, M.E.: An extendable approach to computer-aided software requirements engineering, IEEE Trans. Softw. Eng. 3,1 (1977)

Black, R.: Effects of modern programming practices on software development costs, IEEE Compcon Fall (1977)

Boehm, B.W. et at.: Some experience with automated aids to the design of large-scale software systems. Conf. Reliable Softw. ACM/IEEE (1975)

Boehm, B.W.: Software engineering, IEEE Trans. Computers 25,12 (1976)

Brooks, F.P.: The mythical manmonth, Reading, Mass.: Addison-Wesley (1975)

Brown, H.M.: Support software for large systems In *Buxton/Randell* (1969)

Buxton, J.N. and Randell, B. (eds): Software engineering techniques, Brussels: NATO Scient. Affairs (1969)

Caine, S.H. and Gordon, E.K.: PDL - a tool for software design, Nat. Comp. Conf. AFIPS (1975)

Daly, E.B.: Management of software development, IEEE Trans. Softw. Eng. 3,2 (1977)

Dijkstra, E.W.: Goto considered harmful, Comm. ACM 11,3 (1968a)

Dijkstra, E.W.: A constructive approach to the problem of program correctness, BIT 8 (1968b)

Dijkstra, E.W.: The structure of the THE multi-programming system, Comm. ACM 11,5 (1968c)

Dijkstra, E.W.: Notes on structured programming, Report EWD 219, Einhoven Technical University (1969)

Dijkstra, E.W.: Guarded commands, nondeterminacy and formal derivation of programs, Comm. ACM 18,8 (1975)

Elshoff, J.L.: An analysis of some commercial PL/I programs, IEEE Trans. Softw. Eng. 2,2 (1976)

Elshoff, J.L.: The influence of structured programmming on PL/I program profiles, IEEE Trans. Softw. Eng. 3,5 (1977)

Elspas, B. et al.: An assessment of techniques for proving program correctness, ACM Comp. Surveys, 4,2 (1972)

Endres, A.: Fehleranalyse und Fehlerursachen in Systemprogrammen, In *Hackl* (1974)

Endres, A.: Analyse und Verifikation von Programmen, München: Oldenbourg (1977)

Endres, A. and Glatthaar, W.: A complementary appraoch to program analysis and testing, IBM report GTR 05.215 (1977)

Fagan, M.E.: Design and code inspections to reduce errors in program development, IBM Syst. J. 15,3 (1976)

Floyd, R.W.: Assigning meaning to programs, Symp. Applied Math. 19, Providence R.I. (1967)

Fosdick, L.D. and Osterweil, L.J.: Data flow analysis in software reliability, ACM Comp. Surveys 8,3 (1976)

Gerhart, S.L. and Yelowitz, L.: Observations of fallibility in applications of modern programming methodologies, IEEE Trans. Softw. Eng. 2,3 (1976)

Gewald, K., Haake, G. und Pfadler, W.: Software engineering, München: Oldenbourg (1977)

Goodenough, J.B. and Gerhart, S.L.: Toward a theory of test data selection, IEEE Trans. Softw. Eng. 1,2 (1975)

Gotlieb, C.C.: Performance measurement In *Bauer* (1973)

Graham, R.M.: Performance prediction, In *Bauer* (1973)

Hackl, C. (ed): Programming methodology, Lecture Notes Comp. Science 23 Berlin: Springer (1974)

Hamming, R.W.: One man's view of computer science, J. ACM 16,1 (1969)

Hanford, K.V.: Automatic generation of test cases, IBM Syst. J. 9,4 (1970)

Haslinger, E., Meßerer, F. und Wolters, M.F.: Planung und Durchführung von EDV-Projekten, Düsseldorf: ECON (1975)

Hice, G.F., Turner, W.S. and Cashwell, L.F.: System development methodology, Amsterdam: North Holland (1974)

Hoare, C.A.R.: An axiomatic basis for computer programming, Comm. ACM 12,10 (1969)

Holton, J.B.: Are the new programming techniques being used? Datamation 23,7 (1977)

Howden, W.E.: Methodology for generation of program test data, IEEE Trans. Computers 24,5 (1975)

Howden, W.E.: Reliability of the path analysis testing strategy, IEEE Trans. Softw. Eng. 2,3 (1976)

Huang, J.C.: An approach to program testing, ACM Comp. Surveys 7,3 (1975)

IBM: HIPO - A design aid and documentation technique, Publ. Nr GC20-1851 (1974)

Infotech: Software reliability, Maidenhead: Infotech Ltd. (1977)

Jackson, M.: Principles of program design, London: Academic Press (1975)

Jones, T.C.: Measuring programming quality and productivity, IBM Syst. J. 17,1 (1978)

King, J.C.: A new appraoch to program testing, In *Hackl* (1974)

Kleine, K.: Selected anotated bibliography on software engineering, ACM Softw. Eng. Notes 3,1 (1978)

Kohli, O.R.: High-level design inspection specification, IBM Techn. Report TR21.601 (1975)

Kohli, O.R. and Radice, R.A.: Low-level design inspection specification, IBM Techn. Report TR21.629 (1976)

Komarnicki, O.: Programmiermethodik, Berlin: Springer (1971)

Larson, R.R.: Test plan and test case inspection specification, IBM Techn. Report TR21.586 (1975)

Liskov, B.H. and Zilles, S.N.: Programming with abstract data types, ACM SIGPLAN Notices 9,4 (1974)

London, R.L.: A view of program verification, Int. Conf. Reliable Softw. ACM/IEEE (1975)

Lucas, H.C.: Performance evaluation and monitoring, ACM Comp. Surveys 3,3 (1971)

Metzger, P.W.: Managing a programming project, Englewood Cliffs, N.J.: Prentice-Hall (1973)

Miller, E.F. and Paige, M.R.: Automatic generation of software test-cases, EUROCOMP Uxbridge (1974)

Miller, E.F.: Program testing: art meets theory, IEEE Computer 10,7 (1977)

Mills, H.D.: Top-down development in large systems, In *Rustin* (1971)

Mills, H.D. and Baker, F.T.: Chief programmer teams, Datamation 19, 12 (1973)

Myers, G.J.: Reliable software through composite design, New York: Petrocelli/Charter (1975)

Myers, W.: The need for software engineering, IEEE Computer 11,2 (1978)

Nassi, I. and Shneiderman, B.: Flowchart techniques for structured programming, ACM SIGPLAN Notices 8,8 (1973)

Naur, P.: Proof of algorithms by general snapshots, BIT 6,4 (1966)

Naur, P. and Randell, B. (eds): Software engineering, Brussels: NATO Scient. Affairs (1968)

Parnas, D.L.: A technique for software module specification with examples, Comm. ACM 15,5 (1972a)

Parnas, D.L.: On the criteria to be used in decomposing systems into modules, Comm. ACM 15,12 (1972b)

Ramamoorthy, C.V. and Ho, S.F.: Testing large software with automated software evaluation systems, IEEE Trans. Softw. Eng. 1,1 (1975)

Raver, N. and Hubbard, G.U.: Automatic logical data base design: Concepts and applications, IBM Syst. J. 16,3 (1977)

Robinson, R.A.: National software works: overview & status, IEEE Compcon Fall (1977)

Ross, D.T. and Schoman, K.E.: Structured analysis for requirements definition, IEEE Trans. Softw. Eng. 3,1 (1977)

Rustin, R. (ed): Debugging techniques in large systems, Englewood Cliffs, N.J.: Prentice-Hall (1971)

Schieferdecker, E.: Neue Methoden und Techniken der Programmierung, IBM Nachrichten, Heft 232 (1976)

Shooman, M.: Structural models for software reliability prediction, Proc. 2nd Int. Conf. Softw. Eng. ACM/IEEE (1976)

Stevens, W.P., Myers, G.J. and Constantine, L.L.: Structured design, IBM Syst. J. 13,2 (1974)

Strunz, H.: Entscheidungstabellentechnik , München: Hanser (1977)

Teichrow, D. and Hershey, E.A.: PSL/PSA: Computer-aided technique for structured documentation and analysis of information processing systems, IEEE Trans. Softw. Eng. 3,1 (1977)

Walston, C.E. and Felix, C.P.: A method of programming measurement and estimation, IBM Syst. J. 16,1 (1977)

Wedekind, H.: Systemanalyse, München:Hanser (1973)

Weinberg, G.M.: The psychology of computer programming, New York: Van Nostrand Reinhold (1971)

Wirth, N.: Program development by stepwise refinement, Comm. ACM 14,4 (1971a)

Wirth, N.: The programming language PASCAL, Acta Informatica 1,1 (1971b)

Wirth, N.: MODULA: a language for modular multiprogramming, Softw. Practice & Exp. 7,1 (1977)

Witt, J.: The COLUMBUS approach, Trans. Softw. Eng. 1,4 (1975)

Wolverton, R.W.: The cost of developing large-scale software, IEEE Trans. Computers 23,6 (1974)

Wulf, W.A.: ALPHARD: Toward a language to support structured programs, Comp. Science report, Carnegie-Mellon U.Pittsburgh (1974)

Hinweis Die Kapitelanfangszitate von Graham, Kinslow, Samelson und Van der Poel stammen alle aus *Naur/Randell* (1968)

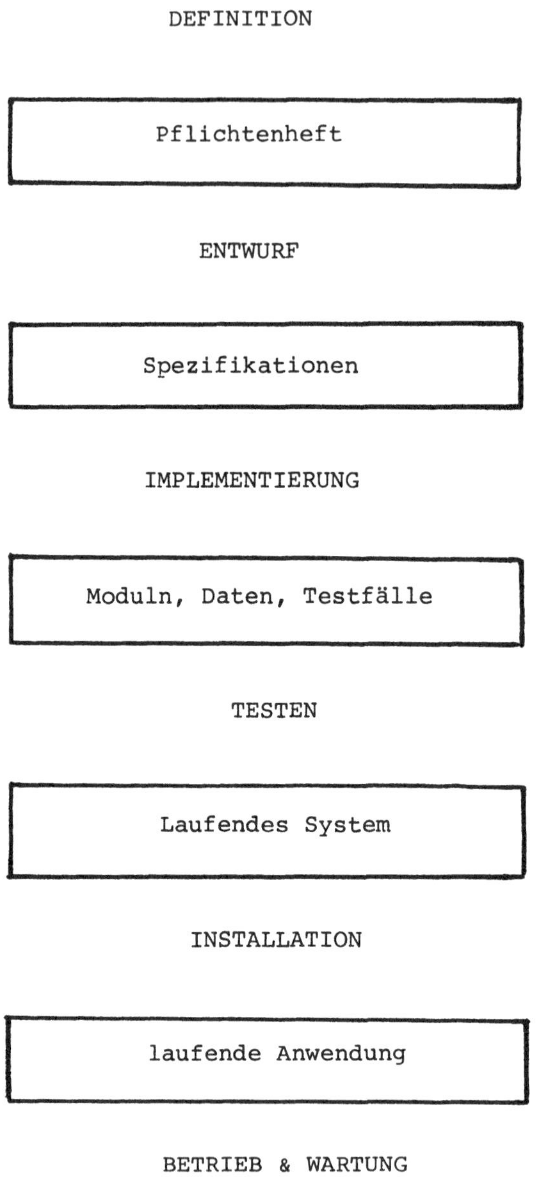

DEFINITION

Pflichtenheft

ENTWURF

Spezifikationen

IMPLEMENTIERUNG

Moduln, Daten, Testfälle

TESTEN

Laufendes System

INSTALLATION

laufende Anwendung

BETRIEB & WARTUNG

Bild 1: Projektphasen und ihre Ergebnisse

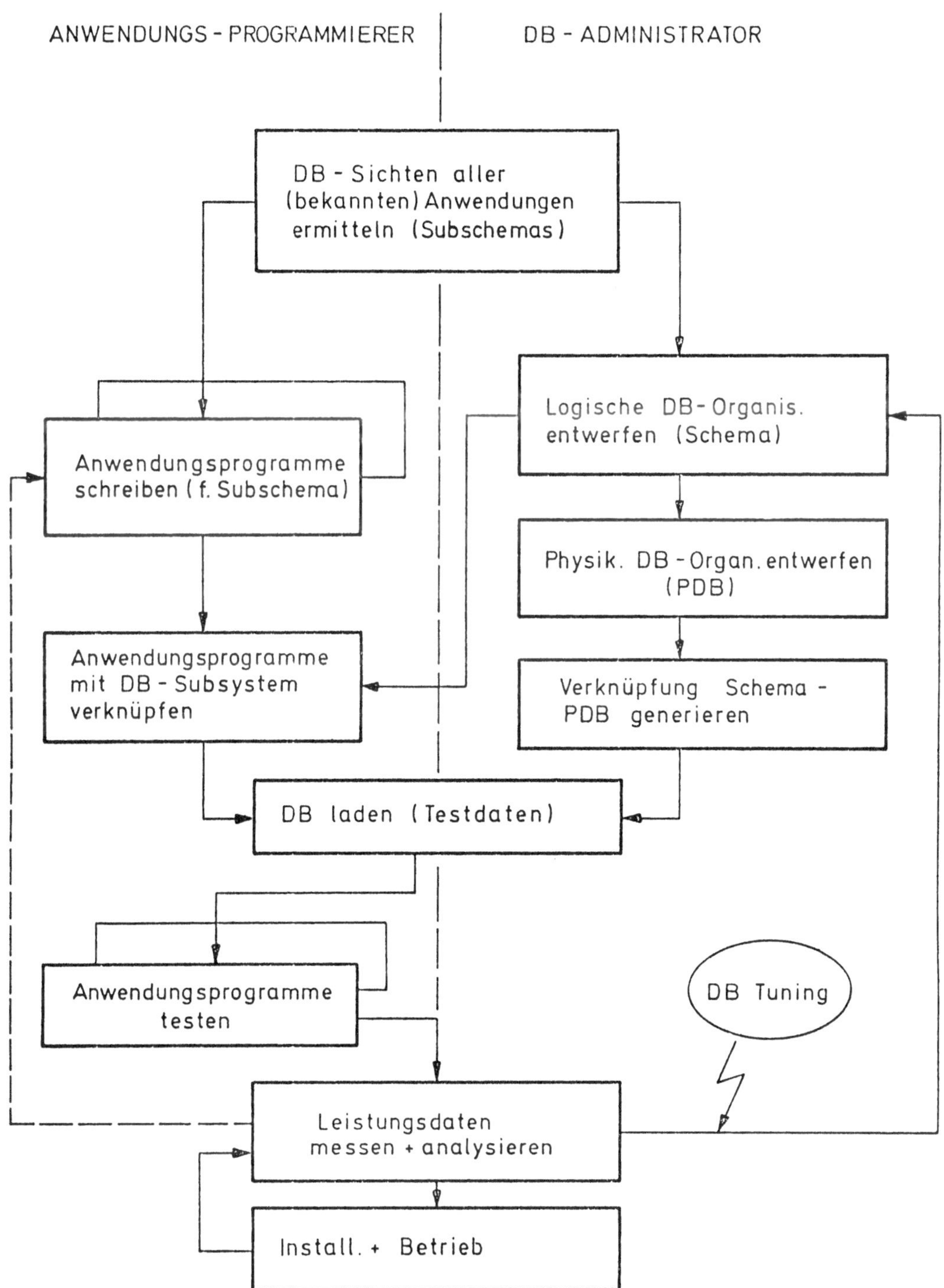

Bild 2: Entwurfs- und Entwicklungsschritte bei einem DB-System

AUFGABEN	METHODEN	HILFSMITTEL
Kostenschätzung	Vergleich mit ähnl. Projekten Extrapolation von einer Aufgabe Detailschätzung	(Daten früherer Projekte) (Faustregeln) Summations- und Listprogramme
Zeitschätzung	Indiv. Schätzung Kritischer Pfad	(Balkendiagramme) Netzplanprogramme
Arbeitsverteilung	Hierarchische Org. Matrixorganisation *Chefprogr. Team* Adaptives Team	
Statuskontrolle	Berichte Konferenzen Indirekte Methoden	} (Graphiken, Tabellen) Diverse Berichte

Tabelle 1: Projektplanung und -organisation

AUFGABEN	METHODEN	HILFSMITTEL
Bedarfsermittlung	Interview Konferenz Fragebogen	} (Audio-visuelle Hilfsmittel) Belegleser, List-programme
Bedarfsdoku-mentation (Pflichtenheft)	Text Datenflußdiagr., HIPO *Definitionssprache*	Text-Editor Graphik-Editor Editor & Bibliothek
Bedarfsprüfung	Präsentation an Auftraggeber & Benutzer Plausibilitätsprüfung *Konsistenz- und Vollständigkeitsprüfung*	(audio-visuelle Hilfsmittel) (Prüflisten) Definitions-Analysator
Bedarfsfort-schreibung	ohne Änderungs-kontrolle mit Änderungs-kontrolle	Text-Editor Änderungsprotokoll

Tabelle 2: Definitionsphase

AUFGABEN	METHODEN	HILFSMITTEL
Entwurf Dialoge & E/A-Formate	ohne Dialog-Simul. mit Dialog-Simul.	(Formulare) Dialogbeschreibg. Spr.
Entwurf DFÜ-Netz	Leitungskostenoptim. Belastungsermittlung	(Tabellen), Netzoptim. Verkehrssimulation
Auswahl Dateiorganis.	Zeitoptimierung Platzoptimierung	Zeitberechnungsprogr. Platzberechnungsprogr.
Auswahl DB-Struktur	Zugriffsoptim. Anwendungsunabh.	Zugriffsberechnung Vollständigkeitsprüfung
Programmentwurf	Entscheidungstabellen *Jackson-Methode* *Myers-Methode* Datenabstraktion	ET-Prüfer & Übersetzer
Entwurfs-dokumentation (Spezifikation)	Text Flußdiagr. (DIN 66001) *Nassi-Shneiderman* *HIPO* *Pseudokode*	Text-Editor Graphik-Editor spez. Zeichenprogr. Programm-Editor
Funktionale Prüfung	Prototyp-Implem. *Entwurfsinspektion*	Simul. od. Progr. Spr. (Prüflisten)
Leistungs-schätzung (allgemein)	Analytische Modelle Simulat. Modelle	Progr.-Sprachen Simul. Spr., Systeme

Tabelle 3: Entwurfsphase

AUFGABE	METHODE	HILFSMITTEL
Erstellung von Bildschirmmasken & Listformaten	generativ interaktiv	(Formulare) Format-Generator Format-Editor
Erstellung von Datenbeschreibgen	sprachorientiert sprachunabhängig	Copy-Bibliothek Datenkatalog
Erzeugung von Daten und Datenstrukturen	Datei-orientiert DB-orientiert	Datei-Initialisierung Lade-, Prüfprogramm DB-Generator
Erstellung von standardisierten Anwendungs- u. Dienstprogr.	Fragebogen-Methode Formularsprachen Normierte Progr. Entscheidungstabellen	Anwendungsanpasser Listprogr. Generator Generator f. norm. Progr. ET-Übersetzer
Erstellung beliebiger Quellprogr.	generativ interaktiv	(Formulare, vorgedruckte Karten) Programm-Editor, Prompter
Dokumentation von Programmen	schritthaltend retrospektiv	(siehe Entwurfsdok.) Dokum. Programme
Kode-Umwandlung und -Optimierg.	auf Zielmaschine auf Gastmaschine	(Macro-)Assembler Kompilierer Kreuz-Assembler Kreuz-Kompilierer

Tabelle 4: Implementierungsphase, Teil 1

AUFGABE	METHODE	HILFSMITTEL
Programmprüfung	Schreibtischtests	(Tischrechner)
	Programm-Analyse (statisch)	Strukturprüfer Standardprüfer Schnittstellenprüfer Bereichsanalysator Pfadanalysator Dekompilierer
	Korrektheitsbeweise	VC-Generator Theorem-Prüfer
	Kode-Inspektion	(Prüflisten) (Org.-Anweisungen)
Verknüpfung mit Betriebssystem und DB-Moduln	Quellprogr. Verkfg.	Vorübersetzer Macro-Assembler
	Objektprogr. Verkfg.	Binder
Programm-Speicherung & -verwaltung	Lochkartenkartei	(Farbkarten, Reiter)
	Magnet-Speicherung (ohne Strukturinfo)	Einfaches Bibliotheks-system
	Magnet-Speicherung (mit Strukturinfo)	Baumstrukt. Entwickl. Bibliothek
Programmkontrolle & Statistik	Statuskontrolle	Vollständigkeitsprüfer Vergleichsprogr. Quantitative Auswertg.
	Änderungskontrolle	Modulbenutzung Fehlerberichte

Tabelle 5: Implementierungsphase, Teil 2

AUFGABEN	METHODEN	HILFSMITTEL
Testfallauswahl	Stichprobe *Strukturierter Test*	Zufallszahlen-Generator Dateigenerator Syntaxmaschine Bereichsanalysator Pfadanalysator
Testdurchführung	Programmierer an Maschine Stapelbetrieb durch Operateur Interaktiver Betrieb d. Programmierer Benützung einer Gastmaschine	Lader, Testmonitor Einzelschrittmodus Testfall-Bibliothek, Treibersystem Interpreter, Symb. Ausf. Testmonitor, Simulator, Emulator Virtuelle Maschine
Auswertung	Ohne bekannte Ergebn. Mit bekannten Ergebn.	(Tischrechner) Autom. Ergebnisvergleich
Fehlersuche	Masch. Sprache Höhere Sprache	Adresstop, Speicherabzug, Protokoll Variablen-, Verzweigungs- Verschachtlungs-Protokoll
Testkontrolle	Abdeckungskontrolle Erfolgskontrolle	Instruktions-, Pfadmarkierer Testberichte

Tabelle 6: Testphase

AUFGABEN	METHODEN	HILFSMITTEL
Datenumstellung	Trägerumstellung Reorganisation	Konversationssystem Daten-Emulator Reorg.-Programm
Programmumstellung	Manuelle Änderung der Quellprogr. Masch. Quellprogr.-umstellung Rekompilierung Verschiebung Biblioth. Umstellung	Programm-Editor Vorübersetzer Kompilierer Binder Bibl. Reorg. Progr.
Systemeinführung	Direkteinführung Stufenweise Einführung Parallelbetrieb	Virtuelle Maschine
Feinanpassung (Tuning)	Datenorganisation Bibliotheks-Org. Gerätezuordnung Prioritätsvergabe Pufferzuordnung Pufferungsmethode	DB Analysator H/W Monitor S/W Monitor

Tabelle 7: Installationsphase

AUFGABEN	METHODEN	HILFSMITTEL
Belegungsplanung	Vordergrund-, Hintergrundbelegung Terminarbeiten	
Datenerfassung & Ablaufsicherung	Direkterfassung Vorbearbeitung Nachbearbeitung	
Leistungsverrechnung	Pauschale Abschätzung Erfassung Betriebsmittelverbrauch je Auftrag	Buchführungsroutine
Datensicherung	Schreib-Leseschutz Redundante Speicherung	Rechnerarchitektur Zugriffsmethoden
Datenschutz	Benützer-Identifizierung Sicherung von Räumen Verschlüsselung	Paßwort, Ausweis Verschlüsselungsgeräte
Rekonstruktion von Dateien	Fixpkt/Wiederanlauf Änderungsjournal	Betriebssystem Zugriffsmethoden
Programmwartung	Zentrale Wartung durch Entwickler Dezentrale Wartung durch Benutzer	Entw. Bibliothek (Service Org.) s. Testphase

Tabelle 8: Betrieb und Wartung

Dr. Reuse - Diskussionsleiter

Podiumsdiskussion über "Berufsaussichten für Informatiker"
8. Jahrestagung der Gesellschaft für Informatik in Berlin

Zeit: Montag, den 2. Oktober 1978, 17.15 Uhr - 18.45 Uhr

Ziel der Veranstaltung:

In der Umfrage "Zur Berufssituation des Diplominformatikers 1977", veröffentlicht in der 23. Folge der GI-Mitteilungen vom 1o. März 1978, wurde erkennbar, daß die bisher ausgebildeten Diplom-Informatiker zu etwa gleichen Teilen in der DV-Industrie, bei DV-Anwendern und im Bereich Lehre/Forschung eingesetzt sind und daß sie ihre eigenen Berufsaussichten positiv sehen.

Ziel der Veranstaltung ist, die Einschätzung der generellen Berufsaussichten für Informatiker und die Trends in den wichtigsten Einsatzgebieten von der Seite der Einstellenden zu beleuchten und eine Prognose über die zukünftigen Berufsaussichten für Informatiker zu versuchen.
Da das Ergebnis der Umfrage der GI nur für den Hochschulbereich vorliegt, zielt die gesamte Veranstaltung vorwiegend auf diesen Bereich (Haupt- und Nebenfachinformatiker) ab.

Formaler Ablauf der Veranstaltung:
In Kurzvorträgen werden von den Podiumsdiskussionsteilnehmern Fakten, Meinungen und Prognosen zur angesprochenen Problematik dargestellt. Daran anschließend und darauf aufbauend findet die Podiumsdiskussion unter sofortiger Beteiligung der Zuhörerschaft statt.

Einzelbeiträge:
1. Viele junge Studenten bewegt die Frage, wie sich die Berufssituation darstellen wird, nachdem Anfang oder Mitte der 8oer Jahre der Vollausstoß an Informatik-Absolventen der Universitäten und die Sättigung des Nachholbedarfes der Industrie erreicht sind.
   In dem ersten Beitrag wird Herr Dipl.-Ing. Dostal, Institut für Arbeitsmarkt- und Berufsforschung der Bundesanstalt für Arbeit, daher versuchen, langfristige Aussagen zu dem qualitativen und quantitativen Bedarf und zum Angebot an Informatikern unter Be-

rücksichtigung des gesamten Arbeitsmarkts zu formulieren.

2. Zur Erinnerung für die Zuhörer und zur Vorbereitung der folgenden 3 Beiträge werden die Ergebnisse der Umfrage der GI von Herrn Professor Hackl, Unternehmensverbindung Wissenschaft der Firma IBM, nochmals kurz dargestellt und anschließend interpretiert.

3.-5. In diesen 3 Beiträgen soll aus der Sicht je eines Vertreters der DV-Anwender (Dr. Faßbender), der DV-Hersteller (Dipl.-Ing. Seßler, Firma Siemens) und des Bereiches Forschung und Lehre (Professor Krüger, Universität Karlsruhe und GfK) dargestellt werden, wie die ersten Erfahrungen mit dem Einsatz der Informatiker in diesen Bereichen sind, welche Wünsche an die Ausbildung sich aus diesen ersten Erfahrungen ableiten lassen und welche Erwartungen bezüglich des zukünftigen Einsatzes von Informatikern bestehen.

Podiumsdiskussion "Berufsaussichten für Informatiker"

Längerfristige Berufsaussichten für Informatiker

Werner Dostal
Institut für Arbeitsmarkt- und Berufsforschung, Nürnberg

Prognoseproblematik

Prognosen über längerfristige Berufsaussichten sind eine Anforderung an die Arbeitsmarkt- und Berufsforschung schon seit jeher, da man allgemein erwartet, eine Berufsberatung sei nur möglich, wenn die Beschäftigungssituation für die nächsten 30 bis 50 Jahre für jeden Ausbildungsberuf als Prognose vorläge. Gewiß gibt es Prognosen über einzelne Berufe, auch längerfristige, doch sind sie meist sehr fein abgegrenzt: es wird ein bestimmtes wirtschaftliches Wachstum unterstellt, die Abgrenzung zu anderen Berufsfeldern wird mit einer Ausschließlichkeit definiert, daß Mobilitätsströme von vorneherein ausgeschaltet werden, und außerdem wird eine Reihe von sonstigen Faktoren mehr oder weniger deutlich fixiert. Meistens dient dann eine derartige Prognose einer Strategie, um z.B. Interessenten von einer bestimmten Ausbildung abzuhalten, indem man behauptet, ein Beruf sei hoffnungslos überlaufen und die Aussichten seien überhaupt sehr schlecht, oder man versucht im Gegenteil durch Schilderung bester Zukunftsaussichten Interessenten für eine Ausbildung zu interessieren.

Die einfachste Methode der Trendextrapolation scheitert bei Trendbrüchen und es sind meist derartige Vorgänge, die zu gänzlich neuen Möglichkeiten für bestimmte Berufsgruppen führen. Die guten Berufschancen für Mathematiker und Physiker in der Datenverarbeitung in den sechziger Jahren waren in keiner Prognose vorhergesagt worden.

Doppelt schwierig wird eine Prognose bei Berufen, die sich in der Berufswelt noch keinen festen Platz erworben haben, die sich für die Beschäftiger noch nicht durchgesetzt haben. Es dauert auch heute noch fast ein Jahrzehnt, bis ein neuer Beruf mit spezieller Berufsbezeichnung und Zertifizierung in der Praxis einen Platz gefunden hat. Da wir noch gar nicht so genau wissen, auf welchen Gebieten und für welche Tätigkeiten sich Informatiker am besten eignen und welche anderen Berufsgruppen in Konkurrenz treten werden, ist es müßig, Zahlenspielereien auszuarbeiten.

Stattdessen seien hier einige Thesen angeführt, die die besondere Situation der Informatiker auf längere Sicht beleuchten sollen:

Thesen

- Informatiker sind nicht für Routinearbeit konzipiert. Mit der perfekten Lösung ist ihre Tätigkeit für eine vorgegebene Aufgabe meist abgeschlossen. Für eine ständige Beschäftigung sollten deshalb die Aufgaben kontinuierlich fließen, eine Forderung die überall schwer zu erfüllen ist.

  Natürlich gibt es Aufgaben kontinuierlicher Art, Wartung und Pflege vorhandener Lösungen, die doch wohl nie das Gewicht der innovativen Aufgaben erreichen werden.

  Die immanente Problematik der Beschäftigung im Informatikbereich wird es sein, den Wunsch nach stetiger Beschäftigung nicht durch die Übernahme von Routinetätigkeit zu erfüllen, sondern immer wieder den Sprung zu neuen Aufgaben zu wagen.

- Der Wunsch, den Platz eines Berufsstandes durch eine standespolitische Absicherung wie durch die Fixierung von Zugangsvoraussetzungen und den Ausschluß anderer (ähnlicher) Ausgebildeten zu schützen, ist verständlich und hat in manchen Fällen funktioniert. Die damit verbundene Problematik liegt darin, daß beanspruchte Claims auch ausgelastet werden müssen und daß der Übergang in andere Bereiche von anderen Seiten ebenso verhindert werden kann.

- Bei der Definition eines Tätigkeitsfeldes für eine neue Berufsgruppe gibt es eine aktive und eine passive Vorgehensweise:

  Aktiv können die Absolventen einer speziellen Ausbildung ihr Aufgabengebiet weitgehend selbst bestimmen, wenn sie ein entsprechendes Personalmarketing betreiben. Dabei können sich Strukturen bilden, die für die Nachfolger derselben Ausbildung noch bessere Chancen eröffnen. (Aufreißen eines Marktes).

  Passiv können die Absolventen warten, bis ihnen Aufgaben zugewiesen werden und bis sie von anderen in bestimmte Tätigkeitsgebiete (ab-)geschoben werden. Dabei bleiben für die Absolventen neuer Ausbildungen meist nur undankbare Randgebiete.

- Die Arbeitsteilung zwischen unterschiedlich Ausgebildeten spielt sich meist individuell ein in einer Konkurrenzsituation, in der Erfahrung und Ausbildung zu einer qualifizierten Struktur führen müssen. Absolventen einer neuen, qualitativ nicht umstrittenen Ausbildung haben zunächst den Ausbildungsvorsprung. Da es aber lange dauert, bis sie auch den Erfahrungsvorsprung haben, kann sich eine neue Ausbildung zwangsläufig nur langsam durchsetzen.

- Vertikale Mobilität, also die Realisierung von Aufstiegschancen, ist für akademisch Ausgebildete leichter zu realisieren, als für nicht akademisch Zertifizierte, da der Leistungsnachweis zumindest bis zu einem bestimmten Grade in der Ausbildung erbracht wurde und nicht mehr dauernd unter Beweis gestellt zu werden braucht.

  Durch die Einkommensnivellierung in bezug auf den Ausbildungsabschluß gibt es von der Kostenseite auch keine Hemmnisse für einen niedrigeren Einstieg bei ungünstigerer Arbeitsmarktlage.

- Regionale Mobilität ist im Bereich der Hochqualifizierten sowieso eine Grundbedingung, sollte aber nicht überbewertet werden. Gerade die moderne Datenverarbeitung wird längerfristig zur Entkoppelung von Arbeitsort und Produktionsort beitragen.

- Bei einer weiteren Penetration aller Lebensbereiche durch Datenverarbeitung, wie ernstzunehmende Prognosen dies längerfristig vorhersagen, kann nicht damit gerechnet werden, daß dies gleichzeitig zu einem entsprechenden Wachstum an Arbeitsplätzen für Informatiker führt. Vielmehr werden dann verstärkt informatikbezogene Arbeitsinhalte in andere Berufsbilder übergehen (Werkzeugcharakter der Datenverarbeitung), während für die Informatiker nur die Kerngebiete mit gesteigerter Problematik übrigbleiben. Ob dies langfristig zu einer Zunahme oder Abnahme der für Informatiker angebotenen Arbeitsplätze führen wird, läßt sich derzeit noch nicht vorher-sagen.

Folgerungen

Ein Informatik-Absolvent mit akademischem Zertifikat dürfte sowohl kurzfristig als auch langfristig gute Beschäftigungsaussichten haben. Diese Beschäftigungsaussichten sind abhängig

- von der globalen Arbeitsmarktlage
- von der weiteren Penetration der Datenverarbeitung in unserer Gesellschaft, die auch langfristig fortschreiten wird
- von dem Bild, das sich die Beschäftiger von dem "Informatiker" machen, das geprägt ist durch die Vorgänger, soweit es schon welche gab
- von den zusätzlich gebotenen persönlichen und fachlichen Qualifikationen des Informatikers auch auf anderen Gebieten.

Im Laufe der Berufskarriere wird dem Einzelnen eine Entscheidung darüber abverlangt, ob er sich zum hochqualifizierten Sachbearbeiter oder zur Führungskraft entwickeln will.

Sollte er Führungskraft werden wollen, dann tritt er zwangsläufig in Konkurrenz mit Anderen, die Ausbildungen anderer Fachqualifikation und anderen Niveaus durchlaufen haben. In dieser Konkurrenzsituation nimmt die Bedeutung der Ausbildung ab und es bleiben oft nur Randbereiche von Ausbildung und Berufserfahrung als entscheidende Elemente übrig. Hierbei ist die Gefahr, in Sackgassen zu geraten, durchaus gegeben. Dies sollte der berücksichtigen, der sein Ziel nicht in der qualifizierten Sachbearbeitung, sondern im Management sieht.

PODIUMSDISKUSSION ÜBER BERUFSAUSSICHTEN DER INFORMATIKER

Interpretation der Ergebnisse der GI-Umfrage zur Berufssituation der Diplom-Informatiker 1977

Prof. C. Hackl, IBM Deutschland GmbH, Stuttgart

Nachdem bis Anfang 1977 etwa 1000 Studierende der Fachrichtung Informatik an Technischen Hochschulen und Universitäten ihr Studium abgeschlossen haben und in das Berufsleben eingetreten sind, hat das Präsidium der Gesellschaft für Informatik die Durchführung einer Umfrage zur Berufssituation der Diplom-Informatiker beschlossen und den Fachausschuß 9/10 Ausbildung mit der Durchführung der Erhebung beauftragt.

Ziel dieser Umfrage war es, festzustellen, in welchen Bereichen der Wirtschaft, der Industrie, der Verwaltung und der Wissenschaft Informatiker Arbeitsplätze gefunden haben, ihre Tätigkeitsfelder zu erfassen und Vorschläge zur Informatik-Ausbildung aus der Sicht der Berufsanforderungen zu erarbeiten.

1. Durchführung der Umfrage

Der Fachausschuß 9/10 Ausbildung der Gesellschaft für Informatik hat im ersten Halbjahr 1977 einen Fragebogen erarbeitet, der Fragen zum Beruf, zur beruflichen Fortbildung, zum Studium und zur Person einschloß. Der Fragebogen wurde in den Mitteilungen der Gesellschaft für Informatik, 23. Folge, März 1978, veröffentlicht.

Der erarbeitete Fragebogen wurde Anfang September 1977 mit Unterstützung durch die Informatik-Institute an den Hochschulen ausgesandt. Um Mitarbeit wurden alle Informatik-Institute gebeten, die im Studien- und Forschungsführer Informatik, Ausgabe 1976, von Brauer, Haacke, Hoffmann, Münch, herausgegeben von GMD und DAAD, aufgeführt waren.

Insgesamt wurden 1200 Absolventen angeschrieben, die zwischen 1972 und 1977 (Sommersemester) ihre Studien abgeschlossen haben. Bei Absolventen des Studienganges Informatik an den Hochschulen betrug die Rücklaufquote 44,4 %. Diese für Fragebogenerhebungen ungewöhnlich hohe Beteiligung ist eine günstige Voraussetzung, um eine repräsentative Datenbasis für die angesprochene Zielgruppe zu gewinnen.

2. Ergebnisse

Die Auswertung der Umfrage ist veröffentlicht in den Mitteilungen der GI, 23. Folge, März 1978, und in der Zeitschrift Informatik-Spektrum, Band 1, Heft 1, August 1978. Aus Platzgründen können an dieser Stelle nur einige wesentliche Ergebnisse kurz aufgeführt werden.

Einsatzbereiche: Die Verteilung der Stichprobe ergab für die gebildeten Bereiche DV-Anwendung 36,1 % der Nennungen, für DV-Industrie 31,7 % und für den Bereich Lehre/Forschung 32,2 %.

Unternehmensgröße: 59 % der befragten Diplom-Informatiker in Industrie und Wirtschaft sind in Unternehmen mit weniger als 5.000 Beschäftigten tätig. Im Bereich DV-Anwendung sind Großunternehmen kaum vertreten.

Position und Vorgänger: Vorwiegend werden berufliche Anfangspositionen ausgeübt. Zwei Drittel aller Befragten gaben an, an einem neu eingerichteten Arbeitsplatz tätig zu sein und keinen Vorgänger gehabt zu haben.

Tätigkeitsfelder: Eine detaillierte Abfrage der Tätigkeiten ergab, daß zwei Drittel aller Nennungen im Bereich der Programmerstellung und der Systemanalyse liegen sowie etwa ein Drittel in den Bereichen der Infrastruktur und der Technik.

Berufe der Datenverarbeitung: Bezüglich der Zuordnung der Diplom-Informatiker zu den Berufen der Datenverarbeitung ergab sich eine breite Streuung, wobei Systemprogrammierer, Systemanalytiker und Anwendungsprogrammierer an der Spitze der Nennungen liegen mit Schwerpunkten im Bereich der Systemprogrammierung in der DV-Industrie und im Bereich der Systemanalyse und Anwendungsprogrammierung in der DV-Anwendung.

Einkommen: Die Einkommenssituation der Diplom-Informatiker entspricht unter Berücksichtigung der beruflichen Anfangssituation der Befragten im wesentlich der vergleichbarer DV-Berufe. Das durchschnittliche Bruttojahreseinkommen 1976 war im Bereich der DV-Industrie am höchsten (DM 40,560), gefolgt vom DV-Anwendungsbereich (DM 38,620) und dem Bereich Lehre/Forschung (DM 36,870).

Zufriedenheit: 48 % der Befragten gaben an, mit ihrer Berufssituation zufrieden zu sein, 45 % sind teilweise zufrieden, 7 % sind nicht zufrieden.

Zusätzliche Ausbildung durch Arbeitgeber: 59 % der Befragten gaben an, von ihrem Arbeitgeber keine zusätzliche Ausbildung zur Ausübung ihrer beruflichen Tätigkeit erhalten zu haben. Das Angebot an fachlicher Weiterbildung ist in der DV-Industrie am höchsten, gefolgt vom Bereich DV-Anwendung und dem Bereich Lehre/Forschung.

3. Bewertung der Umfrageergebnisse

Zusammenfassend kann aufgrund der Umfrageergebnisse gesagt werden, daß zum gegenwärtigen Zeitpunkt die Berufssituation der Diplom-Informatiker als gut bezeichnet werden kann.

Über die Umfrageergebnisse hinaus sind jedoch die folgenden Gesichtspunkte mit zu betrachten:

- Es handelt sich um eine Anfangssituation, sowohl hinsichtlich des Berufsbildes des Diplom-Informatikers als auch der persönlichen Berufspraxis der Befragten, die im Durchschnitt nur etwa 1 - 2 Jahre beträgt.

- Da der Trend zu höheren Anforderungen und zu höherer Qualifikation in den Berufen der Datenverarbeitung weiter anhalten wird, insbesondere in allen Tätigkeiten, die mit den immer komplexer werdenden DV-Systemen selbst in unmittelbarem Zusammenhang stehen, sind die Berufsaussichten für Diplom-Informatiker auch in der nächsten Zeit als gut anzusehen.

- Die Grundlagenorientierung des Informatikstudiums ermöglicht einen guten Einstieg in die breit gefächerten Berufe der Datenverarbeitung. Eine einheitliche Studienregelung, insbesondere für die Grundlagenfächer, sollte nach Möglichkeit beibehalten werden, um die Studiengänge transparent und die Abschlüsse vergleichbar zu machen.

- Im DV-Anwendungsbereich hingegen, insbesondere bei Aufgabenstellungen, die eine Integration der Datenverarbeitung in die einzelnen Fachgebiete oder Fachabteilungen hinein erfordern, wird sich zu den Absolventen anderer Fachrichtungen, etwa Wirtschaftsinformatikern, Ingenieuren, Physikern, Mathematikern, längerfristig gesehen für die Diplom-Informatiker eine gewisse Konkurrenzsituation ergeben.

- Der Konzeption des Nebenfachstudiums der Informatik für andere Fachrichtungen muß daher stärkere Aufmerksamkeit gewidmet werden.

Um zuverlässigere Aussagen über längerfristige Tendenzen gewinnen zu können, sollte in etwa 2 bis 3 Jahren eine Umfrage zur Berufssituation der Informatiker unter Einbeziehung benachbarter Studiengänge wiederholt werden.

Berufsaussichten für Informatiker

Die berufliche Situation der Informatiker im Bereich der DV-Anwendungen.

Dr. Wolfgang Fassbender

Die folgenden Ausführungen sind eine Zusammenfassung der persönlichen Eindrücke des Autors und einzelner Meinungen von Führungskräften aus Industriebetrieben, im wesentlichen des Maschinenbaues, also keine Aussagen im Sinne einer statistischen Repräsentanz. Es sei ferner vorangestellt, dass die Notwendigkeit einer geregelten berufsvorbereitenden Informatik-Ausbildung von den DV-Anwendern nachdrücklich befürwortet wird. Der Beitrag kann sich daher - unter selbstverständlicher Würdigung des breiten Nutzens, den die mit Unterstützung der DV-Förderung der Bundesregierung in Gang gesetzte Informatik-Ausbildung stiftet - auf die Kritik konzentrieren, um so in der gebotenen Kürze möglichst viele Anregungen für Verbesserungen geben zu können.

Die wichtigste Feststellung dürfte sein: Informatik ist wie Mathematik und Statistik in der überwiegenden Zahl aller Berufsfälle eine Hilfsdisziplin. Vor allem die DV-Anwender benötigen betriebswirtschaftlich und technisch vorgebildete Mitarbeiter, die aber ein gutes DV-Zusatzwissen mitbringen sollten. Von den Hauptfachinformatikern müssten also die Anwendungsorientierung und die entsprechenden Nebenfächer zum Schwerpunkt ihres Studiums gemacht werden, wenn sie gute Berufschancen bei DV-Anwendern haben möchten. Am besten dürften dort aber die Aussichten für Nebenfachinformatiker sein. Es sollte deshalb kritisch geprüft werden, ob die zahlenmässige Verteilung der Studierenden auf die verschiedenen Richtungen der Informatik heute bedarfsgerecht ist, und es müssten Einflussmöglichkeiten gesucht werden, welche die Studienanfänger in Richtung der besten Berufschance führen.

Haupt- wie Nebenfachinformatiker dürfen beim DV-Anwender die mittleren Führungsebenen nicht als "unvermeidliche Durchgangsstationen" ansehen, sondern müssen sich besonders auf die Aufgaben dieser Ebene vorbereiten; dazu gehören vor allen Dingen Kenntnisse über Projektmanagement, Mitarbeiterführung, Präsentationstechniken und auch eine gewisse "verkäuferische" Grundschulung.

Das Informatik-Studium darf nicht mehr betrieben werden überwiegend mit Blickrichtung auf Datenverarbeitung mittels grösserer Universalcomputer. Besondere Beachtung muss den sich rasch verbreitenden vielfältigen Formen des "Distributed Processing" - inkl. Textbe- und -verarbeitung - und der ständig wachsenden Integration der verschiedenen sich "computerisierenden" Kommunikationsarten geschenkt werden. Auf diesen Gebieten müssen vor allem die Hochschulen ihr Stoffangebot noch beträchtlich erweitern, denn in fast allen Fachabteilungen eines DV-Anwenders lassen sich diese Kenntnisse in Zukunft gut verwerten.

Seit den Anfängen der Computertechnik werden von Wissenschaftlern und Praktikern gleichermassen die vielfältigen Inkompatibilitäten der Datenverarbeitung, insbesondere das Fehlen der Portabilität und der leichten Anpassungsfähigkeit von Anwendungsprogrammen beklagt. Der Ruf nach dem Einsatz neuer softwaretechnologischer Werkzeuge, die das Übel beheben sollen, schwillt an, aber auf der Ausbildungsseite wird noch zu wenig in dieser Richtung getan. Schon die herkömmlichen Programmierkenntnisse der Informatikabsolventen werden häufig bemängelt, von einer Befähigung zur Anwendung fortschrittlicher computergestützter Methoden zur Erstellung von Anwendungssoftware ist meist nichts vorhanden. Gerade auf diesem für den wirtschaftlichen Einsatz der Datenverarbeitung so entscheidenden Gebiet erwarten die DV-Anwender aber, dass das mit viel Aufwand geschaffene Fachstudium Informatik bald die Fachleute hervorbringt, welche dieses brennende Problem zu lösen imstande sind.

Das Informatik-Studium müsste besonders viele Übungen enthalten, in denen Fälle aus der Praxis behandelt und im Team bearbeitet werden. Auch Seminar- und Diplomarbeiten sollten praxisbezogen sein. Von einem Mitarbeiter mit Informatik-Ausbildung wird bei DV-Anwendern allgemein erwartet, dass er in erster Linie ein fachlicher Problemlöser betriebswirtschaftlicher oder technischer Art ist, sein "DV-Handwerk" muss er ausserdem verstehen, d. h. er benötigt auf diesem Gebiet viel Wissen, aber weniger Kreativität. Für die Mehrzahl der Informatik-Studenten ist deshalb vom Berufsziel her praktische Wissensvermittlung wichtiger als theoretische Denkbefähigung auf diesem Gebiet. In dieser Frage gehen offensichtlich die Ansichten der Universitäten und der DV-Anwender, insbesondere beim Hauptfach Informatik, auseinander. Beide Seiten sollten sich deshalb im Interesse guter Berufschancen der Studierenden durch Schaffung geeigneter Diskussionsgremien möglichst bald um eine Klärung bemühen.

Die Fakultäten der Hochschulen müssten besonders darauf hinwirken, dass wegen des beim DV-Anwender erforderlichen praktischen Wissens eines Informatikers die vermittelten Stoffinhalte aktuell sind und mit der raschen technologischen Entwicklung Schritt halten. Das könnte erreicht werden, indem mehr Praktiker aus Wirtschaft und Verwaltung für Lehraufträge gewonnen werden und indem die Professoren mit ihren Instituten sich noch mehr um praxisnahe Forschungsaufgaben und Gutachten bemühen, die eine enge Verbindung mit den DV-Anwendern herstellen. Durch die grössere Praxisnähe (thematisch und zeitlich) könnte die heute zum Teil recht lange, den Berufsstand des Informatikers mitunter diskreditierende Einarbeitungszeit beim Arbeitgeber stark verkürzt werden.

Ein grosses Problem scheint zu sein, dass die meisten Anfänger des Informatik-Studiums keine rechten Vorstellungen von ihrem zukünftigen Beruf haben und deshalb ihr Studium nicht planvoll auf die späteren Anforderungen ausrichten können. Schon die Studienberatung müsste daher verbessert werden. Die Hochschulen sollten dafür sorgen, dass schon in den beiden ersten Semestern Kontakte zu DV-Anwendern zustandekommen, sei es durch Exkursionen oder durch Informationsseminare mit Referenten aus der Praxis. Eine besonders effektvolle Studienvorbereitung und gleichzeitig auch eine die Berufschancen stark verbessernde Grundlage dürfte eine vor dem Studium liegende betriebliche Informatik-Ausbildung als mathematisch-technischer Assistent oder Datenverarbeitungskaufmann sein. Anstelle der mit einem ordentlichen Abschluss versehenen betrieblichen Ausbildungsgänge könnte auch ein längeres Praktikum gewählt werden.

Wenn die DV-Anwender heute noch relativ selten nach der Qualifikation "Informatik-Absolvent" fragen, sobald sie in ihren Stellenanzeigen DV-Fachleute suchen, so zeigt dies, dass der neue Berufstyp noch nicht voll akzeptiert wird. Das liegt zum einen an einer ungenügenden Kenntnis und vielleicht manchmal auch Voreingenommenheit der Stellenausschreiber, zum anderen dürften aber auch anlaufbedingte Negativa in der Ausbildung - vor allem bei den Hauptfachinformatikern - eine Zurückhaltung oder Ablehnung bewirkt haben. In einer freien Wirtschaft muss der Anbieter einer Leistung den Abnehmer überzeugen. Es ist also Sache der Informatik-Studierenden ein Studium zu absolvieren, das zu einer die Nachfrage steigernden Qualifikation führt. Die Hochschulen müssen ihnen dabei mit einem vollständigen, aktuellen, praxisorientierten Stoffangebot helfen. Andere Stellen wie Regierungen, Behörden und Verbände können durch finanzielle Mittel und Aufklärung nur die Voraussetzungen schaffen; die gebotenen Möglichkeiten wahrnehmen müssen die solcher Art Geförderten selbst. Die Hochschulen und ihre Studierenden dürfen also nicht müde werden, den für ihren Erfolg sehr massgeblichen Dialog mit der Praxis, das sind vor allem die vielen DV-Anwender, immer wieder zu suchen, auch wenn dieser oft schwierig ist, weil gerade heutzutage bei den DV-Anwendern andere Probleme vordringlicher sind als die Informatik-Ausbildung des Nachwuchses und weil auch die Mittel für eine Unterstützung - z. B. durch Praktikanten- und Werkstudentenstellen - knapp sind. Für die Mehrheit der DV-Anwender ist ihr Engagement in dieser Angelegenheit aber nicht eine Frage des Interesses oder Desinteresses, sondern der Gewichtung.

Die Zusammenarbeit zwischen Hochschule und Praxis - oft beschworen und viel beklagt - hat zudem mehrere Aspekte:

- einmal die unmittelbare Beziehung zwischen Hochschule und Betrieb,
- zum anderen die Kontakte der Hochschulen mit den Wirtschaftsverbänden.

Letztere können zu guten Ergebnissen führen, wenn z. B. die Studiengänge bezüglich des stofflichen Inhalts und der Gewichtung der Fächer diskutiert und abgestimmt werden. Von dieser vielfach schon praktizierten Konsultation der Verbände sollte von den Hochschulen weiterhin reger Gebrauch gemacht werden.

Podiumsdiskussion über Berufsaussichten für Informatiker

Die berufliche Situation der Informatiker im Bereich der Dv-Industrie

G. Seßler, Siemens AG, München

Anhand von quantitativen Informationen aus dem Hause Siemens wird untersucht, in welchem Umfang Informatiker seit wann in welche Tätigkeitsbereiche Eingang gefunden haben. Auf der Basis von eigenen Beobachtungen und qualitativen Informationen von mehreren Dv-Beratungsfirmen wird versucht, die Vorbereitung der Informatiker auf die verschiedenen Berufsanforderungen zu bewerten.

Die nachstehenden Aussagen stützen sich auf Informationen von und Erfahrungen mit zahlreichen Dv-Beratungsfirmen sowie konkrete Kenntnisse aus der Siemens AG als großer Dv-Anwender und Dv-Hersteller. Naturgemäß können sich die quantitativen Angaben ausschließlich auf die Verhältnisse in der Siemens AG beziehen. Bei einem Unternehmen dieser Größe sind solche Angaben nur mit einiger Mühe zu gewinnen, daher sind sie vorwiegend auf das Ende des Jahres 77 bezogen.

Zu diesem Zeitpunkt waren in unserem Hause etwa 100 Informatiker als Mitarbeiter tätig. Eine Aufteilung in große Tätigkeitsbereiche gibt folgendes Bild:

Forschung und Grundsatzarbeiten	17%
Software-Entwicklung für Prozeßsteuerung	20%
Software-Entwicklung für MDT	6%
Anwender-Software für Siemens-Aufgaben	20%
Anwender-Software als Dv-Produkt	12%
System-Software als Dv-Produkt	15%
Fachliche Unterstützung von Dv-Kunden	10%

Tab.1: Tätigkeitsbereiche für Informatiker im Hause Siemens

Die anfangs sehr geringe, insbesondere im letzten Jahr jedoch stark angestiegene Einstellquote kommt in dem mittleren Erfahrun salter in industrieller Tätigkeit von etwa 16 Monaten zum Ausdruck. Von Ausnahmen abgesehen, ist festzustellen, daß vor dem Beginn dieser Tätigkeit während des durchschnittlich 11-semestrigen Studiums kaum praktische

Erfahrungen durch Werkstudententätigkeit oder ein Praktikum gesammelt worden sind.

Gleichwohl schneiden Informatiker bei den Dv-orientierten Eignungstests, die unser Haus bei Einstellungen in bestimmten Entwicklungsbereichen obligatorisch durchführt, durchschnittlich mit 0,5 bis 1,0 Notenwert besser ab. Anders ausgedrückt, die Rückweisungsquote der Informatiker aufgrund der Eignungstests ist geringer als die von Hochschulabsolventen anderer Fachrichtungen.

Größere Software-Entwicklungsbereiche haben im eingeschwungenen Zustand einen Anteil von 50% - 65% Akademiker und unter ihnen ein mittleres berufliches Erfahrungsalter von 4 bis 6 Jahren. Die Verteilung auf die verschiedenen Fachrichtungen der Hochschul-Ausbildung ist fast unabhängig von den in Tab.1 gezeigten Tätigkeitsbereichen.

Elektrotechnik	45%
Mathematik	23%
Physik	18%
Maschinenbau	6%
Wirtschaftsingenieur	3%
Informatik	3%
Sonstige Fachrichtungen	2%

Tab.2: Fachrichtungen der Akademiker in Software-Entwicklungsbereichen

Nach diesen allgemeinen Informationen soll versucht werden, den Informatiker in seiner Reaktion auf die verschiedenen Berufsanforderungen zu erkennen und zu beurteilen. Dieses Vorhaben ist schwierig und für den Einzelfall natürlich nicht zutreffend.

Jeder neue Mitarbeiter durchläuft als erstes eine Ausbildungsphase, die in Anpassung an das Einsatzziel und die vorhandenen Voraussetzungen vom verantwortlichen Laborleiter im Kontakt mit dem neuen Mitarbeiter individuell gestaltet wird. Darin wechseln Phasen der Ausbildung in Kursen der Dv-Schule mit produktorientierten Tätigkeiten am Arbeitsplatz unter direkter Anleitung des Laborleiters oder eines anderen erfahrenen Systementwicklers. Die Ausbildung wird im allgemeinen als abgeschlossen bezeichnet, wenn der neue Mitarbeiter die Evolution (Wartung und Weiterentwicklung) einer Systemkomponente verantwortlich und einigermaßen selbständig übernehmen kann. Die gesamte Ausbildungsphase dauert nach vorliegenden Erfahrungen 2 bis 10 Monate, die Kurszeiten darin zwischen 2 und 10 Wochen. In keinem mir bekannten Fall hat ein Informatiker eine längere Ausbildungsphase als 6 Monate benötigt.

In vielen Fällen war jedoch deutlich zu erkennen, daß der neue Mitarbeiter bereits in dieser Phase der Vorbereitung auf vorwiegend <u>fachliche Berufsanforderungen</u> einige Schockerlebnisse verkraften muß. Ihm ist nicht selbstverständlich, daß in der industriellen Software-Entwicklung aus wirtschaftlichen Gründen die Evolution den weitaus größten Arbeitsanteil ausmacht und die Neuentwicklung von Systemen und großen Systemkomponenten der Ausnahmefall ist. Nun kann er das genauso lernen wie Mitarbeiter, die auf das Dv-Fachgebiet nicht so gut vorbereitet sind. Genauso kann er alle anderen Besonderheiten der fachlichen Berufsanforderungen lernen, wie z.B.

- Entwicklung in vorgegebenen Schnittstellen und Randbedingungen;
- Umgang mit extrem großen, gewachsenen Systemen;
- Bedeutung von Anwender-Anforderungen nach Komfort, Stabilität, Performance, Einsatzbreite;
- gleichzeitige Entwicklung von Hardware und Software auf eine vorgeplante gemeinsame Schnittstelle zu;

  usw.

Das eigentliche Problem liegt nicht darin, daß der Informatiker diese Lektionen etwa nicht lernt - im Gegenteil faßt er den intellektuellen Anteil daran außerordentlich schnell auf - sondern es liegt darin, daß diese Verhältnisse nicht mit seinem Selbstverständnis übereinstimmen. Er geht einen langen Weg, bis er versteht, daß die Weiterentwicklung vorhandener Systeme mindestens eine ebenso anspruchsvolle und ehrenhafte Tätigkeit ist wie die Neuentwicklung eines Tasking-Mechanismus oder eines Compilers.

Der Komplex der <u>methodischen Berufsanforderungen</u> (z.B. Software-Engineering) umfaßt Punkte, wie z.B.

- Arbeit im Team, im Team-Verbund;
- Zentrale Planung, Produktion, Steuerung, Kontrolle von Großsystemen;
- Terminorientierung aller Arbeiten nach Netzplänen;

- Anwender-Belieferung und -Betreuung, Diagnose-Tätigkeit;
- Behandlung der Einflußfaktoren: Funktion, Termin, Kosten usw.

Nun gibt es bekanntermaßen gerade im Software-Engineering noch viele verschiedene Meinungen und Praktiken, aber einige Grundkenntnisse sind doch wohl inzwischen gesichert. Zum Beispiel jene, daß ein Großsystem, um produktorientiert handhabbar zu werden, nicht als erstes ein grundsätzlich neues Design, sondern eine angepaßte Produktionsmethode braucht, die erlaubt, die Zeit zu überbrücken, bis ein neues Design realisiert sein kann. In diesem Punkt würde sich die Dv-Herstellerindustrie eine noch bessere Vorbereitung der Informatiker wünschen.

Zum Abschluß möchte ich noch die menschlichen Berufsanforderungen erwähnen, obwohl mir klar ist, wie schwierig gerade dazu eine geeignete Vorbereitung ist. Weil aber immer wieder deutlich wird, wie groß die Überraschung und Hilflosigkeit in Situationen ist, wie z.B.

- Praktiker contra Theoretiker;
- Führung von Personal;
- Kommunikationsengpässe;

  usw.

sollte auf diesen Punkt nochmals intensiv aufmerksam gemacht werden. Informatiker bringen - trotz aller offenen Wünsche - gute Voraussetzungen mit, durchschnittlich schneller als andere Hochschulabsolventen in der Dv-Industrie in Führungspositionen aufzusteigen. Sie sollten auf das Anforderungsprofil dieser Aufgaben möglichst gut vorbereitet sein.

Podiumsdiskussion über "Berufsaussichten für Informatiker"

Die berufliche Situation für Informatiker im Bereich von Lehre und Forschung.

Prof. Dr. G. Krüger

Der vorliegende Beitrag zur Analyse und Prognose der Berufsaussichten der Informatiker in Lehre und Forschung konzentriert sich auf die öffentlich getragenen bzw. maßgeblich beeinflußten Einrichtungen, insbesondere die Universitäten und Fachhochschulen aber auch die hochschulfreien öffentlichen Forschungseinrichtungen (Großforschung, Fraunhofergesellschaft, Bundesanstalten usw.).
Bei dieser Einschränkung darf nicht verkannt werden, daß auch in den DV-Anwendungsgebieten und in der DV-Herstellerindustrie Informatiker im Forschungs- und Entwicklungsbereich und in der Ausbildung in sehr qualifizierter Weise tätig sind und zukünftig sicher in ständig steigender Zahl tätig sein werden.
Man muß jedoch davon ausgehen, daß die Chancen für Informatiker weniger von der Art der ausgeübten Tätigkeiten wie Forschung, Entwicklung, Vertrieb, Beratung oder Feldservice als vielmehr von der Entwicklungsdynamik der jeweiligen "Branche" bestimmt werden.

In diesem Sinne ist auch der öffentliche Bereich außerhalb der eigentlichen Lehr- und Forschungsinstitutionen sicher zukünftig ein wichtiger Nachfrager nach Informatikern, da er in besonderem Maße von den neuen informationstechnologischen Möglichkeiten der Büro- und Verwaltungsautomatisierung, der zukünftigen rechnergestützten Telekommunikationsdienste und der Meß- und Prozeßdatenverarbeitung in dem weiten Feld öffentlicher Aufgaben beispielsweise bei der Rationalisierung der staatlichen Verwaltung, im Gesundheitswesen, im Datenschutz, in der Ver- und Entsorgung und im Verkehrsbereich Nutzen ziehen wird.

Im engeren Bereich von Forschung und Lehre sind die Bedingungen für eine Beschäftigung von Informatikern speziell auf zeitlich unbefristeten Stellen als weniger günstig zu prognostizieren.
In der öffentlich finanzierten Forschung zeichnet sich im Bereich der Förderung moderner Technologien im weitesten Sinne keine weitere Expansion eher eine gewisse Zurückhaltung ab. Da ein Großteil der öffentlichen Forschungsmittel auch des Bundes in anderen technischen Gebieten längerfristig gebunden sind, scheinen die Aussichten für

eine verstärkte Förderung der Informatik, speziell auch der grundlagenorientierten Aktivitäten, nicht sehr günstig.
In der Lehre und ganz speziell im Planstellenbereich der Hochschulen ist, bedingt durch die Haushaltsprobleme der Länder und die ab Mitte der achtziger Jahre beginnenden Auswirkungen des Geburtenrückgangs, eine wesentliche Erweiterung der Langfrist-Beschäftigungsmöglichkeiten ebenfalls recht unwahrscheinlich.

Diese allgemeine Tendenz trifft die jungen Informatikbereiche besonders hart. Trotz der nachdrücklichen Förderung durch Bund und Länder im "Überregionalen Forschungsprogramm Informatik" Anfang bis Mitte der siebziger Jahre, hat die Ausstattung der Informatik an den Hochschulen, insbesondere im Bereich der Nebenfachausbildung noch nicht den ihrer Bedeutung zukommenden Stand erreicht.
Für den Nachwuchs kommt erschwerend hinzu, daß der schnelle Aufbau innerhalb weniger Jahre naturgemäß dazu geführt hat, daß sehr viele Dauerstellen von jüngeren Informatikern besetzt sind, so daß ein merkbarer Ersatzbedarf in absehbarer Zeit nicht besteht. Die GI-Umfrage 77 zeigt ja sehr klar den hohen Grad an "Selbstversorgung" der Forschung und Lehre mit eigenen Absolventen.
Durch die zu erwartenden stabilisierenden Tendenzen in der Wissenschafts- und Forschungspolitik ergibt sich zweifelsfrei, daß sich der prozentuale Anteil der Informatiker in der öffentlichen Forschung und Lehre bei zunehmenden Absolventenzahlen ganz deutlich reduzieren wird.

Positive Aspekte für die Tätigkeitschancen der Informatiker ergeben sich aus der immer stärkeren Durchdringung vieler akademischer Fachrichtungen und der auf sie bezogenen Berufsfelder durch die Informatik. Auslöser für diese Entwicklung sind die in ihren Auswirkungen noch gar nicht überschaubaren technologischen Durchbrüche in der Größtintegration der Mikroelektronik und den zukünftigen Telekommunikationstechniken.
Die Konzeption neuer "informationsgetränkter" Anwendungssysteme erfordert nicht nur die Beherrschung und Strukturierung der informationstechnischen Hardware (Rechner, Speicher, Bediensysteme und modernen Nachrichtenübertragungseinrichtungen) sondern bringt eine "Softwarekomplexität", die nur mit dem sich entwickelnden software- und systemtechnologischen Instrumentarium der Informatik zu bewältigen sein wird.
Durch seine systematische algorithmisch-methodische Schulung und seiner Fähigkeit zur Planung, Entwicklung und Prüfung hochkomplexer Systeme,

erweist sich der Informatiker, auch über sein spezifisches programmier- und rechentechnisches Detailwissen hinaus, als wertvolles, oft unverzichtbares Teammitglied in den Forschungs- und Entwicklungsvorhaben anderer technischer und nichttechnischer Fachrichtungen.
Hier ist deutlich ein bedeutsamer Umdenkprozeß außerhalb der Informatik festzustellen. Bei der Einrichtung des Informatikstudiums wurde besonders von den technischen und betriebswirtschaftlichen Fächern die Ansicht vertreten, daß ein guter Physiker, Maschinenbauer, Elektrotechniker oder Wirtschaftsingenieur das "bißchen Programmieren schon lernen werde" und daß daher Informatiker in den Anwendungen schon wegen der "Sprachschwierigkeiten" wenig Chancen hätten.
Heute wird aus diesen Richtungen anerkannt, daß größere informatikgestützte Anwendungslösungen, wie sie in vielen Fachrichtungen inzwischen vorangetrieben werden, auf erhebliche Schwierigkeiten stoßen, wenn sie in Unterschätzung der Komplexität und des spezifischen Fachwissens von "Amateur-Informatikern" realisiert werden sollen.
Die guten Erfahrungen mit jungen Informatikern, die es im allgemeinen erstaunlich schnell verstanden haben, sich in die Problematik des Anwendungsgebietes einzudenken und die Sprache des Anwendungswissenschaftlers zu sprechen, haben in vielen Bereichen eine bemerkenswerte Bereitschaft erzeugt, Informatiker in Anwendungs-Forschungsgruppen zu integrieren.

Es ist sicher noch zu früh, Voraussagen über die Funktionsübernahmen und gegebenenfalls Aufstiegsmöglichkeiten von Informatikern in wissenschaftlichen Bereichen außerhalb ihres engeren Fachgebietes zu machen. Es wird aber interessant sein zu beobachten, ob das Informatikstudium ähnlich wie das Physikstudium, das den "Generalisten der Natur" mit sehr guten breiten Berufsmöglichkeiten besonders im Forschungs- und Entwicklungsbereich herangebildet hat, in der kommenden informationstechnologisch geprägten Zeit den "Generalisten der Information" mit sehr breiter Verwendbarkeit auszubilden im Stande ist.
Eine Entwicklung in der beschriebenen Richtung könnte bedeuten, daß der Informatiker stärker in andere Ausbildungsgänge, Fachrichtungen und Berufsfelder vordringt als er umgekehrt Konkurrenz von Absolventen anderer Fachrichtungen bekommt.
Voraussetzung dafür ist allerdings, daß das Selbstverständnis der Informatik und damit ihr Ausbildungsangebot und ihre Forschungsprogramme sich offensiv der neuen Herausforderung aus der zukünftigen Integration von Digital-/Rechentechnik, digitaler Nachrichtenübertragung, Datenerfassung, Textverarbeitung und Prozeß- und Fernwirktechniken stellt.

Aus dieser zukünftigen Breite der Informatik als einer fundamentalen Informations- und Systemtechnologie wird ein qualitativ neuer Bedarf an Informatikern entstehen, der durch die gegenwärtig prognostizierten Bedarfszahlen, die im wesentlichen auf das Arbeitsumfeld konventionell gehandhabter DV-Anlagen abgestimmt sind, nur unzureichend erfaßt ist.
Bei genügender fachlicher Breite und intellektueller Mobilität wird daher der Informatiker auch zukünftig im Bereich Forschung und Lehre seine persönlichen Berufschancen wahren können.

BETRIEBSWIRTSCHAFTLICHE ANWENDUNGEN DER INFORMATIK

Joachim Griese
Lehrstuhl für Betriebsinformatik
Universität Dortmund
D-4600 Dortmund 50

1. Einführung

Betriebswirtschaftliche Anwendungen der Informatik liegen im Bereich der Informationssysteme. Es erscheint sinnvoll, die Funktion von Informationssystemen in betriebswirtschaftlichen Anwendungen klarzustellen, bevor eine Unterscheidung von Informationssystemen unter Anwendungsgesichtspunkten erfolgt.

Betriebswirtschaftslehre versteht sich als Entscheidungslehre, Gegenstand wissenschaftlicher Forschung sind betriebliche Entscheidungsprozesse /7/. Als allgemeines Modell betrieblicher Entscheidungsprozesse wird folgender Ansatz (Bild 1) verwendet (vgl. /19/):

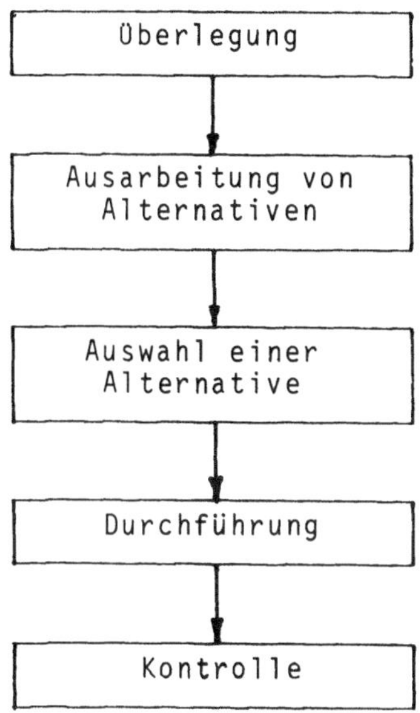

Bild 1: Modell eines betrieblichen Entscheidungsprozesses

Die Phase "Überlegung" bedeutet das Bewußtwerden einer Entscheidungssituation; bei der "Ausarbeitung von Alternativen" wird die Entscheidung vorbereitet, indem die Konsequenzen von Entscheidungsalternativen sichtbar gemacht werden; die "Auswahl einer Alternative" erfolgt unter dem Gesichtspunkt, die im Entscheidungsprozess vorhandenen Ziele des Entscheiders möglichst gut zu erfüllen; schließlich gehören zum Entscheidungsprozeß die "Durchführung" der getroffenen Entscheidung und die "Kontrolle", ob das Ergebnis der Durchführung auch mit den Vorstellungen des Entscheiders übereinstimmt.

Beim Ablauf betrieblicher Entscheidungsprozesse finden Vorgänge der Informationsverarbeitung statt, wobei Informationen hier als Wissen um oder Kenntnis über Sachverhalte verstanden werden. Als betriebliches Informationssystem bezeichnen wir die Menge der Elemente "betriebliche Informationen" und "Informationsverarbeiter" sowie die Beziehungen zwischen diesen Elementen. Es hat die Funktion, die Informationsverarbeitung in betrieblichen Entscheidungsprozessen zu übernehmen. Als Informationsverarbeiter können Menschen und/oder Maschinen eingesetzt werden; bei einem computerunterstützten betrieblichen Informationssystem handelt es sich um ein Mensch-Maschine-System. Ein betriebliches Informationssystem ist kein statisches Gebilde, sondern im Zeitablauf an sich ändernde Strukturen betrieblicher Entscheidungsprozesse anzupassen.

Nach dieser Bestimmung der Funktion von Informationssystemen in betriebswirtschaftlichen Anwendungen werden in der Folge einige Eigenschaften von computerunterstützten betrieblichen Informationssystemen dargestellt, wobei eine Gliederung nach dem zeitlichen Bezug von Entscheidungsprozessen erfolgt.

2. Eigenschaften betrieblicher Informationssysteme

Es werden hier die folgenden Eigenschaften betrieblicher Informationssysteme betrachtet:

- Arbeitsteilung zwischen Mensch und Maschine bei der Informationsverarbeitung in Entscheidungsprozessen
- Standardisierungsmöglichkeiten
- Rechtfertigung für die Einführung computerunterstützter Informationssysteme
- mit der Einführung verbundenes Ausmaß an Reorganisation
- Besonderheiten bei der Gestaltung
- Stand der Realisierung in der Praxis

Um unterschiedliche Ausprägungen dieser Eigenschaften sichtbar zu machen, werden Informationssysteme für verschiedene Arten von Entscheidungsprozessen betrachtet; eine Einteilung erfolgt nach dem zeitlichen Bezug in

- Administrationsentscheidungen,
- Dispositionsentscheidungen und
- Planungsentscheidungen.

Innerhalb einer Organisationshierarchie sind Administrationsentscheidungen der durchführenden Ebene zuzuordnen, Dispositionsentscheidungen der mittleren und Planungsentscheidungen der oberen Managementebene. Die Algorithmisierbarkeit nimmt in der Reihenfolge Administrations-, Dispositions-, Planungsentscheidungen ab /2/. Die für diese Darstellung hilfreiche Gliederung darf jedoch nicht darüber hinwegtäuschen, daß in vielen Fällen Informationssysteme für verschiedene Arten von Entscheidungsprozessen starke Abhängigkeiten aufweisen.

2.1. Informationssysteme für Administrationsentscheidungen

Administrationsentscheidungen beziehen sich auf die Gegenwart; das in Abschnitt 1. dargestellte Modell ist dabei im Normalfall auf die Phase "Durchführung" zusammengeschrumpft. Beispiele für betriebliche Administrationsentscheidungen sind die Finanzbuchhaltung, die Lagerbestandsführung oder die Lohn- und Gehaltsabrechnung (weitere Beispiele findet man z.B. in /14/). Nur in Sonderfällen sind weitere Schritte des Entscheidungsprozesses vorhanden, so die Phase "Auswahl einer Alternative" bei einer Tarifänderung für die Lohn- und Gehaltsabrechnung oder die Phase "Kontrolle" bei der Inventur im Rahmen einer Lagerbestandsführung.

Administrationsentscheidungen sind in hohem Maße algorithmisierbar, die Frage der Arbeitsteilung bei der Informationsverarbeitung zwischen Mensch und Maschine kann stark zugunsten der Maschine entschieden werden. Zusätzlich gilt für Administrationsentscheidungen, daß ihr Ablauf nicht unternehmensindividuell, sondern in Anlehnung an allgemeine Grundsätze (z.B. Grundsätze ordnungsgemäßer Buchführung), vertragliche (z.B. Tarifvertrag) oder rechtliche (z.B. Bewertungsvorschriften für Lagerbestände im Steuerrecht) Bindungen strukturiert ist. Damit sind Voraussetzungen einer Standardisierung von Informationssystemen für Administrationsentscheidungen gegeben.

Die Einführung computerunterstützter Informationssysteme für Administrationsentscheidungen wird allgemein mit einem Streben nach erhöhter Wirtschaftlichkeit, hier definiert als das Verhältnis von Leistung (z.B. Buchungen pro Monat) zu Kosten (z.B. Personalkosten), gerechtfertigt; die Wirtschaftlichkeit erhöht sich hier insbesondere dadurch, daß Kosten reduziert werden (z.B. durch Freisetzung von Mitarbeitern). Wem eine solche Rechtfertigung problematisch erscheint, der sollte sich auch vergegenwärtigen, daß hierbei u.U. Tätigkeiten vom Menschen auf die Maschine verlagert werden, deren Anspruchsniveau und Arbeitsinhalt gering sind.

Bei der Gestaltung eines computerunterstützten Informationssystems für Administrationsentscheidungen werden im Normalfall die bisher vom Menschen durchgeführten Abläufe ohne inhaltliche Änderungen auf die Maschine verlagert, es findet also keine Reorganisation statt. Am Beispiel einer Off-line- bzw. On-line-Finanzbuchhaltung (vgl. /18/ und /8/) läßt sich zeigen, daß Ausnahmen meist technologiebedingt sind. Die frühere konventionelle Durchführung der Finanzbuchhaltung ist in Bild 2 dargestellt: Urbelege, z.B. Überweisungsträger, werden mit Kontennummern für Buchung und Gegenbuchung versehen ("kontiert"); für Teilmengen der täglich eintreffenden Belege, z.B. die Überweisungsträger einer Bank, sind Zwischensummen vorhanden ("Abstimmstreifen"), die

Urbeleg,
z.B. Überweisungsträger
Abstimm-
streifen
Kontieren
und Abstimmen
Verbuchen, z.B. in Form
einer Durchschreibebuchfüh-
rung

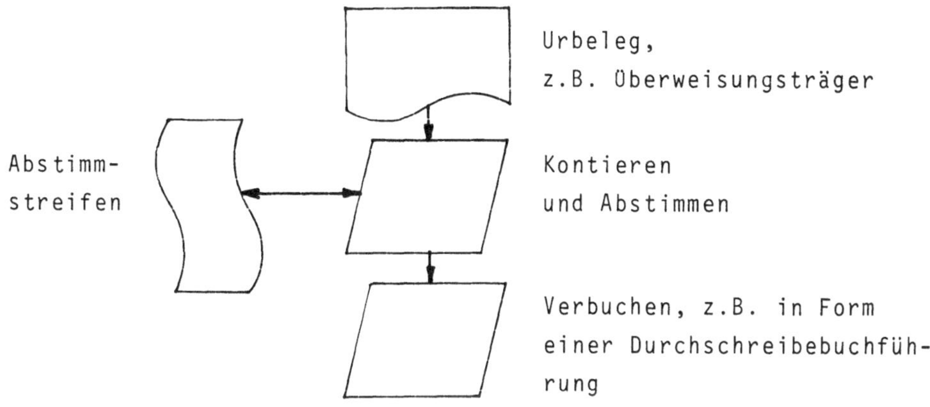

Bild 2: konventionelle Finanzbuchhaltung

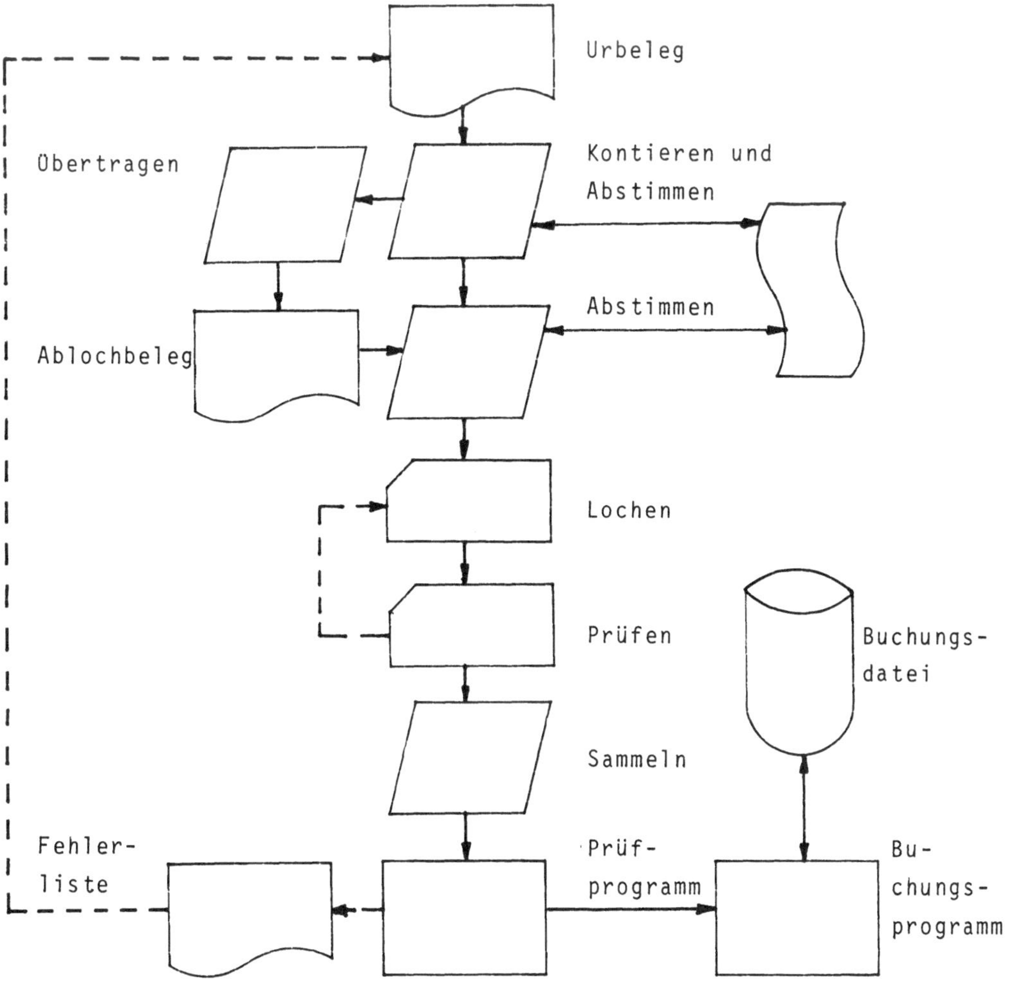

Urbeleg
Übertragen
Kontieren und
Abstimmen
Abstimmen
Ablochbeleg
Lochen
Prüfen
Buchungs-
datei
Sammeln
Fehler-
liste
Prüf-
programm
Bu-
chungs-
programm

Bild 3: Off-line-Finanzbuchhaltung

bei der Kontierung kontrolliert werden können; anschließend werden die Buchungen, z.B. in Form einer Durchschreibebuchführung, auf dem Journal und den Konten vorgenommen. Bild 3 zeigt den Ablauf bei einer Off-line-Finanzbuchhaltung: Durch die Form der Datenerfassung (über Lochkarten) und die damit verbundene Wiederholung von Tätigkeiten, z.B. das Abstimmen, sowie durch die Organisationsform des Stapelbetriebes ist der Prozeßablauf wesentlich komplizierter geworden; es kommt hinzu, daß nicht wenige Buchungssätze zwar alle formalen Prüfungen erfolgreich durchlaufen, aber innerhalb der Buchungsdatei nicht zugeordnet werden können (z.B. weil der Betrag des Zahlungseingangs nicht mit dem der noch offenen Rechnung eines Kunden übereinstimmt); die nicht zuordenbaren Buchungen werden auf einer Datei "Offene Posten" abgelegt, die sehr schnell wächst und meist wöchentlich ausgedruckt wird mit dem Ziel, die Zahl der offenen Posten durch menschliche Intervention - eine Feierabendbeschäftigung für die Buchhaltungsabteilung - zu verringern. Erst die in Bild 4 skizzierte On-line-Finanzbuchhaltung nähert

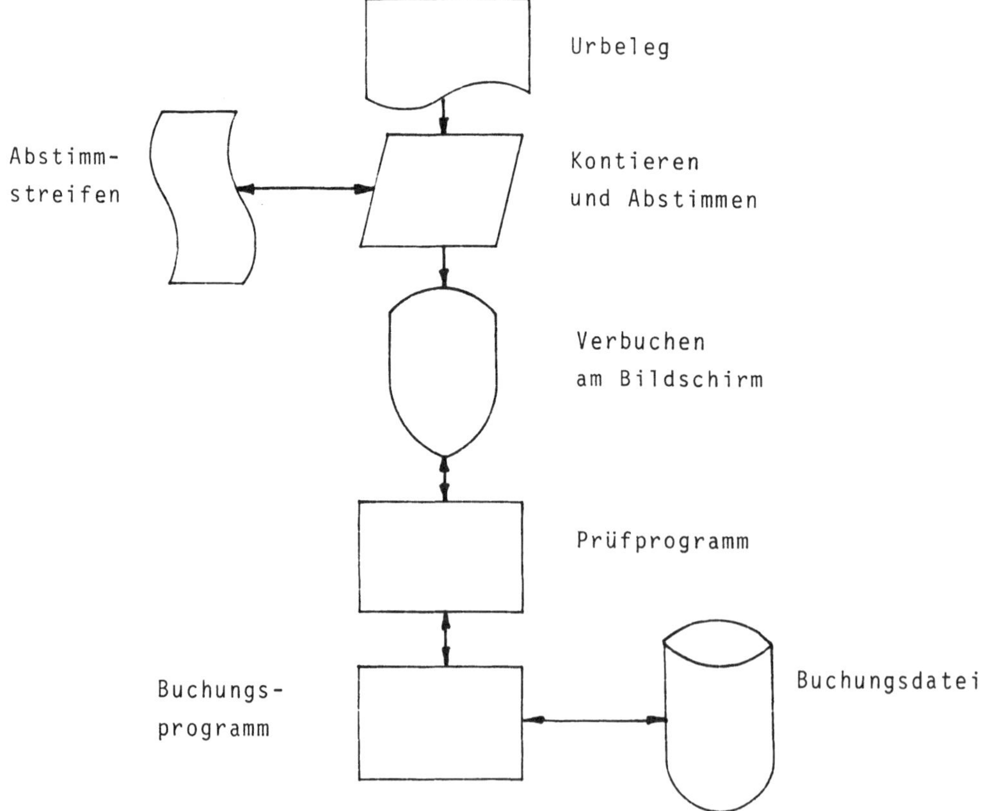

Bild 4: On-line-Finanzbuchhaltung

den Prozeßablauf wieder dem konventionellen Verfahren an: Das Verbuchen - also die Datenerfassung - geschieht am Bildschirm; durch leistungsfähige Prüfroutinen läßt sich im Dialog mit dem Buchhalter in der Fachabteilung sicherstellen, daß nicht nur formale Fehler (z.B. eine falsche Kundennr., die über einen Matchcode richtiggestellt werden kann), sondern auch inhaltliche Mängel (z.B. der Ausgleich von Soll- und Habenbuchung, falls die Differenz einen vorgegebenen Wert nicht überschreitet) in den meisten Fällen sofort behoben werden können.

Bei computerunterstützten Informationssystemen für Administrationsentscheidungen tauchen im Gestaltungsprozeß wenig Besonderheiten auf. Hiermit soll nicht gesagt sein, daß die Gestaltungsprozesse in jedem Fall wenig anspruchsvoll sind: Es können durchaus komplexe Fragestellungen, z.B. bei der Stücklistenauflösung hinsichtlich der Datenstrukturen, vorhanden sein. Die Gestaltungsvorgaben sind jedoch klar formulierbar, so daß eine Übermittlung von der (betriebswirtschaftlichen) Fachebene an den Systemgestalter nahezu keine Probleme mit sich bringt. Ferner decken sich die Qualifikationsanforderungen an den Informationsverarbeiter Mensch als Element des Informationssystems mit den in der Praxis anzutreffenden Eigenschaften der Benutzer dieser Systeme.

Von den etwa 2 Mio. Unternehmen in der BRD und Westberlin setzen ca. 45.000 eigene Rechner ein, ca. 840.000 nehmen Datenverarbeitungsleistungen externer Organisationen in Anspruch. Bei einer Betriebsgröße von mehr als 50 Beschäftigten setzen 51% der Unternehmen Datenverarbeitung ein, 75% davon besitzen eine eigene EDV-Anlage (/5/ /9/). Man kann davon ausgehen, daß computerunterstützte Informationssysteme für Administrationsentscheidungen den Beginn des Einsatzes der Datenverarbeitung in jedem Unternehmen darstellen. Daraus folgt, daß der Stand der Realisierung für diese Informationssysteme schon weit fortgeschritten ist; gleichzeitig sind aber für die nähere Zukunft noch erhebliche Wachstumsraten, vor allem bei mittleren und kleinen Unternehmen, zu erwarten.

2.2. Informationssysteme für Dispositionsentscheidungen

Dispositionsentscheidungen beziehen sich auf die kurzfristige Zukunft; sie stehen meist in regelmäßigen Abständen an, so daß die Phase "Überlegung" des Modells in Abschnitt 1. für diesen Fall entfällt. Als Beispiele seien die Lagerdisposition und der Einsatz von Absatzinstrumenten genannt (weitere Beispiele findet man z.B. in /14/). Bei der Lagerdisposition geht es darum, zu entscheiden, wann und in welcher Menge ein Lager zu bevorraten ist; beim Einsatz von Absatzinstrumenten für kurzfristige Verkaufsaktivitäten muß festgelegt werden, in welchem Ausmaß einzelne Absatzinstrumente (z.B. Preisgestaltung, Werbung) zur Geltung kommen sollen.

Der Grad der Algorithmisierbarkeit ist bei Dispositionsentscheidungen unterschiedlich, z.B. im Fall der Lagerdisposition hoch, im Fall des Einsatzes von Absatzinstrumenten gering. Dadurch sind einer Verlagerung der Informationsverarbeitung vom Menschen auf den Rechner Grenzen gesetzt. Das Maß der möglichen Arbeitsteilung zwischen Mensch und Maschine kann auch in den einzelnen Phasen von Dispositionsentscheidungen unterschiedlich sein; so sind etwa beim Einsatz von Absatzinstrumenten computerunterstützte Informationssysteme bekannt, die sich nur auf die Phase "Kontrolle" beschränken /3/.

Die Standardisierungsmöglichkeiten von Informationssystemen für Dispositionsentscheidungen sind wesentlich geringer als bei Administrationsentscheidungen. Bei der Lagerdisposition z.B. wird in einem Unternehmen die Bestellmenge über "den Daumen" ermittelt, in einem anderen Unternehmen nach der Andler-Losgrößenformel, in einem dritten nach der gleitenden wirtschaftlichen Losgröße, in einem vierten nach einem Verfahren der dynamischen Programmierung usw. (vgl. zu den genannten Verfahren /14/). Man kann entweder bei einer Standardisierung den verschiedenen Varianten Rechnung tragen (für die Lagerdisposition vgl. /17/) oder ganz darauf verzichten.

Die Rechtfertigung für die Einführung von computerunterstützten Informationssystemen bei Dispositionsentscheidungen liegt zwar auch hier in einem Streben nach erhöhter Wirtschaftlichkeit, die jedoch durch eine Verbesserung der Leistung, in diesem Fall der Entscheidungsqualität, bei möglicherweise gleichbleibenden Kosten erreicht werden soll; Fälle eines nennenswerten Personalabbaus durch Einsatz der EDV bei Dispositionsentscheidungen sind bisher nicht bekannt geworden. So führten computerunterstützte Informationssysteme zur Lagerdisposition durch bessere Entscheidungen zu einer Verringerung der Lagerbestände - und damit des dort gebundenen Kapitals - um 20 bis 30%.

Das Ausmaß der Reorganisation bei der Einführung von Informationssystemen für Dispositionsentscheidungen kann beträchtlich sein. Unter der

Zielsetzung einer Verbesserung der Entscheidungsqualität wird man geneigt sein, zusammen mit der Einführung eines Informationssystems auch die Entscheidungsabläufe zu verändern. Hierbei tauchen jedoch häufig große Probleme auf, die zum Scheitern eines Systems führen können. Es ist deshalb einerseits zu erheben, welchen qualitativen Stand die Entscheidungsabläufe vor der Einführung haben, und andererseits im Einzelfall zu prüfen, welches Ausmaß an qualitativer Veränderung und damit Reorganisation des Entscheidungsprozesses für die betroffenen Mitarbeiter tragbar ist.

Die Gestaltung von computerunterstützten Informationssystemen für Dispositionsentscheidungen weist einige Besonderheiten auf. Hierzu zählen insbesondere Verfahren zur Erfassung von Entscheidungsabläufen, die sich noch im Entwicklungsstadium befinden (vgl /6/) sowie die Notwendigkeit einer intensiven Zusammenarbeit zwischen Systemgestaltern und Fachleuten, die eine Aussage über zumutbare Reorganisationsspannen machen können.

Computerunterstützte Informationssysteme für Dispositionsentscheidungen führen ein gewisses Schattendasein zwischen der großen Zahl von realisierten Informationssystemen für Administrationsentscheidungen und den eher spektakulären Erfolgen - und Mißerfolgen - bei Informationssystemen für Planungsentscheidungen. Die Zahl der in der Praxis realisierten Systeme ist nicht in der Summe, sondern nur für einige Dispositionsentscheidungen, z.B. die Lagerdisposition, feststellbar; die Zuwachsraten dürften jedoch für die Zukunft beträchtlich sein.

2.3. Informationssysteme für Planungsentscheidungen

Der Zeithorizont von Planungsentscheidungen ist die mittel- bis langfristige Zukunft; sie enthalten alle Phasen des in Abschnitt 1. dargestellten Modells. Gegenstand von Planungsentscheidungen sind Teilbereiche (z.B. Absatzplanung, Produktionsplanung, Investitionsplanung) oder der Gesamtbereich eines Unternehmens in Form einer Unternehmensgesamtplanung (Beispiele findet man in /15/).

Die Algorithmisierbarkeit von Planungsentscheidungen ist gering. Hinzu kommt, daß Planungsprozesse unternehmensindividuell ausgelegt sind und die Menge der betrieblichen Informationen für Planungsentscheidungen in vielen Fällen nur schwer abgrenzbar ist. Deshalb sind nahezu keine "geschlossenen" Lösungen für computerunterstützte Informationssysteme bei Planungsentscheidungen bekannt, d.h. Systeme, die die Informationsverarbeitung des gesamten Ablaufs übernehmen. Vielmehr herrschen "Insellösungen" vor in der Form, daß die Informationsverarbeitung einzelner Phasen, z.B. "Ausarbeitung von Alternativen" oder "Kontrolle", in einer Arbeitsteilung zwischen Mensch und Maschine vollzogen wird; die Integration einzelner Phasen bleibt dem Informationsverarbeiter Mensch überlassen.

Informationssysteme für Planungsentscheidungen haben unter dem Stichwort "Management-Informations-Systeme" (MIS) einen steilen Aufstieg und einen fast ebenso steilen Fall erlebt /1/. Der wichtigste Grund für folgenschwere Fehlschläge lag darin, daß die ersten MIS-Ansätze wenig oder gar keinen Bezug zu Entscheidungsprozessen hatten. Die heute festzustellende Renaissance von MIS-Überlegungen kann auf besseren technologischen und methodischen Voraussetzungen aufbauen. Zu den technologischen Voraussetzungen zählen On-line-Systeme, die eine Informationsverarbeitung im Dialog zwischen Mensch und Maschine ermöglichen; als Pionierarbeit hierzu ist die Einführung einer kombinierten Absatz- und Produktionsplanung bei der Fa. Westinghouse anzusehen /16/. Bessere methodische Voraussetzungen sind z.B. durch den "Decision-calculus"-Ansatz /13/ geschaffen worden, mit dessen Hilfe Entscheidungsalgorithmen, die vielleicht nur implizit in den Köpfen der Entscheider vorhanden sind, sichtbar gemacht werden können.

Standardisierungsmöglichkeiten für Informationssysteme bei Planungsentscheidungen sind gering. Sie beschränken sich auf den Einsatz von allgemein verwendbaren Werkzeugen, z.B. Berichtsgeneratoren oder Planungssprachen /21/.

Eine Rechtfertigung für computerunterstützte Informationssysteme bei Planungsentscheidungen erfolgt wie bei Dispositionsentscheidungen dadurch, daß man sich hiervon eine bessere Entscheidungqualität verspricht. Im Gegensatz zu Dispositionsentscheidungen ist jedoch die Qualität von Planungsentscheidungen nur schwer meßbar.

Das mit der Einführung von Informationssystemen für Planungsentscheidungen verbundene Maß an Reorganisation ist sehr groß. Vielfach wird die Einführung sogar bewußt als Reorganisationsmaßnahme angesehen: In einer empirischen Untersuchung bei allen deutschen Firmen mit über 1000 Beschäftigten und einer Stichprobe aus Firmen mit 100 bis 900 Beschäftigten gaben 39,7% der ersten Gruppe und 51,2% der zweiten Gruppe an, die Einführung von Planungssystemen als Reorganisation zu betreiben /11/.

Besonderheiten der Gestaltung von Informationssystemen für Planungsentscheidungen liegen einmal im generellen Vorgehen. Boulden /4/ unterscheidet drei Perioden:

- 1. Periode (1956-1963): In einem Bottom-up-Vorgehen wurde die Gestaltungsarbeit überwiegend von OR-Spezialisten durchgeführt, die Modelle aus der administrativen und dispositiven Ebene auch für Planungszwecke einsetzen wollten. Aus Mißerfolgen ließ sich die Lehre ziehen, daß OR-Fachleute als Außenstehende zu wenig von Planungsentscheidungen verstehen.
- 2. Periode (1964-1969): Systemgestalter übernahmen in einem Top-down-Vorgehen die Hauptarbeit unter Verwendung von Time-sharing-Systemen und Planungssprachen. Die Informationssysteme wurden zu komplex und unflexibel.
- 3. Periode (ab 1970): In einem Projektteam arbeiten nach einem Inside-out-Ansatz Manager, OR-Fachleute und Systemgestalter zusammen. Es zeigt sich, daß Manager in den Gestaltungsprozeß erfolgreich eingebunden werden können, daß es nützlich ist, mit kleinen Ansätzen zu beginnen und diese nicht als Endprodukte, sondern als Entwicklungsstufe aufzufassen.

Zum anderen werden die schon bei Dispositionsentscheidungen geschilderten Besonderheiten noch ergänzt durch die Notwendigkeit, besondere Implementierungsstrategien zur Überwindung von Reorganisationswiderständen zu entwickeln.

Über den Stand der Realisierung von computerunterstützten Informationssystemen für Planungsentscheidungen gibt es empirische Untersuchungen u.a. auch für die BRD /11/ /12/. Bild 5 zeigt für 1975 die Anzahl von praktisch einsetzbaren Teilsystemen in verschiedenen Bereichen von 107 Unternehmen, die aus der jährlich erscheinenden Übersicht über die größten (Dimension: Umsatz) Unternehmen stammen. Auch hier ist davon auszugehen, daß die Zahl der praktisch eingesetzten Systeme zunehmen wird - diese Tendenz läßt sich aus einem Zeitvergleich 1970-1975 /12/ ablesen. Darüber hinaus ist anzunehmen, daß mit der Einführung von Informationssystemen für Planungsentscheidungen auch ein Personalausbau

Aufgabenbereiche	praktisch einsatzfähige Teilsysteme
Marketing/Vertrieb/Verkauf	47
Fertigung	32
Kosten- und Leistungsrechnung	26
Materialwirtschaft, Logistik	24
Finanzbuchhaltung	21
Personal	21
Auftragsabwicklung	11
Finanzen	10
Unternehmensplanung	8
Investition	4
Forschung und Entwicklung	4
Einkauf	2

Bild 5: praktisch einsatzfähige Teilsysteme für Planungsentscheidungen /12/

verbunden sein wird, da in vielen Unternehmen bisher die Planung noch stark vernachlässigt wird und entsprechende Abteilungen personell unterbesetzt sind.

3. Schlußbemerkung

Bei der Darstellung betriebswirtschaftlicher Anwendungen der Informatik ist sichtbar geworden, daß im Rahmen der Gestaltung von Informationssystemen anwendungsspezifische Besonderheiten auftauchen. Hierfür werden aus der Anwendungsdisziplin Verfahren entwickelt, die diesen Besonderheiten Rechnung tragen. Das Feld der Gestaltungsverfahren, z.B. in dem Teilbereich Software Engineering Arbeitsgebiet der Informatik, wird damit um anwendungsspezifische Teilbereiche ergänzt. Es liegt im Bereich des Möglichen, daß sich in Zukunft ein fachdisziplinübergreifendes Arbeitsgebiet einer Gestaltungsmethodik und -technologie für Informationssysteme entwickelt.

Literaturzitate:

/1/ Ackoff, R.L.: Management Misinformation Systems, Management Science 14(1967), S. B-147 ff.

/2/ Anthony, R.N.: Planning and Control Systems - A Framework for Analysis, Boston 1965.

/3/ Becker, H.: Information nach Maß, Düsseldorf-Wien 1974.

/4/ Boulden, J.B.: Computer-Assisted Planning Systems - Management Concept, Application, and Implementation, New York u.a. 1975.

/5/ Diebold Deutschland GmbH (Hrsg.): Einsatz software-technologischer Methoden mit Normungseffekt. Studie im Auftrag des BMFT, Frankfurt/Main 1976.

/6/ Griese, J. und Österle, H.: Techniken zur Bedarfsanalyse kommerzieller Informationssysteme. Arbeitsbericht Nr. 3 des Lehrstuhls für Betriebsinformatik der Universität Dortmund, Dortmund 1978.

/7/ Heinen, E.: Betriebswirtschaftslehre heute. Die Bedeutung der Entscheidungstheorie für Forschung und Praxis, Wiesbaden 1966.

/8/ IBM (Hrsg.): IFB - Integrierte Finanzbuchhaltung - Anwendungsbeschreibung, IBM-Form GE12-1282-0.

/9/ Infratest-mbp (Hrsg.): Stand und Entwicklung des Marktes für mehrfach verwendbare Anwendungssoftware in der gewerblichen Wirtschaft, München-Dortmund 1976.

/10/ Kirsch, W. und Klein, H.K.: Management-Informationssysteme I - Wege zur Rationalisierung der Führung, Stuttgart u.a. 1977.

/11/ Köhler, R.: Informationssysteme für die Unternehmensführung, Zeitschrift für Betriebswirtschaft 41(1971), S. 27 ff.

/12/ Köhler, R. und Heinzelbecker, K.: Informationssysteme für die Unternehmensführung - Zur MIS-Entwicklung in der Praxis im Zeitraum 1970/1975, Die Betriebswirtschaft 37(1977), S. 267 ff.

/13/ Little, J.D.C.: Models and Managers: The Concept of a Decision Calculus, Management Science 16(1970), S. B-466 ff.

/14/ Mertens, P., Industrielle Datenverarbeitung. Band 1: Administrations- und Dispositionssysteme, Wiesbaden 1972.

/15/ Mertens, P. und Griese, J.: Industrielle Datenverarbeitung. Band 2: Informations- und Planungssysteme, Wiesbaden 1972.

/16/ Morton, M.S.S.: Management-Entscheidungen im Bildschirmdialog, Essen 1972.

/17/ Siemens (Hrsg.): Wirtschaftliche Lagerhaltung mit HOREST - Grundlagen, data-praxis D 14/4053.

/18/ Siemens (Hrsg.): Softwareprodukt FIBAS - Finanzbuchhaltung im Bausteinsystem (BS 1000) - Kurzbeschreibung, Bestell-Nr. D15/5219-01.

/19/ Simon, H.A.: The New Science of Management Decision, New York-Evanston 1960.

/20/ Szyperski, N.: Realisierung von Informationssystemen in deutschen Unternehmungen, in: Müller-Merbach, H. (Hrsg.): Quantitative Ansätze in der Betriebswirtschaftslehre. Bericht von der wissenschaftlichen Tagung des Verbandes der Hochschullehrer für Betriebswirtschaft e.V. 1.-3. Juni 1977 in Darmstadt, München 1978, S. 67 ff.

/21/ Tilemann, T., Roden, H., Emde, W.B. und Klütsch, H.P.: Betriebswirtschaftliche Analyse- und Planungssoftware. Struktur von Angebot und Bedarf in der Bundesrepublik Deutschland, Köln 1977.

SYNERGETISCHE ORDNUNGSPRINZIPIEN IN PHYSIK UND DATENVERARBEITUNG

H. Haken
Institut für theoretische Physik
der Universität Stuttgart
Pfaffenwaldring 57

1) Einleitung. Synergetik

Zwischen Informatik und Physik gibt es wichtige Berührungspunkte auf verschiedenen Ebenen. Zum einen ist die Datenverarbeitung an physikalische Prozesse geknüpft, was eine genaue Kenntnis der physikalischen Erscheinungen erfordert. In meinem Vortrag will ich jedoch einen zweiten Aspekt ansprechen. Ich will nämlich versuchen, gemeinsame Prinzipien herauszuarbeiten. Die Wissenschaft geht sehr oft so vor, daß sie ihre Untersuchungsobjekte in immer mehr Einzelteile zerlegt, um dadurch Aufschluß über die Eigenschaften der Untersuchungsobjekte zu erhalten. Hierbei zeigt es sich zumeist, daß die Eigenschaften der Objekte nicht durch eine statistische Überlagerung von Eigenschaften der Untersysteme verstanden werden können. Ganz im Gegenteil arbeiten die Untersysteme in einer wohlgeordneten, ja direkt sinnvollen Weise zusammen. Beim Zusammenwirken kommen Prinzipien ins Spiel, die auf dem Niveau der Untersysteme noch gar nicht in Erscheinung treten können. Die hier auftretenden Fragestellungen haben zur Schaffung einer neuen Disziplin, der Synergetik, Anlaß gegeben [1]. Sie untersucht in ganz verschiedenen Gebieten, wie durch Zusammenwirken von Einzelteilen (etwa Atomen, Molekülen, Zellen, Tieren) neuartige Strukturen in selbstorganisierter Weise entstehen und funktionieren. In meinem Vortrag will ich die hierbei auftretenden Erscheinungen und zu ihrer Erklärung geschaffenen Begriffsbildungen am Beispiel der Physik erläutern, um sodann auf Fragestellungen in der Informatik einzugehen.

2) Kurzer historischer Rückblick

Analogien auf der Ebene verwandter Begriffsbildungen hat es schon früher zwischen Physik und Informatik gegeben. Ein besonders bekanntes und interessantes Beispiel ist der Zusammenhang zwischen Entropie und Information.

2.1 Der Entropie-Begriff in der Physik

Ein Gebiet mit sehr breiten Anwendungsmöglichkeiten auch in Nachbargebieten, etwa der Chemie, ist die Thermodynamik, die durch die breite Gültigkeit ihrer Prinzipien besticht. Bei ihrer theoretischen Durchdringung spielt der Begriff "Ordnung und Unordnung" eine wesentliche Rolle. Wichtige Beispiele für die scheinbare Allgemeingültigkeit von Erscheinungen sind die in den Bildern 1 und 2 beschriebenen und uns allen geläufigen Ausgleichsvorgänge. Hierbei

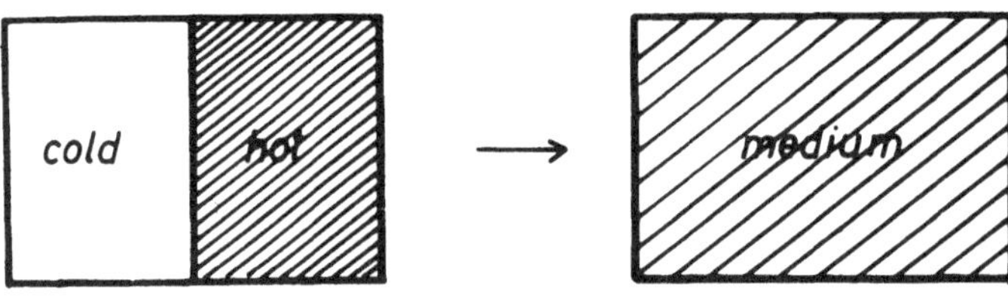

Fig. 1 Irreversibler Wärme-Austausch

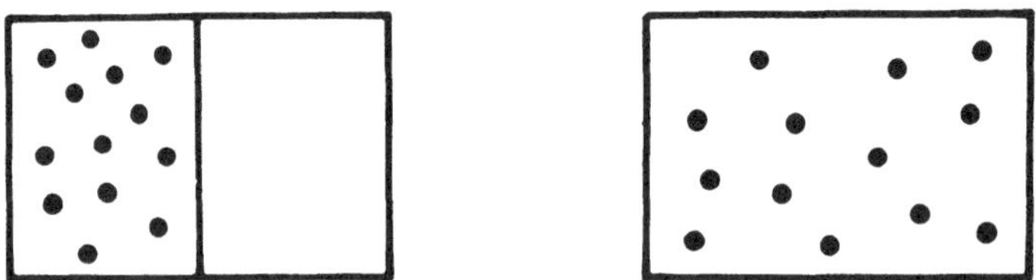

Fig. 2 Irreversible Ausdehnung eines Gases

zeigt es sich, daß die miteinander in Verbindung gebrachten Systeme, die insgesamt abgeschlossen sind, einem eindeutig definierten Endzustand zustreben. Zur adäquaten mathematischen Beschreibung dient der Entropiebegriff [2], der sich auf mikroskopischer Basis mit Hilfe der wahrscheinlichkeitstheoretischen Methoden definieren läßt. Diese Entropie ist durch $S = k \ln W$ definiert. W ist darin die Zahl der möglichen Konfigurationen unter bestimmten Nebenbedingungen, z.B.

festes Volumen, feste Energie usw. Nach dem Grundpostulat der statistischen Physik und Thermodynamik nimmt ein abgeschlossenes System den Zustand mit der größten Entropie an. Um dies zu erläutern denken wir uns 2 Kästen, gewissermaßen in Analogie zu den Fig. 1 und 2, die mit insgesamt 4 Kugeln gefüllt werden können. Offenbar gibt es nur eine Konfiguration, in der alle Kugeln im linken Kasten sind. Hingegen gibt es, wie man leicht abzählen kann, 6 Möglichkeiten, um die verschiedenen Kugeln, die wir uns mit Nummern 1 - 4 versehen denken können, auf die zwei Kästen mit jeweils gleicher Besetzungszahl zu verteilen. Das gleiche Prinzip gilt auch für viel

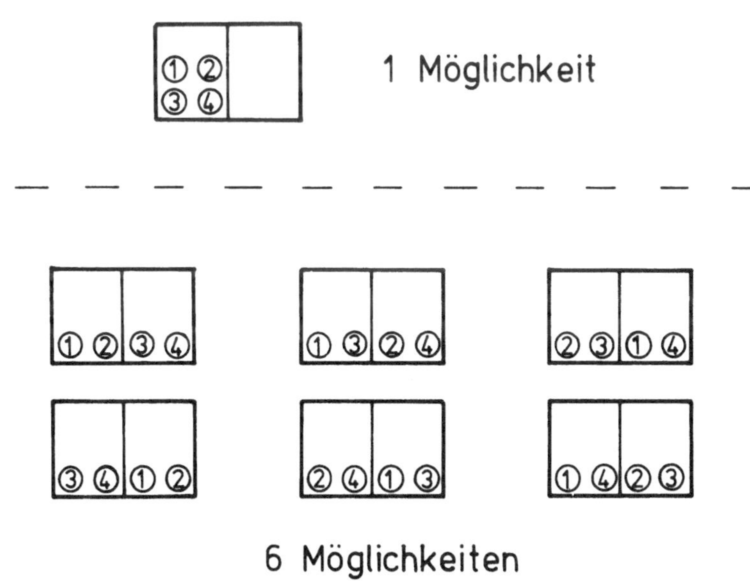

Fig. 3 Beispiele für Verteilung von 4 Kugeln auf 2 Kästen

kompliziertere Fälle. Ganz allgemein können wir diesen Sachverhalt so ausdrücken, daß das Gesamtsystem einem Zustand maximaler Unordnung = maximaler Zahl möglicher Konfigurationen zustrebt. Damit wird also $S = S_{max}$ realisiert. Wichtig ist dabei, Nebenbedingungen zu beachten, z.B., wie bereits gesagt, eine feste Gesamtenergie.

Ein zweites Beispiel für dieses Prinzip sind Spins, die wir uns als kleine Magnetchen vorstellen können. Zeigen die Spins alle in eine Richtung, so gibt es nur eine Möglichkeit, diesen Zustand zu realisieren. Lassen wir hingegen z.B. 4 Spins je zur Hälfte in die eine und die andere Richtung zeigen, so erhalten wir wieder 6 Möglichkeiten. Fordern wir, daß ganz allgemein N_1 Spin nach oben, N_2 Spin nach unten

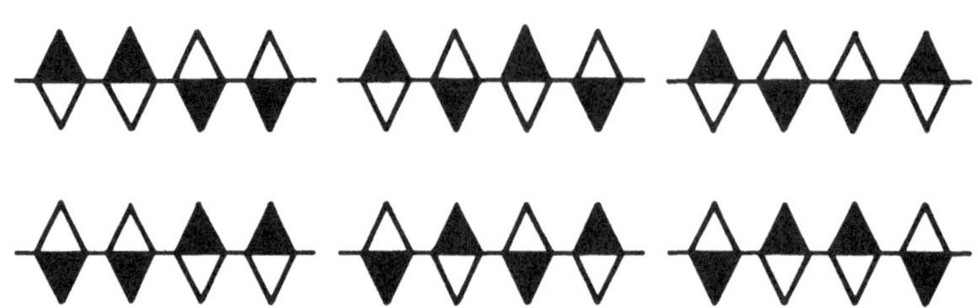

6 Möglichkeiten

Fig. 4 Beispiele für Spin-Einstellungen

zeigen, so daß die Gesamtzahl $N_1+N_2 = N$ erhalten bleibt, so gibt es für eine derartige Konfiguration $W = N!/(N_1!N_2!)$ verschiedene Realisierungen. Bei einer großen Zahl von Spins gibt es entsprechend viele Realisierungsmöglichkeiten.

Während Boltzmann den Begriff der Entropie und ihrer Wahrscheinlichkeitsdeutung bereits im letzten Jahrhundert einführte, wurde der in der Informatik parallele Begriff der Information erst Mitte dieses Jahrhunderts von Shannon [3] eingeführt.

2.2 Informatik: Der Begriff der Information I

Zur Erläuterung denken wir uns ein vereinfachtes Morsealphabet, das nur aus Strichen und Punkten, aber ohne Pausen, besteht. Wir stellen uns nun ein Papierband mit dem Morsealphabet vor, das insgesamt N Elementarzeichen, Punkt oder Strich, enthält. Wir können dann danach fragen, wie viele solcher Ausdrücke man bilden kann, wenn wir die Zahl der Punkte, N_1, und die Zahl der Striche, N_2, jeweils für sich festhalten, wobei $N_1 + N_2 = N$ gilt. Es gibt dann natürlich $W = N!/(N_1!N_2!)$ Möglichkeiten. Indem wir Spin nach oben mit Strich und Spin nach unten mit Punkt identifizieren, erhalten wir eine völlige Analogie zwischen Spins und Zeichen im Morsealphabet. Dies suggeriert natürlich, eine der Entropie entsprechende Größe $I = K \ln W$ einzuführen.

Die Zahl der Stellen, die je zwei Besetzungsmöglichkeiten haben, nennt man in der Informatik übrigens "bit". Das Spin-System von Fig. 4 hat also 4 bit. Führt man noch die relative Häufigkeit $p_j = N_j/N$ ein und läßt Zähler und Nenner sehr groß werden, so läßt sich eine Vereinfachung für I finden, indem wir die Information pro Zeichen einführen. Durch die Definition $i = I/N$ ergibt sich nach einigen Umformungen unter Verwendung der Stirlingschen Formel $i = -K \sum_j p_j \ln p_j$. In der Information wird übrigens K meist so festgelegt, daß I sich als bit-Zahl ergibt. Man kann sich leicht vorstellen, daß die formale Analogie zwischen Information und Entropie zu einer Reihe wertvoller Entwicklungen geführt hat, z.B. beim Problem des Rauschens in der Nachrichtenübermittlung. Der Begriff der Information gestattet es, eine meßbare Größe anzugeben, wieviele Nachrichten über einen Übertragungskanal geschickt werden können, oder genauer, wie viele bits pro Sekunde übertragen werden können. Obwohl sich somit der Begriff der Information als sehr wertvoll erwiesen hat, ist er doch zuweilen überstrapaziert worden und stößt an bestimmte Grenzen. Dies erkennen wir sofort, wenn wir anstelle des Morsealphabets das Alphabet unserer Sprache verwenden. So können wir z.B. aus bestimmten Buchstaben die folgende Kombination bilden:

a a a d e i i l n s s t (1)

Dies ist offensichtlich völlig sinnlos. Ordnen wir hingegen die Buchstaben anders an, etwa zu

da ist ein saal, (2)

so ergibt sich hier plötzlich ein Sinn. Wir kommen hier direkt zur Semantik und stehen vor der Frage, warum der Ausdruck (2) plötzlich vor dem Ausdruck (1) ausgezeichnet ist. Im Zusammenhang mit der Thematik meines Vortrags entsteht die Frage, ob es auch in der Physik Erscheinungen gibt, wo eine Konfiguration vor einer anderen plötzlich in bestimmter Weise ausgezeichnet ist, obwohl bei einer reinen Abzählung diese Zustände völlig gleichbedeutend waren. Dies ist in der Tat der Fall und im nächsten Kapitel soll über einige Beispiele solcher neuen Strukturen gesprochen werden.

3) Geordnete Strukturen offener Systeme in der Physik

3.1 Beispiele

In der Physik sind schon lange geordnete Strukturen bekannt. Hierbei ist es jedoch wichtig, zwischen zwei Arten zu unterscheiden. Die eine Art von Strukturbildung ist mit Phasenübergängen von Systemen im thermischen Gleichgewicht verknüpft. Beispiele hierfür sind der Ferromagnetismus, wo unterhalb einer kritischen Temperatur sich die Spins ausrichten und sich so eine makroskopische Magnetisierung ergibt. Ein anderes Beispiel ist die Supraleitung, bei der unterhalb einer bestimmten kritischen Temperatur die Leitfähigkeit unendlich wird.

Bei der Datenverarbeitung spielen beide Prozesse bei Kernspeichern und Josephson junctions eine entscheidende Rolle. Ich brauche sie wohl kaum hier zu erörtern. Ich will mich vielmehr einer zweiten Sorte von Strukturbildungen zuwenden, die in offenen Systemen weit entfernt vom thermischen Gleichgewicht vorkommen und die, wie wir sehen werden, begrifflich eine Brücke zu Vorgängen in der Datenverarbeitung schlagen werden. Derartige Strukturbildungen gibt es in Flüssigkeiten, in Plasmen, beim Laser, bei chemischen Reaktionen verschiedener Art usw. Ich will hier als konkretes Beispiel den Laser erörtern. Ich tue dies nicht deshalb, weil ich mich selbst sehr inten-

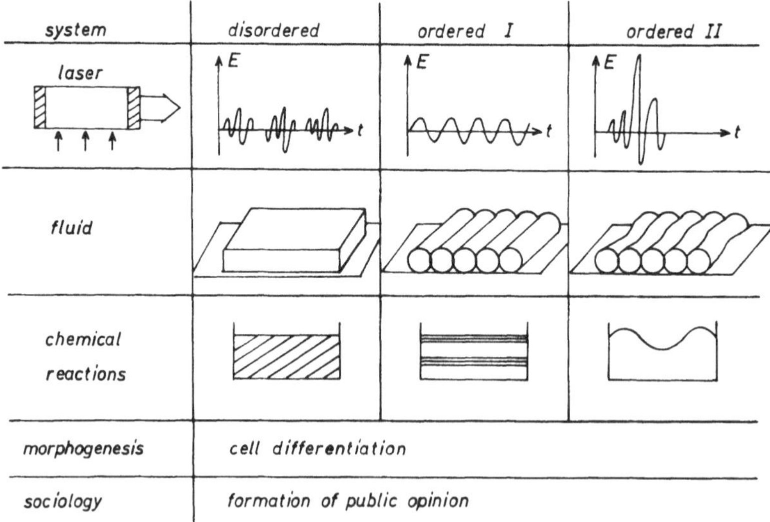

Fig. 5 Beispiele dynamischer Strukturen

siv mit der Theorie des Lasers befaßt habe [4] , sondern weil ich beim Vergleich aller dieser Systeme herausgefunden habe, daß der Laser ein ideales Modellsystem zur Erörterung der neuen Begriffsbildungen der Synergetik ist.

3.2 Der Laser

Der Laser ist, wie wir alle wissen, eine neuartige Lichtquelle. In seiner Grundform besteht der Laser aus einem aktiven Material, unter dem man sich z.B. das Gas einer Leuchtstoffröhre vorstellen kann.

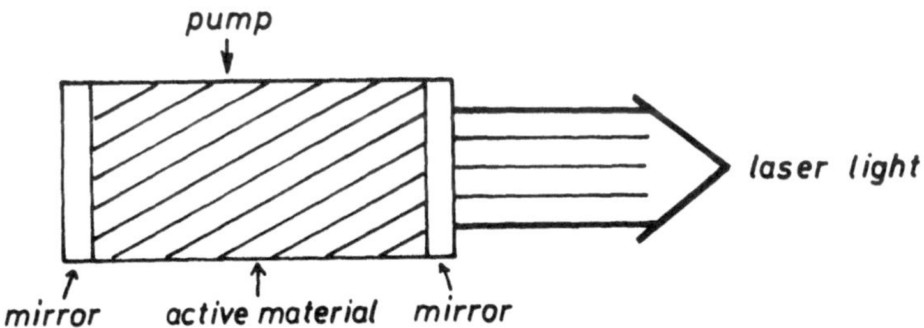

Fig. 6 Typischer Aufbau eines Lasers:
Zentraler Teil: laser-aktives Material
Endflächen verspiegelt

Der Laser wird an den Endseiten von zwei Spiegeln begrenzt, die das in ihm erzeugte Licht immer wieder hin- und herwerfen und somit das Licht in axialer Richtung selektieren. Da die Spiegel nicht völlig reflektieren, kann das in axialer Richtung laufende Licht schließlich in dieser Richtung entweichen. Die Gasatome oder sonstigen laseraktiven Atome werden durch Energiezufuhr von außen angeregt und können dann Licht emittieren. Die physikalischen Eigenschaften des Laserlichts und die dramatische Änderung dieser Eigenschaften an der sogenannten Laserschwelle zeigen die Abbildungen 7a, b.
Auf dem linken Bild ist nach oben die ausgestrahlte Leistung in Abhängigkeit von der zugeführten Pumpleistung aufgetragen. Bei Einsetzen der Lasertätigkeit ändert sich die Neigung der Kurve sprunghaft. Da die Neigung eine Größe für den Wirkungsgrad ist, heißt das, daß der Wirkungsgrad des Lasers plötzlich sprunghaft gegenüber der

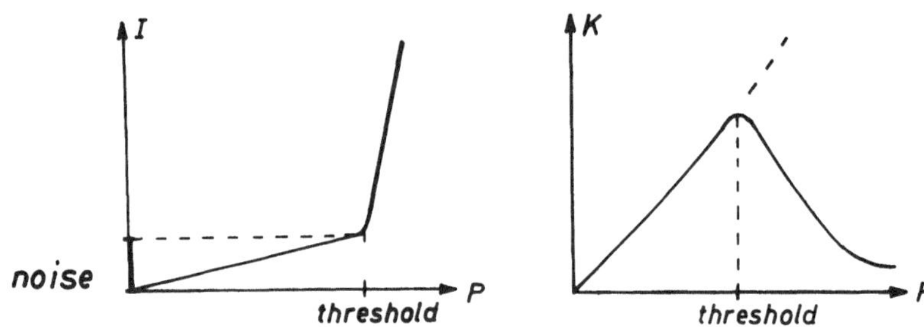

Fig. 7 links: Die Ausgangsleistung eines Lasers in Abhängigkeit von der zugeführten Pumpleistung. Bei der Laserschwelle setzt mit einem starken Knick die Laserausstrahlung ein.
rechts: Die Intensitätsfluktuation normiert auf die Ausgangsleistung als Funktion der Pumpleistung.

Lampe angestiegen ist. Das rechte Bild zeigt die Abhängigkeit der Intensitätsfluktuationen, d.h. des Rauschens in Abhängigkeit von der zugeführten Pumpleistung. Ersichtlich nimmt das Rauschen im Laser gegenüber der Lampe enorm ab. Diese Änderungen der Eigenschaften des Laserlichts gegenüber dem einer Lampe können qualitativ wie folgt verstanden werden. Unterhalb der Schwelle senden die einzelnen Atome unkorrelierte Wellenzüge aus, oberhalb der Laserschwelle hingegen einen amplituden-stabilisierten Wellenzug. Die Problematik, die dieses Verhalten des Lasers bei der Erklärung aufwirft, geht aus folgender Analogie hervor. Symbolisieren wir die Atome durch Männchen und das Lichtfeld durch Wasser, so würde dem Licht von Lampen eine unkorrelierte Wellenbewegung des Wassers entsprechen. Diese wird dadurch erzeugt, daß die Männchen unabhängig voneinander Stöcke in das Wasser stoßen und so individuelle Wellenzüge erzeugen. Dem Laserlicht hingegen entspricht eine gleichmäßige Wasserwelle, die nur dadurch zustandekommen kann, daß die Männchen, wie auf ein Kommando hin, ihre Stöcke in korrelierter Weise in das Wasser stoßen. Beim Laser gibt es natürlich niemanden, der den

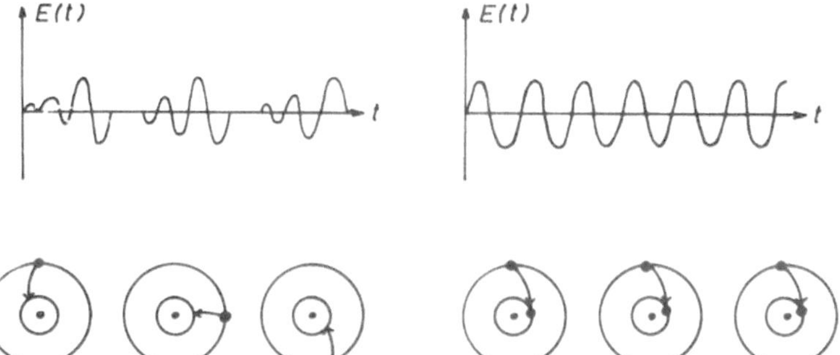

Fig. 8 Die elektrische Feldstärke als Funktion der Zeit bei einer Lampe (links) mit einzelnen Wellenzügen und bei dem Laser (rechts) mit einem fast unendlich langen Wellenzug.

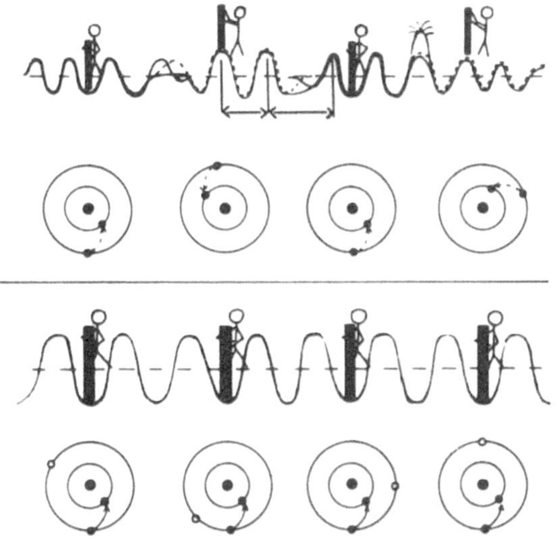

Fig. 9 Männchen an einem Kanal, die Stöcke in das Wasser stoßen und so Wellen erzeugen. Die Männchen symbolisieren die Atome, das Wasser das Lichtfeld.
oben: ungeordnete Bewegung
unten: organisierte Bewegung

Atomen befiehlt, in korrelierter Weise abzustrahlen. Wir stehen vor dem echten Problem einer Selbstorganisation, die, wie aus den Bildern 7a und 7b hervorgeht, äußerst effizient ist. Wenn es also gelingt, Einblick in die Selbstorganisation beim Laser zu erhalten, so öffnen sich auch Perspektiven für ganz andere Systeme. In der Tat hat sich gezeigt, daß die beim Laser entwickelten Begriffsbildungen und Methoden es gestatten, auch die Strukturbildungen in ganz anderen Systemen adäquat zu behandeln.

4) Ordnungsprinzipien der Synergetik

4.1 Das Laserbeispiel

Anhand des Lasers können wir in einfacher Weise das Zustandekommen der Selbstorganisation der Atome verstehen. Um das Prinzip herauszuschälen betrachten wir die auf das nötige Maß zugeschnittenen Lasergleichungen. Das Lichtfeld beschreiben wir durch seine elektrische Feldstärke, deren langsam veränderlicher Anteil der folgenden Gleichung genügt

$$\frac{dE}{dt} = -\kappa E + g(p_1+p_2+\ldots+p_N) + F \qquad (1)$$

Die zeitliche Änderung von E ist gegeben durch die Spiegelverluste $-\kappa$ E. Das Licht wird erzeugt durch Oszillationen der Dipolmomente p_μ der einzelnen Atome, $\mu = 1,2,\ldots,N$. g beschreibt die Ankopplung der Atome an das Lichtfeld, F beschreibt Fluktuationen, die etwa die Spiegel auf das Lichtfeld ausüben. Die Gleichungen für die Dipolmomente der Atome lauten wie folgt:

$$\frac{dp_\mu}{dt} = -\gamma p_\mu + g E D_\mu \qquad (2)$$

Hierin ist γ eine Zerfallskonstante, mit der das Dipolmoment p_μ exponentiell abklingt. Die Dipole werden zur Oszillation durch E angetrieben. D_μ beschreibt den inneren Besetzungszustand des Atoms, ob es nämlich im oberen oder unteren Niveau ist. Die Inversion D_μ genügt einer weiteren Gleichung, die wir hier nicht anschreiben.

Ein zentraler Begriff der Synergetik ist die <u>Versklavung</u>. Zu ihr gelangen wir im vorliegenden Beispiel wie folgt. Nehmen wir an, daß die Zerfallskonstante κ viel kleiner als die Zerfallskonstante γ

ist. Wir werden dann näherungsweise erwarten, daß das Feld E sich viel langsamer ändert als p_μ, wenn wir keine Kopplungen zwischen Feld und Dipolen hätten. Wenn nun aber gemäß Gl.(2) das sich langsam verändernde Feld E das Dipolmoment p_μ antreibt, so wird sich letzteres auch nur sehr langsam ändern. Dies bedeutet aber, daß wir $\dot{p}$ gegenüber γp vernachlässigen können. Dies gestattet es, Gl.(2) sofort nach p_μ aufzulösen.

$$p_\mu(t) \propto E(t)\ D_\mu(t) \tag{3}$$

Der Bewegungszustand des Dipolmoments ist damit eindeutig und instantan durch den Wert von E zur Zeit t gegeben. Wir drücken dies so aus, daß das Dipolmoment p_μ von E versklavt wird. Dies bedeutet, daß E die p's kommandiert oder, mit anderen Worten, den Zustand der Atome ordnet. Wir bezeichnen daher E als Ordnungsparameter. Dies hat eine entscheidende Konsequenz. Wenn nämlich einmal die einzige Variable E bekannt ist, so ist der Ordnungszustand des Systems mit seinen ungeheuer vielen Freiheitsgraden, z.B. 10^{14} bis 10^{18} Variable, festgelegt. Da die p's eindeutig durch E bestimmt sind (und ebenso die Inversionen), können wir p_μ und D_μ eliminieren. Es entsteht dann eine Gleichung für E allein

$$\frac{dE}{dt} = (G-\kappa)E - C\ E^3 + F \tag{4}$$

$$C = \text{const.}$$

Darin ist G der sogenannte Gewinnfaktor, der von der zugeführten Leistung abhängt. Die Bedeutung dieser Gleichung ist am einfachsten zu verstehen, wenn wir E mit der Koordinate q eines Massepunktes identifizieren und auf der linken Seite dieser Gleichung noch einen Beschleunigungsterm in der Form $m\ddot{q}$ hinzufügen

$$m\ddot{q} + \dot{q} = (G - \kappa)q - Cq^3 + F \tag{5}$$

Die Gleichung hat dann die Bedeutung: Masse mal Beschleunigung plus Reibungskraft = äußere Kraft. Die Kraft auf der rechten Seite läßt sich als Ableitung einer potentiellen Energie V schreiben. Diese potentielle Energie ist in Abhängigkeit der Teilchenkoordinate q in Fig. 1o dargestellt. Ersichtlich gibt es qualitativ zwei verschiedene Bereiche. Für $G < \kappa$ gilt die gestrichelte Kurve. Die Gleichgewichtslage des Teilchens und damit auch die elektrische

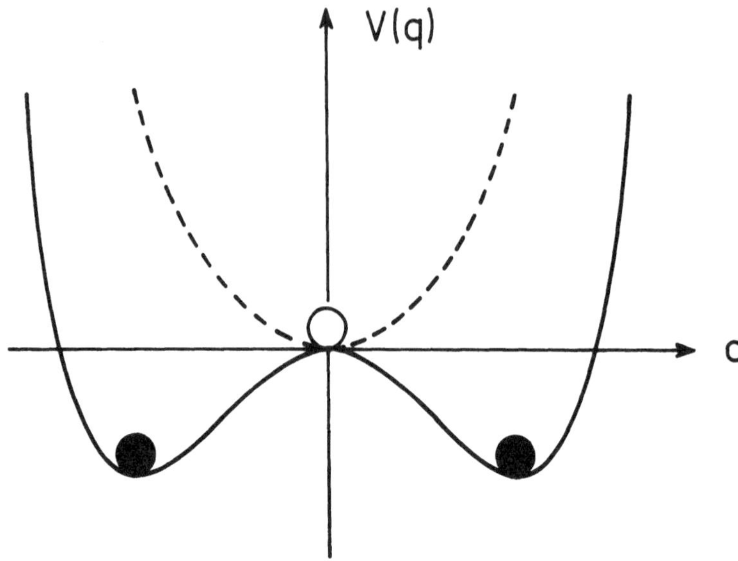

Fig. 1o Das Potential eines fiktiven Teilchens, das das Verhalten der Laseramplitude symbolisiert. Gestrichelte Kurve: unterhalb der Laserschwelle, die mittlere Ausstrahlungsfeldstärke verschwindet, ausgezogene Kurve: oberhalb der Laserschwelle, die Feldstärke nimmt jetzt endliche Werte an.

Feldstärke des Lichts ohne Fluktuationen ist gleich Null. Für $G > \kappa$ gilt die ausgezogene Kurve. Hier gibt es gleich zwei Gleichgewichtslagen, von denen nur eine realisiert werden kann. Man spricht daher von einer <u>gebrochenen Symmetrie.</u> Der makroskopische Zustand des Systems kann daher in verschiedener Weise realisiert werden. Geben wir ferner eine Anfangsbedingung vor, bei der der Ordnungsparameter E noch nicht die Gleichgewichtslage erreicht hat, so wird er vom System in die Gleichgewichtslage hineingezogen werden, d.h. es findet eine <u>Selbstkorrektur</u> statt. Beeinflußt man die Atome durch äußere Felder, so kann die Potentialkurve verformt werden. Je nach Pumpstärke kann man so z.B. die Kurvenscharen von Fig. 11 erhalten. Diese beinhalten eine Hysterese, wie man sich an dem mechanischen Beispiel sofort klar macht. Geht man in Richtung der Kurven von 1 nach 3, so bleibt das Teilchen in der Ruhelage $q = 0$, bis es schließlich bei Kurve 3 zum tieferen Wert springt. Ist es umgekehrt zu Anfang in dem tiefsten Punkt der Kurve 3, so bleibt es in dieser Lage auch dann, wenn die Kurvenscharen sich von 3 nach 2 ändern. Erst wenn die Lage 1 erreicht ist, fällt das Teilchen in den ursprünglichen Zustand zurück. Man muß sich dabei im klaren sein, daß, obwohl wir nur von einer einzigen Variablen reden, damit jeweils das Verhalten eines ganzen Systems, in unserem Falle der Atome, bestimmt

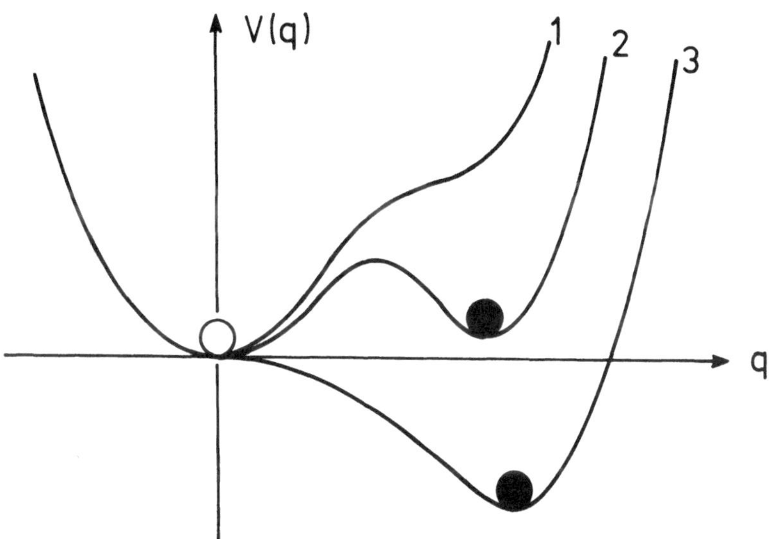

Fig. 11 Beispiel für das Hysterese-Verhalten (vgl. Text)

ist. Im vorliegenden Falle wird also der Zustand eines komplexen Systems von einer einzigen Variablen, dem Ordnungsparameter, bestimmt.

4.2 Der allgemeine Fall

Am Beispiel des Lasers hatte ich gezeigt, wie die Atome durch das Versklavungsprinzip vom Laserlicht gezwungen werden, sich kohärent zu verhalten. Wesentlich ist dabei, daß das Laserlicht umgekehrt von den Atomen erzeugt wird. Die hier aufgefundenen Sachverhalte gelten auch für viel allgemeinere Systeme. Wegen der zugehörigen Mathematik muß ich auf mein Buch über Synergetik [1] verweisen. Ich will mich hier mit der qualitativen Diskussion begnügen.

Im allgemeinen können wir bei einem komplexen System nicht von vornherein sagen, daß gewisse Teile schneller als andere relaxieren (s.oben (1) und (2)). Es läßt sich aber im allgemeinen in einem ersten Schritt eine lineare Analyse durchführen, bei der das System in charakteristische kollektive Prozesse (Bewegungsformen) zerlegt wird. Die Kopplung zwischen diesen Bewegungsformen denkt man sich weggelassen. Es ergeben sich dann zwei typische Bewegungsformen: erstens solche, deren Amplitude immer mehr anwächst. Diese werden wir als Ordnungsparameter betrachten. Zweitens gibt es Bewegungsformen, die, für sich allein gelassen, zerfallen würden. Berücksichtigen wir nunmehr in einem zweiten Schritt die Kopplung zwischen den Bewegungsformen (charakteristische Prozesse), so werden die zerfallenden Bewegungsformen von den Ordnungsparametern versklavt. Bei praktischen Systemen gibt es an "Instabilitätspunkten" zumeist nur wenige Ordnungsparameter, die dann wegen des Versklavungsprinzips die Bewegungsformen der Untersysteme festlegen. Die Ordnungsparameter selbst befinden sich in einer gegenseitigen Wechselwirkung. Je nach System und äußeren Bedingungen kann dies zu einer Konkurrenz oder zu einer Zusammenarbeit zwischen den Ordnungsparametern führen.

Die Systeme können sich wieder, ähnlich wie oben beim Laser, selbst korrigieren. In einer Reihe von Fällen ergibt sich das Phänomen der gebrochenen Symmetrie und der Hysterese. Wichtig auch im Hinblick auf unsere folgende Diskussion für die Anwendung in der Datenverarbeitung ist, daß es in Physik und Chemie einen Algorithmus gibt, der es gestattet, die sich neu bildenden Strukturen zu berechnen und zu klassifizieren. Hierbei sind die Ordnungsparameter die langlebigen Bewegungsformen, die das System beherrschen.Hiermit können wir die Frage beantworten, ob es in der Physik ausgezeichnete Konfigurationen gibt. Wie wir gesehen haben, gibt es diese und wir können sie, und das ist eben wichtig, berechnen. Wenden wir uns nun Problemen der Datenverarbeitung zu.

5) Datenverarbeitung : Mustererkennung (pattern recognition)

Die am höchsten entwickelte Vorrichtung zur Mustererkennung ist nach wie vor unser Gehirn. Deshalb will ich hier mit zwei Beispielen beginnen, die sich auf die menschliche Mustererkennung beziehen. Zugleich mag dies als Überleitung zu anderen Problemen der Mustererkennung dienen. Betrachten wir Fig. 12 und nehmen an, daß der mittlere Teil den Vordergrund darstellt, so erkennen wir eine Vase. Im anderen Fall, wo die beiden Seitenteile den Vordergrund

Fig. 12 Symmetriebrechung bei der Mustererkennung (vgl. Text)

Fig. 13 Hysterese bei der Mustererkennung (vgl. Text)

darstellen sollen, erkennen wir zwei Gesichter. Wir haben somit die Erscheinung der gebrochenen Symmetrie, auf die wir im Zusammenhang mit Fig. 1o bereits eingegangen waren. Ähnlich gebrochene Symmetrien haben wir auch in der Sprache, z.B. wenn wir das Wort Schloß sagen, kann dies ein Türschloß bedeuten, andererseits aber auch einen Herrensitz. Oder das Wort Hahn kann Wasserhahn oder Gockelhahn bedeuten. Ganz offensichtlich muß hier durch eine zusätzliche Information die Symmetrie gebrochen werden. So trivial, da leicht ersichtlich, diese Probleme erscheinen, so werden wir ihnen sogleich wieder bei der Mustererkennung durch Computer wiederbegegnen. Ein zweites Beispiel betrifft die Hysterese bei der Mustererkennung. Betrachten wir die Bilder von Fig. 13 von links oben nach rechts unten, so erkennen wir zuerst ein Männergesicht und erst zuletzt eine Mädchengestalt. Durchlaufen wir die Kette in umgekehrter Richtung, so tritt die Umschaltung von einem Sinneseindruck zum anderen erst an einer späteren Stelle auf. Eine Hysterese kann man auch bei Satzbildungen beobachten. Hier habe ich ein Beispiel aus dem Englischen genommen, bei dem man an sich selbst das Umschalten an verschiedenen Stellen beobachten kann, je nachdem, in welcher Richtung die Sätze nacheinander gelesen werden.

This is a guy
This is a gy
This is a gi
This is a gir
This is a girl

Kommen wir nun zur Mustererkennung durch Computer. Ich will hier nur diejenigen Dinge aufführen, die von unmittelbarem Belang bei dem jetzigen Thema sind. Bei der syntaktischen Mustererkennung werden die Muster in einzelne "Primitive" zerlegt, die selbst von Maschinen in relativ einfacher Weise erkannt werden können [5]. Ein Beispiel hierfür ist etwa die Zerlegung einzelner Buchstaben in Schleifen, wie es in Abb. 14 angegeben ist. Diese Primitive stellen gewissermaßen die Wörter einer Sprache dar. Die Grammatik wird von den Bezeichnungen, die durch räumliche Anordnung gegeben sind, hergestellt. Es handelt sich nun für den Computer darum, bei gegebenen Anordnungen von Primitiven herauszufinden, um welches Objekt es sich handelt. Eine andere Möglichkeit der Mustererkennung besteht darin, den Objekten bestimmte charakteristische Merkmale (features)zuzuordnen. Diesen Merkmalen werden dann Zahlen zugeordnet, die einen Punkt in einem abstrakten Raum definieren.

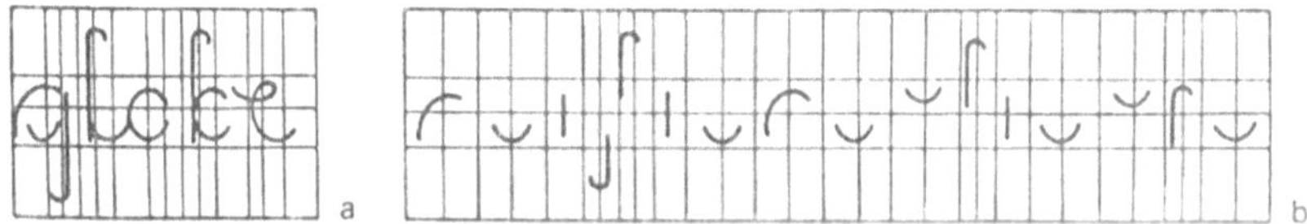

Fig. 14 Die Zerlegung von Handschrift in Primitive. Die Primitiven sind diejenigen Zeichen, die im rechten Teil b) der Abbildung einzeln erscheinen.

Jeder Punkt in diesem abstrakten Raum stellt somit ein Objekt dar. Es liegt nahe, diese Objekte mit den Ordnungsparametern in Analogie zu setzen. Die Gesamtheit der versklavten Systeme bestimmt ja den Ordnungsparameter und dieser wiederum, sobald er bekannt ist, bestimmt die Konfiguration der Untersysteme. Genauso ist es auch hier. Die Konfigurationen, z.B. die einzelnen typischen Merkmale, bestimmen das Objekt. Umgekehrt sind die Konfigurationen festgelegt, falls das Objekt vorgegeben ist. In praktischen Anwendungen sind natürlich nie alle Merkmale einwandfrei identifiziert oder die Primitiven einwandfrei erkannt. Es handelt sich also darum, bei einer unvollständigen Information, um welches Objekt (Ordnungsparameter) es sich handelt. Hier kommt wieder die Analogie, die wir oben erläutert hatten, zum Tragen. Dort hatten wir gesehen, daß das physikalische System bei einem Anfangszustand, der von der Gleichgewichtslage des Ordnungsparameters abweicht, in der Lage ist, das System in den richtigen Gleichgewichtszustand zu ziehen. Genauso ist es bei der Mustererkennung. Aufgrund der vorhandenen Daten muß der Computer entscheiden, um welches Objekt (Ordnungsparameter) es sich handelt. Hierbei kommen nun gerade auch Fragen der Symmetriebrechung ins Spiel. Computer-Experimente an der Universität Tübingen [6] , in denen die Mustermerkmale bereits digital verschlüsselt dem Computer vorgelegt wurden ergaben, daß Situationen auftreten, in denen der Computer das Problem der gebrochenen Symmetrie nicht lösen konnte, sondern einen neuen Punkt im Objektraum bei q = 0 schuf. Im Sinne der Betrachtungsweise der Synergetik würde hier die Lösung so aussehen, daß man dem Computer nur die beiden stabilen Lösungen als erlaubte Objektpunkte gibt. Durch Zufallsfluktuationen oder durch andere äußere Brechungen der Symmetrie wird er sodann gezwungen, einen der beiden Punkte anzulaufen. Falls es nicht möglich ist a priori zu entscheiden, welchen der beiden Punkte er anlaufen muß, muß er nunmehr einen Algorithmus erhalten, der im ersten Durchgang die Symmetrie in der einen Richtung, im zweiten Durchgang in der anderen Richtung bricht.

Kehren wir zu der Frage zurück, wie die in der Physik aufgezeigten synergetischen Ordnungsprinzipien in der Datenverarbeitung verwendet werden könnten. Hier drängt sich die Frage auf, wodurch in der Datenverarbeitung die Ordnungsparameter ausgezeichnet werden könnten, so wie wir in der Physik eine Methode hatten, die Ordnungsparameter zu bestimmen. Das dortige Prinzip war, daß die Ordnungsparameter am längsten, im Idealfall unendlich lang leben. Dies bedeutet: Wiederholen wir einen Versuch mehrmals, so treffen wir immer den gleichen Ordnungsparameter an. "Ordnungsparameter" bedeutet natürlich eine ganz bestimmte Konfiguration der Untersysteme. Damit ergibt sich ein möglicher Schlüssel, Ordnungsparameter bei der Datenverarbeitung einzuführen. Es handelt sich um diejenigen Konfigurationen von Merkmalen oder Primitiven, die immer wieder auftreten. Damit kann man einen Lernprozeß kombinieren. Dem Computer werden immer wieder die in der Praxis vorkommenden Kombinationen gezeigt, darunter natürlich auch fehlerhafte oder nur mangelhaft identifizierbare, z.B. Schriftzeichen des Alphabets. Man kann dann den Computer so programmieren, daß er nur die am häufigsten vorkommenden Kombinationen als Ordnungsparameter (Objekte) beibehält und diese verschlüsselt speichert. Werden ihm nun Muster vorgelegt, so kann er diese im Selbstkorrekturverfahren zu den entsprechenden Ordnungsparametern führen. Umgekehrt, ist ein Ordnungsparameter (auch bei unvollständiger Informationszugabe) bestimmt, so sind damit gleichzeitig alle Untersysteme mit der entsprechenden Konfiguration aufgerufen (assoziatives Gedächtnis). Vielleicht mag man hier nach wie vor den Mangel an Semantik beklagen. Immerhin sollte man darauf hinweisen, daß auch im Nervensystem die Sinneseindrücke einheitlich verschlüsselt in Form von Nervenimpulsen weitergeleitet werden. Die Verschlüsselung mittels Zahlen verbaut so keineswegs den Weg zu einer Semantik. Es kommt vielmehr darauf an, die Zahlenkombinationen mit Gewichten zu versehen.

Natürlich kann es auch zur Bildung verschiedener Ordnungsparameter kommen, die miteinander in Wettbewerb treten. Diese Konkurrenz führt dann dazu, daß Objekte diskriminiert werden aufgrund eines Wettbewerbs von Konfigurationen der Untersysteme. Auch hier scheint ein interessanter Gesichtspunkt sich aus der Synergetik zu ergeben. Die Konkurrenz der Ordnungsparameter wird umso stärker, je unterschiedlicher die Wachstumsraten der einzelnen Ordnungsparameter sind und man dafür sorgt, daß das Wachstum eines Ordnungsparameters auf Kosten eines anderen Ordnungsparameters geht.

6) Schwach gekoppelte Computer-Systeme (losely distributed computers)

Auf dem Computerbau herrschte wohl bis vor kurzem die Tendenz vor, immer größere Computer zu bauen. In neuerer Zeit zeichnet sich hingegen die Tendenz ab, statt eines Großcomputers eine Reihe kleinerer, miteinander in Wechselwirkung stehender Computer aufzubauen. Hierbei treffen wir auf typische Problemstellungen der Synergetik. Zunächst müssen wir prinzipiell zwischen zwei Anordnungen unterscheiden.

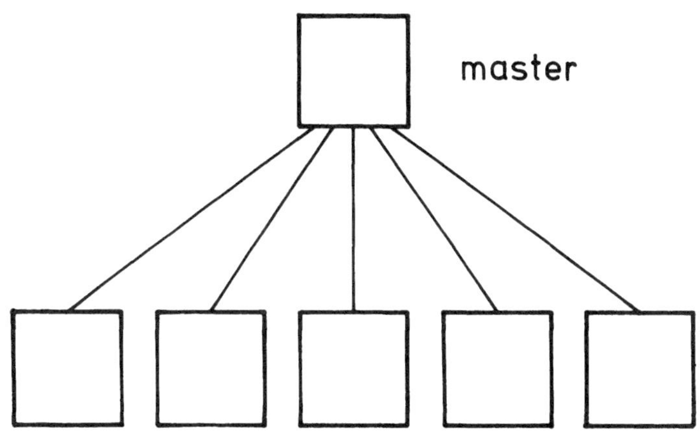

Fig. 15 Computer-Anordnung mit einem Master-Computer

In Fig. 15 wirkt ein Computer als Master, der die anderen Computer steuert und somit versklavt. Das andere typische Beispiel, das in Fig. 16 dargestellt ist, entspricht typischerweise einem synergetischen System. Es wirken viele Computer gleichberechtigt zusammen, ohne daß sie einem äußeren Master unterworfen sind. Bei dem Bau von

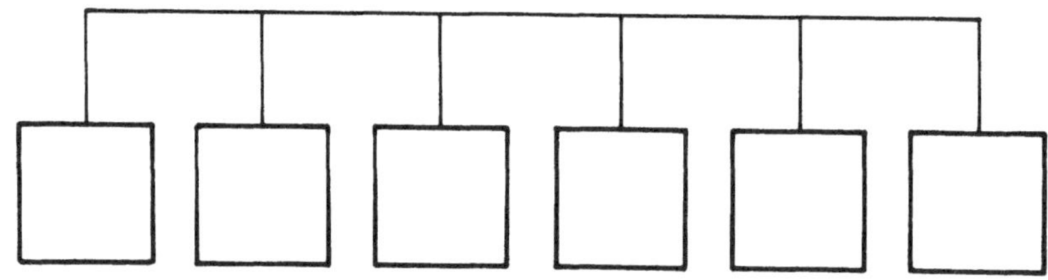

Fig. 16 Ein synergetisches Computersystem

Computer-Netzwerken, wobei die Computer "demokratisch" zusammenwirken, entsteht nun die Aufgabe, die Computer in genau zu definierender Weise optimal zu gestalten. Hierzu muß man passende Größen einführen. Als eine solche bietet sich der Informationsfluß oder der Instruktionsfluß zwischen je zwei Computern an [7] . Aus der Computertechnik ist bekannt, daß es relativ einfach ist, innerhalb eines Computers eine feste Verbindung herzustellen, es jedoch wesentlich schwieriger ist, Verbindungen zwischen zwei verschiedenen Computern in Gang zu setzen. Dies hängt u.a. mit der Frage des zuweilen zeitraubenden Programms zwischen den Computern zusammen, da diese sich gegenseitig die Aufforderung zur Durchführung von Rechenprogrammen, die Bereitschaft, dieses Programm durchzuführen usw., mitteilen müssen ("Protokoll"). Auf diese Weise ergeben sich Probleme optimaler Auslegung,z.B. möglichst wenig Informationsverbindungen zwischen verschiedenen Computern. Nun können aber die einzelnen Computer verschiedene Benutzer haben oder mit bestimmten speziellen Funktionen behaftet sein, etwa Ausgabe durch Bildschirm usw. Hier sind in letzter Zeit auf Graphentheorie gegründete Rechnungen durchgeführt worden, um optimale Computerverbindungen herzustellen (z.B.[7]).

Der Nachteil davon ist, daß in einer Reihe häufig vorkommender Anwendungen die Aufgaben wechseln, so daß jedesmal neue Wege der Informationsübertragung und des Computereinsatzes berechnet werden müssen. Zur Lösung dieses Problems gibt es meiner Ansicht nach zwei grundsätzlich verschiedene Möglichkeiten:
Vorschlag 1 ist bereits von anderer Seite diskutiert worden (etwa [7]), nämlich ein Computerprogramm und damit einen Computer dafür einzusetzen, der die entsprechende Steuerung der einzelnen Computer vornimmt. Dies bedeutet natürlich Rückkehr zum Master-Computer der Fig. 15, also keine echte Selbstorganisation.
Vorschlag 2: Das Computersystem wird ganz ähnlich wie das Lasersystem als sein eigener Analog-Computer verwendet. Dies bedeutet, daß die einzelnen Informationsflüsse innerhalb und außerhalb der Computer gemessen werden und zu einer selbstorganisierten Steuerung der Computer führen. Hierzu werden zur Zeit im Rahmen der Synergetik entsprechende Methoden entwickelt. In welche Richtung dabei vorgegangen wird, sei wie folgt angedeutet. Eine Aufgabe wäre es, etwa zwei Computer zu betreiben. Die eine Möglichkeit ist, die Aufgaben gleichmäßig auf die Computer zu verteilen. Aus verschiedenen Gründen, z.B. Wartung etc., ist es jedoch wünschenswert, den einen Computer für eine Zeitlang ganz, den anderen gar nicht zu belasten. Können die Computer dies in einer selbstorganisierten Weise tun? Im vorliegenden Fall gibt es zweifellos direktere Lösungen als die hier vorgeschlagene, die aber den Vorzug bietet, auf komplexe Fälle verallgemeinerbar zu sein. Wie bei der Frage der Morphogenese in der Biologie von Turing [8] gezeigt wird, kann die Zelldifferentiation dadurch zustandekommen, daß man zwei Zellen, in denen zunächst gleichartige Prozesse ablaufen, durch Materialaustausch miteinander koppelt. Hierbei kann die Symmetrie zwischen den Zellen gebrochen werden und eine Zelle kann nun ganz aktiv werden, die anderen hingegen inaktiv. Auf die hier vorliegenden Gleichungen will ich nicht näher eingehen. Sie treten jedoch (in viel allgemeinerer Form) in vielen synergetischen Problemen auf. Die Problematik, die ich in 4.2 schilderte, kann im folgenden Sinn umgekehrt werden. Dort ging es darum, bei einem vorgegebenen System die lang lebenden Konfigurationen aufzufinden und zu sehen, wie eine Konfiguration in die andere umschlägt. Hierbei sind die Eigenschaften und Kopplungen der Systeme untereinander vorgegeben. Man kann aber nun die Problematik umdrehen und fragen: ich will bestimmte makroskopische Verhaltensmuster, d.h. bestimmte Ordnungsparameter realisieren. Wie muß ich die Kopplungen und Eigenschaften der Untersysteme wählen,

damit das Verhaltensmuster entsteht? Läßt sich das System durch gekoppelte nichtlineare Differentialgleichungen beschreiben (die sich im Falle der Computer etwa auf den Informationsfluß zwischen diesen und die inneren Zustände der Computer beziehen), so läßt sich diese Aufgabe in einem gewissen Rahmen, der zur Zeit Objekt der Forschung ist, in der Tat lösen. Wichtig ist allerdings dabei, daß man bei Änderung äußerer Bedingungen von einer optimalen Konfiguration praktisch stetig in eine neue Konfiguration gelangen kann. Die Frage, wie sich ein System verhält, bei dem das Optimum durch eine Hystereseschleife (vgl. die Diskussion in bezug auf Fig. 11) von dem Istwert getrennt ist, muß andererseits im Rahmen dieser Betrachtungen vorläufig als ungelöst angesehen werden, zumindest wenn der Übergang von einem Zustand in den anderen zu viele Zwischenschritte erfordert.

7) Abschließende Bemerkungen

In dem voranstehenden Vortrag habe ich versucht, einige Grundtendenzen und Begriffsbildungen der Synergetik aufzuzeigen. Um das Verständnis der Leser, die ja aus ganz verschiedenen Bereichen kommen, nicht zu sehr zu strapazieren, habe ich mich auf einfache Beispiele und qualitative Diskussionen beschränken müssen. Hinter diesen steht natürlich der mathematische Apparat, den ich auch schon aus Raumgründen hier nicht darstellen konnte. Ich hoffe aber doch, daß der Leser zumindest ein Gefühl für die tiefgreifenden Analogien erhalten hat, die zwischen dem Verhalten komplexer Systeme in ganz verschiedenen Gebieten bestehen. Das Bindeglied zwischen diesen Erscheinungen stellt die Synergetik im folgenden Sinne dar. Früher wurde die Funktion eines Systems dadurch zu beschreiben versucht, daß man es in seine Einzelteile und deren Funktionen zerlegte, also eine Reduktion auf einzelne Untersysteme vornahm. Auch die Synergetik nimmt eine Reduktion vor, nämlich auf die Ordnungsparameter, d.h. eine Reduktion auf ausgezeichnete kollektive Prozesse. Wie es scheint, sind damit adäquate Begriffsbildungen und Methoden zur Behandlung komplexer Systeme eingeführt worden. Die Betrachtung kollektiver Prozesse schließt natürlich nicht aus, daß in bestimmten Fällen auch einzelne Teilsysteme bevorzugt werden können. Wenngleich mein Vortrag vielleicht auch keine fertigen Lösungen von Problemen der Datenverarbeitung gebracht hat, so hoffe ich doch, daß er Anlaß zum weiteren Nachdenken gegeben hat.

[1] Haken, H., Synergetics. An Introduction,
Springer Verlag Berlin, Heidelberg, New York, 1977
Second edition to appear September 1978

Conference Proceedings:
Haken, H. ed. , Synergetics, Proceedings of an International Symposium on Synergetics, Elmau 1972, B.G.Teubner, Stuttgart 1973

Haken, H. ed. , Cooperative Effects. Progress in Synergetics (Proceedings of a Summerschool at Erice, Sicily 1974)
North Holland, Amsterdam 1974

Haken, H. ed. , Synergetics. A Workshop.
Proceedings of an Internat. Symposium on Synergetics, Elmau 1977, Springer Verlag Berlin, Heidelberg, New York, 1977

[2] Boltzmann, L., Vorlesungen über Gastheorie, 2 Vols.
Leipzig 1896, 1898

[3] Shannon, C.E., A mathematical theory of communication
Bell Syst.Techn.Journ. 27, 37o-423, 623-656 (1948)

Shannon, C.E., Bell System Techn.Journ. 3o, 5o (1951)
Shannon, C.E., W. Weaver, The mathematical theory of communication
Univ. of Illinois Press, Urbana,1949

[4] Haken, H., in Encyclopedia of Physics, Vol. XXV/2c
Laser Theory, Springer Verlag, Berlin, Heidelberg, New York 197o

[5] siehe z.B.
Fu, K.S. ed., Syntactic Pattern Recognition, Applications
Springer Verlag, Berlin, Heidelberg, New York 1977
Fu, K.S. ed., Digital Pattern Recognition,
Springer Verlag, Berlin, Heidelberg, New York, 1976

[6] Brause, R., M. Dal Cin, E. Pfaffelhuber
unveröffentlicht, Mai 1978

[7] siehe z.B. Jenny, Chr., Vortrag Stuttgart 1978

[8] Turing, A.M. Phil.Trans.Roy.Soc. B 234, 37 (1952)

ENTWICKLUNGSLINIEN IN DER INFORMATIK

K. Samelson
Institut für Informatik
Technische Universität München

0. Einleitung

Die Informatik ist eine junge Wissenschaft. Selbst weitherzigste Interpretation kann ihr nicht mehr als ein Alter von etwa 30 Jahren zusprechen. Aber schon in dieser kurzen Zeit hat sie sich in einer Breite entwickelt, die sich in einem gedrängten Überblick auch nicht annähernd vollständig wiedergeben läßt. Die hier getroffene Auswahl an Themen aber ist notwendig subjektiv, durch persönliche Interessen und Vorlieben, gefärbt. So werden viele Leser hochwichtige Themen vermissen.

Informatik ist Studium der Möglichkeiten, Methoden und Hilfsmittel zur automatischen, nach vorgegebenen Regeln ablaufenden Verarbeitung symbolischen, durch Abstraktion aus der Realität gewonnenen Materials, d.h. zur Mechanisierung von Tätigkeiten, die bisher gemeinhin als geistig bezeichnet wurden. Gegenstand der Untersuchungen sind demgemäß einmal die abstrakten Beschreibungen möglichst weiter Klassen solcher Arbeitsvorgänge, also Algorithmen im weitesten Sinne, zum anderen Geräte zur Durchführung ebenfalls möglichst weiter Klassen solcher Vorschriften, also Rechen- oder Datenverarbeitungsanlagen.

Mit diesen beiden Themen kann die Informatik auf eine lange Vorgeschichte zurückblicken. Jedes Rechnen ist Ausführung von Algorithmen. Schon die Antike kannte leistungsfähige Vorschriften, etwa den altägyptischen (im Grunde binären) Multiplikationsalgorithmus. Der mathematisch Beschlagene assoziiert das Wort Algorithmus wohl automatisch mit den beiden großen Namen Euklid und Gauss. Die Entwicklung von Algorithmen gehörte also von jeher zu den Aufgaben der Mathematik, der "rechnenden" Mathematik. Die Frage nach der Möglichkeit von Algorithmen bzw. nach dem universellen Algorithmus zur Lösung "aller denkbaren Fragen", aufgeworfen schon von Raymundus Lullus mit seiner "Ars Magna", danach von Leibniz mit den "Characteristica Universalia", wurde zu einem zentralen Problem der Logik, dem Entscheidungsproblem, das in den dreißiger Jahren dieses Jahrhunderts im negativen Sinne, als "in Allgemeinheit unlösbar", gelöst wurde. Als Weiterentwicklung und Verfeinerung der Entscheidbarkeitstheorie in Richtung auf wirkliches Rechnen kann man die Analyse des Arbeitsaufwands und damit der tatsächlichen Bestimmung von Lösungen theoretisch lösbarer Probleme, die Komplexitätstheorie, betrachten, eine wichtige Disziplin der theoretischen Informatik, auf die hier aber nicht näher eingegangen werden soll.

Die Geschichte der Rechenmaschinen schließlich, als der ersten Geräte zur Ausführung gewisser Algorithmen, beginnt erst (!) im 17. Jahrhundert mit dem Tübinger Professor der biblischen Sprachen, später auch der Mathematik, Wilhelm Schickard. Auch sie weist zwei der größten Namen der Mathematik auf, Pascal und Leibniz, die sich beide als Konstrukteure von Tischrechnern betätigt haben.

Das Konzept der Rechenanlage im modernen Sinne wurde bereits in der ersten Hälfte des 19. Jahrhunderts von Charles Babbage entwickelt, vom technologischen Standpunkt aus um das eine Jahrhundert zu früh, das Babbage von Konrad Zuse trennt, der dieses Konzept seit etwa 1936 selbständig wieder entwickelte und 1941 mit der Z3 als erster verwirklichte. Wegen des Krieges und seiner Folgen aber blieb er in den entscheidenden Jahren unbeachtet. Daher muß man auch ihn, wie Babbage, als großen Vorläufer der Entwicklung ansprechen, die in den späten vierziger Jahren in den USA begann und gemeinhin an den Namen John v. Neumanns geknüpft wird, neben dem allerdings noch zahlreiche andere Namen, wie etwa H.H. Aitken, J. Eckert und J.P. Mauchly, zu nennen wären.

1. Anfänge: Flußdiagramm-Programme und die v. Neumann-Maschine

Tatsächlich kann man die Schriften v. Neumanns zur Rechnerentwicklung und -benützung, insbesondere die Arbeit von Goldstine - v. Neumann "Planning and Coding Problems for an Electronic Computing Instrument" [7], als Anfangspunkt der Informatik betrachten. Hier sind im übrigen die beiden wesentlichen Bereiche, der technisch-konkrete des funktionalen Rechneraufbaus (konstruktiv auf Bausteine und Hilfsmittel der Elektrotechnik gestützt) und der abstrakt-methodische der Entwicklung von Algorithmen und ihrer Darstellung als Programme nebeneinander behandelt. Das in dieser Abhandlung entwickelte Rechnerkonzept der sog. IAS- (Institute of Advanced Studies-) Maschine als wortorientierter Einadreßbefehlsmaschine mit im wesentlichen drei Rechenregistern und einheitlichem Befehls- und Datenspeicher ist bis in die neueste Zeit Richtschnur für den Bau von Rechnern geblieben. Analog kann der hier eingeführte Begriff des Flußdiagramms als Ausgangspunkt für die Entwicklung der Programmiersprachen betrachtet werden.

2. Programmiersprachen und Programmiersysteme

Die Entwicklung von sog. höheren Programmiersprachen mit den zugehörigen Übersetzern oder Programmiersystemen kann als der erste größere Versuch der Informatik betrachtet werden, die Rechenanlage als Hilfsmittel bei der Aufstellung von Algorithmen bzw. Programmen zur Entlastung des menschlichen Benützers einzusetzen. Dabei ging es in erster Linie um die Verständlichkeit des Programmtextes und die Ausschaltung konstruktionsbedingter Maschinendetails aus der Darstellung der Algorithmen.

Den ersten derartigen Vorschlag machte 1952 Rutishauser, der in seiner Arbeit "Automatische Rechenplanfertigung" [14] bereits ein praktikables Verfahren zur Umsetzung seiner Sprache in die Maschinensprache (der Zuse-Z 4) angab, während etwa das nahezu gleichaltrige "Algebraic Coding System" für den "Whirlwind" von Laning und Zierler voll interpretierend arbeitete.

Die erste in großem Umfang zur Anwendung gekommene 'höhere' Programmiersprache war (1957) FORTRAN, die wohl auch heute noch meist verwendete Sprache im naturwissenschaftlich-technischen Bereich. Eine entsprechende Rolle spielt in der kommerziellen Datenverarbeitung das wenig jüngere COBOL. Aus dem ständig wachsenden babylonischen Turm weiterer Programmiersprachen seien hier nur ALGOL 60, ALGOL 68, APL, Basic, PL/I und Pascal genannt. Bei APL, Basic und PL/I ist der Umfang der Anwendung mit Unterstützung großer Hersteller in ständigem Anwachsen begriffen. ALGOL 60 dagegen, eine internationale Gemeinschaftsentwicklung mit dem expliziten Ziel einer Sprache zur Beschreibung von Rechenprozessen für den in dieser Sprache wenig geschulten Leser ebenso wie auch zur mechanischen Übersetzung in Maschinenprogramme, erlangte weitreichende Bedeutung für die Entwicklung der Informatik als Wissenschaft. Die von Backus angegebene Formalisierung des Sprachaufbaus, der Syntax, in der sog. Backus Normal Form BNF (einen vereinfachten Ausschnitt zeigt Fig. 1) und die für und an ALGOL 60 entwickelten Übersetzungsmethoden stellten wesentliche Fortschritte auf dem Gebiet der Programmiersprachen dar. Mit ihnen gab ALGOL 60 den entscheidenden Anstoß zu der raschen Entwicklung eines neuen Forschungsgebiets, der formalen Sprachen und ihrer syntaktischen Analyse, zu dem allerdings die Mathematik, vor allem in der Theorie der Ableitungssysteme, wesentliche Beiträge schon bereithielt. Die bei ALGOL 68 verwendeten Beschreibungsmethoden stellten einen weiteren bedeutenden Fortschritt dar, fanden aber keine ähnliche Resonanz, vielleicht wegen ihrer als übermäßig eingeschätzten Esoterik.

```
<A>      ::=  <A> <ADD> <T> |
              <ADD> <T> |
              <T>
<T>      ::=  <T> <MULT> <F> |
              <F>
<F>      ::=  <V> |
              ( <A> )
<V>      ::=  a | b | ... | z
<ADD>    ::=  + | -
<MULT>   ::=  × | /
```

Fig. 1
BNF-Syntax für arithmetische Ausdrücke

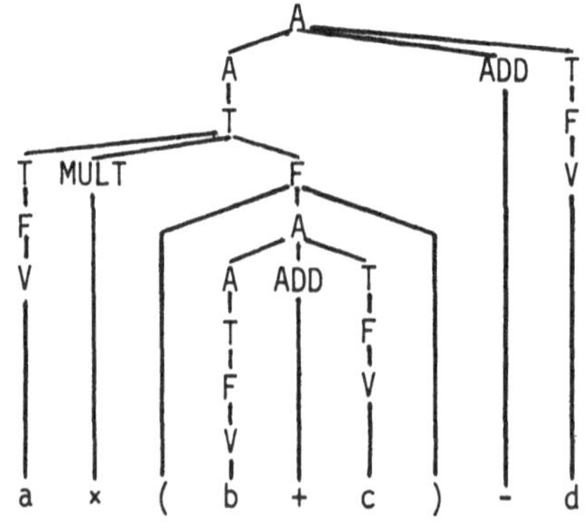

Fig. 2
Syntaxbaum eines einfachen Ausdrucks

Eine ALGOL 60 vergleichbare Bedeutung hat in jüngeren Jahren die Sprache Pascal von Wirth [18] gewonnen, in erster Linie wohl, weil sie von Hoare und Wirth als Träger eines Modellbeispiels für das von Hoare entwickelte axiomatische System [8] zur Herleitung formaler Beweise für die inhaltliche Korrektheit von Programmen benutzt wurde [9]. Wir kommen auf dieses Thema in Abschnitt 8 noch einmal zurück.

3. Formale Sprachen und Syntaxanalyse

Formale Sprachen sind Mengen von Texten, (von deren Bedeutung abstrahiert wird,) die nach den Regeln einer gemeinsamen Grammatik gebildet sind. Unter den oben schon erwähnten, nach formalen Gesichtspunkten gebildeten Klassen sind für das Gebiet Programmiersprachen in erster Linie die kontextfreien oder Chomsky 2-Sprachen von Bedeutung, wie sie zur Beschreibung von ALGOL 60 benützt wurden. Der syntaktische Aufbau eines Textes in einer solchen Sprache läßt sich, wie in dem Beispiel von Fig. 2 dargestellt, durch 'baumartige' gerichtete Graphen veranschaulichen. Die einen maßgeblichen Teil jeder Übersetzung darstellende Syntaxanalyse ist die Ableitung dieser Syntaxbäume, soweit vorhanden, für einen beliebig vorgelegten Text, aus den Regeln der Grammatik, wobei man im allgemeinen im Programmiersprachenbereich auf Eindeutigkeit der Ableitung Wert legt. Für die Anwendung wichtig war die Entwicklung von Methoden mit praktisch tragbarem Aufwand bzw. von Sprachklassen, die solchen Methoden zugänglich sind. 'Tragbarer Aufwand' bedeutet hier insbesondere Sackgassenfreiheit, d.h. die Sicherheit, daß jeder einmal gemachte Reduktionsschritt wirklich auf das Ziel hinführt und nicht als schädlich später wieder rückgängig gemacht werden muß.

Als besonders geeignet haben sich zwei Analysestrategien erwiesen, die sog. "top down"-Methode, bei der man den Baum von der Wurzel, dem Axiom, auf die Blätterfolge des zu analysierenden Worts herabwachsen läßt, und die sog. "bottom up"-Methode, bei der der Baum umgekehrt von den Blättern zur Wurzel hinaufwächst. Diesen Strategien entsprechen die Klassen der sog. LL(k)- bzw. LR(k)- und Präzedenz-Sprachen.[1]

4. Übersetzererzeugende Systeme und Semantikbeschreibung

Eigentliches Ziel bei der Entwicklung solcher generellen Analysemethoden war und ist die Erstellung "übersetzererzeugender" Systeme, die die mühsame umfangreiche Arbeit der Übersetzererstellung ihrerseits automatisieren soll. 'Automatisieren' heißt dabei genauer Reduzieren auf vollständige Beschreibungen der Programmier-(Quell-) Sprache und der zu verwendenden Maschine sowie eine funktionale Charakterisierung der Zuordnung. Hier ist die Syntaxanalyse, deren Erzeugung für Sprach-

---

[1] Das k besagt, daß der jeweils erreichte Analysezustand zusammen mit den nächsten (von links nach rechts gelesenen) k noch nicht verarbeiteten Zeichen des zu analysierenden Worts die nächste beim Aufbau des Baums zu verwendende Ableitungsregel eindeutig festlegt, was die Sackgassenfreiheit garantiert.

klassen wie die obengenannten man seit längerer Zeit gut beherrscht, nur der erste Schritt. Es folgen die sog. semantische Analyse und der (wieder meist mehrstufige) Übergang zur Maschinensprache, die Codeerzeugung. Dieser letzte Teil der Übersetzererstellung ist noch nicht systematisch entwickelt und muß infolgedessen in 'herkömmlicher' Weise von Hand angefertigt werden. Darüber hinaus wird im allgemeinen die Entstehungsweise des sog. Laufzeitsystems, also des als Programm gefertigten Teils der Maschine, die die erzeugten "Maschinenprogramme" verarbeitet, (die praktisch niemals der 'nackte' Rechner ist,) stets schamhaft verschwiegen.

Zur Beschreibung der Semantik, also der Bedeutung der Texte von Programmiersprachen, wurden im Zusammenhang mit der Sprachdefinition, der Übersetzung und der Übersetzererzeugung verschiedene Methoden entwickelt, von denen hier nur die sog. Wiener Definitionsmethode [12], die zweischichtigen v. Wijngaarden-Grammatiken [19] und die Knuthschen attributierten Grammatiken [10] genannt werden sollen. Die Wiener Methode wie die Methode der zweischichtigen Grammatiken definieren die Semantik letztlich durch Interpretation auf einer "abstrakten Maschine".

Attributierte Grammatiken schließlich sind im Grunde kontextfreie Grammatiken mit einer Art 'Rahmenprogramm' in einer spezialisierten Programmiersprache, bestehend aus Aktionen und Bedingungen auf Daten, die als Attribute (der syntaktischen Variablen) bezeichnet werden, das die Verarbeitung von Programmen der zu definierenden Sprache steuert und damit ihre Bedeutung festlegt. Die Attribute bzw. ihre Werte können auch zur Steuerung von Transformationen des Quellprogramms bzw. einer durch die Syntaxanalyse erstellten, der abstrakten Syntax entsprechenden Normalform zum Zwecke der Optimierung und zur Codeerzeugung verwendet werden (vgl. Wilhelm [17]).

Über Systeme, die eine Beschreibung nach der Wiener Methode etwa durch Transformation des Übersetzers und der abstrakten Interpretiermaschine mechanisch zu einem Übersetzersystem verarbeiten, ist nichts bekannt, das gleiche gilt für Beschreibungen mittels zweischichtiger Grammatiken. Dem Ziel der automatischen (und damit sicher korrekten) Übersetzererstellung aus einer Beschreibung der Quellsprache und der Zielmaschine heraus kommt also die Methode der attributierten Grammatiken am nächsten, aber auch nur deshalb, weil sie eben Züge der Übersetzererstellung beinhaltet.

Das Interesse an Semantikdefinitionen im Bereich der Programmiersprachen ist in den letzten zehn Jahren ständig angestiegen, großenteils wohl unter dem Eindruck des auf Scott und Strachey [16] zurückgehenden Ansatzes der sog. mathematischen Semantik und der von Floyd [5] und später von Hoare [8] vorgeschlagenen axiomatischen Systeme, die ebenfalls allgemein als Charakterisierung der Semantik betrachtet werden.

Versteht man unter Semantik nach dem klassischen Vorbild der Logik die Interpretation oder Modellierung formaler Ausdrücke (hier der Programme) in einem als real betrachteten Objektbereich (einer heterogenen, aus mehreren 'Arten' bestehenden Algebra), dann scheint das Vorgehen weitgehend klar: man hat entsprechend den vorgesehenen Typen und Arten Individuenbereiche als Mengen möglicher Wertebelegungen von Variablen einzuführen, Funktionen darüber als Interpretationen der Funktions- oder Operationssymbole und Verknüpfungen als Bilder der ablaufregelnden Elemente.

Programme werden damit schließlich (grob vereinfacht) interpretiert als Funktionen von der Menge der möglichen Wertebelegungen der freien Variablen (der Anfangswerte) in die Menge der Bewertungen der Resultatvariablen. Um diese nicht klar definierten Variablenbegriffe zu vermeiden, führt man Zustände, im wesentlichen partielle Wertebelegungen der Variablen, konkret auf Rechner bezogen Speicherbelegungen, ein. Jede Wertbelegungs- oder Bindungsoperation einer Variablen ist eine Zustandsänderung. Damit werden die Programmschritte als Zustandsübergänge interpretiert, und ein Programm stellt eine Funktion aus der Menge der Anfangszustände in die Menge der Endzustände dar.

Der Ansatz, von Scott noch bereichert um eine ordnungstheoretische Präzisierung des grundlegenden Begriffs der rekursiven Funktion (Fixpunkttheorie), wirkt überzeugend. Die volle Durchführung für eine konkrete Programmiersprache verlangt einen beträchtlichen Aufwand an Detailarbeit. Eine Vorstellung der Darstellungsweise soll Fig. 3 vermitteln.

Syntax: $\langle A\rangle := t \mid f \mid v \mid \langle A_0\rangle \to \langle A_1\rangle, \langle A_2\rangle \mid (\langle A\rangle)$

Semantik: $S[t] = P(true)$ $\quad S[f] = P(false)$

$S[v] = (some\ given\ function)$ $\quad S[(\langle A\rangle)] = S[A]$

$S[\langle A_0\rangle \to \langle A_1\rangle, \langle A_2\rangle] = Cond(S[A_1], S[A_2]) * S[A_0]$

Fig. 3 Semantische Gleichungen nach Scott und Strachey

Eine solche Beschreibung legt zunächst die einer Programmiersprache zugedachte Bedeutung fest und impliziert gleichzeitig eine begriffliche Überprüfung der beschriebenen Sprache. Solange die Beschreibung aber nicht unmittelbar in die tatsächliche Interpretation der Programme auf dem Rechner, also in das zu der Sprache gehörige Programmiersystem, eingeht, stellt sie eigentlich nur ein (äußerst schwer lesbares) Pflichtenheft für den Übersetzerbauer dar. Hat man aber neben der die Semantik der Quellsprache L_q beschreibenden Abbildung $S \mid L_q \to M$ in den Modellbereich M eine entsprechende Semantikabbildung S_z der Zielsprache L_z in den gleichen Modellbereich, so bedeutet für einen Übersetzer $T \mid L_q \to L_z$ die Gleichung

$$S_q = S_z \circ T$$

die semantische Korrektheit, die durch Nachweis des Bestehens dieser Gleichung bewiesen wird.

Das damit skizzierte Programm von der Definition der Sprache bis zum Beweis der Korrektheit ist (mit beispielhaften, aber nicht übersimplifizierten Sprachen) Inhalt des zweibändigen Werks von Milne und Strachey [13], an dem sich der Umfang der Aufgabe ermessen läßt.

Wenn ein solches Definitions- und Beweisverfahren nicht vollständig formalisiert und damit mechanisch nachprüfbar ist, liefert es zwar den Beweis der begrifflichen Korrektheit des Übersetzers. Lokale Fehler (wie etwa Schreibfehler) sind immer noch in beliebigem Umfang möglich. Dessen ungeachtet ist ein Korrektheitsbeweis von hohem Wert. Problematisch ist nur, daß er eben nur für einen korrekten Übersetzer zu führen ist. Bei fehlerhaften Übersetzern versagt die Methode. Daher erschiene es angemessener, die "Korrektheitsgleichung" als eine den Übersetzer definierende Bedingungsgleichung zu betrachten und einen Übersetzer als Lösung dieser Gleichung zu entwickeln, wie das schon 1962 in [15] angedeutet wurde.

Im übrigen muß man sich natürlich darüber klar sein, daß es sich bei diesem Problemkreis zunächst um prinzipielle Fragestellungen von primär wissenschaftlich-begrifflichem Interesse handelt. Bis es zu konkreten praktischen Anwendungen 'im Felde' kommt, wird noch viel Zeit und Mühe aufzuwenden sein.

Anzumerken wäre noch, daß die Verwendung des Worts Semantik im Grunde irreführend ist. Das Bild der Quellsprache unter der "semantischen" Abbildung ist ja nicht wirklich der Objektbereich, sondern eine allein faßbare sprachliche Darstellung in einer "Objektsprache". Die Abbildung ist also eine Sprachübersetzung, und das Interpretationsproblem stellt sich sofort wieder. Hier wird nun unterstellt, daß die (in der Umgangssprache gewohnte) unmittelbare Identifizierung von Objekt durch Bezeichnung zulässig ist, da alle Beteiligten die Objektsprache 'verstehen' - und dieses Verständnis ist die eigentliche Semantik.

5. Rechnersysteme

Bei J. v. Neumann ebenso wie bei dem englischen Rechnerpionier M. Wilkes, dem Erbauer der EDSAC in Cambridge, finden sich bereits die Begriffe Programmbibliothek und Ladeprogramme. Sie kann man als Ursprung der Systeme von Hilfsprogrammen für den Rechenbetrieb betrachten, aus denen im Laufe der Zeit sich die Betriebssysteme entwickelten, die zu den umfangreichsten und komplexesten Systemen gehören, die bisher überhaupt erstellt worden sind. Die Grobgliederung eines solchen Systems nach [11] gibt Fig. 4.

Mit diesen Systemen entstand eine neue Klasse von Sprachen, mit denen der Benützer der Maschine seine Aufträge unter Angabe der dafür vermutlich benötigten Betriebsmittel mitteilt, die im Englischen als Job Control Languages, deutsch ganz farblos als Kommandosprachen bezeichnet werden.

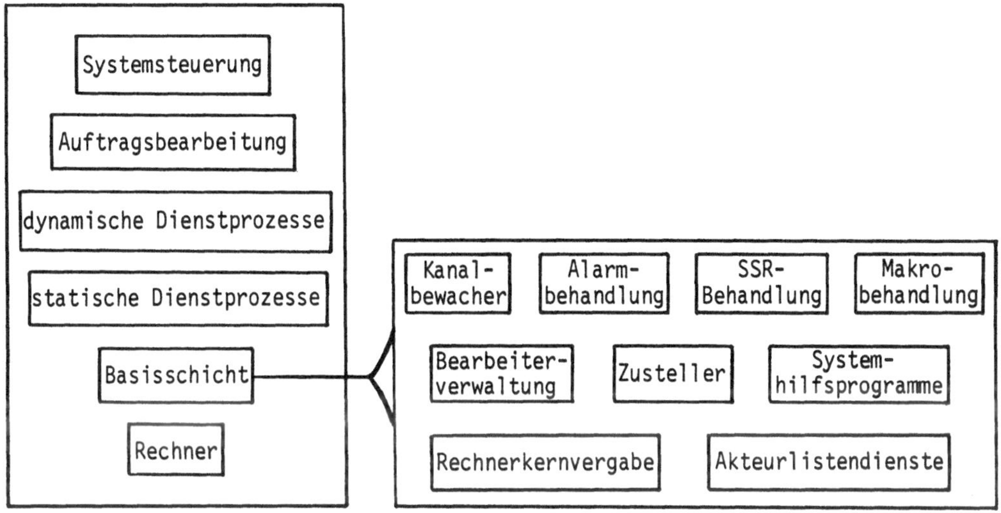

Fig. 4. Zerlegung des Betriebssystems BSM

Leider sind Betriebssystementwicklungen und die das Leistungsangebot an den Benützer widerspiegelnden Kommandosprachen existierender Maschinen stark herstellerspezifisch und daher in den Einzelheiten stark unterschiedlich, obwohl im Grunde alle etwa das gleiche beinhalten. Im Interesse der Benützer erscheint hier eine Vereinheitlichung, besser eine Normung des Funktionsangebots der Betriebssysteme und damit der Kommandosprachen, also der sog. Benutzerschnittstelle, dringend notwendig.

Es ist eine alte Forderung der Informatik, daß ein Rechnersystemkern zumindest funktional als "abstrakte Maschine" aus einem Guß entworfen werden sollte, unter weitestmöglicher Einbeziehung von Erfahrungen aus Programmierung und Betrieb, und daß die Aufteilung dieser Maschine in Apparatur und darauf zu erstellende Programmatur aller gewünschten Härtegrade anschließend an Hand von Kosten-Nutzen-Überlegungen festgelegt werden sollte. Tatsächlich hat bisher stets der Ingenieur mit der Apparaturentwicklung den Vortritt, und der Betriebssystembauer muß von dem ihm vorgesetzten Produkt aus die Brücke zu der von ihm konzipierten oder ihm vorgeschriebenen Benützerschnittstelle bauen, obwohl die Entwicklung eigentlich in umgekehrter Richtung, mit der durch Funktionsanforderungen beschriebenen Benützerschnittstelle als Ausgangspunkt, vor sich gehen sollte.

Eine Konsequenz dieser tatsächlichen Arbeitsteilung ist, daß auch die Rechner der dritten Generation bei allen spektakulären, durch Halbleiterphysik und Elektronik erzielten Leistungssteigerungen funktionell im wesentlichen v. Neumann-Maschinen sind, mit ganz wenigen Erweiterungen.

Der erfolgreiche Aufbau von Großverbundnetzen wie etwa des amerikanischen ARPA-Netzes oder des französischen CYCLADES-Netzes einerseits, die technologische Entwicklung der letzten Jahre andrerseits lassen es möglich erscheinen, daß die herkömmlichen Ein-, Zwei- oder gelegentlich Drei-Prozessor-Großanlagen in nicht zu ferner Zukunft durch Systeme mit stark verteilter Prozessorkapazität abgelöst werden, was auch einen neuen Typ von Betriebssystemen verlangen dürfte. Die Umkehrung der Verhältnisse könnte sogar soweit gehen, daß der bisherige Zeitmultiplexbetrieb des Einzelprozessors, der auf viele konkurrierende Prozesse verteilt werden muß, ersetzt wird durch ein 'Raummultiplexen' e i n e s Prozesses, dem viele konkurrierende Prozessoren Arbeit anbieten, d.h. eine Auflösung des Prozesses in minimale unabhängige Teilprozesse (mit der gröbsten mit der Aufgabenstellung verträglichen Teilordnung), wobei die Beschränktheit der Anzahl verfügbarer Prozessoren ein zusätzliches Problem darstellt. Parallelrechner wie ILLIAC IV, Pipeline-Rechner wie STAR, oder der Cray-Rechner, sind da wohl noch zu schematisch starr. Allerdings dürften Zugang zu und Austausch von gemeinsamen Daten bei größerer Prozessoranzahl zu einem gewichtigeren Vermittlungsproblem als die Prozessorzuteilung werden, mit dem zusätzlichen Handicap des Engpasses, der in dem noch immer nicht vervielfachbaren Speicherzugang liegt.

Die Struktur der gängigen Mikroprozessoren ist wie die der größeren Rechner noch immer im wesentlichen die v. Neumannsche, bereichert um ein Eingriffswerk und evtl. einen kleinen Programmrückkehrkeller. Die Frage liegt nahe, ob die moderne LSI-Technologie nicht die kostenmäßig tragbare Entwicklung von unkonventionellen Maschinen gestatten würde, die dem geplanten Verwendungszweck besser angepaßt sind als die heutigen wortorientierten 'universellen' Befehl-Register-Maschinen. So könnte z.B. die heute eigentlich nur psychologisch erklärbare Separation der Prozeßrechnerentwicklung durch wesentliche funktional bedingte konstruktive Besonderheiten begründet werden.

Im Bereich der Vielzweckrechner etwa könnten nicht zu extravagante höhere Programmiersprachen als Richtschnur dienen. Zu denken wäre an echte Kellermaschinen mit einer passenden Postfixsprache (heute schon in billigen Taschenrechnern verwirklicht), also höhere Strukturierung der Verarbeitungswerke, oder an stärker speicherstrukturierte Maschinen, 'Datenstrukturrechner', mit in gewissem Umfang frei strukturierbarem (wirklich 'assoziativem') Speicher.

Ein in dieser Richtung hochinteressantes Konzept jüngsten Datums ist das STARLET von Giloi [6], das eben diese Strukturierbarkeit des Speichers in hohem Grade besitzt, allerdings beschränkt auf Felder, deren Darstellung augenscheinlich an die von der Verarbeitung von ALGOL 60-Deklarationen her bekannte, in ALGOL 68 explizit eingeführte Deskriptortechnik anknüpft, während die eingeführten Operationen an APL orientiert sind.

6. Anwendersysteme, Daten- und Methodenbanken

Bibliotheken von allgemeinem Interesse standen, wie schon bemerkt, am Anfang der Betriebssystementwicklung. Daß auch Daten, also allgemeiner Information, die keine Arbeitsvorschrift darstellt, von übergreifendem Interesse sein können und deshalb ebenfalls in allgemein zugänglichen 'Bibliotheken' zusammengefaßt werden sollen, ist eine etwas spätere Erkenntnis. Aber schon die Betriebssysteme der ersten Generation enthielten sowohl Programmbibliotheken als auch öffentliche Dateien.

Programmbibliotheken waren ursprünglich Erweiterungen der verfügbaren Programmiersprachen um komplexe Standardoperationen. Mit dem Eindringen der Datenverarbeitung in Wirtschaft und Verwaltung wurden zunehmend Kreise potentieller Benützer angesprochen, die wohl an den erzielbaren Ergebnissen interessiert waren, nicht aber an den Arbeitsmethoden der Datenverarbeitung, und die insbesondere nicht willens oder fähig zu selbständiger Programmierung in größerem Umfang waren. Für solche Benützer, im allgemeinen aus einem bestimmten, relativ engen Anwendungsbereich, wurden aus den Programmbibliotheken Systeme entwickelt, die die für den betreffenden Bereich wesentlichen Standardprogramme in hinreichend parametrisierter Form bereithalten. Die Benützung solcher Anwendersysteme beschränkt sich daher auf die Angabe der auszuführenden Programme als Komplexoperationen unter Spezifizierung der Parameter.

Das komplementäre Gegenstück sind Informationssysteme mit einer Datenbank als Kernstück. Hier werden Datenmengen in großem Umfang als Informationsmaterial verfügbar gehalten, an denen über Eintragung und Löschung, Auffindung und Zugänglichmachung hinaus eine Weiterverarbeitung größeren Stils nur selten stattfindet. Allbekannte Beispiele sind etwa die Flugbuchungssysteme.

Vergleicht man eine Datenbank mit der durch die Objektdeklarationen dargestellten "lokalen Datenbasis" eines üblichen Programms, so zeigt sich ein qualitativer Unterschied. Die Datenbasis des Programms besitzt *eine* feste Struktur. Die elementaren Datenobjekte gehören logisch wie physisch jeweils *einem* vereinbarten festen Datenaggregat (Variable, Struktur, Verbund, Record, Feld) mit eigener Bezeichnung an, das von allen anderen völlig separiert ist und nur durch Operationen mit anderen verknüpft werden kann. Mathematisch gesehen sind alle diese Datenaggregate Elemente von Relationen über den elementaren Objektmengen, und die Aussage ist, daß jedes elementare Datenobjekt Komponente *eines* Elements *einer* festen Relation ist. Querverbindungen zwischen Datenobjekten werden durch Werte von Zeigern hergestellt und sind aus den Deklarationen nicht abzulesen.

In Informationssystemen dagegen gehören die elementaren Datenobjekte im allgemeinen mehreren verschiedenartigen Relationen an, und neue Relationen könn(t)en ständig gebildet, alte aufgelöst werden. Diese Querbeziehungen stellen ja gerade einen wesentlichen Anteil des Informationsgehalts des Systems dar. So sollen die Objekte in durchaus unterschiedlichen Datenaggregaten gleichzeitig auftreten, physisch aber, zur Vermeidung von schwer beherrschbaren Inkonsistenzen bei Änderungen, nur ein einziges Mal in der Datenbank vorhanden sein. Der Umfang, in dem die Querbeziehungen für den Benützer und den Verkehr zwischen Benützer und der Verwaltung des Informationssystems in den externen Schemata für die Relationen (den Typdeklarationen) dargestellt werden, unterscheidet die bekannten Datenbankstrukturmodelle Relationen-, hierarchisches und Netzwerk-Modell.

Abstrakt ist eine Datenbank also ein System von Mengen mit Relationen, ein heterogenes Relativ und damit eine Verallgemeinerung der heterogenen Algebra, der Abstraktion eines Programmiersystems. Die Datenbank läßt sich folglich in gleicher Weise als formales System betrachten, das einen Ausschnitt der realen Welt als Modell[1] besitzt. Der Individuenbereich besteht aus den den Stammdaten entsprechenden Objekten. Den in der "Welt" vorgegebenen Relationen entsprechen wie üblich im formalen System Prädikate als nichtlogische Axiome. Die Menge der daraus mit Hilfe einer formalen Logik ableitbaren Sätze stellt im Grunde den gesamten Informationsgehalt der Datenbank dar. Hier könnte sich möglicherweise eine Anwendung der bislang von ihrer eigentlichen Zielsetzung überforderten mechanischen Beweissysteme als interne Steuermechanismen für die Suche in Datenbanken geben. Die Frage nach der Form der externen Datenbeschreibungs-, Datenmanipulations- und Anfragesprachen, mittels derer Benützer und Verwalter mit dem System verkehren, ist davon weitgehend unabhängig.

Wie das Entwickeln von Information in einem Informationssystem wird auch die Behandlung von Datenverarbeitungsaufgaben in Anwendersystemen zu einem mathematisch-logischen Problem, wenn dem Benützer zugestanden wird, seinen Arbeitsauftrag nur noch durch eine hinreichend präzise Formulierung des Problems ohne Angabe eines Lösungsweges zu erteilen. Systeme, die derartige Aufträge übernehmen und das Programm zur Lösung anhand der Problembeschreibung aus ihrer Programmbibliothek selbst zusammenstellen, werden als Methodenbanken bezeichnet, sind aber derzeit wohl mehr Vorstellung als Realität, die sich auf Modellversuche beschränkt.

Daten- und Methodenbanken sind eigentlich Spezialfälle aus der Klasse der Systeme zur rechnergestützten Entwicklung (und, als nächster Schritt, Fertigung) von Produkten irgendwelcher Art. Diese Systeme stoßen verständlicherweise auf ständig zunehmendes Interesse, haben allerdings den Experimentier- und Modellstatus erst recht noch nicht überwunden. Hierher gehören in erster Linie Systeme des rechnergestützten Entwerfens und Konstruierens, wie sie in allen technischen Disziplinen derzeit diskutiert und entwickelt werden. Einsatzfähige Systeme liegen nur für spezielle Aufgaben vor. Am weitesten fortgeschritten sind wohl Systeme zum Entwurf elektrischer

---

1 im Sinne der Logik; im Sinne der Umgangssprache würde man wohl umgekehrt die Datenbank als Modell der realen Welt bezeichnen

Schaltkreise, die sich im logisch-funktionellen Teil auf eine mathematisch mit booleschen Algebren gut fundierte Theorie stützen können, die in anderen Bereichen fehlt. So bieten heutige Systeme zunächst eine Entlastung des Konstrukteurs von mechanischen Arbeiten wie Erstellung von Zeichnungen und Buch- und Listenführung. Das Ziel aber sind Systeme, die eine Enzyklopädie des technischen Wissens und Könnens vereint mit einem Lexikon der relevanten technischen Daten umfassen, mit einem automatischen Bibliothekar, der über die Inhalte seines Systems so gut "Bescheid weiß", daß er alle beantwortbaren Fragen sofort erledigen kann. Dem entspräche im Fall der rechnergestützten Fertigung das echt automatisierte Werk, in dem alles von der Idee für ein Produkt über Entwicklung, Aufbau der Fertigungsstätten und -mittel und Produktion selbst bis hin zur Auslieferung voll rechnergestützt abläuft.

Erwünscht erschiene in dem gesamten Bereich des rechnergestützten Entwerfens und Fertigens eine engere Zusammenarbeit zwischen den prospektiven Anwendern und den Informatikern, die mit ihren in der Praxis z.B. an den obenerwähnten Programmier- und Rechnerbetriebssystemen gewonnenen Erfahrungen wesentliche Beiträge liefern könnten. Bisher hat es oft den Anschein, als ob die Anwender auf Eigenentwicklung der von der Informatik für die Systemprogrammierung entwickelten Methoden und auf Nachvollzug aller dabei gemachten Fehler beträchtlichen Wert legen.

7. Systementwicklung

Tatsächlich entwickeln sich Entwurf und Konstruktion von Programmsystemen 'an sich' zu einer zentralen Aufgabe der Informatik. Dabei ist der Begriff System so vage wie der Begriff Information. Üblicherweise wird er auf Komplexität und Unüberschaubarkeit im Ganzen abgestützt, als formales Kennzeichen könnte man, in Abgrenzung von Algorithmus oder Programm (deren Ausführung definitionsgemäß nach endlich vielen Schritten beendet ist), das 'Nicht-terminieren' betrachten. Aufgabe des Systementwurfs ist es gerade, aus den Anforderungen an das funktionale Verhalten des Systems zu einer adäquaten Zerlegung in einzelne Algorithmen zu kommen.

So betrachtet ist Systementwurf 'top down'-Entwurf par excellence, Entwicklung von den funktionalen Anforderungen an die Wirkungen des Systems durch Zerlegung in Teilprobleme (zur Veranschaulichung kann Fig. 4 dienen) so lange, bis sich Lösungen dieser Probleme mit Hilfe eines Satzes vorgegebener Werkzeuge oder Operationen angeben lassen. Trotzdem ist das Wort 'top down' eigentlich irreführend, und zwar nicht nur, weil darin im allgemeinen unvermeidliche Fehlentwicklungen, die zu einer Art iterativem Vorgehen führen, ignoriert werden. Davon abgesehen ist schon die Aufgabenstellung im Grunde eine Art Randwertproblem mit den Anforderungen an das System am 'oberen', den verfügbaren Operationen als elementaren Bausteinen am 'unteren' Rand. Und so wie man durch Zerlegung des Problems in Teilprobleme die Formulierung des operativen Lösungswegs 'von oben her' erleichtert bzw. ermöglicht, so kann man diesem

Lösungsweg 'von unten' durch Aufbau komplexerer Bausteine aus den elementaren näher kommen, kurz, Analyse und Synthese stehen sich gleichberechtigt gegenüber.

Schließlich sind ja die Bemühungen der Informatik um Programmierungserleichterungen, wie sie z.B. die höheren Programmiersprachen darstellen, nichts anderes als eine solche 'bottom up'-Entwicklungshilfe für die Programmierung, in der aus den wirklich primitiven Bausteinen, den Maschinenoperationen, komplexere aber übersichtlichere und den erwarteten Aufgaben angepaßtere Operationen zusammengesetzt werden.

Eben diesen Zielen dienen auch die in den letzten Jahren im Bereich der Programmiersprachen aktuell gewordenen abstrakten Datentypen oder Rechenstrukturen, im Grunde Konkretisierungen des Algebrenbegriffs der modernen universellen Algebra. Tatsächlich ist ja eine Programmiersprache ein System, das aus vorgegebenen Rechenstrukturen (etwa der Booleschen Algebra der Wahrheitswerte, dem Integritätsbereich der ganzen Zahlen, der Halbgruppe der Wörter über dem lateinischen Alphabet) und Mitteln zur Definition neuer besteht, mit einigen wenigen zusätzlichen, Abläufe (d.h. Ordnung auf der Menge der Operationsanweisungen eines Programms) beschreibenden Elementen.

8. Methodologie des Programmierens und Systeme zur rechnergestützten Programmierung

Die oben skizzierte Vorgehensweise der Reduktion eines Problems auf einfachere Teilprobleme ist vor nunmehr einem Jahrzehnt unter dem Eindruck der enormen Schwierigkeiten und Fehlschläge, die allenthalben bei der Entwicklung großer Programmsysteme eintraten, unter den Bezeichnungen "Strukturiertes Programmieren" bzw. "Methode der schrittweisen Verfeinerung" von Dijkstra formuliert und in die Literatur eingeführt worden [3]. Daß Dijkstras Darstellung der Methode auch Konkreta umfaßt, wie die Beschränkung auf einige wenige "sichere" sprachliche Ausdrucksmittel unter Unterdrükkung "schädlicher" Befehle wie des go to, hat häufig zu dem Mißverständnis geführt, daß dies *der* Inhalt der Methode sei. Das Wesentliche ist aber vielmehr die Forderung nach methodischer Zerlegung des Gesamtproblems in funktional geschlossen beschreibbare sinnvolle Teilprobleme in einer Weise, die stets auch den Zusammenhang und damit den gesamten Lösungsweg überschaubar hält. Die sprachlichen Beschränkungen sind hier nur Hilfsmaßnahmen, um Verstöße gegen diese Forderungen als Folge mißbräuchlicher Verwendung zu verhindern.

Ein anderer Weg zur Bewältigung der Programmentwicklungsprobleme wurde etwas früher von Floyd [5] vorgeschlagen: die Einführung formaler Methoden zum Beweis der inhaltlichen Korrektheit von Programmen (informell eingeführte Elemente der Floydschen Methode finden sich allerdings schon bei v. Neumann). Das klarste formale System zur Führung von Korrektheitsbeweisen wurde von Hoare entwickelt und, wie oben erwähnt, am Beispiel von Pascal exemplarisch verwirklicht. Grundlage ist dabei die Interpretation eines Programms oder Programmschritts als Zustandsübergang. Ein semantischer

Korrektheitsbeweis verlangt eine unabhängige Charakterisierung der zu realisierenden Zustandsübergangsfunktion und den Nachweis, daß das Programm diese Funktion darstellt. Eine vom Programm unabhängige explizite Darstellung ist meist nicht angebbar, sondern nur eine implizite Definition, also Bedingungen, denen die zu berechnenden Werte, die Endzustände, unter gegebenen Voraussetzungen über die Argumentwerte, die Anfangszustände, genügen müssen. Bedingungen und Voraussetzungen formalisiert man als Aussagen in einer Prädikatenlogik, die Anfangs- und Endzustände des Programms charakterisieren.

Dementsprechend sind die Axiome (richtiger Axiomenschemata) des Hoareschen Systems elementare Anweisungstypen der zugrunde liegenden Programmiersprache, umrahmt von einer "Vorbedingung" und einer "Nachbedingung", die die durch die als Zustandsübergang interpretierte Anweisung verknüpften Zustandsmengen (und damit implizit die Bedeutung der Anweisung selbst) charakterisieren.

Die Ableitungsregeln des Systems beschreiben den Aufbau von entsprechend von Bedingungen eingerahmten zusammengesetzten Anweisungen aus einfacheren. Ein Korrektheitsbeweis ist die Angabe einer formalen Ableitung des Programms mit durch die Problemstellung vorgegebener Vor- und Nachbedingung aus Axiomen mit Hilfe der Ableitungsregeln. Eine komprimierte Beweisskizze zeigt Fig. 5.

Voraussetzungen $(x,y \in N_+)$

$$\begin{cases} (1) & ggt(x,x) = x \\ (2) & ggt(x,y) = ggt(y,x) \\ (3) & ggt(x,y) = ggt(x-y,y) \quad \text{falls } x > y \end{cases}$$

$\{x>0 \wedge y>0\} \rightarrow \{x>0 \wedge y>0 \wedge ggt(x,y) = ggt(x,y)\}$

a := x; b := y;

$\{a>0 \wedge b>0 \wedge ggt(a,b) = ggt(x,y)\}$

<u>while</u> a ≠ b <u>do</u> <u>if</u> a > b <u>then</u> a := a - b <u>else</u> b := b - a <u>fi</u>;

$\{a>0 \wedge b>0 \wedge ggt(a,b) \overset{(2,3)}{=} ggt(x,y) \wedge a=b\} \overset{(1)}{\rightarrow} \{a = ggt(x,y)\}$

g := a;

$\{g = ggt(x,y)\}$

Fig. 5. Partielle Korrektheit eines Programms (größter gemeinsamer Teiler)

Bei einer solchen Anwendung des formalen Systems besteht wieder die schon früher erwähnte Problematik fehlerhafter Programme. Weiter wird ignoriert, daß das Programm ja nicht vom Himmel fällt, sondern eben aus Vor- und Nachbedingung heraus entwickelt werden muß. Daß das System eine solche Entwicklung als Lösung einer Art logisch-algorithmischer Randwertaufgabe, nämlich den Algorithmus zwischen Vor- und Nachbedingung zu 'interpolieren', geradezu verlangt, hat als erster wohl wieder Dijkstra [4] festgestellt. Er erkannte auch, daß die Konstruktion von der signifikanten, der Nachbedingung aus rückwärts erfolgen sollte. So faßt er Anweisungen als Transformationen der Nach- in die Vorbedingung auf und baut darauf ein System der Programmentwicklung als Konstruktion der entsprechenden 'Prädikattransformation' auf.

Das Vorgehen ist ohne Zweifel bestechend. Trotzdem läßt sich noch ein methodischer Einwand anmelden: hier werden zwei Aufgaben nicht nur gleichzeitig angegangen, sondern auch vermengt, die ganz unterschiedlichen Charakter haben und deshalb wohl besser zu trennen wären. Die Aufgaben sind einmal die mathematische Lösung des gestellten Problems, ein konstruktiver Existenzbeweis durch Angabe einer expliziten (u.U. rekursiven) Lösungsfunktion, zum anderen die Entwicklung eines effizienten Algorithmus als operativer Darstellung dieser Funktion.

Für Probleme dieser Art, Auswahl eines besten Elements aus einer Klasse zulässiger, die Bedingungen erfüllender, hat sich ein Vorgehen in zwei Schritten eingeführt, zunächst Bestimmung eines 'Normal'-repräsentanten der Klasse, danach Optimierung (oft wohl nur Meliorierung) mit Hilfe vorgegebener Algorithmen oder Transformationen.

Programmentwicklung in diesem Sinne der Separation der mathematischen und der programmiertechnischen Seite der Gesamtaufgabe ist (wenigstens aus der Sicht des Verfassers) das Anliegen für in neuester Zeit entwickelte bzw. in Entwicklung befindliche wirkliche Programmiersysteme, also Systeme zur rechnerunterstützten Programmentwicklung, wie etwa das Edinburgher System von Darlington und Burstall [2], oder das Münchner System CIP von Bauer und Mitarbeitern [1].

Neben Ansätzen zur Formalisierung der Lösung des mathematischen Problems, die wohl nur sehr langfristig angelegt zu sehen sind, enthalten diese Systeme als Kern eine Bibliothek von Transformationsschemata für Programmteile (meist in der abstrakten Baumform), wie sie zum Teil schon im Bereich des modernen Übersetzerbaus für sog. Quelloptimierungen verwendet werden. Ein Beispiel gibt Fig. 6.

```
proc f = (λ x) μ :
 if B(x) then if B'(x) then f(A(x)) else f(A'(x)) fi
          else C(x)                                   fi

        ↑      Bedingung: A,B,A',B',C sind Formeln, in denen
       ───     weder f noch globale Bezeichnungen vorkommen
        ↓

proc f = (λ x) μ :
 ⌈λ y := x;
  while B(y) do y := if B'(y) then A(y) else A'(y) fi;
  C(y)                                                 ⌋
```

Fig. 6. Beispiel für Transformationsschema zur Entrekursivierung

Tatsächlich ist ja, wie schon früher erwähnt, Übersetzung nichts anderes als semantiktreue Transformation, bei üblichen Übersetzern allerdings von einer festen Quellsprache in eine feste Zielsprache mit Optimierungsschritten nach festen, schon dem Einblick des Programmierers versperrten Strategien.

Demgegenüber ist die hinter den Programmentwicklungssystemen stehende Philosophie, daß der Programmierer, ausgehend von einer möglichst 'hohen', abstrakt-funktionalen und damit leserfreundlichen Version des Algorithmus, durch gezielte Anwendung von als korrekt nachgewiesenen Transformationen nach selbstgewählter Strategie das Programm schrittweise in zunehmend effizientere, zuverlässig semantisch äquivalente Versionen umformt und selbst bestimmt, welche Version er der vollmechanischen Weiterbehandlung überläßt.

Die Bewährungsprobe für die Dijkstrasche Entwicklungsmethode ebenso wie für die Programmentwicklungssysteme und die dahinter stehenden Vorstellungen zur Methodologie der Programmierung steht noch aus. Noch lange Zeit wird vergehen, bis man zu fundierten, aus der Erfahrung gewonnenen Beurteilungen kommen kann. Allerdings legt die deutliche, auch aus dem Typ der bisher behandelten Beispiele ersichtliche stark mathematische Ausrichtung der Vorgehensweisen die Frage nahe, ob ein Einsatz in mathematikfernen, nicht mathematisierten Anwendungsbereichen möglich und ratsam ist. Hierauf läßt sich jedoch erwidern, daß jede Programmierung von Arbeitsabläufen im Grunde eine, wenn auch möglicherweise nur in den Überlegungen des Programmierers implizite, Mathematisierung der zu behandelnden Aufgabe darstellt, die unter derartigen Umständen vermutlich unzureichend ist. Ein Zwang zur expliziten Mathematisierung vor dem Eintreten in das Stadium des Programmierens dürfte für alle Anwendungsbereiche zumindest nützlich sein. Für die Informatik aber bedeutet eine konstruktive Mathematisierung die Basis für das zentrale Anliegen, wie es eingangs genannt wurde, die Algorithmisierung aller nach codifizierbaren Regeln ablaufenden anscheinend geistigen Tätigkeiten und damit den Versuch, durch Kontrastwirkung herauszuarbeiten, was Geist wirklich bedeutet.

Literaturverzeichnis

[1] Bauer, F. L.: Programming as an Evolutionary Process. In: Proc. 2nd Int. Conf. on Software Reliability, pp. 223-234. San Francisco 1976

[2] Darlington, J., Burstall, R. M.: A System which Automatically Improves Programs. Acta Informat. 6, 41-60 (1976)

[3] Dijkstra, E.: Notes on Structured Programming. In: Structured Programming (O. J. Dahl, E. W. Dijkstra, C. A. R. Hoare, eds.) pp. 1-82. New York: Academic Press 1972

[4] Dijkstra, E.: Guarded Commands, Nondeterminacy and Formal Derivation of Programs. Comm. ACM 18, 453-457 (1975)

[5] Floyd, R.W.: Assigning Meaning to Programs. In: Mathematical Aspects of Computer Science, Proc. Symp. Appl. Math. Vol. XIX (J. T. Schwartz, ed.) pp. 19-32, Providence: AMS 1967

[6] Giloi, W. K.: STARLET, die Realisierung einer Datenstruktur-Architektur. TU Berlin, Fachber. 20 - Informatik, Bericht 78-09, März 1978

[7] Goldstine, H. H., v. Neumann, J.: Planning and Coding Problems for an Electronic Computing Instrument. In: Collected Works of John v. Neumann (A. H. Traub, ed.) pp. 8-235. London: Pergamon Press 1963

[8] Hoare, C. A. R.: An Axiomatic Basis for Computer Programming. Comm. ACM 12, 576-581 (1969)

[9] Hoare, C. A. R., Wirth, N.: An Axiomatic Definition of the Programming Language Pascal. Acta Informat. 2, 335-355 (1973)

[10] Knuth, D.E.: Semantics of Context-free Languages. Math. Syst. Theory 2, 127-145 (1968)

[11] Lagally, K. (Hrsgb.): Das Projekt Betriebssystem BSM. TU München, Inst. f. Informatik, Bericht Nr. 7509, Mai 1975

[12] Lucas, P., et al.: Formal Definition of PL/I. IBM Lab. Vienna, Techn. Rep. TR 25.071

[13] Milne, R., Strachey, Ch.: A Theory of Programming Language Semantic. London: Chapman and Hall 1976

[14] Rutishauser, H.: Automatische Rechenplanfertigung bei programmgesteuerten Rechenmaschinen. Mitteilg. a.d. Inst. f. Angew. Math. der ETH Zürich Nr. 3. Basel: Birkhäuser 1952

[15] Samelson, K.: Programming Languages and their Processing. In: Information Processing 1962, Proc. IFIP Congr. 62 (C. M. Popplewell, ed.) pp. 487-492. Amsterdam: North-Holland 1963

[16] Scott, D., and Strachey, Ch.: Toward a Mathematical Semantics for Computer Languages. In: Proc. Symp. Computers and Automata, MRI Symp. Ser. Vol. 21. Brooklyn, N.Y.: Polytechnic Inst. 1972

[17] Wilhelm, R.: Codeoptimierung mittels attributierter Transformationsgrammatiken. In: GI - 4. Jahrestagung, Lect. Notes Comp. Sci., Vol. 26, pp. 257-266. Heidelberg: Springer 1974.

[18] Wirth, N.: The Programming Language Pascal. Acta Informat. 1, 35-63 (1971)

[19] v. Wijngaarden, A., et al.: Revised Report on the Algorithmic Language ALGOL 68. Acta Informat. 5, 1-236 (1975)

GRENZEN DER GROẞINTEGRATION DURCH DETERMINISTISCHE UND STOCHASTISCHE PROZESSE

K.U. Stein
Siemens AG, Bauelemente, München

1. Einleitung

Seit knapp 20 Jahren befindet sich die Elektronik durch die Technik der integrierten Halbleiterschaltungen in einer überwältigenden Weiterentwicklung. Die Einführung dieser Technik ist dabei als Basisinnovation zu sehen, die ähnlich wie die Einführung der Dampflokomotive im Verkehr eine neue Epoche in der Evolution einleitete /1/.

Vor diesem Hintergrund wird im vorliegenden Aufsatz die Weiterentwicklung dieser Technik behandelt. Dazu wird ein für die Beurteilung der Weiterentwicklung relevantes Kriterium erarbeitet und verfolgt. Exemplarisch werden einige bei der Weiterentwicklung auftretende physikalische und technische Grenzen erläutert. Über diese Grenzen gibt es eine Vielzahl von Publikationen, die zunächst neben den physikalischen Elementargrößen /2/ - /4/ vorwiegend Grenzen durch deterministische Prozesse /5/ - /11/ betreffen. Die Bedeutung stochastischer Prozesse /12/ - /14/ wurde im Laufe der Entwicklung immer deutlicher.

Ziel des Aufsatzes ist eine pauschale Aussage im Sinne einer technischen Vorhersage (technological forecasting) /15/ für die Weiterentwicklung des Integrationsgrades als wichtigstes Beurteilungskriterium.

Als Ausgangspunkt für die Ableitung von elementaren Beurteilungskriterien werden die Investitions- oder Benutzerkosten von Anlagen herangezogen, die die Großintegration nutzen. Es sind dies Anlagen in digitaler Technik, insbesondere Zentraleinheiten von Großrechnern, Prozeß- und Kleinrechnern und Geräte mit Mikroprozessoren.

Geht man von den Investitionen aus, so bekommt man als normierte Größe die Kosten je Funktionseinheit. Die elementare Funktionseinheit in einer Halbleiterschaltung ist die Transistorfunktion.

Die Kosten je Transistorfunktion sind mit folgenden technischen Einzelkriterien verknüpft:

- Integrationsgrad (d.h. Anzahl der Transistorfunktionen, die in einem Baustein, Chip genannt, enthalten sind)
- Operationsgeschwindigkeit
- elektrische Verlustleistung
- Zuverlässigkeit
- Herstellaufwand je Chip.

Wie Bild 1 zeigt, besteht eine gute Korrelation der Kosten je Transistorfunktion mit der Anzahl der Transistorfunktionen, die je Chip integriert sind. Dabei werden die jeweils günstigsten integrierten Schaltungen herangezogen. Während sich diese Korrelation im Verlauf von mehr als 15 Jahren über vier Zehnerpotenzen bei den Kosten und 5 Zehnerpotenzen beim Integrationsgrad verfolgen lässt, streuen die übrigen, oben angeführten Einzelkriterien gleichzeitig im wesentlichen nur im Bereich einer 10er-Potenz. Daher wird als Hauptkriterium für die späteren Betrachtungen die Anzahl der Transistorfunktionen je Chip herangezogen.

Geht man von den Benutzerkosten aus (die über Nutzungsgrad, Betriebs- und Kapitalkosten mit den Investitionskosten verknüpft sind), so erhält man als normierte Einheit die Kosten je Elementaroperation. Vergleicht man Anlagen verschiedener Größe aus dem Herstellzeitraum von 1960 bis heute, so findet man, dass die Betriebs- und Kapitalkosten je Zeiteinheit in etwa proportional zur elektrischen Leistungsaufnahme einer Anlage sind. Dies ist verständlich, wenn man das Bauvolumen, die Leistungsabführung und die Stromversorgung mit den daraus resultierenden Kosten betrachtet. Mit diesem empirischen Zusammenhang findet man, dass die Kosten je Operation proportional zur Energie je Operation sind. Die Energie je Operation ist die zugeführte elektrische Energie, die je Elementaroperation in Wärme umgesetzt wird. Als Elementaroperation ist eine logische Inversion in einer Inverterschaltung anzusprechen. Die Energie je Operation entspricht in etwa dem technisch gebräuchlichen Produkt aus Verlustleistung und Verzögerungszeit, dem "Power-Delay-Produkt" /16/. Die Energie je Operation wird als zweites wichtiges Einzelkriterium gegen Ende der folgenden Ausführungen behandelt.

Betrachtet man zur Bestimmung unseres heutigen Standortes in der Entwicklung den zeitlichen Verlauf der Anzahl an Transistorfunktionen je Chip und der Energie je Operation bei digitalen Anlagen in Halbleitertechnik und in anderen Technologien, so stellt man bislang exponentiell anwachsende Verbesserungen fest. Dieses exponentielle Wachstum darf man als ersten Teil der üblichen Wachstumskurven - wie beispielsweise der in Bild 2 dargestellten Pearl--Kurve /15/ - interpretieren. Für eine Vorhersage über die mögliche Weiterentwicklung im Sinne der in Bild 2 dargestellten Wachstumskurve benötigt man eine Aussage über die Grenze des Wachstums. Diese Grenze soll im folgenden für die herausgestellten beiden Einzelkriterien erarbeitet werden /17/.

2. Integrationsgrad

Als Ausgangspunkt für die Behandlung der Entwicklung des Integrationsgrades bietet sich wegen ihrer generellen Gültigkeit und technischen Klarheit die von Moore /18/ bereits 1975 publizierte Darstellung (Bild 3) an. Drei Faktoren tragen zum Anstieg der Anzahl an Transistorfunktionen je Chip bei:

- Vereinfachung von Device und Schaltung
- Verringerung der Abmessungen der Device-Strukturen
- Vergrößerung der Halbleiterfläche je Chip.

Unter Device wird ein integriertes Schaltelement wie beispielsweise ein Transistor verstanden.

Nimmt man die Anzahl der Transistorfunktionen je Chip als wichtiges Einzelkriterium für die Weiterentwicklung, so unterstellt man, dass die Korrelation zwischen Kosten je Transistorfunktion und unserem Einzelkriterium so weiterläuft wie in der Vergangenheit. Diese Annahme ist sicher nicht ganz unvernünftig, man muss jedoch im Auge behalten, dass man damit die wirkliche Situation umkehrt: der Integrationsgrad wächst nämlich nicht um seiner selbst willen an, sondern vor allem deshalb, weil er im Laufe der

Zeit wirtschaftlich günstigere Lösungen bietet.

Die drei Hauptfaktoren werden im folgenden anhand Tabelle 1 behandelt, die Einzelfaktoren, funktionelle Zusammenhänge und wichtige begrenzende Prozesse darstellt.

2.1 Verbesserung von Device und Schaltung

Beispiele für das Erhöhen der Device-Dichte und das Vereinfachen von Schaltungen aus der Vergangenheit sind in Tabelle 2 aufgeführt. Zwei begrenzende Faktoren sind daraus abzuleiten, die in Grundzügen deterministischer Natur sind:

- Device-Verdichtung und Schaltungsvereinfachung dürfen nur so weit getrieben werden, daß mit den vorliegenden Device-Eigenschaften noch eine sichere Schaltungsfunktion gewährleistet ist. (Die dabei ins Spiel kommenden stochastischen Prozesse werden in einem späteren Abschnitt behandelt.)

- Die Herstelltechnologie von Halbleiterschaltungen ist planar. Eine Nutzung der dritten Dimension zur Steigerung der Device-Dichte ist im wesentlichen nur durch die konsekutive Anwendung von planaren Prozessen übereinander voraussehbar. Heutige Schaltungen nutzen nur eine Ebene. Die in Tabelle 2 angeführten Beispiele sind derzeit noch Experimente für das Nutzen der vertikalen Device-Möglichkeiten mit einer zweiten Ebene.

Wie lange können noch Schaltungs- und Device-Vereinfachungen im selben Maße wie bisher einen Beitrag zur Steigerung des Integrationsgrades liefern? Berücksichtigt man die bereits derzeit verfügbaren CCD-Strukturen (Charge-Coupled Device /23/) für Speicher, die eine ideale Nutzung einer gegebenen Fläche der derzeitigen planaren Halbleiter-Technologie erlauben, so sind keine wesentlichen weiteren Beiträge nach dem Jahr 1980 von dieser Arbeitsrichtung zu erwarten /18/. Werden darüber hinaus durch die Erweiterung des Planarprozesses auf viele Ebenen Beiträge erbracht, so sind aufgrund einer sinkenden Herstellausbeute geringere (pauschale) Beiträge bei der im folgenden Abschnitt behandelten Chip-Fläche zu erwarten.

2.2 Vergrößerung der Chip-Fläche

Trägt man die Kosten je Transistorfunktion über der Chip-Fläche auf, so ergibt sich ein Kostenminimum bei der optimalen Chip-Fläche, das durch folgenden Zusammenhang erklärt ist: Bei kleinen Chip-Flächen, d.h. bei nur wenigen Transistorfunktionen je Chip, ergeben sich relativ hohe Kosten je Funktion aus den Montage- und Verpackungskosten des Chips. Bei großen Chips mit vielen Transistorfunktionen sinkt die Ausbeute an fehlerfreien Chips bei der Herstellung. Damit steigen die Kosten je Transistorfunktion an. Die Vergrößerung der Chip-Fläche ist also durch die Wirtschaftlichkeit der Herstellung begrenzt, die ihre Ursachen in den statistisch über die Halbleiterscheibe verteilten Fehler hat. Boltzmann- und Bose-Einstein-Verteilungen sind geeignet, um die Auswirkungen der Fehler auf die Ausbeute zu beschreiben /24/, /25/, /26/. Als Zusammenfassung der Auswirkung stochastischer Prozesse der Fehlerentstehung kann für die Ausbeute

$$Y = \left(1 + \frac{A\,D}{r}\right)^{-r}$$

abgeleitet werden. Dabei ist A die Chip-Fläche und D die aus allen Herstellschritten resultierende Fehlerdichte. Der Anpassungsfaktor r an die Prozeßkomplexität ergibt bei Werten um 3 eine gute Übereinstimmung mit Fertigungsergebnissen /27/. Für unser Vorgehen sagt die Formel, daß unter Erhaltung einer wirtschaftlichen Ausbeute eine Vergrößerung der Chip-Fläche A nur in dem Maße erlaubt ist, wie die Prozeßfehlerdichte D gesenkt werden kann. Da derzeit keine Ansätze für eine physikalische Grenze bei der Prozeßfehlerdichte vorliegen, erscheint eine Extrapolation des bisherigen Trends für die Weiterentwicklung der Chip-Fläche bei gleichbleibenden Anstrengungen zur Reduktion der Prozeßfehlerdichte angemessen (Bild 3). Eine technische Grenze zeichnet sich heute unter dem Gesichtspunkt der Verpackungskosten ab, die bei Chips mit ca. 1 cm² Fläche liegen dürfte. Sie hätte bereits im Jahre 1983 eine Limitierung des Trends zur Folge (Bild 3). Da diese technische Barriere jedoch durch Entwicklung überwunden werden kann, ist eine Vergrößerung der Chip-Fläche bis zur vollen Bedeckung einer Halbleiter-Scheibe von ungefähr 10 cm Durchmesser denkbar. Setzt sich der gegenwärtige Trend fort, so wird diese Zahl im Jahre 2005 erreicht. Bei den

Maßnahmen zur Senkung der effektiven Prozeßfehlerdichte, die bis dahin getroffen werden müssten, sind neben beträchtlichen Prozeßverbesserungen auch fehlertolerierende Schaltungen und Systeme anzuführen.

2.3 Verringerung der Abmessungen

Die wichtigsten Größen und begrenzenden Prozesse, die bei der Verringerung der Abmessungen von Bedeutung sind, sind in Tabelle 1 aufgeführt.

Die Strukturerzeugung erfordert eine Reihe von Prozeßschritten, die derzeit aus der

- Erzeugung von Photoresist-Strukturen mit Belichten und Entwickeln und aus dem
- Erzeugen der Device-Strukturen mit Ätz- und Dotierschritten

bestehen. Die Zwischenergebnisse einer derartigen Strukturerzeugung und die dabei auftretenden begrenzenden Effekte sind in allgemeiner Form in Tabelle 3 zusammengefaßt. Ein rechnerisch ermitteltes Beispiel für die Querschnitte im Laufe einer Prozeßfolge bei der Resist-Strukturerzeugung mit der noch vor der Einführung stehenden Elektronstrahlbelichtung zeigt Bild 5. Bild 5a zeigt die örtliche Verteilung der einfallenden Energie des Elektronenstrahls, die in diesem Fall begrenzt ist durch die Apertur der Elektronenoptik. Bild 5b zeigt die Verteilung der Energie im Resist, insbesondere die Wirkung der rückgestreuten Elektronen aus dem unter dem Resist liegenden Silizium. Das Ergebnis der Resist-Entwicklung nach verschiedenen Zeiten, das auf unterschiedlich schnellem Abtrag je nach Energiedichte beruht, zeigt Bild 5c.

Eine mit dem Rasterelektronenmikroskop gemachte Aufnahme einer lichtoptisch hergestellten Resist-Struktur, die den weit unter 1 µm liegenden Einfluß der lichtoptischen Apertur und die Auswirkung von stehenden Lichtwellen bei der Belichtung zeigt, illustriert Bild 6 (s. Kante der Resist-Struktur im linken Bildteil).

Beim nächsten Schritt, der Erzeugung von Schichtprofilen, existieren Verfahren, die eine weitgehend naturgetreue Übertragung der Resist-Profile gestatten /28/. Ein Beispiel für die Streuung bei der Maskierung eines Dotierverfahrens, in diesem Fall der Ionimplantation, zeigt Bild 7 /29/. Aus diesem Beispiel ist zu entnehmen, ebenso wie aus einer Vielzahl von vorliegenden Experimenten, daß Prozesse für die Erzeugung von Abmessungen bis in den Bereich unter 1 µm verstanden werden.

Als physikalische Grenzen in dieser Prozeßfolge hat Wallmark /13/ den Einfluß der Wellenlänge der Strahlung aufgrund der Ungenauigkeitsrelation, die Rückstreueffekte auf die Verteilung der Energie im Resist und die Molekular-Struktur von Foto-Resists herausgestellt. Dabei verwendet er für die Kantenunsicherheit ΔL die von Brillouin /2/ aus der Unschärferelation abgeleiteten Beziehungen

$$\Delta L \geq \frac{\lambda}{2} \qquad \text{bzw.} \qquad \Delta L \geq h \left(\frac{2}{mE}\right)^{1/2}$$

(λ: Wellenlänge der Strahlung, m: Masse und E: Energie der Teilchen). Er findet eine elementare Abmessung im Bereich um ΔL=2nm, in dem Unschärferelation, Rückstreueffekt und Resist-Struktur günstig zusammenwirken. Als resultierende Genauigkeit mehrerer Kanten zueinander ermittelt Wallmark 6 nm. In einem Analogieschluß zum heutigen Stand der Technik bei 5-µm-Abmessungen kann man sich vorstellen, daß alle weiteren Prozesse so weiterentwickelt werden können, daß man mittlere Strukturbreiten bis herab zum 5fachen Wert der Kantengenauigkeit, das sind 30 nm, erreichen kann. Dieser Wert ist in Bild 8 als Mittelwert der Mindestabmessung, der aus dem Resist abgeleitet werden kann, eingetragen. Soweit die Begrenzung bei der Strukturerzeugung.

Betrachtet man im weiteren Vorgehen nach Tabelle 1 die elektrischen Eigenschaften der Devices - und hier insbesondere die Streuung der elektrischen Eigenschaften - und stellt dabei an eine Vielzahl von Devices relativ hohe Toleranzanforderungen, wie sie z.B. in linearen integrierten Schaltungen üblich sind, so ergeben sich Mindestabmessungen, die deutlich über 1 µm liegen. Als Beispiel dafür ist in Bild 8 ein Wert von 2 µm angegeben. Dieser Wert wurde von Wallmark /13/ für einen Widerstand in einer inte-

grierten Schaltung berechnet, der mit 0,1 µm Kantengenauigkeit hergestellt wird und dessen Widerstandswert 10% streuen darf, wenn man zuläßt, daß bei 10^5 Elementen die Werte von einem Element außerhalb der Streugrenze liegen.
Aus diesem Zahlenbeispiel wird deutlich, daß man mit der Verringerung der Mindestabmessungen beträchtliche Zugeständnisse an Streuung der elektrischen Parameter der Devices machen muß. Dies ist bei digitalen Schaltungen relativ einfach möglich. Als Ausnahme davon sind die dynamischen Halbleiterspeicher anzuführen. Sie stellen an eine Reihe von Devices hohe Toleranzforderungen. (Seltene sporadische Fehler, die bei diesen Speichern beobachtet wurden, sollen von Kernstrahlungseffekten herrühren /30/ und wären demnach als externe Störempfindlichkeit einzuordnen.)

Betrachtet man die heute in bipolaren und MOS-Schaltungen genutzten Effekte zu den physikalischen Minimalabmessungen der Devices, so gibt sich als elementare Strukturgröße die Sperrschichtdicke

$$d = \sqrt{\frac{2 \varepsilon_o \varepsilon_{si} U}{q N}} .$$

Dabei ist U die am pn-Übergang anliegende Spannung einschliesslich der sogenannten Diffusionsspannung von 0,7 V. $\varepsilon_o \cdot \varepsilon_{si}$ ist die Dielektrizitätszahl von Silizium, q die Elementarladung und N die Dotierung des schwächer dotierten Gebietes des pn-Überganges. Diese Formel zeigt, daß durch kleine Spannungen und hohe Dotierungen die Elementargröße der Sperrschichtdicke klein gehalten wird. Als Zahlenbeispiel sei für U = 1,7 V und $N = 2 \times 10^{18}$ cm $^{-3}$ die Dimension von d = 0,03 µm als Wert für eine kleine Spannung und eine hohe Dotierung angeführt.

Hoeneisen und Mead /9/ haben gezeigt, daß aufbauend auf dieser Elementargröße unter Berücksichtigung von Durchbruchseffekten im Halbleiter in Bereichen höherer Feldstärke und des Durchbruchs durch dünne Oxide (Mindestdicke für Si-Dioxid 50 nm) bei MOS--Transistoren für 2 V Betriebsspannung die Mindestabmessung um 0,25 µm bereits aufgrund der deterministischen Prozesse ohne Berücksichtigung von Streuungen liegt.

Swanson und Meindl /10/ haben die Überlegungen über die Mindestabmessungen durch die Betrachtung der elektrischen Eigenschaften von MOS-Transistoren und einfachen Schaltungen (Invertern) in Betrieb bei sehr kleinen Versorgungsspannungen vorangetrieben. Bild 9 zeigt ein Ergebnis ihrer Arbeiten. Aus ihm kann qualitativ abgeleitet werden, daß auch bei Versorgungsspannungen unter 0,2 V eine ausreichende Nichtlinearität für die sichere Funktion von elementaren logischen Schaltungen vorliegt. Eine detaillierte Analyse der dabei verwendeten MOS-Transistoren ergab Einsatzmöglichkeiten für Kanallängen bis zu 0,05 µm, die in Bild 8 als Mittelwert der Mindestabmessungen eingetragen sind.

Will man im Grenzbereich der oben behandelten physikalischen Minimalabmessungen und elektrischen Eigenschaften Schaltungen realisieren, so muß man natürlich die Streuung der zugrunde gelegten Parameter wie z.B. die der elektrischen Durchbruchseigenschaften und der elektrischen Device-Parameter berücksichtigen. Sie haben ihre Ursache in stochastischen Prozessen bei der Herstellung wie z.B. bei der Dotierung durch Diffusion oder Implantation, bei der Oxidation, bei der Resist-Belichtung und bei der Strukturerzeugung durch Ätzen.

Als Beispiel für den Einfluß eines elementaren stochastischen Prozesses wird im folgenden das thermische Rauschen angeführt /14/. Dazu wird aus dem Inverter ein Ersatzschaltbild abgeleitet (Bild 11a), das den von der Eingangsspannung V_I gesteuerten Schalter, den Widerstand R als Ersatzwert aller im Leitungszug auftretenden Widerstände und die Kapazität C als Ersatzwert für alle Kapazitäten enthält. Betreibt man dieses Ersatzschaltbild z.B. mit der Betriebsspannung $V = 3\sqrt{\frac{kT}{C}}$, so ergeben sich aufgrund des thermischen Rauschens die in Bild 11b eingezeichneten Wahrscheinlichkeitsdichten für die Ausgangsspannung /14/. Für die Fälle in den schraffierten Bereichen A_1 und A_0 wird dabei ein falsches Ergebnis erzielt. Bei Erhöhung der Betriebsspannung wandert die rechte Verteilung weiter nach rechts: die Fehlerrate wird geringer. Mit dem Zusammenhang $W_I = CV^2/2$ zwischen Betriebsspannung V und Energie W_I je Operation lässt sich die Fehlerrate A in Abhängigkeit von der Energie je Operation auftragen (Bild 12). Zieht man für ein Zahlenbeispiel ein digitales System mit etwa 300 Elementaroperationen je Nanosekunde heran, bei dem ein Fehler je

Jahr toleriert wird, so hat man eine Fehlerrate von 10^{-19} zu fordern.

Aus Bild 11 entnimmt man dafür eine Mindestenergie je logische Operation von 165 kT. Zum Vergleich mit den von Swanson und Meindl errechneten Grenzen ist dieser Wert in Bild 10 eingetragen. Man entnimmt aus dem Vergleich, daß bei den von Swanson und Meindl angegebenen Grenzwerten bereits eine höhere Fehlerrate toleriert werden müßte.

Als weitere elementare Größen sind in Bild 10 noch eingetragen:

- die Energie von 1 eV (bei der für eine Versorgungsspannung von 0,1 V noch 10 Elektronen am Schaltvorgang beteiligt sind!)
- die durch die Quantisierung der Energie gegebene Grenze h/t_I /4/.

Zusammenfassend wird aus diesen Überlegungen zum Mittelwert der Mindestabmessungen folgender Schluß gezogen: in Fortsetzung des heutigen Trends ist eine Begrenzung der Mindestabmessungen im Bereich zwischen den Jahren 2000 (Durchbruch bei 2-V-Transistoren) und 2015 (0,1-V-CMOS-Inverter), aufgrund der heutigen Kenntnisse, zu erwarten. Die bis dahin extrapolierte Strukturverfeinerung in dem Bereich von 0,25 bis 0,05 µm setzt natürlich die Entwicklung von neuen Resist-Belichtungstechniken - wie z.B. mit Elektronen - ebenso voraus wie eine Weiterentwicklung aller Herstellschritte, wobei auch die Anwendung von bis heute noch nicht bekannten Verfahren für die Erzeugung von feinen Device-Strukturen einzuplanen ist.

2.4 Resultierende Steigerungen des Integrationsgrades

Einen zusammenfassenden Eindruck und eine Vorstellung von der Begrenzung des exponentiellen Wachstums unter Berücksichtigung der erarbeiteten Einzelergebnisse vermittelt Bild 13. Demnach ist eine erste Trendwende um das Jahr 1980 bei ca. 10^6 Transistorfunktionen je Chip zu erwarten. Nach 1983 erfolgt ein Aufspalten. Im resultierenden Streubereich wird zwischen dem Jahr 2000 und dem Jahr 2015 in eine Sättigung zwischen 10^8 und 10^{11} Transistorfunktionen je Chip erreicht.

Es muß nochmals hervorgehoben werden, daß diese Extrapolation nur für die am weitesten entwickelten höchstintegrierten Schaltungen gilt. Des weiteren dürfen sich die technischen und wirtschaftlichen Randbedingungen nicht ändern.

3. Schluß

Abschließend werden noch weitere Einzelkriterien im Zusammenhang mit den beim Integrationsgrad erreichten Werten überprüft.

Die Operationsgeschwindigkeit ist beispielhaft aus der in Bild 10 angegebenen Dauer je Logikoperation zu entnehmen. Diese Dauer verringert sich in etwa proportional zu den Strukturabmessungen. Die in Bild 10 eingetragenen Zeiten sind nur durch die Umladung der parasitären Schaltungskapazitäten gegeben. Die Trägerlaufzeiten in den Schaltelementen spielen noch keine entscheidende Rolle. In komplexen Anordnungen können sich die Operationsdauern vergrößern, da hier noch die Umladezeiten von langen Leitungen bzw. die Laufzeiten von ungefähr 1 ns je 10 cm Leitungslänge berücksichtigt werden müssen. Diese Zeiten sind nach heutigem Wissen auch für viele Anwendungen in sehr großen Systemen tragbar.

Die elektrische Verlustleistung und insbesondere ihre Abführung ist auch in der Halbleitertechnik eine den Aufbau wesentlich bestimmende Größe. Hier gilt es nun zu überprüfen, ob die Wärmeabfuhr die in Bild 13 gemachten Extrapolationen überhaupt realisierbar erscheinen läßt. Dazu ist in Bild 14 der Trend der Energie je logische Operation samt den Grenzen aus den Analysen von Swanson und Meindl und der Grenze aus dem thermischen Rauschen aufgetragen. Die Extrapolation aus dem Trend der vergangenen Jahrzehnte, der sich in den verschiedenen Technologien fortsetzte, führt erst gegen Ende unseres Jahrhunderts bei einem Wert um 10^{-17} Joule zu den ermittelten Grenzen. Auf einem Chip mit mehr als 10^{11} Transistorfunktionen, dem Sättigungswert von Bild 13, die in etwa 10^{11} Inverterfunktionen entsprechen, können bei 100 cm^2 Fläche 1 W/cm^2 oder 100 W insgesamt abgeführt werden. Bei 100 W abführbarer

Leistung und 10^{-17} Joule je logische Operation sind 10^{19} logische Operationen je Sekunde durchführbar. Bei 10^{11} Inverterfunktionen je Chip sagt dies, daß jeder Inverter im Mittel 10^{8} mal je Sekunde geschaltet werden kann. Diese Zahl erscheint für die heute denkbaren Systemstrukturen - wie z.B. Multiprozessoranordnungen mit Speichern - bei weitem ausreichend.

Zur Zuverlässigkeit: bei unserem vorigen Zahlenbeispiel ergaben sich 10^{19} mögliche Operationen je Sekunde. Den Reziprokwert dieser Zahl hatten wir zuvor dem Zahlenbeispiel für die Fehlerrate durch thermisches Rauschen zugrunde gelegt. Die Gleichheit der Werte besagt, daß allein durch thermisches Rauschen bei unserer beispielhaften Anordnung ein Fehler je Sekunde auftritt. Dies macht deutlich, daß die aus den Extrapolationen ermittelten Werte ohne tiefgreifende Maßnahmen seitens des Systementwurfs in Richtung fehlerorientierender Systeme nicht realisierbar sind. Diese und ähnliche Maßnahmen, die aus heutiger Sicht bei der weiteren Steigerung des Integrationsgrades angewandt werden, sind unter den Begriffen "neue Herstellprozesse" und "Redundanz auf dem Chip" in Tabelle 4 angeführt. Falls sie nicht ausreichen, sind weitere Maßnahmen einzuleiten, für die in Tabelle 4 Beispiele angeführt sind - wie der Betrieb von Halbleitertechniken bei tiefen Temperaturen und die Anwendung von Phänomenen, die sich bis heute aus Kostengründen gegenüber der Halbleitertechnik nicht durchsetzen konnten.

Tabelle 1 Steigerung des Integrationsgrades

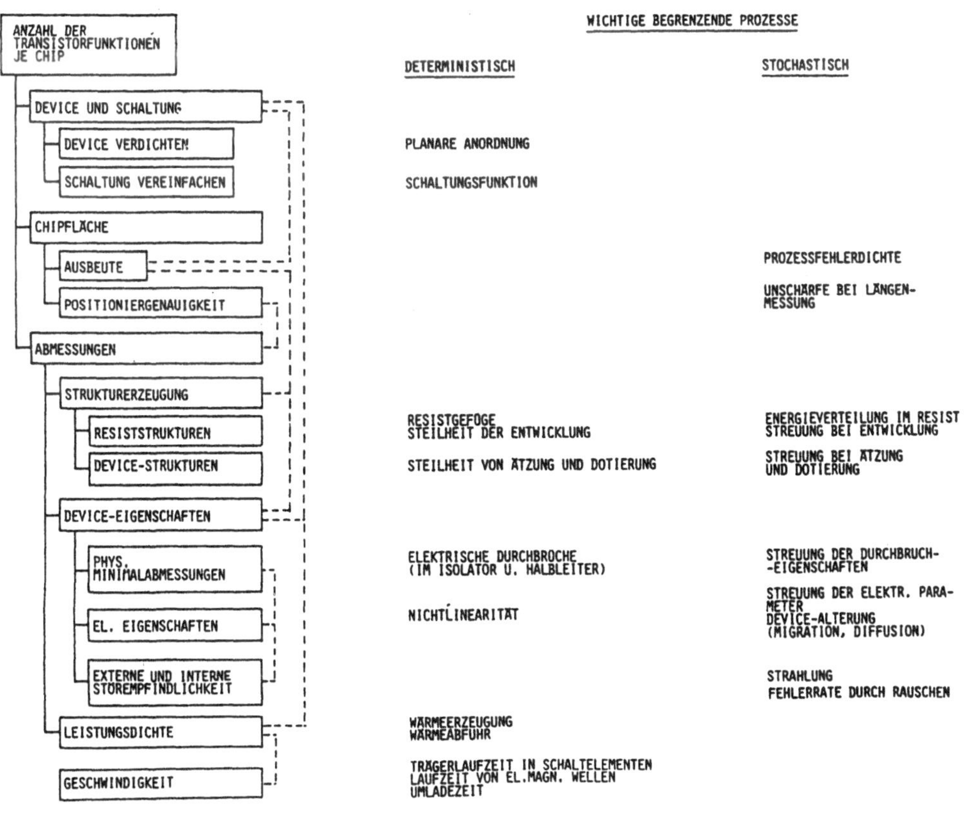

TABELLE 2

BEISPIELE FÜR DAS ERHÖHEN DER DEVICE-DICHTE
UND DAS VEREINFACHEN DER SCHALTUNG

- TRANSISTORFUNKTIONEN OHNE SPEZIELLE ISOLATIONSMASSNAHMEN (MOS-TRANSISTOREN, INVERTIERTE TRANSISTOREN BEI I^2L (19))

- VERSCHMELZEN VON TRANSISTORFUNKTIONEN (LAST- UND SCHALTTRANSISTOR BEI I^2L, WEITERENTWICKLUNG DER DYNAMISCHEN RAM-SPEICHERELEMENTE IN SILIZIUM-GATE-TECHNIKEN (20))

- NUTZEN DER VERTIKALEN DEVICEMÖGLICHKEITEN (SUBSTRATE-FED-I^2L (21), V-MOS-DYNAMISCHES SPEICHERELEMENT (22))

- VEREINFACHEN DER SCHALTUNG (ENTWICKLUNG DER DYN. RAM-SPEICHERELEMENTE (20), EINSATZ VON CCD ANSTELLE DYN. RAM (23), 1-ELEKTRODE-PER-BIT CCD (23))

TABELLE 3

ZWISCHENERGEBNISSE BEI DER STRUKTURERZEUGUNG UND BEGRENZENDE EFFEKTE

ÖRTLICHE VERTEILUNG DER EINFALLENDEN ENERGIE	- WELLENLÄNGE DER STRAHLUNG, APERTUR
VERTEILUNG DER ENERGIE IM RESIST	- STEHENDE WELLEN STREUUNG NACHBARSCHAFTSEFFEKTE
RESIST-PROFILE NACH DER ENTWICKLUNG	- "STEILHEIT" DES ENTWICKLUNGS-PROZESSES
SCHICHT-PROFILE NACH DER SCHICHTSTRUKTUR-ERZEUGUNG	- ABTRAG BZW. AUFBAU-GESCHWINDIGKEITEN
DOTIERPROFILE	- STREUUNG BEI DER MASKIERUNG DER DOTIERVERFAHREN

TABELLE 4

MÖGLICHE MAẞNAHMEN BEI DER WEITEREN STEIGERUNG DES INTEGRATIONSGRADES

NEUE HERSTELLPROZESSE

REDUZIERENDE PROJEKTIONSBELICHTUNG, ELEKTRONEN- UND RÖNTGENVERFAHREN
VERBESSERTE DOTIER- UND ÄTZVERFAHREN
GESCHICHTETE PLANARTECHNOLOGIEN
→ 3-DIMENSIONALE STRUKTUREN

REDUNDANZ AUF DEM CHIP

CODES MIT REDUNDANZ
FUNKTIONSEINHEITEN VIELFACH ANBRINGEN
FAULT TOLERANT COMPUTING
RESERVEEINHEITEN, DIE NACH EIGENÜBERPRÜFUNG BEI BEDARF EINGESCHALTET WERDEN (SPEICHERFELDER, PROZESSOREN, PROZESSOR-SPEICHER-EINHEITEN)

ANWENDUNG NEUER PHÄNOMENE

MAGNETISCHE PHÄNOMENE
SPEICHER- UND SCHALTPHÄNOMENE IN AMORPHEN HALBLEITERN
BETRIEB VON HALBLEITERSCHALTUNGEN BEI TIEFEN TEMPERATUREN
SUPRALEITENDE U. JOSEPHSON-PHÄNOMENE
OPTISCHE PHÄNOMENE

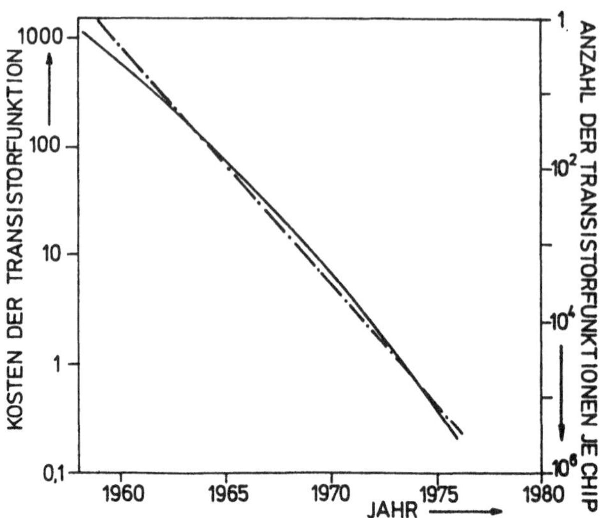

Bild 1 Korrelation der Kosten je Transistorfunktion mit der Anzahl* der Transistorfunktionen, die je Chip integriert sind, bei den jeweils günstigsten Integrierten Schaltungen.

* (-.-.-.)

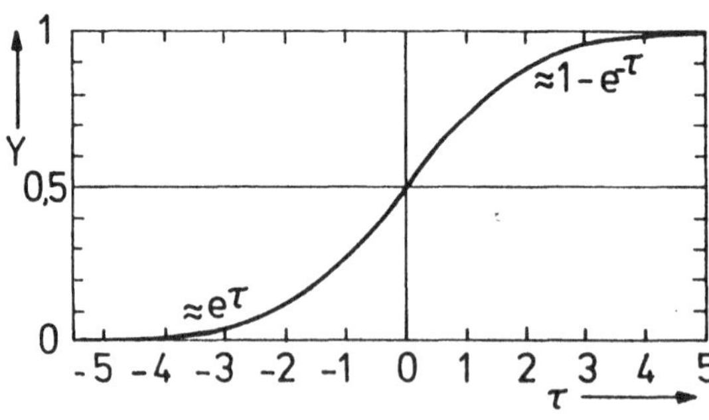

Bild 2 Die meist gebrauchte Wachstumskurve für Vorhersagen über technische Entwicklungen /15/
(PEARL-Kurve; $Y = (1 + a\,e^{-\tau}$; τ: normierte Zeit, a = 1 im Bild)

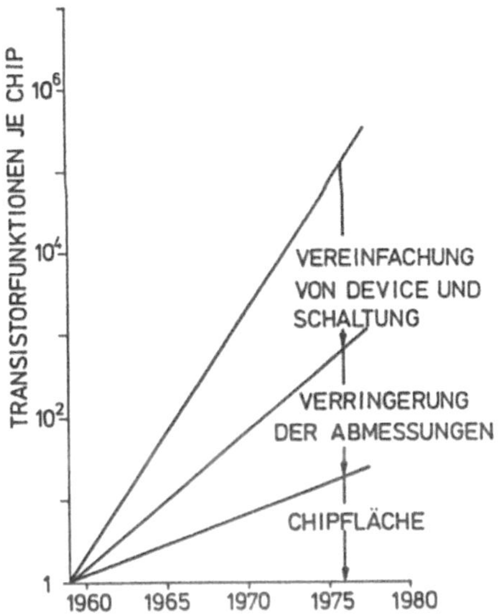

Bild 3 Anzahl der Transistorfunktionen je Chip bei den jeweils größten integrierten Schaltungen und die dazu eingesetzten Beiträge /18/.

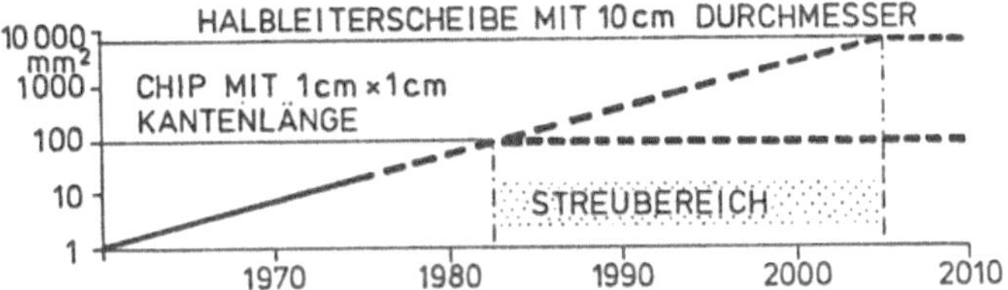

Bild 4 Anwachsen der Chip-Fläche der jeweils größten integrierten Schaltungen auf dem Markt
(Werte von 1960 bis '65 /18/)

Bild 5 Beispiel für die Erzeugung von Resist-Strukturen mit Elektronenstrahlen (berechnete Werte)

a) einfallende Strahlenenergie
b) Energieverteilung im Resist (PMMA)
c) Konturen im Querschnitt nach verschiedenen Entwicklungszeiten.

/31/

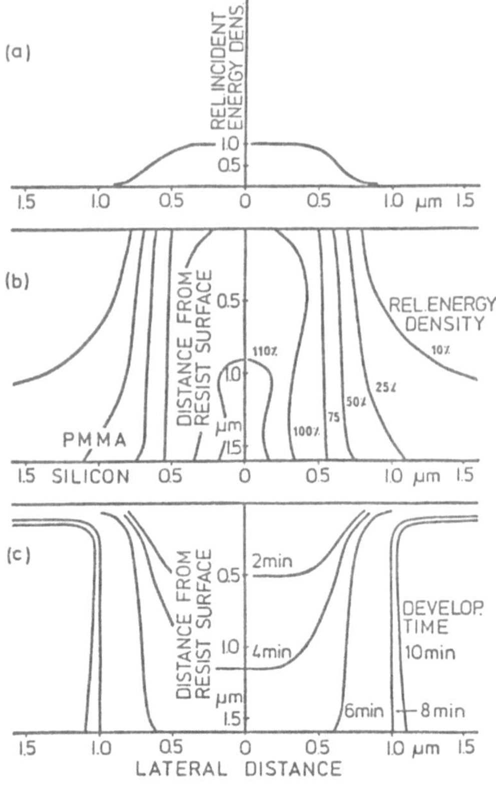

Bild 6 Rasterelektronenmikroskopische Aufnahme einer entwickelten Foto-Resist--Struktur.

Bild 7 Zweimensionale Verteilung der Dotieratom-Konzentration C nach einer teilweise durch Silizium-Dioxid maskierten Bor-Implantation in Silizium /29/

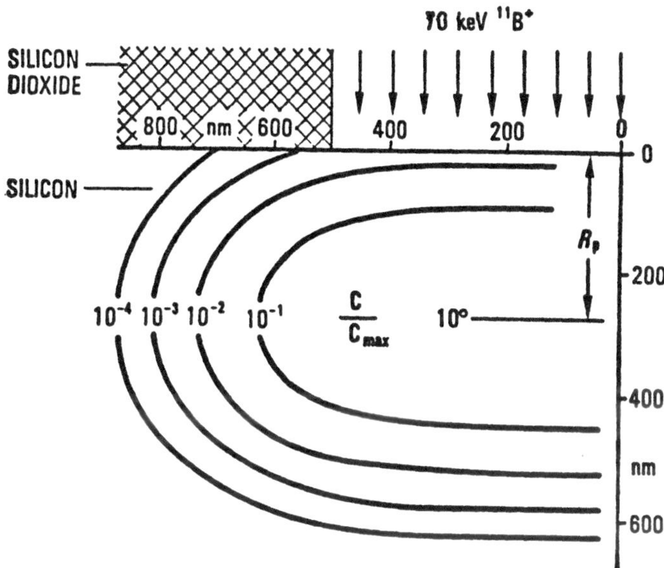

Bild 8 Verringerung des Mittelwertes der Mindestabmessungen der Strukturen auf, z.B. Leiterbahnbreiten, integrierten Schaltungen
• Werte nach /18/

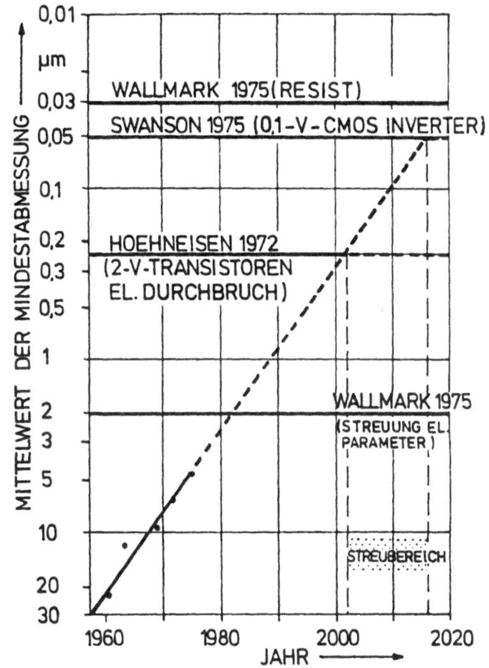

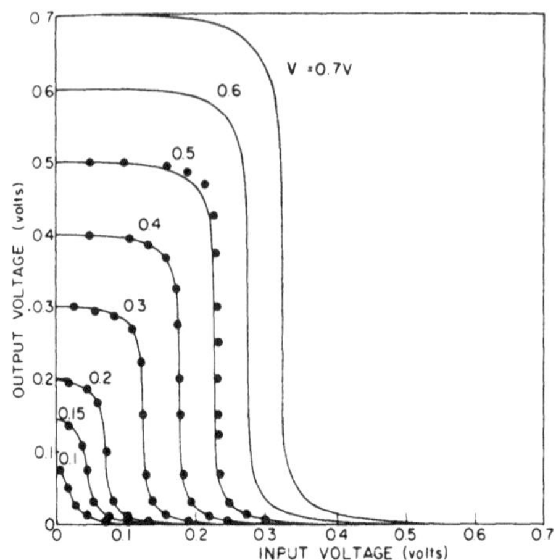

Bild 9 Übertragungskennlinien (gemessen und berechnete Punkte) von CMOS-Invertern bei sehr kleinen Versorgungsspannungen V. /32/

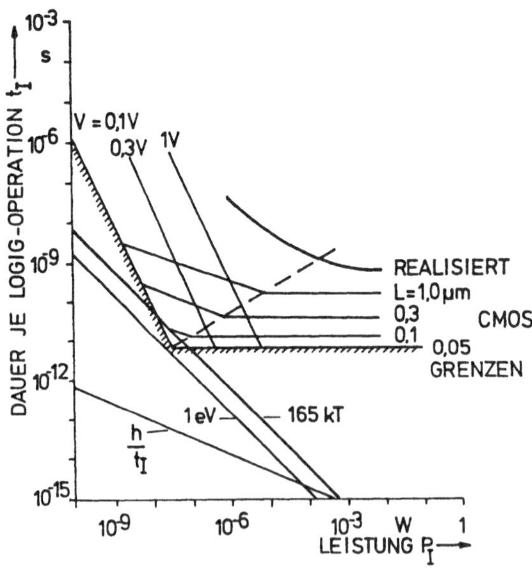

Bild 10 Leistungsaufnahme und Dauer je Logikoperation von realisierten und berechneten CMOS-Invertern.
Physikalische Grenzen: 165 kT - beispielhafter Wert für das thermische Rauschen bei Zimmertemperatur, h/t_I - Quantengrenze.

a)

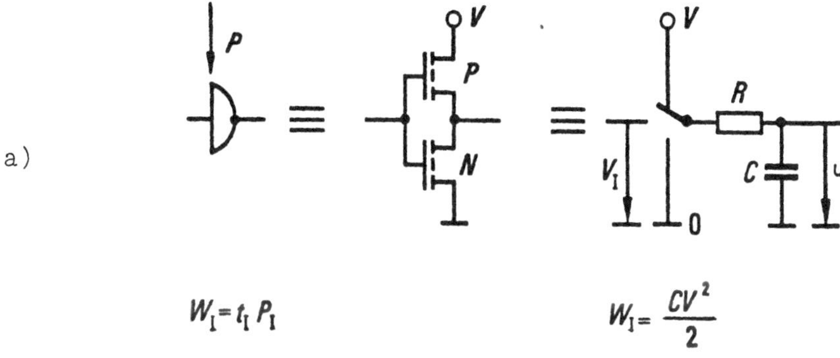

b)

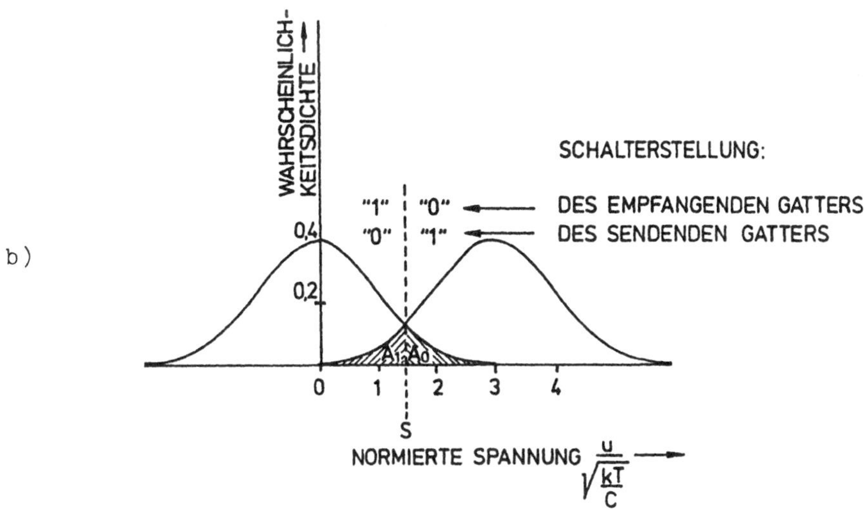

Bild 11 a) Ersatzschaltbild eines Inverters und

b) Beispiel für die Verteilung der Ausgangsspannung für $V = 3\sqrt{\frac{kT}{C}}$ aufgrund des thermischen Rauschens.

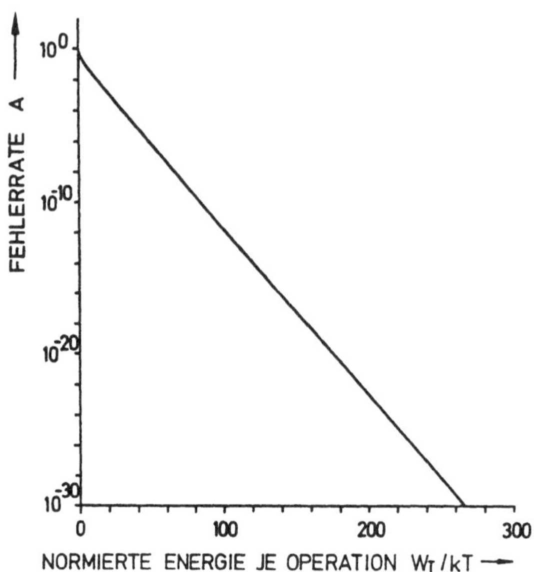

Bild 12 Abhängigkeit der Fehlerrate von der Energie je logische Operation.

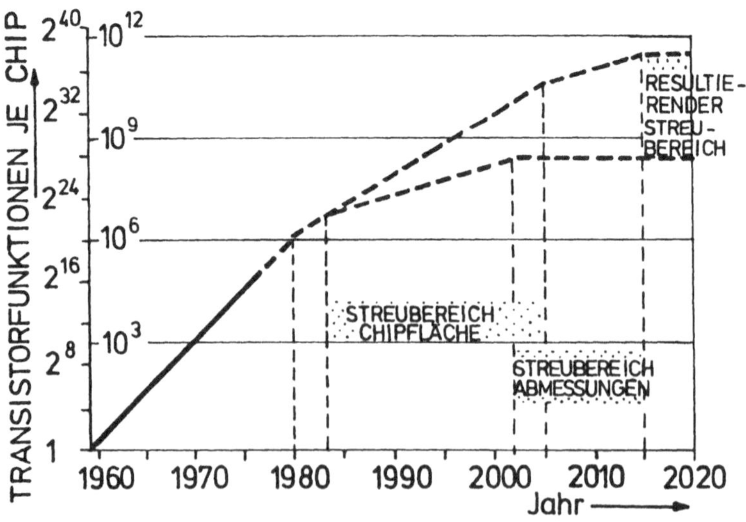

Bild 13 Mögliche Weiterentwicklung der Anzahl der Transistorfunktionen je Chip für die größten integrierten Schaltungen.

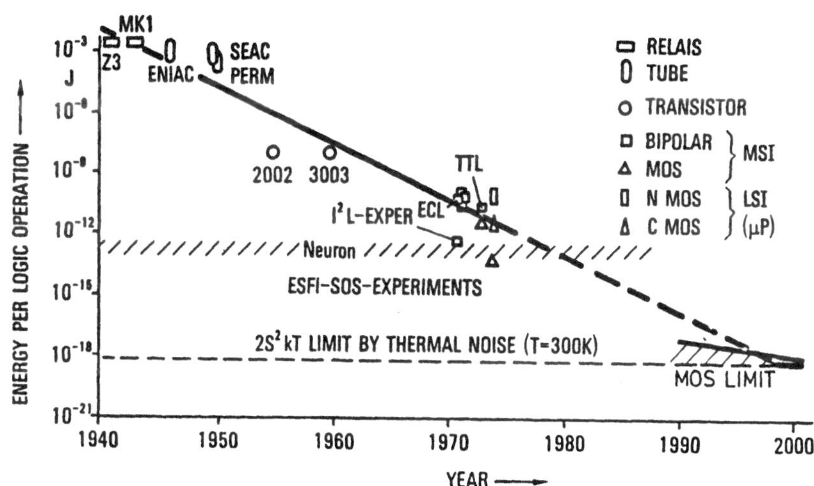

<u>Bild 14</u> Bisheriger Verlauf und mögliche Weiterentwicklung der Energie je logische Operation sowie ihre Grenzen. Neuron: Vergleichswert der Energie beim Aktivieren eines Neurons. MOS LIMIT nach dem Werten von Bild 8 und 10.

L i t e r a t u r

/1/ Mensch, G., Das technologische Patt, Fischer-Taschenbuch-Verlag (1977)

/2/ Brillouin, L., Science a. Information Theory, 2nd Edition, Academic Press Inc. Publishers, New York (1971)

/3/ Landauer, R., Irreversibility and Heat Generation in the Computing Process, IBM J. Res. Dev. 5, pp. 183-191 (1961)

/4/ Kaufmann, H., Zukunftsentwicklung der Informationstechnik, Systems 69, Int. Symposium über Zukunftsfragen, Dt. Verlagsanstalt, Stuttgart, S. 143-161 (1969)

/5/ Keyes, R.W., On power dissipation in semiconductor computing elements, Proc. IRE, Vol. 50, p. 2485 (1962)

/6/ Keyes, R.W., Physical problems and limits in computer logic, IEEE spectrum, pp. 36-45, May (1969)

/7/ Keyes, R.W., Physical Problems of Small Structures in Electronics, Proc. of the IEEE, Vol. 60, No. 9, pp. 1055-1062 (1972)

/8/ Keyes, R.W., Power-Dissipation in Planar Digital Circuits, IEEE Journal of Solid-State Circuits, Vol. SC-10, p. 181, June (1975)

/9/ Hoeneisen, B. und Mead, C.A., Fundamental Limitations in Microelectronics, Solid-State Electronics, Vol. 15, pp. 819-829 (1972)

/10/ Swanson, R.M. und Meindl, J.D., IEEE Int. Solid-State Circuits Conference, Digest of Technical Papers, pp. 110-111 (1975)

/11/ Folberth, O.G. und Bleher, J.H., Grenzen der digitalen Halbleitertechnik, ntz, Bd. 30, Heft 4, S. 307-314 (1977)

/12/ Swanson, J.A., Physical versus Logical Coupling in Memory Systems, IBM Journal, July, pp. 306-310, July (1960)

/13/ Wallmark, J.T., Fundamental physical limitations in integrated electronic circuits, Inst. Phys. Conf., Ser. 25, London, pp. 133-167 (1975)

/14/ Stein, K.U., Noise-Induced Error Rate as Limiting Factor for Energy per Operation in Digital IC's, IEEE Journal of Solid--State Circuits, Vol. SC-12, No. 5, pp. 527-530 (1977)

/15/ Martino, J.P., Technological Forecasting, American Elsevier Publ. Co. Inc., New York (1972)

/16/ Müller, R., Pfleiderer, H.J. und Stein, K.U., Energy per Logic Operation in Integrated Circuits: Definition and Determination, IEEE Journal of Solid-State Circuits, Vol. SC-11, No. 5, pp. 657-661, Oct. (1976)

/17/ Garbrecht, K. und Stein, K.U., Perspectives and Limitations of Large-Scale Integration, Siemens Forsch.- u. Entwickl.-Ber., Bd. 5, Nr. 6, S. 312-318 (1976)

/18/ Moore, G.E., Progress in Digital Integrated Electronics, IEDM Techn. Digest, pp. 11-13 (1975)

/19/ Berger, H.H. und Wiedmann, S.K., Merged transistor logic - a low-cost bipolar logic concept, IEEE Journ. of Solid-State Circuits, SC-7, pp. 340-346, Oct. (1972)

/20/ Hoffmann, K. und Stein, K.U., Trends in Dynamic RAMs, Digest European Solid-State Circuits Conference (ESSCIRC '78) (erscheint demnächst)

/21/ Blatt, V., Walsh, P.W. und Kennedy, L.W., Substrate fed logic, IEEE Journ. of Solid-State Circuits, Vol. SC-10, pp. 336-342, Oct. (1975)

/22/ Rodgers, T.J. et al., V-MOS Memory Technology, IEEE Journ. of Solid-State Circuits, Vol. SC-12, No. 5, pp. 515-524 (1977)

/23/ Séquin, C.H. und Tompsett, M.F., Charge Transfer Devices, Academic Press, New York (1975)

/24/ Murphy, B.T., Comments on "A new look at yield of integrated circuits", Proc. IEEE, p. 1128, July (1971)

/25/ Stapper, C.H., Defect density distribution for LSI yield calculation, IEEE Trans. Electron Devices, vol. ED-20, pp. 655-657, July (1973)

/26/ Price, J.E., Yield and cost analysis of bipolar LSI, Proc. IEEE (Proc. Letters), pp. 1290-1291, August (1970)

/27/ Hodges, D.A., Semiconductor Memories, IEEE Press, New York, p. 175 (1972)

/28/ Widmann, D. und Stein, K.U., Semiconductor Technologies with Reduced Dimensions, Edition du Journal de Physique, Paris, pp. 29-49 (1977)

/29/ Furnkawa, A., Matsumura, H. und Ishiwara, H., Japanese Journ. Appl. Phys. 11, p. 134 (1972)

/30/ - , Dynamic Memories racked by radiation, Electronics Int., pp. 42-43, June 8 (1978)

/31/ Kyser, D.F. und Viswanathan, N.S., J. Vac. Sci. Technol. 12, p. 1305 (1975)

/32/ Swanson, R.M. und Meindl, J.D., Ion-Implanted Complementary MOS Transistors in Low-Voltage Circuits, IEEE Journ. of Solid--State Circuits, Vol. SC-7, No. 2. pp. 146-153, Apr. (1972).

EINFLUSS DER GROSSINTEGRIERTEN SCHALTUNGEN AUF HARDWARE UND SOFTWARE

Helmut Berndt
Siemens Aktiengesellschaft
Bereich Datenverarbeitung*
München

Der technologische Fortschritt führt einerseits zu einem Ersatz bisher software-mäßig realisierter Funktionen durch Hardware. Dabei werden nicht nur Kosten gesenkt, meist kommt es auch zu Leistungssteigerungen Der Einfluß der Großintegration hat andererseits aber auch einen Ersatz von Hardware durch Software zur Folge. Hierfür sorgen vor allem die Einsatzmöglichkeiten von Mikroprozessoren. Sie erlauben ausgefeilte Software-Problemlösungen anstelle von Hardware. Für diese scheinbar gegenläufigen Tendenzen gibt es eine einfache Erklärung. Die mikroprozessororientierte Entwicklung der Großintegration von Schaltungen bedingt zwar mehr Intelligenz bei einfachen Anwendungen aber auch weniger Hardware bei komplexeren Systemen.

1. Einführung

Aus der Sicht ihrer Benutzer bieten informations- wie datenverarbeitende Systeme gegenwärtig einen Funktionsumfang, der - subjektiv betrachtet - die Intensionen der Anwender weitgehend widerspiegelt. Hierbei ist es zunächst uninteressant, welche Funktionen in Hardware oder in Software - sowie in der dazwischen angesiedelten Firmware - realisiert sind. Ausschlaggebend sind allein der angebotene Funktionsumfang und die damit verbundenen Kosten.

Aus technischer - wie auch herstellerbezogener - Sicht handelt es sich dabei aber um die Lösung eines mehrschichtigen Problems: Welche Funktionen sind *wo* anzusiedeln. Im Laufe der nunmehr gut dreißigjährigen Entwicklungsgeschichte der Datenverarbeitung haben sich

---

* Jetzt Bereich Fernsprechsysteme

hierfür Schichten herausgebildet, die durch sprachliche Ausdrucksmittel charakterisiert werden können. Diese *Funktionsschichten* - oder *Betrachtungsebenen* - in einem datenverarbeitenden System konnten bisher ganz eindeutig der Hardware, Firmware und Software zugeordnet werden. Die Verfügbarkeit großintegrierter Schaltungen signalisiert aber bereits heute ein Verschwinden dieser klaren Grenzen.

Der technologische Fortschritt führt einerseits zu einem Ersatz von bisher software-mäßig realisierten Funktionen durch Hardware. Hierdurch werden nicht nur die Kosten gesenkt. Hand in Hand erfolgt meistens auch eine erhebliche Ausweitung der Leistungsfähigkeit. Diese Entwicklungseinrichtung ist vor allem in der eigentlichen Datenverarbeitung zu beobachten. Hier befinden wir uns sogar noch in einer Frühphase. Der Einfluß der Großintegration von Schaltungen hat andererseits aber auch einen Ersatz von Hardware durch Software zur Folge. Dies gilt vor allem in der Regelungs- und Steuertechnik, für die das Funktionsschichtenmodell bisher nur bedingt galt. Meist waren Software-Schichten gar nicht vorhanden. In dem rasanten Umstellungsprozeß von Hardware im Sinne von Mechanik zur Elektronik taucht aber sehr schnell die Software-Komponente auf. Die Mikroprozessoren haben hierfür gesorgt. Auf diesem Gebiet befinden wir uns in einer Umbruchsituation.

Für diese - nur scheinbar - gegenläufigen Tendenzen gibt es eine recht einfache Erklärung. Die mikroprozessororientierte Entwicklung der Großintegration von Schaltkreisen bedingt zwar mehr Intelligenz bei einfachen Anwendungen aber auch weniger Hardware für komplexere Systeme. Das *Mehr* führt zu einer starken Ausweitung der Anwendungsgebiete; das *Weniger* ist eine potentielle Erleichterung. Deshalb ist letztlich eine Bewältigung der Software-Problematik - auch für den Erfolg großintegrierter Schaltungen - ausschlaggebend.

2. Funktionsschichten

Schon für den Betroffenen - als nur mittelbaren Anwender der elektronischen Datenverarbeitung - ergibt sich ein mehrschichtiges Bild. Meist hat er die in unaufdringlich gestaltete Schränke verpackte Hardware schon einmal zu Gesicht bekommen. Zum anderen weiß er um die Software, als den Programmen, die ihm zu maschinell erstellten - aber leider oft weniger gut gestalteten - Belegen unterschiedlichster Art verhelfen.

Der unmittelbare Benutzer sieht sich jedoch einem weit vielschichtigeren Gebilde gegenüber. Ist er Betreiber, Systemadministrator oder Operateur interessiert er sich primär für das Systemverhalten auf der *Bedienungsebene*. Als Anwenderprogrammierer sind für ihn die Eigenschaften auf der *Programmiersprachenebene* maßgebend. Zwar sieht ein Benutzer, z. B. der höheren Programmiersprache PASCAL, durchaus andere Eigenschaften und Funktionen als ein kommerzieller COBOL-Programmierer, doch bedienen sich beide äquivalenter Sprachmittel wie Vereinbarungen, Anweisungen, Prozeduraufrufe und dergleichen. Die nächst tieferen Schichten fallen bereits in den Verantwortungsbereich des Herstellers.

Benutzt man den Wechsel sprachlicher Ausdrucksmittel [1] als Ordnungsprinzip, so lassen sich die Funktionsschichten gängiger Datenverarbeitungssysteme in die folgenden Betrachtungsebenen E_b, mit $b = -3,...,4$, einordnen [1]:

E_4: Bedienungsebene

E_3: Programmiersprachenebene

E_2: Betriebssystemebene

E_1: Maschinenebene

E_0: Mikroprogrammebene

E_{-1}: Logikkomplexebene

E_{-2}: Gatterebene

E_{-3}: Schaltungsebene

Aufbauend auf der *Schaltungsebene* E_{-3}, in der Transistoren, Widerstände und Kondensatoren unmittelbar sichtbar sind, gelangt man über die *Gatterebene* E_{-2} zur *Logikkomplexebene* E_{-1}. Sie ist heute noch am schlechtesten definierbar, da fast ausschließlich herstellerspezifische Darstellungsformen wie auch Namen im Gebrauch sind. Gemeint sind aber stets die auf *Mikroprogrammebene* E_0 ansprechbaren Verarbeitungsmöglichkeiten durch Addierer, Verschiebenetzwerke und dergleichen. Auf E_0 baut die Realisierung der *Maschinen*sprach*ebene* E_1 auf. Die *Betriebssystemebene* E_2 erweitert den bei E_1 gebotenen Funktionsumfang durch zusätzliche Sprachmittel und Dienstleistungen, die in der *Proprammiersprachenebene* E_3 und letztlich der *Bedienungsebene* E_4 erforderlich sind.

Bis E_0 reicht - fast müßte man schon sagen: reichte - üblicherweise die Hardware. Auf E_1 bauen die Software-Schichten auf. Die Maschinenebene E_1 selbst ist heute fast durchweg mikroprogrammiert, d. h. durch Firmware realisiert. In Bild 1 ist diese Zuordnung skizziert.

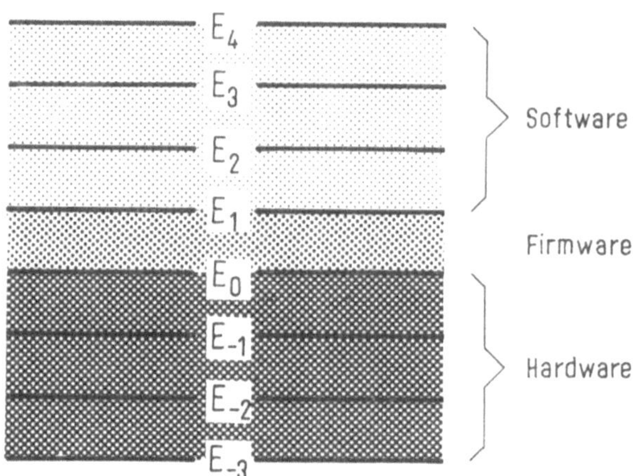

Bild 1: Zuordnung der Betrachtungsebenen b, b = -3,..., 4, in gegenwärtigem Datenverarbeitungs- wie Prozeßrechnersystemen zu Hardware, Firmware und Software. Die Funktionsschichten stimmen mit den Betrachtungsebenen überein.

Dieses Funktionsschichtenmodell hat seit - etwa - Mitte der 60er Jahre für die kommerzielle wie technisch-wissenschaftliche Datenverarbeitung Gültigkeit. Zwischenzeitlich wurde es auch auf die Prozeßrechentechnik anwendbar. Lediglich in der klassichen Regelungs- und Steuertechnik bestand lange Zeit kein Bedarf für solch eine abstrahierende Betrachtungsweise. Die Software-Komponente fehlte gänzlich. Bis zur Bedienungsebene - repräsentiert durch Tasten, Schalter, Anzeigen und dergleichen - war alles hardware-mäßig realisiert. Bild 2 zeigt diesen Zustand unter Zugrundelegung der gleichen Betrachtungsebenen wie in Bild 1.

Die aus Hardware, Firmware, oder Software bestehenden Funktionsschichten entsprechen zunächst den jeweiligen Betrachtungsebenen. Werden etwa bestimmte Betriebssystemfunktionen in Firmware oder gar Hardware verlagert, so ändert sich dadurch im Grunde nur der Funktionsumfang der zugehörigen Betrachtungsebenen. E_2 bietet gewisse Funktionen

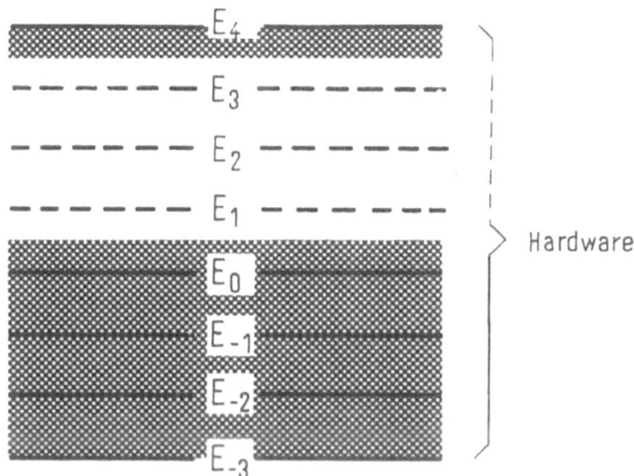

Bild 2: Anwendung des Betrachtungsebenenkonzepts auf die klassische Regelungs- und Steuertechnik. Die Software- und Firmware-Komponenten fehlen. Zwischen E_{-1} und E_4 herrscht keine Zuordenbarkeit zum Funktionsschichtenmodell

nicht mehr originär an, sie sind schon auf E_1 oder gar E_0 realisiert. Im zeitlichen, technologisch bedingten Wandel verändert sich also die Zuordnung der Realisierung einzelner Funktionen zu den Schichten. Um dies anschaulich zeigen zu können, halten wir für die folgenden Betrachtungen an der Funktionsaufteilung auf einzelne Ebenen fest, die sich bis etwa 1975 herausgebildet hatte und - pauschal gesehen - auch heute noch gilt. Veränderungen wie der Einfluß der Großintegration werden dann als Umschichtungen klar erkennbar.

3. Software-Ersatz

Zunächst fällt die Dominanz der Software im heutigen Datenverarbeitungsgeschehen ins Auge. Sie ist einmal bedingt durch die relativ hohen Hardware-Kosten der Vergangenheit, die zu einem spartanischen Umfang mit Hardware bei der Rechnerkonzeption zwangen. Zum anderen fordert der Benutzer Kompatibilität, um beim Übergang zu einem neuen System seine Software-Investitionen unverändert nutzen zu können. Eine Starrheit wesentlicher Systemschnittstellen ist die unmittelbare Folge.

Der technologische Fortschritt von den ersten mit monolithischen Schaltkreisen, sog. SSI-Bausteinen (SSI steht für *Single-Scale Integration*), ausgerüsteten Rechnern Mitte der 60er Jahre, über die gegenwärtig angebotenen Datenverarbeitungssysteme auf der Basis von MSI-Technologie (MSI bedeutet *Medium-Scale Integration*), bis hin zu den neuesten Anlagen, die großintegrierte, d. h. LSI-Bausteine (LSI für *Large-Scale Integration*) enthalten, wurde vorwiegend zur Steigerung der Verarbeitungsleistung genutzt. Darüber hinaus wurde viel für die Verfügbarkeit der Systeme getan. Die Hardware wurde also "schneller" wie auch sicherer. Die Software bleibt hiervon unberührt, sie wuchs nur in sich, wurde dadurch schwerfälliger und auch nicht unbedingt sicherer.

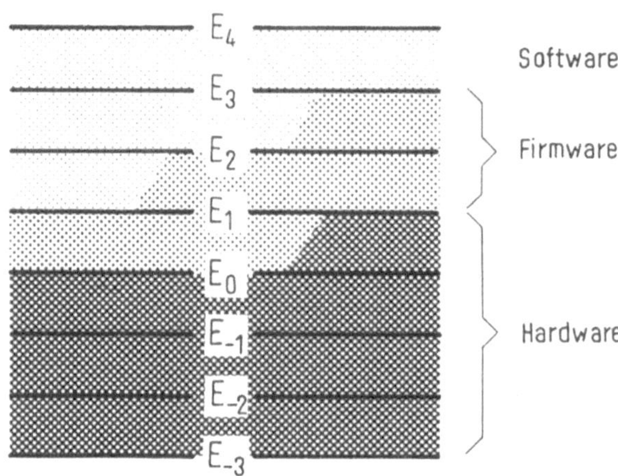

Bild 3: Veränderungen der Funktionsschichten beim Software-Ersatz

Erst in jüngster Zeit ist auch eine Funktionsverlagerung erkennbar. Bild 3 zeigt diesen Trend. Funktionen der Betriebssystemebene E_2 und auch der Programmiersprachenebene E_3 werden zunächst in Firmware verlagert. Dafür gibt es auch schon eine ganze Reihe relevanter Beispiele [1]. Im Vordergrund steht auch hier die mögliche Leistungssteigerung. Sie wird erreicht durch das Verfügbarwerden von Speicherbausteinen, deren Kapazität sich - fast unabhängig von der jeweiligen Technologie - etwa alle 2 Jahre vervierfacht. Damit werden Festwertspeicher (ROM vom Englischen *Read-Only Memory*), einstellbare Festwertspeicher (PROM für *Programmable Read-Only Memory*), änderbare Festwertspeicher (EAPROM von *Electrically Alterable Read-Only Memory*) und beschreibbare Steuerspeicher (englisch WCM für *Writable Control Memory*) in einem Maße verfügbar, das es erlaubt, die Vorteile der Mikroprogrammierung [1] in immer weiteren Bereichen der eigentlichen Datenverarbeitung wie auch der Prozeßrechentechnik zu nutzen. Die unmittelbaren Folgen sind distributive Systeme [2] mit verteilter Intelligenz (Funktionen aus E_2 und E_3 in Firmware) aber auch die Bewältigung der Kompatibilitätsproblematik für E_1.

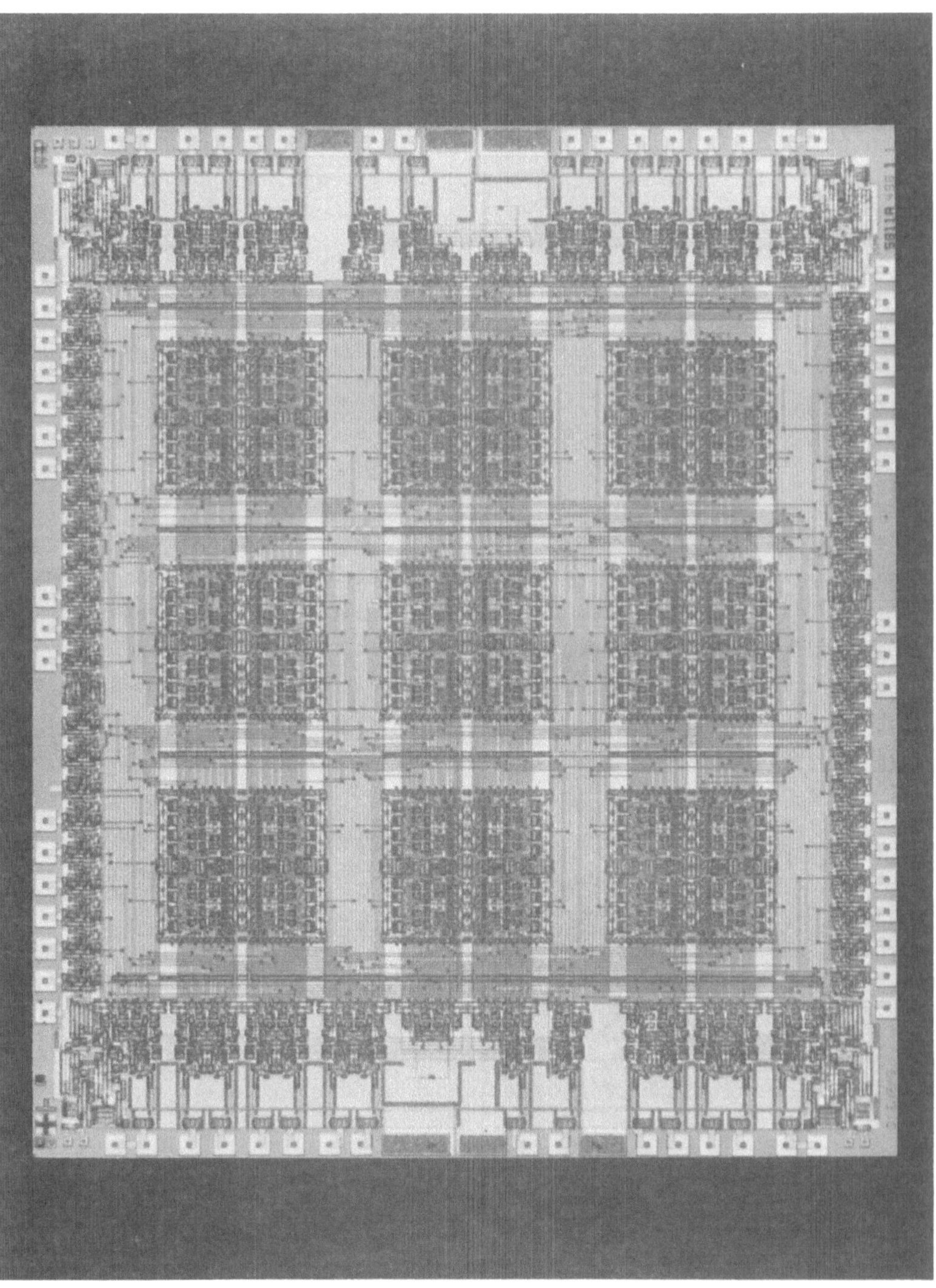

Bild 4: Matrix-LSI in Master-Slice-
Technik mit 36 Logikzellen

In einem zweiten Schritt erscheint jedoch auch eine Anhebung des Funktionsumfangs von E_0 durch reine Hardware-Maßnahmen möglich (Bild 3). Neben der relativ geringen Anzahl standardisierbarer LSI-Bausteine, zu denen die *Bit-Slice*-Mikroprozessoren zählen und die einen gewissen Bitschnitt durch Verarbeitungseinheiten darstellen, kommen hierfür vor allem großintegrierte Bausteine in Frage, die anwendungsspezifische Logikschaltungen auch bei relativ kleinen Stückzahlen ermöglichen. Hier bietet sich beispielsweise die *Master-Slice*-Technologie an, bei der Bausteine bis auf die Verdrahtungsschichten vorgefertigt werden. Matrixartig angeordnete Logikzellen werden dann entsprechend ihrer gewünschten Funktion zusammen mit den anwendungsspezifischen Zellenverbindungen aufgebracht [3]. Bild 4 zeigt als Beispiel einen solchen Baustein mit 36 Logikzellen auf einer Fläche von (im Original) 5,5 mm x 6,5 mm.

Derartige Nutzungen der Großintegration von Bauelementen für Speicher- wie auch Logikbausteine führen zu einem Software *Ersatz* durch Firmware und letztlich auch Hardware. Der Trend ist nicht nur klar erkennbar, der Einsatz kann auch beobachtet werden. Ein "eingeschwungener Zustand" zeichnet sich jedoch für die nähere Zukunft noch lange nicht ab.

4. Hardware-Ersatz

Betrachtet man das Gebiet etwas mehr aus der Sicht der Regelungstechnik, so dominiert dort der Ersatz von Hardware (Schütze, Relais, u. a. m.) durch Software im Zusammenhang mit dem Einsatz von Mikroprozessoren. Sie sind fast schon den VLSI-Technologien (VLSI steht für V*ery* L*arge*-S*cale* I*ntegration*) zuzuordnen. Die Verarbeitungsgeschwindigkeit ist zwar - dank der vorherrschenden MOS-Technologie - noch relativ bescheiden (einige us), aber für die meisten Anwendungsgebiete mehr als ausreichend. Bei den modernsten Mikroprozessoren wird z. Z. eine 16-bit-Verarbeitung mit Befehlsausführungszeiten von wenigen Mikrosekunden geboten.

Dank der Verfügbarkeit solcher Prozessoren im Zusammenspiel mit gleichermaßen großintegrierten Speicherbausteinen, hat sich - fast schlagartig - die in Bild 2 gezeigte Funktionsaufteilung der Hardware auf die Betrachtungsebenen geändert. Die Software-Kompenente kam hinzu. Bild 5 illustriert diesen Übergang. Die bisher nicht (explizit) vorhandenen Betrachtungsebenen E_1 bis (*fast*) E_4 werden nunmehr softwaremäßig realisiert. Sie sind also vorhanden. Und damit existiert auch auf diesem Anwendungsgebiet das Software-Wartungsproblem. Man sollte es nicht unterschätzen.

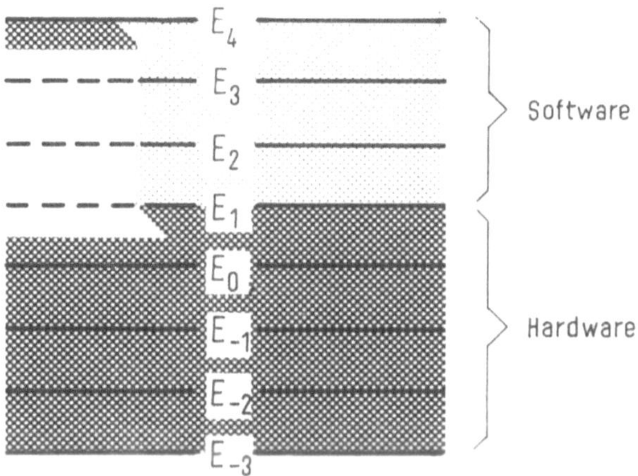

Bild 5: Veränderung der Funktionsschichten beim Hardware-Ersatz

Bild 6 zeigt die Variante mit Bit-Slice-Mikroprozessor-Hardware. Sie kann in vielen Anwendungsfällen den Übergang von der Mechanik zur Elektronik erleichtern, weil die Firmware-Schicht anpassend wirkt. Das gleiche gilt für einen Prozeßrechnerwechsel. Doch darf man in solchen Situationen das Reaktionsvermögen (Ebene E_1) nicht außeracht lassen.

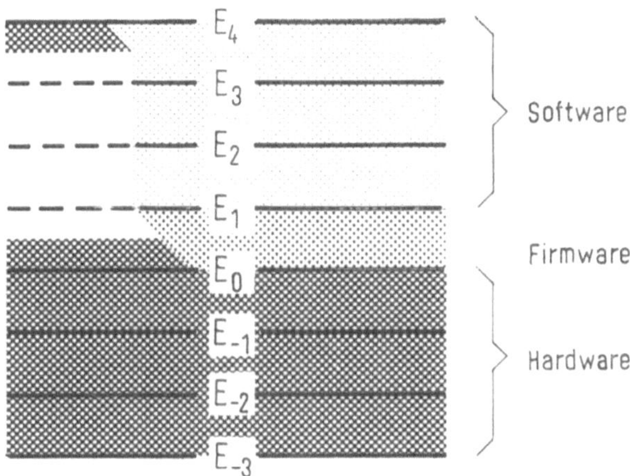

Bild 6: Veränderung der Funktionsschichten beim Hardware-Ersatz unter Einbeziehung von Firmware

Der Hardware-Ersatz durch Software ist mit den üblichen Problemen eines straffen *Software-Engineering* eng verknüpft. Denn eine Optimierung des Realzeitverhaltens widerspricht den Konsequenzen einer strukturierten Programmierung in hohem Maße. Eine pragmatische Vorgehensweise verbunden mit Entwicklungsdisziplin ist deshalb erforderlich, um die anstehenden Aufgaben zufriedenstellend lösen zu können.

Software-Schichten als Hardware-*Ersatz* sind deshalb keinesfalls problemlos. Man muß stets das gesamte Systemgeschehen im Auge halten, um sinnvolle Entscheidungen über Funktionsangleichungen fällen zu können.

5. Ausblick

Anhand eines Funktionsschichtenmodells mit seinen Betrachtungsebenen wurde gezeigt, wie sich prinzipielle Funktionszuordnungen von der Hardware zur Software - über Firmware - und umgekehrt verlagern, wenn man die immanenten Möglichkeiten der Großintegration von Schaltungen nutzt. Differenziert nach Anwendungsgebieten - allgemeine Datenverarbeitung, Prozeßrechnertechnik und Regelungstechnik - wurden die scheinbar gegenläufigen Tendenzen Software-*Ersatz* wie Hardware-*Ersatz* behandelt.

Wie eingangs bereits erwähnt, bedingt und führt dies *Mehr* an Hardware-Intelligenz in mikroprozessorgesteuerten Systemen zu einer Ausweitung im Anwendungsbereich. Ein *Weniger* für die traditionellen Einsatzfälle stellt aber ebenso eine fühlbare Erleichterung dar. Damit ist ein greifbarer Erfolg stets von der Beherrschung der zugehörigen Software-Problematik abhängig.

Schrifttum

[1] Berndt, H.: Was ist Firmware? Elektron. Rechenanl. 19 (1977) H. 2, S. 77-80.

[2] Donner,H.: Tendenzen für die Architektur von Rechensystemen. In: Struktur und Betrieb von Rechensystemen, NTG-Fachberichte, Band 62, T. Einsele, Herausg., Berlin: VDE-Verlag, S. 21-38.

[3] Bräckelmann, W., Fritzsche, H. J., Krcos, F. K., Trinkl, W., Wilhelm, W.: A Master-Slice LSI for Subnanosecond Random Logic. Proc. ISSCC, Philadelphia, Pa., Februar 1977, S. 108-109, 242.

Experimentsteuerung durch Rechengeräte

J. Gaßmann
Max Planck-Institut für Biochemie

1. Einleitung

Rechengeräte werden routinemäßig zur technischen Prozeßsteuerung und -kontrolle eingesetzt [1]. Für physikalische und auch chemische Experimente ist jedoch eine flexiblere Anpassung und Abänderung dieser reinen Automatisierung notwendig, welche erhebliche zusätzliche Aufwendungen bei Hardware und vor allem bei Software benötigen kann. Die entstehenden Gesamtkosten sind dabei ein wesentlicher, wenn nicht gar der entscheidende Faktor bei derartigen Installationen. Diese Aufwendungen müssen in einem annehmbaren Verhältnis zu den Gesamtaufwendungen des Experimentes liegen.

Daher ist es ganz natürlich, daß der Einsatz von Rechnern für Experimentsteuerungen in einigen finanziell aufwendigen Forschungsgebieten bereits lange Tradition aufweist (Hochenergiephysik, Kernphysik) [2]. In anderen Forschungsgebieten, wo vor allem einfachere, nicht derart kostenintensive Experimente anfallen, erhebt sich die Frage, ob eine derartige Steuerung überhaupt sinnvoll und vertretbar ist, und in welcher Form sie erfolgen kann. Diese Frage der Steuerung einfacher Experimente soll im folgenden betrachtet und Möglichkeiten der Durchführung aufgezeigt werden. Dabei soll besonderes Augenmerk auf das Systemkonzept zur Durchführung einer derartigen Steuerung gelegt werden.

Was wird von der Rechnersteuerung eines Experimentes verlangt und erwartet?

Die Gründe sind vielfältig und variieren von Experiment zu Experiment:

- simultane Steuerung von Parametern, d.h. aktive, komplexe Beeinflussung des Experimentablaufs;
- Verringerung und Vereinfachung der manuellen Interventionen, leichte Handhabung, Verkürzung der Experimentierzeit;

- umfangreiche Datenerfassung, Verbesserung der Datengenauigkeit;
- Verkürzung des Experimentaufbaus;
- Reproduzierbarkeit des Experimentablaufs;
- flexibler Experimentaufbau und -ablauf;
- Überwachung, Fehleranzeige, Notabschaltung und Hilfsmittel zum Aufsuchen von Fehlern;
- isolierte Erprobung verschiedener Experimentkomponenten, Simulation des Gesamtexperiments;
- sofortige Datenanalyse, Wiedergabe von Kontrollresultaten und dadurch mögliche Beeinflussung der Steuerparameter, optische Darstellung von Daten für den Anwender;
- Weiterverwendung des Systems bei analogen Experimenten, leichte Reproduzierbarkeit durch einmalige Programmentwicklung.

Je nach Art des Experimentes müssen daher extreme Anforderungen an die Rechnerleistung, Datenübertragungsrate, Datenspeicherung, Datenwiedergabe und das Realzeitverhalten gestellt werden. Neben diesen technischen Gegebenheiten für die Beurteilung eines speziellen Rechnersystems sind es, wie schon erwähnt, hauptsächlich Kostenbetrachtungen, welche das Systemkonzept entscheidend beeinflussen [3]. Dazu gibt es eine Vielzahl geradezu widersprüchlicher Argumente.

2. Systemkonzepte

2.1 Einzelsysteme

In der Anfangszeit der Experimentsteuerung war der Anschluß an Großrechner die einzige Möglichkeit. Auch heute noch sind derartige direkte Kopplungen an Großrechner in Verwendung [4].

Durch die zunehmende Verfügbarkeit von Mini- und Mikrorechnern sind diese Steuerfunktionen jedoch heute überwiegend getrennt von Großrechnern. Die reine Rechenleistung dieser kleineren Rechner ist nicht nur ausreichend, sondern in vielen Fällen derart überdimensioniert, daß ein Anschluß oder eine Kopplung an ein leistungsfähigeres Zentralsystem völlig überflüssig erscheint. Wie auch für Großrechner steht dasselbe Spektrum von Peripheriegeräten zur Verfügung, so daß derartige Rechnersteuerungen als verkleinerte Großrechnersysteme erscheinen. Das Betriebssystem besitzt eine Komplexität und Organisationsstruktur, welche auch auf Großrechnern nicht übertroffen wird. Diese Überdimensionierung erlaubt daher auch den Anschluß mehrerer, möglicherweise ähnlicher Experimente, um den Rechner effektiv und ökonomisch zu nutzen.

Die Vorzüge derartiger unabhängiger Einzelsysteme sind offensichtlich:

- dauernde Verfügbarkeit für den individuellen Benutzer;
- Unabhängigkeit von anderen Einflüssen und Benutzern;
- direkte, spezifische Programmierung;
- relativ geringe Kosten;
- überschaubar in Hardware und Software.

2.2 Gekoppelte Systeme

Die dazu konträren Entwicklungen von gekoppelten Rechnersystemen für Experimentsteuerung existieren jedoch auch heute noch und werden weiterentwickelt.

Unter gekoppelten Rechnersystemen soll ein hierarchischer, radialer Verbund mehrerer Experimentrechner zu einem Zentralsystem verstanden werden, wobei die folgenden Entwurfsziele berücksichtigt wurden:

- gemeinsame Peripherie- und Dateinutzung, meist realisiert durch Peripheriekonzentration am Zentralsystem;
- Bereitstellung hoher oder spezifischer Rechenleistung;
- geringe Kosten durch minimale Vervielfachung von Hardware und Software;
- Verwendung umfangreicher Systemsoftware für Programmerstellung und Datenanalyse.

2.2.1 Stark gekoppelte Systeme

Weshalb sollte diese Tendenz zur Verwendung von alleinstehenden Einzelsystemen durchbrochen werden zugunsten anderer Konzepte, wie zum Beispiel verteilter, aber gekoppelter Rechnersysteme?

Die Analyse der angeführten Argumente zeigt folgendes:

2.2.1.1 Gemeinsame Peripherie- und Dateinutzung

Um die Nutzung aufwendiger Peripheriegeräte, wie Massenspeicher, Magnetbandeinheiten, graphische Terminals, zu optimieren, werden diese Geräte nur zentral angeboten.

Dieses Vorgehen wird jedoch in Zukunft immer mehr an Bedeutung verlieren. Die Kosten für die unmittelbar zum Experiment in Realzeit benötigte Peripherie werden immer geringer, so daß der Anschluß direkt an der Experimentsteuerung sinnvoll ist. Billige Geräte genügender Kapazität (z.B. Diskette) und neue Produkte (z.B. Charge-coupled-devices, Plasma-Displays) werden diesen Trend zu billiger, vielseitiger Peripherie noch weiter verstärken. Mit vertretbaren Kosten wird es daher in Zukunft möglich sein, sämtliche Peripherie, die unmittelbar notwendig für den Ablauf des Experiments ist, direkt an einen einzelnen Experimentrechner anzuschließen. Als weiterer Vorteil kann dabei die sonstige rein serielle Datenaufnahme von einer sofortigen geordneten Datenarchivierung abgelöst werden.

Auch die immer wieder angeführte zentrale oder gemeinsame Dateinutzung für Vergleichszwecke oder Informationsaustausch wird kein Grund bleiben, ein gekoppeltes Rechnersystem zu entwickeln. Im Gegenteil, die Übertragung in ein zentrales Dateiarchiv kann einfacher durch Transfer des kompatiblen Speichermediums nach Experimentablauf erfolgen, ohne auf zeitlich konkurrierende Prozesse im Experimentrechner Rücksicht nehmen zu müssen.

2.2.1.2 Extreme Anforderungen an Realzeitrechenleistung

Derartige Bedürfnisse fallen bei verschiedenen Experimenten (z.B. mehrdimensionale Signalerfassung) an. Neben einer schnellen Zentraleinheit, möglichst mit Gleitkomma-Verarbeitung, ist dann vor allem ein großer Hauptspeicher mit genügend physikalischem und logischem Adreßraum angebracht. Darüber hinaus können spezielle Prozessoren für Vektor- und Matrix-Operationen oder Integral-Transformationen (FFT, Faltung) erforderlich sein. Die Bereitstellung dieser Rechnerleistung in einem zentralen, angekoppelten System ist jedoch für Realzeitanforderungen nicht ausreichend oder vorteilhaft. Der Datentransport der meist umfangreichen Daten zwischen Zentralrechner und Experimentrechner über einen schnellen Datenkanal ist dabei das hauptsächliche technische Problem.

Extrem schnelle Leitungen (5oo KBytes/sec) werden dann benötigt, um diese Datenmengen schnell genug zum Zentralprozessor und zurück zum Experiment zu transportieren.

Der Einsatz von Gleitkomma-Prozessoren oder Spezialprozessoren direkt am Experimentrechner ist nicht nur technisch einfacher, sondern wird auch durch das Ansteigen der allgemeinen Experimentrechnerleistung für immer weniger Anwendungsfälle notwendig sein. Daher erscheint auch das Argument der extremen Rechnerleistung für eine Kopplung von Experimentsteuerrechnern kein ausschlaggebender Grund zu sein.

2.2.1.3 Bereits installiertes, gekoppeltes Rechnersystem

Diese Voraussetzung ist vor allem bei größeren Institutionen oder Instituten gegeben, in denen seit langem Experimentsteuerungen durch Rechner praktiziert werden. Durch die wissenschaftlichen Anforderungen und die technischen Realisierungsmöglichkeiten hat sich üblicherweise mit der Zeit eine Rechnertopologie entwickelt. Die unzweifelhaften Vorzüge, wie umfangreiche Hardware und Software, standardisierte Übertragungswege und die Unterstützung einer neuen Experimentsteuerung durch die Systemgruppe, erleichtern die Implementierung. Andererseits darf nicht übersehen werden, daß solche Systeme entwicklungsbedingte Nachteile aufweisen.

Die Architektur der Experimentrechner sowie die Programmierung entsprechen häufig nicht dem Stand der Technik. Eigenentwickelte Hardware- und Software-Standards bei der Datenübertragung erschweren den Übergang auf neue Übertragungsmöglichkeiten (Industriestandards, Kommunikationsprotokolle). Um den verschiedenen Systemen gerecht zu werden, müssen dann wenig geeignete Experimentrechner und Peripherie beschafft werden. Das bedingt eine Unausgewogenheit und Überdimensionierung des Gesamtsystems, bezogen auf individuelle Steuerungsansprüche. Häufig wird dies noch verstärkt durch die Festlegung auf einen bestimmen Typ von Steuerrechnern (Monokultur). Dies berührt zwar den Einzelbenutzer unmittelbar wenig, da er nur seine Experimentsteuerung in diesem System schnell und für ihn kostengünstig durchführen möchte. Für das gekoppelte System jedoch führt dies zu einem Effizienzverlust.

So ist das Einzelsystem kaum optimal ausgelegt. Überdimensionierung von Rechnerleistung und Unterdimensionierung von Speicher- und Datentransferraten sind normalerweise vorhanden.

Typische Installationen bestehen aus einem zentralen Großrechner, der mit sämtlicher Peripherie ausgestattet ist. Zur besseren Datenübertragung werden als Konzentratoren Frontendrechner eingesetzt, welche den Datentransfer zu den Experimentrechnern durchführen. Diese lokalen Experimentrechner werden über schnelle Datenübertragungskanäle angekoppelt. Als Datenübertragungsmodule werden häufig Standards eingesetzt (z.B. CAMAC, NIM) [5]. Bei Beschränkung auf wenige Typen von Experimentrechnern ergibt sich für Experimente mit einfachen Anforderungen (z.B. niedrige Datenraten) eine Überdimensionierung des angeschlossenen Rechners. Zur besseren Ausnutzung werden dann mehrere Experimente mit ähnlichem Charakter an denselben Rechner angeschlossen.

Charakteristisch für alle diese Systeme ist die Beteiligung sämtlicher Rechnerkomponenten (Zentral-, Frontend-, Experimentrechner) bei der Durchführung eines Experiments. So wünschenswert die Ziele dieses Systemkonzepts auch sind

- lokale Datenerfassung, zentrale Datenspeicherung;
- zentrale Datenanalyse;
- zentrale Software-Erstellung;
- Einführung von Hardware- und Software-Standards,

die starke und starre Kopplung dieser Systeme erfordert das gleichzeitige Funktionieren sämtlicher Komponenten für den Ablauf eines Experiments. Die Zwischenspeicherungsmöglichkeiten des lokalen Experimentrechners sind meist so klein ausgelegt, daß bereits nach kurzer Zeit ein Datenüberlauf eintritt. Für hohe Datenübertagungsraten müssen aufwendige Verbindungen hergestellt werden, um einen ungestörten Datenverkehr zu ermöglichen.

Dies mag für relativ kleine, oft lokal konzentrierte Systeme zu geringen Ausfällen und Störungen führen, ist jedoch bei umfangreichen Systemen oder begrenzter Experimentierzeit oder Einmaligkeit des Experimentiermaterials kaum anwendbar.

Die zur Rechtfertigkeit dieses Systemkonzepts mitunter angegebenen hohen Werte für Systemverfügbarkeit sollten nicht darüber hinwegtäuschen, daß Systemverfügbarkeit meist nicht Totalverfügbarkeit bedeutet. Batch-Verarbeitung bzw. interaktive Verarbeitung brauchen vom Ausfall einer Teilkomponente kaum betroffen zu sein, für ein Experiment ist in diesem Falle eine Wiederholung meist unvermeidbar.

2.2.2 Schwach gekoppelte Rechnersysteme

Aus den dargelegten Gründen werden stark gekoppelte Experimentrechner in Zukunft auf wenige Systeme beschränkt bleiben. Der hohe technische und finanzielle Aufwand sowie die lange Entwicklungszeit beschränken dieses Systemkonzept auf bereits bestehende Konfigurationen. Für ein neu einzurichtendes Experiment ist ein ungestörter Experimentierbetrieb mit minimaler Beeinflussung oder Abhängigkeit des Experimentrechners von anderen Systemkomponenten wünschenswert. Die Kopplung eines Experimentrechners an ein Zentralsystem muß daher während des Experimentablaufs wesentlich schwächer sein.

Dagegen ist die Experimentvorbereitung und auch Experimentmodifikation als auch die nachträgliche Datenanalyse ohne Zweifel vorteilhaft mit Hilfe eines gekoppelten Zentralsystems abzuwickeln. Die Kopplung beschränkt sich im wesentlichen auf Programmentwicklung und -erzeugung für den lokalen Experimentrechner vor dem Experiment und die Datenübertragung und Datenanalyse nach dem Experiment.

Diese Programmentwicklung durch den zentralen Rechner ermöglicht es, den lokalen Experimentrechner gerade nur mit der Peripherie auszurüsten, welche für das Experiment unmittelbar benötigt wird und nicht für die Progammerstellung und nachträgliche Datenanalyse. Die von einem Cross-Compiler erstellten Programme werden dabei im Zentralrechner in ladbare Form gebracht und über ein kleines Ladeprogramm direkt im Experimentrechner abgesetzt.

2.2.2.1 Terminalartiger Experimentrechner

Bei der großen Zahl der umfangreichen Terminalsysteme, welche normalerweise mit einem Großrechner verbunden sind, erscheint es äußerst vorteilhaft, diese Art des Terminalanschlusses auch für die Kopplung von Experimentrechnern zu verwenden. Dies hat vor allem eine minimale Systemkomplexität und geringe Entwicklungszeit zur Folge. Ein Experimentrechner wird demnach als normales Terminal an den Zentralrechner angeschlossen. Für Programmarbeiten ist dabei der ohnehin mit einem Display ausgestattete Experimentrechner völlig transparent. Für das Laden von Programmen in den Experimentrechnern ist dann der als Terminal verwendete Experimentrechner vom Editmodus in einen interaktiven Modus umzuschalten. Die nachträgliche Experiment-Datenübertragung zum Zentralrechner kann ebenfalls im interaktiven Modus geschehen, eine Übertragung im Editmodus wäre aber ebenfalls möglich.

Steuerungsspeicher-Terminals

Äußerst einfache Formen dieser "Terminal"-Ankopplung von Experimentrechnern an ein Zentralsystem werden auch kommerziell angeboten [6]. Der "Experimentrechner" ist dabei ein äußerst einfacher Steuerungsspeicher, welcher die Aktivitäten der angeschlossenen Ein-/Ausgabegereäte des Experiments steuert.

Natürlich sind die Programmierungsmöglichkeiten gering und die lokalen Datenspeicher dieser Steuerungsspeicher auf einfache Medien beschränkt (Kassette, Diskette). Für einfache Experimente mit niedrigen Datenraten reichen derartige Systeme jedoch aus. Die für eine flexible Experimentsteuerung geforderte schwache Kopplung zum Zentralrechner ist bei diesem System in doppelter Weise erfüllt.

Erstens können Steueranweisungen vom Rechner geladen und dann ohne weitere Rechnerbeeinflussung ablaufen. Die aufgenommenen Meßdaten werden lokal gespeichert und nach Ablauf des Experiments an den Zentralrechner übergeben.

Zum zweiten ist das Laden des Steuerungsspeichers vom angeschlossenen Display-Gerät ohne Rechnerunterstützung möglich. Damit können äußerst bequem einzelne Phasen oder Einzelgeräte des Experiments getestet werden. Der Anschluß des Gerätes ist bei jedem üblichen Terminal-System eines beliebigen Zentralrechners möglich, die völlige Gleichsetzung mit einem normalen Terminal-Anschluß erfordert keinerlei spezielle Programmierung.

Mikroprozessor-Terminals

Eine anspruchsvollere Lösung durch die Verwendung von Mikroprozessoren anstelle von Steuerungsspeichern ist offensichtlich. Die Architektur von Mikroprozessoren ist im allgemeinen für den Gebrauch von höheren Programmiersprachen gut geeignet. Dies ist unter anderem durch die Stackeigenschaften dieser Prozessoren bedingt. Es existiert bereits genügend Cross-Software für höhere Programmiersprachen, um logische Programmstrukturen in verschiedenen Mikroprozessoren zu erstellen. Leider wird dabei jedoch oft übersehen, daß eine Experimentsteuerung zum großen Teil aus Unterbrechungsbearbeitung, Ein-/Ausgabe-Aktivitäten und Fehlerbehandlungen besteht. Diese Unterstützung wird durch Compiler höherer Progammiersprachen leider nur sehr unvollständig und rudimentär gegeben [7]. Nur so ist zu verstehen, daß spezielle Programmiersysteme - welche die Software-Erstellung wieder auf das Assembler-Niveau bzw. unstrukturierte, interpretative Sprachen zurückdrängt - sehr häufig für Mikroprozessoren verwendet werden.

Bei kommerziell vertriebenen Systemen dieses Typs können dabei noch gesamte Programmteile durch Knopfdruck abgerufen werden. Dieser anfängliche Komfort fixiert jedoch den Anwender auf bestimmte Vorgehensweisen und beschränkt seine Flexibilität bei der Erstellung neuer Experimentier- und Steuerungstechniken.

Minirechner-Terminals

Bei hoher lokaler Anforderung an Rechenleistung oder bei hohen Datenraten ist die Leistung von Mikroprozessoren heute noch nicht ausreichend. Auch wird die notwendige Echtzeit-Rechenleistung oft unterschätzt, wenn eigentlich geringe Auswertung von statistisch eintreffenden, etwa Poisson-verteilten Ereignissen durchzuführen ist, welche jedoch möglichst viele dieser Ereignisse erfassen soll. Dagegen ist das schnelle Abspeichern großer Datenmengen über Hauptspeicher, direkten Speicherzugriff und lokalen Massenspeicher (Platte, Band) weniger problematisch.

Die für Mikroprozessor-Terminals erwähnte eigenständige Programmierung ist für Minirechner noch weit mehr verbreitet. Jedoch auch hier ist Cross-Programmierung ein wesentlicher Faktor, um die für Programmerstellung notwendige Hardware und Software, insbesondere auch das Betriebssystem im Experimentrechner so zu minimalisieren, daß trotzdem die spezifischen Bedürfnisse des Experiments optimal erfüllt werden [8].

Multiple Terminal-Kopplung

Bei der Leistungsfähigkeit der Minirechner läßt sich dieses Prinzip der schwachen Rechnerkopplung weiter ausdehnen.

Einmal kann ein genügend ausgebauter Minirechner die Funktionen eines Zentralrechners übernehmen. Zum anderen kann ein an einen Zentralrechner gekoppelter Minirechner seinerseits schwach gekoppelte Mini- oder Mikrorechner unterstützen [9,1o]. So ergibt sich durch die Kopplung von Rechnern für einzelne Ein-/Ausgabegeräte oder Instrumente zum gesamten Experimentrechner und dessen weitere Kopplung zum Zentralrechner eine zweistufige Rechnerhierarchie. Für derartige Systeme muß auch Software spezifisch ausgelegt werden. Derartige Untersuchungen werden zwar schon seit einiger Zeit durchgeführt [11], aber kaum zur Implementierungsreife gebracht, welche erst dem Anwender wirklich von Nutzen sein könnte.

3. Zusammenfassung

Es wurde versucht, aufzuzeigen, daß durch starke Kopplung von Experimentrechnern mit Zentralrechnern die beabsichtigte Optimierung heute kein ausreichender Grund mehr für ein derartiges Systemkonzept sein kann. Durch schwache Kopplung von Experimentrechnern mit Zentralrechnern resultieren Vorteile vorwiegend auf dem Gebiet der Programmierung und Datenanalyse. Der Zugriff und Anschluß von Experimentrechnern geschieht dabei über normale Terminalanschlüsse, wie sie jedes Großrechnersystem verfügt.

Die Initiative zu dieser Kopplung muß vom Zentralsystem ausgehen, um dem Einzelbenutzer die entsprechenden Vorteile

- Programmiererleichterung durch Cross-Software mit höheren Programmiersprachen;
- Datenarchivierung und -analyse;
- Flexibilität und Mobilität des Kopplungsanschlusses;
- minimale Hardware- und Software-Ausrüstung des Experimentrechners

zu demonstrieren.

Durch weitere technische Entwicklungen ist eine Weiterführung dieses Systemaufbaus möglich, wobei jedoch stets die einfache Integration eines Einzelexperiments im Vordergrund stehen muß.

Literatur

[1] Trends in on-Line computer control systems (1975)
IEE (ed.) Colmore Press, London

[2] On-Line computing in the laboratory (1976)
R.A. Rosner (ed.) Advance publications Ltd.

[3] Prozeßautomatisierung (1976), Kapitel 2
R. Lauber, Springer Verlag, Berlin,

[4] Computer in der instrumentiellen Analytik (1973)
E. Ziegler, Akad. Verlagsanstalt, Frankfurt

[5] Peatfield A., Spurling K., Zacharov B.,
IEEE Trans. Nucl. Sci. NS21, 867

[6] Guido A., Cole H., Kreighbaum L.B. (1975)
Proc. IEEE 63, 15o9-1513

[7] Ross D. (1972) Control Engineering 19, 44

[8] Stenson J. (1972) in: Computing with Real Time systems,
vol. 2, Transcripta Books, London

[9] Syrbe M. (1974) Regelungstechnik 22, 264

[1o] Strait B., Thuot M., Hong J. (1977) Computer 1o, 36

[11] J. Nehmer (1977) Angew. Informatik, 1, 1

SYMBOLIC COMPUTATION: PAST, PRESENT AND FUTURE

Anthony C. Hearn

Department of Computer Science
University of Utah
Salt Lake City, Utah, USA

ABSTRACT

During the past decade, symbolic computation has become an important problem solving tool for many algebraic calculations in physics and engineering. In this paper, we describe the nature of the field along with some of the characteristics of presently available symbolic computation systems. Some typical applications to physical problems are then considered. Analytic integration by computer is also discussed. We conclude with some considerations about the future of the field.

1. INTRODUCTION

It is now nearly 26 years since the first attempts at doing algebra by computer were reported [1,2]. These experiments involved simple polynomial differentiation, which by current standards is a trivial task. From these humble beginnings, systems and programs for algebraic computation have been developed which can routinely perform not only straightforward polynomial manipulation but also such complex tasks as the analytic integration of highly complicated expressions. It is my aim in this paper to review this field from the point of view of a potential user and describe some of the characteristics of the systems which are used for algebraic computation as well as their main applications.

Algebraic computation might be most easily described as taking an expression and transforming it by computer into another expression by means of a set of mathematical rules, so that the result is in some sense simpler or more tractable than the input. Apart from the aesthetic appeal of such calculations, it is natural to ask why one should be interested in using a computer for doing them since, after all numerical computation by computer is so well understood. There are three main reasons why such algebraic computation is desirable and necessary. First, there are several problems where an analytic form for the result is important. For example, in calculating molecular levels in chemical physics, the cost of computing each level is often measured in terms of the cost of numerical evaluation of the integrals which occur in the theory. Often a whole set of levels can be defined in terms of a parametric form for such integrals, so that if one can obtain a closed form for this expression, the cost of computation of such levels can decrease by orders of magnitude. As a result, one is able to compute many more levels for the same amount of computing resources.

A second reason for doing algebraic computations is that in many cases a numerical computation contains several steps which are so ill-conditioned that the final results are meaningless. If one can perform the ill-conditioned part of the calculation algebraically, then one can often obtain a much more meaningful result. For example, if one is interested in calculating the stability of a plasma in a device such as a Tokamak, then the problem can be reduced to determining whether a certain function has a zero in a given region. However, some of the intermediate steps are so ill-conditioned that a complete numerical computation of this problem can take several hours on the largest computers and still be so approximate that the presence or absence of a zero cannot be resolved. By performing these intermediate steps algebraically, the complete problem can be solved successfully in a matter of minutes.

Finally, there are many calculations in celestial mechanics or quantum electrodynamics, for example, where an analytic result is required, but the algebra is so tedious that hand calculations, besides being error-prone, are too lengthy to contemplate. We shall look at such calculations in more detail later.

Because of the exact nature of algebraic calculations, there are several major problems in numerical computation, such as those connected with roundoff, stability and convergence, which are of no concern to us here. On the other hand, algebraic computation has its own set of difficulties arising from the fact that one is working with expressions rather than only numbers. A major concern to users of algebraic computation systems is a phenomenon known as intermediate expression swell. We find that many algebraic calculations produce extremely large expressions during intermediate stages of the computation, even though the final result may be quite small. Because most algebraic systems keep such expressions in main memory during execution, there is the possibility of exceeding the memory allocation for the job and thus aborting the calculation. Another important problem in algebraic computation is that many of the algorithms used are exponential in nature, whereas the corresponding numerical algorithms satisfy power laws. For example, the product of two numerical matrices is an operation which grows as n^3 with the order of the matrix. Because of the growth in the size of expressions in the corresponding algebraic calculation (whereas numbers always remain with the allotted precision), this law no longer applies in the algebraic case. As a result of such growth it is very difficult to place accurate estimates on the computing time associated with any algebraic calculation. One can, of course, develop theoretical upper bounds, but in many cases these are so large that, if they were believed, one would not begin the calculation in the first place! For example, suppose one is interested in calculating the determinant of a 10 x 10 matrix with algebraic entries. If every element of the determinant is different, then the number of terms produced in an expanded answer is 10!, that is, over three million terms. To produce such a result may take a considerable amount of computing time. Furthermore, who wants to see three million terms anyway? On the other hand, one may be interested in calculating this determinant because one expects the result to be compact. In the most extreme case the result may be 0. Although there are better ways to determine whether a matrix is exactly 0, the use of a general purpose symbolic determinant program could also discover this fact in a very short time. Thus, the range of computing times associated with determinant calculations can vary considerably with the structure of the determinant, and, in the worst case, the calculation may take an impossibly long time. Finally, we have the related problem that the size of the output of symbolic calculations may not be easily estimated. The determinant example above is a good illustration of this. The results may in fact vary in size from that of a number such as 0 all the way to the presentation of an expanded expression involving millions of terms.

The existence of such difficulties in algebraic computations has prompted much activity in the algebraic algorithm area during the past decade in an attempt to solve or at least ameliorate some of these problems. Considerable progress has in fact occurred during the last five to ten years and as a result we can now routinely perform calculations which even five years ago would have been well nigh impossible with systems then available.

2. GENERAL CHARACTERISTICS OF ALGEBRA SYSTEMS

I have mentioned that there are several systems available for doing algebraic computations and I shall refer to those most widely used when considering their applications. However, before looking at such applications in detail, a few remarks about the programming styles and general characteristics of these systems are appropriate.

A study of the most widely used systems shows that the dominant languages upon which these systems are based are LISP, FORTRAN, and various assembly languages. However, the language with which a user communicates with these programs may bear little relationship to the language used for the implementation. Some systems, such as ALTRAN [3] have a FORTRAN-like form with suitable extensions to provide for the special algebraic facilities offered. For example, the following program segment in ALTRAN will compute and print the first eleven Legendre polynomials using the standard recurrence relation:

```
ALGEBRAIC (X:10) ARRAY (0:10) P
INTEGER N
P(0)=1
P(1)=X
DO N=2,10
   P(N)=((2*N-1)*X*P(N-1)-(N-1)*P(N-2))/N
   WRITE P(N)
DOEND
```

Other systems have an ALGOL-like style and as an example of this we see below a similar program segment in the language REDUCE [4]:

```
OPERATOR P;
P(0) := 1; P(1) := X;
FOR N := 2:10 DO
   WRITE P(N) := ((2*N-1)*X*P(N-1)-(N-1)*P(N-2))/N;
```

On the other hand, in the SCRATCHPAD system [5], an attempt has been made to develop a completely new language as near as possible to the form which a mathematically trained person would use to write expressions. For example, the following SCRATCHPAD program will also perform the same calculation:

```
p<0>= 1
p<1>= x
n in (2,3,...,10)
p<n>= ((2*n-1)*x*p<n-1>-(n-1)*p<n-2>)/n
n in (0,1,...,10)
p<n>
```

The output styles of algebraic computation systems also vary considerably. Some adopt a notation which is again essentially FORTRAN or ALGOL-like in form. Others make some attempt at producing output which looks more mathematical in form by putting exponents on another line and so on. For example, the following is the first few lines of the output produced by REDUCE when running the program shown above:

```
                 2
P(2) := 3/2*X  - 1/2

                 3
P(3) := 5/2*X  - 3/2*X

                  4          2
P(4) := 35/8*X  - 15/4*X  + 3/8

                  5          3
P(5) := 63/8*X  - 35/4*X  + 15/8*X

                 ...
```

The most sophisticated examples of such line printer or teletype compatible output styles may be found in MACSYMA [6] and SCRATCHPAD. However, the ultimate output form is surely that of text editing systems such as the one developed by Kernighan and collaborators [7]. This is a program running under the UNIX operating system on a DEC PDP-11 which can produce output of textbook quality for a photo typesetting machine. Examples of such output in an algebraic computation may be found in Ref. [8].

The range of facilities offered by algebraic computation systems can also vary considerably from system to system. All systems offer users the ability to do polynomial manipulation and most offer some form of rational function manipulation. Additional facilities can range from such general capabilities as pattern matching to sophisticated application packages for problems in areas such as general relativity. A prospective user of such systems must therefore be sure that his problem matches the capabilities of the system to be used in order to avoid considerable frustration with an inappropriate choice.

To illustrate these facilities in more detail, let us now turn to some specific applications of algebraic computation programs which have been performed during the last decade or so.

3. SPECIFIC APPLICATIONS

There are now over 600 papers which consider some aspect of algebraic computation and its applications. It is therefore clear that we can only hope to review a limited subset of these in a paper this size. So application examples will be chosen which illustrate some important aspects of the subject, and references will be made to published reviews so that the reader can fill in the gaps. Although it is six years old now, a review which comes closest to covering the whole applications area is that of Barton and Fitch [9], to which we shall often refer. The list of particular application areas is also quite long and includes celestial mechanics, quantum electrodynamics, general relativity, plasma physics, fluid mechanics, electrical network theory and design engineering, to name a few. However, a study of the majority of these applications reveals that they involve problems solved by means of perturbation theories. This in itself is not hard to understand because, after all, nearly all our techniques for solving physical problems, either analytical or numerical, involve a perturbative approximation to the true physical theory. A further study of these applications shows that hand calculations which can be tractably taken to a given order are then extended one or two more orders by computer. Because of the exponential nature of the algebraic techniques, expressions grow so large at this point using currently available systems that the computational time and sheer incomprehensibility of the output limit any further extension. In addition, most of the calculations have been an adjunct to a numerical calculation. In other words, part of the calculation was done algebraically and the results of this were then used to determine a final numerical solution for the problem.

Consider, for example, the field of celestial mechanics, where much use has been made of algebraic systems in the past decade. Here the most tedious task to be considered is in the construction of the analytic perturbation theory; in other words, a formula for calculating the position or rotational properties of a body at any instant in time. The body might be the Moon, a planet or, of even more topical interest, a satellite or space station. To construct such theories requires solving the differential equations that describe the motion or rotational characteristics of the body. Since solutions rarely exist in closed form, one solves them by a technique of repeated approximation and expresses the solution as a power series in terms of the small parameters of the theory such as the orbital eccentricities.

Although the relevant physics is well understood, the parameters cannot be determined with sufficient accuracy until the results of the computation are compared with observations. It is therefore imperative to obtain first the coefficients of the perturbation series as symbolic functions of the parameters, so that as the observational evidence accumulates, the parameter values can be refined and numerical predictions will become increasingly more reliable.

The most famous such calculation is surely Delaunay's work in the Lunar Theory [10], in which the coordinates of the Moon are computed to very high order in the small quantities of the theory. Like most hand calculations of this type, this investigation involved working with thousands of terms. In Delaunay's case the computations took 20 years. When Deprit, Henrard and Rom [11] repeated this calculation by computer in 1970, they found only one error in Delaunay's computation of the secularized Hamiltonian up to the ninth order, a major part of the work; certainly a great tribute to Delaunay's skill and dedication.

An even more challenging problem is posed by the computation of the orbits of the moons of Saturn because of phase-locking among these orbits. Jefferys and Ries [12] have developed a theory of Enceladus and Dione, which can also be applied with small modifications to Mimas-Tethys and Titan-Hyperion. To test the theory and to refine its parameters, the series are generated symbolically and then fitted numerically to the observed data.

What types of manipulation are involved in these calculations? The most frequently considered series in celestial mechanics turn out not to be power series, but Poisson series, which have the form:

$$Q(\underset{\sim}{x},\underset{\sim}{y}) = \Sigma\, P_{\underset{\sim}{j}} \cos(\underset{\sim}{j}\cdot\underset{\sim}{y}) + Q_{\underset{\sim}{j}} \sin(\underset{\sim}{j}\cdot\underset{\sim}{y}), \qquad (1)$$

where $\underset{\sim}{x}$ is a vector of polynomial variables, $\underset{\sim}{y}$ a vector of trigonometrical variables and $\underset{\sim}{j}$ is a vector of integers. $P_{\underset{\sim}{j}}$ and $Q_{\underset{\sim}{j}}$ are polynomials, indexed by $\underset{\sim}{j}$, in the polynomial variables $\underset{\sim}{x}$ whose coefficients may be rational or floating point numbers. It is clear that by the use of the trigonometrical identities

$$\begin{aligned} \sin x \sin y &= \frac{1}{2}\cos(x-y) - \frac{1}{2}\cos(x+y) \\ \sin x \cos y &= \frac{1}{2}\sin(x+y) + \frac{1}{2}\sin(x-y) \qquad (2) \\ \cos x \cos y &= \frac{1}{2}\cos(x+y) + \frac{1}{2}\cos(x-y) \end{aligned}$$

such series are closed under the operations of addition, subtraction, multiplication and differentiation. By making suitable assumptions about the size of the parameters in the series, we can also define operations of division, integration and substitution which do not lead outside this class. Finally, an important theoretical consideration is that Poisson series can be written in a unique canonical form, in other words, a form to which all equivalent expressions can be uniquely reduced. This form can then be used to define the simplification of Poisson series expressions. This means we can avoid many of the problems associated with general expression manipulation which we shall return to later. Such problems arise for example in recognizing that

$$\log \tan (x + \frac{1}{4}\pi) - \sinh^{-1} \tan 2x = 0 \qquad (3)$$

The importance and mathematical simplicity of Poisson series has led to the construction of many systems for their manipulation, including that of Rom [13] used in repeating the Delaunay calculations, Jeffreys' system TRIGMAN [14] which is written in FORTRAN and fairly portable, and CAMAL [15] which has also been used extensively for calculations in general relativity, is well documented and easily obtainable. Further examples are given in the reviews by Jeffreys [16] and Barton and Fitch [9].

To see how Poisson series arise in a natural way in celestial mechanics calculations, let me repeat Barton and Fitch's discussion of the computation of the series solution to Kepler's equation by repeated approximation, which is the starting point for many of these calculations. We are interested in obtaining the solution for E, as a function of u and e, of the implicit equation

$$E = u + e \sin E \qquad (4)$$

where e is to be regarded as a small quantity, typically the eccentricity of an elliptic orbit. Although the problem is capable of a formal solution in terms of Bessel functions, since we normally require the solution correct to a given order in e (say tenth) it is computationally easier if we adopt a repeated approximation procedure. From the Kepler equation, it is obvious that $E = u$ to zero order in e. Then, supposing that $E = u + A_k$ is the solution correct to order k in e, we can easily see that A_{k+1} satisfies the equation

$$A_{k+1} = e \sin(u + A_k), \qquad (5)$$

where the right hand member of Eq. (5) is to be taken to order $k + 1$ in e. Thus, an approximation algorithm may be stated as follows:

$$E = u + \lim_{n\to\infty} A_n \qquad (6)$$

where

$$A_0 = 0$$

$$A_{k+1} = \left[e\sin u \left\{ 1 - \frac{A_k^2}{2!} + \frac{A_k^4}{4!} \cdots \right\} + e\cos u \left\{ A_k - \frac{A_k^3}{3!} + \cdots \right\} \right]_{k+1}.$$

The outer brackets in the above expression indicate that terms of degree greater than $k + 1$ are to be ignored in the calculation. By using the trigonometrical relations given in Eq. (2), we can express the result of this computation as a linear expression in the trigonometrical functions; that is in the form of a Poisson series.

This computation is clearly only a small part of say the complete Delaunay result, but does illustrate the types of expressions to be manipulated. Barton and

Fitch [9] go on to consider the steps involved in the remainder of the Delaunay calculation, as well as looking at other examples of the application of Poisson series processors. The reader is encouraged to study these calculations in order to gain some idea of the sheer enormity of the computations involved.

The second application I would like to consider is in the field of quantum electrodynamics (or QED), an area where one tries to understand the detailed interactions of electrons and photons by means of relativistic quantum mechanics. The most commonly used calculational method is due to Feynman [17] who showed that one could develop a perturbation theory of such interactions with an expansion parameter of about 1/137 (the so-called fine structure constant). The starting point for this method is a diagramatic representation of the particular process under study. From this representation, Feynman developed a method of calculating the contribution of any given diagram to the determination of a physical quantity. The order of perturbation is related very simply to the number of vertices in a diagram. Therefore, since the most important contributions come from the simplest diagrams one can quickly get a rough approximation to the answer. However, as the accuracy of experiments has increased, the need for more and more precise calculations has required more and more complicated diagrams to be studied. To understand the complexity of such calculations it is necessary to look in some detail at the way they are done.

Feynman's method gives you a one-to-one mapping between such diagrams and expressions like

$$\sum_{\mu,\nu} \text{Trace } \{(\gamma\cdot p2 + M)\gamma_\mu \; (\gamma\cdot p2 + \gamma\cdot k2 + M)\gamma_\nu \qquad (7)$$
$$\times(\gamma\cdot p1 + M)\gamma_\nu(\gamma\cdot p2 + \gamma\cdot k2 + M)\gamma_\mu\},$$

which, apart from some simple multiplicative factors, is the lowest order contribution to a physical process known as Compton scattering. The rules for this mapping are quite straightforward and may be found in any suitable textbook on relativistic quantum mechanics, e.g. [18].

In the above expression, γ_μ represents a set of four 4 x 4 noncommuting matrices known as Dirac matrices which satisfy the relation

$$\gamma_{\mu\nu} + \gamma_{\nu\mu} = 2\,\delta_{\mu\nu}\,I. \qquad (8)$$

The Greek indices range from 1 to 4, I is the unit 4 x 4 matrix and $\delta_{\mu\nu}$ is the Kronecker delta function defined by

$$\delta_{\mu\nu} = \begin{cases} 1 \text{ if } \mu = \nu \\ 0 \text{ if } \mu \neq \nu. \end{cases} \qquad (9)$$

M is the electron mass multiplied by a unit 4 x 4 matrix, and $p1$, $p2$, $k1$ and $k2$ are four-component vectors representing the electron and photon momenta in the process. Thus, $\gamma\cdot p1$ represents the sum

$$\gamma_1 \, pl_1 + \gamma_2 \, pl_2 + \gamma_3 pl_3 + \gamma_4 pl_4 . \qquad (10)$$

However, because of the relativistic invariance of the result, one rarely has to study the individual components of the vectors, but only their scalar products, so calculations are less complicated than they might be.

Thus, the result of taking the trace of the 4 x 4 matrix expression in the curly brackets in Eq. (7) and summing over the tensor indices is a scalar. In principle, this computation is straightforward. Equation (8) implies that the trace of the product of an odd number of gamma matrices is zero and the trace of the product of 2n such matrices may be expressed in terms of the trace of 2n-2 products by a simple recurrence relation, given for example in Ref. [18]. However, a naive calcula- can be disastrous. For example, the trace of a single product of 14 gamma matrices generates over 100,000 terms, many of which prove to be equal when contraction over the tensor indices is taken. This problem has motivated the development of more sophisticated algorithms, most of which involve summation over the repeated tensor indices before taking the trace. A description of one such algorithm, due to Kahane [19], may be found in Ref. [9]. Fairly complete reviews of the symbolic calculations which have been done in QED may be found by studying Refs. [20], [21], [22], and [23].

From a computational point of view, such calculations involve quite straightforward through lengthy symbol manipulation. Like Poisson series, the rules for simplification are well defined although a little more exotic than those for polynomial manipulation. In addition, one needs a mechanism for substitution for variables and simple expressions. Although denominators occur in some expressions, rational algebra is not necessary, because the denominators have a simple structure and can therefore be replaced by variables in the numerator. The most widely used systems for such calculations have been REDUCE [4] and SCHOONSCHIP [24]. The former is a LISP-based system mentioned earlier which is also well suited to more general calculations than just QED and has a large number of published applications in many fields to its credit. The latter system is written in COMPASS for the CDC 6000 and 7000 series computers and also has a long application list, though all essentially in QED. A third system of note is a FORTRAN-based program ASHMEDAI [25], which also has been used in some important calculations.

To give one a feel for the scope of current calculations in this area, it is worth looking at the most important such calculation undertaken during the past few years. This is undoubtedly the computation of the sixth order corrections to the anomalous magnetic moment of the electron. The analytic form for the fourth order contribution was completed by hand in 1957 [26]. Because of the sheer magnitude of the calculation, the sixth order result, which involves looking at 72 diagrams, has been completed by a group effort involving many different groups, usually with different algebra programs. The complete answer is still not known analytically because some of the integrations involved were performed numerically. Such integrals arise from the application of the various conservation laws which occur in the theory. The analytic evaluation of these integrals tends to be messy and tedious, rather than sophisticated, as one usually starts with rational functions. However, as integration over several variables is required, the results come out in terms of generalized Spence functions in most cases. Examples of such integrations are given in Refs. [27] and [28], which describe programs in SCHOONSCHIP and REDUCE for evaluating integrals of the form

$$I(k,m,n,r,s) = \int_0^1 dy \int_0^1 dx \int_0^1 dw \int_0^1 dz\; z^r w^s x^{2k-3+n-m} \times y^{k-2+n}\, \Delta^m/\beta^n\Gamma^k$$

where

$$\beta = 1 - xy(1-wz + w^2z^2)$$
$$\Delta = 1 - x(1-wz(1-w)) \qquad (11)$$
$$\Gamma = w^2\, x\beta + y\Delta^2\ ,$$

which arise in some fourth order computations in QED. For example

$$I(1,0,2,2,3) = \frac{1}{6}\pi^2 - \frac{1}{3}\pi^2 \log 2 + \frac{1}{2}\zeta(3) + \frac{1}{3} \qquad (12)$$

where $\zeta(3)$ is the Riemann zeta function. Currently, two groups [29] are trying to find the whole sixth order result analytically by computer and considerable progress has been made. Although their methods are different, the procedure involves expanding expressions in partial fractions and integrating term by term. To give you an idea of the relative times involved in this work, Levine, Perisho and Roskies [29] give statistics for the analytic evaluation of one of the more difficult of the 72 graphs in the sixth order calculation. Their method involved trace evaluation, two straightforward integrations, a partial fraction expansion of the result followed by two further integrations. Using the ASHMEDAI program, the times on a UNIVAC 1108 were 2 minutes for the traces and first two integrals, 18 minutes for the partial fraction expansion and 15 minutes for the two final integrations. It is interesting to note that the trace taking, the original stumbling block for the hand calculations which motivated the development of such computer programs in the first place, is now only a small part of the whole computer calculation.

In fact, it is interesting to see that once the basic trace problem was solved, researchers in this area started looking at other ways of using symbolic computation in their work. Analytic integration is one such example. Another application involved looking at ways to actually generate and manipulate the diagrams which occur in a given problem. Once such a diagram is written down, it is a fairly simple procedure to generate the matrix elements which were the starting point of the previous discussion [30]. The most difficult problem here is to recognize topologically equivalent diagrams, but a recently developed program [31] seems to have solved this problem in an efficient manner. Some earlier programs are described in Ref. [23]. If one is ever interested in looking at eighth order calculations, where over 1000 diagrams contribute to the magnetic moment correction, such graphical programs should be essential even if only used as a bookkeeping device.

These two very successful applications of symbolic computation, celestial mechanics and quantum electrodynamics, are prototypical of a large number of the successes in this field. Both are problems with well-defined rules of simplification, even if the non-standard algebra was responsible for the early development of special purpose systems to handle this. Major application successes were already in evidence five years ago, and the work during the past five years has been concerned with extending the earlier successes to harder and harder problems, or tackling new problems, such as the integration example in QED. At the same time, problems in other areas such as fluid mechanics, plasma physics, electrical network theory and queuing theory, which were amenable to solution by polynomial or power series manipulation were being solved by systems such as ALTRAN (and its predecessor ALPAK), FORMAC [32] and REDUCE which possessed the necessary facilities for performing these tasks. A considerable number of applications of these programs have been described in the literature. Another convenient system for such calculations is Engeli's SYMBAL [33].

There was, however, another group of important calculations being carried out at the same time which involved the manipulation of more general expressions than the examples so far. Since there is no canonical form for a sufficiently large class of expressions [34] the designers of algebra systems for such applications must either try to solve a very complicated simplification problem for which often no clear cut solution exists, (see for example, [35]) or provide sufficiently general substitution facilities so that users can input their own set of rules for simplification. A particularly good example of such calculations, and one for which good reviews exist [9,36] is general relativity, where the calculations considered are concerned with a very large set of elementary functions for which many complicated simplification rules exist.

Applications in this area have been mainly concerned with the field equations which express the relationship between the geometrical structure of the four dimensional space and the distribution of mass and energy within it. These field equations are very complicated even for physically simple cases and involve exponential and circular functions in their description. An account of the systems which have been used to solve such problems is given in the cited references. Among the most widespread in use are FORMAC, CAMAL and LAM and its predecessors [37]. Each of these systems, as is true for the other systems mentioned earlier in this paper, take a different approach to the problem of simplification, and an amusing review of this subject may be found in Ref. [38].

4. ANALYTIC INTEGRATION

Another application of algebraic manipulation involving general expressions is the problem of analytic integration. This is different from our previous applications in that it is in mathematics rather than physics or related areas. However, its importance in many branches of physics is obvious, not only in its own right, but also as an essential step in solving other systems such as differential and integral equations. The problem remains of much research interest currently and considerable progress has been made in finding a solution during the past decade. Most of the effort has been directed toward the problem of indefinite integration, although some work on definite integration has also been reported [39,40]. We can of course always find the value of a definite integral if we have the indefinite form. However, closed form solutions for many definite integrals can be found even when the indefinite form does not exist, and methods for handling such cases are considered in the cited references.

Although earlier programs existed, the first relatively practical program in this area was the SIN program of Moses, whose structure is described in detail in Moses' review of symbolic integration [41]. It is worth looking at this structure because most general purpose integration programs in existence today followed it fairly closely, although the algorithms used are much improved. SIN works very much like a scientist when presented with an expression to be integrated. It first of all tries a cheap general method which gives the result very quickly if it succeeds. One component of this general method is the so-called "derivative divides" test which determines if the integral can be written in the form

$$\int c\, f(u(x))\, u'(x)\, dx.$$

If this test succeeds, then we can immediately write down the required result if the integral of f is known. For example,

$$\int 3 \sin^2 x \cos x\, dx$$

is of this form and therefore such a technique would immediately determine that the integral is $\sin^3 x$. Another general method of considerable importance is integration by parts which can often transform an unknown integral into one which is already known. A third method employed involves reducing the complexity of integrand by expanding it to its fullest extent and then expressing the integral of the resulting sum as the sum of integrals.

Another general method commonly used by most integration programs involves table lookup or pattern matching. In other words, one has a table of general integrals in the computer, much like a book of tables of integrals, and checks by simple transformations on the integrand, such as the renaming of variables, whether the given integral can be expressed in a form given by the table. This method tends to be more time consuming than those considered earlier because of the additional searching and testing involved. However, it is interesting to note that many of the integration problems which occur in QED can be solved by such techniques and results can therefore be obtained in closed form by relatively straightforward programs.

If these methods fail, special methods which are specific to a certain class of integrals are usually tried. For example, if the integrand contains trigonometrical functions the substitution $t = \tan \Theta/2$ would be attempted. If it is a rational function, then the well-known Hermite's method [42] would be used. Again, even though these methods are narrow in scope they provide efficient solutions when they are applicable.

Clearly a large class of interesting integrals will not be evaluated by the above methods and at this point an entirely different approach to the problem is required based on an algorithmic approach to integration developed by R. Risch [43]. This particular method requires a radical transformation of the integrand; for example, sines and cosines would be converted into complex exponentials. Since, as has been pointed out by Moses [38], users prefer to see their answers in terms of the same sort of functions as those used in the problem statement, such transformations should only be used when there is no other more straightforward way to evaluate the given integrals.

The complete Risch algorithm is of extreme importance because it provides a procedure for deciding if an integral exists within a given class of functions. If the integral exists in closed form the algorithm finds it; if it does not exist, the algorithm states this. It is very important to understand the difference between such a decision procedure and the usual hand methods for integration which either find the value of an integral or leave us not knowing if a closed form exists.

The Risch algorithm involves some rather complicated mathematics in its statement as well as its proof, so we can only hope to suggest its structure here. The algorithm is based on Liouville's Theorem which states that if f is a function in a field of rational functions F then

$$\int f\, dx = g + \sum_{i=1}^{n} c_i \log r_i, \qquad (13)$$

where $g, r_i \in F$ and the c_i are constants.
Suppose now that F is the field of rational expressions in x, and that we wish to integrate a given function $f(x, \log x)$, which is a rational function in $\log x$ whose coefficients are in F. The function $\log x$ is used to form a new field Φ, an extension of F. Since $\log x$ is not the root of an algebraic equation in F it is called a *transcendental* extension of F, as opposed to *algebraic* extensions arising from new functions (such as square roots) which are solutions of algebraic equations in F. The latter extensions are considered separately in the algorithm. The Risch algorithm now takes advantage of the rational property of f in $\log x$ over F to assert that

$$\int f(x,\log x)\, dx = g(x,\log x) + \sum_{i=1}^{n} c_i \log r_i, \qquad (14)$$

where g, $r_i \in \Phi$ and c_i are constants.

The algorithm now proceeds to determine, if possible, the functions g and r_i together with the constants c_i by a method similar to the Hermite algorithm. Examples of the application of this method to specific integrals are given in Ref. [41].

Recently, an improved version of this algorithm has been developed by Risch and Norman [44]. The major difference between the new algorithm and the older version is that instead of solving the problem recursively over the successive extensions of the rational field, one solves simultaneously for all such extensions. This method generates a set of linear equations for the unknown coefficients in the solution which can be solved by conventional means. The absence of a consistent solution to these equations again implies the nonexistence of the integral. An initial implementation of this particular algorithm has been made in REDUCE at the University of Cambridge [45], although work continues on both the underlying algorithm and the implementation, so as to improve the range of problems that can be solved. A system using both the Cambridge program and pattern matching for the cases which the program cannot yet handle has also been developed [46].

To extend the Risch-Norman method to algebraic extensions of F requires that we find a basis for expansion of the integral, as in Eq. (15), so that the terms are independent. This is a very difficult computational problem which has so far prevented the complete implementation of the whole algorithm. This particular problem is however currently under study at Cambridge and MIT and the results are encouraging. However, there is still a lot of work to be done before we have a complete algorithmic integration program.

5. FUTURE TRENDS

The examples that we have considered in this paper are fairly representative of the problems which have been tackled so far by existing algebra systems. However, it is important to note that as users have gained more experience with such systems, not only have the number of application areas increased, but the systems have been used more and more for casual calculations on an everyday basis. This has been expecially true for systems used on computers such as the DECsystem 10 or 20 which offer a true timesharing environment for computations. For example, it is now easier for me to turn to a terminal by my desk, log onto our local DECsystem 20, load the algebra program REDUCE and evaluate an indefinite integral, than to get a book of integrals from my bookshelf and look up the result. For one thing, the integration program is quite fast and convenient to use, but for another, the integrand in the table book is nearly always expressed in a different representation from the one I am using, so that some additional work is required in using the tables. The computer program on the other hand can take the integrand in any reasonable representation.

It is also important to realize that during the past few years, research in algebraic algorithms and system design has not seemed as dramatic as in the early days in spite of the tremendous activity in the area. The reason for this is not hard to find. It is exciting to discover that Dirac gamma matrix algebra or indefinite integration for example can be done by computer, but we knew this over ten years ago. The fact that we can now do such things significantly better in more compact and more portable systems is not as glamorous to report. For example, the version of REDUCE which is now being distributed is a far better one than that of three years ago. It has a more modular, portable design, is more efficient and has many more facilities. However, it is hard to get excited about an improved program when having any algebra program at all can mean a completely different way of looking at calculations.

So when will the next really dramatic step take place in this field? To answer this question, it is necessary to understand the problems which limit the availability of today's algebra systems. An important current limitation is the large resource requirements of the more sophisticated programs. As has been discussed in detail by Campbell [23], one needs large memories and much machine time to solve most non-trivial problems, and so anyone without access to a relatively large computer is prevented from doing such calculations. In addition, because of the obvious need for interaction in algebraic computations, an interactive system is essential for successful casual use. It is clear that the rapidly decreasing costs of hardware will have an important effect on solving this problem. In fact, a fairly cheap experimental computer has already been built [47] which can support quite sophisticated algebra systems. It is therefore my belief that the next major advance in this field will occur when the more sophisticated systems become readily available on relatively cheap personal computers or computers shared by a small number of people in a research group. At this point the number of researchers who can get access to such systems will be orders of magnitude greater than at present.

One should also remember that such a personal algebra machine will have a fairly comprehensive numerical function library, so that it will serve as a powerful numerical computation device as well. In fact, many problems even now are best solved by a combination of numerical and symbolic techniques [48], and it is expected that this will become even more apparent as algebraic computation systems become more readily available.

Just as desk and pocket calculators have made most numerical table books obsolete, such personal algebra systems will as surely replace many of our standard algebraic tables. Of course, before we reach this point there remains a lot of work to be done not only on the underlying algorithms but also on the most appropriate system design for such a personal environment. However, I see no reason why such systems should not be available within three to five years from now. After that, who can guess what their impact will be?

ACKNOWLEDGEMENTS

I wish to thank my colleagues in the Utah Symbolic Computation Group for providing continual new insights into this subject. This work has been supported in part by the U. S. National Science Foundation under Grant No. MCS 76-15035.

REFERENCES

[1] KAHRIMANIAN, H.G., *Analytical Differentiation by a Digital Computer*, M.A. Diss, Temple University, Philadelphia, PA, 1953.

[2] NOLAN, J., *Analytical Differentiation on a Digital Computer*, M.A. Diss, MIT, Cambridge, MA, 1953.

[3] BROWN, W.S., *ALTRAN User's Manual*, Third Edition, Bell Laboratories, 1973.

[4] HEARN, A.C., *REDUCE User's Manual*, Second Edition, University of Utah, 1973.

[5] JENKS, R.D., *The SCRATCHPAD Language*, *SIGPLAN Notices*, ACM, New York, *9* (1974) 101-111.

[6] BOGEN, R., et al., *MACSYMA Reference Manual*, Project MAC, M.I.T., Cambridge, MA, 1974.

[7] KERNIGHAN, B.W., and CHERRY, L.L., Comm. ACM *18* (1975), 151-157.

[8] FELDMAN, S.I., *An Application of Symbolic Computation to Crystal Physics*, *SIGSAM Bulletin*, ACM, New York, No. *34* (1975) 19-24.

[9] BARTON, D., and FITCH, J.P., *Rep. Prog. Phys. 35* (1972) 235-314.

[10] DELAUNAY, C., *Théorie du Mouvement de la Lune* (Extraits des Mém. Acad. Sci.), Mallet-Bachelier, Paris, 1860.

[11] DEPRIT, A., HENRARD, J., and ROM, A., *Science 168* (1970) 1569-1570.

[12] JEFFERYS, W.H., and RIES, L.M., *Astronomical Journal 80* (1975) 876-884.

[13] ROM, A., *Celest. Mech. 3* (1971) 331-345.

[14] JEFFREYS, W.H., *Celest. Mech. 2* (1970) 474-480.

[15] FITCH, J.P., *CAMAL User's Manual*, Computer Lab., Cambridge, U.K. (1975).

[16] JEFFREYS, W.H., *Comm. ACM 14* (1971) 538-541.

[17] FEYNMAN, R.P., *Phys. Rev. 76* (1949) 769-789.

[18] BJORKEN, J.D., and DRELL, S.D., *Relativistic Quantum Mechanics*, McGraw-Hill, New York, 1964.

[19] KAHANE, J., *J. Math. Phys. 9* (1968) 1732-1738.

[20] CAMPBELL, J.A., *Comp. Phys. Comm. 1* (1970) 251-264.

[21] HEARN, A.C., *Comm. ACM 14* (1971) 511-516.

[22] HEARN, A.C., *Computer Solution of Symbolic Problems in Theoretical Physics*, *Computing as a Language of Physics*, IAEA, Vienna (1972) 567-596.

[23] CAMPBELL, J.A., *Acta Phys, Austriaca Suppl. XIII* (1974) 595-647.

[24] STRUBBE, H., *Comp. Phys. Comm. 8* (1974) 1-30.

[25] PERISHO, R.C., *ASHMEDAI User's Guide*, U.S.A.E.C. Rep. No. C00-3066-44 (1975).

[26] PETERMANN, A., *Helv. Phys. Acta 30* (1957) 407-408.

[27] MAISON, D., and PETERMANN, A., *Comp. Phys. Comm. 7* (1974) 121-134.

[28] FOX, J.A., and HEARN, A.C., *J. Comp. Phys. 14* (1974) 301-317.

[29] LEVINE, M.J., REMIDDI, E., and ROSKIES, R., $g_e - 2$, *The Current Status, Proc. of the Fourth Intern. Colloq. on Advanced Comp. Methods in Theor. Phys*, St. Maximin, France (1977) 178-192.

[30] CAMPBELL, J.A., and HEARN, A.C., *J. Comp. Phys. 5* (1970) 280-327.

[31] SASAKI, T., *Automatic Generation of Feynman Graphs in QED*, Rikagaku Kenkyosho, Wako-Shi, Saitama, Japan, Preprint 1975.

[32] TOBEY, R.G., et al., *PL/I-FORMAC SYMBOLIC MATHEMATICS INTERPRETER*, SHARE Contributed Program Library, No. 360 D-0.3.3.004 (1969).

[33] ENGELI, M., *An Enhanced SYMBAL System, SIGSAM Bulletin*, ACM, New York, No. *36* (1975) 21-29.

[34] RICHARDSON, D., Ph.D. Thesis, University of Bristol, (1966).

[35] CAVINESS, B.F., *Methods for Symbolic Computation with Transcendental Functions, Proc. of the Fourth Intern. Colloq. on Advanced Comp. Methods in Theor. Phys*, St. Maximin, France (1977) 16-43.

[36] BARTON, D., and FITCH, J.P., *Comm. ACM 14* (1971) 542-547.

[37] D'INVERNO, R.A., *Comp. J. 12* (1969) 124-127.

[38] MOSES, J., *Comm. ACM 14* (1971) 527-537.

[39] WANG, P., *Symbolic Evaluation of Definite Integrals by Residue Theory in MACSYMA, Proc. IFIP Congress 74* (1974) 823-827.

[40] CAMPBELL, J.A., *Applications of Symbolic Programs to Complex Analysis, Proc. ACM Annual Conf. 72* (1972) 836-839.

[41] MOSES, J., *Comm. ACM* (1971) 548-560.

[42] HARDY, G.H., *The Integration of Functions of a Single Variable*, Second Edition, CUP, Cambridge, England (1916).

[43] RISCH, R., *Trans. AMS 139* (1969) 167-189.

[44] NORMAN, A.C., and RISCH, R., to be published.

[45] NORMAN, A.C., and MOORE, P.M.A., *Implementing the New Risch Integration Algorithm, Proc. of the Fourth Intern. Colloq. on Advanced Comp. Methods in Theor. Phys*, St. Maximin, France (1977) 99-110.

[46] HARRINGTON, S.J., *A New Symbolic Integration System in REDUCE, Comp. J.*, to be published.

[47] SCHOICHET, S.R., *The LISP Machine*, Mini-Micro Systems, Boston, MA, Vol. *11*, No. *5* (June 1978) 68-74.

[48] BROWN, W.S., and HEARN, A.C., *Applications of Symbolic Algebraic Computation, Comp. Phys. Comm.*, to be published.

Parallel Programming

by

David Gries
Cornell University

Abstract

A survey is given of various important concepts and notations that are under development in order to deal reliably with concurrently executing programs. The bounded buffer problem is used throughout.

Table of Contents

1. Introduction

My purpose today is to discuss current ideas on harnessing and putting to reliable use the vast amount of parallelism in today's computer systems. I will certainly not discuss all ideas, but will focus on those that seem most important to me and that will introduce you as fully but as simply as possible (I hope) to problems with parallelism.

There are many physicists in the audience who perhaps use the computer as a tool but are not up-to-date in the latest research ideas in computer science. I will attempt to address these physicists, for I would like to demonstrate that "programming methodology", or "software construction", is indeed an intellectually sound and satisfying research area.

Computer science is a relatively new field, and some even question its existence. Particularly in the area of practical programming, many look askance at the opinion that there can and should be mathematical underpinnings that deserve attention. For example, some programmers and managers view "structured programming" as an attempt to "deskill" the industry -- to make programming so simple that any one can do it provided he or she follows a few simple rules. If some of those who spend their lives with computers think that way, how do others with little contact with computers think?

On the other hand, I view the past ten years as an exciting, important period in which we have learned (1) that the traditional programming process, with its emphasis on debugging, is not only inadequate but to some extent unnecessary, and (2) that to some extent mathematical proof of correctness during the programming process is possible and extremely helpful. Whether the proof methods are used formally or not, they have yielded tremendous insight into programming and programming language design. In fact, programming is slowly changing from an _art_ to a _science_, where these words are used in the following sense:

> the term science denotes a department of practical work that depends on the knowledge and conscious application of principles; an art, on the other hand, requires merely knowledge of traditional rules and skill acquired by habit.

I hope to give you some idea of why I feel this way. In the next section I will _briefly_ outline some basic ideas concerning normal sequential programs, their development, and their correctness proofs. The rest of the lecture will deal with parallel, or concurrent, programs. Parallel programming is much, much harder than sequential programming because of the interaction between the concurrently executing programs, and the "methodology" is not as far advanced. Complicating the picture are the many different computer architectures available today, each of which allows parallelism in a different way that seems to require different concepts and notation. Nevertheless, I think we are making progress.

One point that crops up often is the need for concise, understandable notation to express algorithmic ideas, even if that notation is at odds with current programming and computers. The point to remember is that, while the computers may inspire us, we should not let them enslave us; _reliable_ programming requires notations and concepts that are designed for _human_ understanding.

I will not directly reference any reports or publications. Following the last section are a list of publications for further study.

2. The logic of sequential programs

We define a small programming language in terms of how it can be understood, i.e. how it can be proved correct. Thus, each construct is defined by an axiom or inference rule, and a correct program is a theorem that can be proved using these axioms and inference rules together with those of conventional logic. This puts the language on a firm mathematical basis and allows us to concentrate on correctness and understanding, rather than how a program is executed.

Let P and R be assertions about variables used in a statement S -- i.e., P and R are logical sentences, which are either true or false at any moment, about the values of the program variables. Then the notation

$$\{P\}\ S\ \{R\}$$

is interpreted as: suppose execution of S is begun in a machine state in which P is true. Then execution of S is guaranteed to halt in a state in which R is true.

We gave definitions of the null statement skip and the assignment statement x:=e, where x is a simple variable and e is an expression whose type is the same as the type of x. The notation P[e→x] denotes the predicate P, but where every occurrence of x has been simultaneously, textually replaced by e. Examples will be given later.

Axiom Scheme for skip: {P} skip {P} (for all P)

Axiom Scheme for Assignment: {P[e→x]} x:=e {P} (for all P)

We now state two inference rules that allow us to use normal logic to simplify assertions and to combine statements. The notation a,b,.../c means: if a,b,... are true in the system, then so is c.

Rule of Consequence: $\dfrac{P \Rightarrow Q1,\ \{Q1\}\ S\ \{Q2\},\ Q2 \Rightarrow R}{\{P\}\ S\ \{R\}}$

Rule of Composition: $\dfrac{\{P\}\ S1\ \{Q\},\ \{Q\}\ S2\ \{R\}}{\{P\}\ S1;S2\ \{R\}}$

An an example, we have, where all variables have type integer:

(1) (in-out < n) ⇒ (in+1-out ≤ n) (implication)

(2) {in+1-out ≤ n} in:=in+1 {in-out ≤ n} (assignment)

(3) {in-out < n} in:=in+1 {in-out ≤ n} (consequence, 1,2)

Generally, we place assertions at the place in the program where they are supposed to be true; two successive assertions denote the use of implication. Thus the above would be written

```
{in-out < n}
{in+1-out ≤ n}
in:=in+1
{in-out ≤ n}
```

As another example, we consider the <u>bounded buffer problem</u>. Suppose a program stores values in an array, or buffer, b[0:n-1] and later extracts them for processing, in the order inserted. Variable <u>in</u> will contain the total number of values inserted, variable <u>out</u> the number of values extracted. Hence in-out is the number of values inserted but not yet extracted. We define a relation I that indicates what is currently in the buffer; it is partially in mathematical notation, partly in English.

I: 0≤in-out≤n, (1)
The values inserted but not yet extracted are, in order,
b[out <u>mod</u> n], b[out+1 <u>mod</u> n], ..., b[out+in-out-1 <u>mod</u> n].

Statements to establish the truth of I are: "in:=0, out:=0". We give below the obvious statements to insert a new value x in b and to extract the next value. Note how the first assertion of each indicates the set of conditions under which it makes sense to execute the sequence:

```
insert x: {I and in-out<n}                              (2)
          b[in mod n]:=x;
          {I and in-out<n and b[in mod n]=x}
          in:=in+1
          {I}
```

```
extract y:  {I and 0<in-out }                                        (3)
            y:=b[out mod n];
            {I and 0<in-out and y = next value to be extracted}
            out:= out+1
            {I and y = last value extracted }
```

One can of course give similar definitions for conditional statements and loops, and for completeness we give them below. They need not be understood for further understanding; we won't actually need them since we will be concentrating on parallelism. The important point about this section is that an assertion is inserted just before each statement (and after the last) in order to indicate what is true about the program variables at that point, and the truth of these assertions at these points is determined by the logical, mathematical definition of the constructs.

Dijkstra's alternative statement. Let the Bi be logical expressions, the Si statements, and n≥1. The interpretation of the following is: at least one Bi must be true; choose one Bi that is true and execute the corresponding statement Si.

```
B1 or B2 or ... or Bn,
{Bi and P} Si {R}          for 1≤i≤n
-------------------------------------
{P} if B1→S1 [] B2→S2 [] ...[] Bn→Sn fi {R}
```

The loop. Again the Bi are logical expressions and the Si are statements. The interpretation of the following is: repeat until no longer possible: find a true Bi and execute the corresponding Si.

```
{Bi and P} Si {P},           1≤i≤n  (P is the loop invariant)
(Bi and P) ⇒ t≥0,            1≤i≤n  (t an integer function)
{Bi and P} T:=t;Si {t≤T-1},  1≤i≤n  (T a new variable)
----------------------------------
{P} do B1 → S1 []... [] Bn → Sn od {P and not B1 and ... and not Bn}
```

3. Parallel programs sharing variables

The heart of many computer systems is a large random-access store and a central processor (or two, or three) together with an operating system that supports interleaving of execution of several programs or processes. Interesting problems arise if these processes are allowed to share variables (i.e. they communicate via a shared portion of memory) -- in fact, the various parts of the operating system can themselves be considered as separate parallel processes. We need, then, a way of understanding such concurrently executing processes, of knowing that they perform reliably without interfering with each other.

3.1. Simple statements for expressing parallelism

For simplicity, let us assume there are two processes S1 and S2. We classify their variables into three groups: the local variables of S1 (which are not referenced by S2), the local variables of S2, and the shared variables, which may be referenced and changed in both S1 and S2. The following denotes concurrent execution of S1 and S2, with no knowledge being expressed as to how fast they execute.

<u>cobegin</u> S1 // S2 <u>coend</u>

As a simple example, we give a segment that purports to add both 1 and 2 to x, which is initially 0, to result in x=3:

{x=0} <u>cobegin</u> x:=x+1 // x:=x+2 <u>coend</u> {x=3?} (4)

Would execution of (4) in a reasonable implementation on a reasonable machine result in x=3 ? Not necessarily, if we assume that an assignment like x:=x+1 will typically require 2 or 3 machine instructions, for consider the following sequence of actions:

1. S1 evaluates x+1 to yield 1;
2. S2 evaluates x+2 to yield 2;
3. S2 stores 2 in x, so that x=2;
4. S1 stores 1 in x, so that x=1!

The problem is that concurrent execution of one assignment can interfere with the other. To be understandable, we would like concurrent execution of the two to yield the same result as sequential execution of first one and then the other (or vice versa). We can achieve this if we adhere to the following:

> each expression or assignment may contain at most one reference to at most one shared variable that can be changed by another concurrent process.

Note that (4) is now syntactically illegal, since each assignment contains two references to x, which is changed in both S1 and S2. We give up some flexibility for a notation that can be better understood and easily implemented. We could rewrite (4) using local variables t1 and t2 as follows, but of course it will still terminate with x=1, 2 or 3:

{x=0} <u>cobegin</u> t1:=x+1; x:=t1 // t2:=x+2; x:=t2 <u>coend</u> (5)

Further study of possible execution of (5) will reveal another problem with some of today's machines. Suppose that the value of t1 is assigned to x at the same time that execution of t2:=x+2 is retrieving the value of x from the store. Which value of x is retrieved? We do not care whether it is the old value of x or the new value t1, but <u>it may not be garbage caused by fluctuation of the store during the assignment</u>. That is, we require that retrieval and storage be indivisible operations.

On many machines, changing the value in the store is indeed an indivisible operation, but on some it may not be. Consider, for example, the IBM 360 series, where one fullword is four individual bytes. It is certainly possible that writing all four bytes will not be performed indivisibly. Also, for values that take more store, such as a string of characters or a PASCAL record, implementation of assignment to such a variable may take several instructions, which certainly will not be executed indivisibly. Thus, one must be extremely careful in using complete concurrency with such shared variables.

Let us return to program segment (4) again. There are certainly cases where a program must be able to change some shared variable x without interference by another process. Thus we invent a new notation to express it. The statement

<u>await</u> B <u>then</u> S

where B is a logical expression and S a statement, has the following intuitive, operational meaning: delay until B is true, then directly stop execution of all parallel processes; execute S; and upon completion allow the parallel processes to continue. S is called a <u>critical</u> <u>region</u>.

The <u>await</u> statement allows for <u>synchronization</u> of processes (wait until B is true) and <u>exclusion</u> (no other process is allowed to execute while S is executing). The intent of (4) can then be realized by

```
{x=0}                                              (6)
cobegin await true then x:=x+1
     // await true then x:=x+2
  coend
{x=3}
```

In this section, we have discussed basic problems with conventional machines in connection with parallelism. We have introduced a simple notation for expressing parallelism, synchronization, and exclusion. The notation is easier to understand than it is to implement, especially the <u>await</u> (how does one stop all other processes?) but after all it is human understanding that is most important!

3.2. Formal understanding of *await* and *cobegin*

It is quite easy to give a rule of inference for the *await*; notice how it implies that B is assumed to be true when S is executed, and thus no other process may be allowed to falsify B:

Rule of await: $\dfrac{\{P \text{ and } B\}\ S\ \{R\}}{\{P\}\ \textbf{await}\ B\ \textbf{then}\ S\ \{R\}}$

Consider the *cobegin* statement. Suppose we have already proved {P1} S1 {R1} and {P2} S2 {R2}. It would be nice to conclude that during concurrent execution of S1 and S2 the same results hold, that there is no interference between S1 and S2:

{P1 *and* P2} *cobegin* S1 // S2 *coend* {R1 *and* R2}

Unfortunately, if S1 and S2 share variables they can interfere with each other -- for example execution of S2 could change a variable that would make R1 false. One way to check for interference is tc investigate all possible interleavings of execution sequences of S1 and S2, but there is a better way. Instead, one can investigate whether execution of S2 could somehow invalidate the *proof* of {P1} S1 {R1} (and vice versa), for if the proofs are not invalidated then both R1 and R2 will still be true upon termination, even under parallel execution!

How could a "proof be invalidated?" Remember, a proof consists of interleaved assertions and statements (e.g. see (2) and (3)) in which, besides the final assertion R1, each (sub)statement Si is preceded by an assertion, which we call the precondition of Si, pre(Si). The proof of {P1} S1 {R1}assumes that the precondition of each Si is true when Si is ready to begin or is in the middle of execution. Thus, we can say that {P1} S1 {R1} and {P2} S2 {R2} do not interfere with each other -- we say they are *interference-free* -- if execution of S2 cannot falsify R1 or any precondition in the proof {P1} S1 {R1} and vice versa.

Obviously, S2 can only falsify a precondition if it changes a variable referred to in that precondition, and hence we must show that execution of any of S2's assignments or *await* statements do not falsify R1 or any of the precondition of the proof {P1} S1 {R1}. This sounds like a tall order, but in a well-structured proof it is simple enough. Note that in checking for interference-freeness, we need not check for falsification of preconditions of substatements of an _await_, since the _await_ is an indivisible action and hence no other process is executing. Similarly, we only have to consider whether execution of assignments and _awaits_, but not substatements of an _await_, falsify preconditions of the other proof.

Rule for cobegin: {P1} S1 {R1}, {P2} S2 {R2} interference-free
{P1 _and_ P2} _cobegin_ S1 // S2 _coend_ {R1 _and_ R2}

As a first example, we show that program (6) does indeed terminate with x=3. We first introduce assertions; the reader should check that they are correct. Interference-freeness will be shown in a moment. We need not really worry about falsifying the precondition of x:=x+1 or x:=x+2, since they are within _awaits_, so we have not written those preconditions.

```
{x=0} cobegin  {x=0 or x=2}                                  (7)
               await true then x:=x+1
               {x=1 or x=3}
           //  {x=0 or x=1}
               await true then x:=x+2
               {x=2 or x=3}
      coend
{(x=1 or x=3) and (x=2 or x=3)}
{x=3}
```

The derivation of an assertion like {x=0 _or_ x=2} above may seem magical, as if it had been pulled out of a hat. It was created by thinking about possible concurrent execution (e.g. of x:=x+2) and the states the machine might be in because of it.

Let us show that execution of "_await_ true _then_ x:=x+2" in S2 cannot falsify precondition {x=0 _or_ x=2}. We notice that this statement is _executed_ only if {x=0 _or_ x=1}, and so we have:

```
{(x=0 or x=2) and (x=0 or x=1)}
{x=0}
await true then x:=x+2
{x=2}
{x=0 or x=2}
```

To show that the other assertions are not falsified is just as easy and is not done here.

As a second example, let us return to the so-called bounded buffer problem discussed in Section 2. Relation I in (1) describes the buffer, while (2) and (3) show how to insert and extract values. Suppose one process acts as a "producer," computing values and inserting them in the buffer, while another process acts as a "consumer," extracting values and using them for some other purpose. Use of the buffer means that the producer and consumer can execute at their own speeds, as long as they get no further than n values apart (n is the size of the buffer).

The question is: can the sequences (2) and (3) for inserting and extracting values be executed concurrently, without interfering with each other? We write them as parts of parallel programs, where b, in, out, and n are the shared variables and are referenced only where indicated, x is local to S1, and y is local to S2.

```
{I}
cobegin ... {I} await in-out<n then skip;
            {I and in-out<n} b[in mod n]:=x;
            {I and in-out<n and b[in mod n]=x} in:=in+1
            {I} ...
// ...      {I} await 0<in-out then skip;
            {I and 0<in-out} y:=b[out mod n];
            {I and 0<in-out and y=b[out mod n]} out:=out+1
            {I} ...
coend
```

We show that the assertions of S1 cannot be falsified by execution of S2, and leave the other way round to the reader. Therefore, parallel execution of the two is okay. First, I is not falsified since it is everywhere true in S2. Secondly, in-out<n cannot be falsified since execution of out:=out+1 leaves it true, and in, out and n are not elsewhere changed in S2. Finally, b[in mod n]=x cannot be falsified since S2 does not change b, in, n or x.

The first example in this section, (7) shows the use of the await for exclusion or indivisibility only; no synchronization is necessary. The second example shows the use of the await for synchronization only; one parallel program may have to wait because the buffer is full, the other because it is empty. There are cases where one uses the await for both synchronization and exclusion at the same time.

3.3. Resources and the with-when statement

In the last section we outlined a formal system for proving parallel programs correct. A very fine degree of interleaving of actions was allowed -- only the memory reference had to be indivisible. The ideas have been used to develop and prove correct a number of quite complicated algorithms.

One main problem with the method is the freedom given the programmer -- he can refer to shared variables anywhere within his program. Quite often, restricting the programmer's freedom will yield a notation that is more easily understood and that allows more checks on consistency by a compiler. While a little efficiency may be lost, the gain in reliability and understanding is well worth the little loss in efficiency.

In this section we restrict the programmers freedom by restricting where and how shared variables may be used. This will make interference-freeness a syntactic property, which can be checked by a compiler.

We first require that each shared variable be assigned to one (*and* only one) named *resource*. A resource is a set of variables that represent some logical entity, like a buffer, or disk, etc. For example, the buffer resource used in the bounded buffer problem would be declared as

resource buffer: b, n, in, out

Secondly, we introduce a new statement

with r *when* B *do* S

where r is a resource, B a logical expression and S a statement, and restrict references to shared variables of a resource r to the B and S of statements *with* r *when* B *do* S. S is called a *critical region*.

The *with-when* statement acts as an indivisible unit. Execution of it is delayed until B is true and no other program is using resource r. Then S is executed; during this execution, no other program is allowed to use the resource.

The *with-when* is easier to implement then the *await*, since during its execution other programs may also execute; only programs that desire to use the resource must wait.

We give proof rules for the *cobegin* and *with-when* statements. We give them for one resource only. Some restrictions on the use of variables in assertions have not been given; in this brief introduction the basic ideas should suffice. The proof rules make use of a <u>resource invariant</u> Ir, which describes the set of states the variables of resource r can be in when no <u>with-when</u> for r is being executed -- like the buffer invariant I of (1). Note that the interference-freeness condition is no longer necessary, since shared variables can only be referenced within a <u>with-when</u> statement.

<u>Rule for resource cobegin</u>:

$$\frac{\{P1\}\ S1\ \{R1\},\ \{P2\}\ S2\ \{R2\}}{\{Ir\ \underline{and}\ P1\ \underline{and}\ P2\}\ \underline{cobegin}\ \underline{resource}\ r\text{: shared variables; } S1\ //\ S2\ \underline{coend}\ \{Ir\ \underline{and}\ R1\ \underline{and}\ R2\}}$$

<u>Rule for with-when</u>:

$$\frac{\{Ir\ \underline{and}\ P\ \underline{and}\ B\}\ S\ \{Ir\ \underline{and}\ R\}}{\{P\}\ \underline{with}\ r\ \underline{when}\ B\ \underline{do}\ S\ \{R\}}$$

We give the solution to the bounded buffer problem in this notation. Only one program may insert or extract at a time. On the other hand, any number of programs could use the buffer; in the earlier case, only one consumer and one producer was allowed:

```
{I (from (1))}
cobegin resource buffer: b, n, in, out;
        ...
        with buffer when in-out<n do
             begin b[in mod n]:=x; in:=in+1 end;
        ...
//      ...
        with buffer when 0<in-out do
             begin y:=b[out mod n]; out:=out+1 end;
        ...
coend
```

3.4. Monitors

We outline one more restriction on parallel programs. In the last section we discussed the use of the resource and the with-when statement as a means for making clear where shared variables are used. Here we take the direct use of shared variables out of the programmer's hands completely. He will only invoke procedures that reference them.

When a resource such as a buffer is being designed, the designer will typically create all necessary operations on that resource. He knows the reasons for designing the resource, and it should be safe to assume he will do his job correctly. Thus we let him collect together in the form of a monitor all the necessary declarations, any initialization, and all required actions (in the form of procedures or subroutines).

Only one procedure of the monitor may execute at a time; other invoked procedures are delayed until the one executing is finished. Thus we have exclusion. There is also a need for synchronization. If an executing procedure must delay until some condition is met, some signal must be sent to allow another procedure to execute. For this, we introduce condition variables, and allow the two statements

```
conditionvariable.wait     [delay]
conditionvariable.signal   [signal for any one delayed
                            process to continue]
```

Typically, there will be one condition variable for each reason for a delay. This is shown in the following translation of the bounded buffer problem into the monitor notation. There are two reasons for waiting: (1) no insertion can be made because the buffer is full (delay until condition variable nonfull is signalled) and (2) no extraction can be made because the buffer is empty (delay until condition variable nonempty is signalled).

```
monitor buffer;
  var b:  array [0:n-1] of somevaluetype;
      in, out:  integer;
      nonempty, nonfull:  condition;
  procedure insert(x:somevaluetype);
      begin if in-out≥n then nonfull.wait;
            {in-out<n}
            b[in mod n]:=x;
            in:=in+1;
            nonempty.signal
      end;
  procedure extract(y:somevaluetype);
      begin if 0≥in-out then nonempty.wait;
            {0<in-out}
            y:=b[out mod n];
            out:=out+1;
            nonfull.signal
      end;
  initialization:  in:=0, out:=0
  endmonitor
```

Any parallel process may invoke procedures insert and extract, but only one of the procedures will execute at a time. Thus, insertion and extraction may not be performed simultaneously. This is a *very* small price to pay for the additional structure that the notation imposes, especially when one considers that these operations will only consume a small part of the total time.

4. Communicating sequential processes

In section 3 we discussed three approaches for dealing with parallelism when there is a shared memory. There also exists systems composed of several (many) individual processes with no shared memory. To communicate, processes "send messages" to each other. Advances in hardware technology -- the cheapness of chips -- promises to increase the use of such systems.

A number of notations have been developed for such message passing systems. We will outline one briefly. This one is chosen because, though based on a small number of basic primitives, it is surprisingly versatile. It can be used to define most other programming language constructs, such as procedures and coroutines. And it completely obviates the need for worrying about interference of parallel processes. The notation has not been implemented; it remains a tool for _thinking_ about parallel programming and programming language design.

A process has only local variables. (Thus there is no need for an explicit exclusion notation.) It consists of declarations and a sequence of statements. Possible statements are the null statement _skip_, the assignment statement, and the alternative and repetitive statements of Section 2. Note that the latter two statements are non-deterministic. For example, execution of

```
i:=2;
do i>1 → i:=i-2
 [] i≥1 → i:=i-1
od
```

will terminate with i=0, but will take either 1 or 2 iterations to do so, depending on whether i:=i-2 or i:=i-1 is executed the first time. As another example, the following stores the maximum of x and y in z:

```
if x≥y → z:=x
 [] y≥x → z:=y
fi
```

In addition to these statements, communication among processes is done via input-output statements: Execution of

```
P1!name(x,y)
```

in process P2 sends process P1 the two values x and y, while execution of

```
P2?name (a,b)
```

in P1 is a request for P2 to send two values for the parameters a and b. The odd point is that these two operations ! and ? also provide *synchronization*. Execution of P1!name(x,y) in P2 is *delayed* until P1 has executed P2?name(a,b), where *name* is the same identifier in both cases, and the number of parameters and their types must match as usual. When *both*

```
P1!name(x,y) and P2?name(x,y)
```

have been begun, the values in x and y are stored in a and b, and *then* both processes proceed. It is this synchronization that provides the necessary flexibility, and simplicity, to the approach.

One last point. One input command, like P2?name(a,b), may appear just after a condition (guard) in a loop or alternative statement. Thus, execution of

```
if in-out<n, P1?insert(x) → S1
 [] 0<in-out, P1?more()    → S2
fi
```

is delayed until one of the guards in-out<n or 0<in-out is true and the corresponding input command (P1?insert(x) or P1?more()) has a waiting output command from process P1.

As a first example, we write a process that can be called from process P1 any number of times to compute the maximum of two arguments

```
process max::
        var x,y:  integer;
        do true, P1?send(x,y)→
                if x≥y → P1!return(x)
                 [] y≥x → P1!return(y)
                fi
        od
```

To store the maximum of 8 and 5 (say) in a variable z, process P1 must execute an output operation to send max the values, and an input operation to receive the result:

```
process P1::
        var z:  integer;
        ...
        max!send(8,5); max!return(z);
        ...
```

As a second example, we give the bounded buffer problem in this notation. Process buffer will contain the buffer, process producer will execute

```
buffer!insert(x)
```

to insert value x, and process consumer will execute

```
buffer!more(); buffer?extract(y)
```

to extract the next value y. The buffer has size 100.

```
process buffer:
        var b[0..99]:  some valuetype;
            in, out:  integer;
        in:=0; out:=0;
        {0≤in-out≤100}
        do in-out<100, producer?insert(b[in mod 100])
                        →in:=in+1
         [] 0<in-out, consumer?more()
                        →consumer!extract(b[out mod 100]);
                         out:=out+1
        od
```

We have barely touched on important implications of these concepts. For example, we have not discussed termination of process, we have not indicated how a process like buffer could receive insert commands from a variable number of processes. Nevertheless, I hope this slight introduction is enough to whet your appetites for more information on this topic of communicating sequential processes.

5. Concluding remarks

I have briefly surveyed some of the notations used to express parallelism in conventional computer architectures, both with and without shared memory. For comparison, one example, the bounded buffer problem, has been written in all four notations. The notations have been developed for human understanding first and machine imple-second, with an eye for capturing as simply as possible the necessary concepts, such as synchronization, critical regions, mutual exclusion, and the resource as a logical entity. If the ideas seem too simple, it is because I glossed over many important points, or because my examples were too trivial, or perhaps because the researchers have done such a remarkable job in understanding parallelism and making it _appear_ simple.

As mentioned earlier, parallel programming can be an order of magnitude more difficult than sequential programming and yet it is essential, even if just for operating systems, that we learn to control parallelism in a reliable manner. If one compares earlier development for expressing parallelism (e.g. PL/I's task and event facilities, or even Dijkstra's primitive construct, the semaphore) with the developments described in this lecture, one sees a vast improvement in our ability to write and understand parallel programs.

The various ideas in Section 3 were presented not in the order in which they were developed, but from most general to most specific. Thus I have attempted to show how concern for understanding could lead to "restrictions" on the programmer, restrictions that he should gladly follow in order to manage the complexity of parallel programs more easily.

Of prime importance is the development of formal methods for proving programs correct, as illustrated in Sections 2 and 3. This is one of the high points of research in the past ten years.

The lecture has been concerned with parallelism in conventional architectures, both with and without shared memory. Other forms of parallelism exist, for which the methods surveyed are not yet of too much use. We mention the parallelism in the ILLIAC IV in the CDC STAR-100, and in some new "array processors" that are already on the market. It is evident (to me, at least) that the hardware designers are far ahead of us -- they can produce new machines faster than we can devise methods for controlling the complexity that these new machines engender.

References

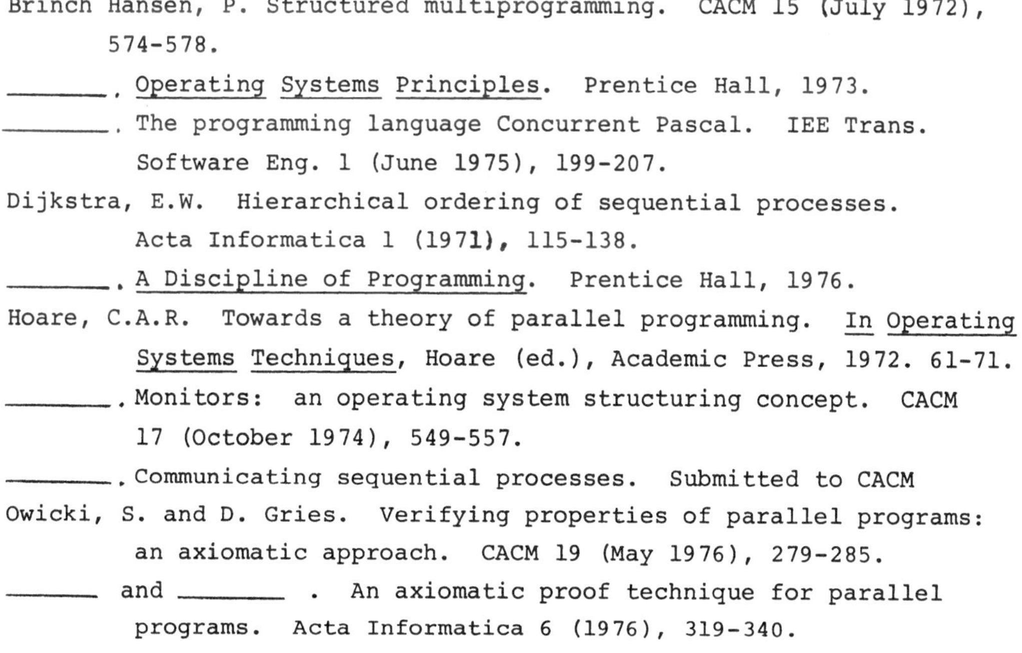

Brinch Hansen, P. Structured multiprogramming. CACM 15 (July 1972), 574-578.

———. *Operating Systems Principles*. Prentice Hall, 1973.

———. The programming language Concurrent Pascal. IEE Trans. Software Eng. 1 (June 1975), 199-207.

Dijkstra, E.W. Hierarchical ordering of sequential processes. Acta Informatica 1 (1971), 115-138.

———. *A Discipline of Programming*. Prentice Hall, 1976.

Hoare, C.A.R. Towards a theory of parallel programming. *In Operating Systems Techniques*, Hoare (ed.), Academic Press, 1972. 61-71.

———. Monitors: an operating system structuring concept. CACM 17 (October 1974), 549-557.

———. Communicating sequential processes. Submitted to CACM

Owicki, S. and D. Gries. Verifying properties of parallel programs: an axiomatic approach. CACM 19 (May 1976), 279-285.

——— and ——— . An axiomatic proof technique for parallel programs. Acta Informatica 6 (1976), 319-340.

Grundlagen der neuronalen Informationsverarbeitung in den Sinnesorganen und im Gehirn

O.-J. GRÜSSER

Physiologisches Institut der Freien Universität Berlin

Inhaltsverzeichnis

1. Ein allgemeines Schema der Wahrnehmung

Die für uns wahrnehmbare Welt ist die Menge aller *Gegenstände* und ihrer *Sachverhalte*. Sachverhalte sind die physikalisch meßbaren Eigenschaften der Gegenstände, die Veränderung der Gegenstände, die Relationen der Gegenstände zueinander, die Relationen der Gegenstände zum wahrnehmenden Menschen und die Veränderung dieser Relationen. Zu den Sachverhalten gehören auch unsere Erfahrung mit den Gegenständen und die Veränderung der Gegenstände durch den wahrnehmenden Menschen.

Die allgemeine Sinnesphysiologie unterscheidet vier Kategorien, durch die sich alle Wahrnehmung gliedern läßt: *Raum, Zeit, Qualität und Intensität*. Die Objekte und ihre Sachverhalte werden in der kategorialen Ordnung von Raum und Zeit wahrgenommen. Folgt man dem reduktionistischen Vorgehen der Sinnesphysiologie, so kann man die durch die Objekte bewirkten Sinneswahrnehmungen auch nach ihren Qualitäten und Intensitäten beschreiben.

Aus zahlreichen sinnespsychologischen Untersuchungen ist bekannt, daß für die phänomenale Ordnung der Wahrnehmung die zeitliche Auflösung eine untere Grenze von 50 bis 80 ms hat. Allerdings ist diese *Präsenz-*

zeit, also die Zeit zwischen dem „Vorher" und dem „Nachher", umso länger, je komplexer der wahrgenommene Sachverhalt ist (bis zu einigen s). Die älteren Sinnesphysiologen haben die Präsenzzeit das *Moment* genannt.

1.1 Die räumliche Ordnung der Wahrnehmung

Unsere Wahrnehmungen haben meist eine *räumliche Ordnung* und beziehen sich entweder auf den *eigenen Leib* oder auf Gegenstände und Sachverhalte im *extrapersonalen* Raum. Die räumliche Präzision des „Hier" oder „Da", mit der eine Wahrnehmung am eigenen Leib erfolgt, kann eine Genauigkeit von weniger als 1 mm erreichen, wenn man z.B. versucht, den Ort einer leichten Berührung mit einer Nadelspitze an der Fingerkuppe festzustellen („Zweipunktschwelle"). In den *Allgemeingefühlen* (z.B. Hunger, Durst, Atemnot, Empfindung muskulärer oder allgemeiner Abgeschlagenheit) wird die räumliche Lokalisation der Wahrnehmung am eigenen Körper unbestimmt, bleibt jedoch phänomenal innerhalb der äußeren Grenzen des Leibes.

Der *extrapersonale Raum* (bzw. dessen Gegenstände und Sachverhalte) läßt sich in vier „Schichten" gliedern (Abb. 1):

(1) Die Objekte im *Greifraum* können meist mit mehreren Sinnesorganen wahrgenommen werden (*multimodale* Objektperception). Mit Hilfe von Instrumenten kann der Greifraum erweitert werden. Jedem ist aus der alltäglichen Erfahrung bekannt, daß Objekte, die mit Instrumenten berührt werden, richtig im Raum lokalisiert werden und nicht dort, wo die Instrumente die Mechanoreceptoren der Handoberfläche erregen.

(2) Im *Nahwirkraum* nehmen wir die Objekte und Sachverhalte meist ebenfalls mit mehr als einem Sinnesorgan wahr; meist sind dies Augen und Ohren. Daneben spielen kinästhetische und tactile Informationen für die Wahrnehmung im Nahwirkraum eine Rolle. Das Gedächtnis ist für die Strukturierung des Nahwirkraumes von erheblicher Bedeutung. Wenn man in einem Zimmer sich visuell beim Umhergehen orientiert hat, so bleibt dieser Nahwirkraum für einige Zeit in der Wahrnehmung *verfügbar*. Man orientiert sich in diesem Raum meist auch dann richtig, wenn man die Augen schließt. Ist man andererseits in einem unbekannten, völlig dunklen Zimmer vorsichtig und hinreichend lange hin- und hergegangen und hat die Gegenstände betastet, so kann man sich ein „Bild" dieses Zimmers machen, ohne es je gesehen zu haben. Für die Wahrnehmung der Objekte und Sachverhalte im Nahwirkraum spielt demnach die unmittelbar zurückliegende Erfahrung eine wichtige Rolle. Die Wahrnehmung vertrauter Räume wird auch durch das Langzeitgedächtnis beeinflußt. Betritt man einen solchen Raum, in dem die gewohnte Lage eines Gegenstandes verändert wurde, so fällt diese Veränderung als erstes auf („die Lampe steht nicht an der gewohnten Stelle").

(3) An den Nahwirkraum schließt sich der *Fernwirkraum* an (Abb. 1). Er wird im wesentlichen visuell erfaßt und besitzt in der Wahrnehmung räumliche Tiefe. Mit Hilfe auditorischer Signale aus dem Fernwirkraum können wir die Gegenstände meist nur sehr ungenau lokalisieren („dort oben auf dem Baum singt die Amsel"). Die auditorische Lokalisation im Nahwirkraum und im Fernwirkraum ist durch Übung wesentlich verbesserbar. Blinde Menschen können sich durch genaue Analyse der Schallreflexion erstaunlich gut in ihrer Umwelt orientieren.

(4) Die äußerste Schicht des extrapersonalen Raumes bildet der *visuelle Hintergrund*. Er hat in der Wahrnehmung keine räumliche Tiefe (z.B. eine Bergkette am Horizont oder der nächtliche Sternenhimmel).

Die Lage der Grenzen dieser verschiedenen, phänomenal unterscheidbaren Schichten des extrapersonalen Raumes ist variabel und kann nur näherungsweise angegeben werden. Der Greifraum ist durch die Größe und Beweglichkeit des Körpers und der Extremitäten bzw. durch die Reichweite der benutzten Instrumente begrenzt. Beim neugeborenen Kind wird der Greifraum zunächst durch den *oralen Greifraum* dominiert. Die Ausdehnung des Nahwirkraumes läßt sich abschätzen, wenn man eine Versuchsperson mit geschlossenen Augen in einem Raum hin- und hergehen läßt, den sie vorher betrachten konnte. Innerhalb des Nahwirkraumes findet sie sich zurecht, ohne unsicher zu werden.

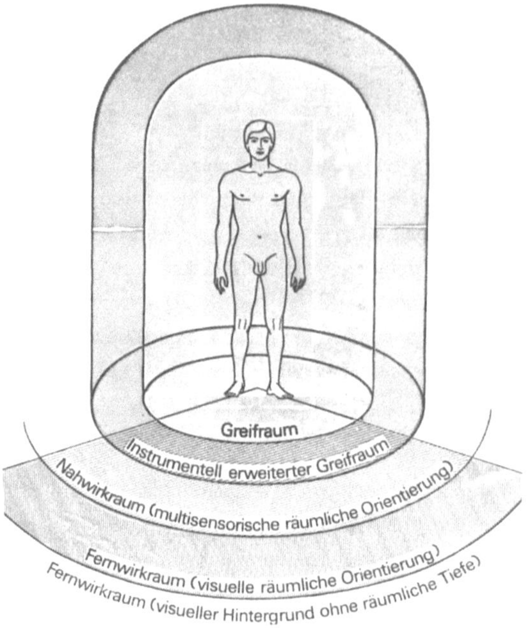

Abb. 1

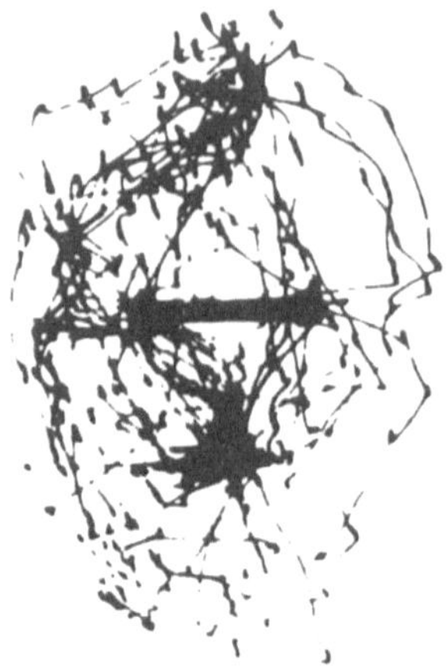

Abb. 2a Augenbewegungen beim Betrachten eines Gesichtes (YARBUS, 1967)

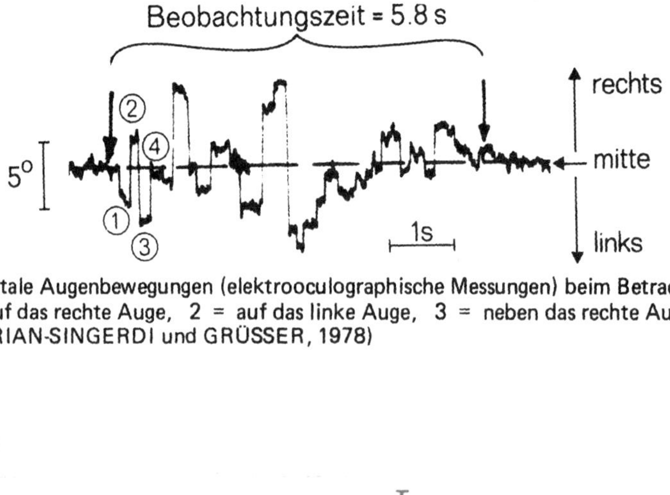

Abb. 2b Horizontale Augenbewegungen (elektrooculographische Messungen) beim Betrachten eines Gesichtes. 1 = Blick auf das rechte Auge, 2 = auf das linke Auge, 3 = neben das rechte Auge, 4 = auf den Mund. (GHAZARIAN-SINGERDI und GRÜSSER, 1978)

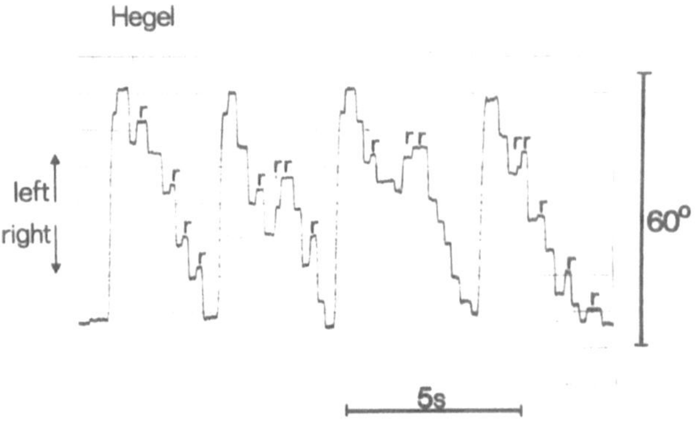

Abb. 2c Augenbewegungen beim Lesen eines sprachlich einfach strukturierten, inhaltlich jedoch schwierigen Textes. (Hegel: Einführung in die Philosophie) Zahlreiche Regressionssaccaden = r (GHAZARIAN und GRÜSSER)

Der Fernwirkraum ist vorwiegend visueller Raum mit *Tiefenstruktur*. Da außer der *Querdisparation* der Bilder auf der Netzhaut beider Augen vor allem *parallaktische* Verschiebungen für die Wahrnehmung der Tiefe eine Rolle spielen, weitet sich der Fernwirkraum aus, wenn der Beobachter hohe Geschwindigkeiten erreicht (z.B. bei einer raschen Fahrt mit der Eisenbahn, dem Automobil oder dem Flugzeug vor einer Berglandschaft).

Der Greifraum und der Nahwirkraum besitzen phänomenal eine einigermaßen euklidische Struktur. Für den Fernwirkraum gilt dies nur mit Einschränkung. Er scheint in vertikaler Richtung stärker ausgedeht zu sein als in horizontaler: Steht man auf einem 100 m hohen Turm und betrachtet Menschen oder Automobile auf dem Boden, so scheinen die Menschen kleine Puppen, die Automobile kleine Spielzeugautos zu sein. Sieht man dagegen die gleichen Objekte und Menschen in 100 m horizontaler Entfernung, so erscheinen sie in „richtiger" Größe, obgleich die Winkelgröße der Netzhautbilder in beiden Betrachtungsweisen natürlich gleich ist.

1.2 Die motorischen Komponenten bei der Wahrnehmung

Unsere Erfahrung mit den Gegenständen der Welt ist in der Regel ein *aktiver* Prozeß. Für viele Bereiche der Wahrnehmung ist die *aktive Zuwendung* (Bewegung in Relation auf das wahrgenommene Objekt, z.B. Betasten, Greifen) eine notwendige Bedingung für die Perception. Dies wurde schon von den Physiologen des 19. Jahrhunderts erkannt (z.B. Hermann von HELMHOLTZ, 1866; SECHENOV, 1878). Die *motorische* Komponente der Wahrnehmung wird auch in den von unserer Sprache benutzten Begriffen deutlich: „Wahr*nehmen*", „Be*greifen*". Unter normalen Bedingungen sind bei der Wahrnehmung motorische und perceptorische Komponenten eng miteinander verschränkt. In Abb. 2a sind die Augenbewegungen beim Betrachten der Photographie eines Gesichtes registriert (YARBUS, 1967). Die zeitlich ruckförmigen Augenbewegungen (Saccaden) dauern 10 bis 80 ms, sie werden durch Fixationsperioden von 0.15 bis maximal 1 s Dauer unterbrochen. Man erkennt an der Registrierung der Abb. 2a leicht, daß die Augenbewegungen und die Fixationspunkte nicht zufällig über das betrachtete Bild verteilt sind: *Hell-Dunkel-Kontraste, Konturen* und *Konturunterbrechungen* sind offenbar bevorzugte Fixationsstellen. Die Registrierung läßt jedoch auch erkennen, daß die *Bedeutung* eines visuellen Signals offenbar die Abtastbewegungen der Augen mitbestimmt. Bei der Betrachtung eines menschlichen Gesichts sind Augen und Mund bevorzugte Fixationsstellen (YARBUS, 1967), die rechte Gesichtshälfte des betrachteten Menschen wird häufiger und länger angeblickt als die linke. In der Regel fällt der erste Blick beim Betrachten eines Gesichts auf ein Auge (rechts > links), danach auf das andere Auge und den Mund (Abb. 2b).

Auch die Messung der Augenbewegungen beim *Lesen* lehrt, daß nicht nur die äußeren Merkmale der visuellen Reize die Abtastbewegungen der Augen bestimmen. Liest man einen zusammenhängenden Text (Abb. 2c), so bewegen sich die Augen in mehreren horizontalen Saccaden über die Zeile. Zwischen den Saccaden treten Fixationsperioden von 0.15 - 0.5 s Dauer auf. Ist das Zeilenende erreicht, so bewegen sich die Augen in einer große Saccade nach links zurück zum nächsten Zeilenanfang. Die Saccadenfolge wird einerseits von der äußeren Struktur des Textes (Zeilenanfang, Wortanfänge, Großbuchstaben, Satzzeichen) bestimmt, andererseits auch vom *Textverständnis*. Die gleichen Versuchspersonen lesen einen Text aus häufig benutzten Worten und von einfacher Struktur schneller als einen Text mit kompliziertem Satzbau und seltenen Worten. Für den Leser in der Regel unbewußt nehmen mit dem Schwierigkeitsgrad des Textes die Amplituden der Saccaden ab sowie die Dauer der Fixationsperioden und die Häufigkeit von rückwärtsgerichteten *Regressionssaccaden* zu. Gleiches gilt, wenn bei etwa gleicher grammatikalischer Struktur eines Textes und gleichem Bekanntheitsgrad der Wörter die ausgedrückten Gedankeninhalte komplizierter werden (Abb. 2c).

Die beiden angeführten Beispiele lehren also, daß bei der visuellen Wahrnehmung nicht nur ein aktiver, intentionaler Aspekt zu berücksichtigen ist, sondern daß auch cognitive Prozesse die Abtastbewegungen der Augen mitbestimmen und daher einen Einfluß darauf haben, was zu jedem Augenblick wahrgenommen wird.

1.3 Multimodale Wahrnehmung und Invarianz der Objekte

Aus *methodischen Gründen* werden in der experimentellen Sinnes- und Neurophysiologie die motorischen und die sensorischen Komponenten der Wahrnehmung getrennt untersucht. Diese oft nicht vermeidbare Aufteilung verführte vor allem die älteren Assoziationspsychologen dazu, einen Gegenstand nur als Summe von Sinnesreizen zu interpretieren. Die Abb. 3 gibt ein vereinfachtes Schema der Operationen wieder, die bei der Wahrnehmung eines Gegenstandes von Bedeutung sind. Gegenstand im Beispiel ist ein Apfel. Er ist die Quelle von verschiedenen Klassen von *Signalen* S(0); S(1), ..., S(j), ... S(n), die sich in zwei große Gruppen gliedern: Die Nullklasse S(0) faßt alle Signale zusammen, die wir nicht direkt mit den Sinnesorganen wahrnehmen können. Solche Signale sind z.B. die temperaturabhängige Infrarotstrahlung des Apfels, die durch ihn verursachte Veränderung des lokalen elektromagnetischen Feldes oder chemische Stoffe, die aus dem Apfel in die umgebende Luft diffundieren und mit den Molekularreceptoren in den Sinneszellen der Riechschleimhaut unserer Nase keine Reaktion eingehen. Daneben gibt es die Gruppe der vom Apfel ausgehenden Signale S(j), die von den Physilogen als *Reize* bezeichnet werden. Diese Signale lösen in *spezialisierten Receptorzellen* unserer Körperoberfläche Reaktionen aus, wenn die *Reizstärke* eine minimale *Reizschwelle* überschritten hat. Die vom Apfel reflektierten Photonen erregen z.B. die Photoreceptoren unseres Auges, die Geruchstoffe des Apfels die Geruchsreceptoren unserer Nasenschleimhaut. Betasten wir den Apfel, so werden die Mechanoreceptoren der Haut erregt. Die zentralnervöse Interaktion der von den Tastreceptoren ausgehenden Signale mit den innerhalb des Nervensystems zurückgemeldeten Signalen, die der motorischen Kontrolle beim Betasten des Apfels dienen, vermittelt die Form und die mechanischen Qualitäten des Apfels. Geschmacks- und Mechanoreceptoren des Mundraumes werden aktiviert, wenn wir in den Apfel beißen. Schließlich wird das charakteristische Geräusch, das durch den Biß in den Apfel entsteht, mit Hilfe der Receptoren des Innenohres wahrgenommen.

Die in den Receptoren der Körperoberfläche entstehenden nervösen Signale werden in den *perceptorischen Systemen* des Gehirns weiter verarbeitet. Diese zentralnervösen Sinnessysteme bestehen jeweils aus vielen Millionen Nervenzellen. Der Apfel ist je nach der Qualität und Modalität der von ihm ausgehenden Reize *gleichzeitig* im neuronalen Erregungsmuster der Nervenzellen unterschiedlicher zentraler perceptorischer Systeme „abgebildet". Man kann vereinfachend sagen, daß der wahrgenommene Gegenstand „Apfel" im Prozeß der Wahrnehmung zunächst in ein „Tastbild", „Riechbild", „Sehbild" usw. zerlegt wird.

Die alltägliche Erfahrung lehrt jedoch, daß der Apfel als Objekt der Wahrnehmung ein hohes Maß von *Invarianz* im Verhältnis zu den zur Wahrnehmung benutzten Receptoren hat. Er bleibt der gleiche Apfel, wenn er mit dem linken oder mit dem rechten Auge gesehen wird, mit der linken oder rechten Hand betastet, sein Duft mit der Nase gerochen wird, er mit den Lippen berührt und mit der Zunge geschmeckt wird. Auch wenn der Apfel vorübergehend überhaupt nicht wahrgenommen wird, wenn er z.B. hinter dem Beobachter auf dem Tisch liegt, so kann er dennoch mit Hilfe des Gedächtnisses präsent und invariant als „hinter mir" liegend erlebt werden. Die Invarianz der wahrgenommenen Objekte gilt auch für die höheren Stufen der symbolischen Abstraktion, so etwa wenn wir „Apfel" sagen oder schreiben und damit den Apfel meinen, der wirklich kurz zuvor oder vor Tagen in unserer Hand war.

Zum Verständnis der Objekt- und Zeichenerkennung hat die Neurobiologie also neben den elementaren Prozessen in den Sinnesorganen und den perceptorischen Systemen auch die Frage zu untersuchen, wie trotz mannigfaltiger und variabler Erregung verschiedener Sinneskanäle ein *invarianter* Gegenstand wahrgenommen wird. Schließlich ist zu klären, durch welche zentralnervösen Prozesse eine *symbolische Repräsentation* von Gegenständen und ihren Sachverhalten entsteht.

Im Blockdiagramm der Abb. 3 ist daher berücksichtigt, daß es in der Großhirnrinde neben den sogenannten primären Projektionsfeldern für das Sehen, Hören, Riechen und Schmecken usw. ausgedehnte Areale gibt, die als *multimodale* (multisensorische) *Assoziations- und Integrationssysteme* bezeichnet werden. In diesen aus

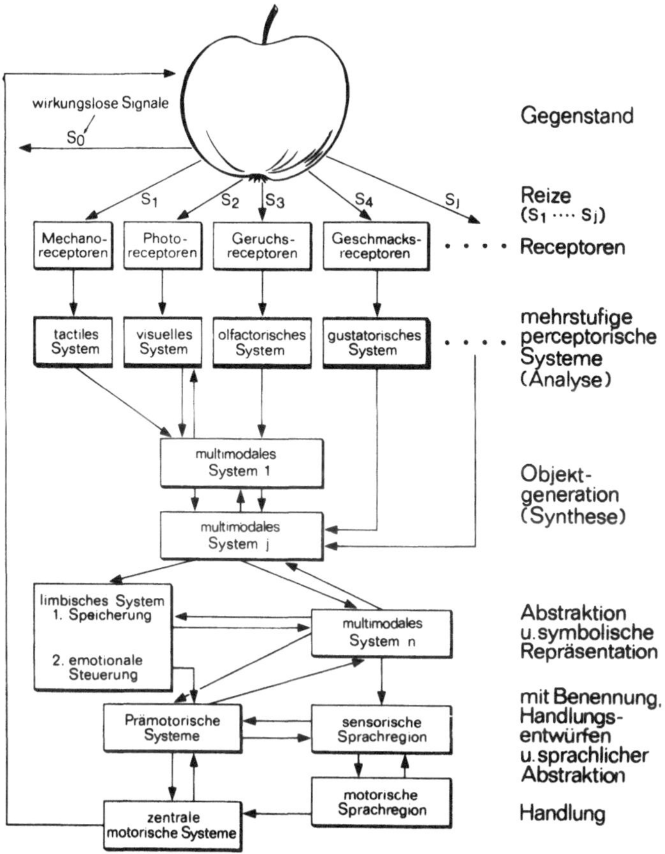

Abb. 3 (GRÜSSER, 1977)

vielen Millionen Nervenzellen zusammengesetzten neuronalen Systemen konvergieren die Signale aus den „primären" sensorischen Projektionsfeldern. Die Nervenzellen dieser Region können also durch visuelle Reize, auditorische Reize oder durch Berühren der Haut usw. erregt werden. Darüber hinaus erhalten die multimodalen Assoziationsfelder der Großhirnrinde „Rückmeldungen" aus den motorischen und prämotorischen Regionen des Gehirns und werden so über die motorischen Akte informiert, die sich auf die jeweils wahrgenommenen Objekte im extrapersonalen Raum beziehen: Das Ergreifen des gesehenen Apfels, den Wechsel des Apfels aus der linken in die rechte Hand, den Biß in den Apfel ... Die verschiedenen multimodalen Assoziationssysteme in der Großhirnrinde des Menschen sind miteinander verbunden und hierarchisch gegliedert. Sie sind nur z.T. in den beiden Hälften der Großhirnrinde gleichartig ausgeprägt.

Die neuronalen Integrationssysteme, die für die *symbolische Repräsentation* der Gegenstände eine besonders wichtige Rolle spielen (z.B. die für die Sprache, das Schreiben, Lesen und Rechnen zuständigen Regionen der Großhirnrinde) sind späte Errungenschaften der Entwicklungsgeschichte und überwiegend in der *dominanten* Großhirnhälfte lokalisiert. Beim Rechtshänder ist in der Regel die linke Großhirnhälfte dominant, während beim Linkshänder mit etwa gleicher Häufigkeit keine der beiden Großhirnhälften, die linke oder die rechte Großhirnhälfte dominant sind.

Ein weiteres wahrnehmungsphysiologisches Problem ist noch kurz zu erwähnen: Auch bei der Wahrnehmung scheinbar neutraler „Objekte" im extrapersonalen Raum kommt es meist zu einer *emotionalen Reaktion*, die für den Physiologen sichtbar wird durch Messung des *elektrischen Hautwiderstandes* oder der *Pupillenweite*. Dieses sind einfache Indikatoren vegetativer Reaktionen. Die *vegetativen Begleitreaktionen* bei der Wahrnehmung werden besonders deutlich, wenn von den Objekten und ihren Sachverhalten erfreuliche oder bedrohliche Signale ausgehen. Die emotionalen Reaktionen sind hierbei nicht nur von den objektiven Signalbedingungen abhängig, sondern auch und oft vor allem *von unserer Erfahrung mit den Gegenständen* und ihren Sachverhalten. Emotionale Begleitreaktionen treten auch auf, wenn das Wahrgenommene eine symbolische Zeichensequenz oder ein einzelnes Zeichen ist. So kann z.B. die emotionale Reaktion beim Lesen eines Berichtes größer sein als beim direkten Wahrnehmen und Miterleben des berichteten Ereignisses. Eine vollständige neurobiologische Beschreibung der Wahrnehmung müßte also auch die emotionalen und z.T. sehr individuellen Komponenten erfassen.

Die Regionen des Großhirns, die für die emotionale Steuerung und die emotionalen Begleitreaktionen bei der Wahrnehmung zuständig sind (das sogenannte „limbische System"), sind die phylogenetisch ältesten Teile des Großhirns. Sie spielen eine nicht unerhebliche Rolle bei der Gedächtnisbildung und der Erinnerung. Für die Nervenzellen des limbischen Systems ist die multimodale Signalintegration ein wesentliches Merkmal.

2. Die Signalaufnahme und Signalverarbeitung durch Receptorzellen

Sinneszellen oder Receptoren sind Zellen an der Körperoberfläche oder im Körper, deren *Reizschwelle* für bestimmte Energieformen oder Signale im Verhältnis zu den übrigen Zellen des Organismus besonders niedrig ist. In der Regel haben Receptorzellen nervöse Verbindungen mit dem Zentralnervensystem (ZNS). Jene Signale, zu deren Aufnahme eine bestimmte Receptorzelle spezialisiert ist, heißen *Reize im engeren Sinn* oder *adäquate Reize*. Die Menge aller adäquaten Reize bildet den *Signalbereich* eines Receptors. Werden Sinneszellen oder die ihnen nachgeschalteten Nervenzellen durch äußere Signale erregt, die nicht zum Signalbereich gehören, dann werden diese Signale als *inadäquate Reize* bezeichnet. Für die Receptorzellen des Auges ist z.B. die elektromagnetische Strahlung in einem Wellenlängenbereich von 400 bis 700 nm (Photonen) der adäquate Reiz, der eine Lichtwahrnehmung hervorrufen kann. Bekanntlich sieht man jedoch auch Licht, wenn man das Auge elektrisch reizt oder im Dunkeln auf das Auge drückt (*Phosphene*). Druck ist also ein inadäquater Reiz für die Receptoren oder Nervenzellen des Auges, während der gleiche Druck für die Mechanoreceptoren der Hautoberfläche ein adäquater Reiz ist.

(a) Die Sinneszellen, mit denen Objekte und Sachverhalte im extrapersonalen Raum wahrgenommen werden, heißen *Exteroreceptoren*. Die *Fernreceptoren* in Auge und Ohr können hierbei Signale aus größerer Entfernung aufnehmen, während die Haut-, Geruchs- und Geschmacksreceptoren als *Nahreceptoren* Signale aus der unmittelbaren Umgebung aufnehmen.

Die Receptorzellen an der Körperoberfläche sind meist zu *Sinnesorganen* (z.B. Auge, Ohr, Geschmacksknospen auf der Zunge) zusammengeschlossen. Sie können jedoch auch (Hautreceptoren) weit verstreut liegen. Funktionell gesehen bildet jedoch auch die Haut ein zusammenhängendes Sinnesorgan, da die Objekte beim Betasten erst durch die sequentielle Erregung mehrerer, örtlich unterschiedlich lokalisierter Mechanoreceptoren der Haut wahrgenommen werden können.

(b) Die *Enteroreceptoren* messen Signale innerhalb des Körpers. Ein Teil der Information, die das Zentralnervensystem aus den Enteroreceptoren erreicht, bleibt unbewußt. Enteroreceptoren sind z.B. Chemoreceptoren, Mechanoreceptoren oder Schmerzreceptoren in den inneren Organen. Spezialisierte Nervenzellen im Gehirn haben ebenfalls Receptorfunktion, so z.B. die für die Regulation der Atmung wichtigen Chemoreceptoren des Hirnstammes.

(c) Die *Proprioceptoren* sind Receptororgane, die Stellung, Länge und Spannung von Muskeln, Sehnen und Gelenken messen. Diese Receptorzellen und die *Schmerzreceptoren* an der Körperoberfläche nehmen eine gewisse Mittelstellung zwischen den eigentlichen Enteroreceptoren und den Exteroreceptoren ein. Einerseits vermitteln diese Receptoren Information über die Objekte im extrapersonalen Raum beim Greifen und Betasten, andererseits auch Signale, die auf den Zustand des eigenen Körpers bezogen sind.

(d) Eine ähnliche Zwischenstellung kommt auch den *Gleichgewichts- und Beschleunigungsreceptoren* des Innenohrs zu. Sie vermitteln nicht nur die Information über die Lage und Lageänderung des Körpers bzw. Kopfes im Raum, sondern bestimmen (neben den Receptoren des Auges) auch die wahrgenommenen Koordinaten des extrapersonalen Raumes, das „Oben" und „Unten", „Links" und „Rechts", „Vorne" und „Hinten".

Im folgenden wird die Signalaufnahme und Signalverarbeitung durch Receptorzellen und perceptorische Systeme am Beispiel des *Sehens* erläutert. Ich folge hierbei dem reduktionistischen Verfahren der „klassischen" experimentellen Receptor- und Sinnesphysiologie, das den Vorteil hat, nicht nur quantitative Daten für die Beziehung zwischen „Reiz" und biologischer Reaktion zu liefern, sondern andererseits auch zu Modellen über die Signalverarbeitungsprozesse in den Sinnesorganen und Nervensystemen führt, die experimentell überprüfbar sind.

2.1 Transformation der Reize

Ehe ein Umweltsignal die Receptorzelle erreicht, unterliegt es in der Regel einem *Transformationsprozeß*. Dieser läßt die *Energieform* unverändert, stellt jedoch ein zeitliches und/oder räumliches Filter für das ursprüngliche Umweltsignal dar. Der dioptrische Apparat des Wirbeltierauges transformiert den Umweltreiz, wobei er ein stark verkleinertes und umgekehrtes Bild der Umwelt auf dem Receptorenraster der Netzhaut entwirft (Abb. 4a). Die räumliche Filterfunktion des optischen Systems der Wirbeltieraugen (Cornea-Kammerwasser-Linse-Glaskörper) schwankt von Species zu Species. Zwei Beispiele sind in Abb. 4b dargestellt. Wichtig zum biologischen Verständnis der *Modulationsübertragungsfunktion* (MTF) des optischen Systems im menschlichen Auge ist der Umstand, daß die Sehschärfe des normalen Auges nicht durch die MTF begrenzt wird, sondern durch die räumliche Dichte des Receptorenrasters und die neuronalen Verarbeitungsprozesse. Diese Behauptung folgt aus dem Resultat eines eleganten Experimentes: Durch Laser-Interferenztechnik wurde unter „Umgehung" der MTF ein Gittermuster variabler räumlicher Frequenz direkt auf der Netzhautoberfläche erzeugt und die psychophysische MTF gemessen.

2.2 Der Transduktionsprozeß

Durch einen sinnesspezifischen Transduktionsprozeß in den Receptorzellen werden Umweltsignale (adäquate Reize) in einen körpereigenen Prozeß umgesetzt, der schließlich zu einer Veränderung des elektrischen Membranpotentials der Receptorzellen führt.

Nach den Signalbereichen, auf die der Transduktionsprozeß spezialisiert reagiert, können die Receptoren in folgende große Klassen eingeteilt werden:

(a) Photoreceptoren
(b) Mechanoreceptoren
(c) Chemoreceptoren
(d) Elektroreceptoren
(e) Thermoreceptoren
(f) Osmoreceptoren

Die *Schmerzreceptoren* lassen sich nicht eindeutig einer bestimmten Klasse von physikalischen Reizen zuordnen (überwiegend Chemoreceptoren). Sie werden auf Grund des subjektiven Reizerfolges zu einer eigenen Klasse zusammengefaßt.

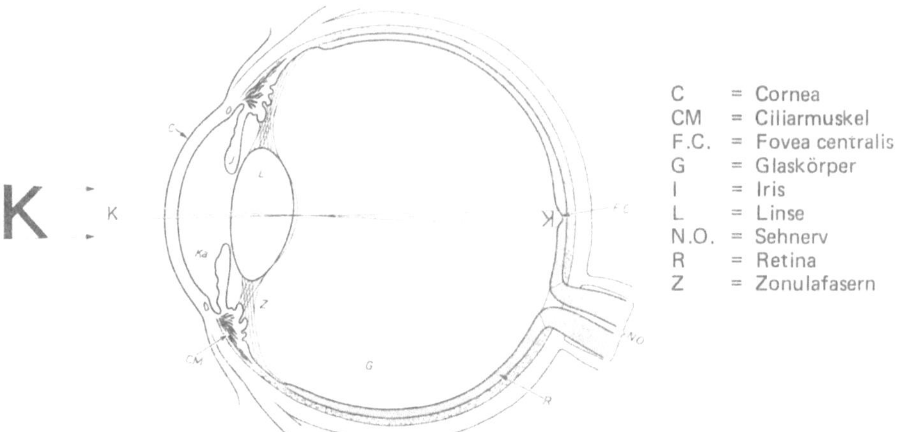

Abb. 4a Schematischer Querschnitt durch das Auge des Menschen. Die Projektion eines Buchstaben (K) auf den Bereich der Fovea centralis (Stelle des schärfsten Sehens) ist eingezeichnet.

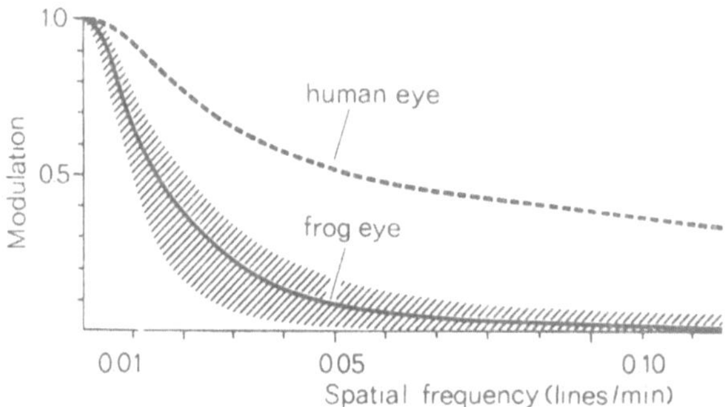

Abb. 4b Modulationsübertragungsfunktion MTF des menschlichen Auges (nach RÖHLER u. Mitarb., 1969) und des Froschauges (*R. esculenta*; nach KRÜGER und MOSER, 1972)

Im *menschlichen Auge* gibt es etwa 126 Millionen Receptorzellen (Photoreceptoren). 120 Millionen sind Stäbchen für das Dämmerungs- und Nachtsehen, 6 Millionen sind Zapfen für das Tageslichtsehen. Die Receptordichte (Receptoren/mm^2) ist für die Zapfen in der Mitte der fovea centralis, für die Stäbchen neben der fovea centralis am größten.

Der *Transduktionsprozeß in den Photoreceptoren* beginnt mit der *Absorption* eines Photons ($400\ nm \leqslant \lambda \leqslant 700\ nm$) durch ein *Sehfarbstoffmolekül*. Die Sehfarbstoffmoleküle sind in den Scheibchen bzw. Membraneinfaltungen der *Außenglieder* der Photoreceptoren in die Lipid-Doppelschicht der Plasma- bzw. Scheibchenmembran regelmäßig eingelagert (Abb. 5a, b). Die Sehfarbstoffe bestehen aus einer chromophoren Gruppe und einem Glykoprotein, dem Opsin. Am besten ist der Sehfarbstoff der Stäbchen analysiert, das *Rhodopsin*. Die drei verschiedenen Zapfentypen im menschlichen Auge haben Sehfarbstoffe, die sich in ihren spektralen Absorptionskurven untereinander und vom Rhodopsin unterscheiden. Die chromophore Gruppe der Sehfarbstoffe des Säugetierauges ist 11-cis-Retinal (Abb. 5c). Durch Absorption eines Photons im π-Elektronenbereich der konjugierten Doppelbindungen des Retinals erreicht das Rhodopsinmolekül eine höhere Energiestufe und beginnt stärker zu schwingen. Dies leitet den *Transduktionsprozeß* ein: Mit einer Wahrscheinlichkeit (*Quantenausbeute*) von 0.5 - 0.65 tritt eine Stereoisomerisation des Retinals auf. Aus der 11-cis-Form entsteht in einem *mehrstufigen Zerfallsprozeß* die all-trans-Form (Abb. 5c, e). Auf der Stufe der Umwandlung von Metarhodopsin I in Metarhodopsin II erfolgt eine *Konformationsänderung* des Sehfarbstoffmoleküls,

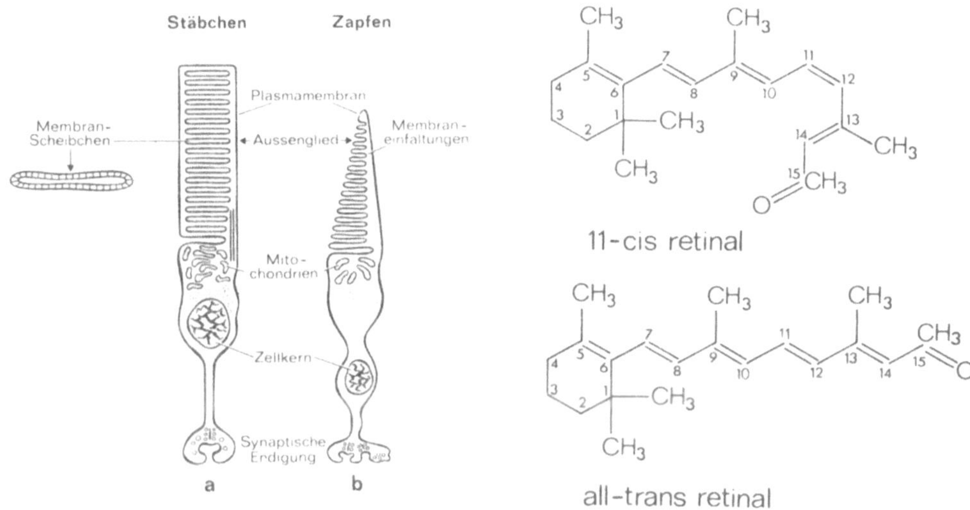

Abb. 5a, b Aufbau eines Stäbchens (a) und eines Zapfens der Wirbeltiernetzhaut (b), stark schematisiert.
Abb. 5c Chromophore Gruppe des Rhodopsins.

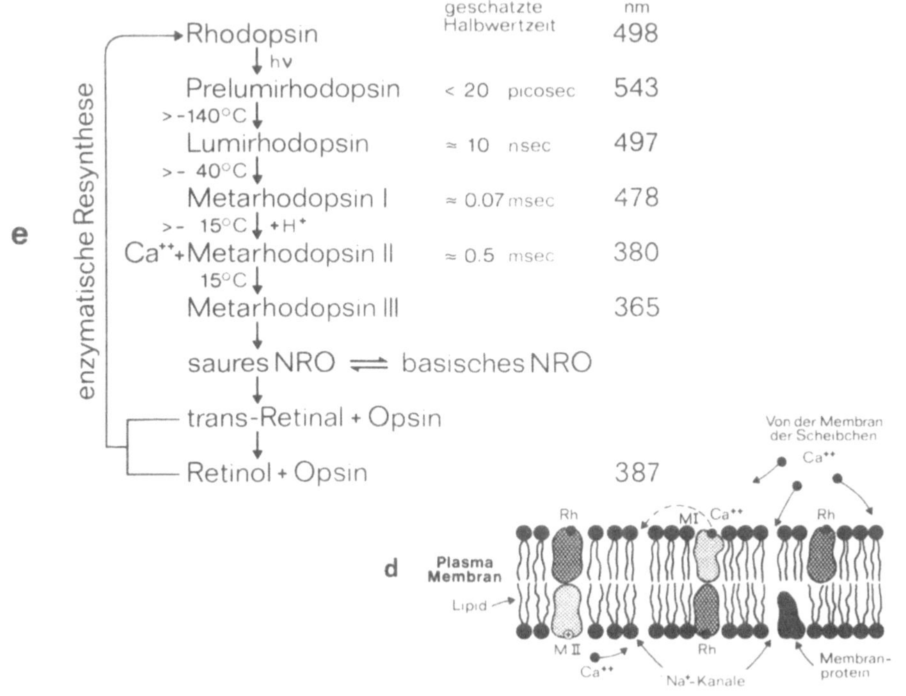

Abb. 5d Schema des Aufbaus der Scheibchen- bzw. Plasmamembran von Photoreceptoren. Ob Rhodopsin doppelt (linke Seite) oder nur einfach (rechte Seite) in die Lipiddoppelschicht eingelagert ist, scheint noch ungeklärt zu sein.
Abb. 5e Zerfall des Rhodopsins nach Photonenabsorption.

durch die wahrscheinlich Calciumionen „aktiviert" werden. Diese sind entweder am Metarhodopsin oder an benachbarten Proteinmolekülen der Membran locker gebunden. Anstelle der freigesetzten Calciumionen nimmt (nach der Modellvorstellung von HAGINS bzw. EMRICH und REICH) das Metarhodopsin-II-Molekül Protonen auf. Die Calciumionen diffundieren von den Membranscheibchen der Stäbchen zur Plasmamembran der Stäbchenaußenglieder bzw. von einer Stelle der Plasmamembran der Zapfen zu anderen Stellen (Abb. 5d). Dort bewirken die Calciumionen eine *Verminderung* des Leitwertes für kleine Ionen, insbesondere für Natrium. Belichtung des Photoreceptors bewirkt also eine Abnahme des *Natrium-Leitwertes* der Plasmamembran. Dies erklärt die unten besprochene Entstehung des sekundären Receptorpotentials.

Die *Konformationsänderung* der Sehfarbstoffmoleküle bewirkt ein auch bei extracellulärer Ableitung meßbares elektrisches Potential, wenn sehr kurze Lichtblitze hoher Intensität auf das Auge gegeben werden. Wegen der gleichzeitigen Konformationsänderung zahlreicher Sehfarbstoffmoleküle ist die Änderung des elektrischen Feldes in der Receptorschicht groß genug, so daß am ganzen Auge das *primäre Receptorpotential* (*early receptor potential*, ERP, Abb. 6) meßbar wird. Das ERP läßt sich auch durch intracelluläre Ableitung mit ultrafeinen Mikropipetten aus einzelnen Receptorzellen registrieren. Es besteht aus verschiedenen Komponenten, die durch unterschiedlich tiefe Temperaturen isolierbar sind. Bei Temperaturen unter 0° wird jene Komponente isoliert, die als Ausdruck der ersten durch Stereoisomerisation bedingten Konformationsänderung der Sehfarbstoffmoleküle angesehen wird.

Der mehrstufige Zerfallsprozeß des Sehfarbstoffmoleküls (Abb. 5e) endet schließlich beim Retinol und Opsin. Über eine Enzymkette wird unter Energieverbrauch aus Retinal bzw. Retinol und Opsin das Rhodopsin wieder aufgebaut. Bei konstantem mittleren Photoneneinfall in das Auge stellt sich ein *Gleichgewicht* zwischen dem lichtinduzierten Sehfarbstoffzerfall und der vorwiegend enzymatisch kontrollierten Regeneration des Sehfarbstoffes ein. Die Lage dieses dynamischen Gleichgewichtes verschiebt sich zu immer höheren Sehfarbstoffkonzentrationen, je geringer der Lichteinfall auf die Netzhaut ist. Dies ist der *photochemische Anteil* der jedem aus dem Alltag bekannten *Dunkeladaptationsprozesse* des Auges, die man an sich selbst z.B. beim Übergang aus einem hell erleuchteten Raum in einen nächtlichen Garten beobachten kann.

2.3 Das sekundäre Receptorpotential

Als *sekundäres Receptorpotential* (late receptor potential, *LRP*) wird bei den Photoreceptoren der Wirbeltiere die durch Belichtung bewirkte *Hyperpolarisation* des normalerweise im Dunkeln -25 bis -35 mV betragenden Membranpotentials der Stäbchen oder der Zapfen bezeichnet. Alle anderen bekannten Receptoren des Organismus reagieren auf adäquate Reizung ebenfalls mit einer Änderung ihres Ruhemembranpotentials (-70 bis -80 mV). Das Receptorpotential dieser Sinneszellen *depolarisiert* jedoch die Membran (Einzelheiten s. SCHMIDT-THEWS, 1977). Für die Entstehung des hyperpolarisierenden Receptorpotentials der Stäbchen und Zapfen läßt sich folgende Modellvorstellung entwickeln:

Durch die Konformationsänderung der Sehfarbstoffmoleküle werden Ca-Ionen aktiviert, die unter dem Einfluß des nicht zerfallenen Rhodopsin-Moleküls an diesem oder benachbarten Lipoprotein-Molekülen der Zellmembran sowohl außen als auch innen locker gebunden sind. Erreicht ein Ca-Ion einen „Na-Kanal" (Abb. 5d), so wird dieser durch die Interaktion von Ca-Ionen mit den Lipoprotein-Molekülen entlang der Na-Kanäle „verstopft". Daher nimmt der Membranleitwert für Natrium (g_{Na}) ab.

Das Membranpotential MP von Receptor- und Nervenzellen kann in guter Näherung durch die *Goldman-Gleichung* beschrieben werden:

$$MP = \frac{RT}{F} \ln \frac{P_K [K^+]_e + P_{Na} [Na^+]_e + P_{Cl} [Cl^-]_i}{P_K [K^+]_i + P_{Na} [Na^+]_i + P_{Cl} [Cl^-]_e} \; [mV] \qquad (1)$$

P kennzeichnet die Permeabilität der Zellmembran für die entsprechenden Ionen und [] die Konzentration

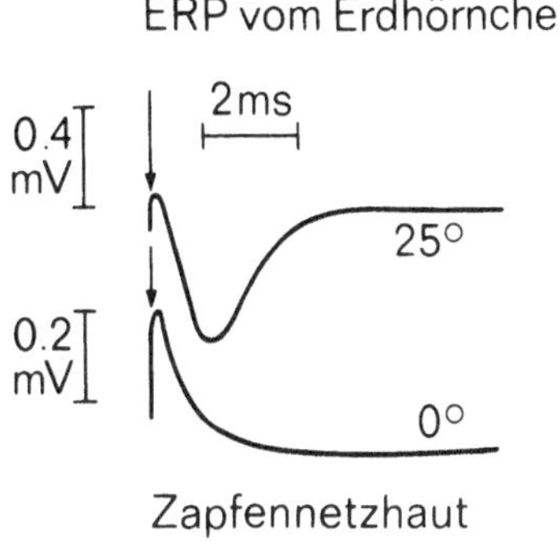

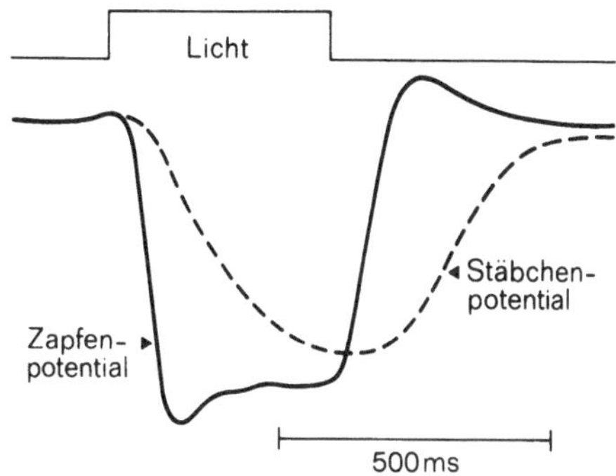

Abb. 6 ERP einer Zapfennetzhaut (nach PAK und EBREY, 1966)

Abb. 7a LRP eines Affen (Makaken) aus der fovealen Zapfenregion und der parafovealen Stäbchenregion der Netzhaut. Umgezeichnet nach WHITTEN und BROWN (1972).

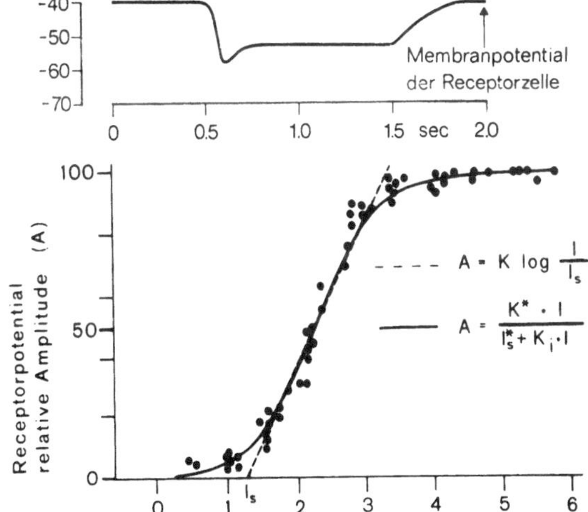

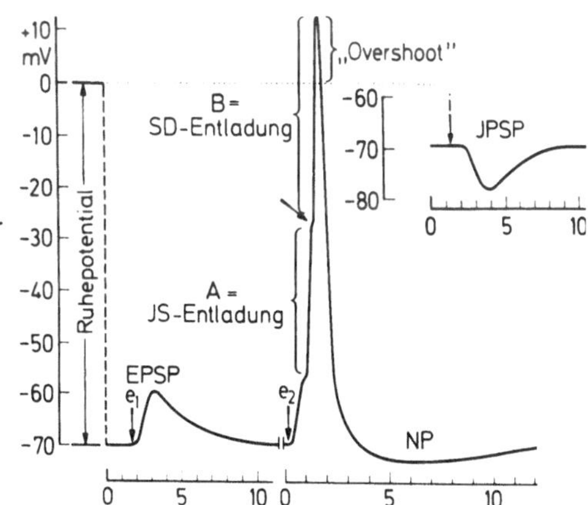

Abb. 7b Schema des Verlaufs des Receptorpotentials eines Zapfens. Abhängigkeit der Amplitude des Receptorpotentials eines Zapfens der Schildkrötenretina von der Reizstärke (umgezeichnet nach BAYLOR und FUORTES, 1970).

Abb. 7c Postsynaptische Potentiale (EPSP, IPSP) und Aktionspotential (AP) einer Nervenzelle.

dieser Ionen im Intracellulärraum (i) bzw. Extracellulärraum (e), der die Receptor- bzw. Nervenzellen umgibt.

Im Vergleich zu anderen Nervenzellen ist der „Ruhewert" (= Dunkelwert) des P_{Na} für die Photoreceptoren der Wirbeltiernetzhaut verhältnismäßig hoch, so daß im Dunkeln ein durch Na-Ionen getragener Dunkelstrom entsteht. Durch Belichtung vermindert sich dieser Dunkelstrom, das hyperpolarisierende Receptorpotential entsteht (Abb. 7).

Die hier geschilderte Variante der Calcium-Hypothese für die intracelluläre Übertragung des Transduktionsprozesses auf die Plasmamembran der Receptoraußenglieder hat den Vorzug, daß sie auch erklärt, warum das sekundäre Receptorpotential der Zapfen eine *kürzere Latenzzeit* hat und insgesamt rascher verläuft als jenes der Stäbchen (Abb. 7a), obgleich die Sehfarbstoffkonzentration in den Stäbchen höher zu sein scheint: Da bei den Zapfen die Sehfarbstoffmoleküle nur in der Plasmamembran vorkommen, sind die Diffusionsstrecken für die aktivierten Ca-Ionen zu den benachbarten Na-Kanälen kürzer als bei den Stäbchen. Bei diesen ist die überwiegende Anzahl von Sehfarbstoffmolekülen in die Membran der Scheibchen des Außengliedes eingelagert (Abb. 5a). Die an dieser Membran spätestens 1 - 2 ms nach Photonenabsorption freigesetzten Ca-Ionen müssen eine längere Strecke zur Außenmembran diffundieren als bei den Zapfen.

Die Amplitude und der zeitliche Verlauf des sekundären Receptorpotentials hängt von der Leuchtdichte und der spektralen Zusammensetzung der Lichtreize ab. Ist die letztere konstant, so gilt folgende Beziehung zwischen Reizstärke I (Photoneneinfall pro Zeiteinheit und Fläche) und der Amplitude A_{RP} des sekundären Receptorpotentials:

$$A_{RP} = \frac{K^{*}I}{1 + k_i I} \; [mV] \qquad (2)$$

Diese Hyperbelgleichung kann für den mittleren Intensitätsbereich durch eine logarithmische Funktion angenähert werden, die in der Sinnesphysiologie gelegentlich auch als Weber-Fechner'sches Gesetz bezeichnet wird (Abb. 7b):

$$A_{RP} = k \ln I/I_s \; [mV] \qquad (3)$$

Die Konstanten K^{*} und k in Gl. (2) und (3) ändern sich bei monochromatischem Licht nach einer Funktion der Wellenlänge, die näherungsweise den spektralen Absorptionskurven der in den Stäbchen bzw. Zapfen vorhandenen Sehfarbstoffe entspricht.

3. Die Signalverarbeitung im Neuronennetz der Retina

3.1 Die synaptische Signalübertragung

Das Membranpotential der Außenglieder der Receptorzellen wird *elektrotonisch* direkt zur Membranregion der synaptischen Kontakte geleitet, die von den Fortsätzen der Receptorzellen mit den nachgeschalteten Nervenzellen gebildet werden (Abb. 8). Ehe ich die Signalübertragung innerhalb des recht komplexen Neuronennetzes der Retina bespreche, möchte ich im folgenden einige „Leitsätze" zur synaptischen Signalübertragung zwischen Nervenzellen (Neuronen) formulieren, die heute als zweckmäßige Arbeitshypothesen die Verarbeitungsprozesse innerhalb von neuronalen Netzen verständlich machen.

Das Membranpotential von Receptorzellen wird entweder direkt *elektrotonisch* zur Membranregion der synaptischen Kontakte geleitet oder zunächst in eine Folge von *Aktionspotentialen* (Impulse von 0.6 bis 1.5 ms Dauer und 60 bis 90 mV Amplitude) umgewandelt. Dies ist der Fall, wenn zwischen dem Ort der Transduktion und dem Ort der synaptischen Signalübertragung sich ein langer Fortsatz (Axon) der Receptorzellen befindet. Die Receptorzelle bildet mit den nachgeschalteten Nervenzellen *synaptische Kontakte*. Synaptische Kontakte werden auch zwischen den Fortsätzen der Nervenzellen (*Axone, Dendriten*) untereinander gebildet.

A. *Die Signalübertragung durch synaptische Kontakte erfolgt entweder durch einen chemischen oder einen elektrischen Übertragungsprozeß. Chemische Synapsen sind gekennzeichnet durch:*
   (a) *unidirektionale Signalübertragung;*
   (b) *eine chemische Transmittersubstanz (Neurotransmitter), die in den synaptischen Bläschen der synaptischen Endigungen akkumuliert ist;*
   (c) *einen subsynaptischen Spalt zwischen der „präsynaptischen" Membran und der „postsynaptischen" Membran;*
   (d) *Molekularreceptoren, die im subsynaptischen Membranbereich der nachgeschalteten Nervenzelle vorhanden sind. Sie reagieren mit dem Neurotransmitter, der an der präsynaptischen Membran freigesetzt wird.*
   (e) *Die Interaktion zwischen Neurotransmitter und Molekularreceptoren bewirkt eine kurzfristige Änderung des Leitwertes der subsynaptischen Membran für kleine Ionen (K^+, Na^+, Cl^-).*
   (f) *Wird durch den Neurotransmitter der Leitwert für alle kleinen Ionen erhöht, so kommt es entsprechend Gl. (1) zu einem depolarisierenden excitatorischen postsynaptischen Potential (EPSP). Die*

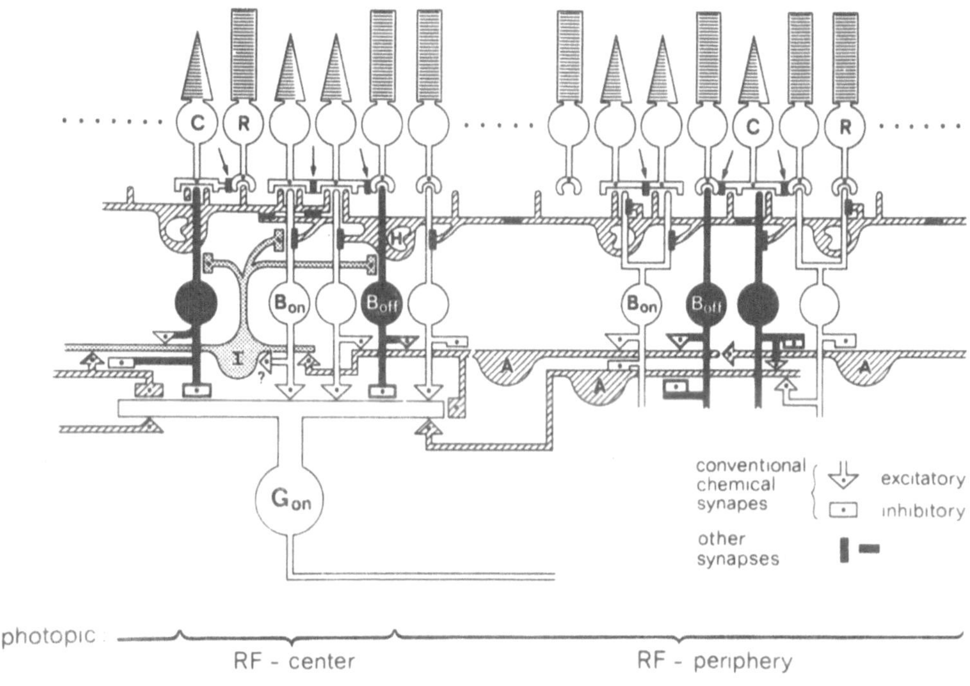

Abb. 8 Schema der Säugetiernetzhaut A = Amacrinen, B = Bipolarzellen, C = Zapfen, G = Ganglienzelle, H = Horizontalzellen, R = Ganglienzellen.

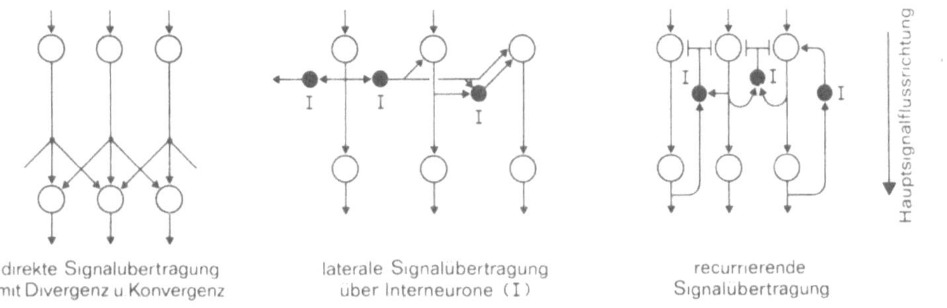

Abb. 9 Signalfluß in einem Neuronennetz.

Synapse wirkt dann erregend. Überschwellige EPSPs lösen Aktionspotentiale aus (Abb. 7c).

(g) *Wird vorwiegend* g_K *und/oder* g_{Cl} *erhöht, so kommt es zu einem hyperpolarisierenden inhibitorischen Potential (IPSP). Die Synapse wirkt dann hemmend.*

B. *Bei den elektrischen Synapsen ist für einen kleinen Bereich der Kontaktstelle zwischen den Fortsätzen benachbarter Nervenzellen der elektrische Widerstand der Membran relativ niedrig, so daß eine direkte Übertragung des Membranpotentials von einer Nervenzelle zur anderen möglich wird. Normalerweise wird diese direkte, „elektrotonische" Signalübertragung zwischen Nervenzellen durch die extracellulären Spalten zwischen den Receptor- bzw. Nervenzellen verhindert.*

Chemische Synapsen sind im elektronenoptischen Bild dadurch gekennzeichnet, daß in der Synapse zahlreiche synaptische Bläschen und im Bereich der subsynaptischen Membran elektronenoptische Verdichtungen zu erkennen sind. Elektrische Synapsen entstehen meist durch eine Verschmelzung der Doppelmembran benachbarter Nervenzellen in einem sehr kleinen Bereich.

C. *Nervenzellen bilden in der Regel durch vielfache synaptische Kontakte neuronale Netze, in denen eine raum-zeitliche Integration der Signale erfolgt. Man kann an solchen neuronalen Netzen im Prinzip drei Signalflußrichtungen unterscheiden (Abb. 9):*

(1) *Die direkte Signalübertragung in einer Neuronenkette in Vorwärtsrichtung;*

(2) *die laterale Signalübertragung in einer Ebene senkrecht zur direkten Hauptsignalflußrichtung. An diesen lateralen excitatorischen oder inhibitorischen Prozessen sind in der Regel Interneurone beteiligt.*

(3) *Die recurrierende Signalübertragung entgegengesetzt zur Hauptsignalflußrichtung. Dadurch werden positive oder negative Rückkopplungsmechanismen möglich.*

3.2 Die synaptische Signalübertragung in der Netzhaut

Die Kontakte zwischen den Receptorzellen der Retina und den nachgeschalteten Nervenzellen (Bipolarzellen und Horizontalzellen, Abb. 8, 10) sind chemische Synapsen. Die Menge des pro Zeiteinheit freigesetzten Transmitters hängt vom jeweiligen Membranpotential des Receptors ab. Im elektronenoptischen Bild sieht man einerseits eine Ansammlung von synaptischen Bläschen um eine *Bandstruktur* in der Mitte der synaptischen Endigung, andererseits auch in einem seitlichen Bereich der synaptischen Endstruktur. Zur Zeit wird zur Erklärung der Signalübertragung zwischen Receptorzellen und den nachgeschalteten Nervenzellen die Hypothese bevorzugt, daß an den synaptischen Kontakten von Stäbchen oder Zapfen umso mehr Transmittersubstanz pro Zeiteinheit abgegeben wird, je weniger negativ das elektrische Potential der Membran ist.
Das hyperpolarisierende Receptorpotential würde bei Belichtung also eine *Abnahme* der Transmitterausschüttung bewirken. Die alternative Hypothese, daß nämlich die ausgeschüttete Transmittermenge mit der Hyperpolarisation ansteigt, erscheint mir jedoch ebenso wahrscheinlich. Beide Hypothesen sind möglich, da man noch nicht weiß, ob die Transmittersubstanz(en) an den Bipolarzellen depolarisierend oder hyperpolarisierend wirken.

Wichtig zum Verständnis der signalübertragenden Prozesse ist, daß bei *Belichtung* jene Bipolarzellen, deren Fortsätze in den zentralen Bereich der Receptorsynapsen reichen, *depolarisiert* werden, während die Bipolarzellen, die im seitlichen Bereich der Receptorsynapsen Kontakte haben, *hyperpolarisiert* werden. Die ersteren werden *On-Bipolarzellen* genannt, die letzteren *Off-Bipolarzellen*.

Die *Horizontalzellen* (Abb. 8) werden durch Belichtung mit „weißem" Licht in der Regel hyperpolarisiert, jedoch fand SVAETICHIN bei farbtüchtigen Fischen Horizontalzellen, die durch rotes Licht depolarisiert, durch grünes hyperpolarisiert wurden (Horizontalzellen des Rot-Grün-Systems) bzw. durch gelbes Licht depolarisiert und durch blaues Licht hyperpolarisiert wurden (Horizontalzellen des Gelb-Blau-Systems). Daneben gibt es noch Horizontalzellen, die im gesamten sichtbaren Spektrum durch monochromatisches Licht hyperpolarisiert werden (Horizontalzellen des Hell-Dunkel-Systems, Abb. 11).

Das Membranpotential der Horizontalzellen beeinflußt seinerseits entweder durch elektrische oder durch chemische Synapsen den Erregungszustand der Bipolarzellen (Abb. 10). Hierbei ist der Einfluß der Horizontalzellen jenem der direkten Erregungsübertragung zwischen Receptoren und Bipolarzellen *entgegengesetzt*. So kommt es zur funktionellen Organisation eines antagonistisch strukturierten „receptiven Feldes": Die Bipolarzellen reagieren auf Belichtung eines größeren Bereiches der Netzhautoberfläche, in dem sich mehrere Receptorzellen befinden. Die On-Bipolarzellen werden durch Belichtung im *Feldzentrum* depolarisiert, durch Belichtung der receptiven *Feldperipherie* infolge des synaptischen Einflusses der Horizontalzellen hyperpolarisiert; die Off-Bipolarzellen reagieren dagegen umgekehrt (Abb. 11).

Die Interaktion zwischen lateralen Signalverarbeitungsprozessen und direkten Signalverarbeitungsprozessen läßt sich auf einer zweiten Stufe bei der Signalübertragung zwischen Bipolarzellen und Ganglienzellen beobachten. Auf dieser Stufe bilden die *Amacrinen* (Abb. 8) das Netzwerk aus Interneuronen für den lateralen Signalfluß. Auch ihre Wirkung ist in der Regel antagonistisch zu der direkten Erregungsübertragung von On- oder Off-Bipolarzellen auf On-Zentrum- bzw. Off-Zentrum-Ganglienzellen. Die Signalübertragung zwischen Amacrinen, Bipolarzellen und Ganglienzellen erfolgt über sogenannte synaptische Triaden (Abb. 12b). Diese bilden „local circuits", durch die in einem Bereich von wenigen um eine offensichtlich differenzierte und heute noch nicht vollständig verstandene Kontrolle des Erregungsflusses zwischen Bipolarzellen und Ganglienzellen möglich ist.

Ein Resultat dieser Verarbeitungsprozesse im Netzwerk der Säugetierretina (Abb. 8) ist durch ein einfaches Schema dazustellen: Es gibt zwei große Neuronenklassen in der Schicht der Ganglienzellen, die *On-Zentrum-Neurone* und die *Off-Zentrum-Neurone*. Während die Signalverarbeitung in den vorausgeschalteten Nervenzellen durch elektrotonische Leitung und entsprechende Verrechnung des Membranpotentials erfolgt, ohne daß Aktionspotentiale gebildet werden, wird am Abgang des Axons der Ganglienzellen das Membranpotential in eine Serie von Aktionspotentialen umgesetzt. Je stärker die Ganglienzellmembran depolarisiert ist, umso höher ist die momentane Impulsrate der Ganglienzellen.

Abb. 12a gibt ein Schema der receptiven Felder (RF) der „einfachen" On-Zentrum- bzw. Off-Zentrum-Ganglienzellen wieder. Im Gegensatz zu Abb. 11 ist jetzt der Erregungsprozeß durch eine *Zunahme* der Rate der Aktionspotentiale („Impulsfrequenz"), der Hemmungsprozeß durch eine *Abnahme* der momentanen Impulsrate gekennzeichnet. Man erkennt an diesem Schema die antagonistische Organisation zwischen Feldzentrum und Feldperipherie, deren Bedeutung in Kap. 3.4 besprochen wird.

Außer diesen einfachen On-Zentrum- und Off-Zentrum-Neuronen des Hell-Dunkelsystems gibt es auf der Ebene der Ganglienzellen der Retina jedoch noch eine komplexere Signalverarbeitung:

(a) Bei farbtüchtigen Tieren kommen farbspezifische Reaktionen vor; die Ganglienzellen haben z.T. auch eine farbspezifisch unterschiedliche Organisation von RF-Zentrum und RF-Peripherie.

(b) Vor allem bei niederen Wirbeltieren (besonders ausführlich untersucht wurden Frösche und Lurche, s. GRÜSSER und GRÜSSER-CORNEHLS, 1976; GRÜSSER-CORNEHLS und HIMSTEDT, 1974) gibt es eine ganze Reihe von Ganglienzellen, an deren Reaktion schon hochspezialisierte neuronale Verarbeitungsprozesse erkennbar sind. Diese retinalen Ganglienzellen antworten nur auf kleine bewegte Reize, wobei die Reizgeschwindigkeit und die Reizgröße, z.T. auch die Richtung der Reize kritische Faktoren sind. Bei einem Teil dieser Ganglienzellen sind Farbspezifität und Bewegungsempfindlichkeit kombiniert (GRÜSSER-CORNEHLS und SAUNDERS, 1977). Es ist wahrscheinlich, daß bei den höheren Säugetieren in der Netzhaut keine so hochspezialisierten Verarbeitungsprozesse stattfinden, sondern erst im zentralen visuellen System.

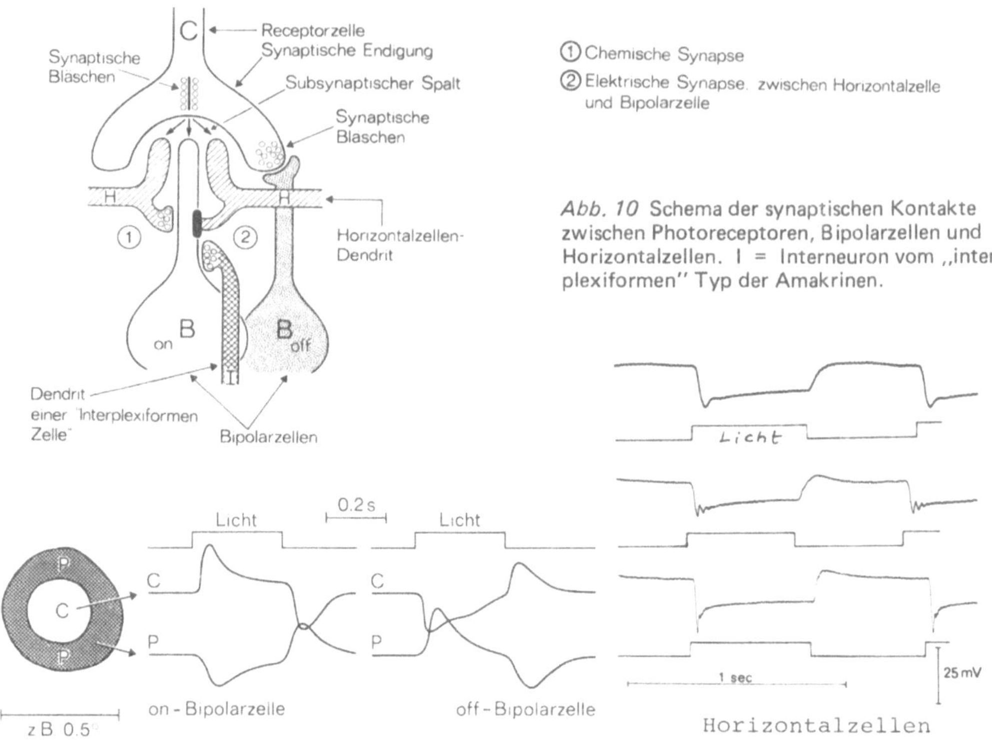

Abb. 10 Schema der synaptischen Kontakte zwischen Photoreceptoren, Bipolarzellen und Horizontalzellen. I = Interneuron vom „interplexiformen" Typ der Amakrinen.

Abb. 11 Schema der Reaktion einer on- und einer off-Bipolarzelle bei Belichtung von RF-Zentrum (C) oder RF-Peripherie (P). Hyperpolarisierende Potentiale von 3 verschiedenen Horizontalzellklassen. Belichtung des receptiven Feldes mit weißem Licht (FOERSTER et al. 1977).

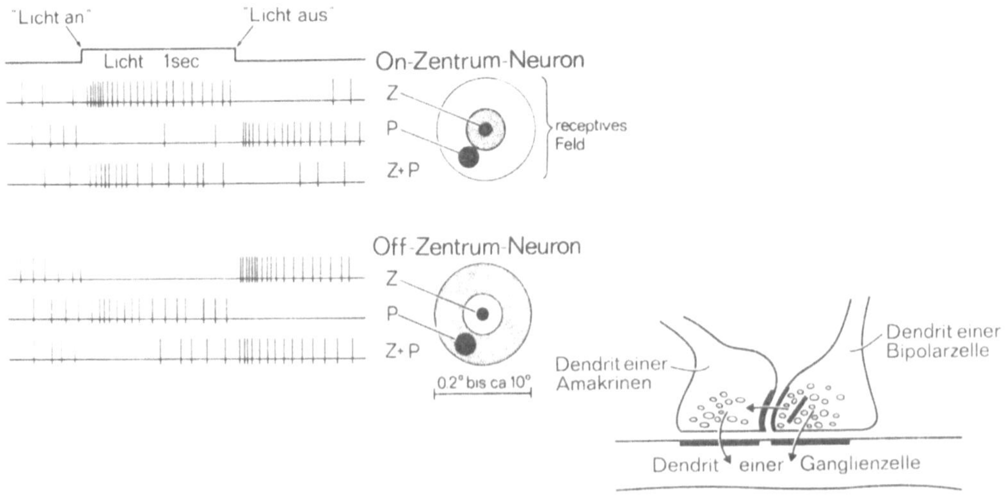

Abb. 12a Schema der Reaktion retinaler Ganglienzellen bei Belichtung des RF-Zentrums (Z), der RF-Peripherie (P) und beider Teile zusammen (Z + P).
Abb. 12b Synaptische Triaden zwischen Amakrinen, Bipolaren und Ganglienzelle.

3.3 Deterministische und probabilistische Prozesse bei der Signalübertragung durch Nervenzellen

Am Beispiel der retinalen Ganglienzellen lassen sich noch weitere für die allgemeine Theorie des Nervensystems wichtige Prinzipien erläutern. Hier sei die Frage besprochen, inwieweit eine Nervenzelle eine deterministische Maschine darstellt und ob probabilistische Prozesse eine Rolle bei der Signalübertragung spielen. Das letztere ist der Fall. Es scheinen folgende allgemeine Regeln zu gelten (Einzelheiten s. GRÜSSER, HELLNER und GRÜSSER-CORNEHLS, 1962; GRÜSSER, 1972):

Unter exakt gleichen Reizbedingungen zeigt das Impulsmuster von Nervenzellen des Zentralnervensystems eine oft erhebliche statistische Variabilität. Diese statistische Unsicherheit bei der Signalübertragung ist bedingt durch spontane Transmitterfreisetzung, Fluktuation der Erregbarkeit bestimmter Triggerzonen in den Dendriten, synaptische Erregung durch Neurone, die nicht reizgekoppelt sind („unspezifische Aktivierung") und stoffwechselbedingte spontane Schwankungen des Membranpotentials der Nervenzellen. Für die Interpretation der meisten Impulsmuster können diese „Rauschfaktoren" nicht vernachlässigt werden. In der Regel nimmt die probabilistische Komponente innerhalb einer Sequenz hintereinandergeschalteter Nervenzellen (Neuronenkette) umso mehr zu, je länger diese Kette ist.

Abb. 13 zeigt, daß schon auf der Ebene der retinalen Ganglienzellen diese probabilistische Komponente festzustellen ist. Die Impulsmuster von Ganglienzellen der Katzennetzhaut wurden unter exakt gleichen Reizbedingungen gemessen, wobei entweder zeitlich periodische Lichtreize (Belichtung des ganzen receptiven Feldes) oder aperiodische Lichtreize („Pseudorauschen" mit Perioden zwischen 2 und 10 Sekunden) benutzt wurden. Die Impulse der Ganglienzellen sind als Punktfolgen durch den Computer dargestellt. Man erkennt leicht, daß individuelle Schwankungen des Impulsintervalls unter exakt gleichen Reizbedingungen auftreten. Diese statistischen Schwankungen werden umso deutlicher, je weniger die Reizstärke von dem Schwellenwert abweicht.

3.4 Die Bedeutung der lateralen Inhibition für die Entstehung des Simultankontrastes

Aus der Organisation der receptiven Felder der retinalen On-Zentrum- und Off-Zentrum-Neurone kann die Entstehung des *Simultankontrastes* abgeleitet werden. Der visuelle Simultankontrast kann im Alltag einfach beobachtet werden: Ein graues Feld auf weißem Hintergrund erscheint z.B. dunkler als ein gleichgraues Feld auf schwarzem Hintergrund. Die Eigenschaften des Hintergrunds bestimmen also die subjektive Helligkeit des grauen Feldes (*Flächenkontrast*). Simultankontrast ist besonders deutlich an Hell-Dunkelgrenzen zu sehen (*Grenzkontrast*): Entlang einer Hell-Dunkelgrenze erscheint der helle Teil aufgehellt, der dunkle Teil dunkler als die jeweils weitere Umgebung. Abb. 14a zeigt schematisch nach Untersuchungen von BAUMGARTNER die Veränderung der Aktivierung eines retinalen On-Zentrum-Neurons, wenn eine Hell-Dunkelgrenze auf verschiedene Stellen des antagonistisch organisierten receptiven Feldes projiziert wird. Die angegebenen Zahlen sind Relativwerte für die neuronale Erregung (+) bzw. Hemmung (-). Abb. 14b zeigt am Beispiel einer On-Zentrum-Ganglienzelle, wie stark eine solche Aktivierungszunahme entlang einer Hell-Dunkelgrenze sein kann. In diesem Beispiel wurde die Hell-Dunkelgrenze langsam über das receptive Feld verschoben und die neuronale Aktivierung als Funktion der *Positionen* der Hell-Dunkelgrenze gemessen. Die räumliche Verteilung dieser Aktivierung kennzeichnet zugleich den mittleren Aktivitätszustand in einem Neuronennetz aus On-Zentrum-Neuronen, wenn eine stationäre Hell-Dunkelgrenze an eine Stelle der Netzhautoberfläche projiziert wird.

Für das Sehen hat der Simultankontrast die Bedeutung, daß *Hell-Dunkelkonturen* besonders stark im neuronalen Erregungsmuster abgebildet werden, während homogene Flächen eine geringere neuronale Aktivierung bewirken. Dies ist ein offenbar sinnvoller Mechanismus, da die *wesentliche Information visueller Gestalten in den Konturen, Konturunterbrechungen und Konturüberschneidungen enthalten ist* (Abb. 15b).

Die funktionelle Organisation der receptiven Felder ändert sich mit dem *Adaptationszustand* der Netzhaut, da die excitatorischen und die inhibitorischen Prozesse unterschiedliche Schwellen und Intensitätsfunktionen

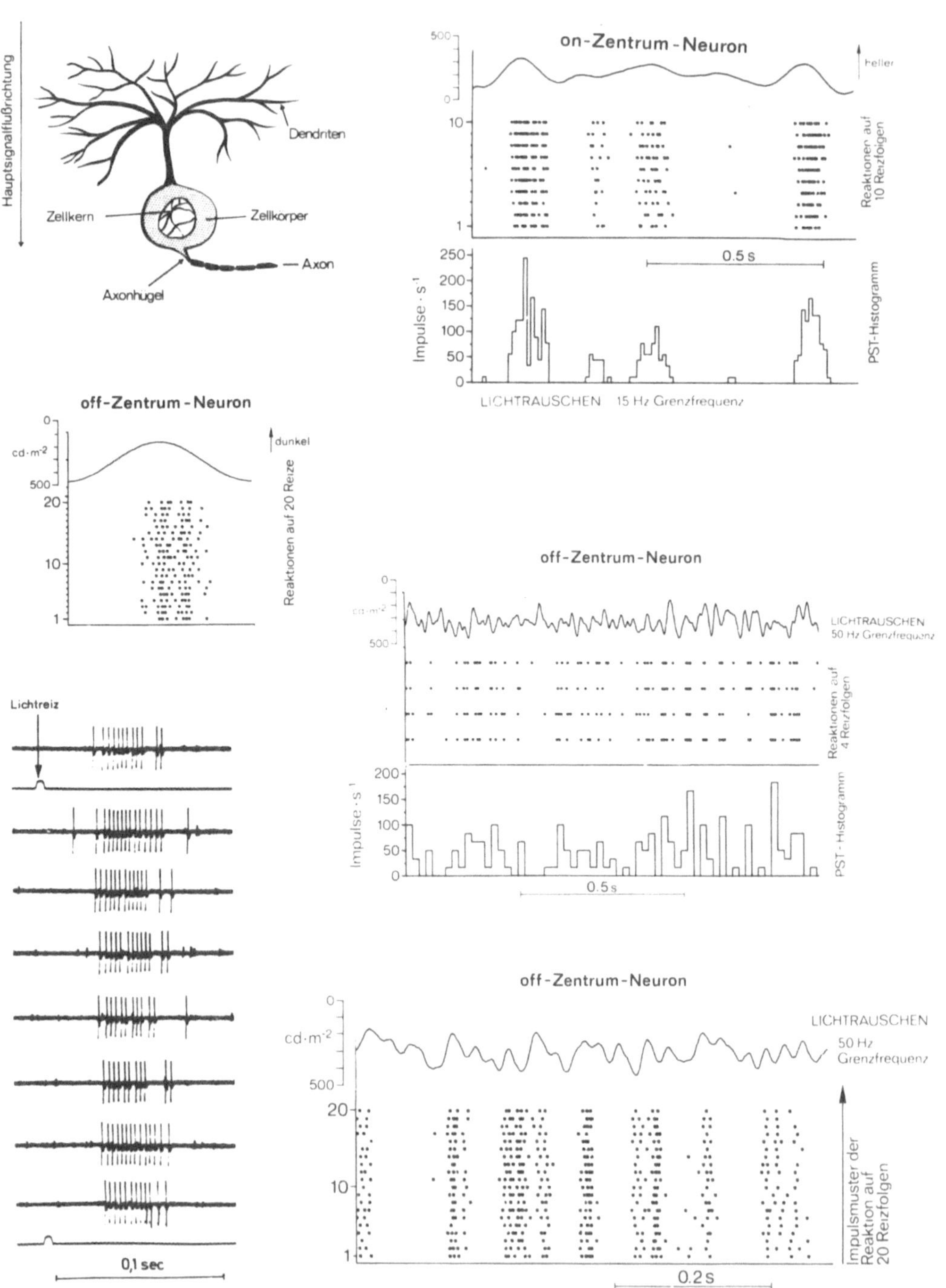

Abb. 13 Struktur einer retinalen Ganglienzelle (schematisiert). Reaktion retinaler Ganglienzellen der Katze auf Belichtung des receptiven Feldes mit periodischen und nichtperiodischen Lichtreizen. Mittlere Leuchtdichte ≈ 90 cd/m², Durchmesser des runden Lichtreizes = 3.2°. In den Diagrammen ist jedes Aktionspotential durch einen Punkt dargestellt. Links: Impulsmuster eines On-Zentrum-Neurons der Katzenretina auf gleiche Lichtblitze. Blitzintervall 2.4 Sekunden.

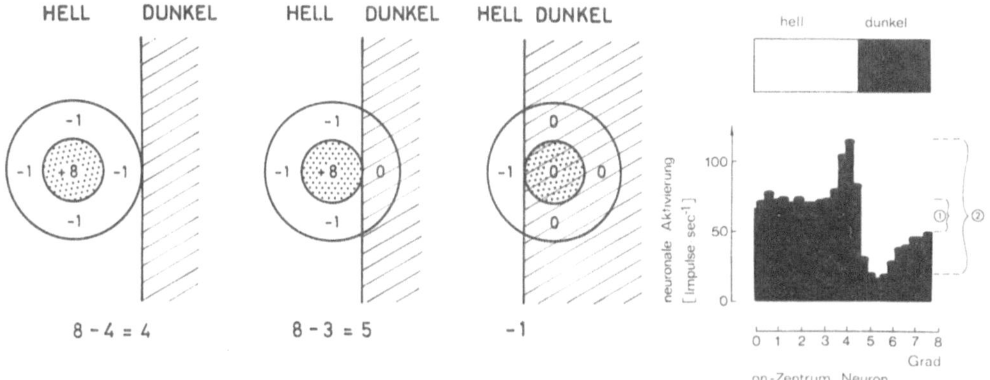

Abb. 14a Schema zur Entstehung des Simultankontrastes. Die Aktivierung des on-Zentrum-Neurons hängt von der Position der Hell-Dunkelgrenze im RF ab.
Abb. 14b Aktivierung eines retinalen on-Zentrum-Neurons als Funktion der Position (Abszisse) einer Hell-Dunkelgrenze. 1 = Aktivierungsdifferenz durch Helligkeitskontrast, 2 = Aktivierungsdifferenz durch Grenzkontrast.

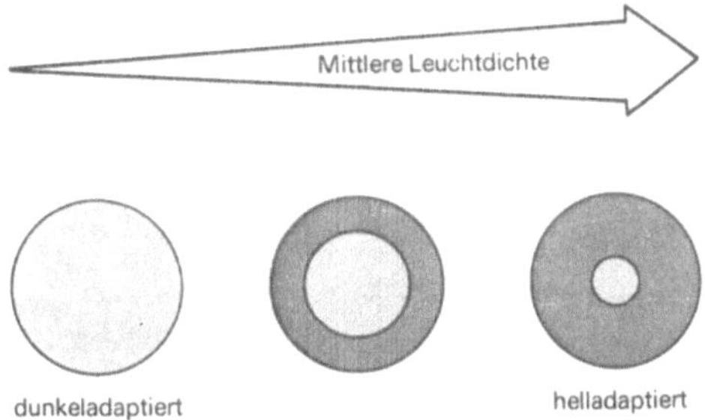

Abb. 15a Veränderung der RF-Organisation eines On-Zentrum-Neurons mit dem Adaptationszustand (aus SCHMIDT-THEWS, 1977).

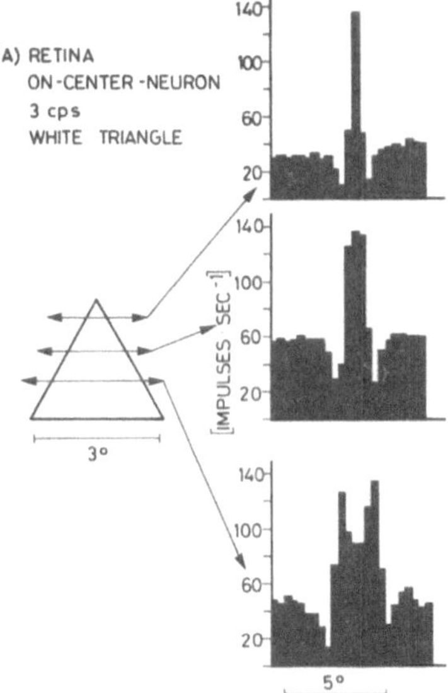

Abb. 15b PST-Histogramme eines On-Zentrum-Neurons der Katzenretina. Reizmuster war ein weißes Dreieck, das in verschiedener vertikaler Position durch das receptive Feld bewegt wurde.

haben. Bei geringem Photoneneinfall auf die Netzhaut (z.B. Sehen in einer sternenklaren Nacht, *skotopisches Sehen*) wird die RF-Organisation durch die excitatorischen Prozesse dominiert; das ganze receptive Feld der On-Zentrum- oder Off-Zentrum-Ganglienzellen reagiert einheitlich. Beim Dämmerungssehen (*mesopisches Sehen*) erkennt man bereits die antagonistische receptive Feldorganisation, die inhibitorischen Prozesse sind jedoch noch relativ schwach. Erst beim Tageslicht-Sehen (*photopisches Sehen*) stellt man eine deutliche antagonistische RF-Organisation fest, wobei funktionell das receptive Feldzentrum umso kleiner wird, je heller (unterhalb der Blendungsgrenze) die Lichtreize sind. Da die Größe des recpetiven Feldzentrums das räumliche Auflösungsvermögen der signalverarbeitenden Prozesse in der Netzhaut bestimmt, kann man aus dem Schema der Abb. 15 auch verstehen, daß die Sehschärfe umso besser ist, je größer die Beleuchtungsstärke der betrachteten visuellen Strukturen unterhalb der Blendungsgrenze ist. Jeder kennt dies aus der alltäglichen Erfahrung; wer einen kleingedruckten Text lesen will, sorgt für ausreichende Beleuchtung.

4. Die Signalverarbeitung im zentralen visuellen System

4.1 Subcorticale Signalverarbeitung

Die Signale aus der Netzhaut werden als Impulsfolgen durch die Axone der Ganglienzellen über den Sehnerven in das zentrale visuelle System übertragen. Ihre Endigungen bilden synaptische Kontakte vorwiegend an folgenden subcorticalen Strukturen in der Tiefe des Gehirns:
Corpus geniculatum laterale, Colliculus superior, prätectale Region, Nucleus des Tractus opticus accessorius
Die Signalverarbeitung im Corpus geniculatum laterale (CGL), das die synaptische Schaltstation auf dem Weg zur *Sehrinde* ist, dient vor allem der visuellen Mustererkennung. Die anderen genannten visuellen subcorticalen Regionen sind vorwiegend für die Steuerung der *Augenbewegungen* sowie die *Accommodation* und die *Pupillenreaktionen* zuständig.

Im Impulsmuster der Ganglienzellen, deren Axone synaptische Kontakte an Nervenzellen des CGL bilden, ist die Reizverteilung auf der Netzhaut unterschiedlich codiert (On-Zentrum-Neurone des Hellsystems, Off-Zentrum-Neurone des Dunkelsystems, farbspezifische Neurone). In der Signalverarbeitung durch die Nervenzellen des CGL wiederholen sich Konvergenz und Divergenz und die RF-Organisation, die oben für die retinalen Ganglienzellen beschrieben wurde: Man findet einen antagonistisch organisiertes RF mit Zentrum und Peripherie. Die unterschiedlichen Neuronenklassen der Hell-Dunkelsysteme und der Farbsysteme bleiben erhalten. Entsprechend der Wiederholung der lateralen Inhibitionsmechanismen nehmen bei einem Teil der Neurone des CGL die Simultankontrasteffekte (Abb. 16b) im Vergleich zu der Antwort der Ganglienzellen der Retina deutlich zu. Insgesamt bleiben jedoch die Funktionsprinzipien erhalten, die für die Ganglienzellschicht der Retina schon beschrieben wurden. In den 6 Zellschichten des CGL bleibt die Information aus dem linken und rechten Auge noch weitgehend getrennt. Die Schichten 1, 4 und 6 verarbeiten Signale aus dem contralateralen Auge, die Schichten 2, 3 und 5 aus dem ipsilateralen Auge (Abb. 16a).

4.2 Die funktionelle Organisation der Sehrinde

(a) Die Projektion der Retina in die Sehrinde. Die Nervenzellen des CGL übertragen auf ihren Axonen die visuelle Information in die *Sehrinde* (visueller Cortex, Area 17), die im Hinterhauptsbereich (Occipitallappen) des Großhirns liegt (Abb. 17, 20). Wie für die Abbildung der Netzhaut in das CGL, so gilt auch für die Projektion in den visuellen Cortex eine *topologische Organisation*: Es besteht eine streng geometrische, genetisch bestimmte Beziehung zwischen jedem Ort der Netzhaut und dem Projektionsort im visuellen Cortex. Benachbarte Orte in der Netzhaut sind durch benachbarte Orte im CGL und im visuellen Cortex repräsentiert. Dies hat zur Folge, daß ähnlich der Abbildung einer Landschaft auf einer Landkarte die Reizverteilung in der Netzhaut im räumlichen Erregungsmuster der Nervenzellen des visuellen Cortex widergespiegelt wird. Die topologi-

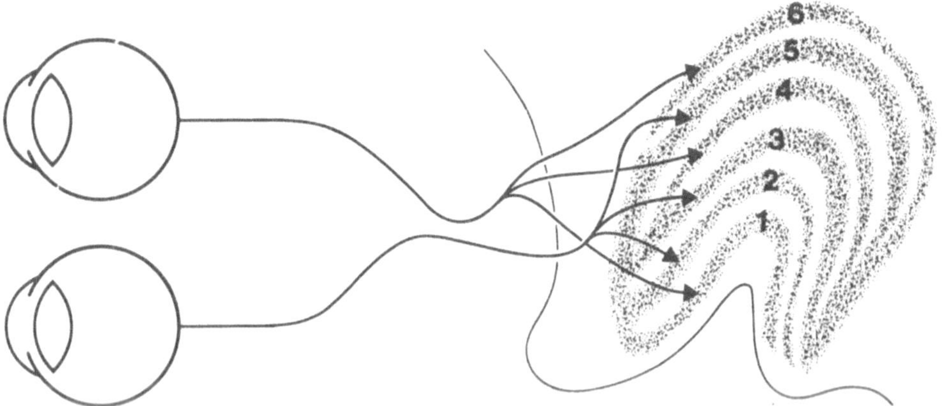

Abb. 16a Schema der 6 Nervenzellschichten des Corpus geniculatum laterale vom Rhesusaffen und die Projektion der Axone aus dem contralateralen und ipsilateralen Auge in diese 6 Schichten.
Abb. 16b Reaktionsmuster eines On-Zentrum-Neurons im CGL der Katze, das durch Bewegung eines weißen Kreises durch das receptive Feld ausgelöst wurde. Stärkere Grenzkontrastaktivierung im Vergleich zur Reaktion retinaler Neurone (Abb. 15b). Abszisse: Reizposition relativ zum receptiven Feld (EYSEL und GRÜSSER, 1968).

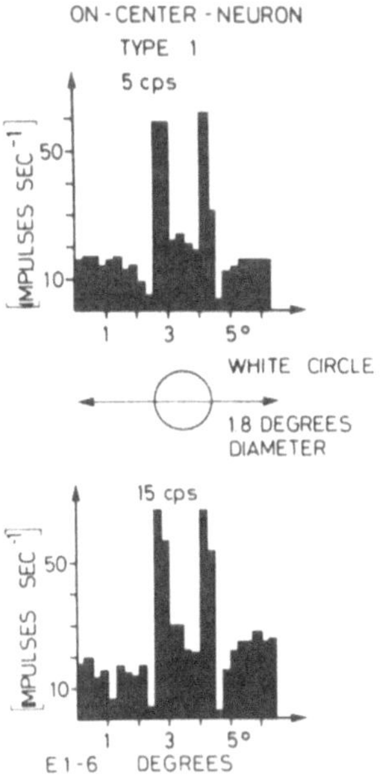

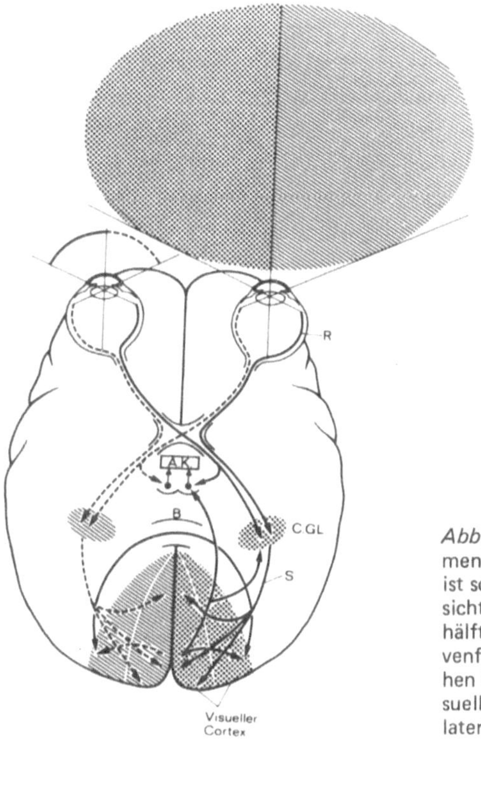

Abb. 17 Schema des Verlaufs der zentralen Sehbahn im menschlichen Gehirn. Das Gesichtsfeld des rechten Auges ist schematisch eingezeichnet. Die linke Hälfte des Gesichtsfeldes bildet sich jeweils auf der rechten Netzhauthälfte des rechten und des linken Auges ab. Die Sehnervenfasern aus der rechten Netzhauthälfte jedes Auges ziehen in die rechte Gehirnhälfte. Von den subcorticalen visuellen Zentren des Gehirns sind das Corpus geniculatum laterale und die Colliculi superiores eingezeichnet.

sche Projektion ist hierbei jedoch – im Unterschied zu den meisten Landkarten – *nichtlinear* verzerrt. Der kleine Bereich der *Fovea centralis* – also der Bereich der Stelle schärfsten Sehens – projiziert sich auf einen relativ großen Teil des CGL und der Sehrinde, während die Projektion der Netzhautperipherie im Verhältnis dazu einen geringeren Raum einnimmt. Wie oben schon erwähnt wurde, ist die Receptordichte (und auch die Dichte der Ganglienzellen) für den Bereich der Fovea centralis wesentlich größer als für die periphere Retina. Die verstärkte neuronale Repräsentation der Fovea centralis in der Sehrinde entspricht auch ihrer Aufgabe: Mit der Fovea centralis werden differenzierte Operationen der *Gestaltwahrnehmung* ausgeführt, während die Verarbeitung der Signale aus der Netzhautperipherie vor allem dazu dient, neu in das Gesichtsfeld eintretende Objekte wahrzunehmen und Augenbewegungen zu diesen neuen Objekten hinzusteuern.

(b) Die funktionelle Architektonik der Sehrinde. Die Nervenzellen in der Sehrinde sind wie in den meisten Gebieten der Großhirnrinde in 6 deutlich unterscheidbare Schichten *parallel* zur Großhirnoberfläche gegliedert (Abb. 18). Die afferenten Axone aus dem CGL endigen in allen Schichten, besonders dicht jedoch in der Schicht IV, die in die Unterschichten a, b, c unterteilt wird. Der Haupterregungszufluß aus dem CGL erfolgt nach Schicht IVc, in der die Verarbeitung der Signale für das rechte und linke Auge fast vollständig noch getrennt ist. Die Nervenzellen dieser Schicht werden also nur monocular aktiviert. An Neuronen der anderen Schichten endigen zwar ebenfalls synaptische Kontakte der Axone aus dem CGL, jedoch erreicht der größere Teil der visuellen Information diese Neurone erst nach der Verarbeitung in den Nervenzellen der Schicht IV. Die Nervenzellen in der Schicht IV haben *einfache receptive Felder*, die entweder denen des Corpus geniculatum laterale sehr ähnlich sind (konzentrische Organisation von RF-Zentrum und RF-Peripherie) oder aus parallel angeordneten On- oder Off-Zonen aufgebaut sind (Abb. 19a).

Neben der horizontalen Organisation der Schichten I bis VI kennt man vor allem durch die ausführlichen Untersuchungen von HUBEL und WIESEL eine *vertikale Organisation* des Neuronensystems der Sehrinde. Zwei Funktionsprinzipien für diese vertikale Organisation wurden bisher näher erforscht:

(α) In regelmäßiger Folge wechseln sich im visuellen Cortex *„oculäre Dominanzsäulen"* (*ocular dominance columns*) miteinander ab. Darunter verstehen HUBEL und WIESEL meist schichtförmige Regionen senkrecht zur Cortexoberfläche. Die Nervenzellen in einer oculären Dominanzsäule werden durch die Signale eines Auges stärker erregt als durch die Signale des anderen Auges. Schichten mit einer Dominanz des contralateralen oder des ipsilateralen Auges wechseln sich in regelmäßiger Folge ab (Abb. 20). In jeder oculären Dominanzsäule gibt es jedoch auch einige Nervenzellen, an denen die binoculare Signalkonvergenz derart organisiert ist, daß das linke und rechte Auge etwa eine gleich starke Erregung auslösen.

(ß) Die Nervenzellen der Schichten II, III, V und VI von Area 17 haben überwiegend „komplexe" receptive Felder. Man kann an diesen receptiven Feldern keine On- oder Off-Zonen mehr unterscheiden, findet jedoch, daß die visuellen Reize bestimmte einfache Eigenschaften haben müssen, um eine optimale Aktivierung dieser Nervenzellen auszulösen. Corticale Nervenzellen mit komplexen receptiven Feldern reagieren z.B. nur auf *Hell-Dunkel-Konturen bestimmter Orientierung*, die in einer bestimmten Richtung durch das RF bewegt werden, oder auf *Konturunterbrechungen, Doppelkonturen* oder *Winkel* (Abb. 19). Besonders die Orientierung einer Hell-Dunkel-Grenze scheint ein weiteres wichtiges Merkmal zu sein, das die vertikale Organisation der Nervenzellen im primären visuellen Cortex bestimmt. HUBEL und WIESEL fanden eine regelmäßige Folge von Säulen untereinander liegender Nervenzellen, die alle etwa die gleiche optimale Orientierung eines Lichtreizes innerhalb ihres receptiven Feldes haben (orientation columns). Benachbarte orientation columns zeigen eine systematische Änderung dieser Vorzugsrichtung (Abb. 21). Nervenzellen, die binokular aktiviert werden, haben gleichartige receptive Felder in korrespondierender Lokalisation in dem Gesichtsfeld jedes Auges.

Die Signale aus dem primären visuellen Cortex werden in die benachbarten corticalen Regionen (Area 18, 19) übertragen, in denen eine weitere visuelle Signalverarbeitung stattfindet. Die Nervenzellen dieser Region sind durch eine receptive Feldorganisation zunehmenden Komplexitätsgrades gekennzeichnet. Neuerdings wurden

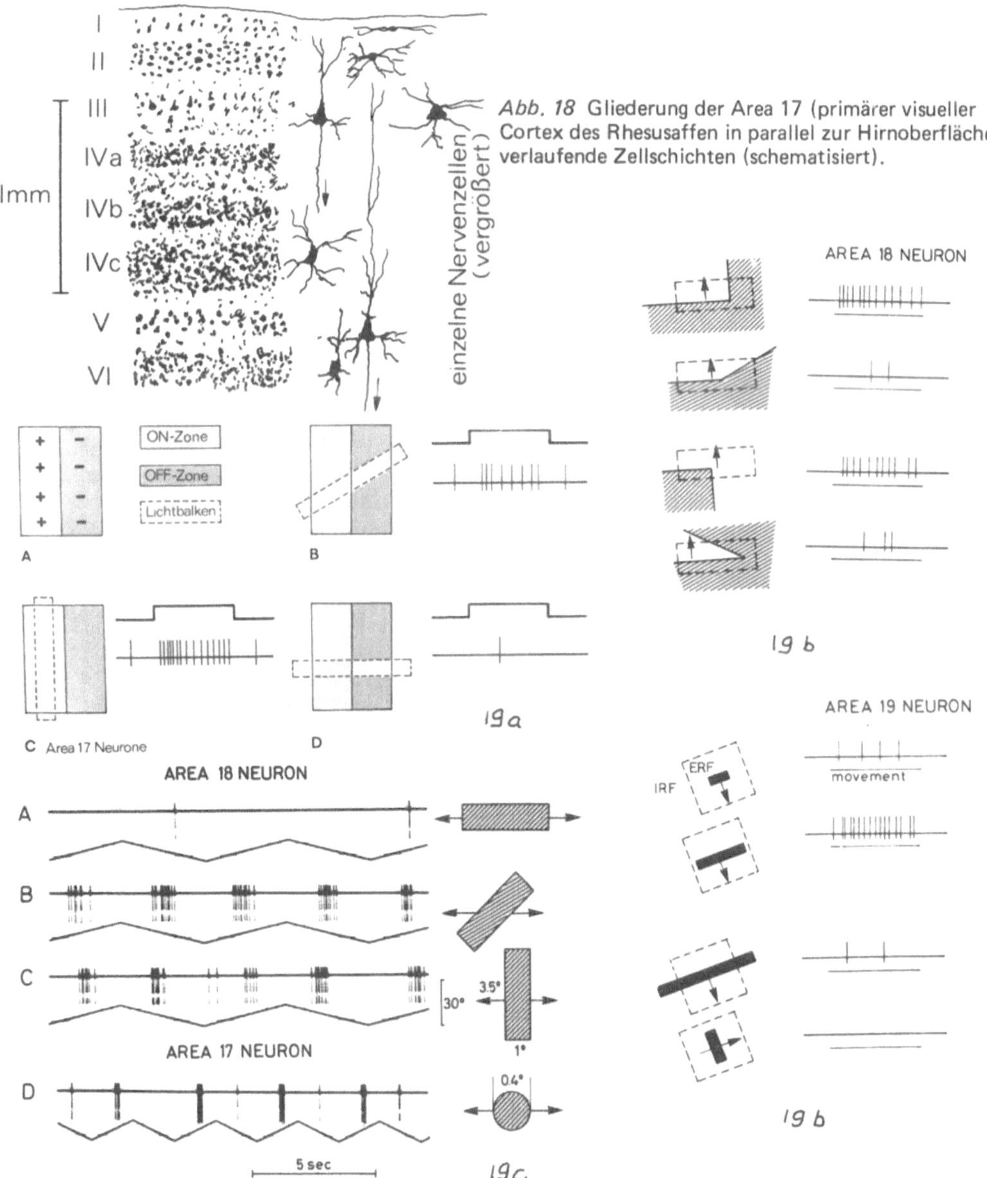

Abb. 18 Gliederung der Area 17 (primärer visueller Cortex des Rhesusaffen in parallel zur Hirnoberfläche verlaufende Zellschichten (schematisiert).

Abb. 19a Funktionelle Organisation eines „einfachen" receptiven Feldes eines Neurons der Schicht IV im primären visuellen Cortex.

Abb. 19b Schema der Reaktion von zwei Neuronen mit „komplexen" receptiven Feldern in der sekundären und tertiären Sehrinde der Katze. Die Aktivierung ist durch eine Zunahme der Frequenz der Aktionspotentiale charakterisiert. Die Nervenzelle A reagiert auf Kontrastbalken bestimmter Orientierung und begrenzter Ausdehnung, die Zelle B auf zwei aufeinanderstoßende Konturen, deren Winkel für die neuronale Aktivierung kritisch ist (schematisiert nach HUBEL und WIESEL).

Abb. 19c Reaktion einer „orientierungsabhängigen" Nervenzelle im sekundären visuellen Cortex der Katze (Area 18) und einer „richtungsabhängigen" Nervenzelle im primären visuellen Cortex. Horizontale Bewegung des Reizmusters.

Area 17 des Rhesusaffen

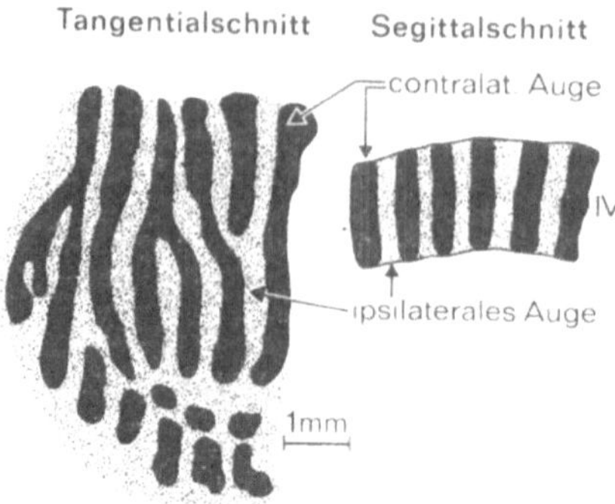

Abb. 20 Schema der Verteilung der oculären Dominanzsäulen in Area 17 des Rhesusaffen nach anatomischen Untersuchungen von HUBEL und WIESEL (1977). Im linken Teil Darstellung eines Tangentialschnittes parallel zur Cortexoberfläche, rechts eines Sagittalschnittes senkrecht zur Cortexoberfläche

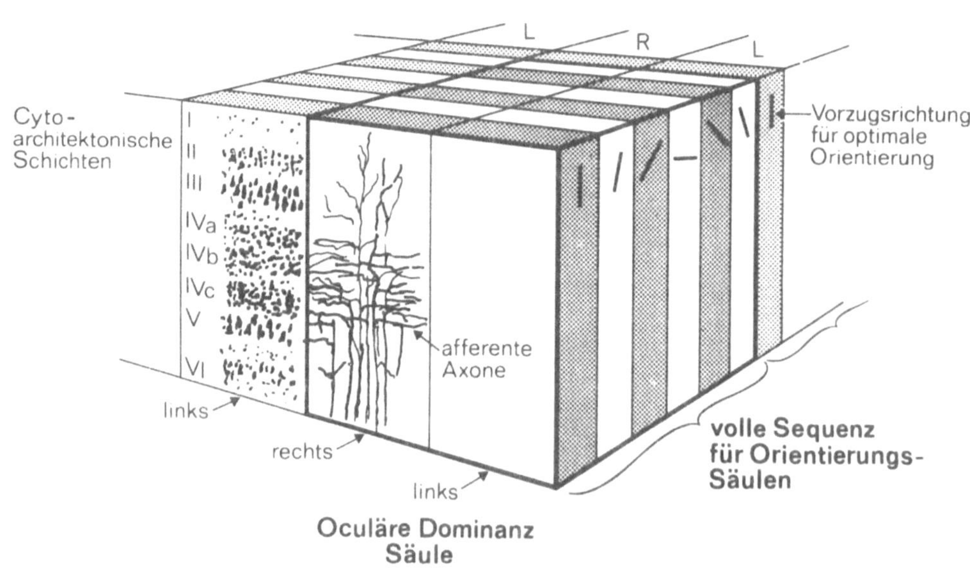

Abb. 21 Regelmäßige Anordnung der „orientation columns" in benachbarten Regionen der Area 17 im Sagittalschnitt (links) und auf die Cortexoberfläche (rechts) projiziert (schematisiert nach HUBEL und WIESEL).

von ZEKI auch cortikale Regionen gefunden, in denen bevorzugt eine Analyse der visuellen Signale nach Farbqualitäten erfolgt.

Die Verarbeitung visueller Signale in der occipitalen Hirnregion soll schematisch anhand des Beispiels der Abb. 22 nochmals zusammenfassend erläutert werden: In diesem Schema sei ein Leuchtbuchstabe „K" für 300 ms auf die Fovea centralis eines Auges projiziert. Während im räumlichen Erregungsmuster der Receptoren der Netzhaut „K" näherungsweise linear geometrisch abgebildet wird, sind die Kontrastgrenzen des „K" im räumlichen Erregungsmuster der Neuronennetze der On-Zentrum- und Off-Zentrum-Neurone der retinalen Ganglienzellschicht und der Nervenzellen des Corpus geniculatum laterale infolge der oben beschriebenen Simultankontrastprozesse bereits verstärkt ausgeprägt. In den Neuronennetzen der Area 17, 18 und 19 ist „K" entsprechend seinen Gestalteigenschaften mehrfach abgebildet, wobei die Richtung der Kontrastgrenzen des „K", die Winkel und die Konturunterbrechungen jeweils zu einer verstärkten Aktivierung bestimmter Neurone führen. Die „Teilbilder" des „K" werden offenbar auf einer späteren Verarbeitungsstufe wieder zu einer einheitlichen Gestalt „zusammengesetzt". Wie dies im einzelnen erfolgt, ist noch unbekannt. Daß solche „Gestalt-generierenden" Prozesse jedoch auch aus unvollständigen Konturen möglich sind, zeigt Abb. 23 vertretungsweise für eine ganze Reihe ähnlicher Phänomene der visuellen Gestaltergänzung. Unvollständige Konturen reichen offensichtlich aus, um in der Wahrnehmung vollständige Gestalten zu erzeugen.

5. Visuelle Gestalterkennung, Objektidentifikation und symbolische Abstraktion

5.1 Neuronale Reaktionen in der parietalen Assoziationsregion

Die Nervenzellen der Sehrinde haben mannigfache Verbindungen mit den integrativen Regionen im Bereich der occipitalen und parietalen Großhirnrinde (Abb. 24). Störungen dieser Hirnregionen bei Menschen infolge von Schädelverletzungen oder einer lokalen Unterbrechung der Blutversorgung („Schlaganfall") können eine Beeinträchtigung der Raumorientierung, der visuellen Objekterkennung, der Objektbenennung, Farbenwahrnehmung und Farbenbenennung und des visuellen Gedächtnisses zur Folge haben. *Mikroelektrodenuntersuchungen* von einzelnen Nervenzellen der parietalen Assoziationsregion (Area 7) des Rhesusaffen haben ergeben, daß diese Nervenzellen *multimodal* erregt werden können: visuelle, akustische oder tactile Reize bewirken eine Aktivierung oder Hemmung der Nervenzellen. Durch chronisch implantierte Mikroelektroden kann man auch am wachen Affen von einzelnen Nervenzellen dieser Assoziationsfelder der Großhirnrinde registrieren, während die Tiere spontane oder erlernte Interaktionen mit Objekten innerhalb des Greifraumes (Abb. 1) ausführen. Abb. 25 zeigt das Schema der Reaktion einer Nervenzelle in Area 7 des wachen Rhesusaffen: Wurde ein für das Tier „interessantes" Objekt in der Nähe der Hand bewegt, so löste diese Bewegung des visuellen Reizes unabhängig von der Augenstellung des Tieres eine Aktivierung der Nervenzelle aus. Blickte das Tier auf das Objekt, so nahm die Aktivierung zu. Die stärkste Aktivierung war zu registrieren, wenn das Tier nach dem Objekt griff und es auch erreichte.

MOUNTCASTLE und Mitarbeiter haben in der parietalen Assoziationsregion der Großhirnrinde des Affen zahlreiche Neurone gefunden, deren Aktivierung von Augenbewegungen abhängig war oder diesen vorausging. Zahlreiche experimentelle Resultate sprechen dafür, daß die Aktivität der Nervenzellen dieser Assoziationsregion von der Intension bzw. Aufmerksamkeit der Versuchstiere abhängig war.

Die Abb. 25 weist ferner darauf hin, daß für die Lage der visuellen receptiven Felder dieser Neurone zum Teil eine Invarianz von der Abbildung auf der Netzhaut gilt: das visuelle receptive Feld des in Abb. 25 gezeigten Neurons blieb an der gleichen Stelle des Raumes, wenn das Tier auf das Objekt blickte (und damit das Bild des Objektes auf der Netzhaut verschob), es bewegte sich jedoch mit der Hand im Raum. Dieser Befund läßt die Hypothese zu, daß die Aktivität solcher Neurone in der parietalen Assoziationsregion der Großhirnrinde das neuronale Substrat für die Repräsentation von Objekten im Greifraum darstellt. Dafür spricht auch die

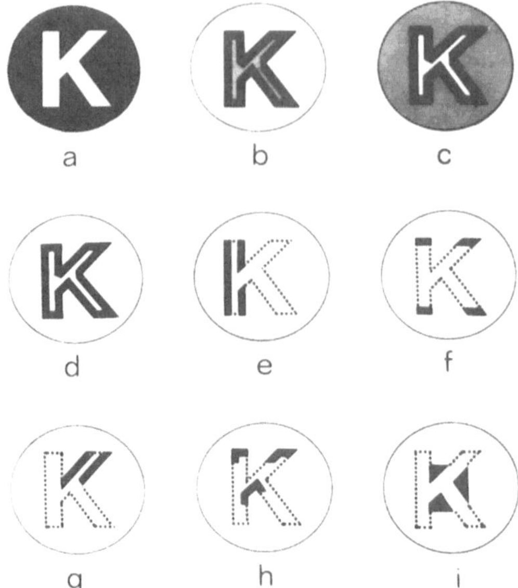

Abb. 22 Schema der Erregungsprozesse, die ein Leuchtbuchstabe „K" in verschiedenen neuronalen Schichten der Netzhaut und des zentralen visuellen Systems auslöst.
a: Bild des Leuchtbuchstaben auf der Netzhaut und räumliches Erregungsmuster in der Receptorschicht der Netzhaut. b und c: Erregungsmuster in der Ausgangsschicht der Netzhaut (Ganglienzellen). In b bis i ist die Erregung durch dunkle Balken charakterisiert, b: On-Neurone, c: Off-Neurone, d: Erregungsmuster in der Neuronenschicht des Corpus geniculatum laterale und einem Teil der Neurone der Sehrinde. Die Konturen des Leuchtbuchstaben lösen eine Erregung der Nervenzellen aus. e bis i: Erregungsmuster in verschiedenen Neuronenschichten von unterschiedlichen Nervenzellklassen in der Sehrinde des Gehirns. Die Nervenzellen werden nur noch durch Konturen bestimmter Orientierung, Winkel- oder Konturenunterbrechungen erregt. Die Darstellung vereinfacht die neurobiologischen Verhältnisse, da die räumliche Verteilung der Erregung in den verschiedenen Nervenzellschichten der Hirnrinde im Verhältnis zum Reizmuster nichtlinear „verzerrt" ist.

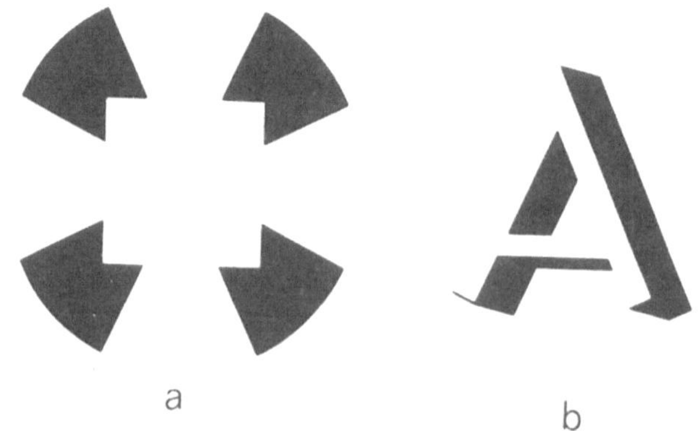

Abb. 23 Beispiele für Gestaltergänzung und Entstehung von „Scheingestalten".
a: Ein weißes Quadrat wird vollständig wahrgenommen, obgleich nur die Ecken des Quadrats als Konturen vorhanden sind.
b: Ein räumlich ausgedehntes „A" wird wahrgenommen, obgleich nur drei gewinkelte schwarze Flächen als Reiz vorhanden sind.

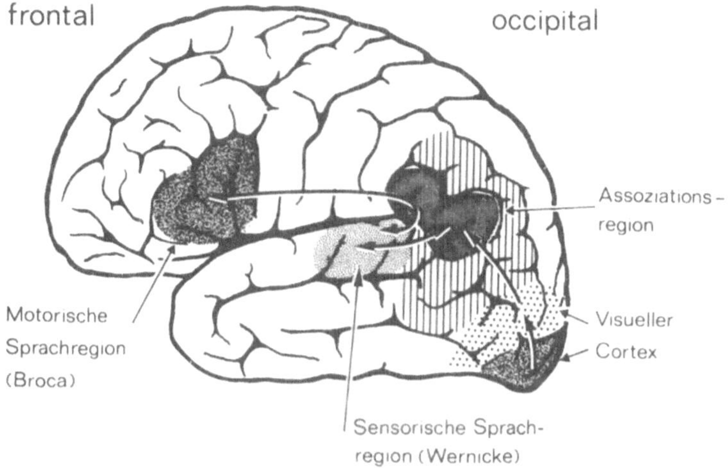

Abb. 24 Dominante (linke) Großhirnhälfte des Menschen. Von den Assoziationsregionen, die zum Teil visuelle Aufgaben haben, ist der Gyrus supramarginalis und Gyrus angularis dunkler und schräg schraffiert, der übrige Teil heller und senkrecht.

multimodale Signalkonvergenz in diesem Neuronensystem, die die neuronale „Objektgeneration" wenigstens teilweise von den einzelnen Sinnesorganen unabhängig macht. Dementsprechend sind die adäquaten Reize für eine optimale Aktivierung dieser Nervenzellen nicht bestimmte Reizqualitäten oder Intensitäten, sondern jeweils reale Objekte, deren Effizienz zur Aktivierung offensichtlich von ihrer *Bedeutung* für das Tier abhängt.

Besteht einerseits in den perceptorischen Systemen die oben geschilderte Hierarchie *analytischer Operationen*, die eine vielfache Abbildung der Objekte nach Gestaltmerkmalen im Erregungsmuster neuronaler Netze zur Folge hat, so kann man andererseits auch eine ähnliche Hierarchie sequentieller *synthetischer Operationen* als Leistung der multimodalen Assoziations- und Integrationsregionen der Großhirnrinde postulieren. Deren neurobiologische Leistung ist ein mehrstufiger Signalverarbeitungsprozeß, der schließlich zur Objektinvarianz führt, wobei von Qualitäten und Intensität der Reize weitgehend „abstrahiert" wird.

5.2 Neurobiologie sprachähnlicher Leistungen

Die entwicklungsgeschichtlich jüngsten Leistungen dieser neuronalen Abstraktionsprozesse sind die Sprachfunktionen. An die Stelle der neuronalen Repräsentation von Objekten tritt in den Neuronensystemen, welche für die Sprache und sprachähnliche Funktionen zuständig sind, die Repräsentation von Zeichen, Zeichenfolgen und Zeichenkomplexen auf, die entweder visuell (Lesen-Schreiben) oder auditorisch (Hören-Sprechen) verarbeitet werden. Diese in der Entwicklungsgeschichte des Gehirns erst im Übergangsfeld des Hominiden zum Menschen erworbenen Leistungen sind wie die meisten mit der Sprache oder sprachähnlichen psychologischen Leistungen verknüpften Funktionen in der *dominanten Hälfte* der Großhirnrinde lokalisiert. Für die meisten Rechtshänder und etwa ein Drittel der Linkshänder ist dies die linke Großhirnhälfte (Abb. 24).

Bis vor kurzem hat man geglaubt, daß die eng mit allgemeinen Sprachfunktionen verknüpften Abstraktionsstufen der visuellen Signalverarbeitung (Verstehen von abstrakten Zeichen und Satzstrukturen aus visuellen Zeichen) nur dem Menschen zukommen. In den letzten 10 Jahren wurden jedoch außerordentlich überraschende Befunde über sprachähnliche Leistungen bei Schimpansen erhoben, die eine gewisse Revision dieser Auffassung erforderlich machen. Diese Tiere sind auf Grund des Baues ihres Kehlkopfes, Rachens und Gau-

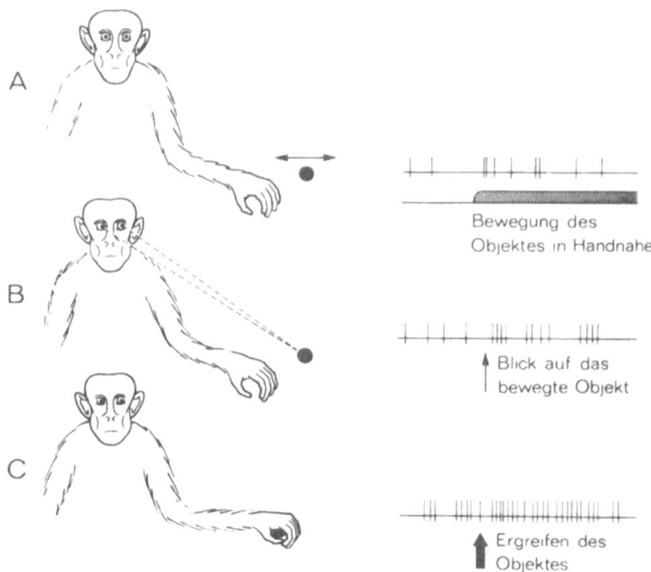

Abb. 25 Schema der Reaktion eines Neurons in Area 7 des wachen Rhesusaffen. A: In der Nähe der Hand, also im Greifraum, wird ein Objekt (z.B. eine Nuß) bewegt. Die Objektbewegung löst eine Aktivierung (Zunahme der Impulsfrequenz) des Neurons aus.
B: Das Tier blickt auf das Objekt, die Impulsfrequenz steigt an.
C: Das Tier greift nach dem Objekt, sehr starke Aktivierung. (Nach unveröffentlichten Untersuchungen von BÜTTNER, GRÜSSER und HENN, 1975.)

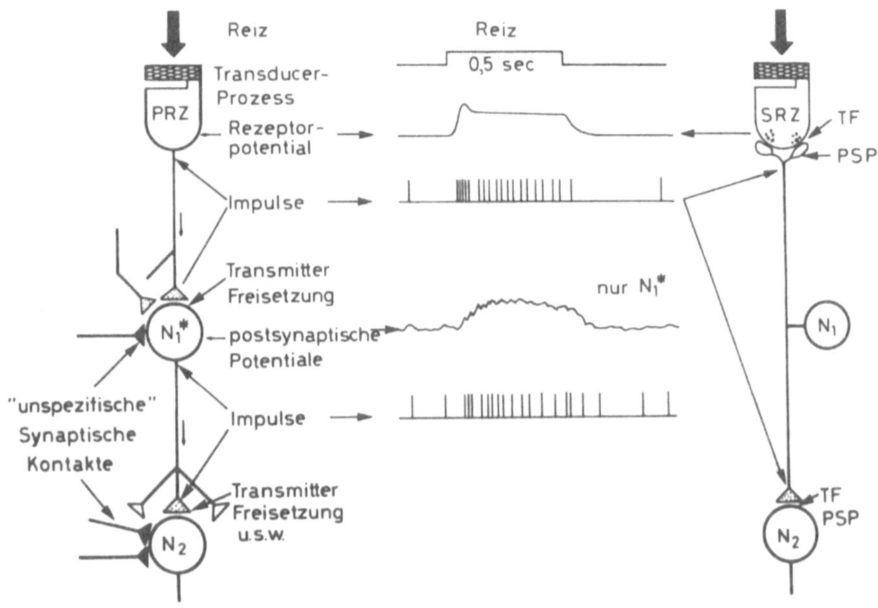

Zusammenfassende Darstellung der Signalerarbeitung durch Nervenzellen

mens nur sehr begrenzt überhaupt in der Lage, artikulierte Laute zu produzieren (s. VAN LAVICK-GOODALL, 1971). Nur im Märchen sind Affen zu artikulatorischen Leistungen befähigt, die sich der menschlichen Sprache annähern (Wilhelm Hauff: „Der Affe als Mensch" in „Der Scheik von Alessandria und seine Sklaven", 1827). Aufgrund des Mangels der zum Sprechen erforderlichen Artikulationsfähigkeit hat man bis vor kurzem geglaubt, daß daher auch die eng mit allgemeinen Sprachfunktionen verknüpften Abstraktionsprozesse der visuellen Signalverarbeitung beim Schimpansen nicht vorhanden seien. Die im folgenden geschilderten Befunde aus drei amerikanischen Arbeitsgruppen zeigen jedoch, daß Schimpansen in der Lage sind, mit schriftähnlichen Zeichen sinnvoll umzugehen, eine ideographische „Schrift" zu erlernen und einfache grammatikalische Strukturen richtig anzuwenden.

R.A. und B.T. GARDNER haben einen Schimpansen erfolgreich in der Anwendung eines Teils der Zeichensprache für Taubstumme unterrichtet. Das Tier kommunizierte mit Hilfe dieser Zeichen mit den Experimentatoren und drückte Wünsche und Bedürfnisse aus, soweit diese durch das Zeichenrepertoire darstellbar waren. Wichtig war, daß auf einer bestimmten Entwicklungsstufe neue, sinnvolle Sätze und Begriffe gebildet wurden.

A.J. und D. PREMACK benützten Plättchen verschiedener Form und Farbe als Symbole (Schriftzeichen) für Gegenstände in der Welt des Schimpansen und für einfache sprachliche Operationen. Diese Schriftzeichen wurden auf einer magnetischen „Schreibtafel" zu Sätzen angeordnet. Nach dem Erlernen der Schriftzeichen und des Umgangs mit denselben (enthalten waren im Repertoire z.B. ein Zeichen für das Tier selbst, Ideogramme für Futter und einfache Gegenstände, Verben und Beziehungswörter) „schrieben" die Tiere neue Sätze, um ihre Bedürfnisse auszudrücken. Auch in diesen Versuchen wurden durch neue Kombinationen der Schriftzeichen neue sinnvolle Begriffe für Objekte spontan durch das Versuchstier „erfunden".

D.M. RUMBAUGH und seine Mitarbeiter haben schließlich ein computer-gesteuertes Schreib- und Lesesystem aus 125 verschiedenen Zeichen entwickelt, durch die eine Interaktion zwischen dem Tier und den Experimentatoren möglich war und dem Tier die Kontrolle über einen futtergebenden Automaten, das Öffnen eines Fensters, Betrachten von Diapositiven usw. gegeben wurde. Es wurde eine im Computer eindeutig abbildbare Sprache mit Ideogrammen (Abb. 26) und syntaktische Regeln formuliert, die zu Ehren des amerikanischen Primatenforschers Yerkes „Yerkish" genannt wurde. Diese Sprache hatte alle formalen Eigenschaften einer einfachen menschlichen Sprache. Schon nach Erlernen einiger Grundregeln und Symbole für Objekte und Handlungszusammenhänge bildete das Tier neue Sätze, was darauf hinwies, daß es den sprachlichen Abstraktionsvorgang begriffen hatte. Der Vorteil dieser Versuchsserien war die Objektivität, mit der die Interaktionen zwischen Experimentator und Tier über das Schreibsystem (Tastenfeld) und das Lesesystem (Feld, in dem die von dem Tier bzw. dem Experimentator zur Kommunikation benutzten Schriftzeichen aufleuchteten) durch den Computer kontrolliert und ausgewertet wurden.

Zur Veranschaulichung gebe ich im folgenden einen Dialog zwischen dem weiblichen Schimpansen als Versuchstier (Lana) und dem Trainer (Tim) wieder. Das Tier kannte den Namen für Apfelsine nicht, hatte jedoch eine Anzahl von Farbnamen erlernt und diese, sowie auch Namen für Ball und Apfel richtig in anderen Zusammenhängen vielfach benützt. Es kannte Apfelsinen als Teil des nicht über den Futterautomaten gegebenen Futters. Der Dialog begann, als der Trainer, für das Tier sichtbar eine Apfelsine in der Hand hatte. „Orange" bedeutet im Dialog der Name für die entsprechende Farbe. „?" hat im Dialog die Bedeutung von „Bitte".

LANA: ? Tim give which-is orange.
TIM: What which-is orange?
LANA: ? Tim give apple which-is green. (Die Farben orange und grün wurden häufig verwechselt)
TIM: No apple which-is green.
LANA: ? Tim give apple which-is orange.
TIM: Yes. (Lana erhielt auf die von ihr erfundene „richtige" Bezeichnung „apple which is orange" die Apfelsine und benützte später weiterhin diesen Begriff für Apfelsine). (nach RUMBAUGH, 1977).

Zeichen - Elemente

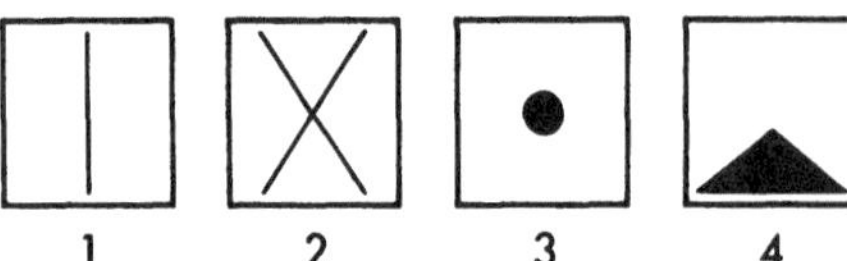

1 2 3 4

Lexigramme

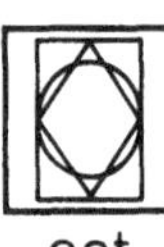

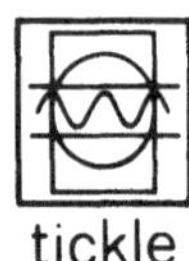

Abb. 26 Elemente und ideographische Zeichen (Lexigramme), die in den Lese- und Schreibexperimenten mit der Schimpansin Lana benützt wurden. Sätze mit maximal 6 (aus 125) Lexigrammen waren möglich und mußten mit einem „period"-Zeichen jeweils abgeschlossen werden, um „gültig" zu sein (nach RUMBAUGH, 1977).

5.3 Schlußfolgerung

Diese Beispiele zeigen nach meiner Einschätzung überzeugend, daß auch im Gehirn höherer Primaten Abstraktionsprozesse, die über die einfache Objekterkennung hinausgehen,möglich sind. Damit besteht für die experimentelle Neurophysiologie für die fernere Zukunft die Chance, die neuronalen Strukturen solcher Prozesse auch auf der Ebene einzelner cortikaler Nervenzellen untersuchen zu können.

Aufgrund von Beobachtungen an Patienten mit Lese- und Sprachstörungen nach Läsionen im Bereich der temporalen, parietalen und frontalen Region der dominanten Großhirnrinde kann man jedoch auch heute schon einige Hypothesen über die Neurobiologie sprachähnlicher Abstraktionsprozesse machen:

(a) Objekte und Sachverhalte sind nicht durch die Aktivität *einzelner* Nervenzellen repräsentiert. Es gibt also keine Neurone, die als Klasse eine bestimmte Universalie abbilden.

(b) Objekte und Sachverhalte sind durch die neuronale Aktivität großer, vermutlich über weite Regionen des Gehirns zerstreuter Netze aus Nervenzellen repräsentiert.

(c) Für ein gegebenes Objekt (z.B. den Apfel der Abb. 3) ist der Erregungszustand in dem dafür „zuständigen" Neuronennetz keineswegs konstant, sondern nur näherungsweise ähnlich.

(d) Für die symbolische Repräsentation verschiedener Objekte oder Begriffe sind vermutlich häufig die gleichen Neuronensysteme zuständig. Unterschiedliche sprachliche Begriffe sind somit durch unterschiedliche Erregungsverteilungen in einem ausgedehnten Neuronennetz der Sprachregionen der Hirnrinde gekennzeichnet.

(e) Aufgrund der Resultate von Untersuchungen an Patienten mit Sprachstörungen (sensorische oder motorische Aphasie) kann postuliert werden, daß ein Ausfall eines Teils der für sprachliche Funktionen zuständigen Hirnregion durch „Umwege" über andere Regionen kompensierbar ist; diese Umwege lassen sich an den verlängerten Entscheidungszeiten für bestimmte sprachliche oder komplexe nichtsprachliche Leistungen erkennen.

Vorausgesetzt, daß ich mich bei der Deutung der neurobiologischen Befunde aus den Assoziationsregionen der Großhirnrinde und den neuropsychologischen Befunden an hirngeschädigten Patienten nicht ganz erheblich irre, so folgt aus dem eben Gesagten, daß die reduktionistische Methode der klassischen Sinnesphysiologie, die sich bei der analytischen Funktion in den Sinnesorganen und in den perceptorischen Systemen des Gehirns als vorzügliches Instrument zur Erforschung der Signalverarbeitung im Nervensystem erwiesen hat, bei der Erforschung der synthetischen (integrativen) Prozesse der Informationsverarbeitung im Gehirn ungeeignet ist. Für die Zukunft wird es eine reizvolle Aufgabe der Neurophysiologie sein, für diese Probleme eine gedanklich klare Experimentalmethode zu entwickeln, die zu experimentell überprüfbaren (falsifizierbaren) Ergebnissen und Modellen führt.

6. Summary

Principles of the neuronal information processing in the sense organs and the brain

(a) Using the visual system as an example, the signal processing properties of receptors, nerve cells and neuronal nets are described. A general scheme of the properties of object and space perception is provided. The extrapersonal space is divided into four regions: the grasping space, the nearby action space, the distant action space and the visual background (Fig. 1). Active motor components are shown to be essential determinants of the multimodal object perception (Fig. 3).

(b) It is demonstrated that the classical „analytical" approach of sensory physiology leads to useful models of signal processing properties in the receptors and the afferent perceptor systems. Nevertheless, it is a reductionistic technique neglecting some essential components of perception.

(c) Applying this analytical procedure, the signal *transformation* and signal *transduction* in the sense organ is described. Transduction of sensory signals in the *photoreceptors* is an optoelectric process initiated after photons are absorbed by photopigment molecules located in the disk-shaped structures of the photoreceptor outer segments (Fig. 5). About 1 to 3 ms after absorption of a photon, metarhodopsin I is transformed into metarhodopsin II and Ca^{++} is released during the confirmation change of the molecules.

(d) The activated Ca^{++} probably reaches the receptor cell membrane by diffusion and decreases the conductivity of the plasma membrane for Na^{+}. This leads to the hyperpolarizing receptor potential (late receptor potential, LRP), with a latency > 8 ms in cones and > 30 ms in rods (Fig. 7). The confirmational changes of the photopigment molecules, on the other hand, lead to a shift in charges across the photopigment layers and thus induce the early receptor potential (ERP) with a latency < 0.05 ms (Fig. 6).

(e) The LRP of the single photoreceptors controls the transmitter release at the synaptic contacts between photoreceptors and bipolar cells or horizontal cells (Fig. 8, 10).

(f) The neuronal signal processing initiated by this transmitter release is described. Bipolar cells, horizontal cells and amacrines are neurons of the retina which process signals mainly by changes in the slow membrane potential. A receptive field organization with a spatially antagonistic structure appears at the level of bipolar cells (Fig. 10, 11).

(g) The output signals of the retina are sequences of action potentials generated at the axon hillocks of retinal ganglion cells. These impulses are conducted along the optic nerve axons to the subcortical visual centers. An essential property of the retinal signal processes is the multiple mapping of the receptor signals into different classes of neurons (on-center neurons and off-center neurons of the black-white system, red-green neurons, yellow-blue neurons of the colour-specific system). Substantial accomplishments of the retinal network are the simultaneous contrast effects, which can be explained by the antagonistic organization of retinal receptive fields (Figs. 12, 14, 15).

(h) The signal processing in the lateral geniculate body and the visual cortices (Area 17, 18, 19) located in the occipital region of the cerebral cortex is described. There exists a non-linear mapping of the retinal surface onto the surface of the visual cortex. The functional architecture of the visual cortex is discussed: 6 cytoarchitectonic laminae parallel to the surface (Fig. 10) and at least two vertical columnar organizations were found. The vertical columns are organized into ocular dominance columns, whereby slabs of neurons are activated predominantly by the contralateral or alternately by the ipsilateral eye. Besides the ocular dominance columns, a second vertical columnar organization was found by HUBEL and WIESEL. These are columns of orientation of the optimal stimulating contrast border moving through the respective receptive fields of cortical neurons (orientation columns). The optimal orientation changes regularly within a ,,hypercolumn'' consisting of orientation and ocular dominance columns (Fig. 20,21).

(i) The receptive field properties of cortical neurons are, except for layer IV, rather different from the concentric center-surround receptive fields of retinal or geniculate body neurons. Elongated receptive fields with separate on- and off-zones (simple receptive fields) are found as well as ,,complex'' receptive fields. To activate neurons with complex receptive fields, moving contrast borders with a specific orientation or even two contrast borders are necessary (Fig. 19).
The result of these neuronal operations within the visual cortex is a multiple mapping according to elementary Gestalt-properties. This is illustrated by Fig. 22.

(j) The information from the visual cortex is projected to higher order association and integration cortices located in the parieto-occipital or parietal region of the cerebral cortex. Microelectrode recordings from these regions in rhesus monkeys revealed the existence of neurons activated by ,,interesting'' objects moving in the grasping space. The activity of many of these parietal association cortex neurons depends on visual, auditory and tactile input as well as on eye and hand movements.

(k) It is assumed that beyond the visual cortices, the visual information is integrated into signal processing properties of neural networks which are described as ,,synthetic'' in contrast to the multiple mapping properties of the afferent visual system, revealing ,,analytical'' functions.
A further step in synthetic neuron networks is attributed to the regions of the cortex which serve language or language-similar functions. Experiments in chimpanzees are described which demonstrated that the visual input is used to characterize language by ideograms. It is therefore conjectured that the basis of language-similar functions will in future be accessible to neurophysiological studies at the single neuron level.
Finally, some observations in patients with aphasia are mentioned, indicating that object recognition and object naming are not properties of single neurons but of large neuronal networks. The difference in recognition of different objects (universals) is considered not to be the activity of different classes of neurons attributed to one respective universal, but rather a functional change of the activity level in a large network of neurons distributed over a considerable part of the cerebral cortex in the dominant half of the brain.

7. Literaturhinweise

Kapitel 1:

(1) Eckmiller, R., Galley, N. und Grüsser, O.-J.: Neurobiologische und nachrichtentechnische Grundlagen des Lesens. In: ,,Lesen und Leben'', Herausgeber: H.G. Göpfert, R. Meyer, L. Muth und W. Ruegg, Buchhändlervereinigung GmbH: Frankfurt a.M. 1975, p. 36-81.
(2) H. Ghazarian und O.-J. Grüsser: Unveröffentlichte Untersuchungen, 1977.
(3) H. Ghazarian-Singerdi und O.-J. Grüsser: Unveröffentlichte Untersuchungen, 1978.
(4) Grüsser, O.-J.: Neurobiologische Grundlagen der Zeichenerkennung. In: Zeichenprozesse, Hrsg.: R. Posner und H.P. Reinecke, Akademische Verlagsgesellschaft Athenaion: Wiesbaden 1977, p. 13-45.
(5) Hensel, H.: Allgemeine Sinnesphysiologie, Hautsinne, Geschmack, Geruch. Berlin-Heidelberg-New York: Springer 1966.
(6) Helmholtz, H. von: Handbuch der Physiologischen Optik, Hamburg, Leipzig: L. Voss, 1866 (1896).
(7) Sechenov, I.: The elements of thought (1878), übersetzt in ,,The lectured works'', E.J. Bonset, Amsterdam 1968.
(8) Yarbus, A.L.: Eye movements and vision. New York: Plenum Press, 1967.

Kapitel 2:

(9) Baylor, D.A. und M.G.F. Fuortes: Electrical responses of single cones in the retina of the turtle. J. Physiol. **207**, 77-92 (1970).

(10) Daemen, F.J.M.: Vertebrate rod outer segment membranes. Biochemica et Biophysica Acta **300**, 255-288 (1973).

(11) Dartnall, H.J.A. (Hrsg.): Photochemistry of Vision. Handbook of Sensory Physiology, Vol. VII/1 Springer: Berlin-Heidelberg-New York, 1972, 810 p.

(12) Ehrhardt, W. und Ch. Baumann: The spatial distribution of currents in the receptor layer of the frog retina. Biol. Cybernetics **25**, 155-162 (1977).

(13) Emrich, H.M. und R. Reich: Über Primärreaktionen beim Sehvorgang. Z. Naturforsch. **29c**, 577-591 (1974).

(13a) Emrich, H.M. und R. Reich: The effect of Ca^{2+} on the metarhodopsin I/II transition. I. Experiments. Pflügers Arch. Europ. J. Physiol. **364**, 17-21 (1976).

(14) Emrich, H.M. und R. Reich: Indication of the metarhodopsin I/II transition by absoption changes of eriochromblack T. Biophys. Struct. Mechanism **2**, 371-333 (1977).

(15) Hagins, W.A., Penn, R.D. und Yoshikami, S.: Dark current and photocurrent in retinal rods. Biophys. J. **10**, 380-412 (1970).

(16) Kaneko, A.: Physiological studies of single retinal cell and their morphological identification. Vision Res. Suppl. **3**, p. 17-26 (1971).

(17) Langer, H. (Hrsg.): Biochemistry and physiology of visual pigments. Springer: Berlin-Heidelberg-New York, 1973, 366 p.

(17a) Pak, W. und R.A. Cone: Isolation and identification of the initial peak of the early receptor potential. Nature **204**, 836-838 (1964).

(18) Reich, R. und Emrich, H.M.: The effect of Ca^{2+} on the metarhodopsin I/II transition. II. Model calculations and hypothesis on a molecular mechanism of visual excitation. Pflügers Arch. Europ. J. Physiol. **364**, – (1976).

(19) Tomita, T.: Electrical response of single photoreceptors. Proc. IEE **56**, 1015-1023 (1968).

(20) Whitten, D.N. and K.T. Brown: The time courses of late receptor potentials from monkey cones and rods. Vision Res. **13**, 107-135 (1973).

Kapitel 3:

(21) Baumgartner, G. und Hakas, P.: Neurophysiologie des simultanen Helligkeitskontrastes. Pflügers Arch. **274**, 489-504 (1962).

(22) Dowling, J.E.: Organization of vertebrate retinas. Invest. Ophthal. **9**, 655-680 (1970).

(23) Eccles, J.C.: The physiology of synapses. Springer: Berlin-Göttingen-Heidelberg 1964, 316 p.

(24) Famiglietti, E.V. und H. Kolb: Structural basis for on- and off-center responses in retinal ganglion-cells. Science **194**, 193-195 (1976).

(25) Foerster, M.H., van de Grind, W.A. und O.-J. Grüsser: Frequency transfer properties of three distinct types of cat horizontal cells. Exp. Brain Res. **29**, 347-366 (1977).

(26) Foerster, M.H., van de Grind, W.A. und O.-J. Grüsser: The response of cat horizontal cells to flicker stimuli of different area, intensity and frequency. Exp. Brain Res. **29**, 367-385 (1977).

(27) Grüsser, O.-J.: Informationstheorie und die Signalverarbeitung in den Sinnesorganen und im Nervensystem. Naturwissenschaften **59**, 436-447 (1972).

(28) Grüsser, O.-J. und U. Grüsser-Cornehls: Neurophysiology of the anuran visual system. In: Frog Neurobiology (R. Linas und W. Precht, Hrsg.) Springer: Berlin-Heidelberg-New York, 297-385 (1976).

(29) Grüsser, O.-J., Hellner, K.A. und Grüsser-Cornehls, U.: Die Signalübertragungen im afferenten visuellen System. Kybernetik **1**, 175-192 (1962).

(30) Grüsser-Cornehls, U. und Himstedt, W.: The urodele visual system. In: The amphibian visual system. A multidiciplinary approach. Academic Press: New York, San Francisco, London, p. 203-266 (1976).

(31) Grüsser-Cornehls, U. und R.McD. Saunders: Unveröffentlichte Untersuchungen, 1975-1977.

(32) Kuffler, S.W.: Discharge pattern and functional organization of mammalian retina. J. Neurophysiol. **16**, 37-68 (1953).

(33) Schmitt, R.F. und G. Thews (Hrsg.): Einführung in die Physiologie des Menschen, 18. Aufl. Springer: Berlin-Heidelberg-New York, 1977, 721 p.

(34) Svaetichin, G.: Spectral response curves from single cones. Acta Physiol. Scand. **39**, Supl. **134**, 17-46 (1956).

Kapitel 4:

(35) Grüsser, O.-J. und Grüsser-Cornehls, U.: Neurophysiologie des Bewegungssehens. Bewegungsempfindliche und richtungsspezifische Neurone im visuellen System. Erg. Physiol. **61**, 178-265 (1969).

(36) Grüsser, O.-J. und R. Klinke (Hrsg.): Zeicherkennung durch biologische und technische Systeme. Berlin-Heidelberg-New York: Springer 1971.

(37) Jung, R. (Hrsg.): Central processing of visual information. A.: Integrative function and comparative data. Handbook of visual physiology. Band VII/3a Berlin-Heidelberg-New York: Springer, 1973.

(38) Hubel, D.H. und Wiesel, T.N.: Receptive fields and functional architecture in two non-striate visual areas (18 and 19) of the cat. J. Neurophysiol. **28**, 229-289 (1965).
(39) Hubel, D.H. und Wiesel, T.N.: Receptive fields and functional architecture of monkey striate cortex. J. Physiol. (Lond.) **195**, 215-243 (1968).
(40) Hubel, D.H. und Wiesel, T.N.: The uniformity of monkey striate cortex: a parallel relationship between field size, scatter and magnification factor. J. Comp. Neurol. **158**, 295-306 (1974).
(41) Hubel, D.H. und Wiesel, T.N.: Functional architecture of macaque monkey visual cortex. Proc. R. Soc. Lond. B. **198**, 1-59 (1977).
(42) Spekreijse, H. und L.H. van der Tweel (Hrsg.): Spatial contrast. North Holland Publishing Company: Amsterdam 1977.
(43) Zeki, S.M.: Convergent input from the striate cortex (Area 17) to the cortex of the superior temporal sulcus in the rhesus monkey. Brain Res. **28**, 338-340 (1971).
(44) Zeki, S.M.: The projections to the superior temporal sulcus from area 17 and 18 in the rhesus monkey. Proc. R. Soc. Lond. (Biol.), **193**, 199-207, 1975.

Kapitel 5:

(45) Gardner, R.A. und Gardner, B.T.: Teaching sign language to a chimpanzee. Science **165**, 664-672 (1969).
(46) Hyvärinen, J. and Poranen, A.: function of the parietal association area 7 as revealed from cellular discharges in alert monkeys. Brain **97**, 673-692 (1972).
(47) Lynch, J.C., Mountcastle, V.B., Talbot, W.H. und Yin, T.C.T.: Parietal lobe mechanisms for directed visual attention. J. Neurophysiol. **40**, 362-389 (1977).
(48) Mountcastle, V.B., Lynch, J.C., Georgopoulos, A., Sakata, H. und Acuna, C.: Posterior parietal association cortex of the monkey: Command functions for operations within extrapersonal space. J. Neurophysiol. 871-907, 1975.
(49) Premack, D.: On the assessment of language competence in the schimpanzee. In A.M. Schrier und F. Stollnitz (Hrsg.): Behavior of non-human primates: modern research trends. Vol. 4, Academic Press, New York, 1971.
(50) Premack, D.: Intelligence in ape and man. 1977
(51) Rumbaugh, D.M.: Language Learning by a Chimpanzee: the Lana project. Academic Press: New York-San Francisco-London, 1977, 312 p.
(52) Van Lawick-Goodall, J.: Wilde Schimpansen,Rowohlt, Hamburg, 1975.

Unsere eigenen Untersuchungen wurden aus Mitteln des Universitätshaushaltes, durch Sachbeihilfen der Deutsche Forschungsgemeinschaft (Gr 161) und der Stiftung Volkswagenwerk sowie ein ETP-Twinning Grant unterstützt. Frau Priv.Doz. Dr. U. Grüsser-Cornehls und Dr. R. McD. Saunders danke ich für die Einsicht in unpublizierte Resultate, Herrn J. Kröller und Frau Dr. U. Schreiter für ihre Hilfe bei den Experimenten, aus denen Abb. 13 stammt. Für sorgfältige technische Assistenz möchte ich auch an dieser Stelle Frau J. Dames und Frau M. Klingbeil danken.

Unsere wissenschaftlichen Forschungsprojekte wurden erheblich beeinträchtigt durch negative Personalentscheidungen des für die Universitäten zuständigen Senators für Wissenschaft und Forschung des Landes Berlin (Dr. P. Glotz), wodurch mehrere meiner Mitarbeiter arbeitslos wurden. Ich danke diesen Kollegen, daß sie trotz dieser der Forschung schadenden Entscheidungen der zuständigen Behörde ihren Enthusiasmus für die wissenschaftliche Arbeit nicht verloren haben.

Anhang

8. Informationstheorie und Signalverarbeitung im Nervensystem

(a) Codierungsformen neuronaler Impulsmuster

Vor der Anwendung informationstheoretischer Überlegungen zur Deutung der Signalübertragung durch Nervenzellen muß eine Hypothese gebildet werden, welcher *Code* innerhalb des betrachteten Neuronennetzes gültig ist und was als *Zeichen* in einer Impulsfolge aus Aktionspotentialen betrachtet wird. Die experimentellen Neurophysiologen sind heute meist der Auffassung, daß in unterschiedlichen neuronalen Systemen unterschiedliche Codierungsformen gültig sein können.

Abb. 27 zeigt ein Schema der drei hauptsächlich diskutierten Codierungsformen: (1) Binär-Code, (2) Impuls-Intervall-Code, (3) „Impulsfrequenz" bzw. Impulsraten-Code. Die Codierungsformen (2) und (3) können zusätzlichen Einschränkungen unterliegen, etwa derart, daß nur jene Intervalle als informationsübertragende Zeichen eine Rolle spielen, deren Länge unter 5 ms und über 2 ms liegen, oder daß gemittelte Impulsfrequenzen nur dann signalübertragende Zeichen sind, wenn ihre Werte um einen bestimmten Betrag oberhalb der Spontanaktivität liegen. Eine Reihe solcher spezieller neuronaler Codes sind in Tabelle 1 zusammengestellt. Formal lassen sich diese Codes jeweils auf einen Impulsintervall-Code oder einen Impulsraten-Code mit bestimmten Einschränkungen zurückführen. Die dem Code digitaler Rechenanlagen entsprechende Binärcodierung (1) kommt bei der Signalübertragung von Nervenzellen nach allen bisher vorliegenden experimentellen Resultaten nicht vor.

Tabelle 1. Codes, die zeitliche Eigenschaften des neuronalen Impulsmusters verwerten (nach PERKEL und BULLOCK, 1968)

1) Zeitliches Auftreten eines Impulses
   a) Augenblick der Entladung
   b) Phasenkoppelung zwischen Entladung und periodischem Reiz
2) Codes, die Intervallstatistik verwerten
   a) Gewichtete und gemittelte Impulsfrequenzen
   b) Momentane Frequenz (Kehrwert der Einzelintervalle)
   c) Zunahme der Impulsfrequenz oberhalb der spontanen Frequenz
   d) Änderung der Impulsfrequenz in der Zeit
   e) Verhältnis von Entladung und Fehlen von Entladungen in bestimmten Intervallen
   f) Variationskoeffizient der Entladungsfolge
   g) Höhere Momente von Intervallverteilungen
3) Zeitliches Muster einer Impulsfolge
4) Zahl der Impulse oder Dauer einer frequenten Impulsfolge
5) Änderung der Leitungsgeschwindigkeit im Axon

Schon bei den ersten Registrierungen einzelner Neurone (Ableitungen von Axonen peripherer Mechanoreceptoren) haben ADRIAN und ZOTTERMANN, 1926 eine sinnvolle Beziehung zwischen der Reizstärke und der neuronalen Antwort gefunden, wenn sie die Reizstärke mit der *mittleren Impulsrate* korrelierten. Der Impulsraten-Code hat sich seither als außerordentlich brauchbar erwiesen und zur sinnvollen Darstellung experimenteller Daten geführt. Meist wird in einem Experiment die Mittelung auf gleiche Reize wiederholt: es entsteht so ein „Peri-Stimulus-Time-Histogramm" oder „Post-Stimulus-Time-Histogramm" (PSTH, Abb. 13). Dieser Auswertung liegt die Hypothese zugrunde, daß bei der Verarbeitung im Zentralnervensystem eine zeitliche Mittelung der Impulsrate durch einzelne Nervenzellen oder durch ein Netz von Nervenzellen mit einer bestimmten *Zeitkonstante* ausgeführt wird. Aus Gründen der Einfachheit der Auswertungen wird diese Zeitkonstante zu einem *„Integrationsintervall"* t_i vereinfacht, d.h.,die neuronale Impulsfolge wird durch ein zeitliches Fenster betrachtet. Dieses zeitliche Fenster kann entweder kontinuierlich gleiten (dann ist der Computeraufwand bei der Auswertung etwas größer) oder eine Folge diskreter Zeitabschnitte sein. Die erhaltenen Resultate sind meist sehr ähnlich.

Die Informationskapazität eines Neuronenkanals in einem perceptorischen System mit Impulsraten-Code kann durch folgende Grenzen angegeben werden:

$$\frac{1}{t_i} \ \mathrm{ld}\,(d + t_i\, f_{max}) \leqslant IK < \frac{1}{t_i} \ \mathrm{ld}\,(1 + t_i\, f_{max}) \ [\mathrm{bit/s}] \tag{4}$$

wobei $0.4 < d < 0.7$ ist, t_i ist das Integrationsintervall, f_{max} die maximale Impulsrate, die während der Zeit t_i auftreten kann. Die Abschätzung der Gl. (4) geht davon aus, daß die Zeichen sich gerade um einem Impuls pro Integrationsintervall t_i unterscheiden. Dieses ist keineswegs zwingend. Es kann notwendig sein, einen erheblich größeren Zeichen-Abstand anzunehmen, so daß Zeichen durch 2, 3 ... μ Impulse pro t_i sich unterscheiden müssen. Dann folgt aus Gl. (4):

$$IK < \frac{1}{t_i} \ \mathrm{ld} \ \frac{(1 + t_i\, f_{max})}{\mu} \quad [\mathrm{bit/s}] \tag{5}$$

Das Integrationsintervall t_i ist das neurophysiologische Korrelat der in Kap. 1 erwähnten Präsenzzeit, das Moment der alten Sinnesphysiologen.

Betrachtet man die Impulsfolge an einem präsynaptischen Eingang zu einer Nervenzelle, also auf einem afferenten Axon, das synaptische Kontakte mit der Nervenzelle hat, deren Impulsfolge ebenfalls registriert wird, so kann man für diesen Neuronenkanal den Transinformationsfluß T* bestimmen. Er entspricht in der Kopplung der beiden betrachteten Neurone der *Nutzinformation*, die am Ausgang der Nervenzelle durch *Störinformation* überlagert wird. Diese Störinformation (*Streuinformationsfluß* H_s) ist der Ausdruck spontaner Schwankungen des Membranpotentials einer Nervenzelle und des Einflusses der nicht betrachteten synaptischen Kontakte an der Nervenzelle.

In ähnlicher Form kann man auch den Informationsfluß zwischen dem Signal (z.B. einem weißen Lichtrauschen mit Gauss'scher Amplitudenverteilung (Abb. 13)) und dem Impulsmuster einzelner Nervenzellen der Netzhaut oder des Corpus geniculatum laterale bestimmen. Wendet man hierzu wie ECKHORN und PÖPEL die Entropie-Funktion an,

$$\begin{aligned} T = \text{Transinformation} = &- \sum_{j_0,\dots,j_{n-1}} p(y_{j_0},\dots,y_{j_{n-1}})\,\mathrm{ld}\,p(y_{j_0}|y_{j_1},\dots,y_{j_{n-1}}) \\ &+ \sum_{\substack{j_0,\dots,j_{n-1}\\ i_0,\dots,i_{m-1}}} p(y_{j_0},\dots,y_{j_{n-1}},x_{i_0},\dots,x_{i_{m-1}}) \cdot \mathrm{ld}\,p(y_{j_0}|y_{j_1},\dots,y_{j_{n-1}},x_{i_0},\dots,x_{i_{m-1}})\,. \end{aligned} \tag{6}$$

so läßt sich zunächst frei von Hypothesen über den neuronalen Code der maximal mögliche Informationsfluß einschließlich der Streuinformation bestimmen. Geht man davon aus, daß für die Signalübertragung im afferenten visuellen System ein Impulsintervall-Code gelten würde, so werden nach Gl. (6) 90 Prozent des Informationsflusses durch eine retinale Ganglienzelle Störinformation. Dieser Schluß aus den Messungen von ECKHORN und PÖPEL weist nach meiner Einschätzung darauf hin, daß nicht der Impuls*intervall*-Code, sondern der Impuls*raten*-Code die Signalübertragung im afferenten visuellen System adäquat beschreibt.

(b) Die Änderung der Informationskapazität einer Nervenzelle bei Änderung des Erregungszustandes.

Die Impulsentstehung am Axonhügel einer Nervenzelle kann als ein etwas komplizierter Abtastprozeß betrachtet werden: Überschreitet das Membranpotential die Schwelle zur Entstehung von Aktionspotentialen (Abb. 28), so entsteht ein Impuls. Gleichzeitig erhöht sich jedoch die Schwelle weit über den möglichen Depolarisationsbereich der Membran hinaus und fällt dann näherungsweise hyperbolisch mit der Zeit wieder auf den „Normalwert" ab. „Schneiden" sich Schwellenverlauf und Membranpotential, so entsteht ein neues Aktionspotential. In einigen Systemen kommt es bei diesem Prozeß zu einer sogenannten „Rest-

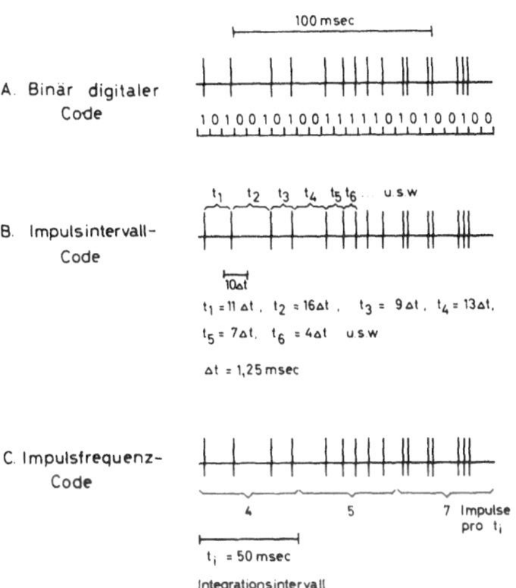

Abb. 27 Schema der verschiedenen Codes, die zur Interpretation des gleichen neuronalen Impulsmusters benutzt werden können.

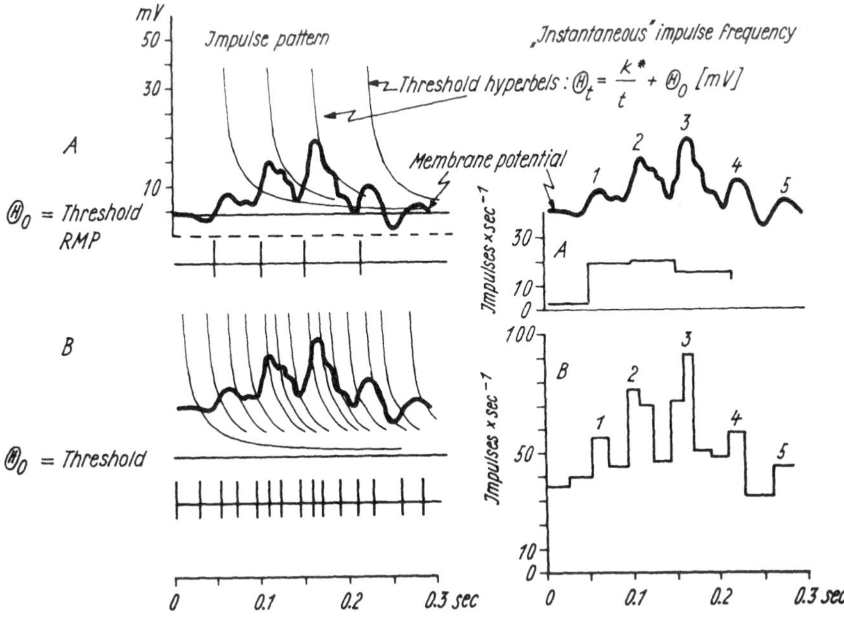

Abb. 28 Änderung des neuronalen Impulsmusters, das durch das gleiche postsynaptische Potential ausgelöst wird, wenn sich das Gleichspannungsniveau des Membranpotentials ändert. A) die mittlere Membrandepolarisation ist nahe der Schwelle (Θ_0). Rechts ist die aus dem Impulsabstand resultierende „momentane" Impulsfrequenz aufgezeichnet. Die 5 Amplitudenmaxima des postsynaptischen Potentials sind in der momentanen Impulsfrequenz nicht mehr zu erkennen. Die Schwelle ändert sich nach jedem Impuls entsprechend der angegebenen Hyperbelgleichung. B) Gleiches postsynaptisches Potential wie in A. Die mittlere Depolarisation des Membranpotentials ist jedoch um einen konstanten Betrag höher. Infolge der höheren „Abtastfrequenz" durch die Schwellenhyperbeln erhöht sich die mittlere Impulsrate am Ausgang der Nervenzelle. Die Amplitudenmaxima des postsynaptischen Potentials sind jetzt im Verlauf der momentanen Impulsfrequenz (rechts) erhalten.

schwellensummation" (EYSEL und GRÜSSER), wodurch eine sequentielle Kopplung aufeinanderfolgender Impulsintervalle entsteht. Für das afferente visuelle System scheint diese Kopplung jedoch unter 5 Prozent zu liegen, so daß sie vernachlässigt werden kann. Im folgenden soll gezeigt werden, wie man die von SHANNON angegebene Formel zur Berechnung der Informationskapazität eines Kanals *kontinuierlicher* Signale auf die neuronale Signalverarbeitung und die Impulsentstehung anwenden kann. Nach SHANNON gilt:

$$IK = B \, ld \, (1 + \frac{P_S}{P_R}) \; [bit/s] \qquad (7)$$

Hierbei sind B die Bandbreite (Differenz zwischen oberer und unterer Grenzfrequenz) des betrachteten Kanals, P_S und P_R die Leistungen des Signals bzw. des Rauschens. Diese können aus den effektiven Spannungen des Signals bzw. der Streuung σ^2_S und σ^2_R der Amplitudendichteverteilung für Signal und Rauschen bestimmt werden. Man erhält dann:

$$IK = B \, ld \, (1 + \frac{\sigma^2_S}{\sigma^2_R}) \; [bit/s] \qquad (8)$$

Gl. (8) kann direkt auf die Signalübertragung von Receptoren, Bipolarzellen oder Horizontalzellen angewandt werden, wenn Lichtrauschen mit Gauss'scher Amplitudenverteilung als Signal benützt wird. Allerdings sind (7) und (8) nur dann streng gültig, wenn Signal und Rauschen voneinander statistisch unabhängig sind.

Auf eine Nervenzelle angewandt, wird der Term $ld \, (1 + \sigma^2_S / \sigma^2_R)$ in Gl. (8) weitgehend durch die synaptischen Membranprozesse bestimmt. B in Gl. (8) ist für die Nervenzelle jedoch nicht identisch mit der Grenzfrequenz der synaptischen Prozesse, sondern meist kleiner. B_n hängt von der neuronalen Impulsfrequenz ab und läßt sich aufgrund folgender Überlegungen abschätzen: Nach dem Abtasttheorem der Nachrichtentheorie kann ein Analogsignal mit der Bandbreite B durch eine Abtastung mit der Tastfrequenz $F_t > 2B$ übertragen werden. Die Amplitude der Abtastimpulse gibt hierbei die Amplitude des Analogsignals wieder. Durch Tiefpaßfilterung kann das abgetastete Analogsignal ohne Informationsverlust wieder hergestellt werden. Die Signalübertragung durch die Impulsfolgen von Nervenzellen kann jedoch nur mit Einschränkung als ein einfaches Abtastverfahren betrachtet werden.

(α) Nimmt man an, daß die Aktionspotentiale selbst die Abtastimpulse der post-synaptischen Potentialschwankungen darstellen, so wird bei direkter Anwendung des Abtasttheorems ein Fehler gemacht, weil die *Amplitude* des Abtastimpulses konstant ist.

(ß) Wird angenommen, daß die maximale Impulsrate (Kehrwert des kleinsten Impulsintervalles) das Abtastsignal ist, dann ist zwar die Amplitude der Abtastsignale variabel, jedoch ändert sich auch die Abtastfrequenz F_t mit der Amplitude der post-synaptischen Potentialschwankungen. Für die Bandbreite B_n gilt

$$B_n < \frac{f^*_{max}}{2} \qquad (9)$$

Man kann aus Gl. (8) eine Abschätzung der Informationskapazität erhalten, wenn man einen mittleren Wert von f^*_{max} zur Bestimmung von B_n annimmt. Diese mittlere Impulsrate hängt von der mittleren Depolarisation D oberhalb der Impulsschwelle Θ_0 ab, dann gilt:

$$IK \approx \frac{(D - \Theta_0)}{2} \; ld \, (1 + \frac{\sigma^2_S}{\sigma^2_R}) \; [bit/s] \qquad (10)$$

σ_S kennzeichnet das Signal, σ_R faßt alle Rauschfaktoren zusammen, die bis zum postsynaptischen Potential sichtbar werden.

Fig. 28 zeigt anschaulich, daß die Schwankungen des postsynaptischen Membranpotentials durch eine Folge von Aktionspotentialen umso frequenzgetreuer übertragen werden, je höher die mittlere Depolarisation D des Membranpotentials und damit die mittlere Impulsrate ist. Dieser empirisch durch Messungen an verschiedenen Neuronensystemen gesichtete Befund folgt unmittelbar aus dem Schwellenverlauf, da die Häufigkeit,mit der die Schwellenhyperbel das Membranpotential ,,schneidet'', umso höher ist, je höher der Wert $(D - \Theta_0)$ ist.

Systemtheoretisch betrachtet, enthalten neuronale Impulsfolgen noch Frequenzkomponenten, die wesentlich höher sind als der Kehrwert der Impulsintervalle. Für die neuronale Signalübertragung können solche Frequenzkomponenten meist jedoch vernachlässigt werden, da die Zeitkonstante der synaptischen Integrationsprozesse hinreichend groß ist.

Aus Gl. (10) kann man schließen, daß die Informationskapazität einer Nervenzelle durch Änderung des mittleren Membranpotentials bei konstantem σ^2_S und σ^2_R verändert werden kann. Aus dieser Überlegung läßt sich auch die Bedeutung der ,,unspezifischen'' Eingänge für die Signalübertragung an Nervenzellen der afferenten Sinnessysteme ableiten. Die Aktivierung dieser unspezifischen erregenden Synapsen depolarisiert das Membranpotential. Bei gleichen spezifischen Eingangssignalen wird dadurch die zeitliche Auflösung der Signalübertragung durch die Nervenzelle verbessert, wenn die Zunahme von σ^2_R in Grenzen bleibt, und die Informationskapazität der Nervenzelle steigt entsprechend Gl. (10) an. So kann durch eine interne Kontrolle der signalübertragenden Prozesse Information aus der Umwelt unterdrückt oder "verbessert" werden.

Ich habe in diesem Abschnitt nur einige Betrachtungen zur Anwendung der Informationstheorie auf die Signalverarbeitung in den Sinnesorganen und im Nervensystem zusammengestellt. Der interessierte Leser sei auf folgende Zusammenfassungen hingewiesen, in denen auch noch weitere Codierungsprobleme besprochen werden: Stein, 1967; Färber, 1968, Grüsser, 1972; Holden, 1976; Eckhorn und Pöpel, 1974, 1975; Eckhorn et al., 1976.

Literatur:

(53) Eckhorn, R. and B. Pöpel: Rigorous and extended application of information theory to the afferent visual system of the cat. I. Basic concepts. Biol. Cybernetics **16**, 191-200 (1974).
(54) Eckhorn, R. and B. Pöpel: Regorous and extended application of information theory to the afferent visual system of the cat. II. Experimental results. Biol. Cybernetics **17**, 7-17 (1975).
(55) Eckhorn, R. Grüsser, O.-J., Kroeller, J., Pellnitz, K. und Pöpel, B.: Efficiency of different neuronal codes: information transfer calculations for three different neuronal systems. Biol. Cybernetics **22**, 49-60 (1976).
(55a) Eysel, U.Th. und Grüsser, O.-J.: The impulse pattern of muscle spindle afferents. Pflügers Arch. **315**, 1-26 (1970).
(56) Färber, G.: Berechnung und Messung des Informationsflusses der Nervenfaser. Kybernetik **5**, 17-29 (1968).
(57) Grüsser, O.-J.: Die Informationskapazität einzelner Nervenzellen für die Signalübermittlung im Zentralnervensystem. Kybernetik **1**, 209-211 (1962).
(58) = (29)
(59) Holden, A.V.: Models of the stochastic activity of neurons. Springer: Berlin-Heidelberg-New York (1976), 368 p.
(60) Perkel, D.H. und Bullick, T.H.: Neural Coding. N.R.P. Bulletin **6**, 221-348 (1967).
(61) Shannon, C.E.: A mathematical theory of communication. Bell Systems Techn. J. **7**, 379-423, 623-653 (1948).
(62) Stein, R.B.: The information capacity of nerve cells using a frequency code. Biophys. J. **7**, 797-826 (1967).
(63) Stein, R.B. French, A.S. und A.V. Holden: The frequency response, coherence and information capacity of two neuronal models. Biophys. J. **12**, 295-322 (1972).

Anschrift des Verfassers: Prof. Dr. O.-J. Grüsser, Physiologisches Institut,
Arnimallee 22, 1000 Berlin 33

GRUNDLAGEN, OPERATIONSPRINZIPIEN UND STRUKTUREN VON INNOVATIVEN RECHNERARCHITEKTUREN

W. K. Giloi
Technische Universität Berlin
Fachbereich Informatik

Einleitung

In der gesamten bisherigen Geschichte elektronischer Computer konnte alle 5 bis 6 Jahre eine Leistungssteigerung um eine Größenordnung erzielt werden. Dieser Fortschritt war immer primär ein Fortschritt der Bausteine-Technologie, hinter dem die ebenfalls erzielten Fortschritte der Rechnerorganisation eine sekundäre Rolle spielten. Der Fortschritt der Halbleiter-Technologie in Richtung auf hohe Integrationsdichte, hohe Arbeitsgeschwindigkeit und geringe Kosten war in den letzten Jahren besonders dramatisch. Um diese Fortschritte wirklich nutzen zu können, ist eine Abkehr von der jahrzehntelang dominierenden Architektur der von-Neumann-Maschine unvermeidbar. Aber auch um die neuesten Erkenntnisse der Softwaretechnik hinsichtlich Modularisierung von Software, Datenschutz und -integrität, Anpassungsfähigkeit der Betriebssysteme, Realisierung von Datentypen und Datenmodellen, Realisierung prozeßorientierter Sprachen usw. zu nutzen und hardwaremäßig zu unterstützen, sind neue Wege in der Rechnerarchitektur zu beschreiten. Der so wichtige Aspekt der Fehlertoleranz und Zuverlässigkeit hat Rückwirkungen auf die Architektur einer Maschine. Langsam nähert man sich den physikalischen Grenzen für die Arbeitsgeschwindigkeit von Schaltkreisen und Speicherelementen. Über diese Grenzen hinaus werden nur noch innovative architektonische Lösungen weitere Leistungssteigerungen erbringen können.

Alles dies hat dazu geführt, daß in den USA das Gebiet der Rechnerarchitektur in den letzten Jahren zu einem der wichtigsten Gebiete der Informatik geworden ist (nachdem dieses Gebiet viele Jahre lang als zu "hardwarenahe" mit einer gewissen Geringschätzung betrachtet wurde, da man glaubte, auf dem Gebiet der Rechnerorganisation eine Standardisierung und damit einen stationären Zustand erreicht zu haben). Insbesondere hat in jüngster Zeit aber auch der Mikroprozessor viele Spekulationen über die Struktur zukünftiger Rechnersysteme hervorgerufen, die bis zu der extremen Ansicht gehen, daß in Zukunft ein Rechner aus einer Anzahl von kooperierenden Mikroprozessoren bestehen wird, wobei sich Großrechner und kleinere Systeme nur in der Zahl der Mikroprozessoren unterscheiden werden. Wir werden diese Frage etwas näher beleuchten. Darüber hinaus werden wir uns bemühen, eine Systematisierung des Gebietes der Rechnerarchitektur vorzulegen. Eine solche Systematisierung stand bisher trotz mancher Bemühungen noch aus, was auch das bisherige Überwiegen von ad-hoc-Lösungen erklärt. Es ist aber nötig, daß die Rechnerarchitektur eine ähnliche Entwicklung wie die Softwaretechnik einschlägt, nämlich eine top-down-Entwurfsmethodik zu entwikkeln, die auf abstrakten, allgemeingültigen Prinzipien aufgebaut ist.

1. Was ist Rechnerarchitektur

Rechnerarchitektur ist eine Übersetzung des englischen Begriffes computer architecture. Architecture bedeutet im Englischen Baukunst oder Baustil; aber auch das einzelne Produkt der Baukunst wird als architecture bezeichnet. Die letztgenannte Bedeutung hat das deutsche Wort Architektur nicht. Wenn wir von Rechnerarchitektur sprechen, meinen wir jedoch den vollen Bedeutungsinhalt von computer architecture.

Rechnerarchitektur wie Architektur im allgemeinen dient einem Zweck. Wir zitieren hier die Encyclopaedia Britannica ("Art of Architecture", Macropaedia 1,1089): "The types of architecture are established not by architects but by society, according to the needs of the different institutions. Society sets the goals and assigns to the architect the job of finding the means of achieving them."

Entsprechend ihrem Zweck unterscheidet man in der Baukunst Typen von Architekturen wie die Architektur des Wohnungsbaus, des Fabrikbaus, des Sakralbaus, des Verwaltungsbaus etc.

Die Grundaufgabe einer Rechenanlage ist die Sammlung, Speicherung, Verarbeitung und Darstellung von Information. Diese Grundaufgabe kann auf den verschiedensten Anwendungsgebieten zu erfüllen sein.
Eine Rechenanlage, die auf jedem beliebigen Gebiet einsetzbar sein soll, soll Allzweckrechner genannt werden. Daneben gibt es Anlagen, die für eine spezielle Aufgabe konzipiert wurden und die deshalb Spezialrechner heißen. Dementsprechend werden wir Allzweckrechner-Architekturen und Spezialrechner-Architekturen zu unterscheiden haben.

Der Computer-Architekt hat seine Aufgabe aber noch nicht damit gelöst, daß er ein architektonisches Konzept vorlegt, welches den vorgegebenen Zweck erfüllt. Es wird vielmehr von ihm erwartet, daß dieses Konzept gewisse Forderungen möglichst optimal erfüllt. Solche Forderungen können unter verschiedenen Aspekten gestellt werden, nämlich

- dem Leistungs-Aspekt
- dem Fehlertoleranz-Aspekt
- dem Erweiterbarkeits-Aspekt
- dem pragmatischen Aspekt.

Leistungs-Aspekt. Bei manchen Spezialrechnern für Echtzeitaufgaben kann mitunter die Forderung nach maximaler absoluter Leistung im Vordergrund stehen, hinter der Kostenerwägungen zurücktreten müssen. Dies ist immer dann der Fall, wenn die gestellte Aufgabe nur dann erfüllt werden kann, wenn eine bestimmte Mindest-Rechnerleistung erbracht wird. Wir sprechen hier von Leistung pro Zeiteinheit. Im allgemeinen wird man aber nicht die absolute Leistung sondern das Verhältnis von Leistung zu Kosten zu maximieren trachten, d. h. die Leistung pro Kosteneinheit (wie immer diese messbar sein mag). Es ist dabei zu beachten, daß zwei verschiedene Systeme nur dann in ihrer Leistung verglichen werden können, wenn auch ihre Anwendungsbreite etwa gleich ist. Bei Allzweckrechnern kann es daher nicht darum gehen, die Leistung für eine bestimmte Aufgabe zu maximieren, sondern die mittlere Leistung, betrachtet über alle Anwendungsgebiete.

Fehlertoleranz-Aspekt. Das Optimierungskriterium ist hier die Maximierung der Verfügbarkeit einer Anlage, d. h. die Minimierung der durch Wartung oder auftretende Fehler bedingten Ausfallzeiten. Dies führt zu den fehlertoleranten Systemen, bei denen selbst bei Ausfällen einzelner Komponenten des Systems noch ein betriebsfähiger Kern übrigbleibt, so daß eine bestimmte Mindestleistung zu allen Zeiten zur Verfügung steht.

Erweiterbarkeits-Aspekt. Bei diesem Aspekt handelt es sich darum, ein Rechnersystem so zu entwerfen, daß seine Erweiterbarkeit durch verschiedene Ausbaustufen ermöglicht wird.

Pragmatik-Aspekt. Unter diesem Stichwort fassen wir Architekturen zusammen, bei denen eine höhere Programmiersprache unmittelbar durch die Hardware des Systems interpretiert wird. Das bedeutet, daß die höhere Programmiersprache bereits die Maschinensprache des Systems ist, und daß zwischen der Darstellung eines Programms in der höheren Programmiersprache und der das Programm ausführenden Hardware keine weitere

Zwischendarstellung existiert (siehe den folgenden Abschnitt). Damit sprechen der Anwendungsprogrammierer, der Systemprogrammierer und der Wartungstechniker ein und dieselbe Sprache. Da dieser Aspekt die Beziehung zwischen einem Rechnersystem und den Personen, die mit seiner Programmierung und Wartung betraut sind, betrifft, nennen wir ihn den Pragmatik-Aspekt (wobei wir uns den Begriff Pragmatik aus der Semiotik ausleihen).

Es muß betont werden, daß die genannten Aspekte sich keineswegs gegenseitig ausschließen. Gewisse architektonische Konzepte mögen entwikkelt werden, um zwei oder mehr der genannten Aspekte Genüge zu tun. So mag man bestimmte Betriebsmittel zu einer Rechnerstruktur verbinden, die zunächst fehlertolerant ist, daneben aber auch eine möglichst hohe Rechnerleistung erbringt. Es muß ferner kaum besonders betont werden, daß der Leistungs-Aspekt und der Fehlertoleranz-Aspekt mit Abstand die wichtigsten Aspekte bei der Konzeption von Rechnerarchitekturen sind. Wir wollen hier nicht über die Signifikanz der anderen beiden Aspekte urteilen, aber wir würden kaum heftig widersprechen, wenn jemand die Bedeutung des Pragmatik-Aspektes anzweifeln sollte.

Dem Gebäude-Architekten stehen bestimmte Materialien wie Holz, Stein, Beton, Stahl, Glas zur Verfügung. Aus diesen Materialien bildet er zunächst Strukturelemente oder <u>Komponenten</u> wie Pfeiler und Sturz, Bogen, Gewölbe, Fachwerk usw. Gewisse Konstruktionsprinzipien liefern die Methoden, nach denen Strukturelemente zu Strukturen zusammengesetzt werden können. Das Resultat sind die charakteristischen Strukturen einer Architektur, der Ausdruck der Konstruktionsidee durch die Form. So finden wir zum Beispiel den formalen Ausdruck der speziellen Konstruktionsidee, die beim Gewölbe entstehenden lateralen Kräfte durch Strebpfeiler abzufangen, als ein charakteristisches Merkmal der Architektur gothischer Dome.

Die Materialien des Rechner-Architekten sind die integrierten Halbleiter-Bausteine. Auch hieraus werden zunächst gewisse Komponenten realisiert, die dann nach bestimmten Prinzipien zu einem System zusammengesetzt werden können. Während bei der Baukunst die berühmten drei Forderungen VENUSTAS, UTILITAS, FIRMITAS gelten, steht bei der Rechnerarchitektur primär nur die UTILITAS, der Zweck, die Funktion im Vordergrund. Um den gewünschten Zweck zu erreichen, lassen sich bestimmte Prinzipien aufstellen, nach denen ein Rechner arbeitet. Ein solches Prinzip, das anstelle des Konstruktionsprinzips der Baukunst nun die Vorschriften für das Zusammenfügen bestimmter Komponenten zu einem

Rechnersystem liefert, nennen wir das Operationsprinzip.

Die Festlegung eines Operationsprinzips allein impliziert aber noch nicht die physikalische Struktur eines Rechners. Vielmehr mag es eine Zahl von strukturell verschiedenen architektonischen Lösungen geben, die alle nach dem gleichen Operationsprinzip arbeiten, ebenso wie es für ein bestimmtes Operationsprinzip strukturell verschiedene Realisierungen geben kann.

Wir fassen das Ergebnis unserer Diskussion in der Form von Definitionen zusammen und fügen noch einige ergänzende Definitionen an.

DEFINITION: <u>Rechnerarchitektur</u>
Eine Rechnerarchitektur beinhaltet ein Operationsprinzip, nach dem die Hardware des Rechners arbeitet, sowie die Struktur des Aufbaus des Systems aus den einzelnen Hardware-Betriebsmitteln. Eine Rechnerarchitektur dient einem bestimmten Zweck.□

DEFINITION: <u>Operationsprinzip</u>
Das Operationsprinzip einer Rechnerarchitektur ist die Definition der Informationsdarstellung in der Maschine, nach Art und Struktur der Informationskomponenten, sowie der Art und Weise der Informationsinterpretation und -transformation durch die Maschine.□

DEFINITION: <u>Rechnerstruktur</u>
Eine Rechnerstruktur wird bestimmt durch die Art und Zahl der Hardware-Betriebsmittel (Komponenten) einer Rechenanlage, der Verbindungseinrichtungen zwischen diesen Komponenten, sowie der Art ihres Zusammenwirkens.□

DEFINITION: <u>Rechnerorganisation</u>
Eine Rechnerorganisation definiert die funktionelle Arbeitsweise der einzelnen Hardware-Betriebsmittel einer Rechenanlage sowie ihrer Verbindungseinrichtungen. Insbesondere beinhaltet eine Rechnerorganisation auch die Details von Datenfluß und Kontrollfluß in der Anlage.□

DEFINITION: <u>Rechnerrealisierung</u>
Eine Rechnerrealisierung beinhaltet den logischen Entwurf und die <u>physikalische</u> Realisierung der einzelnen Hardware-Komponenten einer Rechenanlage, berührt also Fragen der Schaltungs-, Packungs- und Verbindungstechnik.□

DEFINITION: Hardware-Betriebsmittel
Hardware-Betriebsmittel sind die hauptsächlichen Komponenten einer Rechnerarchitektur wie Prozessoren, Speicher, Busse oder andere Verbindungseinrichtungen. Diese Komponenten sind in sich abgeschlossene Einheiten in dem Sinne, daß sie über eine eigene Steuerung verfügen. Selbstverständlich müssen sie aber innerhalb eines Rechnersystems miteinander kommunizieren und kooperieren.□

2. Das hierarchische Schichtenmodell eines Rechnersystems

Wir haben im vorhergehenden Abschnitt bewußt nicht das Rechnen als die Grundaufgabe einer Rechenanlage angeführt, sondern das Sammeln, Speichern, Verarbeiten und Darstellen von Information. Betrachten wir zum Beispiel den Einsatz einer Rechenanlage als Datenbank, so ist für den Benutzer nicht explizit erkennbar, wo hier gerechnet wird. Zweifellos sind in einer Datenbank aber Daten zu sammeln, zu speichern und darzustellen. Der Benutzer weiß auch, daß in einer solchen Anwendung intern gewisse Algorithmen, d. h. Rechenabläufe auszuführen sind (z. B. bei der Berechnung von Adressen), aber für den Benutzer stehen diese Operationen nicht im Vordergrund, sondern die für ihn allein wichtigen Funktionen des Speicherns und Wiederauffindens von Daten.

Selbstverständlich gibt es keine nicht-numerische Computer-Anwendung, die nicht intern Berechnungen, d. h. die Ausführung von logischen oder arithmetischen Operationen notwendig machen würde; und es gibt auch keine numerische Anwendung, die nicht in irgendeiner Form den Aufbau und die Manipulation von Datenstrukturen impliziert. Das Berechnen und das Handhaben von Datenstrukturen ist nicht voneinander zu trennen.

Eine sehr allgemeine Definition dessen, was wir Berechnen (computation) nennen, finden wir bei Wegner [1]: "Computation is a sequence of transformations which transform an initial representation through a sequence of intermediate representations into a final representation. ... A representation is a transforming function and its data."

Das, was Wegner 'transformung function' nennt, sind die der Berechnung zugrundeliegenden Rechenabläufe, die Algorithmen. Diese werden vom Programmierer in der Form eines Programms formuliert. Wir übersetzen daher die Wegnersche Definition wie folgt:

DEFINITION: Berechnen
Das Berechnen besteht in einer Folge von Transformationen, durch die eine Quelldarstellung über eine Folge von Zwischendarstellungen in eine Enddarstellung überführt wird. Eine Darstellung ist ein Programm mit den zugehörigen Datenmengen.□

Daten sind die Träger der Information, die von einer Rechenanlage gesammelt, gespeichert, verarbeitet und darsgestellt werden. Knuth [2] definiert Daten als "representations in a precise, formalized language of some facts or concepts, often numeric or alphabetic values, in a manner which can be manipulated by a computational method".

Die in Zusammenhang mit dem Berechnen auftretenden Datenmengen sind üblicherweise in irgendeiner Form strukturiert. Eine solche strukturierte Datenmenge oder Datenstruktur wird von Knuth definiert als "a table of data including struktural relationships".

Die Folge von Transformationen beim Berechnen wird notwendig durch die extreme Verschiedenartigkeit der Quelldarstellung, das ist die Darstellung, die der Programmierer oder die Programmiererin liefert, und der Darstellung, die die Hardware versteht und bearbeiten kann. Die Daten des Programmierers sind strukturierte Mengen von Zahlen oder Zeichen, die transformierenden Algorithmen werden beschrieben als eine Folge von Anweisungen, die zum Teil Organisationsanweisungen sind, zum Teil Ausführungsanweisungen für numerische Operationen. Die Objekte der Maschine sind Bitketten, d. h. Vektoren mit zweiwertigen Elementen, die Operationen sind elementare logische Verknüpfungen. In Abwandlung eines Zitats von Rosin [3] über Mikroprogrammierung[1] können wir sagen, daß die Folge von Transformationen der Quelldarstellung bis zur Enddarstellung notwendig ist, um etwas (vom Standpunkt des Benutzers) Vernünftiges mit (vom Standpunkt des Benutzers) unvernünftigen Mitteln zu erreichen.

Die Folge von Transformationen von Darstellungen bei der Berechnung durch ein Rechnersystem führt auf das Modell eines Rechnersystems als

---

1 Rosins Definition der Mikroprogrammierung lautet: "Microprogramming is the implementation of hopefully reasonable systems through interpretation on unreasonable machines."

eine Hierarchie von abstrakten Maschinen. Dabei definieren wir:

DEFINITION: Abstrakte Maschine
Eine abstrakte Maschine ist ein Paar

$$(L,P),$$

wobei L eine Sprache und P ein (abstrakter) Prozessor ist, durch den Darstellungen in L transformiert werden können. Der Prozessor P kann als Übersetzer oder als Interpreter arbeiten.□

DEFINITION: Geschichtete Hierarchie von abstrakten Maschinen
Eine geschichtete Hierarchie von abstrakten Maschinen ist eine Folge

$$(L_0,P_0)$$
$$(L_1,P_1)$$
$$\dots\dots\dots$$
$$(L_{n-1},P_{n-1}).$$

Dabei gilt: Wenn P_i ein Übersetzer ist, dann besteht die Bearbeitung einer Darstellung in L_i durch P_i in der Erzeugung einer neuen, vollständigen Darstellung in L_{i+1}.

Wenn P_i ein Interpreter ist, dann besteht die Bearbeitung einer Darstellung in L_i durch P_i in der Erzeugung einer Zwischendarstellung in L_{i+1}, die eine Bearbeitung der Darstellung in L_i durch den Prozessor P_{i+1} erlaubt.

Auf irgendeiner Stufe der Hierarchie ist die Grenzlinie zwischen Software und Hardware zu ziehen (die Software-Realisierungen abstrakter Prozessoren sind dabei wieder "Darstellungen" eigener Art). Wo im konkreten Falle diese Grenzlinie zu ziehen ist, hängt von der Architektur eines Rechners ab, während seine Organisation festlegt, wieviel Ebenen von abstrakten Maschinen innerhalb der Rechner-Hardware zu unterscheiden sind.

Typische Sprachebenen eines von-Neumann-Rechners mögen sein: höhere Programmiersprache, Assemblersprache, konventionelle Maschinensprache, Mikroprogrammsprache, Picoprogrammsprache. Im konkreten Falle kann es zweckmäßig sein, noch weitere Schichten zu betrachten. Prinzipiell ist ein Compiler in der Lage, eine höhere Programmiersprache auf jede beliebige konventionelle Maschinensprache abbilden zu können. Das gleiche gilt für die Abbildung einer konventionellen Maschinensprache auf eine bestimmte Hardware durch den Emulator einer mikroprogrammierten Maschine. Diese Freiheit, wonach die Struktur einer Schicht nicht die der darüberliegenden Schicht impliziert, gilt nicht mehr im Verhältnis zwischen Mikroprogrammsprache, Picoprogrammsprache und Hardware. Darin und in der Tatsache, daß auf der Picoprogrammebene echt Parallelarbeit geleistet werden kann, unterscheiden sich beim von-Neumann-Rechner die Schichten des Software-Teils des Systems von den Schichten des Hardware-Teils.

In den letzten Jahren wurde mit Erfolg der Versuch unternommen, durch entsprechende Mikroprogramme gewisse Operationen einer höheren Ebene in die Mikroprogrammebene zu verlagern ("vertical migration"), statt die Software-Hardware-Grenze generell auf eine höhere Ebene zu verlagern. Solche Maßnahmen stellen letztlich aber nur einen Behelf dar, um der Hardware eines von-Neumann-Rechners Aufgaben aufbürden zu können, die sie auf der Basis des zugrundeliegenden Operationsprinzips an sich nicht leisten kann. Die bessere Lösung wird hier sicherlich in der Entwicklung leistungsfähiger Operationsprinzipien liegen. Es mag in diesem Zusammenhang angebracht sein, eine klare Definition der von-Neumann-Architektur zu geben. Diese lautet:

DEFINITION: Von-Neumann-Architektur
Die von-Neumann-Architektur ist eine Rechnerarchitektur, deren Operationsprinzip in der Verarbeitung skalarer Speicherzelleninhalte besteht. Die Struktur der von-Neumann-Architektur ist dadurch gekennzeichnet, daß es nur eine zentrale Recheneinheit (CPU) gibt.□

3. Datenstrukturen und Parallelarbeit

In der Regel sind die Datenmengen, die durch die Ausführung einer Berechnung zu transformieren sind, strukturiert. Allgemein kann eine Menge dadurch strukturiert werden, daß man auf ihr Untermengen bildet, die ihrerseits identifizierbare Einheiten sind. Die Teilmengen-Identifikation geschieht üblicherweise durch Angabe einer definierenden Eigenschaft. Statt dessen kann man nach Knuth [2] auch sagen, daß die Elemente einer bestimmten Teilmenge in der durch die definierende Eigenschaft spezifizierten Relation miteinander stehen. Diese Betrachtung führt uns auf die folgende

DEFINITION: Abstrakte Datenstruktur
Eine abstrakte Datenstruktur [4] ist ein geordnetes Paar

$$(S, \rho)$$

Wobei S eine Menge von Datenobjekten und ρ eine Menge von zweistelligen Relationen auf S ist (d. h. alle Relationen sind Untermengen von $S \times S$).□

Je nach den Eigenschaften der "konstituierenden" Relation kann man bestimmte Strukturklassen unterscheiden. Diese sind: LINEARE ORDNUNG (Strings, Arrays, Keller, Warteschlangen, lineare Listen), PARTITIONIERUNGEN (geschachtelte Mengen, Bäume und binäre Bäume, Wälder) und MENGEN VON UNTERMENGEN (azyklische Graphen, verallgemeinerte hierarchische Listen, assoziative Strukturen).

Zur Darstellung einer zweistelligen Relation in ortsadressierten Speichern ist es notwendig, für jedes Element aus dem Definitionsbereich der Relation die Adresse der Relationspartner (d. h. der zugeordneten Elemente des Wertebereichs) auffinden zu können. Dies kann grundsätzlich dadurch geschehen, daß man

(a) diese Adressen berechnet oder

(b) diese Adressen speichert.

Die Berechnung der Adresse des Relationspartners eines gegebenen Elementes einer linearen Ordnung ist besonders einfach (einfaches Inkrementieren oder Dekrementieren). Aus diesem Grunde ist die eindimensionale lineare Liste, der "Datenvektor", die einfachste und natürlichste Struktur für die Datenspeicherung in ortsadressierten Speichern. Existieren auf der Maschinenebene noch andere Datenstrukturen, so bildet man diese zweckmäßigerweise auf den Datenvektor ab. Die Abbildung, die dies leistet, sei Adressierungsfunktion genannt. Um Konflikte zu vermeiden, sollte diese Funktion injektiv sein.

Die Adressierungsfunktion ist verhältnismäßig einfach für alle Strukturen aus der Klasse der LINEAREN ORDNUNGEN. Für Strukturen aus der Klasse der PARTITIONIERUNGEN ist die Funktion zwar noch bijektiv, ihre Ausführung kann aber recht aufwendig werden. Strukturen aus der Klasse der MENGEN VON UNTERMENGEN können in der Regel nicht durch eine Adressierungsfunktion realisiert werden. Deshalb realisiert man die beiden letztgenannten Klassen gemeinhin dadurch, daß man in den Datensatz eines jeden Elementes einer Struktur eine Informationseinheit aufnimmt, die direkt oder indirekt die Adressen der Relationspartner angibt. Eine Größe, die unmittelbar die Adresse eines Relationspartners darstellt, nennt man einen Zeiger. Bei der indirekten Methode gibt man anstelle eines Zeigers den Namen eines Deskriptors an, der dann seinerseits die zum Auffinden der Adressen nötige Information liefert (z. B. durch Angabe einer Adressierungsfunktion). Die Einführung von Deskriptoren erlaubt es, geordnete Datenmengen auf der Hardwareebene als Einheit zu verarbeiten [5].

Neuerdings hat sich die Anschauung durchgesetzt, daß eine Datenstruktur nicht ohne die zugehörigen Operationen zu ihrem Aufbau und zum Zugriff auf die Elemente gesehen werden kann. Als Bezeichnung für eine Gesamtheit von Strukturen und darauf definierten Operationen hat sich die Bezeichnung Datentyp eingebürgert. Wir definieren daher

DEFINITION: Datentyp
Ein Datentyp ist eine Datenstruktur (oder eine Menge von Strukturen) in Verbindung mit Operationen zum Aufbau oder zur Veränderung der Struktur sowie zum Zugriff auf die bzw. zur Transformation der Elemente der Struktur. Die Elemente der Struktur(en) gehören bestimmten Datensorten wie INTEGER, REAL, BOOLEAN, CHARACTER an.□

Die einzigen Datentypen, die durch die Hardware der von-Neumann-Maschine unterstützt werden, sind Skalare der einschlägigen Datensorten mit den zugehörigen elementaren arithmetischen oder logischen Operationen. Gewisse innovative Rechnerarchitekturen unterstützen komplexere Datentypen (z. B. vektorförmig geordnete Datenmengen und Vektoroperationen).

Die Einführung geordneter Datenmengen auf Maschinenebene eröffent prinzipiell die Möglichkeit, eine Anzahl von Operationen auf den Elementen der Struktur gleichzeitig auszuführen. Geordnete Datenmengen bieten sich daher von Natur aus zur Parallelverarbeitung an. Ferner ergeben sich damit vorgezeichnete Bearbeitungsstrukturen, die prinzipiell dadurch gekennzeichnet sind, daß entweder gleichartige Operationen gleichzeitig auf einer "räumlich" geordneten Menge von Datenelementen ausgeführt werden können und verschiedenartige Operationen zeitlich nacheinander, oder aber daß gleichartige Operationen nacheinander auf einer zeitlich geordneten Folge von Datenelementen, einem Strom, ausgeführt werden und verschiedenartige Operationen gleichzeitig (auf verschiedenen Elementen). Der erste Fall führt auf die Bearbeitung durch ein Array von Bearbeitungselementen (PEs), der zweite auf die Bearbeitung durch eine Pipeline. Die durch die Aufgabenstellung gegebene Bearbeitungsstruktur kann in beiden Fällen durch ein geschlossenes Gebiet in einem Raum-Zeit-Diagramm dargestellt werden [6], wobei die Raumkoordinate die Anzahl der zu einem Zeitpunkt parallel ausführbaren gleichartigen Operationen angibt. Wir nennen ein solches Diagramm das Task-Profil. Ein ähnliches Diagramm läßt sich für den Computer angeben als die Menge der gleichartigen Operationen, die zu jedem Zeitpunkt ausgeführt werden können. Wir nennen dies das Bearbeitungsprofil der Maschine. Es gilt dann trivialerweise, daß eine Task (eine Aufgabe) in der durch ihr Profil gegebenen Form nur dann durch eine Maschine parallel bearbeitet werden kann, wenn das Bearbeitungsprofil der Maschine sie zu jedem Zeitpunkt überdeckt.

Sei M die Zahl der zur Verfügung stehenden gleichartigen Verarbeitungselemente (Prozessoren) der Maschine, d. h. sei ihr Bearbeitungsprofil ein Rechteck der Höhe M. Sei $\hat{H}$ die maximale innere Höhe der Task. Dann kann die Task solange vollständig parallel ausgeführt werden, wie $\hat{H} \leq M$. Für $\hat{H} > M$ muß die Task zunächst dem Bearbeitungsprofil angepaßt werden, so daß ihre innere Höhe an keiner Stelle M überschreitet. In konventionellen Einprozessor-Systemen müssen daher alle Tasks zu einem Streifen der Höhe 1 gestreckt werden, um bearbeitet werden zu können.

Man kann diesen Vorgang auch so betrachten, daß die Teile einer Task, für die $H(i.\Delta t) > M$ ist, nur durch mehrmaliges "Überstreichen" des Task-Profils durch das Bearbeitungsprofil bearbeitet werden können, wobei bei jedem neuerlichen Überstreichen in einer anderen Höhe angesetzt werden muß. Diese mehrfachen Durchläufe erfordern eine gewisse Buchführung; z. B. das Zurückspringen auf den Anfang einer Schleife nach jedem Durchlauf. Die beste Ausnutzung der Maschine ist dann gegeben, wenn die Höhe der Streifen, in die das Task-Profil solcherart zerlegt wird, gleich M ist und wenn außerdem $\hat{H}$ ein ganzzahliges Vielfaches von M ist.

Chen hat eine Reihe von Kenngrößen für parallel ausführbare Tasks definiert [6], die sich aus dem Task-Profil ableiten lassen. Dies sind (PE = Bearbeitungselement):

Vervielfachungsgrad: M = Anzahl der PEs

Parallelitätsgrad: $\rho = \dfrac{\text{Task-Profil-Fläche für } H > 1}{\text{gesamte Task-Profil-Fläche}}$

Wirkungsgrad: $\eta = \dfrac{\text{Task-Profil-Fläche}}{\text{Gesamte von den PEs überstrichene Fläche}}$

Ausnutzungsgrad: $A = \eta \cdot M$

Gewinn: $G = \eta \cdot \dfrac{\text{Ausführungszeit bei einem PE}}{\text{Ausführungszeit bei M PEs}}$

Besonders interessant ist die Betrachtung des Ausnutzungsgrades als Funktion des Vervielfachungsgrades M (Bild 1), wie er für einen idealisierten Verlauf des Task-Profils berechnet werden kann [6].

Trotz aller Idealisierung zeigt diese Funktion die grundsätzliche Tatsache auf, daß der Ausnutzungsgrad (wie auch der Wirkungsgrad) durch den gegebenen Parallelitätsgrad ρ beschränkt ist und nur für $\rho \sim 1$ akzeptable Werte erreicht (im Lichte dieser Aussage überlege man sich, wie allgemeingültig das Konzept eines Vielprozessor-Systems sein kann).

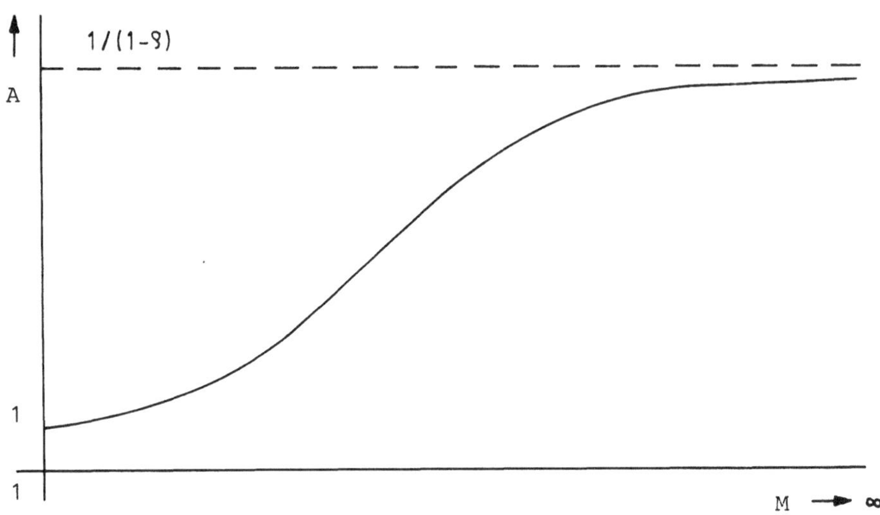

Bild 1: Ausnutzungsgrad als Funktion des Vervielfachungsgrades (für ein Task-Profil)

4. Programmstrukturen und Parallelarbeit

Für die Transformationen, die auf den Daten einer Darstellung auszuführen sind (siehe die Definition des Berechnens), werden Algorithmen, d. h. Rechenabläufe formuliert, die dann vom Programmierer in ein Programm umzusetzen sind. Üblicherweise besteht ein in einer höheren Programmiersprache geschriebenes Programm in einer Menge von Vereinbarungen über die Größen, mit denen gerechnet werden soll, und einer Menge von Anweisungen. In prozeduralen Sprachen ist die Menge der Anweisungen partiell geordnet. Dies bedeutet, daß die Anweisungen eines Programms zum Teil genau in der durch das Programm vorgegebenen Ordnung ausgeführt werden müssen, daß es aber auch Gruppen von Anweisungen gibt, innerhalb derer die Reihenfolge der Ausführung beliebig ist.

Operationen, bei denen die Reihenfolge der Ausführung beliebig ist, können im Prinzip auch gleichzeitig oder "parallel" ausgeführt werden, vorausgesetzt, die vorhandenen "Betriebsmittel" des Systems erlauben eine solche gleichzeitige Bearbeitung.

Die Dichotomie zwischen sequentieller und paralleler Ausführbarkeit, die man im allgemeinen bei den Anweisungen eines Programms findet, findet man auch innerhalb der Ausdrücke, die in den Anweisungen auftreten können. Auch hierzu betrachten wir ein Beispiel: Es sei die Ordinate eines Punktes auf einer Geradenstrecke, deren Endpunkte (X1,Y1) und (X2,Y2) sind, als Funktion der Abszisse zu bestimmen. Hierfür gilt Y←((X-X1)*(Y2-Y1)/(X2-X1))+Y1. Die übliche Darstellung dieses Ausdrucks durch einen Graphen führt auf eine (geordnete) Baumstruktur, in der die Variablen die Blätter und die Operationen die nicht-terminalen Knoten sind (Bild 2). Man sieht unmittelbar, daß im Prinzip alle Operationen einer Ebene des Baums gleichzeitig ausgeführt werden könnten, während das Fortschreiten von Ebene zu Ebene nur sequentiell erfolgen kann. Die Menge der Operationen eines Ausdrucks ist damit ebenfalls partiell geordnet, der geordnete Baum entsteht durch Zerlegung dieser Menge und mehrfache Verfeinerung der Zerlegung, entsprechend der Anzahl der Ebenen des Baums, sowie der Einführung einer Ordnung innerhalb der einzelnen Äquivalenzklassen.

Die Tatsache, daß die Anweisungen eines Programms linear geordnete Teilfolgen bilden, erlaubt auf der Hardwareebene die Anwendung des Befehlszählerprinzips. Die Statusinformation, die bei der Bearbeitung eines Programms angibt, welche Anweisung als nächste auszuführen ist, wird üblicherweise die Programmkontrolle oder kurz Kontrolle (control) genannt. Beim von-Neumann-Rechner ist dies der Inhalt eines Befehlszähler genannten Registers. Eine Programm-Steuerung, die primär durch den durch die Ordnung der Befehle dargestellten prozeduralen Ablauf gegeben ist, nennt man eine Programmfluß-Steuerung (program flow control). Daten spielen dabei nur in dem Maße eine Rolle, wie sie die in einem Algorithmus vorkommenden Fallunterscheidungen beeinflussen.

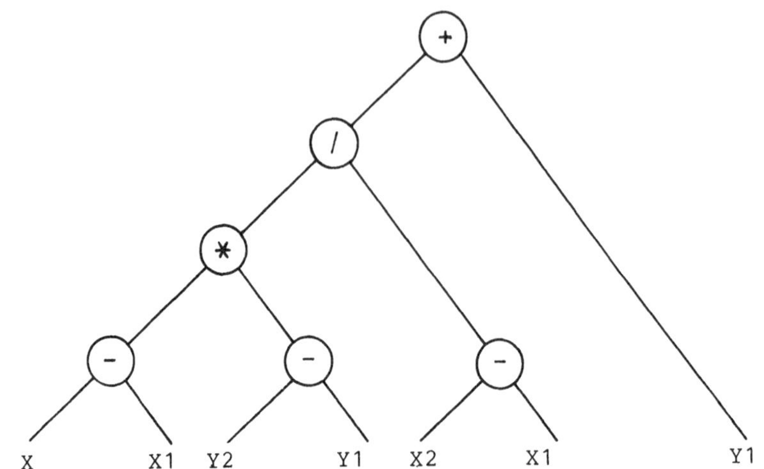

Bild 2: Verarbeitungsbaum des Ausdrucks ((X-X1)*(Y2-Y1)/(X2-X1))+Y1

Die Programmfluß-Steuerung ist sicher das angemessene Arbeitsprinzip in der Mehrzahl aller Computer-Anwendungen. Es gibt aber auch wichtige Anwendungsklassen, wo es primär darum geht, eine (üblicherweise in einem Array geordnete) Menge von Ausgangsdaten (initial values) durch Anwendung einer fest vorgegebenen Folge von Transformationen über eine Folge von Zwischenwerten in eine Menge von Endwerten (final values) zu überführen. Hier steht also nicht der algorithmische Ablauf im Vordergrund dondern der Datenfluß; und eine Programmsteuerung in der Maschine, die primär durch den Datenfluß bestimmt ist, nennt man daher eine Datenfluß-Steuerung (data flow control).

Als abstraktes Modell kann man in beiden Fällen den endlichen Automaten ansehen, der eine Zustandsfolge durchläuft, von einem Anfangszustand zu einem Endzustand. Bei der Programmfluß-Kontrolle sind die Zustände des Automaten als Programmzustände anzusehen (in die natürlich gewisse Datenwerte eingehen mögen), während man bei der Datenfluß-Kontrolle die Zustände des Automaten mit den Zuständen gleichsetzt, in denen sich die zu transformierende Datenmenge befinden kann.

Der Unterschied zwischen Steuerfluß und Datenfluß wird von Wiederhold sehr schön anhand des in Bild 3 gezeigten einfachen Beispiels erläutert[2]. Wie das Bild zeigt, kann man neben dem Steuerfluß und dem Datenfluß noch ein drittes, den Steuerdatenfluß betrachten. Steuerdaten sind diejenigen Werte aus dem Datenfluß, die als sogenannte Zustandsgrößen wiederum den Programmsteuerfluß beeinflussen.

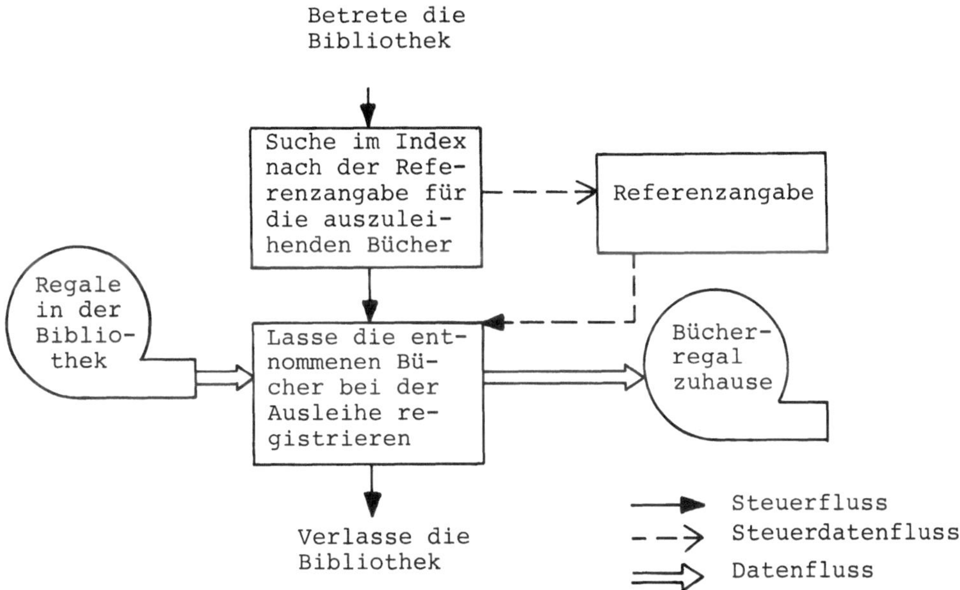

Bild 3: Steuerfluß, Steuerdatenfluß und Datenfluß für die Prozedur der Buchausleihe

Höhere Programmiersprachen geben dem Programmierer eine Reihe von Mitteln zur Strukturierung eines Programms an die Hand. Grundsätzlich wird ein Programm dadurch strukturiert, daß es in Teile zerlegt wird, die bezüglich der Programmkontrolle oder der Datenkontrolle (oder beidem) eine Einheit bilden. Übliche Strukturierungsmittel sind die Blocks bzw. die Prozeduren, verbunden mit einem Mechanismus zur Begrenzung des Gültigkeitsbereichs der darin vorkommenden Variablen. Andere Strukturierungsmittel sind die heute üblichen, modernen Kontrollkonstruktionen. Schließlich bieten manche Sprachen noch Co-Routinen oder gar Prozesse (oft auch 'task' genannt) als Programmkontroll-Mechanismen an.

---

[2] Wiederhold, G.: Database Design, McGraw-Hill, New York 1977.

Wir haben weiter oben darauf hingewiesen, daß der Begriff der "Kontrolle" eng mit der Anwendung des Befehlszähler-Prinzips im von-Neumann-Rechner verknüpft ist. Da wir hier primär nicht am von-Neumann-Rechner interessiert sind, ist es zweckmäßig, den Begriff der Kontrolle durch eine etwas andere Betrachtungsweise zu ersetzen. Ausgangspunkt ist das im vorhergehenden Abschnitt eingeführte Modell einer abstrakten Maschine, die aus einer Sprache und einem Prozessor zur Bearbeitung eines in der Sprache formulierten Programms besteht. Programme, Unterprogramme, Coroutinen - alle benötigen zu ihrer Ausführung den Prozessor. Wenn ein im Besitz des Prozessors befindliches Programm ein Unterprogramm aufruft, so leiht es den Prozessor an dieses für die Dauer seiner Ausführung aus. Einem unterbrochenen Programm ist der Prozessor "gewaltsam" entzogen worden. Eine Coroutine gibt den Prozessor in irgendeinem Zeitpunkt ihrer Ausführung an eine andere Coroutine ab und wartet dann darauf, den Prozessor wieder zurückzuerhalten.

Nun ist es ja prinzipiell möglich, daß eine (abstrakte oder reale) Maschine mehr als einen Prozessor hat. Nennen wir für den Augenblick eine Einheit einer Programmstruktur, die eines Prozessors zu ihrer Ausführung bedarf, einen Prozeß, so können wir sagen, daß in diesem Falle mehrere Prozesse gleichzeitig ausgeführt werden können. Allerdings werden wir sehr schnell feststellen müssen, daß diese Aussage sehr pauschal und eine solche Definition eines Prozesses unzureichend ist. Wir kommen daher nicht umhin, eine konkretere Definition für den Prozeß anzubieten. Dabei ist es sicherlich angebracht, sich möglichst eng an die in der Technik übliche Bedeutung dieses Begriffes zu halten.

DEFINITION: Prozeß
Ein Prozeß ist der zeitliche Ablauf einer Folge von Aktionen, die bezüglich eines bestimmten Zweckes eine funktionelle Einheit bilden. Der Ablauf wird dabei von prozeduralen Regeln bestimmt, die in einem dem Prozeß zugrunde liegenden Programm festgelegt sind. Wesentlich für einen Prozeß ist, daß zu dem zugrunde liegenden Programm noch besondere, zeitlich veränderliche Statusinformationen hinzukommen.□

Ein Prozeß ist solange "ruhend", bis er durch seine Aktivierung in den Zustand "arbeitend" gebracht wird. Ein Prozeß kann auch zeitweilig unterbrochen sein, wenn ihm der Prozessor vorübergehend entzogen worden ist; oder er kann zwar aktiviert worden sein, aber zunächst nichts anderes tun als auf die Zuweisung eines Prozessors warten. Es liegt auf der Hand, daß ein Prozeß seinen Status nicht selbst bestimmen kann, sondern daß dies einer übergeordneten Instanz (monitor, scheduler) überlassen bleibt.

Mit der Einführung des Prozeß-Begriffs wird eine weitere (und höhere) Ebene einer möglichen Parallelarbeit eines Rechnersystems eingeführt: Enthält ein System mehrere Prozessoren, so lassen sich im Prinzip mehrere Prozesse parallel bearbeiten. Wir sprechen hier von parallelen Prozessen im Gegensatz von den konkurrenten (nebenläufigen) Prozessen, wie man sie z. B. bei den Betriebssystemen kennt. Konkurrente Prozesse können Programmteile sein, die miteinander kommunizieren (durch gemeinsam benutzte Daten) oder kooperieren (zur Erzielung eines bestimmten Resultats) und die daher in ihrem zeitlichen Ablauf aufeinander abgestimmt oder synchronisiert werden müssen. In einem Einprozessor-System werden solche Prozesse aber nicht echt parallel sondern in Wirklichkeit abschnittsweise-sequentiell ausgeführt.

Zur Lösung des Problems der Prozeß-Kommunikation (data lockout) bzw. -Kooperation (wait for event) sind sehr wirkungsvolle Synchronisations-Konstrukte entwickelt worden, die sich auch zur Synchronisation echt parallel ablaufender Prozesse anwenden lassen.

5. Die Ebene einer möglichen Parallelarbeit

Schon frühzeitig ging man auch beim von-Neumann-Rechner dazu über, mehrere Programme im Rechner speicherresident zu halten, um die vorhandenen Betriebsmittel (Zentraleinheit, EA-Prozessoren) möglichst gut auslasten zu können (Prinzip des "Multiprogramming"). Man nennt üblicherweise ein speicherresidentes, bearbeitungsfähiges Benutzerprogramm, das eine in sich abgeschlossene Einheit bildet, einen Auftrag oder Job. Genauer gesagt ist ein Job die Gesamtheit aller Verarbeitungsleistungen für diese Programmeinheit (die die Übersetzung, Ein/Ausgabe usw. mit einschließen mag). Ein Job kann aus mehreren Prozessen bestehen. Bei kommunizierenden Prozessen lösen sich unkritische und kritische Abschnitte ab. Prozess-Abschnitte bestehen in einer Folge von Anweisungen, und Anweisungen (genauer die Zuweisung, die aber ca. 50% der Anweisungen ausmacht) können zusammengesetzte Ausdrücke enthalten. Es besteht somit eine Hierarchie, die sich über vier Ebenen erstreckt, auf denen Parallelarbeit stattfinden kann. Diese sind:

1. Multiprogramming-Ebene: mehrere Jobs werden gleichzeitig bearbeitet
2. Job-Ebene: mehrere Prozesse laufen konkurrent ab

3. Prozess-Ebene: mehrere Anweisungen eines Prozeßabschnittes werden gleichzeitig ausgeführt

4. Statement-Ebene: mehrere Operationen eines zusammengesetzten Ausdrucks werden gleichzeitig durchgeführt.

Damit die Hardware eines Rechnersystems Parallelarbeit leisten kann, muß ihr kenntlich gemacht werden, welche Programmeinheiten parallel ausgeführt werden können. Prinzipiell kann diese Information auf zwei Arten geliefert werden:

(1) der Programmierer macht Programmeinheiten, die parallel bearbeitet werden können, explizit als solche kenntlich;

(2) das System erkennt selbst gewisse "Parallelismen", zum Beispiel beim Übersetzen eines Programms.

Eine Parallelarbeit auf der Multiprogramming-Ebene ist verhältnismäßig leicht zu organisieren, aber nur sehr schwer oder gar nicht im Sinne einer maximalen Betriebsmittel-Auslastung zu optimieren. Letzteres erfordert komplizierte Zuweisungsalgorithmen (scheduling), denen detaillierte Informationen über die Aufträge zur Verfügung stehen müssen, wie zum Beispiel: die (geschätzte) Ausführungszeit, die belegten Speicherbereiche, die benötigten Betriebsmittel, die bestehenden Abhängigkeiten von anderen Aufträgen (z. B. über gemeinsam benutzte Datenmengen) usw.

Oft ist nicht die Maximierung der Betriebsmittel-Auslastung das vorherrschende Optimierungskriterium, sondern die Maximierung einer Gewinnfunktion, die sich als Summe der Gewinnfunktionen der einzelnen Aufträge ergibt. Dabei gibt es verschiedene charakteristische Verläufe für den Gewinn eines Auftrags als Funktion der Bearbeitungsdauer. So kann im einfachsten Fall der Gewinn konstant sein; oder aber der Gewinn ist konstant bis zur Erreichung eines Grenzwertes, und von da an null. In anderen Fällen mag der Gewinn umgekehrt proportional zur Bearbeitungsdauer sein. Es gibt eine Reihe von Lösungen solcher Probleme für Systeme mit zwei oder drei Bearbeitungseinrichtungen (servers), die in der Regel unter stark idealisierten Annahmen erhalten werden. Allgemeine Lösungen für Systeme mit beliebig vielen Bearbeitungseinrichtungen gibt es bisher nicht.

Ähnliche Verhältnisse gelten, wenn die Aufträge aus Prozessen bzw. Prozeßabschnitten bestehen, d. h. bei der Parallelarbeit auf der

Job-Ebene. Vor allem die Echtzeitsysteme wie z. B. die Prozeßsteuerungssysteme verlangen, daß im System eine große Zahl unterschiedlicher Prozesse mit unterschiedlichen Prioritäten existieren, die von Zeit zu Zeit durch Anforderungen aus der "Umwelt" des Systems aktiviert werden müssen. Solche Prozesse müssen in der Regel unterbrechbar sein, d. h. es müssen "Wiedereintrittspunkte" (reentry points) geschaffen werden. Da bei einer größeren Zahl von Prozessen nicht alle Prozesse im Hauptspeicher residieren können, wird sich ein Teil davon in einem "Sekundärspeicher" (Plattenspeicher oder Massenspeicher) befinden. Bei Bedarf sind damit bestimmte Prozesse in den Hauptspeicher nachzuladen, wobei sie dann andere, bisher im Hauptspeicher befindliche Prozesse "verdrängen", d. h. deren Stelle einnehmen. In solchen Fällen muß das System entscheiden, welche Prozesse verdrängt werden sollen. Das hierzu am häufigsten angewandte Verfahren ist das LRU-Schema (LRU = least recently used), bei dem diejenigen Prozesse verdrängt werden, die am längsten nicht benutzt worden sind. Durch dynamische Prioritätsänderung kann erreicht werden, daß nicht sogenannte "Kellerleichen" entstehen: Ist ein auf seine Bearbeitung wartender Prozeß für längere Zeit nicht bearbeitet worden, so wird seine Priorität erhöht, um seine Chancen zu verbessern.

Systeme, in denen eine größere Zahl von Prozessen zur Bearbeitung anstehen, bieten sich naturgemäß sehr zur Parallelarbeit mehrerer Hardware-Prozessoren an: Anstelle eines einzigen Prozessors, der nach einem Prioritätenschema nacheinander alle aktiven Prozesse abarbeitet, stehen nun mehrere Prozessoren hierfür zur Verfügung. Ein solches Vorgehen wirft aber sofort auch die Frage der Optimierung (z. B. im Sinne der Maximierung des mittleren Ausnutzungsgrades der Hardware-Betriebsmittel) auf, ein absolut nichttriviales Problem. Aber auch einfachere Probleme wie das der Erkennung bzw. Verhütung von Verklemmungen (deadlocks) (Beispiel: Prozeß A wartet auf Prozeß B und Prozeß B wartet auf Prozeß A) bedürfen einigen Aufwands.

Die Erkennung der parallel bearbeitbaren Prozesse bzw. Prozeßabschnitte ist verhältnismäßig einfach, da der Programmierer die hierzu nötigen Angaben ja in der Form von Deklarationen und Kontroll-Anweisungen liefert. Prozesse werden als solche deklariert. Die Kennzeichnung des parallelen Ablaufs von voneinander unabhängigen Prozessen kann mit so einfachen Konstrukten wie dem FORK-JOIN [7] geschehen. Bei kommunizierenden Prozessen werden Verschließanweisungen wie das bereits besprochene LOCK-UNLOCK benötigt; und bei kooperierenden Prozessen benötigt man Synchronisations-Konstrukte, die im einfachsten Fall aus einem WAIT(<event>) bestehen mögen.

Auf der Programmsegment-Ebene wie auch auf der Anweisungsebene kann ein System verhältnismäßig leicht in die Lage versetzt werden, Parallelismen selbst zu erkennen. Hierfür sind eine Reihe von Verfahren entwickelt worden, die meist darauf beruhen, den Rechenablauf durch einen gerichteten Graphen zu modellieren, in welchem die Knoten die Tasks und die Kanten die Vereinigung aller möglichen Vorgänger-Nachfolger-Relationen angeben (bei jeder bedingten Verzweigung gibt es ja mehr als einen möglichen Nachfolger). Auf der Anweisungsebene, d. h. bei den zusammengesetzten Ausdrücken dient der Verarbeitungsbaum (*expression tree*), für den Bild 2 ein Beispiel angibt, als Ausgangspunkt. Die *Breite* des Baums (Anzahl der Knoten einer Ebene) gibt dabei auf jeder Ebene die mögliche Parallelverarbeitung an, während die *Höhe* (Anzahl der Ebenen) angibt, wieviele Rechenschritte mindestens nacheinander auszuführen sind. Durch Anwendung des Assoziativgesetztes (bei assoziativen Operationen) bzw. des Kommutativgesetzes (bei kommutativen Operationen) kann die Höhe des Baumes oft reduziert und damit die gesamte Bearbeitungszeit verringert werden [8].

Auf der Anweisungsebene lassen sich nicht nur Ausdrücke analysieren und (soweit möglich) Teiloperationen parallel ausführen, sondern man kann auch zu komplexeren Elementaroperationen übergehen, z. B. für die Bearbeitung von ganzen Vektoren oder Matrizen.
Schließlich besteht die Möglichkeit, in immer stärkerem Maße von der Parallelarbeit auf der Mikroprogramm-Ebene Gebrauch zu machen. Dies bedeutet eine Vervielfachung der funktionellen Einheiten der Hardware, was beim heutigen Stand der Großintegration kein Kostenfaktor mehr ist. Auf der Picoprogramm-Ebene, d. h. innerhalb der funktionellen Einheiten der Hardware, ist Parallelarbeit seit langem in hohem Grade üblich, z. B. in den modernen 'Bit slice'-Komponenten. Sowohl die Mikroprogramm-Ebene wie auch die Picoprogramm-Ebene liegen aber unterhalb des Bereiches der Rechnerarchitektur. Der Aufbau eines Systems aus gegebenen Komponenten ist eine Architekturfrage, jedoch nicht der Aufbau der Komponenten selbst.

6. Die Zukunft der Multi-Mikroprozessor-Systeme

Aus den hier betrachteten, geläufigen Programmstrukturen wird man mit Sicherheit keine Möglichkeiten ableiten können, hunderte oder gar tausende von Mikroprozessoren gleichzeitig an der Bearbeitung eines Programms mitwirken zu lassen. Nun hört man oft das Argument, daß die zukünftigen Vielprozessor-Systeme uns dazu zwingen werden, den bisher üblichen Algorithmusbegriff als einen zeitlich geordneten Ablauf von Operationen durch eine radikal andersartige Betrachtungsweise zu ersetzen, bei der die mögliche Gleichzeitigkeit von Datenmanipulationen - nötigenfalls bis in die einzelnen Bits einer binären Zahlendarstellung hinein - im Vordergrund steht, die zeitliche Ordnung also sozusagen durch eine "räumliche" Ordnung ersetzt wird. Daß solche Ersetzungen sequentieller durch parallele "Abläufe" in bestimmten Fällen möglich sind, zeigt das Beispiel des Cooley-Tukey-Algorithmus für die "schnelle Fouriertransformation" (FFT). Solche Ersetzungen sind möglich bei sehr großen, sehr regulär strukturierten Datenmengen (z. B. Matrizen). Betrachtet man aber das gesamte Gebiet numerischer Anwendungen des Computers, so wird man in der Mehrzahl der Fälle nicht solche sehr regulären Strukturierungen der zu verarbeitenden Datenmengen finden, und erst recht nicht bei den nicht-numerischen Anwendungen, die den überwiegenden Teil aller Computer-Anwendungen bilden. Dies bedeutet nicht, daß es nicht sinnvoll sein mag, Vielprozessor-Systeme für spezielle Anwendungen zu bauen wie zum Beispiel: Schnelle Fouriertransformation, Bildverarbeitung, Lösung von Systemen gewöhnlicher oder partieller Differentialgleichungen oder ähnlichem. Nur sind solche Rechner dann Spezialrechner und keine Allzweckrechner; und es ist kein Zufall, daß das hervorstechende architektonische Prinzip solcher Spezialrechner das der Datenfluß-Architektur ist.

Bei den Datenfluß-Architekturen liegt die Struktur des Systems weitgehend fest, d. h. es ist keine große Flexibilität im Aufbau von Datenwegen erforderlich. Die Notwendigkeit einer solchen Flexibilität entsteht aber in dem Augenblick, wo ein Vielprozessor-System als Allzweckrechner eingesetzt werden soll. Diese Flexibilität ist, das weiß man inzwischen, nur durch unverhältnismäßig hohen Aufwand in den Verbindungswegen oder durch untragbar hohe Einbuße im Wirkungsgrad des Gesamtsystems zu erkaufen. Hierzu einige Tatsachen:

(1) Das Verbindungssystem größtmöglicher Flexibilität, der Kreuzschienenverteiler (crossbar switch), der es erlaubt, jede Komponente mit jeder anderen zu verbinden, steigt in seinem Aufwand

in erster Näherung mit $k \cdot N^2$ an, wenn N die Anzahl der zu verbindenden Komponenten ist. Der Proportionalitätsfaktor k hängt zwar von der verfügbaren Technologie ab, die quadratische Komplexität jedoch nicht, so daß, unabhängig von der Bauelemente-Technologie, immer ein Punkt erreicht wird, wo die Kosten der Verbindungseinrichtung die der "aktiven" Komponenten (Prozessoren, Speicher) übersteigen und wegen des quadratischen Anstiegs sehr bald ein Vielfaches ausmachen. Dieser Punkt liegt bei Multi-Mikroprozessor-Systemen bei einem verhältnismäßig kleinen N.

(2) Mit dem linearen Anstieg der Zahl der Prozessoren im System steigt aber die erzielbare Rechenleistung beileibe nicht proportional an. Es gilt hier durch den überproportional ansteigenden Aufwand für die Verwaltung des Systems (overhead) ein "law of decreasing return"; d. h. die Rechenleistung pro Prozessor wird mit jedem hinzukommenden Prozessor geringer. Untersuchungen anhand statistischer Modelle wie auch praktische Erfahrungen zeigen sogar, daß unter gewissen Umständen dieser Zuwachs negativ werden kann.

(3) Eine sehr billige Möglichkeit, von jeder Komponente aus jede andere zu erreichen, besteht darin, alle Komponenten mit einem im Zeitmultiplex arbeitenden Bus zu verbinden. Eine solche Verbindungseinrichtung kann sich jedoch bereits bei einer verhältnismäßig kleinen Zahl von Prozessoren zu einem ausgesprochenen "Flaschenhals" im System entwickeln [9].

Mikroprozessoren werden in wenigen Jahren ubiquitär sein; nicht nur in Autos, Waschmaschinen und "intelligenten" Datenendgeräten, sondern als Bausteine an vielen Stellen des Computers selbst. Es ist typisch, daß das Grundmotiv, welches bei der Firma INTEL zur Entwicklung des ersten Mikroprozessors führte, nicht das war, einen universell einsetzbaren, hochintegrierten Mikrocomputer zu schaffen, sondern ein programmierbares Schaltwerk für Steuerungszwecke. Wir können es aber nach der bisherigen Diskussion getrost dem Urteil des Lesers überlassen, zu entscheiden, wieweit die Vorhersage, wonach in einer vorhersehbaren Zukunft ein Rechner nur noch aus einer Ansammlung von Mikroprozessoren bestehen wird, ernst zu nehmen ist.

7. Das Klassifizierungsproblem der Rechnerarchitekturen

Bei der Einordnung von Rechnerarchitekturen wird sehr häufig eine auf Flynn [10] zurückgehende Klassifizierung verwendet, die auf den Wahrheitswerten der beiden Aussagen beruht

(1) "die Maschine bearbeitet in einem gegebenen Zeitpunkt mehr als einen Befehl" und

(2) "die Maschine bearbeitet in einem gegebenen Zeitpunkt mehr als einen Datenwert".

Flynn beschreibt die vier möglichen Kombinationen der Wahrheitswerte dieser Aussagen wie folgt:

00: single instruction - single data (SISD)
01: single instruction - multiple data (SIMD)
10: multiple instruction - single data (MISD)
11: multiple instruction - multiple data (MIMD).

Die Signifikanz dieser Merkmale ergibt sich aus der Tatsache, daß sie in gewissem Grade die strukturelle Form eines Systems implizieren. So ist SISD die Kategorie des von-Neumann-Rechners, d. h. des rein sequentiell arbeitenden Systems. SIMD enthält die zellularen Systeme, die Pipeline-Systeme und die Systeme, die aus einem Array von Prozessoren bestehen. Um zwischen diesen drei durch die SIMD-Kategorie zusammengefaßten Computertypen unterscheiden zu können, müßten weitere Merkmale betrachtet werden. MISD bedeutet, daß zur Berechnung eines einzigen Datenwertes bereits mehrere Befehle notwendig sind; die Organisationshöhe eines solchen Systems würde noch unter dem des von-Neumann-Rechners liegen. Da dies nicht sinnvoll ist, ist die MISD-Klasse leer.[3] Schließlich enthält die MIMD-Klasse alle Multiprozessor-Systeme, die symmetrischen wie die unsymmetrischen. Ein Multiprozessor-System wird symmetrisch genannt, wenn seine Prozessoren gleichartig sind.

Es zeigt sich, daß die Flynnsche Klassifizierung wenig aussage- und unterscheidungskräftig ist: Nur zwei der vier Klassen sind für innovative Architekturen relevant, die dritte ist die des von-Neumann-Rechners und die vierte ist leer. Versuche, die Aussagekraft dieser Klassifizierung durch die Hinzunahme weiterer Kenngrößen zu verbessern, können diese Schwäche letztlich nicht beheben. Ebensowenig wie zur Klassifizierung sind die Flynnschen Merkmale daher geeignet, eine Hilfe bei der systematischen Suche nach innovativen Architekturen zu bieten.

---

[3] Mitunter findet man - fälschlich - unter MISD die Pipeline-Architekturen eingeordnet

Die entscheidende Schwäche der Flynnschen - oder ähnlicher - Klassifizierung ist, daß sie nur strukturelle Merkmale betrachtet, nicht aber das Operationsprinzip einer Architektur. Nur beides zusammen ergibt einen Merkmalraum, in dem sich Rechnerarchitekturen befriedigend erklären und klassifizieren lassen [11]. Da beide Merkmalklassen - Operationsprinzip und Struktur - weitgehend orthogonal zueinander sind, liegt es nahe, diesen Raum in der Form einer Matrix aufzuspannen, die wir die <u>OS-Matrix</u> nennen.

8. <u>Eine Taxonomie der Leistungsarchitekturen</u>

Die in Abschnitt 1 gegebene Definition von Rechnerarchitekturen läßt sich formalisieren.

DEFINITION: <u>Rechnerarchitekturen</u>
Eine Rechnerarchitektur RA ist ein Tripel

$$RA = (p \in P,\ o \in O,\ s \in S).$$

Dabei bedeutet P eine Menge von Zwecken (<u>purposes</u>), denen die Architektur zu dienen hat, O die Menge der Operationsprinzipien und S die Menge der Strukturklassen.□

Dementsprechend erhalten wir eine Taxonomie einfach als dreidimensionalen Raum mit den durch P, O und S gegebenen Koordinaten. Jeder Punkt des Raumes, d. h. jedes Element des kartesischen Produktes $P \times O \times S$ definiert eine Gruppe von Rechnerarchitekturen.

Im folgenden wollen wir uns auf den Leistungsaspekt beschränken, d. h. nur Leistungsarchitekturen betrachten. In diesem Falle reduziert sich die <u>Taxonomie der Leistungsarchitekturen</u> auf den Raum $O \times S$, den wir in der Form einer Matrix darstellen können. Zunächst müssen wir zu diesem Zweck aber festlegen, was die Mengen O und S sind.

8.1. <u>Die Operationsprinzipien</u>

Wir haben bereits festgestellt, daß man bezüglich des Operationsprinzips zwei Klassen von Rechnerarchitekturen unterscheiden kann

- Rechnerarchitekturen mit speziellem Operationsprinzip
- Rechnerarchitekturen mit allgemeinem Operationsprinzip.

An speziellen Operationsprinzipien kennen wir:

- das Prinzip der Datenfluß-Architekturen (data flow architectures)
- das Prinzip der Verarbeitung von arrayförmig geordneten Datenmengen (array processing)
- das Prinzip der assoziativen Verarbeitung von Daten (associative processing)
- das Prinzip des orthogonalen Zugriffs auf Daten (vertical processing).

Die "Anwendungsbreite" des jeweiligen Prinzips nimmt bei dieser Liste nach unten hin ab. Selbstverständlich lassen sich sicher noch mehr als die genannten Operationsprinzipien finden.

An allgemeinen Operationsprinzipien kennen wir:

- das Prinzip der von-Neumann-Architektur der Speicherung und Verarbeitung völlig unstrukturierter und unspezifizierter Daten, d. h. von skalaren Größen, die entsprechend den Zuständen der Maschine als Befehl oder Datum interpretiert werden.
- das Prinzip der Speicherung und Verarbeitung selbtsbeschreibender Daten (tagged architectures).
- das Prinzip der Speicherung und Verarbeitung strukturierter Datenmengen, auf die über von der Hardware interpretierte Deskriptoren zugegriffen werden kann (data structure architectures).
- das Prinzip der HLL-Architekturen (high-level language architectures).

Sicherlich wird es noch weitere nützliche Operationsprinzipien geben, die aber erst noch gefunden werden müssen (so war auch das Prinzip der Datenstruktur-Architekturen vor kurzem noch unbekannt). Es liegt hier also ein reizvolles Feld für neuartige Ideen vor.

8.2. Rechnerstrukturen

An Strukturklassen können wir unterscheiden

- die Einprozessor-Systeme
- die zellularen Systeme
- die Arrays von gleichartigen Prozessor-Elementen (PEs)
- die Pipelines von verschiedenartigen Prozessor-Elementen
- die symmetrischen Multiprozessor-Systeme
- die asymmetrischen Multiprozessor-Systeme.

Einprozessor-Systeme. Diese Klasse schließt die von-Neumann-Rechner ein, daneben aber auch noch gewisse innovative Architekturen wie die assoziativen Rechner mit einem Prozessor.

Zellulare Systeme (cellular processor systems) bestehen aus einer regulären räumlichen Anordnung von vielen gleichartigen "Verarbeitungszellen", von denen jede eine (oder mehrere) spezielle Operation(en) ausführen kann. Die werteverändernde Operation der Zelle ist in der Regel von relativ einfacher Natur und mit der Funktion des Speicherns integriert. Die Kontrolle kann zentralisiert oder aber dezentral in die Zellen verlagert sein.

Arrays von gleichartigen Prozessor-Elementen seien auch kurz als Prozessor-Arrays bezeichnet. Ein Prozessor-Element (PE) kann üblicherweise die vier arithmetischen Grundrechenarten sowie einige logische Operationen ausführen. Der entscheidende Unterschied zu einem symmetrischen Multiprozessor-System besteht in zwei Punkten:

(1) alle PEs müssen in einem gegebenen Zeitpunkt dieselbe Operation ausführen (als einzige Ausnahme mag zugelassen sein, daß sie stattdessen keine Operation (NOOP) ausführen).

(2) die Datenwege zwischen den PEs sind festgelegt, und zwar so, daß ein PE nur mit bestimmten anderen PEs Daten austauschen kann (z. B. mit seinen beiden Nachbarn im Falle eines eindimensionalen Arrays oder mit seinen vier bzw. acht Nachbarn im Falle des zweidimensionalen Arrays).

Zwischen den zellularen Systemen und den Prozessor-Arrays besteht eine strukturelle Ähnlichkeit. Der Unterschied liegt zum einen in der Komplexität der Operation(en), die von der Zelle bzw. vom PE ausgeführt werden können, zum anderen darin, daß die Verbindungen zwischen den PEs eines Arrays fest sind, während die Zellen eines zellularen Systems u. U. Verbindungswege zwischen den Zellen selbst herstellen können [12].

Pipelines von Prozessor-Elementen (kurz Prozessor-Pipelines) bestehen wie die Prozessor-Arrays aus festen Arrays von PEs. Im Gegensatz zu den Prozessor-Arrays können die PEs einer Pipeline aber nur eine bestimmte Operation ausführen, in der Regel eine der arithmetischen Grundrechenoperationen. Entscheidend ist dabei, daß jedes Element einer Pipeline eine andere Operation ausführt. Das Ergebnis der Operation eines Prozessor-Arrays ist eine Menge von gleichzeitig erhaltenen Werten; das Ergebnis der Operation einer Prozessor-Pipeline ist eine Folge von zeitlich nacheinander erhaltenen Werten. Gewöhnlich bestehen Pipelines nur aus eindimensionalen Arrays, aber diese Beschränkung ist nicht zwingend. Eine gewisse strukturelle Variabilität der Pipeline kann dadurch erzielt werden, daß die PEs der Pipeline von Fall zu Fall verschiedenartig zusammengeschaltet werden können. Eine solche Pipeline nennen wir rekonfigurierbar (re-configurable).

Symmetrische Multiprozessor-Systeme bestehen aus einer Anzahl von Allzweck-Prozessoren, die auf vielfältige Weise miteinander und mit den Speichereinheiten verbunden werden können. Im Extremfall kann jeder Prozessor mit jedem anderen verkehren. Diese Verbindungen können entweder über ein besonderes Koppelfeld (crossbar switch), ähnlich wie in der Fernsprechtechnik, hergestellt werden, oder über einen gemeinsamen multiport-Speicher, oder aber über einen gemeinsamen Bus, der dann im Zeitmultiplex betrieben wird. Die letztgenannte Möglichkeit ist aber nur bei sehr langsamen Prozessoren vertretbar, da ein Zeitmultiplex-Bus sehr schnell zum geschwindigkeitsbegrenzenden Engpaß im System werden kann. Die Allzweck-Prozessoren sind bei den bisher bekannten Systemen dieser Art von-Neumann-Prozessoren. Prinzipiell spricht jedoch nichts dagegen, auch innovative Prozessortypen (Prozessor-Arrays, Prozessor-Pipelines etc.) wiederum zu einem Multiprozessor-System zusammenzuschalten.

Um Mißverständnisse zu vermeiden, soll an dieser Stelle der Unterschied zwischen einem Multiprozessor-System und einem Rechnernetzwerk betont werden. Die Prozessoren eine Multiprozessor-Systems können zwar vollständige Computer sein, die für sich auch autonom arbeiten können (z. B. Minicomputer oder Mikrocomputer). Im Multiprozessor-System arbeiten sie aber unter der Aufsicht eines zentralen Betriebssystems, das für das integrierte Gesamtsystem zuständig ist. Bei einem Rechnernetzwerk hingegen findet man eine Anzahl autonomer Rechenanlagen (die gleichartig oder verschieden sein mögen) mit eigenem Betriebssystem, die im Verbund miteinander arbeiten. Die Kommunikation bzw. Kooperation der einzelnen Anlagen in einem solchen Verbund geschieht durch den Austausch von Protokollen. Rechnernetzwerke sind nicht das Thema unserer Betrachtungen.

Asymmetrische Multiprozessor-Systeme bestehen aus der Zusammenschaltung einer Anzahl von Prozessoren, die im Gegensatz zu den symmetrischen Multiprozessor-Systemen nicht alle Allzweck-Prozessoren sind. Dies bedeutet, daß zumindest einige der Prozessoren für einen speziellen Zweck ausgelegt sind (z. B. durch ihre spezielle Organisation oder durch Emulation). Auch in diesem Falle können bestimmte Prozessoren im System aber auch innovativen Architekturen angehören. Die Art der Prozessoren und ihre Zusammenschaltung wird durch das Operationsprinzip bestimmt, das der Architektur, die strukturell als asymmetrisches Multiprozessor-System realisiert wird, zugrundeliegt. Bild 6 zeigt die durch die genannten Operationsprinzipien und Strukturen aufgespannte OS-Matrix, in die einige der bekanntesten innovativen Rechnerarchitekturen eingetragen sind. Insbesondere findet man in ihr auch die vier Projekte (TARCUS, ABACUS, EGPA, STARLET/DAS), über die im folgenden noch etwas näher berichtet werden soll.

9. Drei innovative Rechnerarchitekturen

9.1. TARCUS - Eine modulare Systemstruktur (Richter)

TARCUS (task attracting reconfigurable computer utility system) ist das Konzept eines Mehrprozessor-Systems, das sich durch eine dezentrale Kontrolle der beteiligten Prozessoren und damit einen hochmodularen Aufbau des Betriebssystems sowie durch innovative Strategien zur Betriebsmittelvergabe auszeichnet. Das System besteht aus einem Speicherprozessor und mehreren Arbeitsprozessoren. Der Speicherprozessor verwaltet eine virtuelle dreistufige Speicherhierarchie mit Segment- und Seitenadressierung. Die Arbeitsprozessoren führen die Benutzerprozesse aus, wobei ein Multiprogramming-Grad von etwa 4 bis 5 angestrebt wird. Die Arbeitsprozessoren müssen dabei nicht einheitlich sein, sondern es können dafür strukturell unterschiedliche Mini- oder Mikroprozessoren eingesetzt werden. Dies wird dadurch ermöglicht, daß durch entsprechende Mikroprogrammierung dieser Prozessoren eine einheitliche Schnittstelle auf der Firmware-Ebene hergestellt wird, auf der sich dann eine einheitliche

Software-Ebene aufbaut. Durch dieses Konzept besteht die Möglichkeit, das System jederzeit zu rekonfigurieren bzw. zu erweitern. Das hierarchisch aufgebaute TARCUS-Betriebssystem besteht aus "wechselseitig einander mißtrauenden" Modulen. Durch die Segmentierung des Speichers lassen sich die einzelnen Module völlig disjunkt halten. Die globalen Strategien des TARCUS-Betriebssystems (TAROS) sowie die Eigenschaften der virtuellen Maschine (TARMIL) und der darauf laufenden Implementiersprache (TARSIL) werden in der Arbeit näher erläutert.

9.2. Das Operationsprinzip des "Descriptor Referenced Autonomous Memory Access" (DRAMA) (Giloi und Berg)

In diesem Beitrag wird das Prinzip des descriptor referenced autonomous memory access (DRAMA) vorgestellt als das Operationsprinzip eines Computers, in dem strukturierte Datenmengen an die Stelle der skalaren Maschinenvariablen des von-Neumann-Rechners treten, d. h. als elementare Informationseinheiten der Maschine identifiziert und verarbeitet werden. Die Grundidee von DRAMA ist es, von einer Variablen als einem Namen-Wert-Paar auszugehen, wobei aber nicht wie bei der von-Neumann-Maschine der Name eine Speicherzellen-Adresse und der Wert deren Inhalt ist. Vielmehr ist der Wert eine strukturierte Datenmenge, die durch ein Paar,bestehend aus einer Struktur-Spezifikation und dem die Elemente der Menge enthaltenden Datenvektor,repräsentiert wird. Die Struktur-Spezifikation wird durch einen von der Hardware interpretierbaren Deskriptor geliefert; und der Name einer solchen Variablen ist somit der Name des Deskriptors. Damit können alle zur Parallelverarbeitung einer strukturierten Datenmenge benötigten Informationen unmittelbar dem Deskriptor entnommen werden; es sind weder Programmstrukturen zu analysieren noch Indexrechnungen durchzuführen, da die Strukturangaben im Deskriptor in der Form von verallgemeinerten Speicherabbildungsfunktionen dargestellt werden, die unmittelbar von der Hardware der Maschine ausgeführt werden können. Ferner wird gezeigt, daß sich dieses Prinzip in optimaler Weise zur Implementierung beliebiger Datentypen aus standardisierten Funktionen, die von der Hardware ausgeführt werden, eignet, sowie zur Definition von durch die Hardware zur Laufzeit überwachten Zugriffsrechten bzw. Software-Capabilities. Damit ist das brennende Problem des Datenschutzes und der Datensicherung auf der Ebene der individuellen Variablen (= strukturierten Datenmenge) lösbar. Alles dies machen das DRAMA-Prinzip zu einer vielversprechenden Alternative zum von-Neumann-Operationsprinzip. Das ihm innewohnende Potential zur Parallelarbeit, auf der Programmfluß-Ebene wie der Datenfluß-Ebene, führt zu einem sehr modularen, asynchronen und asymmetrischen Multiprozessor-System. Es besteht die Absicht, ein solches System an der Technischen Universität Berlin zu realisieren.

9.3. Sprachorientierte Hardware (Bürkle, Frick, Schlier)

Bisherige Fortschritte der Rechner-Architektur haben die Entwicklung von Rechnern, die nicht mehr die typischen Instruktionen des von-Neumann-Rechners haben, sondern den höheren Programmiersprachen in dieser Hinsicht angepaßt sind, sehr vernachlässigt. Im Grenzfall müssen die Anweisungen der höheren Sprache zu "Maschinenbefehlen" werden. Ein solcher Rechner mit BASIC als Sprache wurde gebaut, seine Effizienz ist nicht schlechter als die eines von-Neumann-Rechners vergleichbarer Technologie.

Ein laufendes Projekt untersucht, inwieweit man von der Beschränkung auf eine Programmiersprache abgehen kann, indem man "Grundfunktionen" verdrahtet, die als Maschinenbefehle für mehrere höhere Sprachen dienen können. Die Grundfunktionen selbst werden von einem sprachspezifischen, aber kurzen (BASIC : < 1000 x 64 bit) Mikroprogramm aufgerufen. Die für einen solchen Rechner notwendige Daten-Repräsentation und einige Grundfunktionen werden besprochen.

9.4. Ein flexibler Post-von-Neumann-Rechner und seine Bewertung aufgrund von Warteschlangen-Modellen (Händler, Herzog, Hoffmann, Hofmann)

Die Erlanger Informatik verfolgt - unterstützt vom BMFT - ein Projekt, in dem man sowohl die Züge einer Mehrprozessoranlage als auch die eines Feldrechners erkennen kann. Diese System trägt den Namen EGPA (Erlanger General Purpose Array). Zuerst werden einige Thesen erläutert, z. B. Größenmodularität in Hardware und Software, Datenfluß-Konzept, Standort des Rechnerkonzeptes zwischen "tightly coupled" und "loosely coupled", space-sharing-Komplexität und Flexibilität. Aus diesen Ideen heraus wird ein Gesamtkonzept für das EGPA-Projekt entwickelt. Insbesondere werden die grundlegenden Überlegungen zur Struktur des Betriebssystems und der Koordinierung von Anwender-Prozeß-Systemen erläutert. Schließlich wird noch kurz auf den Stand der Pilotimplementierung eingegangen.

STRUKTUR \ OPERATIONSPRINZIP	von Neumann Prinzip	String/ Array-Verarbeitung	Orthogonale Verarbeitung	Assoziative Verarbeitung	Selbstbeschreibende Daten	Datenstruktur-Architektur	HLL-Architekturen	Datenfluß-Kontrolle
Ein-Prozessor-System	00 von Neumann Rechner	01	02 OMEN	03	04 B 5500, RICE R-2	05	06 B 5500 ABACUS	07
Zellulares System	10 Holland Machine	11	12	13	14	15	16	17
Prozessor-Array	20 ILLIAC IV	21	22	23 STARAN, PEPE	24	25	26	27
Prozessor-Pipeline	30 Makro-Pipeline	31 CDC-STAR-100	32	33	34	35	36	37
Symmetrisches Multi-Prozessor-System	40 C.mmp, EGPA	41	42	43	44	45	46	47
Asymmetrisches Multi-Prozessor-System	50 CDC-6600, TARCUS	51 STARLET	52	53	54	55 STARLET/DAS	56 SYMBOL	57

Bild 4: Taxonomie von Leistungsarchitekturen

Ein wesentliches Problem bei der Parallelverarbeitung ist die Synchronisation asynchroner Prozesse. Ein Teilaspekt ist das Problem, daß ein Prozeß erst dann gestartet werden kann, wenn andere Prozesse beendet sind. Dieser Synchronisationsmechanismus wird mit einer neuen Klasse von Warteschlangenmodellen dargestellt und analysiert. Die Bedienungseinheit (BE) hat dazu L Warteschlangen. Ein Auftrag besteht aus L Teilaufträgen, und die BE entnimmt aus jeder ihrer Warteschlangen genau einen Teilauftrag und bearbeitet sie zusammen. Damit bleibt die BE leer, bis in jeder Warteschlange mindestens ein Auftrag enthalten ist. Geschlossene Modelle mit solchen Bedienungseinheiten werden analytisch behandelt unter verschiedenen Voraussetzungen, insbesondere auch mit verschiedenen Bedienungszeitverteilungen.

Als zweites Grundmodell wird das sogenannte Parallelverarbeitungsmodell behandelt, bei dem mehrere a-Prozessoren unabhängig und parallel arbeiten und dabei von einem b-Prozessor überwacht werden. Mit Hilfe der hierarchischen Technik bei der Modellbildung wird aus den behandelten Grundmodellen anschließend ein Systemmodell entworfen und ausgewertet für ein hierarchisch organisiertes Mehrprozessorsystem (als solches kann die EGPA-Pyramide angesehen werden), mit einem parallelen Algorithmus für das traveling-salesman-Problem als Auftrag. Der Vergleich mit Ergebnissen, die durch eine schrittweise Simulation des parallelen Algorithmus auf solch einem Mehrprozessorsystem erhalten werden, zeigt die Genauigkeit des angegebenen Verfahrens und der Einzelmodelle.

Literaturverzeichnis

[1] Wegner, P.: Programming Languages, Information Structures, and Machine Organization. McGraw-Hill, New York 1971.

[2] Knuth, D.E.: The Art of Computer Programming. Vol. 1., Chapter 2. Addison-Wesley, Reading/Mass. 1975 (2nd. ed.).

[3] Rosin, R.F.: The Significance of Microprogramming. SIGMICRO Newsletter 4,4, Jan. 1974, 24-39.

[4] Giloi, W.K.; Berg, H.K.: Abstract Data Types, Abstract Data Structures, and a Discipline of Structured Specification. Noch unveröffentlicht.

[5] Giloi, W.K.: The DRAMA Principle of Parallel Processing. Noch unveröffentlicht.

[6] Chen, T.C.: Parallelism, Pipelining and Performance Enhancement by Multiprocessing. Hasselmeier/Spruth, Rechnerstrukturen, Oldenbourg, Munich 1974.

[7] Conway, M.E.: A Multiprocessor System Design. Proc. FJCC 1963, 139-146.

[8] Kuck, D.J.: A Survey of Parallel Machine Organization and Programming. Computing Surveys 9,1 (March 1977), 29-59.

[9] Kinney, L.L.: Analysis of a Multiprocessor System with a Shared Bus. Proc. 5th Annual Symposium on Computer Architecture, IEEE Publ. No. 78CH1284-9C.

[10] Flynn, M.J.: Some Computer Organizations and Their Effectiveness. IEEE Trans.on Computers C-21,9, Sept. 1972, 948-960.

[11] Giloi, W.K.: Rechnerarchitekturen. Vorlesungsskript. Technische Universität Berlin 1977.

[12] Holland, J.: A Universal Computer Capable of Executing an Arbitrary Number of Sub-Programs Simultaneously. Proc. EJCC 1959, 108-113.

Konzepte, Probleme und Möglichkeiten von CAD-Systemen in der industriellen Praxis

J. Encarnacao
Institut für Informationsverwaltung
und Interaktive Systeme
Technische Hochschule Darmstadt

E.G. Schlechtendahl
Institut für Reaktorentwicklung
Kernforschungszentrum Karlsruhe

Kurzfassung:

Dieser Aufsatz ist die Einführung zu dem CAD-Fachgespräch während der GI-Jahrestagung 1978. Er dient als Übersichtsbeitrag und wird durch verschiedene Einzelbeiträge während des Fachgesprächs ergänzt und vertieft.

Inhaltlich wird von einer CAD-Struktur ausgegangen, die aus einer Datenbank, aus einer (Anwendungs-) Programmkette und aus einem Kommunikationsmodul besteht. Das CAD-System wird als Informationssystem gesehen, die einzelnen System-Funktionen werden näher erläutert. Es wird auf die verschiedenen Organisationsformen und auf die Problematik der Einführung und Integration von CAD-Systemen in der Praxis eingegangen. Einige in nächster Zukunft für den weiteren Fortschritt im CAD-Bereich erforderliche Entwicklungen werden erläutert.

Inhalt:

1. Einleitung

Das rechnergestützte Entwerfen und Konstruieren wird üblicherweise CAD genannt und ist in (1,2) definiert als "die Nutzung von Computer Hardware und Software für den Entwurf von Produkten, die von der Gesellschaft benötigt werden". Dabei sind Produkte Elemente von Systemen. Systeme können aber sein: ein Automat, ein medizinisches Zentrum, ein Logistik-Plan, ein Stadtentwicklungsprojekt u.v.a.. In (3) wird CAD als "äquivalent zu der Integration von geeigneten Computer Hardware- und Software-Moduln um Entwurfsysteme für besondere Erfordernisse zu erzeugen",beschrieben.

Wie von R. Noppen in (4) eingeführt, kann das CAD-System gesehen werden als das Zusammenwirken zwischen einer Datenbank, einer Anwender-Programmkette und einem Kommunikationsmodul. Wenn wir uns den Kommunikationsmodul näher betrachten, so sehen wir, daß er aufgegliedert werden kann in drei verschiedene Moduln (Bild 1):

a) Dialog
b) Daten-Ein- und Ausgabe
c) Graphik

In dem Dialogmodul finden wir die Kommandosprache des verwendeten Betriebssystems vor, soweit unmittelbar Funktionen des Betriebssystems angesprochen werden. Darüber hinaus bietet das CAD-System selbst eine Dialogsprache zur Kommunikation mit dem Benutzer. Dialogsprache ist hier zunächst im allgemeinen Sinne als Austausch von Anweisungen und Nachrichten zu verstehen, wobei das Zeitverhalten keine Rolle spielt. Mehr und mehr jedoch tritt im CAD-Bereich der langsame "Dialog" des Stapelbetriebs zurück zugunsten der interaktiven Betriebsweise. Die Datenerfassung, die Integritätsprüfung und die Anfragesprache sind Teile des Daten-E/A-Moduls. Die graphische Ein- und Ausgabe und der graphische Dialog werden im Graphik-Modul durchgeführt. Dabei unterscheiden wir zwischen einem Modellierungsteil, der Bestandteil der Programmkette ist und in dem die gewünschte (graphische) Topologie definiert wird, und einem gemeinsamen Kern als Darstellungs- und den graphischen Dialog ausführenden Modul.

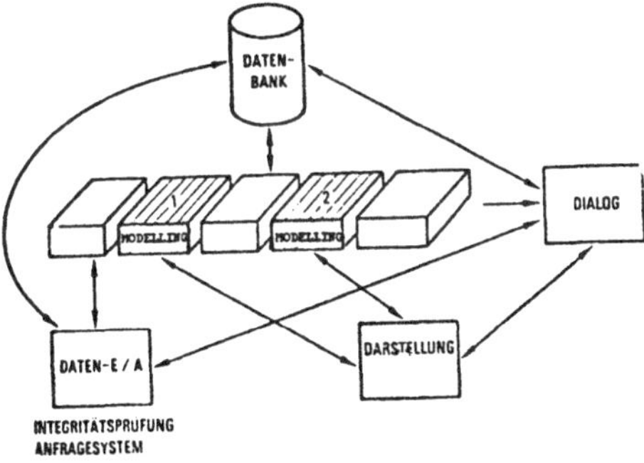

Bild 1: Die Komponenten eines CAD-Systems

Die Programmkette besteht aus den Programmteilen, die über die Methodenbank dem Anwender zur Verfügung gestellt werden. In dieser Methodenbank sind auch Moduln enthalten, die für die Systemfunktionen (Datenbank, Dialog, Daten-E/A, Graphik) verwendet werden. Die einzelnen Bestandteile, d.h. Moduln der Methodenbank selbst können große Anwendungsprogramme sein (z.B.Modul für Finite Elemente).

2. Die Struktur von CAD-Systemen

Die Struktur eines CAD-Systems hat die in Bild 2 angegebene Form. Dabei werden die Daten bzw. die Datenbank zum funktionellen Zentrum des CAD-Systems.

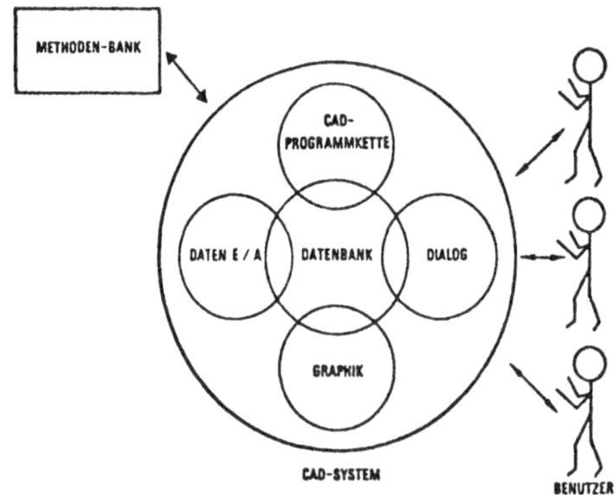

Bild 2: Funktionelle Struktur eines CAD-Systems

Von der Verwendung und Realisierung des CAD-Systems her gesehen, können dabei drei Ebenen betrachtet werden. Die erste entspricht der Verwendung als Informationssystem, d.h. insbesondere der Moduln Datenbank und Daten-E/A einschließlich den zugehörigen Anfragemöglichkeiten. CAD-Systeme werden meistens im Mehrbenutzerbetrieb eingesetzt, sowohl als Teilnehmer- wie als Teilhabersysteme. Der einzelne Benutzer selbst arbeitet an einem interaktiven Arbeitsplatz, der je nach lokaler (Hardware/Software-) Mächtigkeit als einfaches E/A-System, gepuffertes E/A-System, Intelligentes Terminal oder Intelligenter Satellit betrieben wird.

Die jeweilige Hardware-Organisation des CAD-Systems ist im wesentlichen abhängig von den Rechenkosten, von der Antwortzeit im interaktiven Betrieb, von der Systemzuverlässigkeit und von der Programmportabilität.

Durch die fallenden Hardware-Kosten ist es denkbar, daß sich in Zukunft immer mehr Netzwerke von Rechnern mit mehrfachem Zugriff für CAD-Anwendungen durchsetzen werden. Durch die verteilte Organisation wäre dann für den einzelnen Anwender das Potential an Methodenbanken viel größer und die Kommunikation zwischen CAD-Benutzern viel effizienter.

Struktur und Organisationsformen von CAD-Systemen werden von G. Nees (Siemens AG, Erlangen) bei dem CAD-Fachgespräch während der GI-Jahrestagung 1978 vom Gesichtspunkt der bisherigen Praxis aus betrachtet (22). Dabei wird sowohl die Entwicklung bis zu den CAD-Systemen bewertet,die inzwischen in Einsatz gegangen sind, als auch eine Extrapolation der weiteren Entfaltung von CAD unter Einfluß der erkennbaren Faktoren versucht. Im Vordergrund steht die Einführung von CAD in die Entwicklung, Projektierung, Abwicklung und Konstruktion elektrischer Anlagen.

Beeinflußt durch das Hard- und Software-Angebot am Markt schälten sich im wesentlichen drei Strukturen der CAD-Anwendung heraus:
Leistungsfähige Einzelprogramme - Inselsysteme auf der Basis von Kleinrechnern-Terminalsysteme mit Anschluß an Großrechner und den dort residierenden Datenbanken. Für jede dieser Strukturen wird ein Beispiel aus der Praxis zusammen mit der sich jeweils ergebenden Organisationsform erörtert (Finite-Elemente Berechnung,Leiterplattenentwurf,Stromlaufplanerstellung). Es läßt sich zeigen, daß die Organisationsformen u.a. durch Kommunikationsformen des Ingenieurs bestimmt sind: A) Kontakt Ingenieur/Maschine (mit der Möglichkeit unmittelbarer Handlungsalternativen);
B) Ingenieur/Spezialist/Maschine; (Aufbau von Bibliotheken, derzeit noch rationelle Nutzung teuerer Hilfsmittel); C) Ingenieur/Datenerfassungspersonal/Maschine (um Massendaten aufzunehmen).

Die Zukunft von CAD kann man dadurch extrapolieren, oder zu beeinflussen versuchen, daß man geeignete Einflußgrößen ausfindig macht. Zu diesen gehören sicher ein Konsolidierungsfaktor und ein Innovationsfaktor, beide mit verschiedenen Aspekten. Randbedingungen sind das Rentabilitäts- und das Ergonomieproblem. Über alle diese Aspekte werden von G. Nees grundsätzliche Betrachtungen angestellt und aus den bisherigen Erfahrungen dafür Schlußfolgerungen gezogen.

3. Das Dialogsystem

Für die Realisierung von CAD-Systemen braucht man zwei Sprachen:die Kommandosprache und die Programmiersprache. Mit der ersten steuert der Benutzer das System, in der zweiten werden die (Anwendungs-)Programme selbst geschrieben. Nach J. Hatvany et al. in (3) findet man in CAD-Systemen die folgenden vier Typen von Kommandosprachen:

(1) Festes Format
(2) Irregulär Polnisch
(3) Modell des endlichen Automaten
(4) Descriptiver Typ

Der in CAD-Systemen am häufigsten verwendete Typ von Kommandosprachen ist Typ 3. Die Programmiersprache ist meistens FORTRAN. Es ist aber zu erwarten, daß der grösser werdende Einsatz von Rechner-Netzwerken für CAD-Anwendungen dazu führen wird, daß die Popularität von anderen Sprachen durch das dann steigende Kennenlernen ihrer Vorzüge für den Anwender wesentlich steigt. Insbesondere werden Sprachen wie APL und PL/1 sicherlich in Zukunft eine breitere Verwendung im CAD-Bereich finden. Speziell für die Erstellung von CAD-Systemen erweiterte Programmiersprachen finden sich in den sogenannten "integrierten Systemen" wie ICES, IST, GENESYS, REGENT,

DINAS.(Die Bezeichnung "integrierte Systeme" ist historisch bedingt und nicht besondern glücklich). Integrierte Systeme unterscheiden sich zwischen einem Systemkern und den Bausteinen (5). Mit dem Kern wird der Ablauf der Benutzerprogramme, d.h. die Kommandointerpretation, die Datenhaltung und das dynamische Laden von Modulen, gesteuert. Auch besondere Möglichkeiten zur Definition und Verarbeitung neuer fachbezogener Kommandosprachen sowie zur Programmierung von problemorientierten Teilsystemen sind in den integrierten Systemen enthalten. Nach F. Bauhuber (6) hat man dann die folgenden Stufen der Programmierung:

SYSTEMKERNENTWICKLER	SYSTEMKERN SYSTEMVERWALTUNG- UND -ABLAUFSTEUERUNG PRECOMPILER KOMMANDOINTERPRETER
SUBSYSTEMENTWICKLER	FACHBEZOGENE ANWENDERSPRACHE FACHBEZOGENE KOMMANDOSPRACHE
ANWENDER	PROBLEMLÖSUNG

Beispiel für die Realisierung eines solchen Systems ist REGENT (7), das auf PL/1-Basis arbeitet und bei dem jede neudefinierte Kommandosprache selbst wieder als Programmiersprache für weitere Bausteine benutzt werden kann.

Ein interaktives Dialogsystem muß, um die CAD-Forderung nach möglichst schneller Verarbeitung (effizienter Dialog) und möglichst großer Benutzerfreundlichkeit (Übersicht trotz Komplexität der Probleme) zu erfüllen, trotz programmiertem Dialog dem Benutzer die Möglichkeit geben, zu bestimmten Zeitpunkten den Fortgang des Programms aus den vorhandenen Durchläufen frei wählen zu können, die Programmabläufe zu erweitern und zu manipulieren. Dies setzt Möglichkeiten des Löschens, des Kopierens, des Korrigierens und der Definition von Programmsequenzen bzw. Programmabläufen, sowie des Beginns und der Beendigung des Dialoges voraus.

4. Die graphisch-interaktive Komponente

Der Grundgedanke beim Einsatz von graphisch-interaktiven Systemen im CAD-Bereich besteht darin, daß man das graphische System in einen geräteunabhängigen und einen geräteabhängigen Teil aufspaltet und die graphische Aus- und Eingabe vollkommen vom Anwenderprogramm trennt (8,9).

Will man irgendwann den graphischen Teil eines CAD-Systems an neue Aus- und Eingabegeräte anpassen, so braucht man dadurch nur die Programmteile neu zu schreiben, die den Aus- und Eingabeprozess durchführen.

Die interessanten Schnittstellen sind:

a) Schnittstelle zum Anwenderprogramm
b) Codegeneratorschnittstelle
c) logische Eingabeschnittstelle

Trennung zwischen Modellieren und Darstellen

Hinsichtlich des Zweckes, den Programmierer und Anwender mit der graphischen Ausgabe verfolgen, können wir unterscheiden (10) (Bild 3):

(1) "Modellierung". (Aufbau der Topologie)

(2) "Darstellung". ("Kern" des graphischen Systems).

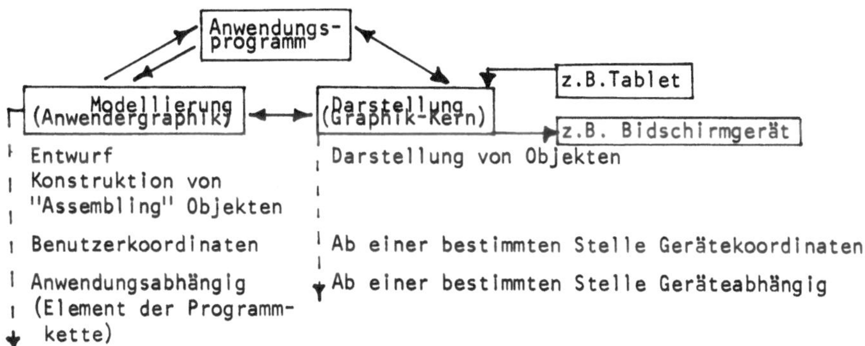

Bild 3: Trennung zwischen "Modellierung" und "Darstellung" im graphischen System

Klassifizierung der Anwendungsformen

Eine graphische Anwendung kann als ein Viertupel gesehen werden.

GA = (I, IM, ST, MT)

mit

I = Interaktivität

IM = Graphische Informationsmenge

ST = Bildstruktur

MT = Meßtreue

Beispiel für eine quantitative Unterscheidung dieser Merkmale ist:

Klassen	1	2	3	4
Interaktivität (Antwortzeit)	0.01 ÷ 0,1 sec	0,1 ÷ 5sec	5sec ÷ 1min	1min ÷ 2h
Graphische Informationsmenge (Anzahl Items)	<100	100 ÷ 1000	1000 ÷ 10000	> 10000
Bildstruktur (Schachtelungstiefe)	0	1	2 - 32	>32
Meßtreue	<1%	1 ÷ 20%	20% ÷ >Faktor 2	>Faktor 2

Graphische Anwendungssysteme kann man dadurch charakterisieren, daß sie für bestimmte Bereiche (Klassen) der Parameterwerte dieser Tupel geeignet sind. R. Lindner klassifiziert und charakterisiert auf der Grundlage dieser Merkmale in (11) die graphischen Anwendungen in

a) Graphische Eingabe: Datengeneration durch den Benutzer mit Korrekturmöglichkeiten unter interaktiver Kontrolle

b) Graphische Datenhaltung: Zugriff zu Daten und ihre Manipulation

c) Graphisches Konstruieren: Zusammenstellung und Manipulieren von Daten

d) Graphische Auswertung: Einbeziehung des Benutzers in Algorithmen auf Datensätzen

e) Graphische Simulation: Alles, wodurch dem Benutzer Realität vorgespiegelt wird.

5. Die CAD-Datenbank

Unter Datenbank wollen wir hier ein System verstehen, mit dem eine große Menge von Daten integriert, organisiert und gesteuert wird. Nach D. Eastman (12) müßten zur Charakterisierung der verschiedenen CAD-Datenbanktypen die folgenden drei Aspekte betrachtet werden:

1) Die Art und Weise, wie die Daten gespeichert sind, und ihre Beziehung zu den verschiedenen Anwendungsprogrammen

2) Die Methode zur Speicherung der geometrischen Information

3) Die bei der Implementierung verwendete Entwicklungsstrategie

Die ersten CAD-Systeme (z.B. ICES (13)) hatten erweiterte Maschinenfähigkeiten für das Laden, Steuern und Ausführen von Analyseprogrammen (Moduln der Programmkette) und für Ein- und Ausgabe aus Sekundärspeichern. Die nächsten Systeme integrieren alle Daten in einer Datenbank. Dies ist in CAD-Systemen grundsätzlich in zwei verschiedenen Formen realisiert worden:

a) Entwicklung von einer Menge von Analyseprogrammen, die auf denselben Daten basieren (z.B. Finite-Elemente-Systeme)

b) Zusammenbringen von allen Daten, die für eine Vielfalt von Analyse- und anderen Anwenderprogrammen gebraucht werden. Das Problem liegt darin, daß die Daten untereinander funktionelle Beziehungen haben. Jede Änderung verlangt auch eine Änderung dieser Relationen und das ist teuer. Dies versucht man zu berücksichtigen, indem feste Abarbeitungsfolgen von Analyseprogrammen festgelegt werden.

Funktionelle Relationen zwischen den Daten können aber auch als Redundanz verstanden werden. Als Folge hiervon ergab sich die Konzeption, bei der aus einer nicht-redundanten Datenbank heraus die vom jeweiligen Anwendermodul gewünschte Daten-Organisation zur Verfügung gestellt wird. Die Reihenfolge bei der Abarbeitung der Analyseprogramme ist dann beliebig.

Die Daten in einer CAD-Datenbank können nach P. Ciampi und J. Nash (14) von den folgenden Typen sein:

1) Topologische Daten
2) Strukturdaten (abhängig vom Anwenderprogramm)
3) Anwendungsbezogene Daten (z.B. Testdaten)
4) Beschreibungsdaten (z.B. Dokumentationsdaten)

Die Daten vom Typ 2 und 3 werden aus Typ 1 heraus generiert. Die Existenz von Daten dieses Typs ist eine wesentliche Neuerung gegenüber den klassischen MIS-Datenbanksystemen. Ein zweiter Unterschied liegt in der größeren Komplexität der Anwendungsprogramme in CAD-Systemen.

6. Die Daten- E/A-Funktion

Durch diese Funktion werden in CAD-Systemen die Datenerfassung, die Integritätsprüfüng und die Anfragesprache realisiert. Über die Datenerfassung selbst kann wenig CAD-spezifisches gesagt werden. Sie ist anwendungs- und systemabhängig; die Erfassung kann syntaxgesteuert vorgenommen werden. Wird dies über Digitalisierungsvorrichtungen realisiert, so muß das CAD-System Möglichkeiten zur Definition von Benutzerprimitives, zum Aufbau einer Benutzerdatenstruktur und zur Digitalisier (-Dialog)-führung zur Verfügung stellen. Beispiele für diese Systemtypen werden in (19) angegeben und erläutert.

Auch bei der Erfassung von nicht-graphischen Daten werden neuerdings verstärkt Bildschirmgeräte verwendet. Dafür benutzt man dann Formularsprachen (15).

7. Interaktive Arbeitsplätze

Ein interaktiver CAD-Arbeitsplatz hat die in Bild 4 angegebene Grundform. Wichtig ist dabei, wie groß die jeweilige Rechnermächtigkeit ("Intelligenz") ist. Dies hängt im wesentlichen von der Anwendung und von der Benutzerforderung ab. Es wird daher hier auf der Grundlage der Arbeiten von R. Lindner (11, 16) die Sichtweite des Benutzers in den Mittelpunkt der Betrachtungen gestellt.

Zur Charakterisierung von CAD-Arbeitsplätzen werden die folgenden Merkmale verwendet und in jeweils 3 Bereiche untergliedert:

a) Interaktionsvermögen : "Niedrige Zykluszeiten","Sofort Antwort", "Echtzeit"
b) Bildinhaltsumfang : "Überblick", "Seite lesen", "Einzelheiten suchen"
c) Bildstrukturfähigkeit: "Keine Struktur", "Gruppenstruktur", "Legendestruktur".

Unter Interaktionsvermögen versteht man den "Kopplungsgrad" zwischen Gerät und Benutzer. Liegt die Wartezeit im Dialog zwischen 1 und 10 Sekunden, so spricht man von "Niedriger Zykluszeit"; wenn sie unter einer Sekunde liegt, spricht man von

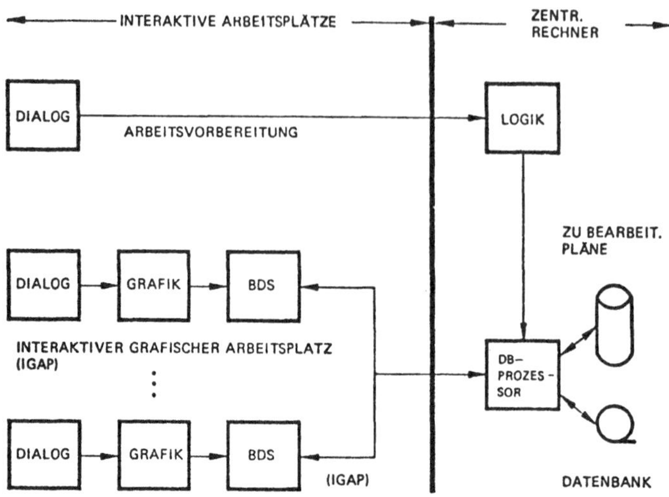

Bild 4: Beispiel eines interaktiven CAD-Arbeitsplatzes (19)

"Sofort Antwort"-Betrieb, wenn der "Kommando-Modus" benutzt wird. Beim "Echtzeit"-Betrieb wird dem Benutzer mit Wartezeiten unter 1/10 Sekunden und ständiger Systemreaktion (im Gegensatz zum Kommando-Modus) der Eindruck eines unmittelbaren Kontaktes zum Arbeitsvorgang vermittelt.

Wenn entsprechend dem Bildinhaltsumfang der Benutzer die gesamte Bildinformation auf einen Blick erfassen kann, spricht man vom "Überblick"-Inhalten; entspricht der Umfang der Information in etwa einer DIN A 4-Seite voll Graphik oder Text, so handel es sich um "Seite lesen"-Inhalte (Beispiele: Diagramme, Blockbilder etc.). Noch größere Bildinhalte interessieren gewöhnlich nicht in allen Details und werden "Einzelheiten suchen"-Bildinhalte genannt.

Der Strukturzusammenhang ist bei der"Gruppenstruktur" auf den ersten Blick deutlich. "Legendestruktur"-Darstellungen bedienen sich der Darstellungsvariationen weniger zur Gliederung als zur Codierung zusätzlicher Information zum Bildelement. Die Bedeutung der Darstellungsweisen ist in einer Legende definiert (Beispiel: Kartographie).

8. Grundtätigkeiten beim Konstruieren

Man unterscheidet dabei die in Bild 5 angegebenen Phasen (17) bei der Entwicklung einer Konstruktionslösung. Für die Durchführung dieser Tätigkeiten hat der Konstrukteur Fähigkeiten erlernt und Erfahrungen gesammelt, die in CAD-Systemen durch den Rechner verwirklicht werden müssen. Eine wichtige Rolle spielt dabei das Zeichnen und das ergonomische Verhalten des CAD-Systems gegenüber dem Benutzer.

Betrachtet man die Elemente, die der Konstrukteur zur Beschreibung einer Lösung benutzt, so sind es in den Konstruktionsphasen der Funktionsfindung und Prinziperarbeitung einfache Symbole. In den Phasen der Gestaltung und Detaillierung sind es geometrische Körper unterschiedlicher Komplexität, aber auch zusammengesetzte Körper.

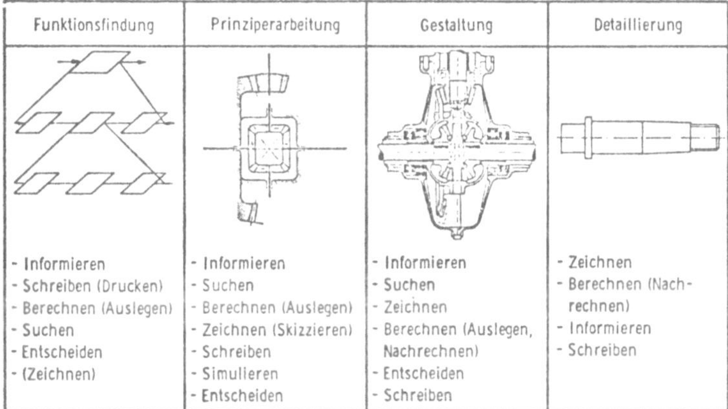

Bild 5: Grundtätigkeiten beim Konstruieren (17)

Aus dieser Sicht ist das CAD-System ein System zur Rechnerunterstützung der Kreativität des Konstrukteurs. In den letzten Jahren versuchten viele Forschungsvorhaben Konzepte der künstlichen Intelligenz (AI) und der Mustererkennung für den Entwurf von CAD-Systemen auszuwerten bzw. zu verwenden. Auf der Grundlage der Ergebnisse der IFIP Working Conference (1978) über "Artificial Intelligence and Pattern Recognition in Computer Aided Design" wird J.-C. Latombe (IMAG, Grenoble, France) bei dem CAD-Fachgespräch während der GI-Jahrestagung 1978 diesen Problemkreis behandeln und dabei die folgenden Aspekte erläutern (23):

(1) Gründe für den AI-Ansatz für CAD-Systeme (Komplexität von CAD-Systemen, Flexibilität der Mensch-Maschine-Kommunikation, Modellierung des Entwurfprozesses);
(2) Ergebnisse der AI-Forschung, die hierfür verwendet werden könnten;
(3) Berichte über Arbeiten, wo AI-Konzepte in CAD-Systemen integriert werden;
(4) Voraussagen über die Folgen hiervon für die CAD-Praxis und das CAD-Denken.

9. Ergonomische Aspekte des CAD-Arbeitsplatzes

Ergonomie ist die Wissenschaft von der Anpassung der Technik an den Menschen zur Erleichterung der Arbeit, mit dem Ziel, die Belastung des arbeitenden Menschen so gering wie möglich zu halten (18).

Das Arbeiten mit modernen technischen Geräten und Methoden nimmt bei CAD-Prozessen einen sehr großen Anteil der gesamten Arbeitszeit in Anspruch. Ergonomische Betrachtungen sind daher gerade bei CAD wichtig.

Will man die Dialoghilfsmittel auf ihre ergonomische Qualität hin untersuchen und vergleichen, so muß zunächst ein meßbares Kriterium gefunden werden. Es wird dabei meist von der Fehlerhäufigkeit, die bei vergleichbarem Test gemessen wird, ausgegangen. Wenn dieses Kriterium auch am eindeutigsten meßbar und daher für Vergleiche am besten geeignet ist, so soll im folgenden eine andere Wertung, die Ermüdung, allen Betrachtungen zugrunde gelegt werden. Der Grund liegt darin, daß die Ermüdung als Ursache, die Fehler als Wirkung betrachtet werden können.

Wird ein Dialoghilfsmittel nach ergonomischer Tauglichkeit überprüft, so müssen eine Fülle von Eigenschaften betrachtet und miteinander abgestimmt werden (26). Im einzelnen sind für gute Arbeitsbedingungen folgende Punkte zu berücksichtigen (am Beispiel eines Sichtgerätes):

a) - Bildschirmabmessung
- Bildschirmkontrast
- Auflösung
- Flackerfreiheit
- Menge der Information

b) - Anordnung des Sichtgerätes
- Arbeitstisch
- Abstell-,Ablagefläche
- Wärme und Geräuschentwicklung
- Benutzung von einem Benutzer oder Gruppen

c) - Antwortzeiten
- Darstellung wichtiger Information
- Komplexität von Einzelsymbolen
- Rückkoppelung
- Fehler und Hilfestellung

Bei der Aufzählung der einzelnen zu berücksichtigenden Eigenschaften wurden drei Gruppen gebildet, und zwar die Geräteeigenschaften (a), die Umgebungsbedingungen (b) und die Eigenschaften des Verfahrens oder der Software (c).

10. Konzipierung und Realisierung eines CAD-Systems

Die Konzipierung und Realisierung eines CAD-Systems sollte in zwei Schritte durchgeführt werden (20):

(1) Strukturierte Forderungsanalyse
(2) Systematische Systementwicklung

Die Definition von Forderungen beinhaltet die Problemanalyse, die zu einer funktionellen Spezifizierung führt. Darüber hinaus müssen die folgenden Fragen beantwortet werden:

(1) Warum wird das System gebraucht?
(2) Welche Systemeigenschaften sind dafür notwendig?

(3) Wie soll das System gebaut werden?

So gesehen muß sich die Definition von Forderungen an ein System mit den drei Themen beschäftigen:

(a) Kontextanalyse (Warum?)

(b) Funktionelle Spezifizierung (Was?)

(c) Entwurfszwänge (Wie?)

Nimmt man alle diese Betrachtungen zusammen, so definieren ihre Antworten bzw. Aussagen die Bedürfnisse, d.h. die Forderungen an das System, vollständig. Beschreibungen dieser Art geben lediglich einen Rahmen für das Problem: sie lösen es noch nicht. Die Definition der Forderungen versorgt lediglich die folgende Spezifizierung, den Entwurf und die Implementierung mit allen notwendigen Randbedingungen.

Die Phasen der systematischen Systementwicklung sind die Spezifikation, der Entwurf (Planung) die Implementierung (Programmierung, Testen) und die Dokumentation. Die Spezifikation ist die exakte Definition der zu lösenden Programmieraufgabe. Bei dem Entwurf, d.h. bei der Implementierungsplanung, wird das System bereits modularisiert betrachtet.

11. Beispiel aus der Praxis

In dem CAD-Fachgespräch während der GI-Jahrestagung 1978 wird von W.Klingenberg (Olympia-Werk AG) die Entwicklung eines CAD-Systems für die Feinwerktechnik, als ein Bericht aus der industriellen Praxis, erläutert (24). Es werden die Gründe für die Einführung von CAD und die Zielsetzungen angegeben, die resultierende Konzeption eines CAD-Systems (OLYKON) begründet, die Probleme bei der Realisierung diskutiert und die Erfolge und Probleme der Anwendung,sowie ihre Rückwirkungen auf das System erläutert. Anhand des Systems OLYKON werden demnach alle bisherigen Betrachtungen dieses Aufsatzes aus einer Anwendungssicht kritisch durchleuchtet und die jeweiligen, praxis-bedingten Entscheidungen angegeben und begründet.

12. Aufgaben bei der Auswahl und Einführung von CAD-Systemen

Bei der Einführung von CAD-Systemen wiederholen sich die bekannten Probleme der Einführung von DV in konzentrierter Form. Im Gegensatz zur kommerziellen DV sind die hier zu unterstützenden Entwurfsprozesse komplexer, die Anforderungen an die Datenbank, als zentralen Teil jedes CAD-Systems, schärfer und die Methoden einer CAD-Systemanalyse noch nicht entwickelt. Kaum eine Firma, als potentieller CAD-Anwender, ist heute aus Kostengründen in der Lage ,auf der Basis von Standard-Hard- und Software mechanische CAD-Systeme selbst zu entwickeln. Damit stellt sich die Aufgabe, Anwendungssoftware auszuwählen. Zwischen Moduln solcher Software verschiedener Hersteller, sowie zwischen Anwendungssoftware und zu verschiedenen Betriebssystemen gibt es praktisch keine brauchbaren Schnittstellen. Eine Ausnahme mit beträchtlichen Einschränkungen ist FORTRAN. Aus diesen Gründen neigen viele potentielle CAD-Anwender zum Kauf umfangreicher, schlüsselfertiger Systeme.

In jedem Fall müssen Maßstäbe entwickelt werden, die es gestatten, den Nutzen des Anwenders abzuschätzen. Bei der Bewertung von CAD-Systemen (Software- und/oder Hardware) können in sinnvoller Weise meist nur die externen Eigenschaften bewertet werden.

Der Anwender muß sich die folgenden Fragen beantworten:
- Wie wirtschaftlich werden die beabsichtigten Konstruktionsaufgaben gelöst?
- Welches Potential zur Lösung weiterer Angaben ist vorhanden?
- Mit welchem Aufwand ist das System durch den Anwender erweiterbar(programmierbar)?
- Welche (dokumentierten) Schnittstellen stehen dem Anwender zum Anschluß zukünftiger oder vorhandener Systeme zur Verfügung?

Dieses Thema wird im CAD-Fachgespräch während der GI-Jahrestagung 1978 von K.Pasemann (Volkswagenwerk AG.,Wolfsburg) ausführlich behandelt (25).

Auf eine wesentliche Konsequenz der Einführung von CAD-Systemen wird in (30) hingewiesen. Während in der Planungsphase des CAD-Systems ein weiter Spielraum hinsichtlich der Gestaltung des durch den Rechner zu unterstützenden Konstruktionsprozesses besteht, ist der Ablauf dieses Prozesses <u>nach</u> Realisierung des konkreten Systems starrer formalisiert und fixiert als zuvor. "An der erreichten, konkret vorliegenden Lösung kann der ausgenutzte oder verspielte Gestaltungsspielraum nicht mehr abgelesen werden"(Zitat). Werden die Anforderungen an das System (siehe Kap.10) nicht treffend genug erfaßt oder bei der Implementierung mißachtet, so muß sich ein Mißerfolg einstellen.

13. Notwendigkeit eines Prozeß-Modells für CAD

Während die vorangegangenen Kapitel mehr den Stand der Technik im CAD darlegen, soll im folgenden stärker auf noch erforderliche Entwicklungen eingegangen werden. Im CAD-Bereich richtet sich das Interesse gegenwärtig überwiegend auf "Systeme", deren Aufbau und Entwicklung (17). Der Entwurfs- und Konstruktionsprozeß selbst jedoch, den diese Systeme unterstützen sollen, ist noch nicht in dem Maße formal beschreibbar, wie es nötig wäre, um im konkreten Fall Hilfen für den Aufbau eines CAD-Systems abzuleiten. Nur in den einfachsten Fällen trifft die Vorstellung eines sequentiellen Ablaufs (evtl. mit Iterationen) zu, wie er sich im Begriff einer "Programmkette"(4) widerspiegelt. Vielmehr laufen - wenigstens bei größeren Produkten - viele Entwurfsteilprozesse parallel (oder zumindest quasi-parallel) ab. Innerhalb der einzelnen Teilprozesse werden neue Unteraufgaben erzeugt, die selbst durch ähnliche CAD-Prozesse gelöst werden müssen.

Auf eine durch den Termindruck hervorgerufene Eigenheit wird in (30) hingewiesen: Oft werden vorzeitig unvollständige oder nicht ausgereifte Informationen aus frühen Stadien des Konstruktionsprozesses an logisch spätere Prozesse weitergereicht (beispielsweise an die Fertigungsvorbereitung), wobei bewußt das Risiko in Kauf genommen wird, daß sich im Änderungsfalle ein größerer Aufwand einstellt, als es bei einem streng sequentiellen Vorgehen der Fall wäre.

Die Koordinierung und Synchronisierung dieser Teilprozesse wirft Probleme auf, wie sie auch im Bereich der Prozeßdatenverarbeitung auftreten. Nach Kenntnis der Autoren ist jedoch bislang kaum ein Versuch unternommen worden, die im Bereich der Prozeßdatenverarbeitung entwickelten und erfolgreich eingesetzten Konzepte (wie z.B. Semaphore für Aufgaben der Synchronisation) auf CAD-Systeme zu übertragen. Selbst wenn man darauf verzichtet, eine CAD-Sprache zu entwickeln, die derartige Konstruktionen enthält (in Analogie zur Prozeß-Sprache PEARL (27)), so erscheint es doch zweckmäßig, bei der Spezifikation von CAD-Systemen diese Hilfsmittel einzusetzen.

14. Die Portabilität von CAD-Programmen

Ein charakteristisches Merkmal der CAD-Praxis ist die Forderung nach kurzer Entwicklungszeit (25). Der modulare Aufbau der CAD-Programmkette ist ein wesentliches Mittel, die Entwicklung zu beschleunigen und frühzeitig Teilerfolge zu erzielen. Dies resultiert aus der Tatsache, daß viele Konstruktions- und Berechnungsmethoden für eine große Klasse von Produkten einsetzbar sind. Typische Beispiele hierfür sind Methoden der Festigkeitsberechnung, der Geometriebehandlung (28), der graphischen Darstellung (8,9) und der Kommunikation. Es muß jedoch deutlich zwischen der Portabilität der Methoden oder Algorithmen und der Portabilität der Programme (siehe Bild 2) unterschieden werden. Während für die Methoden die rechnerinterne Darstellung der Daten irrelevant ist, hängen die Programme immer mehr oder weniger von der Realisierung der Datenstruktur ab.

Durch Einsatz geeigneter Datenbanken (29) kann diese Abhängigkeit reduziert werden, allerdings auf Kosten der Abhängigkeit von dem betreffenden Datenbanksystem, wodurch wiederum die Portabilität von Installation zu Installation beeinträchtigt wird. Auch aus Gründen der Effektivität der Programmausführung ist es - zumindest wenn große Datenmengen zu verarbeiten sind - oft unumgänglich, die Daten in einer für Programme, die jeweilige Datenmenge und die betreffende Rechnerausstattung möglichst günstigen aber natürlich speziellen rechnerinternen Darstellung verfügbar zu halten. Die Konsequenz ist zwangsläufig der Verlust der Portabilität der Programme. Auch die Rechnerausstattung spielt eine wesentliche Rolle. Selbst bei Einsatz identischer Methoden können die Programme sehr verschieden sein, wenn die Betriebsmittel wie Hardwareausstattung (Speichergröße, Externspeicher, graphische Geräte) und Softwareausstattung (virtuelle Speicher, verfügbare Programm- und Unterprogrammbibliotheken) verschieden sind. Selbst Abrechnungsmodalitäten (relative Kosten von CPU, Speicher und Ein/Ausgabe-Vorgängen) sowie unterschiedliche Auslastung und damit unterschiedliche Antwortzeit der Rechenanlage kann dazu führen, daß"im Prinzip" portable Programme sich als nicht übertragbar erweisen.

Der in letzter Zeit spürbare Trend zur Vereinheitlichung von CAD-Arbeitsplätzen (17), CAD-typischen Rechnerkonfigurationen (4) und Kernfunktionen für graphische Ein/Ausgabe (8,9) wird die Portabilität von CAD-Programmen fördern. Dennoch wird es nötig sein, in stärkerem Maße als bisher Verfahren zur Anpassung der Programme an die verfügbaren Betriebsmittel einzusetzen. Dabei ist vor allem an Techniken der Programmgenerierung zu denken. Methoden, die im Bereich von Rechnerbetriebssystemen eingesetzt werden, müssen auf ihre Einsatzfähigkeit im CAD-Bereich überprüft werden. Ansätze hierzu finden sich in den bekannten integrierten Systemen ICES, IST, GENESYS, REGENT und DINAS. Die in diesen Systemen realisierten Konzepte wurden in (21) auf ein Systemkonzept übertragen, das von einer Prozeßdarstellung ausgeht. Es wurden Regeln abgeleitet für

(1) die funktionelle Dokumentation,
(2) die Identifikation und Verwaltung der Teilprozesse,
(3) die Weitergabe von Betriebsmitteln an die Teilprozesse,
(4) die Strategie der Betriebsmittelverwaltung und
(5) die Dokumentation der Betriebsmittelerfordernisse und Betriebsmittelverwaltung.

15. CAD-Sprachen

Wie von G. Nees (22) erläutert muß unterschieden werden zwischen Programmiersprachen, die für die Implementierung von CAD-Systemen benutzt werden,und Benutzersprachen, die der Benutzer des CAD-Systems zur Kommunikation mit dem System und dessen Programmen verwendet. Während es denkbar ist, daß als Implementierungssprache (heute überwiegend FORTRAN IV) in Zukunft einmal eine spezielle CAD-Programmiersprache bereitgestellt wird (ähnlich wie PEARL für Prozeßdatenverarbeitung), so wird es immer nötig sein, die Benutzersprachen - auch bei Einsatz gleicher Methoden und Programme - an die Erfordernisse der einzelnen CAD-Prozesse anzupassen. Bekannte Techniken der Sprachdefinition und der Sprachverarbeitung werden im CAD-Bereich in steigendem Maße eingesetzt und - besonders für die interaktive Kommunikation - weiterentwickelt werden müssen.

Planung der Benutzersprache und Planung des CAD-Prozesses müssen parallel durchgeführt werden. Vor allem der Frage der Bündelung von Information kommt große Bedeutung zu. Benutzersprache und Systemaufbau werden maßgeblich durch die Entscheidung geprägt, welche und wieviele Informationen jeweils als zusammengehörige Pakete vom Benutzer an das System bzw. umgekehrt fließen sollen.

16. CAD als wissenschaftliche Disziplin

Charakteristisch für größere CAD-Systeme ist die Vielfalt der in ihnen zur Anwendung kommenden Methoden der Informatik. Historisch gesehen der älteste Teilbereich umfaßt die numerischen Methoden für die im Rahmen von Entwurf und Konstruktion anfallenden Berechnungen. Diese ebenso wie halbnumerische Methoden (z.B. Sortieren,

Suchen) können heute als voll im CAD integriert angesehen werden. Auch Methoden zur Handhabung komplexerer Datenstrukturen gehören heute zum Handwerkzeug des CAD-Systemerstellers ebenso wie die Beherrschung der graphischen Datenverarbeitung. Es gibt jedoch Bereiche der Informatik, an denen die CAD-Praxis bis heute vorübergegangen ist. Diese für CAD-Anwendungen aufzubereiten und in die Praxis zu überführen, ist als eine der künftigen Aufgaben anzusehen (siehe Kap.15 und 16).
Mit der Vielfalt der Methoden ergibt sich das Problem: Wie können diejenigen, die in der Praxis einsatzfähige CAD-Systeme spezifizieren und erstellen sollen, diese Methoden beherrschen? Akzentuiert wird das Problem durch die Tatsache, daß die CAD-Leute überwiegend als Ingenieure ausgebildet sind und nicht immer bereits existierende Methoden der Informatik kennengelernt haben. So kommt es häufig dazu, daß "das Rad mehrfach neu erfunden wird" und im Prinzip gleiche Verfahren in unterschiedlicher Terminologie beschrieben werden (oder noch schlimmer: gleiche Terminologie wird für verschiedene Dinge eingesetzt). Eine der wichtigsten Aufgaben des CAD in den nächsten Jahren ist das Finden allgemein akzeptierter Konzepte und einer einheitlichen Terminologie; das Finden zu sich selbst. Erst dann wird es eine breite und effektive Ausbildung von CAD-Spezialisten geben, die in der Praxis mehr Gelerntes einsetzen als neue oder alte Methoden entwickeln.

17. Zusammenfassung

In diesem Aufsatz wurde eine einführende Übersicht in CAD-Systeme gegeben. Es wurde davon ausgegangen, daß ein CAD-System als ein spezielles Informationssystem angesehen werden kann, bestehend aus einer Datenbank, einer (Anwendungs-) Programmkette und einem Kommunikationsmodul. Die einzelnen Komponenten sind beschrieben und einige Regeln für den Entwurf von CAD-Systemen entwickelt worden.
Der Aufsatz soll als Einführung für das CAD-Fachgespräch während der GI-Jahrestagung 1978 dienen. Er wird ergänzt durch verschiedene Vorträge, die die Beziehungen zwischen CAD und "künstlicher Intelligenz", die verschiedenen Organisationsformen von CAD-Systemen, die Entwicklung eines CAD-Systems (OLYKON) aus der Sicht der industriellen Praxis und die allgemeine Problematik bei der Einführung von CAD-Systemen, eingehend behandeln werden.

18. Literatur

(1) Diebold Deutschland GmbH: Rechnerunterstütztes Entwickeln und Konstruieren in USA; CAD-Bericht, KFK-CAD 7, Januar 1976

(2) J. Encarnacao: Systemtechnologische Aspekte von CAD-Systemen; Informatik Fachberichte, Band 11, Springer Verlag, 1977; pp.20-51

(3) J. Hatvany, W.M. Newmann and M.A. Sabin: World survey of computer-aided-design; Computer-aided-design, Vol.9, No.2, April 1977, pp. 79-98

(4) R. Noppen: Technische Datenverarbeitung bei der Planung und Fertigung industrieller Erzeugnisse; Informatik Fachbericht,Band 11, Springer Verlag, 1977;pp.1-19

(5) Integrierte Programmsysteme: CAD-Bericht, KFK-CAD 2, Karlsruhe, September 1975

(6) F. Bauhuber: Spezielle Hilfsmittel für die Entwicklung fachbezogener Anwendersprachen; CAD-Mitteilungen 1/1973, pp.301-316, Karlsruhe, August 1973

(7) E.G. Schlechtendahl, G. Enderle, K. Leinemann und R. Schuster: Das Programmsystem REGENT im praktischen Einsatz; Informatik Fachberichte, Band 11, Springer Verlag, 1977; pp. 287-301

(8) Status-Report of the Graphics Standards Planning Committee (GSPC) of ACM/SIGGRAPH Computer Graphics, Vol. 11, No.3, Fall 1977

(9) R. Eckert, F.-J.Prester, E.G.Schlechtendahl und P. Wißkirchen: Functional description of the graphical core system GKS as a step towards standardization; Informatik Fachberichte, Band 11, Springer Verlag, 1977; pp.163-176

(10) R. Guedj et.al.: Preliminary report on the IFIP W.G. 5.2 Workshop on "Methodology in Computer Graphics", Chateau de Seillac, France, May 23-26, 1976

(11) R.Lindner: Aspects of interactive computer graphics - Applications and Systems - Fachgebiet Graphische Datenverarbeitung, Bericht Nr. 75-7; TH Darmstadt

(12) C.M. Eastman: Data bases for physical system design: a survey of US efforts; Proceedings of CAD 76 (IPC Science and Technology Press) London, March 1976, pp. 1-10

(13) D.T. Ross: ICES System Design; MIT Press, Cambridge, 1976

(14) P.L. Ciampi and J.D.Nash: Concepts in CAD Data Base Structures; Proceedings of the 13th Design Automation Conference San Francisco, June 1976, pp.290-296

(15) M. Burmeister, A. Seyferth, H.-J.Teichmann, R. Eckert und J. Encarnacao: Die Formularsprache FOSPRA und ihre Implementierung im REDAS-Datenerfassungssystem; Angewandte Informatik 6/75; pp. 247-255

(16) R. Lindner u. C. Tozzi: Detailed Concept for a Realization of an Advanced TV Raster Display Terminal; Fachgebiet Graphische Datenverarbeitung, Bericht Nr.77-1; TH Darmstadt

(17) H. Grabowski: Entwicklung und Integration von Verarbeitungsbausteinen in CAD-Systemen; Informatik-Fachberichte, Band 11, Springer Verlag, 1977;pp.52-77

(18) E. Hörbst: Technische Aspekte der Kommunikation in CAD-Systemen; Informatik-Fachberichte, Band 11, Springer Verlag, 1977; pp.120-146

(19) R. Konkart, E. Alff und C. Hornung: GRADAS - Graphisches Informationssystem auf der Grundlage einer relationalen Datenbank; Informatik-Fachberichte, Band 11, Springer Verlag, 1977; pp.262-276

(20) J. Encarnacao: Entwurfsverfahren und Werkzeuge der Systementwicklung; Bericht des Forschungssymposiums "Systeme mit Mikroprozessoren" Siemens AG, Zentrale

Forschung u. Entwicklung; Herausgeber: H.Schwärtzel, Juni 1978; pp.135-144

(21) E.G. Schlechtendahl: Rules for designing CAD software machines; Erscheint in den Proceedings of the International Conference "Interactive Techniques in Computer Aided Design"; Bologna, Italy; September 1978

(22) G. Nees: Struktur und Organisationsformen von CAD-Systemen aus der bisherigen Praxis; Erscheint in Beiträge zum CAD-Fachgespräch während der GI'78, Bericht GRIS 78-3; TH Darmstadt, Fachgebiet Graphisch-Interaktive Systeme

(23) J.-C. Latombe: The artificial intelligence approach to computer-aided design; Erscheint in Beiträge zum CAD-Fachgespräch während der GI'78, Bericht GRIS 78-3; TH Darmstadt, Fachgebiet Graphisch-Interaktive Systeme

(24) W. Klingenberg: Entwicklung eines CAD-Systems für die Feinwerktechnik; Erscheint in Beiträge zum CAD-Fachgespräch während der GI'78, Bericht GRIS 78-3; TH Darmstadt, Fachgebiet Graphisch-Interaktive Systeme

(25) K. Pasemann: Aufgaben bei der Auswahl und Einführung von CAD-Systemen; Erscheint zum CAD-Fachgespräch während der GI'78, Bericht GRIS 78-3; TH Darmstadt, Fachgebiet Graphisch-Interaktive Systeme

(26) T.F.M. Steward: Computer terminal ergonomics; Design Techniques for Teleprocessing Tagung; London, 1974

(27) A. Kappatsch, T. Martin: Full PEARL Language Description,Bericht KFK-CAD 130 Kernforschungszentrum Karlsruhe, 1977

(28) G. Spur et.al.: Behandlung technischer Objekte in CAD-Systemen - Geometrieverarbeitung und Zeichnungserstellung, Bericht KFK-CAD 31, Kernforschungszentrum Karlsruhe, Februar 1977

(29) A. Blaser, U. Schauer: Aspects of Data Base Systems for Computer Aided Design. Informatik-Fachberichte, Band 11. Springer Verlag, 1977; pp.78-119

(30) G. Beckmann et.al.: Auswirkungen des Einsatzes informationsverarbeitender Technologien im Bereich CAD/CAM - Eine sozialwissenschaftliche Begleituntersuchung. Wird als KFK-CAD-Bericht veröffentlicht. Kernforschungszentrum Karlsruhe, 1978

THE COMPLEXITY OF COMBINATORIAL COMPUTATIONS: AN INTRODUCTION

L.G. Valiant
Computer Science Department
Edinburgh University
Edinburgh, Scotland

The search for mechanizable procedures or algorithms for solving problems has been an integral part of mathematics from the beginning. Concern about the efficiency of the algorithms discovered was rarely mentioned explicitly, however, until the last few decades. Nevertheless, we must presume that this concern was often present, since such algorithms as Gaussian elimination for solving linear equations, Newton's iteration for algebraic equations, and Euclid's algorithm for greatest common divisors , appear very efficient even now after centuries of further investigation.

The field of study that has developed recently and is known as computational complexity attempts at a systematic study of the efficiency of algorithms. It looks at an old branch of knowledge from a fresh perspective, and in that sense, can claim to be the oldest part of computer science.

This article is intended as a short introduction to the field for computer scientists of other specialities. It takes the single notion of a "search function" as its theme and outlines some of the more important discoveries about combinatorial algorithms that can be discussed in terms of it. It does not attempt to be a survey. Alternative approaches to introducing the subject are taken by Knuth [20], Rabin [27] and Tarjan [33], for example, and these are recommended to the interested reader.

1. Search Functions

Detailed claims about the behaviour or run-time of an algorithm can only be made if we have a precise machine model on which it is to be executed. In contrast, statements of a very general nature can often be made without having to make very specific assumptions about the model of computation. An example of the latter kind is the assertion that an algorithm halts for all inputs. Such an assertion should not depend on the machine model.

For a successful theory of algorithmic efficiency we would like to have notions that bridge the two virtues of being (i) detailed enough to be relevant, and at the same time (ii) general enough to be essentially machine-independent. In discrete computations such notions fortunately exist, and we shall be concerned here with one of them, that of "polynomial time computability".

To formulate the notion we assume that the input is encoded as a sequence of symbols from some fixed finite set, (e.g. the set {0,1}) and that the encoding is reasonably efficient. For example representing the integer m by a sequence of m 1's is not reasonable since with n or fewer symbols we can then encode only n distinct inputs, while we would expect to be able to do an exponential number (e.g. 2^n or $2^{\sqrt{n}}$) of different ones, as we can indeed with binary notation.

Having chosen an encoding we say that the size of an input is the number of symbols needed to represent it. An algorithm runs in time f(n) if for all inputs of size up to n the algorithm takes at most f(n) "basic steps". It runs in polynomial time if for some constants c and k it runs in time $f(n)=cn^k$ for all n.

We have not said what our model of computation is or what a "basic step" is. The point of the polynomial time criterion is that we do not need to be very specific. For all the "reasonable" models of sequential computation that have been considered it can be shown that the classes of problems that are polynomial time computable are the same. (See [1] for more details) Also, in practice, the choice of encoding for a problem influences the size measure by only a polynomial factor. For example for representing a graph the several available representations are all polynomially related to each other, and also to the number of nodes. The conjunction of these two observations allows one to discuss polynomial time computability without having to be too specific about the input representation or the machine model.

In spite of its crudeness, the notion is nevertheless very relevant since the distinction between it and run-times that are worse (typically exponential) appears empiricly to be the most valid divide known between what can be computed in practice and what cannot (c.f. [1] p2). Consequently we will abbreviate the expression "polynomial time" to "fast" from now on.

Suppose we have two sets of objects X and Y with a size measure on each. The size of an object x will be denoted by $|x|$.

Definition. A search function for X and Y is a mapping f:X → subsets of Y s.t. (A) for some integer k, for all $x \in X$ if $y \in f(x)$ then $|y| < |x|^k$, and

(B) there is a fast algorithm that given x and y as input will determine whether $y \in f(x)$.

In words, a search function maps an object x to f(x), the set of solutions of x, under the constraints that (A) the solutions can be at most polynomially larger than the input, and (B) given objects x and y it can be determined fast whether y is indeed a valid solution of x.

Example 1. Let X be the set of positive integers, and Y the set of pairs of integers $\{(u,v) \mid u,v > 1\}$. Define

$f(x) = \{(u,v) \mid$ product of u and v is x$\}$.

Then f(x) consists of all the pairs of factors of x. Clearly the set f(x) is empty if and only if x is a prime number.

Example 2. Let X be the set of undirected graphs, and Y the set of sequences of edges. Let $y \in f(x)$ if y is a Hamiltonian circuit in x (i.e. y is a sequence of edges that forms a circular path that visits every node exactly once.)

The reader can make these examples precise by choosing any reasonable representation for them. Example 1 clearly satisfies both of the conditions of a search function since (A) the factors of a number are smaller than it, and (B) given x, u and v it can be checked fast whether x=uv. Similarly for Example 2.

Given a search function f and an input $x \in X$ the following are all natural questions to ask:

(a) Is f(x) empty? (i.e. do any solutions exist?)

(b) Find a $y \in f(x)$. (i.e. construct a solution to x.)

(c) How many elements are there in f(x)?. (i.e. count the number of solutions of x.)

In Example 1 these would correspond respectively to (a) testing for primality, (b) finding a pair of factors, and (c) counting the number of pairs of factors.

We notice that it follows from the definition that for any search function all three of the questions (a)-(c) can be computed by enumerating every object y allowed by restriction (A) and testing each one for validity by (B). Unfortunately this would take exponential time because there are that many choices of y to be tested. The fundamental questions we ask about a search function are whether (a), (b) or (c) can be computed fast for it, or, in other words, whether a different method that is substantially better than complete enumeration exists for it.

Very large numbers of classical problems can be phrased in terms of search functions. At first sight this concept would appear to be so general that it is surprising that significant new insights can be derived using it. Before showing that this is indeed the case we shall introduce several more examples that are well known and variously motivated.

Example 3: Satisfiability. X is the set of Boolean formulae and f(x) the set of assignments of truth values to the variables of x that make x true. (e.g. if x is "$(p_1+p_2)(\bar{p}_1+\bar{p}_2)$" then f(x) is the set $\{(p_1=T, p_2=F), (p_1=F, p_2=T)\}$.

Example 4: Cliques. Given a graph G and an integer k a solution is set of k nodes of G such that between each pair of these nodes there is an edge in G.

Example 5: Bin-packing. A set of n objects with respective "weights" $A=\{a_1, \dots . a_n\}$ can be "packed" into k bins if they can be distributed among k bins such that the total weight in each bin does not exceed unity. The search function

f(A, k) = set of ways of packing A into k bins

is then well-defined if, for example, the weights $\{a_i\}$ are represented as rational numbers in binary notation.

Example 6: Perfect Matchings. Given a graph with an even number n of nodes a solution is a set M of n/2 edges such that each of the n nodes is the end point of exactly one edge from M .

Example 7: Network Reliability. If G is a graph with nodes V and edge E then a subgraph of G is any graph with the same set of nodes V and some subset of E as edges. Let s and t be two nodes of G. Then define $f(G,s,t) = \{G' | G' \text{ is a subgraph of } G \text{ in which there is a path between } s \text{ and } t\}$. Here the number of solutions, denoted by $||f(G,s,t)||$, is related to network reliability as follows: Suppose in G each edge has probability 1/2 of failure. Then the probability that node s will be connected to node t will be

$$||f(G,s,t)||/2^{||E||}$$

where $||E||$ denotes the number of edges of G.

Example 8: Spanning Trees. If G is a graph a solution is any subgraph that forms a tree (i.e. has no cycles) and connects up all the nodes of G.

The status of these eight examples as far as the existence of fast algorithms is summarized in table 1, where a tick means "yes" and a question mark means "not known".

	existence	construction	counting
1. Primes	?	?	?
2. Hamiltonian C	?	?	?
3. Satisfiability	?	?	?
4. Cliques	?	?	?
5. Bin-packing	?	?	?
6. Matchings	√	√	?
7. Reliability	√	√	?
8. Spanning Trees	√	√	√

Table 1

The existence problem for Examples 7 and 8 are both computationally trivial corresponding, as they do, to the questions of whether the graph is connected or whether two points in it are connected. The reader can verify that any of the obvious algorithms for these problems also construct solutions. That testing for and constructing perfect matchings can be done fast is, however, significant and requires non-trivial algorithms [5,7].

Although counting problems have been extensively investigated for many decades there are very few positive results as far as counting solutions to search functions. One of the few exceptions is our last example, spanning trees, for which a fast algorithm is implicit in the work of Kirchhoff [18].

Until around 1971 the remaining open questions in the table appeared to be a set of diverse problems each of which merited further intensive work in the search for fast algorithms. In this decade, however, spectacular progress has been made in changing this viewpoint, as we describe in the next section.

2. The Hardest Search Functions

Complexity theory has provided an answer to these open problems that is perhaps the simplest and most beautiful imaginable. It asserts that they are not distinct problems that have to be investigated separately, but from large groups of computationally equivalent problems. In fact the eight questions of existence and construction for Examples 2-5 are all equivalent to each other! The six questions of counting for examples 2-7 form another group of equivalent problems. Furthermore this remarkable phenomenon is fairly typical of naturally occurring search functions.

To explain the meaning of "computationally equivalent" we need to introduce some definitions.

Definition A problem P is p-reducible to problem Q if there is a program ρ such that (i) ρ computes a solution to P and (ii) ρ contains calls of a subroutine for solving Q but makes a polynomial number of steps if each call of Q is notionally charged as one basic step (i.e. the actual execution time of the subroutine is not counted).

In other words, if P and Q both really require exponential time separately then "P is p-reducible to Q" means that "nearly all the computational difficulty of computing P can be concentrated in a small number of calls of Q". (N.B. if P can be computed fast by itself then the above reducibility relation is meaningless.)

Definition P and Q are p-equivalent iff P is p-reducible to Q and Q is p-reducible to P. This implies that the inherent complexity of problems P and Q are the same to within a polynomial relation, and if P and Q are hard to compute then they are hard for the same reason.

Definition A search function f is NP-complete iff the existence problem for any search function is p-reducible to the existence problem for f.

If a function is NP-complete it is in a strong sense "the hardest search function". This is a very strong requirement and, at first sight, it may be surprising that such a function exists at all. It was therefore a very significant discovery by Cook [4] that in fact several famous problems turned out to be examples of this hardest search function. The collection of known NP-complete problems was enlarged significantly by Karp [14] and now numbers several hundred.

The practical significance of NP-completeness is due to the empirical fact that for a large variety of previously open combinatorial problems it has turned out that they can be readily proved to be NP-complete. It is a happy fact that with a few exceptions such as our Example 1 natural search-functions have been successfully divided between the two categories of "computable fast" and "NP-complete".

One property that NP-complete problems share with each other is that their construction problem can always be reduced to their existence problem. The reader can easily verify this for the particular case of the cliques problem, for example.

In contrast, no such relation is known between testing a number of primality and finding its factors. Indeed, this apparent dichotomy has found a significant application in a recent scheme for cryptography [29].

One interesting property is shared by all search functions. It can be proved that for all of them there exist essentially optimal algorithms for their construction problems [23,30]. This distinguishes them from various, apparently pathological, functions for which there is no optimal algorithm [3]. Although these optimal algorithms are very simple they do not appear to be useful or their run-time analysable.

It is clear that counting the number of solutions is always at least as hard as determining existence, and hence that the counting problems for NP-complete problems must be difficult. The main negative results here are the ones that show that even where the existence problems are easy (e.g. Examples 6,7) counting is exactly as difficult as for NP-complete problems [34].

Definition A search-function f is #P-complete iff the counting problems for all other search-functions are p-reducible to the counting problem of f.

Examples 2-7 can all be shown to have #P-complete counting problems. The last two of them have not only combinatorial but also algebraic implications. For example, the network reliability problem has a close superficial resemblence to that of computing electrical resistance in a network of resistors, a problem which has an efficient algebraic solution. Similarly matchings are closely related to the permanent function (i.e. the determinant with all minus signs changed to plus). We therefore have explanations of why the search for fast algebraic techniques for these problems have failed.

The one remaining observation is that in the absence of such negative results as those given in [24] for other problems, it is still logically conceivable that all search functions have fast algorithms for existence, construction, and even counting. If that is the case then all the above results would be vacuous. Since the search for fast algorithms for many NP- and #P-complete problems has been pursued for decades, there is substantial historical evidence that these problems are inherently difficult to compute. The complexity theory community is therefore willing to embrace the hypothesis that no fast algorithms exist for them without having concrete proof. The consequences of the contrary would be so sweeping and fortunate that everyone would be glad to be proved wrong.

3. Fast Algorithms

In contrast with the apparent unities found amongst the hard problems, the search for positive results still proceeds by particular analysis. Important techniques of wide applicability in fast algorithms do, of course, exist.

Depth-first search for connectivity and planarity problems in graphs [12,32], augmenting paths for matchings and network flows [8,11], and embedding into linear algebra for counting problems [17,18] are remarkable examples of them. As an illustration consider an instance of the last of these, namely counting spanning trees in undirected graphs. Let the graph G have nodes $\{1,2,\ldots,n\}$ and consider the $(n-1)\times(n-1)$ matrix M^G such that

$$M^G_{ij} = \begin{cases} -1 \text{ if nodes } i \text{ and } j \text{ are joined by an edge} \\ -\sum_{i\neq k} M^G_{ik} \text{ if } i=j \end{cases}$$

Kirchhoff discovered the remarkable relationship that the determinant of M^G is exactly equal to the number of spanning trees of G. This implies a fast algorithm for the latter problem.

For NP-and #P-complete problems the existence of analogous relationships would be so revolutionary that we do not expect that they exist. Nevertheless we still wish to compute them in practice and therefore we have to settle for something short of the ideal, which would be an algorithm that is fast and exact on all inputs. Here we illustrate three approaches that can be taken under these circumstances:

(i) Randomized algorithms

Monte-Carlo methods for obtaining approximate solutions to problems are widely known. If we wanted to determine the probability of connectedness for our reliability problem to one decimal place, then we could do this fast, and with small probability of error, by simulating the random behaviour of the network a small number of times. That such randomization may help in the computation of problems with Yes/No answers, with no notion of approximation, has been appreciated fully only recently. A remarkable illustration of it is Strassen's algorithm for testing primality [31].

Essentially, he exhibits a search function

f: positive integers $\to$ sets of positive integers

such that for any n

$$f(n) = \begin{cases} \text{empty if } n \text{ prime} \\ \text{at least half of the set } \{1,\ldots,n-1\} \text{ if } n \text{ composite.} \end{cases}$$

Given a number n as input consider the following procedure:

"choose an arbitrary number b from $\{1,\ldots,n-1\}$ and test whether $b \in f(n)$"

Clearly, if n is prime the procedure always fails, and if n is composite then the procedure succeeds with probability at least a half. Now suppose this procedure is repeated k times independently. Then if n is prime it will fail all k times. If n is composite it will succeed at least once with large probability, since the probability of failing all k times is less than 2^{-k}. By choosing k large enough, k=100 say, we get a fast algorithm for testing primality that will be correct with overwhelming probability. The one in 2^{100} chance of error is considered acceptable for most purposes. (Note that the algorithm has no "bad inputs" on which it behaves worse than this.)

An important point about the function f is that it is different from the function defined in Example 1. In other words, given a number n a solution exists under the one function if and only if one exists under the other. The solutions themselves, however, are very different and a correct value of b in the above algorithm does not appear to give information about the factors of n.

Whether randomization can give an inherent gain in efficiency in computing primality is unknown since we have no proof that this problem is inherently difficult to compute by an exact algorithm. Results of Miller [25] indicate that the reverse may well be the case. For example, it is possible that with a little more understanding of number theory, we could specify a small subset of $\{1,...,n-1\}$ on which the function f would determine primality with certainty. Examples of other randomized algorithms are given by Rabin [28].

(ii) Algorithms with good probabilistic behaviour.

In the above algorithm for primality probabilities enter only as random computation steps, and the behaviour of the algorithm is good for all inputs. In this section we consider a notion that is weaker but of apparently wider applicability. We assume that inputs are drawn from some distribution and make deductions about the probabilistic performance of the algorithm.

The weakness of such results is that in most practical situations we have little guidance as to what distributions are valid. On the other hand many algorithms that perform well in practice do have very bad worst-case run-times [19], and it is reasonable to expect a probabilistic explanation for this.

A probabilistic distribution for graphs that has been widely studied is the following: $G_{n,N}$ is a random variable whose values are graphs with n nodes and N edges such that each possible such graph has the same probability. On this distribution several remarkable "threshold" phenomena are known. For example, if N is slightly less than $\frac{1}{2}n\log_e n$ then the graph is disconnected with large probability, while if it is even slightly greater, then the reverse holds [6].

The cliques problem offers a good illustration of what the computational questions are. Assuming, for example that a half of the edges are present (i.e. $N= n(n-1)/4$) it can be shown that with large probability the largest clique will be of size very near $2\log_e n$. (See [10] for such results for a slightly different distribution). Thus at no computational cost we can predict the existence of such cliques with some confidence. The computational problem of finding such a clique remains, and is currently unsolved. An "obvious" fast heuristic does have the following behaviour, however: with large probability it will find a clique of half the optimal size (i.e. near $\log_e n$). This algorithm simply initializes a set C to be empty and then looks at the nodes in some order and adds each one to C if it is joined by an edge to every node already in C.

One motivation in pursuing positive probabilistic results is that it may suggest new good heuristics. An example of this is that of finding Hamiltonian circuits. These clearly cannot exist in disconnected graphs, but, again, above a threshold near $N = \frac{1}{2} n \log_e n$ they suddenly occur with overwhelming probability. The work of Posa [24] in establishing this has suggested an algorithm that is efficient ($O(n \log^2 n)$ steps) and finds a Hamiltonian circuit with large probability if N is sufficiently larger than $\frac{1}{2} n \log_e n$[2]. In this case it appears that a non-trivial algorithm is really necessary, since some more immediately obvious heuristics can be shown to fail with large probability.

There is considerable difficulty in analysing the probabilistic behaviour of algorithms that are at all complicated. The problem is that even if the initially assumed distribution is the simplest possible, the progress of the algorithm will have a conditioning effect that is hard to follow. Recent examples of successful analysis can be found in [15,16,21,22].

(iii) Approximation algorithms.

A third way of retreating from the ideal "always exact and fast" algorithm is to modify the problem we are solving. Restricting the class of possible inputs to a subclass is one such modification. Here we shall illustrate a different kind that is valid when we have a notion of approximation.

Consider the bin-packing problem and suppose that instead of trying to find a packing in the optimal number M of bins we are satisfied with cM bins where c is a constant only modestly larger than unity. This is a reasonable aim since in practical situations we can often tolerate underutilization of resources by 5 or 10%,

Johnson et al. [13] analyse several simple heuristics for this problem with great precision. Assume the bins are labelled $B_1, B_2, \ldots$ and consider the following algorithms.

First Fit: The objects $a_1, \ldots, a_n$ are placed successively into a bin as follows:- for each a_i find the smallest j such that a_i can be placed into B_j without overfilling it.

First Fit Decreasing: First sort $\{a_i\}$ into decreasing order and then apply First Fit.

The reader can easily verify that these algorithms do not always find an optimal packing. The question is how far from optimal they may be in the worst case. Consider the case n=30t where for some very small $\varepsilon > 0$, a_i takes the values $\frac{1}{2} + \varepsilon$, $1/4 + 2\varepsilon$, $1/4 + \varepsilon$ or $1/4 - 2\varepsilon$, according to whether i is in the range [1,6t], (6t,12t], (12t,18t] or (18t,30t] respectively. It is straightforward to verify that the second algorithm will use 11t bins while an optimal packing into 9t bins exists. Thus the ratio c can be consistently as large as 11/9.

By very complex arguments it has been shown [13] that this simple example does embody the worst-case behaviour, so that the ratio 11/9 is, in fact, the worst that can happen (except for a small additive constant).

If such a factor of 22% is acceptable then the algorithm can be used with confidence. Also, one can hope that most of the time the performance will be substantially better than this worst case. For other problems, such as the travelling salesman problem there are results that show that for certain input distributions, answers very close to optimal will be obtained with large probability [15,16].

Analysis of the First Fit algorithm shows that it behaves rather badly, with a worst-case ratio of 17/10. In most situations the slightly more complex algorithm is therefore preferable.

Many varieties of approximation algorithms have been studied, and a good bibliography is given in [9]. One variety is the approximation scheme. This is a family of algorithms such that for any $\varepsilon > 0$ we can choose one member that approximates to within a ration of $(1 + \varepsilon)$. To decrease ε we may have to have a longer run-time.

4. Summary

We have given several examples to show that numerous important computational problems can be phrased in terms of search functions. The concepts of NP- and #P-completeness explain with considerable success why for many of these no fast algorithms have been found. Such negative results focus attention on notions of computation that are weaker than that of algorithms that are always fast and correct. We have given three approaches that can be tried if positive results of some such weaker nature are sought.

REFERENCES

1. A. Aho, J. Hopcroft and J. Ullman. The Design and Analysis of Computer Algorithms. Addison Wesley (1974).
2. D. Angluin and L. Valiant. Fast probabilistic algorithms for Hamiltonian circuits and matchings. Proc. 9th ACM Symp. on Theory of Computing. (1977).
3. M. Blum. A machine-independent theory of the complexity of recursive functions. JACM 14 (1967) 322.
4. S. Cook. The complexity of theorem proving procedures. Proc. 3rd ACM Symp. on Theory of Computing (1971) 151.
5. J. Edmonds. Paths, trees and flowers. Can. J. Math 17 (1965) 499.
6. P. Erdos and A. Renyi. On random graphs I, Publ. Math. 6 (1959) 290.
7. S. Even and O. Kariv. An $O(n^{2.5})$ algorithm for maximum matching in general graphs. Proc. 16th IEEE Symp. on FOCS (1975) 100.
8. L. Ford and D. Fulkerson. Flows in Networks. Princeton Univ. Press, (1962).
9. M. Garey and D. Johnson. Performance guarantees for heuristic algorithms. In "Algorithms and Complexity", J.F. Traub (ed), Academic Press (1976).

10. G. Grimmett and C. McDiarmid. On colouring random graphs. Math. Proc. Camb. Phil. Soc. 77 (1975) 313.

11. J. Hopcroft and R. Karp. An $n^{2.5}$ algorithm for maximum matchings in bipartite graphs. SIAM J. Comput. 2 (1973) 225.

12. J. Hopcroft and R. Tarjan. Efficient planarity testing. JACM 21 (1974) 549.

13. D. Johnson et al. Performance bounds for simple one dimensional bin-packing algorithms. SIAM J. Comput. 3 (1974) 299.

14. R. Karp. Reducibility among combinatorial problems. In Complexity of Computer Computations, R.E. Miller and J.W. Thatcher (eds). Plenum Press, N.Y. (1972) 85.

15. R. Karp. Probabilistic analysis of partitioning algorithms for the travelling salesman problem in the plane. Math. of Operations Research, Aug. 1977.

16. R. Karp. A patching algorithm for the nonsymmetric travelling salesman problem. SIAM J. on Comput. (to appear).

17. P. Kasteleyn. Graph theory and crystal physics. In Graph Theory and Theoretical Physics, F. Harary (ed), Academic Press (1967) 43.

18. G. Kirchhoff. Ann. Phys. Chem, 72, (1847) 497.

19. V. Klee and G. Minty. How good is the simplex algorithm? Proc. 3rd Symp. on Inequalities, UCLA. O. Shisha (Ed), Academic Press, (1969) 159.

20. D. Knuth. Mathematics and computer science: coping with finiteness. Science 194 (1976) 1235.

21. D. Knuth and A. Schonhage. The expected linearity of a simple equivalence algorithm. Theoretical Comp. Sci. 6 (1978) 281.

22. A. Korsunov. Solution of a problem of Erdos and Renyi on Hamiltonian cycles in nonoriented graphs. Soviet Math. Dokl. 17 (1976) 760.

23. L. Levin. Universal combinatorial problems. Probl. Peredaci Informacii 9 (1972) 115.

24. A. Meyer and L. Stockmeyer. The equivalence problem for regular expressions with squarring requires exponential space. Proc. 13th IEEE Symp. on SWAT (1972) 125.

25. G. Miller. Riemann's hypothesis and tests for primality. Proc. 7th ACM Symp. on Theory of Computing (1975) 234.

26. L. Posa. Hamiltonian circuits in random graphs. Discrete Mathematics. 14 (1976) 359.

27. M. Rabin. Complexity of Computations CACM 20 (1977) 625.

28. M. Rabin. Probabilistic algorithms. In Algorithms and Complexity, J.F. Traub. (ed) Academic Press (1976) 21.

29. R. Rivest, A. Shamir and L. Adleman. A method for obtaining digital signatures and public-key cryptosystems. CACM 21 (1978) 120.

30. C. Schnorr. Optimal algorithms for self-reducible problems. Proc. 3rd Coll. on Automata, Languages and Programming, S. Michaelson and R. Milner (eds) Edinburgh U. Press (1976) 322.

31. R. Solovay and V. Strassen. A fast Monte-Carlo test for primality. SIAM J. Comput. 6 (1977) 84.

32. R. Tarjan. Depth first search and linear graph algorithms. SIAM J. Computing 1 (1972) 146.

33. R. Tarjan. Complexity of combinatorial algorithms. Tech. Rep. STAN-CS-77-601, C.S. Dept, Stanford University (1977).

34. L. Valiant. Complexity of enumeration and reliability problems. SIAM J. on Comput. (to appear).

ZUM GLEICHEN THEMA:

W. Paul, Universität Bielefeld: "Über die Analyse von Algorithmen".

Ein Formalismus zur Analyse von Rechenzeit und Speicherplatz wird vorgeschlagen.

K. Pasedach, Philips Forschungslaboratorium in Hamburg: "Schnelle Algorithmen für Matrixoperationen".

Viel Rechenzeit wird in Computer-Programmen durch Matrixoperationen wie der Multiplikation einer Matrix A mit einem Vektor verbraucht. Häufig enthält die Matrix A strukturelle Redundanzen, z.B. Rangverminderung, Zirkulanz, direktes Produkt, direkte Summe, Bandstruktur oder Dünnbesetztheit. Bei a-priori-Kenntnis läßt sich das für schnelle Algorithmen ausnutzen und für beliebige Matrizen kann eine Methode der additiven Zerlegung in Redunanztypen angegeben werden, die einen schnellsten Algorithmus liefert.

J. van Leeuwen, Rijksuniversiteit Utrecht: "The Composition of Fast Priority Queues".

Priority queues are datastructures which effectively support INSERT, DELETE, MIN and UPDATE commands in some application environment. In order to achieve fast response times, priority queues have often been designed from balanced or binomial tree structures. We present additional techniques for structuring priority queues which will be useful (or otherwise entertaining) to programmers. First we characterize a class of common algorithms which perform MIN-DELETE-INSERT cycles, where the new element to be inserted is generated by some monotone function from the extracted min. The class includes e.g. Huffman's construction of minimum redundancy codes. We show that the algorithms can be implemented using a simple priority queue structure whose response time is bounded by a constant for each of the commands involved. Next, in a more general approach, we consider ways of composing fast priority queues from simpler, more conventional sub-queues. We obtain a priority queue, for instance, whose response time for INSERT commands is always bounded by a constant. DELETE and MIN commands may take O(log n) time, where n is the number of elements in the queue. The same approach leads to another priority queue organization (which is less efficient in space), whose response time for MIN commands is always bounded by a constant at the expense of a moderate increase in the time for INSERT commands (essentially to loglog n). The constructions shed new light on the structure of binomial queues, and illustrate various techniques and current ideas used for efficient datastructuring.

DATENSCHUTZ UND DATENVERARBEITUNG - EINIGE GRUNDSÄTZLICHE BETRACHTUNGEN ZUM BUNDESDATENSCHUTZGESETZ

Rolf Bayer
Institut für Informatik
Technische Universität München

Kurzfassung[1)]

Das BDSG wird aus der Sicht des Informatikers interpretiert. Es werden konkrete technische und organisatorische Maßnahmen abgeleitet, die zu treffen wären, um die Forderungen des BDSG zu erfüllen. Dabei sich ergebende Schwierigkeiten, einige Unzulänglichkeiten des Gesetzes, sowie einige prinzipielle Grenzen des Datenschutzen werden diskutiert.

Datenschutz erfordert sichere DV-Systeme. Die Frage der Delegation der Verantwortung für die Sicherheit von DV-Systemen wird aufgeworfen.

Notwendige Voraussetzungen für eine Überwachung der ordnungsgemäßen Anwendung von DV-Programmen werden untersucht. Bei der Programmerstellung und Handhabung stimmen diese Voraussetzungen weitgehend mit den Forderungen einer modernen Programmiertechnik überein. Aufgaben und Verantwortungsbereiche der DV-Abteilung und des Datenschutzbeauftragten werden gegeneinander abgegrenzt.

---

1) Die gesamte Arbeit erscheint im INFORMATIK-SPEKTRUM 1, 1. Springer 1978.

MIKROPROGRAMMIERUNG

Helmut K. Berg
Technische Universität Berlin
Fachbereich Informatik

1. Einleitung

Seit der Prägung des Begriffs Mikroprogrammierung durch M. V. Wilkes im Juli 1951 [1] ist die Mikroprogrammierung zu einer Technik für den Entwurf und die Implementierung der Kontrollfunktionen von digitalen Rechnersystemen gereift, ohne dabei eine formale Definition zu erlangen. Wir beabsichtigen nicht, eine derartige Definition zu geben, sondern versuchen, anhand von grundlegenden Definitionen in die Thematik einzuführen, den gegenwärtigen Stand des Fachgebietes Mikroprogrammierung zu beleuchten und Tendenzen der Entwicklung dieses Fachgebietes aufzuzeigen. Als Grundlage dafür unterscheiden wir die folgenden beiden Aspekte der Mikroprogrammierung:

- die systematische Implementierung von Steuerungsabläufen in der Rechnerhardware;
- die Interpretation von spezifischen Maschinenbefehlen durch Mikroprogramme.

Der erste Aspekt repräsentiert die Ideen des von M. V. Wilkes vorgeschlagenen Konzepts der <u>Mikroprogrammierung</u> [1,2] (obwohl auch hier schon auf die Möglichkeiten der Mikroprogrammierung spezifischer Maschinenbefehlsvorräte verwiesen wurde). Der zweite Aspekt, der sich auf die Spezialisierung der Benutzung von Rechnersystemen durch mikroprogrammierte Implementierungen von Maschinenbefehlen bezieht [3], wird gemeinhin als <u>Firmware</u> bezeichnet. Der Begriff Firmware, der im Jahre 1967 von A. Opler eingeführt wurde [4], beschreibt Mikroprogramme für die Interpretation von Maschinenbefehlen.

Zur weiteren Unterscheidung der Begriffe Mikroprogrammierung und Firmware ist es angebracht, die jeweilige Beziehung zur Implementierung von Rechnersystemen zu betrachten. Im Rahmen des Entwurfs von Rechnerhardware und der Implementierung von Steuerungsabläufen stehen z. B. Fragen nach Tendenzen in der Halbleiter-Technologie, Hardware-Kosten, -Zuverlässigkeit und -Wartung im Vordergrund. Aufgrund dieses Hardwarebezugs wird die Mikroprogrammierung gemeinhin mit dem Entwurf und der Realisierung von Mikrobefehlsvorräten und Mikrobefehlsformaten für die effiziente Implementierung von Steuerungsabläufen in Beziehung gebracht. Andererseits ist der Mikroprogrammierer an der Benutzung des gegebenen Mikrobefehlsvorrates interessiert. Für ihn ist die Organisation der Rechnerhardware nur in bezug auf den Kontrollfluß und die funktionellen Charakteristiken der Hardware-Komponenten von Wichtigkeit. Der Mikroprogrammierer ist maßgeblich an den verfügbaren Mikroprogrammierungshilfen und an der Spezifikation der zu implementierenden Funktionen interessiert. Die vorangehende Diskussion deutet an, daß Mikroprogrammierung und Firmware sich an der Grenzlinie zwischen Hardware- und Software-Techniken für den Entwurf und die Implementierung von Rechnersystemen treffen. Deshalb werden wir sowohl die Hardware-Ebene als auch die Software-Ebene von Rechnersystemen betrachten. Unseren Betrachtungen legen wir die folgenden Definitionen zugrunde:

Rechnerarchitektur: Eine Rechnerarchitektur beinhaltet ein Operationsprinzip, nach dem die Hardware des Rechners arbeitet, sowie die Hardware-Struktur des Rechneraufbaus aus Hardware-Betriebsmitteln.

Rechnerorganisation: Eine Rechnerorganisation definiert die funktionelle Arbeitsweise der einzelnen Hardware-Betriebsmittel eines Rechners sowie ihrer Verbindungseinrichtungen.

Rechnerrealisierung: Eine Rechnerrealisierung beinhaltet den logischen Entwurf und die physikalische Realisierung der einzelnen Hardware-Betriebsmittel und ihrer Verbindungseinrichtungen.

Aus den obigen Definitionen läßt sich direkt folgender hierarchischer Zusammenhang ableiten, der in Bild 1 graphisch dargestellt ist. Das Operationsprinzip definiert das funktionelle Verhalten des gesamten Rechnersystems durch die Festlegung der Informationsdarstellung, -interpretation und -transformation in der Maschine sowie durch die Definition von Kontroll-Algorithmen für die Informationsinterpretation und -transformation, die die Kommunikations-Mechanismen zwischen den Hardware-Betriebsmitteln einschließen. Diese Definitionen basieren nur auf einer Spezifikation der Art und Zahl der Hardware-Betriebsmittel und ihrer Verbindungseinrichtungen. Die Definition einer Rechnerorganisation stellt eine funktionelle Implementierung des Operationsprinzips und der Rechnerstruktur dar, die den Daten- und Kontrollfluß in und zwischen den funktionell definierten Hardware-Betriebsmitteln (Prozessoren, Speicher, periphere Einheiten) festlegt. Die Rechnerrealisierung wird durch eine physikalische Implementierung der Rechnerorganisation erhalten. Die Rechnerrealisierung betrifft Fragen der Schaltungs-, Packungs- und Verbindungstechnik, die in diesem Text nicht näher behandelt werden.

RECHNER-	Funktionelle →	RECHNER-	Physikalische →	RECHNER-
ARCHITEKTUR	Implementierung	ORGANISATION	Implementierung	REALISIERUNG

Bild 1: Stufen der Implementierung eines Rechnersystems

2. Grundlegende Definitionen

Die folgenden Definitionen dienen dem Zweck der Festlegung wesentlicher Merkmale, die die Mikroprogrammierung und Firmware als die Schnittstelle zwischen Software und Hardware definieren. Zunächst entwickeln wir ein Modell des geschichteten Aufbaus eines Rechnersystems. Danach wenden wir uns der Arbeitsweise der Rechnerhardware zu und beschreiben die Mikroprogrammierung als eine Alternative für die Implementierung der Steuerungsabläufe in der Rechnerhardware.

2.1. Schichtenmodell eines Rechnersystems

Wir beginnen unsere Betrachtungen mit Wegners Definitionen [5] des Berechnens und eines Prozessors.

Berechnen: Das Berechnen besteht in einer Folge von Transformationen, durch die eine Quelldarstellung über eine Folge von Zwischendarstellungen in eine Enddarstellung überführt wird. Eine Darstellung ist ein Programm mit den zugehörigen Datenmengen.

Prozessor: Ein Prozessor ist eine aktive Komponente eines Rechners, die eine Transformation auf ihren Daten ausführt.

In Abwandlung einer Definition der Mikroprogrammierung von Rosin [6] können wir sagen, daß die Folge von Transformationen der Quelldarstellung bis zur Enddarstellung notwendig ist, um etwas (vom Standpunkt des Benutzers) Vernünftiges mit einem (vom Standpunkt des Benutzers) unvernünftigen Prozessor auszuführen. Die Folge von Transformationen, die bei einer Berechnung durch ein Rechnersystem erzeugt werden muß, führt auf das Modell eines Rechnersystems als eine Hierarchie von abstrakten Maschinen.

Abstrakte Maschine: Eine abstrakte Maschine ist ein Paar

$$(L,P),$$

wobei L eine Sprache und P ein (abstrakter) Prozessor ist, der durch Übersetzung oder Interpretation Darstellungen in der Sprache L transformieren kann.

<u>Geschichtete Hierarchie von abstrakten Maschinen</u>: Eine geschichtete Hierarchie von abstrakten Maschinen ist eine Folge von

$$
\begin{array}{l}
(L_0, P_0) \\
(L_1, P_1) \\
\dots\dots\dots \\
(L_{n-1}, P_{n-1}),
\end{array}
$$

wobei die Transformation einer Darstellung in einer Sprache L_i durch einen Prozessor P_i zu einer Darstellung in der Sprache L_{i+1} führt, $0 \leq i \leq n-2$.

Wenn das "Schichtenmodell" auf Wegners Definition des Berechnens angewandt wird, ergibt sich, daß die Quelldarstellung in L_0 ist, von der eine Enddarstellung in L_n erzeugt wird. Da die Transformation der Darstellung in L_n in der "Identitätstransformation" besteht, braucht die abstrakte Maschine (L_n, P_n) nicht betrachtet zu werden.

Wenn wir ein konventionelles Rechnersystem aus der Klasse der von-Neumann-Architekturen betrachten, mag das in Bild 2 gezeigte Schichtenmodell gelten.

Im Schichtenmodell eines jeden Rechnersystems existiert die Grenzlinie zwischen Software und Hardware, die durch die entsprechende Rechnerarchitektur festgelegt ist. Die Anzahl der existierenden Ebenen im Software-Bereich ist durch die Organisation der Systemsoftware bestimmt, während die Rechnerorganisation die Anzahl der Ebenen im Hardware-Bereich festlegt. Wir beschränken unsere Betrachtungen vorerst auf den Hardware-Bereich, dem Mikroprogrammierung und Firmware von ihrer Definition her zugeordnet sind.

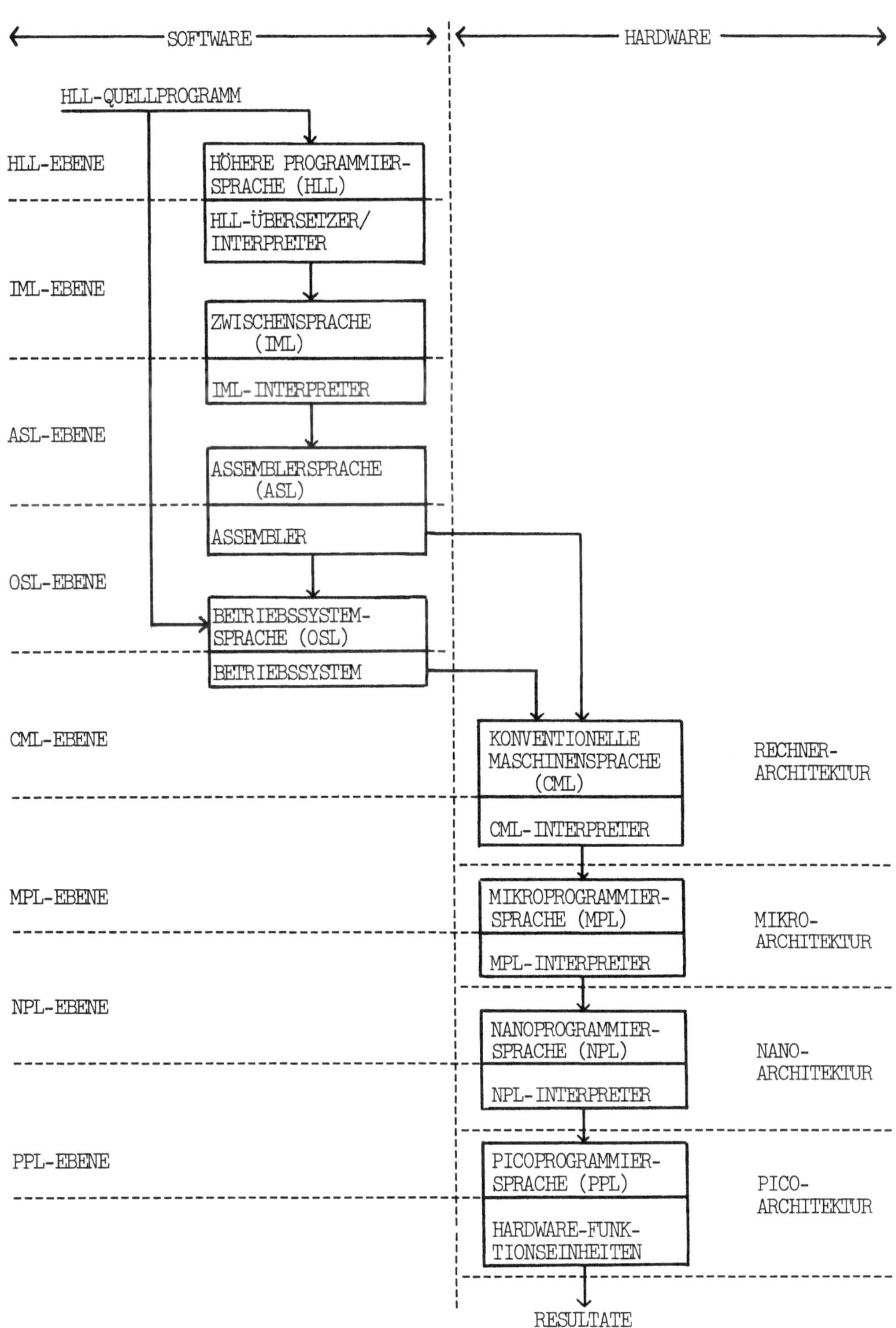

Bild 2: Schichtenmodell eines konventionellen Rechnersystems

Für jede Ebene im Hardware-Bereich kann die Architektur und Organisation der zugeordneten abstrakten Maschinen definiert werden [7].

Architektur einer abstrakten Maschine: Die Architektur einer abstrakten Maschine (L_i, P_i) im Hardware-Bereich des Schichtenmodells beinhaltet ein Operationsprinzip für den Prozessor P_i, das auf der Informationsstruktur der Sprache L_i basiert, und die Hardware-Struktur des Prozessors P_i.

Organisation einer abstrakten Maschine: Die Organisation einer abstrakten Maschine (L_i, P_i) im Hardware-Bereich des Schichtenmodells definiert die funktionelle Arbeitsweise der Hardware-Komponenten des Prozessors P_i und ihrer Verbindungseinrichtungen.

Aus den obigen Definitionen ersehen wir, daß die Organisation einer abstrakten Maschine (L_i, P_i) durch die Architektur und die Organisation der abstrakten Maschine (L_{i+1}, P_{i+1}) definiert ist. Damit lassen sich die Beziehungen zwischen den Architekturen und Organisationen der abstrakten Maschinen im Hardware-Bereich unseres Schichtenmodells wie folgt beschreiben:

RECHNERORGANISATION = MIKRO-ARCHITEKTUR + MIKRO-ORGANISATION
MIKRO-ORGANISATION = NANO-ARCHITEKTUR + NANO-ORGANISATION
NANO-ORGANISATION = PICO-ARCHITEKTUR + PICO-ORGANISATION

Durch Ersetzung erhalten wir die folgende Beziehung:

RECHNERORGANISATION = MIKRO-ARCHITEKTUR + NANO-ARCHITEKTUR + PICO-ARCHITEKTUR + PICO-ORGANISATION

Entsprechend dieser Beziehung schließt die Thematik Mikroprogrammierung und Firmware die Architekturebenen im Hardware-Bereich unseres Schichtenmodells sowie die Organisation der abstrakten Maschine (PPL, HARDWARE-FUNKTIONSEINHEITEN) ein. Rosins Definition der Mikroprogrammierung [6] "microprogramming is the implementation of hopefully reasonable systems through interpretation on unreasonable machines" verweist ebenso auf diese Beziehung, die die Hardware-Funktionseinheiten (ALU, Multiplexer, Shifter usw.) als die Interpreter einer mehrstufigen Implementierung des Operationsprinzips eines Rechnersystems auszeichnet.

Ebenso wie es möglich ist Architekturebenen im Hardware-Bereich des Schichtenmodells einzuführen, können die verschiedenen Ebenen durch die Sprachen der entsprechenden abstrakten Maschinen gekennzeichnet werden.

Darüber hinaus ist jeder Sprache L_i ein Interpreter (Prozessor) P_i zugeordnet, der üblicherweise in der Sprache L_{i+1} implementiert ist.

<u>Konventionelle Maschinensprache (CML)</u>: Die konventionelle Maschinensprache beinhaltet Instruktionen für arithmetische und logische Operationen, unbedingte und bedingte Verzweigungen und andere organisatorische Operationen (z. B. Rotieren und Maskieren von Bitfeldern). Eine konventionelle Maschineninstruktion CIN spezifiziert eine konventionelle Maschinenoperation COP und 0, 1 oder mehrere Operanden.

<u>CML-Interpreter</u>: Ein CML-Interpreter besteht aus einem Befehlsentschlüssler für das Holen und Dekodieren von CML-Instruktionen (CIN) und einer Menge von Mikroprogrammen MP_i für die Ausführung der verschiedenen CML-Operationen COP_i. Der CML-Interpreter steuert die Ausführung eines CML-Programms.

<u>Mikroprogrammiersprache (MPL)</u>: Die Mikroprogrammiersprache beinhaltet Mikroinstruktionen für arithmetische und logische Mikrooperationen, unbedingte und bedingte Mikroprogrammverzweigungen und (Register-)Transfer-Mikrooperationen. Eine Mikroinstruktion MIN spezifiziert eine oder mehrere Mikrooperationen MOP und gegebenenfalls Mikroinstruktionsoperanden.

<u>MPL-Interpreter</u>: Ein MPL-Interpreter besteht aus einem Mikrobefehlsentschlüssler für das Holen und Dekodieren von Mikroinstruktionen und einer Menge von Picoprogrammen PP_j für die Ausführung der verschiedenen Mikrooperationen MOP_j. Der MPL-Interpreter steuert die Ausführung eines Mikroprogramms MP.

<u>Picoprogrammiersprache (PPL)</u>: Die Picoprogrammiersprache beinhaltet Picoinstruktionen für logische Picooperationen. Picoinstruktionen (PIN) spezifizieren üblicherweise nur eine einzige Picooperation POP und sind Anweisungen an Hardware-Funktionseinheiten, die dort bestimmte Transformationen auslösen.

<u>PPL-Interpreter</u>: Jede Hardware-Funktionseinheit interpretiert eine Untermenge der Picoinstruktionen, deren Gesamtheit die Picoprogrammiersprache PPL darstellt.

Die Beziehungen zwischen den abstrakten Maschinen im Hardware-Bereich des Schichtenmodells sind in Bild 3 dargestellt. Dabei haben wir die abstrakte Maschine (NPL, NPL-INTERPRETER) aus folgenden Gründen ausgelassen :

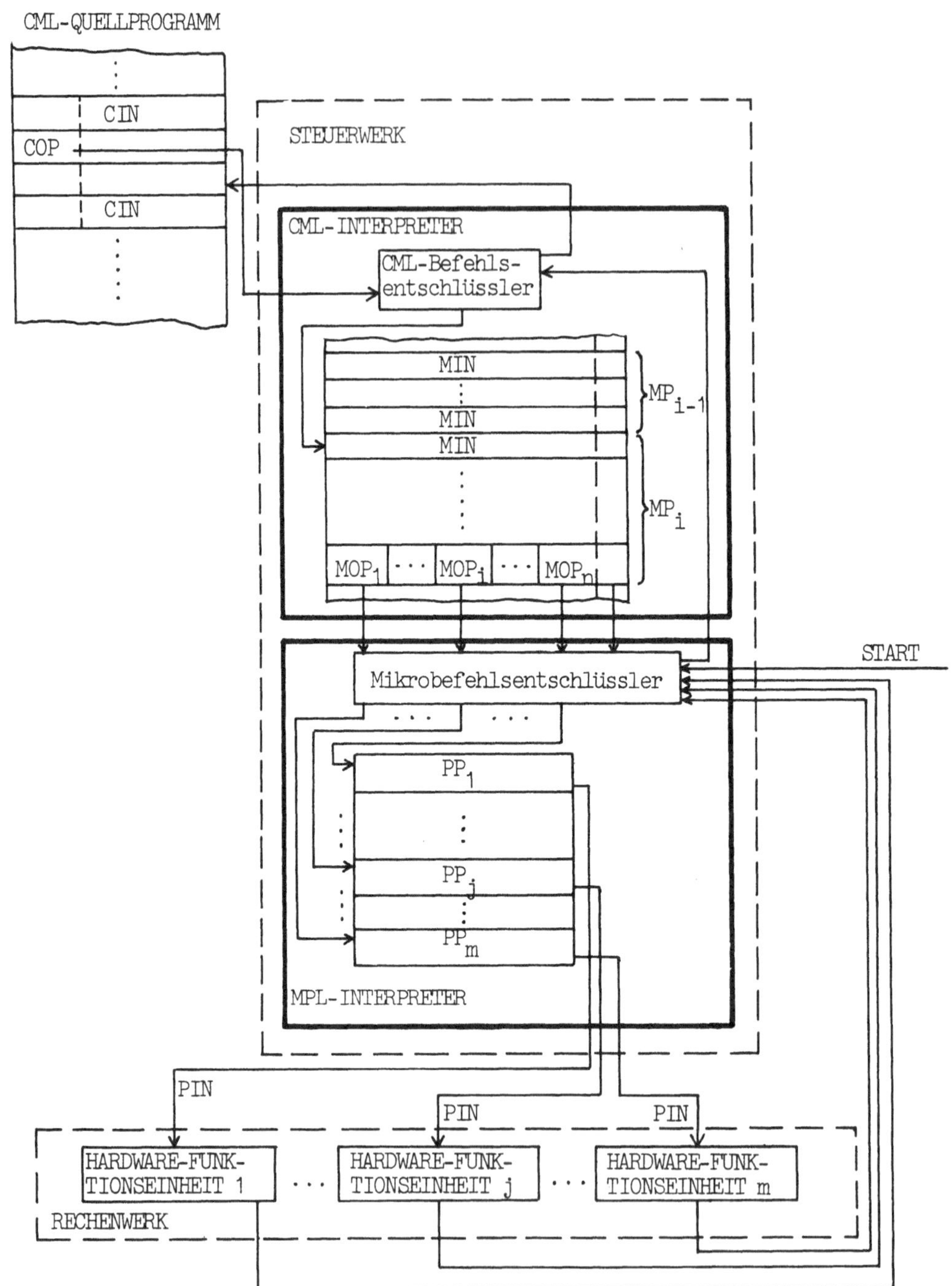

Bild 3: Beziehungen zwischen den abstrakten Maschinen im Hardware-Bereich des Schichtenmodells

Die NPL-Ebene ist funktionell mit der MPL-Ebene gleichzusetzen. Bei Rechnersystemen, die von der Nanoprogrammierung Gebrauch machen, wie z. B. die Nanodata QM1 [8], sprechen wir auch oft von zweistufiger Mikroprogrammierung, um damit auszudrücken, daß der MPL-Interpreter Mikrooperationen nicht direkt in Picoinstruktionen umwandelt, sondern ein Nanoprogramm aufruft, dessen Interpretation zur Erzeugung der Picoinstruktionen führt. Da bei den meisten existierenden Systemen diese Ebene jedoch fehlt, werden wir im folgenden die NPL-Ebene nicht berücksichtigen.

Aus Bild 3 erkennen wir weiterhin die Notwendigkeit, zwischen kontrollierenden und kontrollierten Hardware-Funktionseinheiten zu unterscheiden. Die kontrollierten Hardware-Funktionseinheiten nennen wir das Rechenwerk. Die Hardware-Funktionseinheiten, die den MPL-Interpreter implementieren, stellen die kontrollierenden Hardware-Funktionseinheiten dar. Die Picoinstruktionen, die die Transformationen von Mikrooperationen in Picoinstruktionen im MPL-Interpreter auslösen, werden nicht durch Transformationen des CML-Quellprogramms erzeugt, sondern werden von außen z. B. durch Drücken einer START-Taste an der Prozessorkonsole erzeugt. Die Picoinstruktion START initiiert einen zyklischen Steuerungsablauf im MPL-Interpreter, der nur durch einen speziellen Mechanismus, wie z. B. das Drücken der STOP-Taste an der Prozessorkonsole, beendet werden kann. Das Rechenwerk und das Steuerwerk eines Prozessors lassen sich jetzt wie folgt definieren:

<u>Rechenwerk</u>: RECHENWERK = PPL-INTERPRETER

<u>Steuerwerk</u>: STEUERWERK = CML-INTERPRETER + MPL-INTERPRETER

Mit Bezug auf die Ausführung von CML-Programmen und MPL-Programmen einerseits und PPL-Programmen andererseits muß ein wesentlicher Unterschied beachtet werden. Die Instruktionen eines CML-Programms oder eines MPL-Programms werden sequentiell ausgeführt und ermöglichen damit die Anwendung des Befehlszähler-Prinzips. Dahingegen werden die PPL-Programme für die Ausführung der Mikrooperationen in einer Mikroinstruktion parallel ausgeführt. Für die parallele Ausführung von Picoinstruktionen müssen natürlich getrennte Hardware-Funktionseinheiten zur Verfügung stehen. Dieser Parallelismus erschwert das Mikroprogrammieren und ist eine Quelle charakteristischer Mikroprogrammierungsfehler.

2.2. Mikroprogrammierte Steuerungsabläufe

Ein konventionelles Rechnersystem läßt sich funktionell in vier Untereinheiten aufgliedern: Steuerwerk, Rechenwerk, Hauptspeicher und Ein-/Ausgabe-Einheiten. Das Steuerwerk und das Rechenwerk bilden zusammen den Prozessor (CPU). Die Ein-/Ausgabe-Einheiten umfassen Kommunikationsmedien (z. B. Teleschreiber) und externe Massenspeicher (z. B. Magnetband- oder Plattenspeicher). Das Steuerwerk kontrolliert die Operationen der Untereinheiten und den Informationsfluß in den Verbindungseinrichtungen des Rechnersystems. Die vom Steuerwerk generierte und interpretierte Kontrollinformation setzt sich aus dem Steuerungsvektor und dem Zustandsvektor zusammen.

Steuerungsvektor: Die Komponenten des Steuerungsvektors nennen wir Steuersignale. Der Steuerungsvektor enthält die Steuersignale, die vom Steuerwerk erzeugt werden, um eine Transformation in einer Hardware-Funktionseinheit des Rechnersystems auszulösen. Ein Steuersignal ist die Realisierung einer Picoinstruktion.

Zustandsvektor: Der Zustandsvektor ist ein Indikator spezifischer Zustände der Untereinheiten eines Rechnersystems, der in einem oder mehreren Status-Registern gespeichert ist und durch die Ausführung von Mikroinstruktionen verändert wird. Die Interpretation des Zustandsvektors im Steuerwerk bedingt die Erzeugung von Steuersignalen. Eine Komponente des Zustandsvektors nennen wir ein Zustandsbit.

Auf der Grundlage der obigen Definitionen kann ein Rechnersystem als ein System miteinander verbundener, endlicher Automaten betrachtet werden. Für jede Untereinheit ist dann eine Zykluszeit als das Zeitintervall zwischen zwei aufeinanderfolgenden Zustandsänderungen definiert. Da die Zykluszeiten der möglicherweise gleichzeitig operierenden Untereinheiten normalerweise verschieden sind, ist die Synchronisierung der Interpretation des Zustandsvektors der kontrollierten Untereinheiten mit der Erzeugung von Steuersignalen eine wesentliche Aufgabe des Steuerwerks. Diesbezüglich unterscheiden wir die folgenden Zeitbedingungen für Steuerungsabläufe [7] :

Synchrone Steuerung mit konstanter Zykluszeit: Bei synchroner Steuerung mit konstanter Zykluszeit werden alle in einer Mikroinstruktion spezifizierten Mikrooperationen in einem Steuerwerkzyklus ausgeführt.

Synchrone Steuerung mit variabler Zykluszeit: Bei synchroner Steuerung mit variabler Zykluszeit kann die Ausführung einer Mikroinstruktion mehrere Steuerwerkzyklen betragen. Die Zahl der benötigten Steuerwerkzyklen ist durch den Typ der auszuführenden Mikrooperationen bestimmt und daher für verschiedene Mikroinstruktionen unterschiedlich. Das Steuerwerk ändert seinen Zustand mit dem letzten zur Ausführung benötigten Steuerwerkzyklus.

Asynchrone Steuerung: Bei asynchroner Steuerung arbeiten die kooperierenden Untereinheiten in verschiedenen Zykluszeiten. Nachdem sich der Zustandsvektor einer asynchron gesteuerten Untereinheit stabilisiert hat, wird seine Interpretation mit dem Steuerwerkzyklus synchronisiert und die Untereinheit ist in der Lage, neue Steuersignale zu interpretieren.

Die meisten Hardware-Funktionseinheiten im Rechenwerk und gegebenenfalls auch der Hauptspeicher werden synchron gesteuert. Die Ein-/Ausgabe-Einheiten, der Hauptspeicher und Hardware-Funktionseinheiten im Rechenwerk, die ein selbständiges Steuerwerk beinhalten, werden üblicherweise asynchron gesteuert. Asynchrone Steuerung erfordert eine zusätzliche Hardware-Einrichtung für die Synchronisierung, die wir Interface nennen. Ein Interface kann lediglich aus einigen Speicherbits bestehen, in welchem Fall die kooperierenden Untereinheiten die Synchronisierung selbständig durchführen müssen, oder es kann ein Synchronisierungsschaltwerk beinhalten, das die kooperierenden Untereinheiten weitgehend von der Synchronisierung befreit.

Mit dem Grad der Parallelansteuerung verschiedener Untereinheiten und der Parallelausführung von Mikrooperationen in den Hardware-Funktionseinheiten der einzelnen Untereinheiten erhöht sich die Zahl potentieller Mikroprogrammierungsfehler, die sich aus den Zeitbedingungen für Steuerungsabläufe ergeben. Diese Fehlerquellen lassen sich wie folgt charakterisieren:

- gleichzeitige Erzeugung und Verwertung derselben Daten
- mehrfache und gleichzeitige Benutzung von Datenwegen (Verbindungseinrichtungen)
- Synchronisierungsfehler, die zu (von parallelen Software-Programmen bekannten) Effekten wie "deadlock", "blocking" und "starvation" führen können.

In herkömmlichen Rechnersystemen ist das Steuerwerk in der Form eines Schaltwerks realisiert. In diesem Schaltwerk, das auch oft "controller" genannt wird, sind die Mikroinstruktionen für die Interpretation von CML-Instruktionen zusammen mit dem MPL-Interpreter durch Schaltnetze realisiert, die aus dem gespeicherten Steuerwerkzustand und dem Zustandsvektor der kontrollierten Untereinheiten einen Steuerungsvektor erzeugen. Derartige "hardwired" Steuerwerke sind aufgrund ihrer Komplexität ad hoc in ihrem Entwurf und starr in ihrer Funktionalität, in dem Sinne, daß die Steuerwerkfunktionen fest verdrahtet sind. Demzufolge sind "hardwired" Steuerwerke üblicherweise mit Problemen bezüglich Effizienz, Zuverlässigkeit und Wartung behaftet.

Um die Probleme von "hardwired" Steuerwerken zu reduzieren, schlug Wilkes das Konzept mikroprogrammierter Steuerungsabläufe als eine Systematisierung der Implementierung von Steuerwerkfunktionen vor [1]. Die Grundidee dieses Konzepts ist die Speicherung aller Steuerungsvektoren, die das Steuerwerk für die Interpretation von CML-Instruktionen erzeugt, in einem spezifischen Kontrollspeicher.

Kontrollspeicher (control store): Der Kontrollspeicher wird für die Speicherung ausführbarer Mikroprogramme benutzt.

In einem nach dem "Wilkes scheme" realisierten CML-Interpreter sind Mikroinstruktionen durch Bit-Muster in den Kontrollspeicherwörtern dargestellt. Jede Mikroinstruktion repräsentiert einen bestimmten Wert des Steuerungsvektors, in dem jeder Bit-Position ein Steuersignal zugeordnet ist. Die in einem Steuerwerkzyklus zu erzeugenden Steuersignale lassen sich dann wie folgt ableiten: Die Kontrollspeicheradressen entsprechen den Steuerwerkzuständen. In einem spezifischen Steuerwerkzyklus (d. h. bei der Ausführung einer Mikroinstruktion) werden alle diejenigen Steuersignale erzeugt, für die eine 1 in dem durch den Steuerwerkzustand identifizierten Kontrollspeicherwort gespeichert ist. Mikroinstruktionen werden also als Indikatoren der zu erzeugenden Steuersignale interpretiert. Die Grundprinzipien des Konzepts mikroprogrammierter Steuerungsabläufe lassen sich wie folgt zusammenfassen:

Mikroprogrammiertes Steuerwerk: In einem mikroprogrammierten Steuerwerk sind der CML-Interpreter und der MPL-Interpreter als eigene, miteinander verbundene Einheiten implementiert. Der CML-Interpreter ist durch die Mikroprogramme für die Interpretation der CML-Instruktionen definiert, die im Kontrollspeicher gespeichert sind. Der MPL-Interpreter ist in der Form eines Schaltwerks realisiert, das die Ausführung des MPL-Interpreters steuert.

Einer Realisierung mikroprogrammierter Steuerwerke nach dem "Wilkes scheme" standen vor 1960 technologische Gründe im Wege, da Realisierungen von Kontrollspeichern als Diodenmatrizen einen wesentlichen Geschwindigkeitsnachteil gegenüber "hardwired" Steuerwerken aufzeigten und sich nicht für Implementierungen von umfangreichen CML-Interpretern eigneten. Industriell wurde das Konzept mikroprogrammierter Steuerwerke erstmals in der Rechnerfamilie IBM System /360 [9] angewendet. Allerdings sind die meisten Systeme dieser Rechnerfamilie wie auch die meisten mikroprogrammierten Steuerwerke anderer namhafter Hersteller (von Zentraleinheiten und Peripheriegeräten) lediglich Hersteller-mikroprogrammierbar. Der Kontrollspeicher Hersteller-mikroprogrammierbarer Steuerwerke ist ein Festwertspeicher (ROM), der vom Hersteller mit den Mikroprogrammen für die Interpretation eines festen Maschinenbefehlsvorrates beschrieben wird und vom Benutzer nicht verändert werden kann. Mit der Verfügbarkeit schneller, ladbarer Speicher (RAM) in diesem Jahrzehnt sind die Voraussetzungen für die Realisierung Benutzer-mikroprogrammierbarer (oder kurz mikroprogrammierbarer) Steuerwerke gegeben. Mehrere verschiedene CML-Inerpreter können in einem Benutzer-mikroprogrammierbaren Steuerwerk implementiert werden, indem je nach Bedarf die entsprechenden Mikroprogramme in den Kontrollspeicher der Maschine geladen werden. Die Existenz mikroprogrammierbarer Rechner (meist Kleinrechner) ist die Grundlage dafür, daß Firmware sich als ein wesentliches und rapide an Wichtigkeit gewinnendes Teilgebiet des Fachgebietes Mikroprogrammierung entwickelt hat.

Mikroprogrammierbares Steuerwerk: Ein mikroprogrammierbares Steuerwerk ist ein mikroprogrammiertes Steuerwerk mit einem ladbaren Kontrollspeicher und zusätzlichen Hardware-Einrichtungen für das Laden des Kontrollspeichers.

Als ladbare Kontrollspeicher werden schnelle RAMs, PROMs (programmierbare ROMs) und auch Hauptspeicher benutzt. Letztere scheiden jedoch aufgrund ihrer Geschwindigkeitsnachteile für viele Anwendungen aus. Rechner mit schnellen, ladbaren Kontrollspeichern (schnelle RAMs) werden oft als dynamisch mikroprogrammierbare Rechner bezeichnet. Für alle mikroprogrammierbaren Rechner müssen, neben den Hardware-Einrichtungen für das Laden des Kontrollspeichers, Software-Einrichtungen für die Mikroprogrammerzeugung, -übersetzung und -fehlerbeseitigung zur Verfügung stehen.

Für die Ausführung von Mikroinstruktionen eines Mikroprogramms wird im allgemeinen zwischen der Verkettungs-Methode und der Mikroinstruktionszähler-Methode unterschieden.

<u>Verkettungs-Methode</u>: Die Verkettungs-Methode definiert die Nachfolger-Mikroinstruktion für jede Mikroinstruktion eines Mikroprogramms explizit durch Speicherung von Kontrollspeicheradressen in Mikroinstruktionen. Die Kontrollspeicheradresse der zugehörigen Nachfolger-Mikroinstruktion bestimmt der MPL-Interpreter durch Auswertung einer Verzweigungsbedingung in den Komponenten des Zustandsvektors.

<u>Mikroinstruktionszähler-Methode</u>: Die Mikroinstruktionszähler-Methode definiert die Kontrollspeicheradressen von Nachfolger-Mikroinstruktionen in linearen Mikroinstruktionsfolgen implizit durch das Inkrementieren eines Mikroinstruktionszählers im MPL-Interpreter. Die Nachfolger-Mikroinstruktionen von Verzweigungen sind in speziellen Verzweigungs-Mikroinstruktionen nach der Verkettungs-Methode explizit definiert.

In beiden Methoden kann für die Implementierung von bedingten Verzweigungen zwischen dem Auswahl-Prinzip und dem Modifikations-Prinzip unterschieden werden.

<u>Auswahl-Prinzip</u>: Im Auswahl-Prinzip werden die Kontrollspeicheradressen aller Nachfolger-Mikroinstruktionen gespeichert. Die Auswertung der Verzweigungsbedingungen liefert einen Index für die Auswahl der Kontrollspeicheradresse der zugehörigen Nachfolger-Mikroinstruktion.

<u>Modifikations-Prinzip</u>: Im Modifikations-Prinzip wird ein Nachfolger-Identifikator gespeichert, dessen Bits entsprechend der Verzweigungsbedingung durch logische Verknüpfungen der Komponenten des Zustandsvektors modifiziert werden, um die Kontrollspeicheradresse der zugehörigen Nachfolger-Mikroinstruktion zu erzeugen.

Einige der Probleme beider Prinzipien, wie z. B. die notwendige Erweiterung von Mikroinstruktionen für die Speicherung von Kontrollspeicheradressen im Auswahl-Prinzip, oder die Vergabe von ungenutzten Kontrollspeicherwörtern im Modifikations-Prinzip, können durch PLA-Realisierungen (PLA: programmable logic array) von Teilen des Steuerwerks vermieden werden [7]

Einer der Hauptgründe für die starke Proliferation des Fachgebietes Mikroprogrammierung ist die Tatsache, daß nahezu ebensoviel Mikroinstruktionsformate und dazugehörige Implementierungen von MPL-Intertern zu finden sind wie unterschiedliche Typen von mikroprogrammierten und mikroprogrammierbaren Rechnern existieren. Diese Vielfalt von

Mikroinstruktionsformaten läßt sich in die folgenden drei Kategorien einteilen:

Horizontales Mikroinstruktionsformat: Horizontale Mikroinstruktionen beinhalten eine große Zahl von Mikrooperationen (meist können alle Hardware-Funktionseinheiten der kontrollierten Untereinheiten eines Rechners durch eine einzelne Mikroinstruktion angesteuert werden), die parallel ausgeführt werden. Mikrooperationen sind durch einzelne Bits oder Bit-Felder, die direkt von den Hardware-Funktionseinheiten der kontrollierten Untereinheiten interpretiert werden können (z. B. ein 5-bit-Feld zur Bestimmung einer von 32 ALU-Operationen), repräsentiert. Horizontale Mikroinstruktionen entsprechen dem oben definierten Steuerungsvektor, aus dem die Picoinstruktionen (Steuersignale) ohne Dekodierung abgeleitet werden können. Die Steuerung der Mikroprogrammausführung ist im MPL-Interpreter üblicherweise nach der Verkettungs-Methode implementiert.

Vertikales Mikroinstruktionsformat: Vertikale Mikroinstruktionen beinhalten in der Regel nur eine einzige Mikrooperation und einen oder mehrere Mikroinstruktions-Operanden (z. B. Registeradresse, Hauptspeicheradresse). Die Mikrooperationen, die üblicherweise die Komplexität von ALU-Operationen, Speicherzugriffen oder bedingten Verzweigungsanweisungen haben, sind in einem Mikrooperationskode kodiert. Oftmals findet man eine mehrstufige Kodierung der Mikrooperationen, so daß ein Teil des Mikrooperationskodes (bit steering) oder der Inhalt eines Prozessorregisters (format shifting) die Interpretation des restlichen Operationskodes bestimmt. Vertikale Mikroinstruktionen werden im MPL-Interpreter dekodiert, um die entsprechenden Steuersignale für die Ansteuerung einer einzelnen, komplexeren Hardware-Funktionseinheiten (wenig Parallelismus) zu erzeugen. Die Steuerung der Mikroprogrammausführung ist im MPL-Interpreter üblicherweise nach der Mikroinstruktionszähler-Methode implementiert.

Quasi-horizontales Mikroinstruktionsformat: In quasi-horizontalen Mikroinstruktionen sind die vorteilhaften Charakteristiken vertikaler und horizontaler Mikroinstruktionen zusammengelegt. Sie enthalten mehrere Mikrooperationen, die parallel ausgeführt werden. Mikrooperationen sind üblicherweise einstufig in Feldern kodiert (womit eine höhere Komplexität der Mikrooperationen als im horizontalen Format erzielt wird), die entweder direkt von kontrollierten Hardware-Funktionseinheiten interpretiert oder vom MPL-Interpreter dekodiert werden. Für die Steuerung der Mikroprogrammausführung findet man sowohl Implementierungen nach der Verkettungs-Methode als auch nach der Mikroinstruktionszähler-Methode.

Oftmals wird das quasi-horizontale Format als diagonales Format bezeichnet, um die Position dieses Formates zwischen dem horizontalen und vertikalen Format deutlich zu machen. Aus folgenden Gründen bevorzugen wir die Bezeichnung quasi-horizontales Format [10]: Mit der steigenden Komplexität von LSI-Bausteinen erhöht sich naturgemäß die Komplexität der Picoinstruktionen, die direkt von derartigen Hardware-Funktionseinheiten interpretiert werden können. Der resultierende Komplexitätsanstieg der Mikrooperationen schlägt sich im quasi-horizontalen Format nieder, während die wesentlichste Eigenschaft des horizontalen Formates, die parallele Ausführung von Mikrooperationen, erhalten bleibt. Letztere ist eine Grundvoraussetzung für die effiziente Ausnutzung von Hardware-Einrichtungen, da ständig sinkende Hardware-Kosten die Vervielfachung von Hardware-Funktionseinheiten als eine Standard-Organisationsform der Rechnerhardware in Aussicht stellen.

3. Emulation, Firmware-Entwurfscharakteristiken und Leistungsvergleiche

Die charakteristische Anwendung der Mikroprogrammierung ist die Emulation. Ein Emulator ist die Menge aller für die Interpretation einer konventionellen Maschinensprache bereitgestellten Mikroprogramme. Emulatoren werden auch oft mikroprogrammierte Simulatoren genannt. Die Speicherung eines ausführbaren Emulators im Kontrollspeicher eines Rechners definiert eine abstrakte Maschine der Form (CML, CML-Interpreter).
Der Rechner, auf dem der Emulator ausgeführt wird, wird üblicherweise als das Gastgebersystem (host system) bezeichnet. Ein Emulator definiert die Organisation der abstrakten Maschine durch eine funktionelle Implementierung des Operationsprinzips dieser abstrakten Maschine auf der Hardware des Gastgebersystems.

Das grundlegende Ziel der Emulation, das bereits von Wilkes in Betracht gezogen wurde [1,2], ist es, die Kompatibilität verschiedener Rechnersysteme zu unterstützen. Systeme einer Rechnerfamilie können durch Emulation "upward compatible" oder "downward compatible" gemacht werden. In kompatiblen Rechnerfamilien findet man dann eine gemeinsame Maschinensprache, obwohl die Organisation und die zur Realisierung angewandte Technologie der einzelnen Systeme variiert. Rechnersysteme einer neuen Generation können - durch die Erweiterung der Kontrollspeicherkapazität - neben dem Emulator für die eigene Maschinensprache mit einem Emulator für die Maschinensprache der Vorgängermaschine ausgestattet werden. Durch diese sogenannte "backward compatibility" läßt sich die in einem Rechnergenerationswechsel anfallende Neuprogrammierung über einen längeren Zeitraum verteilen. Kompatibilität zwischen Rechnersystemen verschiedener Hersteller, die ebenso durch Emulation unterstützt werden kann, wird als "sideways compatibility" bezeichnet.

Normalerweise kann Emulation nicht ausschließlich durch Firmware bewerkstelligt werden. Während sich Konzepte und Methoden für die effektive Firmware-Implementierung von Register- und Hauptspeicherzugriffen sowie für die meisten CML-Instruktionen weitgehend etabliert haben [11], ist die Firmware-Emulation von Ein-/Ausgabe-Organisationen und die Verwaltung der Kommunikation zwischen dem Benutzer und dem Gastgebersystem mit erheblichen Schwierigkeiten verbunden. Diese Schwierigkeiten resultieren zum größten Teil daher, daß die meisten kommerziellen Rechnersysteme auf die effiziente Emulation einer bestimmten Maschinensprache ausgerichtet sind. Daher müssen derartige Rechnersysteme oftmals durch zusätzliche Hardware-Einrichtungen für die effiziente Handhabung der Informationsstruktur der zu emulierenden abstrakten Maschine erweitert werden. Weiterhin mag die Software-Implementierung von Steuerprogrammen für die Verwaltung des Gastgebersystems, die gegebenenfalls auch CML-Instruktionen simulieren, notwendig werden. Diese Schwierigkeiten stimulierten die Entwicklung mikroprogrammierbarer Rechnersysteme, die sich in effizienter Weise für die Emulation eines möglichst breiten Spektrums von abstrakten Maschinen eignen. Ein prominentes Beispiel für ein derartiges Forschungsprojekt ist das MATHILDA-System [12]. Mit Systemen dieser Art wurden dynamisch mikroprogrammierbare, mehrsprachige Rechner entwickelt, in denen mehrere CML-Emulatoren sowie andere Anwendermikroprogramme unter Steuerung des Betriebssystems in einer Multiprogramming-Organisation nebeneinander ausführbar sind.

Die folgenden Hardware-Charakteristiken mikroprogrammierbarer Rechnersysteme beeinflussen den Firmware-Entwurf für die Emulation abstrakter Maschinen.

- Hauptspeicher- und Registerwortlänge sowie die Breite der Verbindungseinrichtungen zwischen Hardware-Funktionseinheiten.
- Zahl, Typ und Zugänglichkeit von Hardware-Funktionseinheiten, Prozessorregistern und Verbindungseinrichtungen.
- Zahl und Typ von Interrupt- und Ein-/Ausgabe-Einrichtungen.
- Zahl der für die einzelnen kontrollierten Untereinheiten zur Verfügung stehenden Zustandsbits (d. h. Länge des Zustands-

vektors oder Länge der Statusregister).

- Mikroinstruktionsformat (insbesondere Grad des Parallelismus).

Bezüglich der obigen Charakteristiken besteht ein "tradeoff" zwischen den Kosten eines Rechnersystems und der Emulationsflexibilität einerseits und der Effizienz von Emulatoren andererseits. Ein für die Emulation einer spezifischen Maschinensprache zugeschnittenes Rechnersystem besitzt im allgemeinen nicht die notwendige Flexibilität für effiziente Emulationen beliebiger abstrakter Maschinen, kann aber mit relativ minimalem Hardwareaufwand (Hardwarekosten) entwickelt werden. Andererseits kann durch gezielte Erweiterungen von Hardware-Einrichtungen in den kontrollierten Untereinheiten als auch im Steuerwerk eines Rechnersystems (erhöhte Hardwarekosten), die für die Maschinensprache des Gastgebersystems redundant sein mögen, die Emulationsflexibilität und damit die Effizienz von Emulatoren beträchtlich gesteigert werden. Aus der Wahrnehmung dieser Tatsache und den sich ständig erweiternden Anwendungen des Emulationsprinzips resultieren Forderungen nach standardisierten und modular erweiterbaren LSI-Komponenten.

Leistungsvergleiche verschiedener mikroprogrammierbarer Rechnersysteme, wie z. B. das im folgenden Unterabschnitt beschriebene Projekt, verdeutlichen den erheblichen Einfluß der obigen Firmware-Entwurfscharakteristiken auf die Leistung (per Zeiteinheit) und die Komplexität (Speicherbedarf) von Emulatoren. Dies wird besonders deutlich, wenn die Sprache der zu emulierenden abstrakten Maschine Instruktionen für die Unterstützung von System- oder Anwenderfunktionen beinhaltet, die von den üblichen CML-Instruktionen abweichen und damit das fundamentale Emulationskonzept variieren.

3.1. Vergleich der Implementierbarkeit von Betriebssystemoperationen durch Mikroprogramme auf den Rechnern Nixdorf ZE 1501 und Varian 75 (Niggemann, Röder)

Das in [13] ausführlich beschriebene Projekt vergleicht zwei Mikroprogramm-Implementierungen bezüglich Zeit- und Speicherkomplexität. Außerdem wird untersucht, inwieweit die Architekturen der Rechner Nixdorf ZE 1501 und Varian 75 diese Implementierung unterstützen.

Die Architekturen der beiden Gastgebersysteme sind recht unterschiedlich. Der Nixdorf-Rechner ZE 1501 hat einen lokalen Speicher von 256 Registern. Sein Kontrollspeicher besitzt eine geteilte Struktur zur Aufnahme von vertikalen Mikroinstruktionen und horizontalen Nanoinstruktionen. Die Größe des Registerfiles des Rechners Varian 75 beträgt dagegen nur 16 Register. Sein Kontrollspeicher besteht aus einer Ebene und dient zur Aufnahme von sehr komplex aufgebauten quasihorizontalen Mikroinstruktionen mit teilweise mehrstufiger Kodierung.

Für die Implementierung wurden Mini- und Midiprimitive ausgewählt, die aus dem Betriebssystem-Modell von Bredt und Saxena [14] abgeleitet wurden. Dieses Modell besitzt einige Charakteristiken, die für eine effiziente Implementierung der Midiprimitiven gewisse Anforderungen an die Mikro-Architekturen der Rechner stellen. Dazu zählen z. B. gute Unterprogrammtechniken auf der Mikroprogramm-Ebene und ein großes, flexibel einsetzbares Prozessor-Statusregister. Es zeigt sich, daß keiner der beiden Rechner diese Anforderungen optimal erfüllt. Inwieweit die vorhandenen Mikro-Architekturen die Implementierung jeweils unterstützen, wird in einer Gegenüberstellung gezeigt, die u. a. auf folgende Merkmale eingeht:

- Größe und Adressierbarkeit des lokalen Speichers
- Anzahl und Breite der Datenwege
- Dekodierung der CML-Instruktionen
- Unterprogrammtechniken auf Mikroprogramm-Ebene.

4. Vertikale Verlagerung (vertical migration)

Mit der ständigen Ausweitung von Anwendungsgebieten elektronischer Datenverarbeitung ist eine Absorption der steigenden Fähigkeiten von Rechnersystemen, die aus der Verfügbarkeit schnellerer, billigerer und komplexerer Hardware-Betriebsmittel resultieren, zu beobachten. Trotz dieser kontinuierlichen Verbesserung der Leistungsfähigkeit von Rechnersystemen bleibt die Forderung nach weiterer Leistungssteigerung erhalten. Neben innovativen architektonischen Entwicklungen, die wir in diesem Text nicht betrachten, ist die anwendungsspezifische Spezialisierung von Rechnersystemen durch die Erweiterung des Emulationsprinzips eine der wesentlichsten Methoden, derartige Leistungssteigerungen zu erlangen. Die Grundidee dieser Methode ist es, System- und Anwenderfunktionen, die üblicherweise in Software implementiert sind, durch Firmware zu implementieren.

4.1. Leistungssteigerung durch die Verlagerung von Software-Primitiven in die Firmware

Durch die Implementierung system- und anwendungsorientierter Funktionen in der Firmware können CML-Instruktion bereitgestellt werden, deren Funktionalität der von CML-Programmsegmenten entsprechen. Offensichtlich können derartige CML-Programmsegmente wiederum Primitiven der Sprache einer beliebigen abstrakten Maschine im Software-Bereich des in Bild 2 gezeigten Schichtenmodells repräsentieren. Also lassen sich durch die Verlagerung von Software-Primitiven in die Firmware alle Ebenen des Software-Bereichs eines Rechnersystems durch Anhebung und Spezialisierung der Schnittstelle zwischen Hardware und Software unterstützen. Da diese Schnittstelle durch die Rechnerarchitektur bestimmt ist, entspricht die Firmware-Implementierung von Software-Primitiven der Definition einer Rechnerarchitektur und wird daher auch als "architecture synthesis" bezeichnet.

Die Leistungssteigerung durch die Verlagerung von Software-Primitiven in die Firmware ergibt sich maßgeblich wie folgt: Die Zusammenfassung von CML-Instruktionen spart Speicherzugriffe für das Holen von CML-Instruktionen. Weiterhin kann die Effizienz einer Firmware-Implementierung eines CML-Programmsegmentes gegenüber der sequentiellen Aneinanderreihung der Mikroprogramme für die einzelnen CML-Instruktionen des Programmsegmentes erheblich gesteigert werden. Der Gebrauch der so geschaffenen Software-Primitiven führt ferner auch zu effizienteren Software-Implementierungen von System- und Anwenderprogrammen.

Die beschriebene Methode hat ein breites Feld von Anwendungen, das die direkte Interpretation von höheren Programmiersprachen, die Unterstützung von Laufzeitsystemen höherer Programmiersprachen durch die direkte mikroprogrammierte Interpretation von Zwischensprachen, die Unterstützung von Betriebssystemen, die Unterstützung der Bilderzeugung in graphischen Systemen, die Implementierung von Signalverarbeitungsfunktionen, die Implementierung innovativer Operationsprinzipien in konventionellen Rechnersystemen usw. einschließt. Von all diesen Anwendungsgebieten steht die Unterstützung von Betriebssystemen im Vordergrund. Dies rührt vor allem daher, daß Betriebssysteme üblicherweise als hierarchisch geschichtete Software-Systeme implementiert sind, die über mehrere Interpretationsebenen ausgeführt werden. Die Struktur von hierarchischen Betriebssystemen bietet sich also für die Verlagerung der tieferen Software-Ebenen in die Firmware an. Ein Beispiel für die Anwendung der beschriebenen Methode für die Firmware-Implementierung von Betriebssystemfunktionen ist im folgenden Unterabschnitt beschrieben.

4.1.1. Implementierung und Leistungsmessung eines mikroprogrammierten hierarchischen Betriebssystemkerns (Maier, Burkhardt)

Betriebssysteme heutiger Rechenanlagen benötigen teilweise mehr als die Hälfte der gesamten CPU-Zeit für Verwaltungsaufgaben (BS-Overhead). Die Mikroprogrammierung von Systemkomponenten erlaubt eine Reduzierung dieses Overheads. Bisher bekannt gewordene Untersuchungen haben durch Einführung neuer, leistungsfähiger CML-Instruktionen einzelne Systemfunktionen direkt auf der MPL-Ebene realisiert, ohne damit die Rechnerarchitektur grundlegend zu verändern. Unsere Untersuchungen [15] zeigen jedoch, daß die Ineffizienz heutiger Rechnerarchitekturen vorwiegend aus einer unzureichenden Anpassung zwischen den Hardware- und Software-Bereichen in den untersten Ebenen eines Betriebssystems resultiert.

Als eine Konsequenz unserer Untersuchungen wird der mikroprogrammierte System-Nukleus (Mikro-Nukleus) als Satz elementarer Prozeß- und Prozessorfunktionen mit wechselseitig angepaßten Schnittstellen entworfen und implementiert. Eine Kontrollspeicher- und Mikroprogrammhierarchie ermöglicht die Laufzeit- und Speicheroptimierung der Nukleus-Mikroprogramme.

Die Grundlage für die vergleichende Untersuchung ist die Implementierung des Mikro-Nukleus als funktionsäquivalente BS-Maschine. Über ein System-Modell werden statische und dynamische Leistungsparameter definiert, die reproduzierbare Arbeitsbelastungen des Nukleus ermöglichen. Ein speziell entworfener Firmware/Software-Monitor erlaubt die Bestimmung dieser Parameter für beide Maschinen. Die Ergebnisse zeigen eine signifikante Reduktion des Nukleus-Overhead zwischen 50 und 90 %.

4.2. Die Software/Firmware-Schnittstelle in der Verlagerung von System- und Anwenderfunktionen

Neben vielen Vorteilen hierarchischer Systeme [16] ist die mehrstufige Interpretation, die teilweise erheblichen Overhead erzeugt, ein Nachteil. Dieser Overhead kann durch die Verlagerung ausgewählter Ebenen in der Interpretations-Hierarchie reduziert werden. Dabei eigenen sich insbesondere CPU-intensive Funktionen für die Verlagerung in die Firmware. Der Leistungsgewinn einer derartigen Verlagerung ist damit begründet, daß die entsprechenden Funktionen auf einer zwar primitiveren, aber effizienteren (schnelleren) abstrakten Maschine ausgeführt werden. Allerdings ist bei der Verlagerung von Funktionen in der Interpretations-Hierarchie darauf zu achten, daß die verlagerte Funktion die Funktionalität der tieferen Ebene nicht überschreitet. Ziele und Vorteile der

Verlagerung von Software-Funktionen in die Firmware werden im folgenden Unterabschnitt aufgezeigt.

4.2.1. Verallgemeinerung der Prinzipien mikroprogrammierbarer Rechner (Hartenstein)

Probleme durch Softwarekomplexität, Mangel an Software-Zuverlässigkeit, hohe und steigende Software-Kosten, sinkende Hardware-Kosten und schnell wachsende Hardware-Leistungsfähigkeit erzeugen den Wunsch, beim Systementwurf den Hardware-Anteil zu erhöhen, möglichst viele Funktionen von der Software in die Hardware zu verdrängen, und die Hardware nach Möglichkeit auch für bessere Strukturierung und leichtere Testbarkeit von Software und Gesamtsystem anzuwenden. Die prinzipiellen Mechanismen mikroprogrammierbarer Rechner lassen sich als Hilfsmittel bei der Erreichung dieser Ziele anwenden.

Unter allen bekannten, praktischen Methoden der Formung von Prozeß-Hierarchien in digitalen Systemen haben mikroprogrammierte Rechner folgende Vorteile:

- sie bieten die sauberste und stärkste Trennung zwischen semantischen Funktionen und Mechanismen der Kopplung verschiedener Ebenen in der Prozeß-Hierarchie (dies verbessert die Systemtransparenz und diszipliniert den Entwurfsvorgang).

- sie bieten Möglichkeiten zur Vermeidung von Prozeß-Verdrängungsaktionen (dies verringert die Software-Komplexität und verbessert die Testbarkeit des Systems erheblich).

Die zu diesen Vorteilen führenden Prinzipien lassen sich nicht nur für klassische mikroprogrammierte Systeme, sondern durch Verallgemeinerung auch zum Entwurf größerer Systeme anwenden. Hierbei entstehen "nested machines" bzw. Systeme, deren Hardware-Blockstruktur eine größere Schachtelungstiefe aufweisen kann, wobei auch mehrere "Maschinen" pro Ebene vorkommen können. Hierzu wird eine Struktursprache angegeben und mit PMS verglichen, sowie ein Hardware-Bausteinkonzept skizziert [17].

4.3. "Vertical Migration" Methodik

Für die Verlagerung von Software-Funktionen hat sich in der amerikanischen Literatur der Begriff "vertical migration" eingebürgert. Vertical-migration [18] ist eine Technik zur Verbesserung der Systemleistung durch die vertikale Verlagerung von Software-Primitiven in den

Anwendungssystem-, Betriebssystem- und Firmware-Ebenen eines Rechnersystems (siehe Bild 2). Vertical migration unterscheidet sich damit von "horizontal migration", das sich auf die Verlagerung von Arbeitsbelastungen auf mehrere Systemmoduln auf der gleichen Ebene des Schichtenmodells eines Rechnersystems bezieht.

Für die formale Anwendung dieser Technik wurde eine "vertical migration Methode" vorgeschlagen [18], die auf die Spezialisierung und Optimierung der Firmware, der Anwenderprogramm-Ebenen und der Betriebssystem-Software für eine spezifische Anwendung oder eine Klasse von Anwendungen ausgerichtet ist. Diese Methode kann in der Software-Software-Verlagerung als auch in der Software-Firmware-Verlagerung angewendet werden und besteht aus den folgenden Phasen:

- Durchführbarkeits-Analyse: Untersuchung der Verlagerbarkeit von CPU-intensiven Funktionen.

- Leistungs-Abschätzung: Abschätzung der Leistungssteigerung, die sich aus der Verlagerung ergibt.

- Verlagerungs-Implementierung: Implementierung der verlagerten Funktion auf der entsprechenden Ebene und ihre Integration in das System.

- Leistungs-Verifikation: Bestätigung der Leistungs-Abschätzung durch Tests.

Einige der Voraussetzungen, Kriterien und Entscheidungsprozesse für die Anwendung einer "vertical migration Methode" sind im folgenden Unterabschnitt an einem Beispiel einer Firmware-Implementierung von Betriebssystemfunktionen dargestellt.

4.3.1. Verlagerung von Betriebssystemfunktionen in Mikroprogramme - Voraussetzungen, Kriterien und Entscheidungshilfen (Albrich)

Für die Verlagerung von Funktionen des Betriebssystems MCP V.1 der Rechenanlagen Burroughs B 1700/1800 in Mikroprogramme sind die folgenden Voraussetzungen gegeben:

- Das Betriebssystem besteht aus einer Anordnung von Prozeduren und ist in einer höheren Programmiersprache geschrieben.

- Die Programmiersprache stellt Leerbefehle zur Verfügung (Typ EXECUTE (...)), die eine Übertragung einer variablen Zahl von

Parametern gestatten und zunächst auf Interpretationsebene ignoriert werden. Ein an diese Stelle des Interpreters gesetztes Mikroprogramm soll dann die Ausführung der übertragenen Betriebssystemfunktion veranlassen.

- Der Einbau von Ablaufverfolgungssignalen (Monitorsignalen) in beliebige Software-Ebenen und in die Firmware-Ebene soll durch entsprechende Konstruktionen in jeder Sprache ermöglicht werden.

- Der flexible und schnelle Einbau von Monitorsignalen soll durch die Möglichkeit der Teilübersetzung von Programmen gewährleistet sein.

- Ein System zur Aufnahme und Auswertung solcher Signale (Firmware-Monitor) wurde konstruiert und in Betrieb genommen.

Eines der Anwendungsgebiete dieses Firmware-Monitors ist die Entdeckung von Aktivitätszentren (häufige und zeitaufwendige Prozeduren) in der Menge der Betriebssystemfunktionen und die Bereitstellung von Entscheidungshilfen für die Verlagerung besonders aussichtsreicher Kandidaten in Mikroprogramme.

Im Rahmen der bisher erzielten Ergebnisse (Verlagerung von Funktionen der Hauptspeicherverwaltung in Mikroprogramme) konnten die folgenden Kriterien entwickelt werden:

- Kandidaten zur Verlagerung (Prozeduren) sollten immer so konstruiert sein, daß als Parameter möglichst nur lokale Variablen und keine globalen Variablen übertragen werden müssen.

- Kandidaten zur Verlagerung (Aktivitätszentren) dürfen selbst keine außerhalb liegenden Prozeduren des Betriebssystems aufrufen. Sollte dies dennoch der Fall sein, ist ein geeigneter Zerlegungsprozeß vorzuschalten.

In dem betrachteten Betriebssystem konnten einige Funktionen isoliert werden, die den oben genannten Kriterien genügten und als Kandidaten zur Verlagerung in Frage kamen.

Zur Entscheidung welcher Kandidat verlagert werden soll und ob diese Verlagerung überhaupt ein meßbares Ergebnis an erhöhtem Durchsatz erzielen kann, wurde unter Einsatz des Firmware-Monitors das folgende Vorgehen gewählt:

- Entdeckung von Aktivitätszentren durch die Analyse der Aufrufhäufigkeit sämtlicher Betriebssystemprozeduren.

- Gewichtung der isolierten Kandidaten zur Verlagerung durch Bestimmung der relativen Aufrufhäufigkeit und des absoluten Zeitbedarfs jedes Kandidaten.

- Beurteilung der ausgewählten Kandidaten nach den vorgenannten Kriterien.

- Unterstützung der Entscheidung durch die experimentelle Verlagerung über Leerbefehle und anschließende Sofortaussage über den erzielten Gewinn durch eine Leistungsmessung mit dem Firmware-Monitor.

5. Werkzeuge für die Mikroprogrammentwicklung

Die Mikroprogrammentwicklung kann wie die Software-Programmentwicklung in zwei Phasen zerlegt werden: die Mikroprogrammerzeugung und die Fehlerbeseitigung. Dementsprechend existieren zwei Hauptklassen von Werkzeugen für die Mikroprogrammentwicklung, und zwar Mikroprogrammiersprachen mit zugehörigen Übersetzern, die mnemonische Darstellungen von Mikroprogrammen in die binäre Kontrollspeicherdarstellung transformieren, sowie Test- und Verifikationssysteme, die es erlauben, die Effekte von Mikroprogrammausführungen zu untersuchen. Die Verfügbarkeit solcher Mikroprogrammierhilfen ist eine Notwendigkeit für die Mikroprogrammentwicklung im allgemeinen und insbesondere eine notwendige Grundlage eines dynamisch mikroprogrammierbaren Rechners. Ein typisches Mikroprogramm-Entwicklungssystem besteht aus einem Mikroassembler, einem Mikroprogramm-Lader/Linker und einem Mikroprogramm-Simulator. Hochentwickelte Mikroprogramm-Entwicklungssysteme mögen weiterhin automatische Testgeneratoren, Hardware-Hilfsmittel für die Analyse von Mikroprogrammausführungen, Mikroprogramm-Verifikationssysteme, Übersetzer für höhere Mikroprogrammiersprachen usw. beinhalten.

In einem typischen Mikroassembler sind mnemonische Darstellungen für alle gültigen Mikrooperationen definiert, die zur Beschreibung von Mikroinstruktionen aneinandergereiht werden können. Darüber hinaus erlauben sie den Gebrauch von mnemonischen Marken und unterstützen das Laden von Mikroprogrammen in den Kontrollspeicher. Dazu sind sie entweder direkt mit einem Mikroprogramm-Lader/Linker gekoppelt, der ebenso ausführbaren Kode für einen Mikroprogramm-Simulator erzeugt, oder erzeugen Kode für einen entkoppelten Lader und den Simulator. In fortschrittlichen Mikroassemblern findet man auch Einrichtungen für Makro-Definitionen und Definitionen von zusammengesetzten Anweisungen, die üblicherweise die Form von Register-Transferanweisungen haben. Weiterhin wurden Versuche unternommen, teilweise maschinenunabhängige oder selbstdokumentierende Mikroassembler zu entwickeln. Ebenso wie für Software-Programmierung existieren höhere Mikroprogrammiersprachen, die neben den bekannten Vorteilen gegenüber Assemblersprachen im speziellen Fall der Mikroprogrammierung bisher immer noch erhebliche Unzulänglichkeiten aufweisen, auf die wir im nächsten Abschnitt näher eingehen.

Die Fehlerbeseitigung ist ein wesentlicher Bestandteil der Mikroprogrammentwicklung, die nicht bis nach dem Laden von Mikroprogrammen in den Kontrollspeicher (der ein Festwertspeicher sein kann) verzögert werden darf. Daher müssen Mikroprogrammiersprachen die Fehlerbeseitigung unterstützen. Die grundlegenden Methoden die Fehlerfreiheit von Programmen zu zeigen, sind formale Korrektheitsbeweise und das Testen. Mit Korrektheitsbeweisen beschäftigen wir uns im nächsten Paragraphen. Bezüglich Testmethoden lassen sich statische und dynamische Varianten unterscheiden. Statisches Testen durch Programmanalyse wird in der Mikroprogrammierung kaum angewendet. Syntaxtests, die Mikroassembler zur Überprüfung der Gültigkeit der vom Mikroprogrammierer in einer Mikroinstruktion spezifizierten Mikrooperationen durchführt, können als eine Form des statischen Testens angesehen werden. Dynamisches Testen durch Programmausführungen kann in zwei Kategorien aufgeteilt werden: "soft" (off-line) Testen und "hard" (on-line) Testen.

Die Simulation von Mikroprogrammen ist eine typische Off-line-Testmethode. Ein Mikroprogramm-Simulator ist ein Software-Programm, das die Ausführung von Mikrooperationen in den Hardware-Funktionseinheiten und Verbindungseinrichtungen eines Prozessors nachvollzieht. Simulatoren sind meistens interaktiv und erlauben dem Benutzer die Ausführung von Mikroprogrammen durch das Setzen von "traces" und "breakpoints" sowie durch die Ausgabe von Registerinhalten zu verfolgen. Darüber hinaus ist es möglich, Mikroprogramme durch das Setzen von Registerinhalten (und gegebenenfalls simulierten Kontrollspeicherwörtern) zu initialisieren (und zu korrigieren).

Im allgemeinen können nur statische Fehler, die sich aus einer weitgehend maschinenunabhängigen Überprüfung der Effekte von Mikroprogrammausführungen ableiten lassen, mit einem Mikroprogramm-Simulator entdeckt und lokalisiert werden. Die Möglichkeiten dynamische, maschinenabhängige Fehler zu entdecken, die von Verletzungen spezifischer Zeitbedingungen in den Steuerungsabläufen resultieren (siehe Abschnitt 2.2), sind von der Genauigkeit der Abbildung der Rechnerhardware in der Simulator-Software abhängig. Zugunsten akzeptabler Simulationszeiten ist die Genauigkeit der Rechnerabbildung in der Simulator-Software jedoch normalerweise für die Entdeckung dynamischer Fehler unzureichend. Obwohl die Entdeckung dynamischer Fehler durch geeignete Definitionen des Mikroinstruktionsformates in beschränktem Maße unterstützt werden kann, sind On-line-Testmethoden für die Entdeckung und Lokalisierung dynamischer Fehler notwendig.

Während Off-line-Testsysteme die Fehlerentdeckung meistens auf der Mikroinstruktions-Ebene unterstützen, kann zwischen On-line-Testsystemen auf der Mikroprogramm-, der Mikroinstruktions- und der Mikrooperations-Ebene unterschieden werden. On-line-Testsysteme auf der Mikroprogramm-Ebene sind oft mit Mikroprogramm-Ladern gekoppelt und erlauben die Ausführung von Mikroprogrammen aus dem physikalischen Kontrollspeicher. Mit derartigen Testsystemen, deren Testmöglichkeiten sich auf das Initiieren von vollständigen Mikroprogrammen durch die Ausführung von spezifischen CML-Instruktionen und die Untersuchung von Register- und Speicherinhalten nach Beendigung der Mikroprogrammausführung beschränken, können zwar dynamische Fehler entdeckt, aber nicht lokalisiert werden. Das typische On-line-Testsystem auf der Mikroinstruktions-Ebene ist der interaktive Debugger. Ein Debugger hat im allgemeinen die gleiche Kommandosprache wie ein Mikroprogramm-Simulator, führt diese Kommandos aber mit Bezug auf Mikroprogrammausführungen auf der physikalischen Maschine aus. Mit Debugger können zwar einige dynamische Fehler entdeckt und lokalisiert werden, doch sind sie in der Mehrzahl der Fälle unzureichend für die Lokalisierung der wesentlichsten dynamischen Fehler, die sich aus Konflikten in der Ausführung von Mikrooperationen einer einzelnen Mikroinstruktion ergeben. Für die Lokalisierung dynamischer Fehler auf der Mikrooperations-Ebene sind in der Regel spezifische Hardware-Hilfsmittel für die Analyse von Mikroprogrammausführungen (z. B. Wartungskonsolen) notwendig. Zu diesem Zweck lassen sich Logic State Analyzer sehr effektiv einsetzen [19]. Ein Beispiel eines hochentwickelten Mikroprogramm-Entwicklungssystems ist im folgenden Unterabschnitt beschrieben.

5.1. Ein mikroprozessorunterstütztes Mikroprogramm-Entwicklungssystem für den Nixdorf-Rechner ZE 1501.XX (Fey)

Das Mikroprogramm-Entwicklungssystem besteht aus zwei Komponenten:

- Dem Mikroprozessor, der aus einem F8-Mikroprozessor mit umfangreicher Peripherie (u. a. diversen Schnittstellen zur ZE 1501.XX) besteht.

- Dem Softwaresystem, das aus einem Mikroassembler, einem Hardwaremonitor-Simulator und einem Testmonitor besteht.

Das auf den ersten Blick relativ umfangreich erscheinende Mikroprozessorsystem ersetzt ein für diese Zwecke üblicherweise verwendetes komplettes Rechnersystem oder sogar einen Doppelprozessor (der Nixdorf-Rechner steht dagegen nur als OEM-Version zur Verfügung). Der Mikroassembler ermöglicht das formatfreie Schreiben von Mikroprogrammen in mnemonischer Form. Ein Linker übernimmt die Aufgabe, aus unabhängig erstellten und assemblierten Mikroprogrammen, deren Adressen als "fixed" oder "relocatable" qualifiziert werden können, einen Objektmodul herzustellen. Er ist als Crossassembler auf einer PDP 11/20 implementiert. Der Nixdorf-Rechner besitzt einen Hardwaremonitor, der die externe Taktung des Rechners ermöglicht. Nach jedem Einzeltakt (ein Maschinenzyklus ist in 8 Einzeltakte unterteilt) können bestimmte Register- und Merkerinhalte auf einem Lampentableau angezeigt werden. Es handelt sich dabei nicht um einen Echtzeitmonitoring, sondern um einen Trace auf Einzeltaktebene (Mikroinstruktions-Ebene). Weiterhin lassen sich mit dem Hardwaremonitor Hauptspeicherzellen der ZE 1501.XX lesen und schreiben (der Mikrospeicher wird beim "reset" automatisch aus einem bestimmten Teil des Hauptspeichers geladen).

Die Simulation des Hardwaremonitors erfolgt auf dem F8 und bietet die folgenden Vorteile:

- übersichtliche Darstellung von Register- und Merkerinhalten auf dem Bildschirm/Drucker.

- Statusinformationen von Taktsequenzen können auf dem Drucker ausgegeben werden.

- Register der virtuellen Maschine können strukturiert auf dem Bildschirm/Drucker angezeigt werden.

- zeitlich überlappte Vorgänge können gespeichert und strukturiert dargestellt werden.

Unter Verwendung des Testmonitors ist das automatische Prüfen von "assertions", die in ein Mikroprogramm eingeführt werden können, möglich. Bei Nichterfüllung können bestimmte Aktionen veranlaßt werden

(z. B. Ausdrucken von Taktsequenzen, Mikrospeicherausdruck usw.). Die Formulierung der "assertions" und Aktionen erfolgt in einer Testsprache, deren Kode nicht Bestandteil des Mikrokodes ist, sondern separat auf dem F8 erzeugt und unter Verwendung der Funktionen des Hardwaremonitor-Simulators ausgeführt wird. Der Vorteil gegenüber üblichen Softwaremonitoren besteht darin, daß durch die separate Kodeausführung die Mikroprogrammstruktur nicht verändert wird.

6. Firmware Engineering

Im Gegensatz zur Entwicklung von Techniken und Methoden für die Spezifikation, Produktion, Verifikation und Wartung von Software-Systemen, die im letzten Jahrzehnt weltweit mit enormen Anstrenungen vorangetrieben wurde, sind entsprechende Entwicklungen auf dem Gebiet der Firmware in unvergleichbarem Maße zurückgeblieben. Dieses Mißverhältnis ist um so erstaunlicher, da Firmware sich in vieler Hinsicht nicht von Software unterscheidet und daher vom Fortschritt im Software Engineering hätte profitieren können. Andererseits besteht eine dringende Nachfrage nach fortschrittlichen Werkzeugen für die Mikroprogrammierung. Dieser Bedarf ist nicht nur durch die rapide expandierenden Anwendungen von Firmware im "vertical migration" bedingt, die die Gruppe der traditionellen Mikroprogrammierer auf System- und Anwendungsprogrammierer erweitert, sondern resultiert ebenso aus der Tatsache, daß Mikroprogrammieren detailliert, präzise, zeitaufwendig und teurer als das Software-Programmieren ist. Daraus ergibt sich, ebenso wie für die Software, die Notwendigkeit für eine Engineering-Disziplin, die die Firmware-Entwicklung billiger, schneller und zuverlässiger macht. Wir definieren - in Anlehnung an [20] und die Definition des Software Engineering - Firmware Engineering als die praktische Anwendung einer Engineering-Disziplin für die Spezifikation, Konstruktion, Verifikation und Wartung von Firmware.

6.1. Engineering-Disziplin

Im folgenden fassen wir die Entwicklungsstufen, die Entwicklungsprinzipien und die Zielsetzungen einer Engineering Disziplin für den speziellen Fall der Firmware-Entwicklung zusammen.

Entwicklungsstufen:

System-Analyse: Feststellung des Zwecks des Systems und der Anforderungen an das System.

Spezifikation: Definition des funktionellen Verhaltens und der globalen Struktur des Systems.

Konstruktion: Realisierung des Systems, die die gegebenen Spezifikationen erfüllt.

Verifikation: Beweis der Übereinstimmung des Systems mit den Spezifikationen.

Wartung: Notwendige Arbeitsleistungen für die Aufrechterhaltung der Arbeitsfähigkeit des Systems und Vorkehrungen für Erweiterungen, Korrekturen und Modifikationen des Systems.

Entwicklungsprinzipien:

Modularität: Zerlegung des Systems in Moduln mit wohldefinierten Schnittstellen.

Abstraktion: Bestimmung der wesentlichen Eigenschaften, die von außen sichtbar sind oder in Moduln verborgen werden.

Konformität: Beschränkung der Abstraktion durch die Notwendigkeit, Informationen, die für die Verifikation benötigt werden, sichtbar zu machen.

Verfeinerung: Erweiterung von Abstraktionen oder Transformationen von Abstraktionen.

Zielsetzungen der Firmware-Entwicklung:

Optimalität: Minimisierung von Mikroprogramm-Ausführungszeiten und -Speicherbedarf (Zeitminimisierung ist im allgemeinen wichtiger als Raumminimisierung).

Korrektheit/Zuverlässigkeit: Fehlerfreie (bezüglich der Spezifikationen) Implementierung von mikroprogrammierten Steuerungsabläufen unter Einbeziehung von Fehlerentdeckungs- und Fehlerbeseitigungs-Routinen (microdiagnostics).

Verständlichkeit: Unterstützung der Lesbarkeit und Bereitstellung von Dokumentationen für das Gesamtsystem und die Systemmoduln.

Modifizierbarkeit: Systematische und modulare Strukturierung des Systems, die Erweiterungen, Korrekturen und Veränderungen erleichtert.

6.2. Gegenwärtiger Stand des Firmware Engineering

Entwicklungen im Firmware Engineering beziehen sich im allgemeinen auf Erfahrungen aus der Mikroprogrammierung, dem Hardware Engineering und dem Software Engineering, wobei das Software Engineering offensichtlich die wesentlichste Grundlage ist [20]. Dies wird besonders deutlich durch die große Zahl offener Fragen in Gebieten, in denen Firmware-Konzepte von den entsprechenden Software-Konzepten abweichen. Darüber hinaus liegen nahezu keine Ergebnisse auf dem Gebiet der Wartung von Software oder Firmware vor.

Für die Spezifikation von Firmware-Systemen sind Ansätze zu erkennen, Software-Spezifikationssprachen [21] anzuwenden. Allerdings ergeben sich dabei Probleme, da sich Software-Spezifikationssprachen für die Handhabung von Besonderheiten der Firmware - wie z. B. dem Parallelismus in Mikroinstruktionen, den Zeitbedingungen in Steuerungsabläufen und der Synchronisierung von asynchronen Operationen in Hardware-Interfaces - von ihrer Natur her nicht uneingeschränkt eignen. Firmware-Spezifikationssprachen müssen neben den Fähigkeiten von Software-Spezifikationssprachen vor allem Einrichtungen für die Spezifikation von technologischen Beschränkungen der Hardware-Betriebsmittel, Leistungsangaben, Zeitbedingungen und des Parallelismus besitzen, die die Systemoptimierung unterstützen.

Werkzeuge für die Firmware-Konstruktion sind Werkzeugen des Software Engineering sehr ähnlich (z. B. Assembler, höhere Programmiersprachen). Hier entstehen Konflikte dadurch, daß der Wunsch "high-level"-Werkzeuge zu benutzen nicht unmittelbar mit der Aufrechterhaltung des engen Hardwarebezugs in der Firmware-Entwicklung vereinbar ist. Höhere Mikroprogrammiersprachen versuchen zwar einerseits Maschinenunabhängigkeit und strukturiertes Mikroprogrammieren zu unterstützen, während sie andererseits versuchen, die notwendige Flexibilität des engen Hardwarebezugs, wie man ihn im Mikroassembler findet, beizubehalten. Daher sind die meisten höheren Mikroprogrammiersprachen entweder maschinenabhängig oder zu universell, um effizient einsetzbar zu sein. Darüber hinaus stellt die Erzeugung von optimiertem Mikrokode durch Compiler solcher Sprachen ein äußerst gravierendes Problem dar [20].

Methoden zum Nachweis der Fehlerfreiheit von Mikroprogrammen basieren entweder auf formalen Korrektheitsbeweisen oder Testmethoden. Während Korrektheitsbeweise versuchen, die Abwesenheit von Fehlern zu zeigen, können Testmethoden nur die Anwesenheit von Fehlern aufzeigen. Testmethoden sind im vorangegangenen Paragraphen diskutiert worden.

Im folgenden Unterabschnitt gehen wir in der Beschreibung eines Vorschlags einer Firmware-Engineering-Disziplin auf die Beziehungen zwischen formalen Software- und Firmware-Verifikationsmethoden ein.

6.3. Vorschlag einer Firmware-Engineering-Disziplin (Berg, Franta, Giloi)

Die Prinzipien und Werkzeuge einer Firmware-Engineering-Disziplin müssen alle Zielsetzungen der Firmware-Entwicklung unterstützen. Offensichtlich kann keines der vorangehend besprochenen Werkzeuge diese Forderung alleine erfüllen, sondern dieses Ziel kann nur durch eine Verbindung dieser Werkzeuge erreicht werden, die sowohl auf "high-level"-Methoden als auch auf technolgische Charakteristiken zugeschnitten ist.

Die Grundlage für die Erfüllung der obigen Forderung ist unserer Meinung nach [22] die formale Verifikation der Korrektheit von Mikroprogrammen durch Beweise in einem deduktiven System, das auf einer vollständigen Definition der Semantik einer maschinenunabhängigen, höheren Programmiersprache und der Hardware eines spezifischen Rechners basiert. Diese Aussage beruht auf den folgenden Begründungen:

- Formale Korrektheitsbeweise [21] unterstützen alle Zielsetzungen der Firmware-Entwicklung, außer der Optimalität, und sind notwendig, da fehlerhafte Firmware eine fehlerhafte, operationsunfähige Maschine (Wartungsprobleme) impliziert.

- Formale Spezifikationen der Rechnerhardware unterstützen Korrektheitsbeweise für Mikroprogramme einer spezifischen Maschine, die in einer höheren, maschinenunabhängigen Sprache geschrieben sind, und reduzieren damit die Komplexität von unumgänglichen Tests maschinenabhängiger Bedingungen, die auf der abstrakten Ebene nicht gehandhabt werden können.

- Es existieren konstruktive Verifikationsmethoden [21], die alle Voraussetzungen erfüllen, die zur Erhaltung der auf der abstrakten Ebene bewiesenen Korrektheit bei der Mikrokodeoptimierung im Compiler einer höheren Mikroprogrammiersprache notwendig sind.

Wir schlagen die folgende Strukturierung eines Firmware-Engineering-Systems vor [22]:

- Die Basis des Systems soll ein Verifikationssystem sein, das auf der von Dijkstra vorgeschlagenen konstruktiven Verifikationsmethode [23] basiert. Diese Methode ist für die Handhabung des Parallelismus in

Mikroinstruktionen erweiterbar und profitiert erheblich von der im Vergleich zu Software-Programmen niedrigeren Komplexität von Mikroprogrammen.

- Im deduktiven System dieses Verifikationssystems soll die Hardware eines spezifischen Rechners durch Axiome beschrieben werden. Die Semantik der höheren Mikroprogrammiersprache soll durch Schlußregeln definiert werden. Zeit- und Synchronisationsbedingungen für die spezifische Rechnerhardware sollen durch "Interface"-, "Deadlock"-, Blocking"- und "Starvation"-Invarianten [21] mit der Semantic-Definition gekoppelt werden.

- Die Funktionen der zu implementierenden Firmware sollen in einer Spezifikationssprache, die auf die konstruktive Verifikationsmethode ausgerichtet ist (z. B. SPECIAL) und für die Firmware-Spezifikation erweitert werden muß, spezifiziert werden.

- Die höhere Mikroprogrammiersprache (die einen optimierenden Compiler haben soll) soll durch die Definition abstrakter Datentypen zur Beschreibung der Rechnerhardware und spezifischen Firmware-Datenobjekte maschinenunabhängig und erweiterbar gemacht werden.

- Das Verifikationssystem auf der abstrakten Ebene soll durch ein Testsystem komplementiert werden, das eine Untermenge der Spezifikationssprache interpretieren kann.

Literaturverzeichnis

[1] Wilkes, M.V.: The Best Way to Design an Automatic Calculating Machine. Report of Manchester University Computer Inaugural Conference, Juli 1951, S. 16-18.

[2] Wilkes, M.V.: Microprogramming. Proc. Eastern Joint Computer Conference, Dezember 1958, S. 18-20.

[3] Berndt, H.: Was ist Firmware. Elektronische Rechenanlagen, Vol. 19, No. 2, 1977, S. 77-80.

[4] Opler, A.: Fourth-Generation Software. Datamation, Vol. 13, No. 1, 1967, S. 22-24.

[5] Wegner, P.: Programming Languages, Information Struktures, and Machine Organization. Mcgraw-Hill, Inc., London, 1971.

[6] Rosin, R.F.: The Significance of Microprogramming. SIGMICRO Newsletter, Vol. 4, No. 4, Januar 1974, S. 24-39.

[7] Berg, H.K.: Microprogramming. Vorlesungsskript. Technische Universität Berlin, 1978.

[8] Agrawala, A.K.; Rauscher, T.G.: Foundations of Microprogramming, Architecture, Software, and Applications. Academic Press Inc., New York, 1976.

[9] Tucker, S.G.: Microprogram Control for System/360. IBM System Journal, Vo. 6, 1967, S. 222-241.

[10] Schünemann, C.: Mikro- und Pico-Programmspeicher. (Hasselmeier, Spruth, ed), Rechnerstrukturen, Oldenbourg-Verlag, München, 1974, S. 36-74.

[11] Katzan, H., Jr.: Microprogramming Primer. McGraw-Hill, Inc., Now York, 1977.

[12] Kornerup, P.: Concepts of the MATHILDA System. Proc. 2nd Annual Symposium on Computer Architecture, IEEE Publ. 75CH0916-7C, 1975, S. 159-164.

[13] Röder, H.; Niggemann, H.: Primitiv-Operationen strukturierter Betriebssysteme - Entwurf und Implementierung". Universität Dortmund, Sept. 1977.

[14] Bredt, T.H.; Saxena, A.R.: A Structured Specification of a Hierarchical Operating System. Proc. 1975 Intl. Conference on Reliable Software, ACM SIGPLAN Notices, Vol. 9, No. 6, 1975.

[15] Burkhardt, W.H.; Randel, R.C.: Design of Operating Systems with Micro-programmed Implementations. NTIS Report No. PIT-CS-BU-73-01, Sept. 1973.

[16] Dijkstra, E.W.: The Structure of the THE Multiprogramming System. Comm. ACM, Vol. 11, No. 5, 1968.

[17] Hartenstein, R.W.: Fundamentals of Structured Hardware Design. North-Holland Publ. Comp., 1978.

[18] Stockenberg, J.; van Dam, A.: Vertical Migration for Performance Enhancement in Layered Hardware/Firmware/Software Systems. Computer, Vol. 11, No. 5, 1978, S. 35-50.

[19] Berg, H.K.; Covey, C.R.: A Primer on the Use of a Logic State Analyzer as a Microprogram Debugging Aid. Department of Computer Science, University of Minnesota, Tech. Report 78-12.

[20] Davidson, S.; Shriver, B.D.: An Overview of Firmware Engineering. Computer, Vol. 11, No. 5, 1978, S. 21-33.

[21] Berg, H.K.; Boebert, E.; Franta, W.R.; Moher, T.: Formal Methods in Program Verification and Specification. Noch unveröffentlicht.

[22] Berg, H.K.; Franta, W.R.; Giloi, W.K.: Towards a Firmware Engineering Discipline. Noch unveröffentlicht.

[23] Dijkstra, E.W.: A Discipline of Programming. Prentice-Hall, Inc., Engelwood Cliffs, 1976.

INFORMATIONSTECHNOLOGIE UND GESELLSCHAFTLICHER WANDEL

von Jürgen Reese

Die Gesellschaft für Mathematik und Datenverarbeitung hat von einer interdisziplinär zusammengesetzten Wissenschaftler-Gruppe[1)] eine "Bestandsaufnahme der Wirkungsforschung im Bereich Informationstechnologie" erstellen lassen, die vor knapp zwei Monaten vorgelegt worden ist. In ihrer Auseinandersetzung mit den möglichen oder gar wahrscheinlichen Wirkungen der informationstechnologischen Entwicklung auf die Gesellschaft gelangt die Gruppe unter anderem zu den folgenden, nicht apokalyptischen sondern vielmehr Forschung und Politik herausfordernden Annahmen:

Die vorherrschenden ökonomischen Verwertungsinteressen bemächtigen sich der Informationstechnologie, so wie sie sich zu früheren Zeiten auch anderer Technologien bemächtigt haben, und sie sind dabei dem Staat als Wahrer sozialer Interessen immer ein Stück voraus. Die große Geschwindigkeit, mit der informationstechnologische Potentiale wirtschaftlich zur Entfaltung kommen, und die Tiefe ihres Eingriffs in bestehende soziale Strukturen können zu ungewöhnlich scharfen Problemen des sozialen Wandels führen. Im einzelnen ist zu befürchten, daß die weltwirtschaftliche Verflechtung und die Unternehmenskonzentration voranschreiten, daß der Druck in Richtung neuer Produkte und Märkte steigt und daß sich die fortwährende Substitution von Arbeit durch Kapital erheblich beschleunigt, mit der Folge struktureller Arbeitslosigkeit.

Der ökonomische Druck von Strukturwandel und Rationalisierung führt über die Anwendung der Informationstechnologie im Arbeitsbereich zu einer Verringerung beruflicher Autonomie, zur Polarisierung der Qualifikation und zur innerbetrieblichen Machtkonzentration. Diese sozialen Nachteile wirken wegen des hohen Tempos des wirtschaftsstrukturellen Wandels innerhalb einer Generation, für die sie eine große Belastung darstellen. Verstärkend kommen die psychische Belastung aus

---

1) Jürgen Reese, Herbert Kubicek, Bernd-Peter Lange, Bernd Lutterbeck, Uwe Reese

Arbeitsintensivierung und die Angst vor Verlust des Arbeitsplatzes oder Abgruppierung hinzu. Im sogenannten Freizeitbereich macht sich das als verstärkter Bildungs-, Fortbildungs- und Umschulungsdruck bemerkbar.

Alle diese Belastungen zusammengenommen werden zunehmend als soziale Probleme erlebt, um die sich der Staat zu kümmern hat. So werden die gesetzlichen Regelungsbedürfnisse im Arbeitsleben, der Gewährleistungsanspruch zur sozialen Sicherheit und die Ansprüche an medizinische und psychiatrische Versorgung weiter erheblich steigen. Das politische System selbst wird unter Nutzung der Informationstechnologie bei der Erledigung aller dieser zusätzlichen Aufgaben immer komplexer, und immer wenigere verstehen seine Programme und Gesetze: Es entwickelt sich zum technokratischen Vollversorgungsstaat.

Wie gesagt: Diese Befürchtungen der Wissenschaftler sollen nach ihrem eigenen Verständnis nicht zur Untätigkeit und damit zu einer Self-Fulfilling-Prophecy führen. Sie sollen aufrütteln und sowohl auf den Forschungsbedarf als auch auf die Notwendigkeit frühzeitiger politischer Korrekturen aufmerksam machen. Wie aber soll die Forschung an diesen Gegenstand herangehen?

1.) Vor noch kaum zwei Jahren hätte der Begriff Wirkungsforschung auf einer solchen Jahrestagung wahrscheinlich Rätselraten verursacht, es sei denn, ein Massenkommunikationsforscher hätte der Ungewißheit aus dem Begriffsverständnis seiner Disziplin eine Ende gesetzt. Dort bemüht man sich nämlich seit Jahren um die Analyse von Wirkungen des Fernsehens und anderer Medien auf das Publikum - vor allen Dingen also massenhaft verbreiteter Informationsinhalte - und hat dafür den Begriff Wirkungsforschung geprägt. Hier ist nun von einer anderen Art Wirkungsforschung die Rede. Sie ist umfassender sowohl in Hinblick auf den Auslöser der Wirkungen, die "Informationstechnologie", als auch in Hinblick auf das über diesen Auslöser Bewirkte, die "Veränderung gesellschaftlichen Wandels".

Eine Eingrenzung dessen, was mit Informationstechnologie gemeint ist, kann verhältnismäßig leicht geschehen. Die Autoren der oben zitierten Bestandsaufnahme verstehen darunter vier Technikfamilien: Datenübertragung, Datenverarbeitung, Datenspeicherung und Datenein-/-ausgabe. Jede dieser Familien hat in den vergangenen Jahrzehnten eine geradezu atemberaubende Entwicklung durchlaufen - atemberaubend vor allem für die Ingenieure und Manager in den betreffenden Firmen und nach und nach auch für eine wachsende Zahl von Anwendern der neuen Techniken. Aber die Zahl der in dieser Weise Betroffenen war doch zunächst insgesamt eher begrenzt. Erst in jüngerer Zeit bahnt sich ein Zusammenwachsen der verschiedenen Technikfamilien an mit der Folge, daß völlig neue Technikanwendungen in zum Teil neue Märkte vorstoßen und dadurch einschneidende Veränderungen für eine große Zahl von Menschen, wenn nicht für die ganze Gesellschaft mit sich bringen. Um nur einige dieser Technikanwendungen zu nennen: Elektronische Post, elektronischer Zahlungsverkehr, Kabelfernsehen und Kabeltext, Büroautomation, Industrieroboter, Informations- und Dokumentationssysteme, Telekonferenzsysteme.

Aus systematischen Gründen sei daran erinnert, daß die Massenkommunikationsforschung, die wegen des bislang kaum entwickelten Rückkanals der Medien (Ausnahmen: Leserbriefe, Studiodiskussion, Meinungsforschung, Einschaltquotenerhebung u.a.) präziser Massen<u>informations</u>forschung heißen müßte, nur einen Bruchteil der gesellschaftlichen Veränderungen erfaßt, die in die Wirkungsforschung einzubeziehen sind.

Wenn eine Information viele Adressaten an verschiedenen Orten zugleich und schnell erreichen kann, so ist das ein wichtiger, aber keineswegs der einzige, ja wahrscheinlich nicht einmal der wichtigste Aspekt der Informationstechnologie. Zunehmend bedeutungsvoll erscheint die massenhafte Kommunikation, die massenhafte Informationsspeicherung und Informationsverarbeitung sowie die Automatisierung durch Prozeßsteuerung. Dieser Tatbestand würde schon eher durch das Wort Informationsmassen-Forschung umschrieben, wenn dadurch nicht die Technik zu sehr in den Mittelpunkt der Aufmerksamkeit geraten würde. Das ist ein weiterer Grund, weshalb hier von Wirkungsforschung gesprochen werden soll, denn in diesem Begriff steckt in aller Deutlichkeit, daß es um die Wirkungen der Informationstechnologie in der Gesellschaft geht. Wirkungsforschung im Bereich Informationstechnologie ist also jede Art von Forschung, die zur Aufklärung der Beziehungen zwischen Informationstechnologie und Gesellschaft beiträgt.

2.) Erörterungen dieser Beziehungen haben bisher häufig unter Verwirrung der Kausalitätsannahmen gelitten. Mal hieß es, der Computer habe Auswirkungen auf die Gesellschaft, dann sprach man von seinen Wirkungen; auch wurde die Formel verwendet, der Computer "sei" die gesellschaftliche Wirkung. Dem gegenüber haben viele Fachleute behauptet, der Computer habe gar keine Wirkung, die der Mensch nicht von ihm wolle. Als ein neutrales Werkzeug könne er zwar erwünschte, nicht aber unerwünschte Wirkungen haben. Die Verwirrung scheint komplett, wenn dann von anderen wiederum ausgeführt wird, die gesellschaftlich unerwünschten Wirkungen würden sogar über die erwünschten Effekte dominieren, weshalb man am besten eine

Art Non-Proliferationsabkommen für manche Informationstechniken unter den marktführenden Nationen schließen solle.

In allen diesen Annahmen befindet sich ein Stückchen Wahrheit. Das ist eine kritische und relativierende Aussage, die zunächst einmal selbst der Kritik unterzogen werden muß. Zu fragen ist nämlich, ob Aussagen zur Kausalität im betreffenden Forschungsbereich überhaupt wahrheitsfähig sind. Wirkungen, wie sie hier zur Diskussion stehen, erfolgen überwiegend innerhalb eines weitverzweigten Geflechts sozialer Beziehungen, bei dem unzählige auslösende Faktoren als Ursachen in Betracht gezogen werden müssen. Eine experimentelle Isolierung einzelnen Faktoren ist in aller Regel nicht möglich. Sozialstatistische Analysen können trotz dieser Komplexität zwar eine Häufung des Zusammenfallens zweier oder mehrerer Ereignisse wie zum Beispiel Computereinsatz und Dequalifizierung der betroffenen Arbeitnehmer nachweisen, doch bedürfen sie der Interpretation. Wahrheitsfähig sind sie in Bezug auf Kausalitätsaussagen nicht. In strenger wissenschaftlicher Rede sollte man also nicht von einer Informationstechnik als Urasache einer bestimmten sozialen Veränderung (=Wirkung) sprechen.

Diese Klärung kann nun allerdings nicht darüber hinwegtäuschen, daß im Gefolge des Einsatzes von Informationstechnologie schon heute eine Reihe von Veränderungen in der Gesellschaft vor sich gehen, die man sich ohne die technologischen Möglichkeiten nicht vorstellen kann und die darüber hinaus bei vielen Betroffenen unerwünscht sind. Offenbar - und das ist nun die soziologische Formulierung eines Wirkungszusammenhangs - wird mit der Informationstechnologie vieles bewirkt, das zur Erregung wissenschaftlicher und öffentlicher Aufmerksamkeit führt (zum Beispiel Streik in der Druckindustrie). D.h. die Informationstechnologie ist zur Waffe in der Auseinandersetzung konkurrierender Interessen geworden. Nicht die Informationstechnologie an sich hat also gesellschaftliche Wirkungen, sondern ihre Verwertung in der jeweils vorfindlichen Interessenkonstellation. Bei dieser Konzeption des Wirkungsbegriffs wird auch verständlich, was es bedeutet, wenn von "unerwünschten" Wirkungen der Informationstechnologie gesprochen wird, denn damit ist gemeint, daß sich Betroffene einer Technikanwendung mit deren interessiertem Einsatz auf Grund ihrer ganz anders gearteten Interessenlage nicht einverstanden erklären können.

3.) Wenn Wirkungsforschung nicht nur beschreiben, sondern auch erklären und prognostizieren will, muß sie Kenntnis haben sowohl von technologischen Potentialen - den bei entsprechender Entwicklung technisch möglichen Anwendungen - als auch von der gesellschaftlichen Interessen- und Machtkonstellation ("Verwertungsbedingungen"). Das hat erhebliche Konsequenzen für ihre Organisation, auf die noch zurückzukommen sein wird. Die so verstandene analytische Wirkungsforschung versucht zukünftige Wirkungen auf die Gesellschaft vorauszusagen und schafft Grundlagen für die Bewertung der Entwicklung dadurch, daß sie auf eventuell verletzte Rechtsnormen und Interessen von Betroffenen hinweist. Sie liefert damit den Politikern, Gewerkschaften und Verbänden eine Voraussetzung zur rechtzeitigen Verhinderung unerwünschter Entwicklungen, genauer: Sie liefert die wissensmäßigen Voraussetzungen zur rechtzeitigen Mobilisierung derjenigen, die ihre Betroffenheit sonst erst bemerken würden, wenn die Technikentwicklung von Forschung über Produktion bis hin zum Einsatz in der Praxis schon zu viele Investitionen an Kapital, Organisation und Arbeit in Anspruch genommen hat, als daß die nun an ihrer Verwertung Interessierten die Produktion und den Vertrieb kampflos einstellen würden.

Eine zweite Voraussetzung zur Beherrschung der informationstechnologischen Entwicklung bietet die Wirkungsforschung, indem sie die Wirkung verschiedener Mittel staatlicher Intervention untersucht. Bekanntlich erfordert die zu erwartende Entwicklung im Informationssektor immer umfassendere Datenschutzregelungen - man hat sie auch Datenverkehrsrecht genannt - ferner Normung, arbeitsrechtliche Vorschriften usw. Schließlich rührt ein gewichtiger Einfluß des Staates daher, daß er die Entwicklung der Informationstechnologie mit großen Summen fördert, ein Monopol bei den Netzen unterhält und obendrein einer der bedeutendsten Nachfrager nach Informationstechnik ist. Die zahlreichen Einflußmöglichkeiten führen dazu, daß er faktisch einen erheblichen Teil der Verantwortung für die informationstechnologische Entwicklung im Land trägt. Ihr kann er aber nur gerecht werden, wenn die Eignung unterschiedlicher Instrumente zur Steuerung der Entwicklung genügend bekannt ist. Das ist die Aufgabe der instrumentellen Wirkungsforschung.

Die ungewöhnlich rasche Entwicklung der Informationstechnologie läßt nicht immer genügend Zeit für den prinzipiell zu fordernden analytischen Vorgriff auf die mit ihr verbundenen Probleme, zumal das dafür einzusetzende wissenschaftliche Potention in der Bundesrepublik nicht eben groß ist. Technikanwendungen werden also weiterhin in großem Umfang ohne Rücksicht auf soziale Konsequenzen entwickelt. Sie folgen vorwiegend ökonomischen (volkswirtschaftlichen und betriebswirtschaftlichen) Kalkülen, und die Marktforschung bildet eine für diesen Zweck äußerst nützliche Brücke zwischen hochorganisierter Technologieentwicklung und gesellschaftlichem Bedarf. Hier hat die pragmatische Wirkungsforschung anzusetzen. Sie stellt eine zweite Brücke zwischen Technologieentwicklung und Gesellschaft her, und zwar die zwischen technischer Systementwicklung und Systembenutzern und Systembetroffenen. Im Gegensatz zur Marktforschung knüpft sie nicht an den artikulierten Bedarf organisierter Interessenten, sondern an die seltener artikulierten Bedürfnisse des Bürgers in verschiedenen Lebensbereichen an.

4.) Gemessen an ihren drei umfassenden Aufgaben steckt die Wirkungsforschung im Bereich Informationstechnologie in der Bundesrepublik noch in den Anfängen, und in vielen Fällen wird sie trotz ernsthafter Bemühungen ihren Zielen von der Konzeption her nicht gerecht. Die analytische Wirkungsforschung hat kaum wirklich verwertbare Ergebnisse vorzuweisen: Zu wenig wissen wir über den wirtschaftsstrukturellen Wandel, dessen Bedeutung spätestens seit den Analysen von Edwin Parker und Marc Uri Porat in den USA bekannt ist. Immer noch kann behauptet werden, die Informationstechnologie würde sich auf den Arbeitsmarkt nicht weiter auswirken. Ob die Technologie zu einer verstärkten Unternehmenskonzentration führt und wie der Medienmarkt auf sie reagiert - über derartige Fragen wird zum Teil aus Mangel an Wissen und häufig wegen einer ungeeigneten Organisation des schon vorhandenen Wissens kontrovers diskutiert.

Etwas besser sieht es bei der Analyse des politischen Systems aus. Hier sind insbesondere zum Thema Verwaltungsautomation eine Reihe von Arbeiten entstanden, die über Folgen der Datenverarbeitung für die Beschäftigten in der öffentlichen Verwaltung Aufschluß geben. Auch das Thema Datenschutz hat zu einer größeren Anzahl von Studien geführt, durch die einzelne Probleme staatlicher Nutzung von Datenverarbeitung erkannt worden sind. Generell sind aber auch in diesem Analysefeld überwiegend Lücken festzustellen. So ist der Wandel des Verhältnisses zwischen Bürger und Staat vor dem Hintergrund einer sich ständig ausweitenden technischen Komplexität der öffentlichen Verwaltung noch kaum wahrgenommen, geschweige denn erforscht, und selbst die Wirkungen der Informationstechnologie auf das Gleichgewicht demokratischer Institutionen wie Regierung, Parlament und Rechtsprechung finden sich nur in vereinzelten Reden und Aufsätzen behandelt. Von organisierter Forschung kann kaum die Rede sein.

Im Bereich Arbeit sieht es etwas besser aus. Hier finden sich zahlreiche Forschungsprojekte, in denen der Wandel der Arbeitsplatzbedingungen, der Qualifikation und die Belastungen während des Umstellungsprozesses eingehend untersucht werden. Hinzu kommen ergonomische und psychische Wirkungsforschung, die schon aus Eigeninteresse von den Anbietern der Informationstechnologie selbst durchgeführt werden. Allerdings handelt es sich bei den meisten dieser Arbeiten nur um analytische Wirkungsforschung, die kaum noch zur Verbesserung der Arbeitsbedingungen beitragen kann, obwohl gerade die pragmatische Wirkungsforschung wegen ihrer Verwertungsorientierung größeren Nutzen verspricht.

Schließlich ist der vom Durchschnittsbürger besonders geschätzte Bereich Freizeit bzw. Reproduktion zu erwähnen. Er ist, vom Medienmarkt (insbesondere Fernsehen) abgesehen, bisher noch wenig von der informationstechnologischen Entwicklung erfaßt worden, und deshalb überrascht es kaum, daß er als lohnendes Betätigungsfeld der Wirkungsforschung nocht nicht entdeckt worden ist. Man kann nur hoffen, daß die Zurückhaltung der Forschung bald aufgegeben wird, denn daß der Mensch gerade auch in seiner Freizeit zunehmend von den Notwendigkeiten des rapiden Wandels in der Gesellschaft verfolgt wird, zeichnet sich schon heute, wie bereits bemerkt, durch die Zunahme von Aus- und Fortbildungsaktivitäten in der Freizeit ab, in Zukunft vermehrt wohl auch über "bequeme" Medien wie z.B. Kassettenfernsehen. Der Konkurrenzkampf um die relativ knapper werdenden höherqualifizierten Stellen setzt sich von dem Berufsbereich in den Reproduktionsbereich fort und belastet den Menschen zusätzlich.

Eine pragmatische Wirkungsforschung ist in zahlreichen Ansätzen erkennbar, doch bisher wenig erfolgreich. Das Problem liegt hier vor allem darin, daß das Bewußtsein der Systementwickler immer noch am klassischen Instrumentenansatz ("Werkzeugstil") festhält, wonach eine vom späteren Einsatzfeld isolierte Entwicklung des Systems möglich sei, ohne daß die Nutzung dadurch beeinträchtigt werde. Dieser Standpunkt verliert allerdings umso mehr an Überzeugungskraft, je tiefer die zunehmend komplexen Systeme in die Sozialorganisation des Anwendungsbereichs eingreifen. Wie zuvor schon die Politiker in ihrer Ratlosigkeit bei Bürgerinitiativen in der Stadtentwicklungsplanung, so rufen nun auch zunehmend Systementwickler nach dem rettenden Sozialwissenschaftler - in der Regel einem jungen, unerfahrenen Universitätsabgänger, der in seiner Ausbildung von betrieblicher oder administrativer Wirklichkeit kaum etwas zu hören bekommen hat und von der Informationstechnologie so gut wie nichts weiß. Die Ernüchterung folgt sehr bald.

Pragmatische Wirkungsforschung kann in der Tat nur von interdisziplinären Teams betrieben werden. Aber sie steht noch vor dem nur schwer zu überwindenden Hindernis ihrer Theorie- und Erfahrungslosigkeit. Sie ist deshalb erfolgreich nur als ein organisierter Lernprozeß durchzuführen, in dessen Verlauf Sozialwissenschaftler die von ihnen einzunehmende Vermittlungsfunktion zwischen Systementwicklern und Systemanwendern (Betroffenen) immer wieder von neuem überprüfen und von Projekt zu Projekt theoretisch besser fundieren. Derartige Bedingungen sind in der Wirkungsforschung hierzulande noch nicht anzutreffen, wohl aber in den skandinavischen Ländern, die dabei zum Teil Vorbildliches leisten.

Die instrumentelle Wirkungsforschung schließlich ist nicht einmal in Ansätzen entwickelt. Das muß nicht verwundern, wenn man berücksichtigt, daß auch staatliche Aktivitäten in anderen Politikbereichen erst äußerst zögernd mit Programmevaluierung beginnen. Andererseits ist schwer vorstellbar, daß die anstehenden Steuerungsprobleme zunächst im technischen Kommunikationsbereich, dann aber erneut im Datenschutz und in zahlreichen anderen rechtlich geschützten und ungeschützten Bereichen ohne instrumentelle Wirkungsforschung effektiv gelöst werden können.

Insgesamt ist festzuhalten, daß die bisherige Wirkungsforschung im Bereich Informationstechnologie in der Bundesrepublik trotz entschlossener Bemühungen vereinzelter Wissenschaftler noch weit von einer Bewältigung der gesellschaftlichen Probleme entfernt ist, die die Informationstechnologie ohne rechtzeitiges wissenschaftliches und politisches Handeln sehr wahrscheinlich mit sich bringen wird.

PROZESSAUTOMATISIERUNG UND INFORMATIK

Rudolf Lauber
Institut für Regelungstechnik und Prozess-automatisierung der Universität Stuttgart

Summary

The close relations between process automation and computer science are discussed by investigating three problem areas: process control computer languages, real-time operating systems and specification and design methodologies. It is demonstrated that time-dependent information processing and the development of people-oriented methods and software tools remain to be a challenge to computer science.

Übersicht

Die enge Verbindung zwischen Prozeßautomatisierung und Informatik wird beispielhaft an Hand der folgenden Problemkreise aufgezeigt: Prozeßprogrammiersprachen, Prozeßrechner-Betriebssysteme, Spezifikationssprachen und Entwurfssysteme. Die Schwierigkeiten der zeitabhängigen Datenverarbeitung, wie sie für den Anwendungsbereich der Prozeßautomatisierung typisch sind, und die Erfordernisse, Verfahren und Software-Werkzeuge den Menschen anzupassen, die sie handhaben sollen, werden als Herausforderung an die Informatik hervorgehoben.

Einführung in die Thematik

Die Prozeßautomatisierung (als Ingenieurdisziplin von der Automatisierung technischer Prozesse mit Prozeßrechnern) und die Informatik (als Wissenschaft von der systematischen Verarbeitung von Informationen, insbesondere mit Hilfe von Digitalrechnern [1]) sind im Titel dieses Vortrages im Sinne einer "Konjunktion" verknüpft. Damit kommt zum Ausdruck, daß es Teilmengen von Aufgabenstellungen, Lösungsansätzen und Methoden gibt, die beiden gemeinsam sind. Je nach dem eingenommenen Standpunkt kann man dabei das Gebiet der Prozeßautomatisierung als eigenständiges Fach verstehen, wobei die Informatik, ähnlich wie die Mathematik, den Charakter einer Dienstleistungs-Wissenschaft hat, die unentbehrliche Hilfsmittel liefert - oder aber man kann die Informatik als übergeordnete Wissenschaft sehen, zu deren Zweig der "Technischen Informatik" das Gebiet der Prozeßautomatisierung als eines unter vielen Teilgebieten zu rechnen ist. Man spricht dann gern von der "Prozeßdatenverarbeitung" oder "Prozeßinformatik". Gleichgültig, welchen Standpunkt man nun bevorzugt: In jedem Fall ist festzustellen, daß trotz der engen Verknüpfung das Verhältnis zwischen Prozeßautomatisierung und Informatik eher kühl und wenig entwickelt ist. Selbst dort, wo es um Kerngebiete der Informatik geht, wie z.B. um die Entwicklung von Programmiersprachen, finden Automatisierungsingenieure und Informatiker nur schwer zueinander. Dafür gibt es viele Gründe - nicht zuletzt den Grund, daß der Informatiker sein "Handwerk" in der klimatisierten Atmosphäre eines Rechenzentrums erlernt. Daher ist ihm ein Prozeßrechner, der über elektrische Leitungen an einen technischen Prozeß angeschlossen ist, oft unbekannt und fremd. Um diese Fremdheit zu überwinden, werden im Folgenden beispielhaft einige Problemkreise der Prozeßautomatisierung behandelt. Es soll daran nicht nur deutlich werden, welche typischen Aufgaben aus dem Bereich der Informatik hier zu lösen sind. Vielmehr soll darüber hinaus der Versuch unternommen werden, zu zeigen, daß es auf diesem Gebiet zahlreiche interessante Aufgaben gibt, die gerade auch für den Informatiker reizvoll sein können.

Problemkreis Prozeßprogrammiersprachen

Die Situation auf dem Gebiet der Programmierung von Prozeßrechnern ist dadurch gekennzeichnet, daß bis heute noch mehr als 80% aller Prozeßautomatisierungsprogramme in der Assemblersprache des jeweiligen Zielrechners geschrieben werden. Dies bedingt ein schwerfälliges, zweistufiges Vorgehen bei der Erstellung der Programme: In einer ersten Stufe führen Ingenieure - oft in diesem Zusammenhang etwas herablassend als die "Technologen" bezeichnet - eine Systemanalyse durch und legen die Automatisierungsverfahren aus. In einer zweiten Stufe setzt dann ein erfahrenes Programmiererteam (aus einer Software-Abteilung des Herstellerwerkes oder aus einer Software-Firma kommend) die Automatisierungsabläufe und -Algorithmen in Assemblerprogramme für den Prozeßrechner um.
Als Folge dieses Vorgehens wachsen die Kosten für die Entwicklung und insbesondere für die spätere Pflege und Wartung der Software immer bedrohlicher an. Immer mehr dominieren die Software-Kosten

gegenüber den Hardware-Kosten.
Man fragt zu Recht: Warum werden bei Prozeßrechnern nur so zögernd höhere Programmiersprachen eingesetzt, die es den Ingenieuren ermöglichen würden, selbst die Automatisierungs-Software zu erstellen und die Pflege und Wartung zu übernehmen? Von den vielfältigen Gründen seien zwei wesentliche genannt:

- Bei der Anwendung höherer Programmiersprachen muß im allgemeinen eine gewisse Ineffizienz in Kauf genommen werden, d.h. in aller Regel wird der Speicherbedarf und die Rechenzeit höher sein als bei Assemblerprogrammen. Während dies bei Datenverarbeitungsanlagen für technisch-wissenschaftliche und kommerzielle Anwendungen die Ergebnisse nicht beeinflußt, können sich bei zeitkritischen Automatisierungsprogrammen Schwierigkeiten ergeben. Außerdem geht der Speicherbedarf unmittelbar in die Hardwarekosten ein - ein Gesichtspunkt, der wegen der sinkenden Speicherkosten schon beinahe vergessen schien, der aber jetzt bei den Mikrorechnern wieder aufgetaucht ist.

- Die für Zeit-unabhängige Datenverarbeitungsaufgaben konzipierten höheren Programmiersprachen, wie z.B. ALGOL, FORTRAN usw. sind für Prozeßautomatisierungsprogramme nicht geeignet. Denn bei diesen muß ja, zusätzlich zu den algorithmischen Zusammenhängen, auch die zeitliche und logische Synchronisierung zwischen Programm- und Prozeßgeschehen, der rechtzeitige und parallele Ablauf von Automatisierungsprogrammen und die Ein- und Ausgabe von Prozeßsignalen mit entsprechenden Sprachmitteln formulierbar sein [2].

In den letzten Jahren wurden nun spezielle Prozeßprogrammiersprachen mit solchen Spracheigenschaften entwickelt [3, 4, 5, 6]. Es ist zu erwarten, daß sich diese jetzt verfügbaren Prozeßprogrammiersprachen, insbesondere PEARL, wegen ihrer offensichtlichen Kostenvorteile im Bereich der Prozeßrechner mittlerer und größerer Leistungsfähigkeit allmählich durchsetzen werden. Bei den Mikrorechnern dagegen ist das Bild widersprüchlich. Auf der einen Seite sind die in der Vergangenheit und gegenwärtig noch marktbeherrschenden 8-bit-Typen bezüglich der Software-Erstellung mit den früheren Röhrenrechnern vergleichbar: Sie haben eine so geringe Leistungsfähigkeit und so kleine Speicher, daß nur eine maschinennahe Programmierung in Betracht kommen kann.
In der Zukunft jedoch ist eine grundlegende Änderung dieser Situation abzusehen:

- die neu erscheinenden 16-bit-Mikrorechner versprechen, so leistungsfähig zu sein, daß Betriebssysteme und höhere Programmiersprachen einsetzbar werden.

- gleichzeitig wird diese Mikrorechnergeneration zunehmend in neue Anwendungszweige, z.B. im Maschinenbau, eindringen, wo bisher wenig Hardware- und Software-Kenntnisse vorhanden sind. Damit erwächst die Notwendigkeit, die Handhabbarkeit der Mikrorechner diesen Bedingungen anzupassen.

Diese Verbesserung der Handhabbarkeit (im Sinne von: Möglichkeit zur Erstellung, zum Test und zur Wartung von Mikrorechnersystemen durch Personal mit geringem Ausbildungsstand) mit Hilfe geeigneter Hardware- und Software-Schnittstellen, z.B. mit Programmiersprachen verschiedener Sprachebenen, steht als neue, anspruchsvolle Aufgabe vor uns. Sie sollte von Prozeßingenieuren und Informatikern gemeinsam angepackt werden.

Problemkreis Prozeßrechner-Betriebssysteme

Ein Prozeßrechner-Betriebssystem hat u.a. die Aufgabe, die Durchführung der Automatisierungsprogramme zu steuern, oder anders ausgedrückt, die Betriebsmittel den konkurrierenden Rechenprozessen zuzuteilen. Mit geeigneten Betriebssystem-Strategien muß dabei versucht werden, die vom technischen Prozeß her gestellten Zeitbedingungen einzuhalten.
Da die Zeit-abhängige Datenverarbeitung ein Charakteristikum der Prozeßautomatisierung darstellt, sollen die in der Praxis gestellten Anforderungen bezüglich der Erfüllung von Zeitbedingungen im Folgenden näher erläutert werden, wobei Ergebnisse aus [7] verwendet werden.

Grundsätzlich lassen sich Zeitbedingungen in die beiden folgenden Kategorien einteilen:

- Absolute Zeitbedingungen, d.h. Bedingungen, die - bezogen auf die Uhrzeit - fest liegen.

  Beispiel für die Formulierung einer absoluten Zeitbedingung in PEARL:

  AT 11:45:00 ALL 50 SEC DURING 10 MIN ACTIVATE PUMPE PRIORITY 2 ;
  (Ab 11.45 Uhr soll alle 50 Sekunden während der folgenden 10 Minuten der Rechenprozeß PUMPE mit der Priorität 2 aktiviert werden).

- Relative Zeitbedingungen, d.h. Bedingungen, die relativ zu (noch bevorstehenden) stochastischen Ereignissen gelten.

  Beispiel (in PEARL):

```
WHEN ALARM ALL 1 MIN ACTIVATE BLINKLICHT ;
```

(Nach Eintreffen des Unterbrechungssignals ALARM soll jede Minute der Rechenprozeß BLINKLICHT beauftragt werden).

Sowohl bei den absoluten, als auch bei den relativen Zeitbedingungen kann man wieder 4 Fälle unterscheiden (Bild 1):

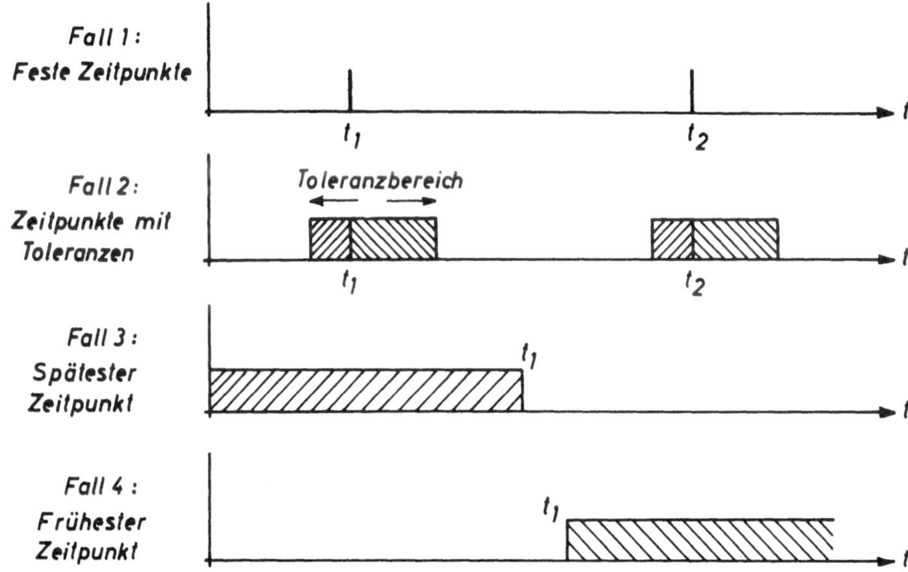

Bild 1: Klassifizierung von Zeitbedingungen nach [7].
Der Nullpunkt der Zeitachsen wird entweder durch eine fest Uhrzeit (bei absoluten Zeitbedingungen) oder durch den Zeitpunkt des Eintretens eines Ereignisses (bei relativen Zeitbedingungen) definiert.

Fall 1: Eine Aktion (z.B. Erfassen eines Meßwertes, Ausgabe eines Stellsignals usw.) hat genau zu bestimmten Zeitpunkten t_i zu erfolgen.

Fall 2: Eine Aktion hat während eines Zeitintervalls zu erfolgen, das durch einen Zeitpunkt t_i und einen oberen und unteren Toleranzbereich gegeben ist.

Fall 3: Eine Aktion hat spätestens zu einem bestimmten Zeitpunkt zu erfolgen.

Fall 4: Eine Aktion darf frühestens zu einem bestimmten Zeitpunkt erfolgen.

In Bild 2 sind zu den so definierten Kategorien und Fällen jeweils typische Beispiele aus der Praxis der Prozeßautomatisierung angegeben.

	Absolute Zeitbedingungen	Relative Zeitbedingungen
Fall 1: "Feste Zeitpunkte"	Kennfeldaufnahme an Prüfständen	Kennfeldaufnahme an Prüfständen
Fall 2: "Zeitpunkte mit Toleranzbereichen"	Erfassung von Regelgrößen bei der direkten digitalen Regelung	Meßwertüberwachung auf gleitende Grenzen
Fall 3: "Spätester Zeitpunkt"	Erfassung von Datentelegrammen bei Linienleitersystemen	Erfassung von Stückgutkennungen
Fall 4: "Frühester Zeitpunkt"	Folgesteuerung bei Chargenprozessen	Anfahrsteuerung bei Turbinen

Bild 2: Typische Anwendungsbeispiele aus der Prozeßautomatisierung für die in Bild 1 angegebenen Zeitbedingungen

Der Fall 1 tritt bei allen Prüfständen auf, z.B. bei der Erstellung von Kennfeldern an Motorprüfständen. Einander zugeordnete Meßwerte müssen jeweils zum gleichen Zeitpunkt erfaßt werden. Je nachdem, ob ein äußeres Ereignis (z.B. der Zündzeitpunkt) oder ein Uhrzeittakt die Meßzeitpunkte bestimmt, handelt es sich um absolute oder relative Zeitbedingungen.
Theoretisch könnte Fall 1 als Sonderfall von Fall 2 aufgefaßt werden, da ja streng genommen die genaue Einhaltung von Sollzeitpunkten nicht zu erzielen ist. Praktisch bedeutet Fall 1, daß die noch erträglichen Abweichungen von den Sollzeitpunkten kleiner als eine Millisekunde und damit klein gegenüber den üblichen Taskverwaltungszeitspannen sind.

Fall 2 tritt in der Praxis am häufigesten auf. Bei dem in Bild 2 genannten Beispiel der direkten digitalen Regelung werden die Regelgrößen im Idealfall zyklisch zu festen Abtastzeitpunkten erfaßt (absolute Zeitbedingungen). Verschiebungen dieser Abtastzeitpunkte führen zu einer Verringerung der Regelgüte [8]. Die noch zulässigen Toleranzbereiche, die sich aus der geforderten Regelgüte berechnen lassen, können - je nach den Zeitkonstanten der Regelstrecken - wenige Millisekunden bis zu einigen Sekunden betragen. Ähnliche Zeitbedingungen, jedoch im allgemeinen relativ zu einem Startereignis, ergeben sich bei der Überwachung des dynamischen Verlaufs von Meßwerten (Überwachung auf gleitende Grenzen). Verschiebungen der Erfassungszeitpunkte können z.B. bei Prüfautomaten dazu führen, daß fehlerhafte Signalverläufe noch als einwandfrei eingestuft werden und damit unerkannt bleiben bzw. daß umgekehrt einwandfreie Verläufe fälschlicherweise beanstandet werden [9].

Fall 3 tritt insbesondere bei Stückprozessen auf, wo entweder nach einem festen Fahrplan (absolute Zeitbedingungen) oder beim Eintreffen eines Objekts an einem Beobachtungspunkt (relative Zeitbedingungen) Aktionen auszuführen sind. Diese Aktionen können z.B. die Übernahme eines Datentelegramms bei der Linienleiterübertragung von Zügen oder die Erfassung einer Stückgutkennung beinhalten. Aus dem in Betracht kommenden Wegstück und der Geschwindigkeit der Objekte läßt sich bestimmen, zu welchem Zeitpunkt die betreffende Aktion spätestens auszuführen ist.

Fall 4 kommt bei Folgeprozessen häufig vor, wo das Eintreten eines neuen Prozeßzustandes abgewartet werden muß, bevor eine bestimmte Aktion ausgeführt werden darf. Beispiele sind Chargenprozesse in der chemischen Verfahrenstechnik oder das Anfahren einer Dampfturbine. Dabei können absolute oder relative Zeitbedingungen auftreten, je nachdem, ob die Steuerungsaktionen nach einem festen Zeitplan oder in Abhängigkeit von der Erreichung eines vorhergehenden Prozeßzustandes erfolgen.

Welche Betriebssystem-Strategien werden nun bei Prozeßrechner-Betriebssystemen verwendet, um diese verschiedenen Fälle von absoluten und relativen Zeitbedingungen zu erfüllen?
Die Antwort ist sehr ernüchternd: Das weithin übliche Verfahren ist die Verwendung konstanter Prioritätszahlen als Grundlage für die Betriebsmittel-Zuteilung. Dieses Verfahren ist zwar einfach zu implementieren, überläßt es aber dem Anwender, durch die Wahl geeigneter Prioritätszahlen zu versuchen, mit den gestellten Anforderungen fertig zu werden. Es läßt sich zeigen, daß ihm dies für Fall 1 garnicht und für die übrigen Fälle nur dann einigermaßen gelingen kann, wenn die Auslastung der Rechenanlage gering ist. Angesichts dieser Nachteile setzen neuere Prozeßprogrammiersprachen Realzeit-Betriebssysteme voraus, bei denen die Prioritätsfestlegung an beliebigen Stellen im

Programm vorgesehen werden kann (dynamische Prioritäten). Die Formulierung einer Prioritätsfestlegung geschieht z.B. in HAL/S durch ein "UPDATE-PRIORITY"- Statement oder in PEARL durch das "PRIORITY"-Attribut beim "ACTIVATE"- bzw. "CONTINUE"-Statement. Theoretisch besteht damit die Möglichkeit, die geforderten Zeitbedingungen durch geeignete Auswahl der Prioritäten zu erfüllen. Praktisch wird damit jedoch dem Anwendungsprogrammierer zugemutet, die Algorithmen, die bei anderen Strategien durch die Taskverwaltung des Betriebssystems ausgeführt werden, jeweils selbst im Programm zu formulieren.

Angesichts dieser unbefriedigenden Sachlage ist es nur schwer verständlich, daß bisher Untersuchungen über andere Betriebssystem-Strategien spärlich sind. In der Arbeit [7] wurden nun die Strategien

- kürzeste Restzeit (auch als "next-deadline-Strategie" bezeichnet)
- kleinster Spielraum ("slack-time-Strategie")

theoretisch und mit Hilfe eines Modellbetriebssystems untersucht. Dabei erwies sich, daß Varianten dieser Strategien die Chance bieten, die geschilderten Zeitbedingungen weitgehend zu erfüllen und daß solche Strategien durchaus implementierbar sind.

Problemkreis Spezifikationssprachen und Entwurfssysteme

Höhere Programmiersprachen, wie etwa die oben erwähnte Prozeßprogrammiersprache PEARL, können einen wichtigen Beitrag zur Senkung der Software-Entwicklungs- und Wartungs-Kosten und zur Erhöhung der Zuverlässigkeit der Prozeßrechnerprogrammsysteme leisten. Doch hilft die beste Programmiersprache nur wenig, wenn die Spezifikation der Anforderungen unvollständig oder gar widersprüchlich ist oder wenn die dem Programmentwurf zugrunde liegenden Lösungskonzepte und Algorithmen ungünstig gewählt sind. Die entscheidenden Weichen für den Erfolg werden nicht erst bei der Programmkonstruktion oder gar bei der Codierung, sondern schon bei der Festlegung der Anforderungen und bei der Konzeption der grundsätzlichen Lösungsverfahren zur Erfüllung dieser Anforderungen gestellt.

Dies gilt selbstverständlich nicht nur für Prozeßautomatisierungssysteme, sondern allgemein für umfangreiche Systeme jeder Art. Gleichfalls allgemein gilt leider, daß in den ersten Phasen der System-Entstehung, in denen dem kreativen, originellen und auf Erfahrung basierenden Handeln eine große Bedeutung zukommt, häufig unsystematisch vorgegangen wird, wo doch gerade hier Systematik besonders nötig wäre!

Wie in Bild 3 gezeigt, läßt sich nach dem Prinzip der schrittweisen Verfeinerung jedes System (in unserem Fall das zu entwerfende Prozeßautomatisierungssystem) in Betrachtungsebenen gliedern - und zwar unabhängig davon, ob bei der Entstehung ein "top-down"-Verfahren oder ein "bottom-up"-Verfahren vorherrschend war, da die Ebenenstruktur ja auch nachträglich definiert werden kann.
Auf jeder Ebene sind Tätigkeiten auszuführen und Dokumente zu erstellen. Diese Dokumente sind gleichzeitig

- das Ergebnis der Tätigkeit auf der betreffenden Ebene
- die Grundlage für die Tätigkeit auf der jeweils darunter liegenden Ebene.

Soweit diese Dokumente die Anforderungen an das Gesamtsystem, an Subsysteme oder an Automatisierungsfunktionen beschreiben, werden sie auch Spezifikationen genannt. Der Begriff "Spezifikation" wird hier also nicht für eine der Betrachtungsebene, z.B. die Ebene 0, reserviert, sondern allgemein im Sinne von "ins Einzelne gehende Angabe" verstanden.

Die "oberste" Betrachtungsebene in Bild 3 ist zunächst die Ebene Nr. 0, da hier die Anforderungen an das gesamte zu entwerfende Prozeßautomatisierungssystem (PAS) und dessen Schnittstellen zu anderen Systemen, die mit diesem zusammen ein "Übergeordnetes System" z.B. einen Fertigungsbetrieb, ein ganzes Unternehmen usw., betrachtet werden. Die Zielsetzung für dieses übergeordnete System und damit auch für das in diesem enthaltene Prozeßautomatisierungssystem ist jedoch häufig nur unter Berücksichtigung der wirtschaftlichen, soziologischen, ökologischen oder gar politischen Zusammenhänge festlegbar. Daher ist als Ebene Nr. -1 das diese Zusammenhänge beschreibende "Umweltsystem" mit eingetragen.

In den letzten Jahren wurden zahlreiche Verfahren und Werkzeuge entwickelt, die darauf abzielen, die in Bild 3 eingezeichneten Tätigkeiten des Spezifizierens und Entwerfens, insbesondere bei komplexen Informationsverarbeitenden Systemen, systematisch und Rechner-gestützt auszuführen [10]. Die "Wünsche", die dabei aus der Sicht der Prozeßautomatisierung an solche Spezifikationen und Entwurfssysteme zu stellen sind, betreffen folgende Gesichtspunkte:

- Formulierbarkeit: Es müssen Verarbeitungsvorgänge, Daten, Prozeßschnittstellen, Prozeß- und Zeitereignisse und die Synchronisierung paralleler Aktivitäten spezifiziert werden können.
- Dokumentation: Sie sollte schritthaltend mit dem Entwurf entstehen und möglichst weitgehend durch einen Rechner automatisch erstellt

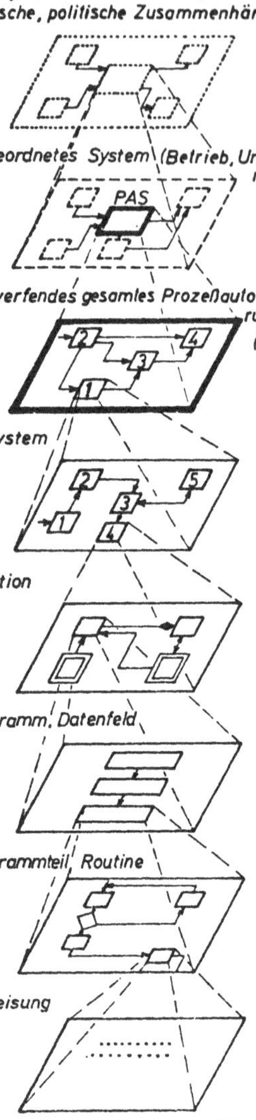

	Betrachtungs-Ebenen	Nr.	Tätigkeiten	Dokumente
Zielsetzung, Spezifikation der Anforderungen	Umweltsystem (Wirtschaftliche, soziologische, ökologische, politische Zusammenhänge)	-1	Zielsetzung für das Gesamtsystem (Prozeßautomatisierungssystem) festlegen	Zielsetzung
	Übergeordnetes System (Betrieb, Unternehmen) PAS	0	Situationsanalyse Klärung der Anforderungen (Requirements)	Spezifikation der Anforderungen (Aufbau des technischen Prozesses, Betriebsbedingungen, Anforderungen bei Störfällen)
Funktions-Entwurf	Zu entwerfendes gesamtes Prozeßautomatisierungssystem (PAS)	1	Aufgliederung des Prozeßautomatisierungssystems in Subsysteme (Systemanalyse I, Grobstruktur-Entwurf)	Spezifikation der "Architektur" des gesamten Prozeßautomatisierungssystems, reguläre und irreguläre Betriebsarten
	Subsystem	2	Aufgliederung der Subsysteme in Funktionen (Systemanalyse II, funktioneller Entwurf)	Spezifikation der Automatisierungsfunktionen
Programm-Entwurf	Funktion	3	Realisierung der Funktionen durch Programme und Datenblöcke bzw. durch Geräte	Beschreibung der Programme bzw. der Geräte
	Programm, Datenfeld	4	Aufgliederung der Programme in Programmteile (Tasks, Prozeduren usw.)	Beschreibung der Programmteile (Tasks, Prozeduren usw.)
	Programmteil, Routine	5	Formulierung der Programmteile als Flußdiagramm	Flußdiagramme bzw. Formulierung in höheren Programmiersprachen
Codierung	Anweisung	6	Programmierung der Anweisungen	Listing der Programme mit Kommentar

Bild 3: Gliederung eines Systems in Betrachtungsebenen.

werden. Unabhängig vom Vorgehen beim Entwurf muß die Dokumentation stets streng hierarchisch aufgebaut werden [11]. Übersichtlichkeit wird sowohl bezüglich der Zusammenhänge innerhalb einer Betrachtungs- bzw. Beschreibungsebene, als auch zwischen den Beschreibungsebenen, gefordert. Wesentlich ist die Beachtung unterschiedlicher Zielgruppen: Die Dokumentation muß so gestaltet sein, daß sie auch als Kommunikationsmittel zwischen dem Management und den System- und Programmentwicklern geeignet ist.

- Möglichkeit für Prüfungen während des Entwurfs: Prüfungen bezüglich Vollständigkeit und Konsistenz sollten auf jeder Betrachtungsebene und zwischen verschiedenen Ebenen möglich sein. Mit Hilfe statischer Tests soll der logische Ablauf sequentieller Teilsysteme überprüfbar sein. Außerdem ist eine Überprüfung des Echtzeitverhaltens des Gesamtsystems mit Hilfe einer dynamischen Simulation anzustreben.
- Behandlung von Änderungen: Änderungen des Entwurfs müssen auf einfache Weise einfügbar sein. Dabei muß gewährleistet werden, daß die gesamte Dokumentation jeweils mit geändert wird und daß alle Auswirkungen einer Änderung erkennbar gemacht werden.
- Rechner-Unterstützung: Sie muß so gestaltet werden, daß sie für die System- und Programmentwickler attraktiv wird, d.h. daß diese den Rechner gerne anwenden, weil er die Arbeit erleichtert und verbessert. Dazu gehört auch, daß das Spezifikations- und Entwurfssystem auf einem leicht zugänglichen Rechner verfügbar sein muß. Da Großrechner diese Bedingung vielfach nicht erfüllen, ergibt sich daraus die Forderung nach Implementierbarkeit auf einem mittelgroßen Prozeßrechner (Minirechner)!
- Lösungsfindung: Es sollten dem Entwerfer Hilfen und Anregungen geboten werden, um zu einem möglichst optimalen Lösungskonzept zu kommen. Dabei sollte eine Gewichtung der Anforderungen möglich gemacht werden (manche Anforderungen müssen erfüllt werden, andere sollten erfüllt werden, wieder andere wären erwünscht).
- Projekt-Management: Als Hilfe für das Projekt-Management sollte die Überwachung von Entwicklungszeiten, sowie die Erstellung, Änderung und Kontrolle von Netzplänen unterstützt werden.

Bei den bisher bekannt gewordenen Spezifikations- und Entwurfssystemen bleiben viele dieser Wünsche offen. Außerdem sind die zugrundeliegenden Methoden für Zeit-unabhängige Informationsverarbeitungssysteme ausgelegt. Da Prozeß- und Zeitereignisse nicht berücksichtigt sind, ist ein Einsatz für die Prozeßautomatisierung nur möglich, wenn entsprechende Änderungen und Erweiterungen eingeführt werden. So wird z.B. in [12] über ein Vorhaben berichtet, bei dem das ursprünglich für Informations-Management-Systeme entwickelte Entwurfssystem PSL/PSA an die Erfordernisse der Prozeßautomatisierung angepaßt wurde.

Am Institut des Verfassers wird gegenwärtig daran gearbeitet, die oben aufgeführten Wünsche, auch bezüglich der Implementierbarkeit auf einem mittelgroßen Prozeßrechner, mit einem neuen Spezifikations- und Entwurfssystem EPOS (Entwurfs-unterstützendes PEARL-orientiertes Spezifikationssystem) zu erfüllen. Außerdem soll dabei die verwendete Spezifikationssprache mit der Prozeßprogrammiersprache PEARL, in der das Ergebnis des Software-Entwurfs formuliert wird, verträglich sein.

Den bisher behandelten rechnergestützten Spezifikations- und Entwurfssystemen lag die Absicht zugrunde, möglichst kostengünstig ein optimal für den vorgesehenen Zweck ausgelegtes und zuverlässig arbeitendes Hard- und Software-System zu erstellen. Bei Anwendungen, in denen darüber hinaus auch Sicherheit gefordert wird (wie z.B. beim Einsatz von Prozeßrechnern für Verkehrssysteme oder in Kernkraftwerken) kommt ein weiteres Anliegen hinzu: Hier muß ein Sicherheitsnachweis geführt werden, d.h. ein Nachweis, daß gefährliche Ausfälle des Prozeßrechensystems - sei es des Hardwaresystems, des Softwaresystems oder des Zusammenwirkens zwischen beiden - ausgeschlossen sind. Bezüglich der Software gibt es zwei Möglichkeiten des Vorgehens:

- entweder es wird nachgewiesen, daß ein redundant oder diversitär ausgelegtes Softwaresystem fehlertolerant ist, d.h. daß es auch im Fehlerfalle keine gefährlichen Ausfälle zeigt
- oder man versucht, mit Hilfe von Verifikations- oder Programmanalyseverfahren die Korrektheit des Softwaresystems zu beweisen.

Bei dem zuletzt genannten Vorgehen beruht der Beweis jedoch stets auf der Annahme, daß die zugrundeliegende Spezifikation der Anforderungen widerspruchsfrei und vollständig ist - eine Annahme, deren Richtigkeit ihrerseits nachgewiesen werden muß. Was liegt näher, als hierfür eine geeignete Spezifikationssprache einzusetzen, die einen solchen Nachweis rechnergestützt ermöglicht?

Erstmals wurde in [13] eine solche Spezifikationssprache vorgestellt, die das Ziel hat, u.a. auch die Vollständigkeit und Widerspruchsfreiheit der gestellten zeitlichen Bedingungen nachzuweisen. Eine Untersuchung dieser Spezifikationssprache [14] zeigt allerdings, daß die Anwendbarkeit auf eine gewisse Klasse von Echtzeitsystemen beschränkt ist. Außerdem muß das zu entwerfende System den Grundkonzepten der Sprache angepaßt werden. Dies bedeutet, daß die wichtige Forderung, daß eine Spezifikation nur Anforderungen festlegen, Entwurfsentscheidungen aber nicht vorwegnehmen soll, verletzt wird.

Es ist also leider festzustellen, daß eine für diesen Anwendungsfall geeignete Spezifikationssprache bisher nicht in Sicht ist. Andererseits offenbart auch dieses Beispiel: Es gibt im Bereich der Prozeßautomatisierung noch zahlreiche ungelöste Problemstellungen, die den Forschergeist der Informatiker herausfordern!

Schlußbemerkungen

Aus der Behandlung der verschiedenen Problemkreise sollte beispielhaft deutlich werden:

- Die Zeit-abhängige Datenverarbeitung, wie sie für den Bereich der Prozeßautomatisierung typisch ist, ist ein interessantes Aufgabengebiet der Informatik.
- Bei der Entwicklung von Verfahren und Software-Werkzeugen für die Prozeßautomatisierung geht es vorrangig darum, diese den Menschen anzupassen, die sie handhaben sollen. Mit der zunehmenden Verbreitung von Mikrorechnern wird diese Problematik immer dringlicher.

Die zuletzt genannte Forderung, Verfahren der Informationsverarbeitung für Digitalrechner so zu entwickeln, daß sie auch für Menschen in der Praxis handhabbar werden, ist eine Herausforderung an die Informatik, die sicher nicht nur auf das Anwendungsgebiet der Prozeßautomatisierung beschränkt ist.

Literatur

1 Brauer W., Haacke W. und Münch S.: Studien- und Forschungsführer Informatik. Herausgeber: GMD und DAAD, Bonn 1978.

2 Eichenauer B.: Prozeßsprachen und Portabilität. Informatik-Fachbericht 12, Springer Verlag 1978, S. 9 - 27.

3 Lauber R.: Prozeßautomatisierung I. Berlin: Springer 1976.

4 Eichenauer B., Haase V., Holleczek P., Kreuter K. und Müller G.: PEARL, eine Prozeß- und Experimentorientierte Programmiersprache. Angew. Informatik 9 (1973) S. 363 - 372.

5 Full-PEARL Language Description. KFK-PDV 130, Karlsruhe 1977.

6 Basic-PEARL Language Description. KFK-PDV 120, Karlsruhe 1977.

7 Rössler R.: Betriebssystemstrategien zur Bewältigung von Zeitproblemen in der Prozeßautomatisierung.
An der Universität Stuttgart als Dissertation eingereicht 1978 (bisher unveröffentlicht).

8 Eichenauer B.: Dynamische Prioritätsvergabe an Tasks in Prozeßrechensystemen. Dissertation Universität Stuttgart 1975.

9 Ghassemi A.: Untersuchung der Eignung der Prozeßprogrammiersprache PEARL zur Automatisierung von Folgeprozessen.
An der Universität Stuttgart als Dissertation eingereicht 1978 (bisher unveröffentlicht).

10 Ludewig J. und Streng W.: Überblick und Vergleich verschiedener Mittel für die Spezifikation und den Entwurf von Software. Bericht KFK Nr. 2506 Karlsruhe 1978

11 Lauber R., Konakovsky R. und Reinshagen K.-P.: Structured Documentation Method for Safety-Related Computer Controlled Systems. IFAC-Congress Helsinki, 12. - 16. June 1978. Preprints pp. 739 - 746

12 Ludewig J. und Streng W.: Erweiterung des Entwurfssystems PSL/PSA für die Entwicklung von Prozeßrechner-Software. GI-Jahrestagung 4. - 6. Oktober 1978, Themenkreis 7: Softwaretechnik

13 Quirk, W.J. and Gilbert R.: The formal specification of the requirements of complex real-time systems. Computer Science and Systems Division, AERE Harwell. Report Nr. R 8602. Oxfordshire, June 1977.

14 Reimann H.-P.: Untersuchung einer formalen Spezifikationssprache für komplexe Echtzeitsysteme auf Anwendbarkeit. Diplomarbeit am Institut für Regelungstechnik und Prozeßautomatisierung der Universität Stuttgart 1978 (unveröffentlicht)

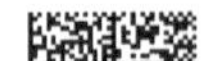